# BERLITZ PHRASE BOOKS

World's bestselling phrase books feature not only expressions and vocabulary you'll need, but also travel tips, useful facts and pronunciation throughout. The handiest and most readable conversation aid available.

| | | |
|---|---|---|
| Arabic | French | Portuguese |
| Chinese | German | Russian |
| Danish | Greek | Serbo-Croatian |
| Dutch | Hebrew | Spanish |
| European | Hungarian | Latin-American |
| (14 languages) | Italian | Spanish |
| European | Japanese | Swahili |
| Menu Reader | Norwegian | Swedish |
| Finnish | Polish | Turkish |

## BERLITZ CASSETTEPAKS

Most of the above-mentioned titles are also available combined with a cassette to help you improve your accent. A helpful 32-page script is included containing the complete text of the dual language hi-fi recording.

# Berlitz Dictionaries

| | |
|---|---|
| **Dansk** | Engelsk, Fransk, Italiensk, Spansk, Tysk |
| **Deutsch** | Dänisch, Englisch, Finnisch, Französisch, Italienisch, Niederländisch, Norwegisch, Portugiesisch, Schwedisch, Spanisch |
| **English** | Danish, Dutch, Finnish, French, German, Italian, Norwegian, Portuguese, Spanish, Swedish |
| **Español** | Alemán, Danés, Finlandés, Francés, Holandés, Inglés, Noruego, Sueco |
| **Français** | Allemand, Anglais, Danois, Espagnol, Finnois, Italien, Néerlandais, Norvégien, Portugais, Suédois |
| **Italiano** | Danese, Finlandese, Francese, Inglese, Norvegese, Olandese, Svedese, Tedesco |
| **Nederlands** | Duits, Engels, Frans, Italiaans, Portugees, Spaans |
| **Norsk** | Engelsk, Fransk, Italiensk, Spansk, Tysk |
| **Português** | Alemão, Francês, Holandês, Inglês, Sueco |
| **Suomi** | Englanti, Espanja, Italia, Ranska, Ruotsi, Saksa |
| **Svenska** | Engelska, Finska, Franska, Italienska, Portugisiska, Spanska, Tyska |

# BERLITZ®

# spanish-english
# english-spanish
## dictionary

## diccionario
# español-inglés
# inglés-español

By the Staff of Editions Berlitz

Revised edition 1979
Library of Congress Catalog Card Number: 78-78079

6th printing 1984
Printed in Switzerland

# Contents

## SPANISH-ENGLISH DICTIONARY 15

## ENGLISH-SPANISH DICTIONARY 189

# Índice

## DICCIONARIO ESPAÑOL-INGLÉS 15

## DICCIONARIO INGLÉS-ESPAÑOL 189

# Preface

In selecting the 12.500 word-concepts in each language for this dictionary, the editors have had the traveller's needs foremost in mind. This book will prove invaluable to all the millions of travellers, tourists and business people who appreciate the reassurance a small and practical dictionary can provide. It offers them—as it does beginners and students—all the basic vocabulary they are going to encounter and to have to use, giving the key words and expressions to allow them to cope in everyday situations.

Like our successful phrase books and travel guides, these dictionaries—created with the help of a computer data bank—are designed to slip into pocket or purse, and thus have a role as handy companions at all times.

Besides just about everything you normally find in dictionaries, there are these Berlitz bonuses:

- imitated pronunciation next to each foreign-word entry, making it easy to read and enunciate words whose spelling may look forbidding

- a unique, practical glossary to simplify reading a foreign restaurant menu and to take the mystery out of complicated dishes and indecipherable names on bills of fare

- useful information on how to tell the time and how to count, on conjugating irregular verbs, commonly seen abbreviations and converting to the metric system, in addition to basic phrases.

While no dictionary of this size can pretend to completeness, we expect the user of this book will feel well armed to affront foreign travel with confidence. We should, however, be very pleased to receive comments, criticism and suggestions that you think may be of help in preparing future editions.

# Prefacio

Al seleccionar las 12 500 palabras-conceptos en cada una de las lenguas de este diccionario, los redactores han tenido muy en cuenta las necesidades del viajero. Esta obra es indispensable para millones de viajeros, turistas y hombres de negocios, quienes apreciarán la seguridad que aporta un diccionario pequeño y práctico. Tanto a ellos como a los principiantes y estudiantes les ofrece todo el vocabulario básico que encontrarán o deberán emplear en el lenguaje de todos los días; les proporciona las palabras clave y las expresiones que les permitirán enfrentarse a las situaciones de la vida diaria.

Al igual que nuestros conocidos manuales de conversación y guías turísticas, estos diccionarios – realizados en computadora con la ayuda de un banco de datos – han sido ideados para llevarse en el bolsillo o en un bolso de mano, asumiendo de este modo su papel de compañeros disponibles en todo momento.

Además de las nociones que de ordinario ofrece un diccionario, encontrará:

- una transcripción fonética tan sencilla que facilita la lectura, aun cuando la palabra extranjera parezca impronunciable

- un léxico gastronómico inédito que le hará «descifrar» los menús en un restaurante extranjero, revelándole el secreto de los platos complicados y los misterios de la cuenta

- informaciones prácticas que le ayudarán a comunicar la hora y a contar, así como a utilizar los verbos irregulares, las abreviaturas más comunes y algunas expresiones útiles.

Ningún diccionario de este formato puede tener la pretensión de ser completo, pero el fin de este libro es permitir que quien lo emplee posea un arma para enfrentarse con confianza al viaje en el extranjero. Sin embargo, recibiremos con gusto los comentarios, críticas y sugestiones que con toda seguridad nos permitirán preparar las futuras ediciones.

# spanish-english
## español-inglés

# Introduction

This dictionary has been designed to take account of your practical needs. Unnecessary linguistic information has been avoided. The entries are listed in alphabetical order regardless of whether the entry word is printed in a single word or in two or more separate words. As the only exception to this rule, a few idiomatic expressions are listed as main entries alphabetically according to the most significant word of the expression. When an entry is followed by sub-entries, such as expressions and locutions, these, too, have been listed in alphabetical order.[1]

Each main-entry word is followed by a phonetic transcription (see guide to pronunciation). Following the transcription is the part of speech of the entry word whenever applicable. When an entry word may be used as more than one part of speech, the translations are grouped together after the respective part of speech.

Whenever an entry word is repeated in sub-entries a tilde (~) is used to represent the full entry word.

An asterisk (*) in front of a verb indicates that the verb is irregular. For details you may refer to the lists of irregular verbs.

The dictionary is based on Castilian Spanish. All words and meanings of words that are exclusively Mexican have been marked as such (see list of abbreviations used in the text).

# Abbreviations

| | | | |
|---|---|---|---|
| *adj* | adjective | *n* | noun |
| *adv* | adverb | *nAm* | noun (American) |
| *Am* | American | *num* | numeral |
| *art* | article | *p* | past tense |
| *conj* | conjunction | *pl* | plural |
| *f* | feminine | *plAm* | plural (American) |
| *fMe* | feminine (Mexican) | *pp* | past participle |
| *fpl* | feminine plural | *pr* | present tense |
| *fplMe* | feminine plural (Mexican) | *pref* | prefix |
| *m* | masculine | *prep* | preposition |
| *Me* | Mexican | *pron* | pronoun |
| *mMe* | masculine (Mexican) | *v* | verb |
| *mpl* | masculine plural | *vAm* | verb (American) |
| *mplMe* | masculine plural (Mexican) | *vMe* | verb (Mexican) |

---

[1] Note that the alphabetical order in Spanish differs from our own in three cases: *ch, ll* and *ñ* are considered independent letters and come after *c, l* and n, respectively.

# Guide to Pronunciation

Each main entry in this part of the dictionary is followed by a phonetic transcription which shows you how to pronounce the words. This transcription should be read as if it were English. It is based on Standard British pronunciation, though we have tried to take account of General American pronunciation also. Below, only those letters and symbols are explained which we consider likely to be ambiguous or not immediately understood.

The syllables are separated by hyphens, and stressed syllables are printed in *italics*.

Of course, the sounds of any two languages are never exactly the same, but if you follow carefully our indications, you should be able to pronounce the foreign words in such a way that you'll be understood. To make your task easier, our transcriptions occasionally simplify slightly the sound system of the language while still reflecting the essential sound differences.

## Consonants

| | |
|---|---|
| **bh** | a rather indecisive **b**, i.e. one verging on **v** |
| **dh** | like **th** in **th**is, often rather indecisive, possibly quite like **d** |
| **g** | always hard, as in **g**o |
| **g** | a **g**-sound where the tongue doesn't quite close the air passage between itself and the roof of the mouth, so that the escaping air produces audible friction; it is also on occasions pronounced as an indecisive **g** |
| **kh** | like **g**, but based on a **k**-sound; therefore hard and voiceless, like **ch** in Scottish lo**ch** |
| **l**<sup>**y**</sup> | like **lli** in mi**lli**on |
| **ñ** | as in the Spanish se**ñ**or, or like **ni** in o**ni**on |
| **r** | slightly rolled in the front of the mouth |
| **rr** | strongly rolled **r** |
| **s** | always hard, as in **s**o |

## Vowels and Diphthongs

| | |
|---|---|
| **ah** | a short version of the **a** in c**a**r, i.e. a sound between **a** in c**a**t and **u** in c**u**t |
| **igh** | as in s**igh** |
| **ou** | as in l**ou**d |

1) Raised letters (e.g. **ay^oo^, ^y^ah**) should be pronounced only fleetingly.

2) Spanish vowels (i.e. not diphthongs) are pure and fairly short. Therefore, you should try to read a transcription like **oa** without moving tongue or lips while pronouncing the sound.

## Latin-American Pronunciation

Our transcriptions reflect the pronunciation of Castilian, the official language of Spain. In Latin America, two of the Castilian sounds are practically unknown:

1) **ll** as in the word ca**ll**e (which we represent by **l^y^**) is usually pronounced like Spanish **y** (as in English **y**et); in the Río de la Plata region, though, both **ll** and **y** are pronounced like **s** in plea**s**ure.

2) The letters **c** (before **e** and **i**) and **z** are pronounced like **s** in **s**o instead of **th** as in **th**in.

# A

**a** (ah) *prep* to, on; at; **a las ...** at ... o'clock

**abacería** (ah-bhah-thay-*ree*-ah) *f* grocer's

**abacero** (ah-bhah-*thay*-roa) *m* grocer

**abadía** (ah-bhah-*dhee*-ah) *f* abbey

**abajo** (ah-*bhah*-khoa) *adv* downstairs; down; **hacia ~** downwards

**abandonar** (ah-bhahn-doa-*nahr*) *v* abandon

**abanico** (ah-bhah-*nee*-koa) *m* fan

**abarrotería** (ah-bhah-rroa-tay-*ree*-ah) *fMe* grocer's

**abarrotero** (ah-bhah-rroa-*tay*-roa) *mMe* grocer

**abastecimiento** (ah-bhahss-tay-thee-m<sup>y</sup>ayn-toa) *m* supply

**abatido** (ah-bhah-*tee*-dhoa) *adj* down

**abecedario** (ah-bhay-thay-*dah*-r<sup>y</sup>oa) *m* alphabet

**abedul** (ah-bhay-*dhool*) *m* birch

**abeja** (ah-*bhay*-khah) *f* bee

**abertura** (ah-bhayr-*too*-rah) *f* opening

**abierto** (ah-*bh<sup>y</sup>ayr*-toa) *adj* open

**abismo** (ah-*bhee*-zmoa) *m* abyss

**ablandador** (ah-bhlahn-dah-*dhoar*) *m* water-softener

**ablandar** (ah-bhlahn-*dahr*) *v* soften

**abogado** (ah-bhoa-*gah*-dhoa) *m* barrister, lawyer, attorney; solicitor; advocate

**abolir** (ah-bhoa-*leer*) *v* abolish

**abolladura** (ah-bhoa-l<sup>y</sup>ah-*dhoo*-rah) *f* dent

**abonado** (ah-bhoa-*nah*-dhoa) *m* subscriber

**abono** (ah-*bhoa*-noa) *m* manure, dung

**aborto** (ah-*bhoar*-toa) *m* miscarriage; abortion

**abrazar** (ah-bhrah-*thahr*) *v* embrace; hug

**abrazo** (ah-*bhrah*-thoa) *m* hug; embrace

**abrecartas** (ah-bhray-*kahr*-tahss) *m* paper-knife

**abrelatas** (ah-bhray-*lah*-tahss) *m* can opener, tin-opener

**abreviatura** (ah-bhray-bh<sup>y</sup>ah-*too*-rah) *f* abbreviation

**abrigar** (ah-bhree-*gahr*) *v* shelter

**abrigo** (ah-*bhree*-goa) *m* coat, overcoat; **~ de pieles** fur coat

**abril** (ah-*bhreel*) April

**abrir** (ah-*bhreer*) *v* open; unlock; turn on

**abrochar** (ah-bhroa-*chahr*) *v* button

**abrupto** (ah-*bhroop*-toa) *adj* steep

**absceso** (ahbhs-*thay*-soa) *m* abscess

**absolución** (ahbh-soa-loo-*th<sup>y</sup>oan*) *f* acquittal

**absolutamente** (ahbh-soa-loo-tah-*mayn*-tay) *adv* absolutely

**absoluto** (ahbh-soa-*loo*-toa) *adj* sheer;
total

**abstemio** (ahbhs-*tay*-mʸoa) *m* teetotaller

*****abstenerse de** (ahbhs-tay-*nayr*-say)
abstain from

**abstracto** (ahbhs-*trahk*-toa) *adj* abstract

**absurdo** (ahbhs-*soor*-dhoa) *adj* absurd;
foolish

**abuela** (ah-*bhway*-lah) *f* grandmother

**abuelo** (ah-*bhway*-loa) *m* grandfather,
granddad; **abuelos** *mpl* grandparents *pl*

**abundancia** (ah-bhoon-*dahn*-thʸah) *f*
abundance, plenty

**abundante** (ah-bhoon-*dahn*-tay) *adj*
abundant, plentiful

**abundar** (ah-bhoon-*dahr*) *v* abound

**aburrido** (ah-bhoo-*rree*-dhoa) *adj* boring, dull

**aburrimiento** (ah-bhoo-rree-*mʸayn*-toa)
*m* annoyance

**aburrir** (ah-bhoo-*rreer*) *v* bore, annoy

**abusar de** (ah-bhoo-*sahr*) exploit

**abuso** (ah-*bhoo*-soa) *m* misuse, abuse

**acá** (ah-*kah*) *adv* here

**acabar** (ah-kah-*bhahr*) *v* end; **acabado**
finished; over

**academia** (ah-kah-*dhay*-mʸah) *f* academy; ~ **de bellas artes** art school

**acallar** (ah-kah-*lʸahr*) *v* silence

**acampador** (ah-kahm-pah-*dhoar*) *m*
camper

**acampar** (ah-kahm-*pahr*) *v* camp

**acantilado** (ah-kahn-tee-*lah*-dhoa) *m*
cliff

**acariciar** (ah-kah-ree-*thʸahr*) *v* cuddle

**acaso** (ah-*kah*-soa) *adv* perhaps

**accesible** (ahk-thay-*see*-bhlay) *adj* accessible

**acceso** (ahk-*thay*-soa) *m* entrance, access; approach

**accesorio** (ahk-thay-*soa*-rʸoa) *adj* additional; **accesorios** *mpl* accessories *pl*

**accidental** (ahk-thee-dhayn-*tahl*) *adj*
accidental

**accidente** (ahk-thee-*dhayn*-tay) *m* accident; ~ **aéreo** plane crash

**acción** (ahk-*thʸoan*) *f* share; action;
deed; **acciones** *fpl* stocks and
shares

**acechar** (ah-thay-*chahr*) *v* watch for

**aceite** (ah-*thay*-tay) *m* oil; ~ **bronceador** suntan oil; ~ **de mesa** salad-oil; ~ **de oliva** olive oil; ~ **lubricante** lubrication oil; ~ **para el pelo** hair-oil

**aceitoso** (ah-thay-*toa*-soa) *adj* oily

**aceituna** (ah-thay-*too*-nah) *f* olive

**acelerador** (ah-thay-lay-rah-*dhoar*) *m*
accelerator

**acelerar** (ah-thay-lay-*rahr*) *v* accelerate

**acento** (ah-*thayn*-toa) *m* accent

**acentuar** (ah-thayn-*twahr*) *v* emphasize, stress

**aceptar** (ah-thayp-*tahr*) *v* accept

**acera** (ah-*thay*-rah) *f* pavement; sidewalk *nAm*

**acerca de** (ah-*thayr*-kah day) about

**acercarse** (ah-thayr-*kahr*-say) *v* approach

**acero** (ah-*thay*-roa) *m* steel; ~ **inoxidable** stainless steel

*****acertar** (ah-thayr-*tahr*) *v* \*hit; guess
right

**acidez** (ah-thee-*dhayth*) *f* heartburn

**ácido** (*ah*-thee-dhoa) *m* acid

**aclamar** (ah-klah-*mahr*) *v* cheer

**aclaración** (ah-klah-rah-*thʸoan*) *f* explanation

**aclarar** (ah-klah-*rahr*) *v* clarify

**acné** (ahk-*nay*) *m* acne

**acogida** (ah-koa-*khee*-dhah) *f* reception

**acomodación** (ah-koa-moa-dhah-*thʸoan*) *f* accommodation

**acomodado** (ah-koa-moa-*dhah*-dhoa) *adj* well-to-do

**acomodador** (ah-koa-moa-dhah-*dhoar*) *m* usher

**acomodadora** (ah-koa-moa-dhah-*dhoa*-rah) *f* usherette

**acomodar** (ah-koa-moa-*dhahr*) *v* accommodate

**acompañar** (ah-koam-pah-*ñahr*) *v* accompany; conduct

**aconsejar** (ah-koan-say-*khahr*) *v* recommend, advise

**\*acontecer** (ah-koan-tay-*thayr*) *v* occur

**acontecimiento** (ah-koan-tay-thee-m*y*ayn-toa) *m* event; happening, occurrence

**\*acordar** (ah-koar-*dhahr*) *v* agree; **\*acordarse** *v* remember, recollect, recall

**acortar** (ah-koar-*tahr*) *v* shorten

**\*acostar** (ah-koass-*tahr*) *v* \*lay down; **\*acostarse** *v* \*go to bed

**acostumbrado** (ah-koass-toom-*brah*-dhoa) *adj* accustomed; customary; **\*estar ~ a** \*be used to

**acostumbrar** (ah-koass-toom-*brahr*) *v* accustom

**\*acrecentarse** (ah-kray-thayn-*tahr*-say) *v* increase

**acreditar** (ah-kray-dhee-*tahr*) *v* credit

**acreedor** (ah-kray-ay-*dhoar*) *m* creditor

**acta** (*ahk*-tah) *f* certificate; **actas** minutes

**actitud** (ahk-tee-*toodh*) *f* attitude; position

**actividad** (ahk-tee-bhee-*dhahdh*) *f* activity

**activo** (ahk-*tee*-bhoa) *adj* active

**acto** (*ahk*-toa) *m* act, deed

**actor** (ahk-*toar*) *m* actor

**actriz** (ahk-*treeth*) *f* actress

**actual** (ahk-*twahl*) *adj* present; topical

**actualmente** (ahk-twahl-*mayn*-tay) *adv* now

**actuar** (ahk-*twahr*) *v* act

**acuarela** (ah-kwah-*ray*-lah) *f* watercolour

**acuerdo** (ah-*kwayr*-dhoa) *m* approval; agreement, settlement; **¡de acuerdo!** all right!, okay!; **\*estar de ~ con** approve of

**acumulador** (ah-koo-moo-lah-*dhoar*) *m* battery

**acusación** (ah-koo-sah-th*y*oan) *f* charge

**acusado** (ah-koo-*sah*-dhoa) *m* accused

**acusar** (ah-koo-*sahr*) *v* accuse; charge

**adaptar** (ah-dhahp-*tahr*) *v* adapt; suit

**adecuado** (ah-dhay-*kwah*-dhoa) *adj* adequate; convenient, appropriate

**adelantar** (ah-dhay-lahn-*tahr*) *v* \*get on; **por adelantado** in advance; **prohibido ~** no overtaking

**adelante** (ah-dhay-*lahn*-tay) *adv* ahead, onwards, forward

**adelanto** (ah-dhay-*lahn*-toa) *m* advance

**adelgazar** (ah-dhayl-gah-*thahr*) *v* slim

**además** (ah-dhay-*mahss*) *adv* moreover, furthermore, besides; **~ de** beyond, besides

**adentro** (ah-*dhayn*-troa) *adv* inside, in; **hacia ~** inwards

**adeudado** (ah-dhay°°-*dhah*-dhoa) *adj* due

**adición** (ah-dhee-th*y*oan) *f* addition

**adicional** (ah-dhee-th*y*oa-*nahl*) *adj* additional

**adicionar** (ah-dhee-th*y*oa-*nahr*) *v* add; count

**¡adiós!** (ah-*dh*°*y*oass) good-bye!

**adivinanza** (ah-dhee-bhee-*nahn*-thah) *f* riddle

**adivinar** (ah-dhee-bhee-*nahr*) *v* guess

**adjetivo** (ahdh-khay-*tee*-bhoa) *m* adjective

**administración** (ahdh-mee-neess-trah-

*th<sup>y</sup>oan*) *f* administration; direction

**administrar** (ahdh-mee-neess-*trahr*) *v* manage; direct; administer

**administrativo** (ahdh-mee-neess-trah-*tee*-bhoa) *adj* administrative

**admirable** (ahdh-mee-*rah*-bhlay) *adj* admirable

**admiración** (ahdh-mee-rah-*th<sup>y</sup>oan*) *f* admiration

**admirador** (ahdh-mee-rah-*dhoar*) *m* fan

**admirar** (ahdh-mee-*rahr*) *v* admire

**admisión** (ahdh-mee-*s<sup>y</sup>oan*) *f* admission; admittance

**admitir** (ahdh-mee-*teer*) *v* admit; acknowledge

**adonde** (ah-*dhoan*-day) *adv* where

**adoptar** (ah-dhoap-*tahr*) *v* adopt

**adorable** (ah-dhoa-*rah*-bhlay) *adj* adorable

**adorar** (ah-dhoa-*rahr*) *v* worship

**adormidera** (ah-dhoar-mee-*dhay*-rah) *f* poppy

**adorno** (ah-*dhoar*-noa) *m* ornament

**adquirible** (ahdh-kee-*ree*-bhlay) *adj* obtainable, available

*\*adquirir** (ahdh-kee-*reer*) *v* acquire; *\*buy

**adquisición** (ahdh-kee-see-*th<sup>y</sup>oan*) *f* acquisition

**aduana** (ah-*dwah*-nah) *f* Customs *pl*

**adulto** (ah-*dhool*-toa) *adj* grown-up, adult; *m* grown-up, adult

**adverbio** (ahdh-*bhayr*-bh<sup>y</sup>oa) *m* adverb

**advertencia** (ahdh-bhayr-*tayn*-th<sup>y</sup>ah) *f* warning

*\*advertir** (ahdh-bhayr-*teer*) *v* caution, warn; notice

**aerolínea** (ah-ay-roa-*lee*-nay-ah) *f* airline

**aeropuerto** (ah-ay-roa-*pwayr*-toa) *m* airport

**aerosol** (ah-ay-roa-*soal*) *m* atomizer

**afamado** (ah-fah-*mah*-dhoa) *adj* noted

**afección** (ah-fayk-*th<sup>y</sup>oan*) *f* affection

**afectado** (ah-fayk-*tah*-dhoa) *adj* affected

**afectar** (ah-fayk-*tahr*) *v* affect; feign

**afeitadora eléctrica** (ah-fay-tah-*dhoa*-rah ay-*layk*-tree-kah) electric razor

**afeitarse** (ah-fay-*tahr*-say) *v* shave; **máquina de afeitar** safety-razor; shaver

**afición** (ah-fee-*th<sup>y</sup>oan*) *f* hobby

**aficionado** (ah-fee-th<sup>y</sup>oa-*nah*-dhoa) *m* supporter

**afilar** (ah-fee-*lahr*) *v* sharpen; **afilado** sharp

**afiliación** (ah-fee-l<sup>y</sup>ah-*th<sup>y</sup>oan*) *f* membership

**afiliado** (ah-fee-*l<sup>y</sup>ah*-dhoa) *adj* affiliated

**afirmación** (ah-feer-mah-*th<sup>y</sup>oan*) *f* statement

**afirmar** (ah-feer-*mahr*) *v* claim

**afirmativo** (ah-feer-mah-*tee*-bhoa) *adj* affirmative

**aflicción** (ah-fleek-*th<sup>y</sup>oan*) *f* grief

**afligido** (ah-flee-*khee*-dhoa) *adj* sad; *\*estar* ~ grieve

**afluente** (ah-*flwayn*-tay) *m* tributary

**afortunado** (ah-foar-too-*nah*-dhoa) *adj* fortunate, lucky

**África** (*ah*-free-kah) *f* Africa

**África del Sur** (*ah*-free-kah dayl soor) South Africa

**africano** (ah-free-*kah*-noa) *adj* African; *m* African

**afuera** (ah-*fway*-rah) *adv* outside, outdoors; **hacia** ~ outwards

**afueras** (ah-*fway*-rahss) *fpl* outskirts *pl*

**agarradero** (ah-gah-rrah-*dhay*-roa) *m* grip

**agarrar** (ah-gah-*rrahr*) *v* grasp, seize; **agarrarse** *v* \*hold on

**agarre** (ah-*gah*-rray) *m* grip, grasp

**agencia** (ah-*khayn*-th<sup>y</sup>ah) *f* agency; ~

**de viajes** travel agency
**agenda** (ah-*khayn*-dah ) *f* diary
**agente** (ah-*khayn*-tay) *m* agent; ~ **de policía** policeman; ~ **de viajes** travel agent
**ágil** (*ah*-kheel) *adj* supple
**agitación** (ah-khee-tah-*th*ᵞ*oan*) *f* excitement; bustle
**agitar** (ah-khee-*tahr*) *v* stir up
**agosto** (ah-*goass*-toa) August
**agotado** (ah-goa-*tah*-dhoa) *adj* sold out
**agotar** (ah-goa-*tahr*) *v* use up
**agradable** (ah-grah-*dhah*-bhlay) *adj* agreeable; enjoyable, pleasing, pleasant; nice
*****agradecer** (ah-grah-dhay-*thayr*) *v* thank
**agradecido** (ah-grah-dhay-*thee*-dhoa) *adj* grateful, thankful
**agrario** (ah-*grah*-rᵞoa) *adj* agrarian
**agraviar** (ah-grah-*bh*ᵞ*ahr*) *v* wrong
**agregar** (ah-gray-*gahr*) *v* add
**agresivo** (ah-gray-*see*-bhoa) *adj* aggressive
**agrícola** (ah-*gree*-koa-lah) *adj* agrarian
**agricultura** (ah-gree-kool-*too*-rah) *f* agriculture
**agrio** (*ah*-grᵞoa) *adj* sour
**agua** (*ah*-gwah) *f* water; ~ **corriente** running water; ~ **de mar** seawater; ~ **de soda** soda-water; ~ **dulce** fresh water; ~ **helada** iced water; ~ **mineral** mineral water; ~ **potable** drinking-water
**aguacero** (ah-gwah-*thay*-roa) *m* shower; downpour
**aguafuerte** (ah-gwah-*fwayr*-tay) *f* etching
**aguanieve** (ah-gwah-*n*ᵞ*ay*-bhay) *f* slush
**aguantar** (ah-gwahn-*tahr*) *v* \*bear
**aguardado** (ah-gwahr-*dhah*-dhoa) due
**aguardar** (ah-gwahr-*dahr*) *v* expect

**agudo** (ah-*goo*-dhoa) *adj* keen; acute
**águila** (*ah*-gee-lah) *m* eagle
**aguja** (ah-*goo*-khah) *f* needle; spire; **labor de** ~ needlework
**agujero** (ah-goo-*khay*-roa) *m* hole
**ahí** (ah-*ee*) *adv* there
**ahogar** (ah-oa-*gahr*) *v* drown; **ahogarse** *v* \*be drowned
**ahora** (ah-*oa*-rah) *adv* now; **de** ~ **en adelante** henceforth; **hasta** ~ so far
**ahorrar** (ah-oa-*rrahr*) *v* save
**ahorros** (ah-oa-*rroass*) *mpl* savings *pl*; **caja de** ~ savings bank
**ahuyentar** (ou-ᵞayn-*tahr*) *v* chase
**aire** (*igh*-ray) *m* air; sky; breath; ~ **acondicionado** air-conditioning; **cámara de** ~ inner tube; \***tener aires de** look
**airear** (igh-ray-*ahr*) *v* air, ventilate
**aireo** (igh-*ray*-oa) *m* ventilation
**airoso** (igh-*roa*-soa) *adj* airy
**aislado** (ighz-*lah*-dhoa) *adj* isolated
**aislador** (ighz-lah-*dhoar*) *m* insulator
**aislamiento** (ighz-lah-*m*ᵞ*ayn*-toa) *m* isolation; insulation
**aislar** (ighz-*lahr*) *v* isolate; insulate
**ajedrez** (ah-khay-*dhrayth*) *m* chess
**ajeno** (ah-*khay*-noa) *adj* foreign
**ajetrearse** (ah-khay-tray-*ahr*-say) *v* labour
**ajo** (*ah*-khoa) *m* garlic
**ajustar** (ah-khooss-*tahr*) *v* adjust
**ala** (*ah*-lah) *f* wing
**alabar** (ah-lah-*bhahr*) *v* praise
**alambre** (ah-*lahm*-bray) *m* wire
**alargar** (ah-lahr-*gahr*) *v* lengthen; renew; hand
**alarma** (ah-*lahr*-mah) *f* alarm; ~ **de incendio** fire-alarm
**alarmante** (ah-lahr-*mahn*-tay) *adj* scary
**alarmar** (ah-lahr-*mahr*) *v* alarm
**alba** (*ahl*-bhah) *f* dawn

**albañil** (ahl-bhah-*ñeel*) *m* bricklayer

**albaricoque** (ahl-bhah-ree-*koa*-kay) *m* apricot

**albergue para jóvenes** (ahl-*bhayr*-gay pah-rah *khoa*-bhay-nayss) youth hostel

**alborotador** (ahl-bhoa-roa-tah-*dhoar*) *adj* rowdy

**alboroto** (ahl-bhoa-*roa*-toa) *m* noise, racket

**álbum** (*ahl*-bhoom) *m* album

**alcachofa** (ahl-kah-*choa*-fah) *f* artichoke

**alcalde** (ahl-*kahl*-dhay) *m* mayor

**alcance** (ahl-*kahn*-thay) *m* reach, range

**alcanzable** (ahl-kahn-*thah*-bhlay) *adj* attainable

**alcanzar** (ahl-kahn-*thahr*) *v* achieve, reach

**alce** (*ahl*-thay) *m* moose

**alcohol** (ahl-*koal*) *m* alcohol; ~ **de quemar** methylated spirits

**alcohólico** (ahl-*koa*-lee-koa) *adj* alcoholic

**aldea** (ahl-*day*-ah) *f* hamlet

**alegrar** (ah-lay-*grahr*) *v* cheer up

**alegre** (ah-*lay*-gray) *adj* cheerful, merry, joyful; glad, gay

**alegría** (ah-lay-*gree*-ah) *f* gaiety; gladness

**alejar** (ah-lay-*khahr*) *v* move away

**alemán** (ah-lay-*mahn*) *adj* German; *m* German

**Alemania** (ah-lay-*mah*-nᵛah) *f* Germany

**\*alentar** (ah-layn-*tahr*) *v* encourage

**alergia** (ah-*layr*-khᵛah) *f* allergy

**alfiler** (ahl-fee-*layr*) *m* pin

**alfombra** (ahl-*foam*-brah) *f* carpet

**alfombrilla** (ahl-foam-*bree*-lᵛah) *f* rug

**álgebra** (*ahl*-gay-bhrah) *f* algebra

**algo** (*ahl*-goa) *pron* something; *adv* somewhat

**algodón** (ahl-goa-*dhoan*) *m* cotton;

cotton-wool; **de** ~ cotton

**alguien** (*ahl*-gᵛayn) *pron* someone, somebody

**alguno** (ahl-*goo*-noa) *adj* any; **algunos** *adj* some; *pron* some

**alhaja** (ah-*lah*-khah) *f* gem

**alharaca** (ah-lah-*rah*-kah) *f* fuss

**aliado** (ah-*lᵛah*-dhoa) *m* associate; **Aliados** *mpl* Allies *pl*

**alianza** (ah-*lᵛahn*-thah) *f* alliance

**alicates** (ah-lee-*kah*-tayss) *mpl* pliers *pl*

**alienado** (ah-lᵛay-*nah*-dhoa) *m* lunatic

**aliento** (ah-*lᵛayn*-toa) *m* breath

**alimentar** (ah-lee-mayn-*tahr*) *v* \*feed

**alimento** (ah-lee-*mayn*-toa) *m* fare; food

**alivio** (ah-*lee*-bhᵛoa) *m* relief

**alma** (*ahl*-mah) *f* soul

**almacén** (ahl-mah-*thayn*) *m* depot, warehouse, depository, store-house; store; ~ **de licores** off-licence; **grandes almacenes** department store

**almacenaje** (ahl-mah-thay-*nah*-khay) *m* storage

**almacenar** (ahl-mah-thay-*nahr*) *v* store

**almanaque** (ahl-mah-*nah*-kay) *m* almanac

**almendra** (ahl-*mayn*-drah) *f* almond

**almidón** (ahl-mee-*dhoan*) *m* starch

**almidonar** (ahl-mee-dhoa-*nahr*) *v* starch

**almirante** (ahl-mee-*rahn*-tay) *m* admiral

**almohada** (ahl-moa-*ah*-dhah) *f* pillow; ~ **eléctrica** heating pad

**almohadilla** (ahl-moa-ah-*dhee*-lᵛah) *f* pad

**almohadón** (ahl-moa-ah-*dhoan*) *m* cushion; pillow

**almuerzo** (ahl-*mwayr*-thoa) *m* lunch, luncheon

**alojamiento** (ah-loa-khah-*mᵛayn*-toa)

*m* accommodation, lodgings *pl*

**alojar** (ah-loa-*khahr*) *v* lodge

**alondra** (ah-*loan*-drah) *f* lark

**alquilar** (ahl-kee-*lahr*) *v* hire; rent, lease, *let

**alquiler** (ahl-kee-*layr*) *m* rent; ~ **de coches** car hire; **de** ~ for hire

**alrededor de** (ahl-ray-dhay-*dhoar* day) around, round; about

**alrededores** (ahl-ray-dhay-*dhoa*-rayss) *mpl* environment, surroundings *pl*

**altar** (ahl-*tahr*) *m* altar

**altavoz** (ahl-tah-*bhoath*) *m* loud-speaker

**alteración** (ahl-tay-rah-*th<sup>y</sup>oan*) *f* alteration

**alterar** (ahl-tay-*rahr*) *v* alter

**alternar con** (ahl-tayr-*nahr*) mix with

**alternativa** (ahl-tayr-nah-*tee*-bhah) *f* alternative

**alternativo** (ahl-tayr-nah-*tee*-bhoa) *adj* alternate

**altiplano** (ahl-tee-*plah*-noa) *m* uplands *pl*

**altitud** (ahl-tee-*toodh*) *f* altitude

**altivo** (ahl-*tee*-bhoa) *adj* haughty

**alto** (*ahl*-toa) *adj* high, tall; **en** ~ overhead

**¡alto!** (*ahl*-toa) stop!

**altura** (ahl-*too*-rah) *f* height

**aludir a** (ah-loo-*dheer*) allude to

**alumbrado** (ah-loom-*brah*-dhoa) *m* lighting

**alumna** (ah-*loom*-nah) *f* schoolgirl

**alumno** (ah-*loom*-noa) *m* scholar, pupil; schoolboy

**alzar** (ahl-*thahr*) *v* raise

**allá** (ah-*l<sup>y</sup>ah*) *adv* over there; **más** ~ beyond; **más** ~ **de** past, beyond

**allí** (ah-*l<sup>y</sup>ee*) *adv* there

**amable** (ah-*mah*-bhlay) *adj* kind, friendly

**amado** (ah-*mah*-dhoa) *adj* dear

**amaestrar** (ah-mah-ayss-*trahr*) *v* train

**amamantar** (ah-mah-mahn-*tahr*) *v* nurse

**amanecer** (ah-mah-nay-*thayr*) *m* sunrise, daybreak

**amante** (ah-*mahn*-tay) *m* lover

**amapola** (ah-mah-*poa*-lah) *f* poppy

**amar** (ah-*mahr*) *v* love

**amargo** (ah-*mahr*-goa) *adj* bitter

**amarillo** (ah-mah-*ree*-l<sup>y</sup>oa) *adj* yellow

**amatista** (ah-mah-*teess*-tah) *f* amethyst

**ámbar** (*ahm*-bahr) *m* amber

**ambicioso** (ahm-bee-*th<sup>y</sup>oa*-soa) *adj* ambitious

**ambiente** (ahm-*b<sup>y</sup>ayn*-tay) *m* atmosphere

**ambiguo** (ahm-*bee*-gwoa) *adj* ambiguous

**ambos** (*ahm*-boass) *adj* both; either

**ambulancia** (ahm-boo-*lahn*-th<sup>y</sup>ah) *f* ambulance

**ambulante** (ahm-boo-*lahn*-tay) *adj* itinerant

**amenaza** (ah-may-*nah*-thah) *f* threat

**amenazador** (ah-may-nah-thah-*dhoar*) *adj* threatening

**amenazar** (ah-may-nah-*thahr*) *v* threaten

**ameno** (ah-*may*-noa) *adj* nice

**América** (ah-*may*-ree-kah) *f* America; ~ **Latina** Latin America

**americana** (ah-may-ree-*kah*-nah) *f* jacket

**americano** (ah-may-ree-*kah*-noa) *adj* American; *m* American

**amiga** (ah-*mee*-gah) *f* friend

**amígdalas** (ah-*meeg*-dhah-lahss) *fpl* tonsils *pl*

**amigdalitis** (ah-meeg-dhah-*lee*-teess) *f* tonsilitis

**amigo** (ah-*mee*-goa) *m* friend

**amistad** (ah-meess-*tahdh*) *f* friendship

**amistoso** (ah-meess-*toa*-soa) *adj* friendly

**amnistía** (ahm-neess-*tee*-ah ) *f* amnesty

**amo** (*ah*-moa ) *m* master

**amoníaco** (ah-moa-*nee*-ah-koa) *m* ammonia

**amontonar** (ah-moan-toa-*nahr*) *v* pile

**amor** (ah-*moar*) *m* love; darling, sweetheart

**amorío** (ah-moa-*ree*-oa) *m* affair, romance

**amortiguador** (ah-moar-tee-gwah-*dhoar*) *m* shock absorber

**amortizar** (ah-moar-tee-*thahr*) *v* \*pay off

**amotinamiento** (ah-moa-tee-nah-*mʸayn*-toa) *m* mutiny

**ampliación** (ahm-plʸah-*thʸoan*) *f* enlargement; extension

**ampliar** (ahm-*plʸahr*) *v* enlarge; extend

**amplio** (*ahm*-plʸoa) *adj* broad

**ampolla** (ahm-*poa*-lʸah ) *f* blister

**amueblar** (ah-mway-*bhlahr*) *v* furnish

**amuleto** (ah-moo-*lay*-toa) *m* charm

**analfabeto** (ah-nahl-fah-*bhay*-toa) *m* illiterate

**análisis** (ah-*nah*-lee-seess ) *f* analysis

**analista** (ah-nah-*leess*-tah) *m* analyst

**analizar** (ah-nah-lee-*thahr*) *v* analyse; \*break down

**análogo** (ah-*nah*-loa-goa) *adj* similar

**anarquía** (ah-nahr-*kee*-ah) *f* anarchy

**anatomía** (ah-nah-toa-*mee*-ah) *f* anatomy

**anciano** (ahn-*thʸah*-noa) *adj* aged; elderly

**ancla** (*ahng*-klah) *f* anchor

**ancho** (*ahn*-choa) *adj* broad; wide; *m* breadth

**anchoa** (ahn-*choa*-ah) *f* anchovy

**anchura** (ahn-*choo*-rah) *f* width

**andadura** (ahn-dah-*dhoo*-rah) *f* walk

**andamio** (ahn-*dah*-mʸoa) *m* scaffolding

**\* andar** (ahn-*dahr*) *v* walk

**andares** (ahn-*dah*-rayss ) *mpl* pace

**andén** (ahn-*dayn*) *m* platform

**anemia** (ah-*nay*-mʸah ) *f* anaemia

**anestesia** (ah-nayss-*tay*-sʸah ) *f* anaesthesia

**anestésico** (ah-ayss-*tay*-see-koa ) *m* anaesthetic

**anexar** (ah-nayk-*sahr*) *v* annex

**anexo** (ah-*nayk*-soa) *m* annex, enclosure

**anfitrión** (ahn-fee-*trʸoan*) *m* host

**ángel** (*ahng*-khayl) *m* angel

**angosto** (ahng-*goass*-toa) *adj* narrow, tight

**anguila** (ahng-*gee*-lah) *f* eel

**ángulo** (*ahng*-goo-loa) *m* angle

**angustioso** (ahng-gooss-*tʸoa*-soa) *adj* afraid

**anhelar** (ah-nay-*lahr*) *v* desire, long for

**anhelo** (ah-*nay*-loa) *m* longing

**anillo** (ah-*nee*-lʸoa) *m* ring; ~ **de boda** wedding-ring; ~ **de esponsales** engagement ring

**animado** (ah-nee-*mah*-dhoa) *adj* crowded

**animal** (ah-nee-*mahl*) *m* beast, animal; ~ **de presa** beast of prey; ~ **doméstico** pet

**animar** (ah-nee-*mahr*) *v* encourage, inspire; animate

**ánimo** (*ah*-nee-moa) *m* mind; courage

**aniversario** (ah-nee-bhayr-*sah*-rʸoa) *m* anniversary; jubilee

**anoche** (ah-*noa*-chay) *adv* last night

**anomalía** (ah-noa-mah-*lee*-ah ) *f* aberration

**anónimo** (ah-*noa*-nee-moa) *adj* anonymous

**anormal** (ah-noar-*mahl*) *adj* abnormal

**anotación** (ah-noa-tah-*thʸoan*) *f* entry

**anotar** (ah-noa-*tahr*) *v* \*write down

**ansia** (*ahn*-sʸah ) *f* anxiety

**ansioso** (ahn-*sʸoa*-soa) *adj* anxious, eager

**ante** (*ahn*-tay) *prep* in front of

**anteayer** (ahn-tay-ah-*ᵞ*ayr) *adv* the day before yesterday

**antecedentes** (ahn-tay-thay-*dhayn*-tayss) *mpl* background

**antena** (ahn-*tay*-nah) *f* aerial

**anteojos** (ahn-tay-*oa*-khoass) *mpl* spectacles, glasses

**antepasado** (ahn-tay-pah-*sah*-dhoa) *m* ancestor

**antepecho** (ahn-tay-*pay*-choa) *m* window-sill

**anterior** (ahn-tay-*r*ᵞoar) *adj* former, prior, previous

**antes** (*ahn*-tayss) *adv* before; formerly; at first; ~ **de** before; ~ **de que** before

**antibiótico** (ahn-tee-*bh*ᵞoa-tee-koa) *m* antibiotic

**anticipar** (ahn-tee-thee-*pahr*) *v* advance

**anticipo** (ahn-tee-*thee*-poa) *m* advance

**anticonceptivo** (ahn-tee-koan-thayp-tee-bhoa) *m* contraceptive

**anticongelante** (ahn-tee-koang-khay-*lahn*-tay) *m* antifreeze

**anticuado** (ahn-tee-*kwah*-dhoa) *adj* old-fashioned; ancient, out of date, quaint

**anticuario** (ahn-tee-*kwah*-rᵞoa) *m* antique dealer

**antigualla** (ahn-tee-*gwah*-lᵞah) *f* antique

**Antigüedad** (ahn-tee-gway-*dhahdh*) *f* antiquity

**antigüedades** (ahn-tee-gway-*dhah*-dhayss) *fpl* antiquities *pl*

**antiguo** (ahn-*tee*-gwoa) *adj* ancient, antique; former

**antipatía** (ahn-tee-pah-*tee*-ah) *f* antipathy, dislike

**antipático** (ahn-tee-*pah*-tee-koa) *adj* nasty, unpleasant

**antiséptico** (ahn-tee-*sayp*-tee-koa) *m* antiseptic

**antojarse** (ahn-toa-*khahr*-say) *v* fancy, *feel like

**antojo** (ahn-*toa*-khoa) *m* fad, whim

**antología** (ahn-toa-loa-*khee*-ah) *f* anthology

**antorcha** (ahn-*toar*-chah) *f* torch

**anual** (ah-*nwahl*) *adj* annual, yearly

**anuario** (ah-*nwah*-ree-oa) *m* annual

**anudar** (ah-noo-*dhahr*) *v* tie; knot

**anular** (ah-noo-*lahr*) *v* cancel

**anunciar** (ah-noon-*th*ᵞahr) *v* announce

**anuncio** (ah-*noon*-thᵞoa) *m* announcement; advertisement

**anzuelo** (ahn-*thway*-loa) *m* fishing hook

**añadir** (ah-ñah-*dheer*) *v* add

**año** (*ah*-ñoa) *m* year; **al** ~ per annum; ~ **bisiesto** leap-year; ~ **nuevo** New Year

**apagado** (ah-pah-*gah*-dhoa) *adj* mat

**apagar** (ah-pah-*gahr*) *v* extinguish; *put out, switch off

**aparato** (ah-pah-*rah*-toa) *m* appliance, apparatus; machine

**aparcamiento** (ah-pahr-kah-*m*ᵞayn-toa) *m* parking; **zona de** ~ parking zone

***aparecer** (ah-pah-ray-*thayr*) *v* appear

**aparejo** (ah-pah-*ray*-khoa) *m* gear; ~ **de pesca** fishing tackle

**aparente** (ah-pah-*rayn*-tay) *adj* apparent

**aparición** (ah-pah-ree-*th*ᵞoan) *f* apparition

**apariencia** (ah-pah-*r*ᵞayn-thᵞah) *f* appearance, semblance

**apartado** (ah-pahr-*tah*-dhoa) *adj* out of the way

**apartamento** (ah-pahr-tah-*mayn*-toa) *m* suite; apartment *nAm*

**apartar** (ah-pahr-*tahr*) *v* separate

**aparte** (ah-*pahr*-tay) *adv* aside; *adj* individual

**apasionado** (ah-pah-sᵞoa-*nah*-dhoa)

*adj* passionate

**apearse** (ah-pay-*ahr*-say) *v* *get off

**apelación** (ah-pay-lah-*th<sup>y</sup>oan*) *f* appeal

**apelmazado** (ah-payl-mah-*thah*-dhoa) *adj* lumpy

**apellido** (ah-pay-*l<sup>y</sup>ee*-dhoa) *m* family name, surname; ~ **de soltera** maiden name

**apenado** (ah-pay-*nah*-dhoa) *adj* sorry

**apenas** (ah-*pay*-nahss) *adv* hardly, barely, scarcely; just

**apéndice** (ah-*payn*-dee-thay) *m* appendix

**apendicitis** (ah-payn-dee-*thee*-teess) *f* appendicitis

**aperitivo** (ah-pay-ree-*tee*-bhoa) *m* aperitif, drink

**apertura** (ah-payr-*too*-rah) *f* opening

**apestar** (ah-payss-*tahr*) *v* *stink

**apetito** (ah-pay-*tee*-toa) *m* appetite

**apetitoso** (ah-pay-tee-*toa*-soa) *adj* appetizing

**apio** (*ah*-p<sup>y</sup>oa) *m* celery

**aplaudir** (ah-plou-*dheer*) *v* clap

**aplauso** (ah-*plou*-soa) *m* applause

**aplazar** (ah-plah-*thahr*) *v* postpone, adjourn, *put off

**aplicación** (ah-plee-kah-*s<sup>y</sup>oan*) *f* application

**aplicar** (ah-plee-*kahr*) *v* apply; **aplicarse a** apply, *be valid for

**apogeo** (ah-poa-*khayoa*) *m* height; zenith; ~ **de la temporada** peak season

**apostar** (ah-poass-*tahr*) *v* *bet

**apoyar** (ah-poa-*<sup>y</sup>ahr*) *v* support; **apoyarse** *v* *lean

**apoyo** (ah-*poa*-<sup>y</sup>oa) *m* support; assistance

**apreciar** (ah-pray-*th<sup>y</sup>ahr*) *v* appreciate

**aprecio** (ah-*pray*-th<sup>y</sup>oa) *m* appreciation

**aprender** (ah-prayn-*dayr*) *v* *learn; **aprenderse de memoria** memorize

**apresar** (ah-pray-*sahr*) *v* hijack

**apresurado** (ah-pray-soo-*rah*-dhoa) *adj* hasty

**apresurarse** (ah-pray-soo-*rahr*-say) *v* hasten, hurry

**apretado** (ah-pray-*tah*-dhoa) *adj* tight

**apretar** (ah-pray-*tahr*) *v* press; tighten

**apretón** (ah-pray-*toan*) *m* clutch; ~ **de manos** handshake

**aprobación** (ah-proa-bhah-*th<sup>y</sup>oan*) *f* approval

**aprobar** (ah-proa-*bhahr*) *v* approve; pass

**apropiado** (ah-proa-*p<sup>y</sup>ah*-dhoa) *adj* appropriate, suitable, proper; fit

**aprovechar** (ah-proa-bhay-*chahr*) *v* profit, benefit

**aproximadamente** (ah-proak-see-mah-dhah-*mayn*-tay) *adv* about, approximately

**aproximado** (ah-proak-see-*mah*-dhoa) *adj* approximate

**aptitud** (ahp-tee-*toodh*) *f* qualification; faculty

**apto** (*ahp*-toa) *adj* suitable; *ser ~ **para** qualify

**apuesta** (ah-*pwayss*-tah) *f* bet

**apuntar** (ah-poon-*tahr*) *v* aim at; point out

**apunte** (ah-*poon*-tay) *m* note; memo; **libreta de apuntes** notebook

**aquel** (ah-*kayl*) *adj* that; **aquellos** *adj* those

**aquél** (ah-*kayl*) *pron* that; **aquéllos** *pron* those

**aquí** (ah-*kee*) *adv* here

**árabe** (*ah*-rah-bhay) *adj* Arab; *m* Arab

**Arabia Saudí** (ah-*rah*-bh<sup>y</sup>ah sou-*dhee*) Saudi Arabia

**arado** (ah-*rah*-dhoa) *m* plough

**arancel** (ah-rahn-*thayl*) *m* tariff; duty

**araña** (ah-*rah*-ñah) *f* spider; **tela de ~**

cobweb

**arar** (ah-*rahr*) v plough

**arbitrario** (ahr-bhee-*trah*-rʸoa) adj arbitrary

**árbitro** (*ahr*-bhee-troa) m umpire

**árbol** (*ahr*-bhoal) m tree; ~ **de levas** camshaft

**arbolado** (ahr-bhoa-*lah*-dhoa) m woodland

**arbusto** (ahr-*bhooss*-toa) m shrub

**arca** (*ahr*-kah) f chest

**arcada** (ahr-*kah*-dhah) f arcade

**arce** (*ahr*-thay) m maple

**arcilla** (ahr-*thee*-lʸah) f clay

**arco** (*ahr*-koa) m arch, bow; ~ **iris** rainbow

**archivo** (ahr-*chee*-bhoa) m archives pl

**arder** (ahr-*dhayr*) v *burn

**ardilla** (ahr-*dhee*-lʸah) f squirrel

**área** (*ah*-ray-ah) f area; are

**arena** (ah-*ray*-nah) f sand

**arenoso** (ah-ray-*noa*-soa) adj sandy

**arenque** (ah-*rayng*-kay) m herring

**Argelia** (ahr-*khay*-lʸah) f Algeria

**argelino** (ahr-khay-*lee*-noa) adj Algerian; m Algerian

**Argentina** (ahr-khayn-*tee*-nah) f Argentina

**argentino** (ahr-khayn-*tee*-noa) adj Argentinian; m Argentinian

**argumentar** (ahr-goo-mayn-*tahr*) v argue

**argumento** (ahr-goo-*mayn*-toa) m argument

**árido** (*ah*-ree-dhoa) adj arid

**arisco** (ah-*reess*-koa) adj unkind

**aritmética** (ah-reet-*may*-tee-kah) f arithmetic

**arma** (*ahr*-mah) f weapon, arm

**armador** (ahr-mah-*dhoar*) m shipowner

**armadura** (ahr-mah-*dhoo*-rah) f frame; armour

**armar** (ahr-*mahr*) v arm

**armario** (ahr-*mah*-rʸoa) m cupboard; closet

**armonía** (ahr-moa-*nee*-ah) f harmony

**aroma** (ah-*roa*-mah) m aroma

**arpa** (*ahr*-pah) f harp

**arqueado** (ahr-kay-ah-dhoa) adj arched

**arqueología** (ahr-kay-oa-loa-*khee*-ah) f archaeology

**arqueólogo** (ahr-kay-*oa*-loa-goa) m archaeologist

**arquitecto** (ahr-kee-*tayk*-toa) m architect

**arquitectura** (ahr-kee-tayk-*too*-rah) f architecture

**arraigarse** (ah-rrigh-*gahr*-say) v settle down

**arrancar** (ah-rrahng-*kahr*) v uproot, pull out; start off

**arranque** (ah-*rrahng*-kay) m starter motor

**arrastrar** (ah-rrahss-*trahr*) v haul, drag; *draw; **arrastrarse** v crawl

**arrecife** (ah-rray-*thee*-fay) m reef

**arreglar** (ah-rray-*glahr*) v settle; tidy up; repair, fix; **arreglarse con** *make do with

**arreglo** (ah-*rray*-gloa) m arrangement; settlement; **con ~ a** in accordance with

**arrendamiento** (ah-rrayn-dah-*mʸayn*-toa) m lease; **contrato de ~** lease

*  **arrendar** (ah-rrayn-*dahr*) v lease

**arrepentimiento** (ah-rray-payn-tee-*mʸayn*-toa) m regret, repentance

**arrestar** (ah-rrayss-*tahr*) v arrest

**arresto** (ah-*rrayss*-toa) m arrest

**arriar** (ah-*rʸahr*) v *strike, lower

**arriate** (ah-*rʸah*-tay) m flowerbed

**arriba** (ah-*rree*-bhah) adv upstairs; up

**arriesgado** (ah-rryayz-*gah*-dhoa) adj risky

**arriesgar** (ah-rrʸayz-*gahr*) v venture, risk

**arrodillarse** (ah-rroa-dhee-*l*ᵛahr-say) *v* *kneel

**arrogante** (ah-rroa-*gahn*-tay) *adj* snooty

**arrojar** (ah-rroa-*khahr*) *v* *throw

**arroyo** (ah-*rroa*-ᵛoa) *m* stream, brook

**arroz** (ah-*rroath*) *m* rice

**arruga** (ah-*rroo*-gah) *f* wrinkle

**arrugar** (ah-rroo-*gahr*) *v* wrinkle

**arruinar** (ah-rrwee-*nahr*) *v* ruin; **arruinado** broke

**arte** (*ahr*-tay) *m/f* art; **artes industriales** arts and crafts; **bellas artes** fine arts

**arteria** (ahr-*tay*-rᵛah) *f* artery; ~ **principal** thoroughfare

**artesanía** (ahr-tay-sah-*nee*-ah) *f* handicraft

**articulación** (ahr-tee-koo-lah-*th*ᵛoan) *f* joint

**artículo** (ahr-*tee*-koo-loa) *m* article

**artificial** (ahr-tee-fee-*th*ᵛahl) *adj* artificial

**artificio** (ahr-tee-*fee*-th*ᵛoa*) *m* artifice

**artista** (ahr-*teess*-tah) *m/f* artist

**artístico** (ahr-*teess*-tee-koa) *adj* artistic

**arzobispo** (ahr-thoa-*bheess*-poa) *m* archbishop

**asamblea** (ah-sahm-*blay*-ah) *f* assembly, meeting

**asar** (ah-*sahr*) *v* roast; ~ **en parrilla** roast

**asbesto** (ahdh-*bhayss*-toa) *m* asbestos

**ascensor** (ah-thayn-*soar*) *m* lift; elevator *nAm*

**aseado** (ah-say-*ah*-dhoa) *adj* tidy

**asegurar** (ah-say-goo-*rahr*) *v* assure, insure; **asegurarse de** ascertain

**asemejarse** (ah-say-may-*khahr*-say) *v* resemble

**asesinar** (ah-say-see-*nahr*) *v* murder

**asesinato** (ah-say-see-*nah*-toa) *m* murder, assassination

**asesino** (ah-say-*see*-noa) *m* murderer

**asfalto** (ahss-*fahl*-toa) *m* asphalt

**así** (ah-*see*) *adv* thus, so; ~ **que** so that

**Asia** (*ah*-sᵛah) *f* Asia

**asiático** (ah-sᵛah-tee-koa) *adj* Asian; *m* Asian

**asiento** (ah-sᵛayn-toa) *m* seat

**asignación** (ah-seeg-nah-*th*ᵛoan) *f* allowance

**asignar** (ah-seeg-*nahr*) *v* allot; ~ **a** assign to

**asilo** (ah-*see*-loa) *m* asylum

**asimismo** (ah-see-*meez*-moa) *adv* also, likewise

***asir** (ah-*seer*) *v* grip

**asistencia** (ah-seess-*tayn*-thᵛah) *f* attendance; assistance

**asistente** (ah-seess-*tayn*-tay) *m* assistant

**asistir** (ah-seess-*teer*) *v* assist, aid; ~ **a** assist at, attend

**asma** (*ahz*-mah) *f* asthma

**asociación** (ah-soa-thᵛah-*th*ᵛoan) *f* association; club, society

**asociado** (ah-soa-*th*ᵛah-dhoa) *m* associate

**asociar** (ah-soa-*th*ᵛahr) *v* associate; **asociarse a** join

**asombrar** (ah-soam-*brahr*) *v* amaze, astonish

**asombro** (ah-*soam*-broa) *m* amazement; wonder

**asombroso** (ah-soam-*broa*-soa) *adj* astonishing

**aspecto** (ahss-*payk*-toa) *m* aspect; appearance, look; sight

**áspero** (*ahss*-pay-roa) *adj* harsh; rough

**aspiración** (ahss-pee-rah-*th*ᵛoan) *f* inhalation; aspiration

**aspirador** (ahss-pee-rah-*dhoar*) *m* vacuum cleaner; **pasar el** ~ hoover

**aspirar** (ahss-pee-*rahr*) *v* aspire; ~ **a** aim at

**aspirina** (ahss-pee-*ree*-nah ) *f* aspirin

**asqueroso** (ahss-kay-*roa*-soa) *adj* disgusting

**astilla** (ahss-*tee*-l<sup>y</sup>ah ) *f* splinter; chip

**astillar** (ahss-tee-l<sup>y</sup>ahr) *v* chip

**astillero** (ahss-tee-l<sup>y</sup>ay-roa ) *m* shipyard

**astronomía** (ahss-troa-noa-*mee*-ah ) *f* astronomy

**astucia** (ahss-*too*-th<sup>y</sup>ah ) *f* ruse

**astuto** (ahss-*too*-toa) *adj* cunning; clever, sly

**asunto** (ah-*soon*-toa) *m* affair, matter; concern, business; topic

**asustado** (ah-sooss-*tah*-dhoa) *adj* afraid

**asustar** (ah-sooss-*tahr*) *v* scare; **asustarse** *v* *be frightened

**atacar** (ah-tah-*kahr*) *v* attack, assault; *strike

**atadura** (ah-tah-*dhoo*-rah ) *f* binding

**atañer** (ah-tah-*ñayr*) *v* concern

**ataque** (ah-*tah*-kay ) *m* attack, fit; stroke; ~ **cardíaco** heart attack

**atar** (ah-*tahr*) *v* tie, *bind; fasten; bundle

**atareado** (ah-tah-ray-*ah*-dhoa) *adj* busy

**atención** (ah-tayn-*th<sup>y</sup>oan*) *f* attention; consideration, notice; **prestar** ~ *pay attention, look out

***atender a** (ah-tayn-*dayr*) attend to, see to; nurse

**atento** (ah-*tayn*-toa) *adj* attentive; thoughtful

**ateo** (ah-*tay*-oa) *m* atheist

**aterido** (ah-tay-*ree*-dhoa) *adj* numb

**aterrador** (ah-tay-rrah-*dhoar*) *adj* terrifying

**aterrizar** (ah-tay-rree-*thahr*) *v* land

**aterrorizar** (ah-tay-rroa-ree-*thahr*) *v* terrify

**Atlántico** (aht-*lahn*-tee-koa) *m* Atlantic

**atleta** (aht-*lay*-tah) *m* athlete

**atletismo** (aht-lay-*teez*-moa) *m* athletics *pl*

**atmósfera** (aht-*moass*-fay-rah) *f* atmosphere

**atómico** (ah-*toa*-mee-koa) *adj* atomic

**átomo** (*ah*-toa-moa) *m* atom

**atónito** (ah-*toa*-nee-toa) *adj* speechless

**atontado** (ah-toan-*tah*-dhoa) *adj* dumb

**atormentar** (ah-toar-mayn-*tahr*) *v* torment

**atornillar** (ah-toar-nee-l<sup>y</sup>ahr) *v* screw

**atracar** (ah-trah-*kahr*) *v* dock

**atracción** (ah-trahk-*th<sup>y</sup>oan*) *f* attraction

**atraco** (ah-*trah*-koa) *m* hold-up

**atractivo** (ah-trahk-*tee*-bhoa) *adj* attractive

***atraer** (ah-trah-*ayr*) *v* attract

**atrapar** (ah-trah-*pahr*) *v* contract

**atrás** (ah-*trahss*) *adv* back

**atrasado** (ah-trah-*sah*-dhoa) *adj* overdue

***atravesar** (ah-trah-bhay-*sahr*) *v* cross, pass through

**atreverse** (ah-tray-*bhayr*-say) *v* dare

**atrevido** (ah-tray-*bhee*-dhoa) *adj* daring

***atribuir a** (ah-tree-*bhweer*) assign to

**atroz** (ah-*troath*) *adj* horrible

**atún** (ah-*toon*) *m* tuna

**audacia** (ou-*dhah*-th<sup>y</sup>ah ) *f* nerve

**audaz** (ou-*dhahth*) *adj* bold

**audible** (ou-*dhee*-bhlay) *adj* audible

**auditorio** (ou-dhee-*toa*-r<sup>y</sup>oa ) *m* audience

**aula** (*ou*-lah) *f* auditorium

**aumentar** (ou-mayn-*tahr*) *v* increase, raise

**aumento** (ou-*mayn*-toa) *m* increase; rise; raise *nAm*

**aun** (ah-*oon*) *adv* (aún) yet; even

**aunque** (*oung*-kay) *conj* although, though

**aurora** (ou-*roa*-rah) f dawn
**ausencia** (ou-*sayn*-thᵞah) f absence
**ausente** (ou-*sayn*-tay) adj absent
**Australia** (ouss-trah-lᵞah) f Australia
**australiano** (ouss-trah-lᵞah-noa) adj Australian; m Australian
**Austria** (ouss-trᵞah) f Austria
**austríaco** (ouss-*tree*-ah-koa) adj Austrian; m Austrian
**auténtico** (ou-*tayn*-tee-koa) adj authentic; true, original
**auto** (*ou*-toa) m car
**autobús** (ou-toa-*bhooss*) m coach, bus
**autoestopista** (ou-toa-ayss-toa-*peess*-tah) m hitchhiker
**automático** (ou-toa-*mah*-tee-koa) adj automatic
**automatización** (ou-toa-mah-tee-thah-thᵞoan) f automation
**automóvil** (ou-toa-*moa*-bheel) m motor-car, automobile; ~ **club** automobile club
**automovilismo** (ou-toa-moa-bhee-*leez*-moa) m motoring
**automovilista** (ou-toa-moa-bhee-*leess*-tah) m motorist
**autonomía** (ou-toa-noa-*mee*-ah) f self-government
**autónomo** (ou-*toa*-noa-moa) adj independent, autonomous
**autopista** (ou-toa-*peess*-tah) f motorway; highway nAm; ~ **de peaje** turnpike nAm
**autopsia** (ou-*toap*-sᵞah) f autopsy
**autor** (ou-*toar*) m author
**autoridad** (ou-toa-ree-*dhahdh*) f authority
**autoritario** (ou-toa-ree-*tah*-rᵞoa) adj authoritarian
**autorización** (ou-toa-ree-thah-thᵞoan) f authorization; permission
**autorizar** (ou-toa-ree-*thahr*) v allow; license
**autoservicio** (ou-toa-sayr-*bhee*-thᵞoa) m self-service
*****hacer autostop** (ah-*thayr* ou-toa-*stoap*) hitchhike
**auxilio** (ouk-*see*-lᵞoa) m assistance; **primeros auxilios** first-aid
**avalancha** (ah-bhah-*lahn*-chah) f avalanche
**avanzar** (ah-bhahn-*thahr*) v advance
**avaro** (ah-*bhah*-roa) adj avaricious
**avefría** (ah-bhay-*free*-ah) f pewit
**avellana** (ah-bhay-lᵞah-nah) f hazelnut
**avena** (ah-*bhay*-nah) f oats pl
**avenida** (ah-bhay-*nee*-dhah) f avenue
**aventura** (ah-bhayn-*too*-rah) f adventure
*****avergonzarse** (ah-bhayr-goan-*thahr*-say) v *be ashamed
**avería** (ah-bhay-*ree*-ah) f breakdown
**averiarse** (ah-bhay-rᵞahr-say) v *break down; **averiado** adj out of order
**aversión** (ah-bhayr-sᵞoan) f aversion, dislike
**avestruz** (ah-bhayss-*trooth*) m ostrich
**avión** (ah-*bhᵞoan*) m aeroplane; aircraft, plane; airplane nAm; ~ **a reacción** jet; ~ **turborreactor** turbojet
**avíos** (ah-*bhee*-oass) mpl kit; ~ **de pesca** fishing gear
**avisar** (ah-bhee-*sahr*) v inform
**aviso** (ah-*bhee*-soa) m notice
**avispa** (ah-*bheess*-pah) f wasp
**aya** (*ah*-ᵞah) f governess
**ayer** (ah-ᵞayr) adv yesterday
**ayuda** (ah-ᵞoo-dhah) f help; relief; ~ **de cámara** valet
**ayudante** (ah-ᵞoo-*dhahn*-tay) m helper
**ayudar** (ah-ᵞoo-*dhahr*) v aid, help
**ayuntamiento** (ah-ᵞoon-tah-mᵞayn-toa) m town hall
**azada** (ah-*thah*-dhah) f spade
**azafata** (ah-thah-*fah*-tah) f hostess; stewardess
**azar** (ah-*thahr*) m chance, luck

**azor** (ah-*thoar*) *m* hawk
**azote** (ah-*thoa*-tay) *m* whip
**azúcar** (ah-*thoo*-kahr) *m/f* sugar; **terrón de** ~ lump of sugar
**azucena** (ah-thoo-*thay*-nah) *f* lily
**azul** (ah-*thool*) *adj* blue
**azulejo** (ah-thoo-*lay*-khoa) *m* tile

# B

**babor** (bah-*bhoar*) *m* port
**bacalao** (bah-kah-*lah*-oa) *m* cod; haddock
**bacteria** (bahk-*tay*-r<sup>y</sup>ah) *f* bacterium
**bache** (*bah*-chay) *m* hole
**bahía** (bah-*ee*-ah) *f* bay
**bailar** (bigh-*lahr*) *v* dance
**baile** (*bigh*-lay) *m* ball; dance
**baja** (*bah*-khah) *f* slump
**bajada** (bah-*khah*-dhah) *f* descent
**bajamar** (bah-khah-*mahr*) *f* low tide
**bajar** (bah-*khahr*) *v* lower; **bajarse** *v* *bend down
**bajo** (*bah*-khoa) *adj* low; short; *prep* under, below; *m* bass
**bala** (*bah*-lah) *f* bullet
**baladí** (bah-lah-*dhee*) *adj* insignificant
**balance** (bah-*lahn*-thay) *m* balance
**balanza** (bah-*lahn*-thah) *f* scales *pl*
**balbucear** (bahl-bhoo-thay-*ahr*) *v* falter
**balcón** (bahl-*koan*) *m* balcony; circle
**balde** (*bahl*-day) *m* pail, bucket
**baldío** (bahl-*dee*-oa) *adj* waste
**balneario** (bahl-nay-*ah*-r<sup>y</sup>oa) *m* spa
**ballena** (bah-*l<sup>y</sup>ay*-nah) *f* whale
**ballet** (bah-*lay*) *m* ballet
**bambú** (bahm-*boo*) *m* bamboo
**banco** (*bahng*-koa) *m* bank; bench
**banda** (*bahn*-dah) *f* band; gang
**bandeja** (bahn-*day*-khah) *f* tray
**bandera** (bahn-*day*-rah) *f* flag; banner
**bandido** (bahn-*dee*-dhoa) *m* bandit

**banquete** (bahng-*kay*-tay) *m* banquet
**bañador** (bah-ñah-*dhoar*) *m* bathing-trunks
**bañarse** (bah-*ñahr*-say) *v* bathe
**baño** (*bah*-ñoa) *m* bath; *mMe* bathroom; ~ **turco** Turkish bath; **calzón de** ~ swimming-trunks; **traje de** ~ swim-suit
**bar** (bahr) *m* bar; saloon, café
**barajar** (bah-rah-*khahr*) *v* shuffle
**baranda** (bah-*rahn*-dah) *f* banisters *pl*
**barandilla** (bah-rahn-dee-*l<sup>y</sup>ah*) *f* rail; railing
**barato** (bah-*rah*-toa) *adj* inexpensive, cheap
**barba** (*bahr*-bhah) *f* beard
**barbero** (bahr-*bhay*-roa) *m* barber
**barbilla** (bahr-*bhee*-l<sup>y</sup>ah) *f* chin
**barca** (*bahr*-kah) *f* boat
**barco** (*bahr*-koa) *m* boat
**barítono** (bah-*ree*-toa-noa) *m* baritone
**barman** (*bahr*-mahn) *m* bartender, barman
**barniz** (bahr-*neeth*) *m* varnish; ~ **para las uñas** nail-polish
**barnizar** (bahr-nee-*thahr*) *v* varnish
**barómetro** (bah-*roa*-may-troa) *m* barometer
**barquillo** (bahr-*kee*-l<sup>y</sup>oa) *m* waffle
**barra** (*bah*-rrah) *f* bar, rod; counter
**barrer** (bah-*rrayr*) *v* *sweep
**barrera** (bah-*rray*-rah) *f* barrier, rail; ~ **de protección** crash barrier
**barril** (bah-*rreel*) *m* barrel, cask
**barrilete** (bah-rree-*lay*-tay) *m* keg
**barrio** (*bah*-rr<sup>y</sup>oa) *m* quarter, district; ~ **bajo** slum
**barroco** (bah-*rroa*-koa) *adj* baroque
**barrote** (bah-*rroa*-tay) *m* bar
**basar** (bah-*sahr*) *v* base
**báscula** (*bahss*-koo-lah) *f* weighing-machine
**base** (*bah*-say) *f* basis, base
**basílica** (bah-*see*-lee-kah) *f* basilica

**bastante** (bahss-*tahn*-tay) *adv* enough, sufficient; fairly, pretty, rather, quite

**bastar** (bahss-*tahr*) *v* suffice

**bastardo** (bahss-*tahr*-dhoa) *m* bastard

**bastón** (bahss-*toan*) *m* cane; walking-stick; **bastones de esquí** ski sticks

**basura** (bah-*soo*-rah) *f* trash, rubbish, garbage; **cubo de la ∼** rubbish-bin

**bata** (*bah*-tah) *f* dressing-gown; **∼ de baño** bathrobe; **∼ suelta** negligee

**batalla** (bah-*tah*-lʸah) *f* battle

**batería** (bah-tay-*ree*-ah) *f* battery

**batidora** (bah-tee-*dhoa*-rah) *f* mixer

**batir** (bah-*teer*) *v* *beat, whip

**baúl** (bah-*ool*) *m* trunk

**bautismo** (bou-*teez*-moa) *m* baptism

**bautizar** (bou-tee-*thahr*) *v* christen, baptize

**bautizo** (bou-*tee*-thoa) *m* christening, baptism

**baya** (*bah*-ʸah) *f* berry

**bebé** (bay-*bhay*) *m* baby

**beber** (bay-*bhayr*) *v* *drink

**bebida** (bay-*bhee*-dhah) *f* drink, beverage; **∼ no alcohólica** soft drink; **bebidas espirituosas** spirits

**beca** (*bay*-kah) *f* grant, scholarship

**becerro** (bay-*thay*-rroa) *m* calf skin

**beige** (*bay*-khay) *adj* beige

**béisbol** (*bayz*-bhoal) *m* baseball

**belga** (*bayl*-gah) *adj* Belgian; *m* Belgian

**Bélgica** (*bayl*-khee-kah) *f* Belgium

**belleza** (bay-*lʸay*-thah) *f* beauty; **salón de ∼** beauty salon

**bello** (*bay*-lʸoa) *adj* fine

**bellota** (bay-*lʸoa*-tah) *f* acorn

***bendecir** (bayn-day-*theer*) *v* bless

**bendición** (bayn-dee-*th*ʸ*oan*) *f* blessing

**beneficio** (bay-nay-*fee*-th*ʸoa*) *m* profit, benefit

**berenjena** (bay-rayng-*khay*-nah) *f* egg-plant

**berro** (*bay*-rroa) *m* watercress

**besar** (bay-*sahr*) *v* kiss

**beso** (*bay*-soa) *m* kiss

**betún** (bay-*toon*) *m* shoe polish

**biblia** (*bee*-bhlʸah) *f* bible

**biblioteca** (bee-bhlʸoa-*tay*-kah) *f* library

**bicicleta** (bee-thee-*klay*-tah) *f* cycle, bicycle

**biciclo** (bee-*thee*-kloa) *m* cycle, bicycle

**bicimotor** (bee-thee-moa-*toar*) *m* moped

**biela** (*bʸay*-lah) *f* piston-rod

**bien** (bʸayn) *adv* well; **¡bien!** all right!; **bien … bien** either … or

**bienes** (*bʸay*-nayss) *mpl* goods *pl*; possessions

**bienestar** (bʸay-nayss-*tahr*) *m* ease; welfare

**bienvenida** (bʸayn-bhay-*nee*-dhah) *f* welcome; ***dar la ∼** welcome

**bienvenido** (bʸayn-bhay-*nee*-dhoa) *adj* welcome

**biftec** (beef-*tayk*) *m* steak

**bifurcación** (bee-foor-kah-*th*ʸ*oan*) *f* road fork, fork

**bifurcarse** (bee-foor-*kahr*-say) *v* fork

**bigote** (bee-*goatay*) *m* moustache

**bilingüe** (bee-*leeng*-gway) *adj* bilingual

**bilis** (*bee*-leess) *f* gall, bile

**billar** (bee-*lʸahr*) *m* billiards *pl*

**billete** (bee-*lʸay*-tay) *m* ticket; **∼ de andén** platform ticket; **∼ de banco** banknote; **∼ gratuito** free ticket

**biología** (bʸoa-loa-*khee*-ah) *f* biology

**biológico** (bʸoa-*loa*-khee-koa) *adj* biological

**bisagra** (bee-*sah*-grah) *f* hinge

**bizco** (*beeth*-koa) *adj* cross-eyed

**bizcocho** (beeth-*koa*-choa) *m* cookie *nAm*

**blanco**[1] (*blahng*-koa) *adj* white; blank

**blanco**[2] (*blahng*-koa) *m* mark, target

**blando** (*blahn*-doa) *adj* soft
**blanquear** (blahng-kay-*ahr*) *v* bleach
**bloc** (bloak) *mMe* writing-pad
**bloque** (*bloa*-kay) *m* block; writing-pad
**bloquear** (bloa-kay-*ahr*) *v* block
**blusa** (*bloo*-sah) *f* blouse
**bobina** (boa-*bhee*-nah) *f* spool; ~ **del encendido** ignition coil
**bobo** (*boa*-bhoa) *adj* silly
**boca** (*boa*-kah) *f* mouth
**bocadillo** (boa-kah-*dhee*-l<sup>y</sup>oa) *m* sandwich
**bocado** (boa-*kah*-dhoa) *m* bite
**bocina** (boa-*thee*-nah) *f* horn, hooter;
**tocar la** ~ hoot
**boda** (*boa*-dhah) *f* wedding
**bodega** (boa-*dhay*-gah) *f* hold
**bofetada** (boa-fay-*tah*-dhah) *f* smack, slap
**boina** (*boi*-nah) *f* beret
**bolera** (boa-*lay*-rah) *f* bowling alley
**boletín meteorológico** (boa-lay-*teen* may-tay-oa-roa-*loa*-khee-koa) weather forecast
**boleto** (boa-*lay*-toa) *mMe* ticket
**bolígrafo** (boa-*lee*-grah-foa) *m* ball-point-pen, Biro
**Bolivia** (boa-*lee*-bh<sup>y</sup>ah) *f* Bolivia
**boliviano** (boa-lee-*bh<sup>y</sup>ah*-noa) *adj* Bolivian; *m* Bolivian
**bolsa** (*boal*-sah) *f* bag; stock market, stock exchange; pocket-book, purse; ~ **de hielo** ice-bag; ~ **de papel** paper bag
**bolsillo** (boal-*see*-l<sup>y</sup>oa) *m* pocket
**bolso** (*boal*-soa) *m* handbag; bag
**bollo** (*boa*-l<sup>y</sup>oa) *m* bun
**bomba** (*boam*-bah) *f* pump; bomb; ~ **de agua** water pump; ~ **de gasolina** petrol pump; fuel pump *Am*
**bombardear** (boam-bahr-dhay-*ahr*) *v* bomb
**bombear** (boam-bay-*ahr*) *v* pump

**bomberos** (boam-*bay*-roass) *mpl* fire-brigade
**bombilla** (boam-*bee*-l<sup>y</sup>ah) *f* light bulb; ~ **de flash** flash-bulb
**bombón** (boam-*boan*) *m* chocolate; candy *nAm*
**bondad** (boan-*dahdh*) *f* goodness
**bondadoso** (boan-dah-*dhoa*-soa) *adj* good-natured, kind
**bonito** (boa-*nee*-toa) *adj* pretty; fair, nice, lovely
**boquerón** (boa-kay-*roan*) *m* whitebait
**boquilla** (boa-*kee*-l<sup>y</sup>ah) *f* cigarette-holder
**bordado** (boar-*dhah*-dhoa) *m* embroidery
**bordar** (boar-*dhahr*) *v* embroider
**borde** (*boar*-dhay) *m* edge, border; verge, rim, brim; ~ **del camino** wayside
**bordillo** (boar-*dhee*-l<sup>y</sup>oa) *m* curb
**a bordo** (ah *boar*-doa) aboard
**borracho** (boa-*rrah*-choa) *adj* drunk
**borrar** (boa-*rrahr*) *v* erase
**borrascoso** (boa-rrahss-*koa*-soa) *adj* gusty
**borrón** (boa-*rroan*) *m* blot
**bosque** (*boass*-kay) *m* wood, forest
**bosquejar** (boass-kay-*khahr*) *v* sketch
**bosquejo** (boass-*kay*-khoa) *m* sketch
**bostezar** (boass-tay-*thahr*) *v* yawn
**bota** (*boa*-tah) *f* boot; **botas de esquí** ski boots
**botadura** (boa-tah-*dhoo*-rah) *f* launching
**botánica** (boa-*tah*-nee-kah) *f* botany
**bote** (*boa*-tay) *m* rowing-boat; ~ **a motor** motor-boat
**botella** (boa-*tay*-l<sup>y</sup>ah) *f* bottle
**botón** (boa-*toan*) *m* button; knob, push-button; ~ **del cuello** collar stud
**botones** (boa-*toa*-nayss) *mpl* bellboy
**bóveda** (*boa*-bhay-dhah) *f* vault, arch

**boxear** (boak-say-ahr) v box
**boya** (boa-Yah) f buoy
**braga** (brah-gah) f briefs pl; panties pl
**bragueta** (brah-gay-tah) f fly
**branquia** (brahng-kYah) f gill
**Brasil** (brah-seel) m Brazil
**brasileño** (brah-see-lay-ño) adj Brazilian; m Brazilian
**braza** (brah-thah) f breaststroke; ~ de mariposa butterfly stroke
**brazo** (brah-thoa) m arm; del ~ arm-in-arm
**brea** (bray-ah) f tar
**brecha** (bray-chah) f breach
**bregar** (bray-gahr) v labour
**brema** (bray-mah) f bream
**breve** (bray-bhay) adj brief; en ~ soon
**brezal** (bray-thahl) m moor
**brezo** (bray-thoa) m heather
**brillante** (bree-lYahn-tay) adj brilliant
**brillantina** (bree-lYahn-tee-nah) f hair cream
**brillar** (bree-lYahr) v glow, *shine
**brillo** (bree-lYoa) m glow, gloss
**brincar** (breeng-kahr) v hop; skip
**brindis** (breen-deess) m toast
**brisa** (bree-sah) f breeze
**británico** (bree-tah-nee-koa) adj British; m Briton
**brocha** (broa-chah) f brush; ~ de afeitar shaving-brush
**broche** (broa-chay) m brooch
**broma** (broa-mah) f joke
**bronca** (broang-kah) f row
**bronce** (broan-thay) m bronze; de ~ bronze
**bronquitis** (broang-kee-teess) f bronchitis
**brotar** (broa-tahr) v bud
**bruja** (broo-khah) f witch
**brújula** (broo-khoo-lah) f compass
**brumoso** (broo-moa-soa) adj foggy; hazy

**brutal** (broo-tahl) adj brutal
**bruto** (broo-toa) adj gross
**bucear** (boo-thay-ahr) v dive
**bueno** (bway-noa) adj good; kind; sound; ¡bueno! well!
**buey** (bway) m ox
**bufanda** (boo-fahn-dah) f scarf
**buffet** (boof-fayt) m buffet
**buhardilla** (bwahr-dee-lYah) f attic
**buho** (boo-oa) m owl
**buitre** (bwee-tray) m vulture
**bujía** (boo-khee-ah) f sparking-plug
**bulbo** (bool-bhoa) m bulb; light bulb
**Bulgaria** (bool-gah-rYah) f Bulgaria
**búlgaro** (bool-gah-roa) adj Bulgarian; m Bulgarian
**bulto** (bool-toa) m bulk
**bulla** (boo-lYah) f fuss
**buque** (boo-kay) m ship; vessel; ~ a motor launch; ~ cisterna tanker; ~ de guerra man-of-war; ~ velero sailing-boat
**burbuja** (boor-boo-khah) f bubble
**burdel** (boor-dhayl) m brothel
**burdo** (boor-dhoa) adj coarse
**burgués** (boor-gayss) adj middle-class, bourgeois
**burla** (boor-lah) f mockery
**burlarse de** (boor-lahr-say) mock
**burocracia** (boo-roa-krah-thYah) f bureaucracy
**burro** (boo-rroa) m ass, donkey
**buscar** (booss-kahr) v look for; look up, *seek, search; hunt for; *ir a ~ *get, pick up, fetch
**búsqueda** (booss-kay-dhah) f search
**busto** (booss-toa) m bust
**butaca** (boo-tah-kah) f armchair, easy chair; stall; orchestra seat Am
**buzón** (boo-thoan) m pillar-box, letter-box; mailbox nAm

# C

**caballero** (kah-bhah-*l<sup>y</sup>ay*-roa) *m* gentleman; knight

**caballitos** (kah-bhah-*l<sup>y</sup>ee*-toass) *mpl* merry-go-round

**caballo** (kah-*bhah*-l<sup>y</sup>oa) *m* horse; ~ **de carrera** race-horse; ~ **de vapor** horsepower

**cabaña** (kah-*bhah*-ñah) *f* cabin, hut

**cabaret** (kah-bhah-*rayt*) *m* cabaret; nightclub

**cabecear** (kah-bhay-thay-*ahr*) *v* nod

**cabeceo** (kah-bhay-*thay*-oa) *m* nod

**cabello** (kah-*bhay*-l<sup>y</sup>oa) *m* hair

**cabelludo** (kah-bhay-*l<sup>y</sup>oo*-dhoa) *adj* hairy

**cabeza** (kah-*bhay*-thah) *f* head; ~ **de turco** scapegoat; **dolor de** ~ headache

**cabezudo** (kah-bhay-*thoo*-dhoa) *adj* head-strong

**cabina** (kah-*bhee*-nah) *f* cabin; booth; ~ **telefónica** telephone booth

**cable** (*kah*-bhlay) *m* cable

**cablegrafiar** (kah-bhlay-grah-*f<sup>y</sup>ahr*) *v* cable

**cablegrama** (kah-bhlay-*grah*-mah) *m* cable

**cabo** (*kah*-bhoa) *m* cape

**cabra** (*kah*-bhrah) *f* goat

**cabritilla** (kah-bhree-*tee*-l<sup>y</sup>ah) *f* kid

**cabrón** (kah-*bhroan*) *m* goat

**cacahuate** (kah-kah-*wah*-tay) *mMe* peanut

**cacahuete** (kah-kah-*way*-tay) *m* peanut

**cacerola** (kah-thay-*roa*-lah) *f* saucepan

**cachear** (kah-chay-*ahr*) *v* search

**cachivache** (kah-chee-*bhah*-chay) *m* junk

**cada** (*kah*-dhah) *adj* every, each; ~

**uno** everyone

**cadáver** (kah-*dhah*-bhayr) *m* corpse

**cadena** (kah-*dhay*-nah) *f* chain

**cadera** (kah-*dhay*-rah) *f* hip

**caducado** (kah-dhoo-*kah*-dhoa) *adj* expired

***caer** (kah-*ayr*) *v* *fall; **dejar** ~ drop

**café** (kah-*fay*) *m* coffee; public house

**cafeína** (kah-fay-*ee*-nah) *f* caffeine

**cafetera filtradora** (kah-fay-*tay*-rah feel-trah-*dhoa*-rah) percolator

**cafetería** (kah-fay-tay-*ree*-ah) *f* snack-bar, cafeteria

**caída** (kah-*ee*-dhah) *f* fall

**caja** (*kah*-khah) *f* box; crate; pay-desk; ~ **de cartón** carton; ~ **de caudales** safe, vault; ~ **de cerillas** match-box; ~ **de colores** paint-box; ~ **de velocidades** gear-box; ~ **fuerte** safe; ~ **metálica** canister

**cajera** (kah-*khay*-rah) *f* cashier

**cajero** (kah-*khay*-roa) *m* cashier

**cajón** (kah-*khoan*) *m* drawer

**cal** (kahl) *f* lime

**calambre** (kah-*lahm*-bray) *m* cramp

**calamidad** (kah-lah-mee-*dhahdh*) *f* disaster

**calcetín** (kahl-thay-*teen*) *m* sock

**calcio** (*kahl*-th<sup>y</sup>oa) *m* calcium

**calculadora** (kahl-koo-lah-*dhoa*-rah) *f* adding-machine

**calcular** (kahl-koo-*lahr*) *v* reckon, calculate

**cálculo** (*kahl*-koo-loa) *m* calculation; ~ **biliar** gallstone

**calderilla** (kahl-day-*ree*-l<sup>y</sup>ah) *f* petty cash

**calefacción** (kah-lay-fahk-*th<sup>y</sup>oan*) *f* heating

**calefactor** (kah-lay-fahk-*toar*) *m* heater

**calendario** (kah-layn-*dah*-r<sup>y</sup>oa) *m* calendar

***calentar** (kah-layn-*tahr*) *v* warm, heat

**calidad** (kah-lee-*dhahdh*) *f* quality; **de**

**primera** ~ first-class

**caliente** (kah-*l*<sup>y</sup>*ayn*-tay) *adj* warm, hot

**calificado** (kah-lee-fee-*kah*-dhoa) *adj* qualified

**calina** (kah-*lee*-nah) *f* haze

**calinoso** (kah-lee-*noa*-soa) *adj* hazy

**calma** (*kahl*-mah) *f* calm

**calmante** (kahl-*mahn*-tay) *m* tranquillizer, sedative

**calmar** (kahl-*mahr*) *v* calm down; **calmarse** *v* calm down

**calor** (kah-*loar*) *m* warmth, heat

**caloría** (kah-loa-*ree*-ah) *f* calorie

**calorífero** (kah-loa-*ree*-fay-roa) *m* hot-water bottle

**calumnia** (kah-*loom*-n<sup>y</sup>ah) *f* slander

**calvinismo** (kahl-bhee-*neez*-moa) *m* Calvinism

**calvo** (*kahl*-bhoa) *adj* bald

**calzada** (kahl-*thah*-dhah) *f* carriageway, causeway; drive

**calzado** (kahl-*thah*-dhoa) *m* footwear

**calzoncillos** (kahl-thoan-*thee*-l<sup>y</sup>oass) *mpl* pants *pl*, briefs *pl*, drawers; shorts *plAm*

**callado** (kah-*l*<sup>y</sup>*ah*-dhoa) *adj* silent

**callarse** (kah-*l*<sup>y</sup>*ahr*-say) *v* \*be silent

**calle** (*kah*-l<sup>y</sup>ay) *f* street; road; ~ **lateral** side-street; ~ **mayor** main street

**callejón** (kah-l<sup>y</sup>ay-*khoan*) *m* alley, lane; ~ **sin salida** cul-de-sac

**callo** (*kah*-l<sup>y</sup>oa) *m* callus; corn

**cama** (*kah*-mah) *f* bed; ~ **de tijera** camp-bed; cot *nAm*; **camas gemelas** twin beds; ~ **y desayuno** bed and breakfast

**camafeo** (kah-mah-*fay*-oa) *m* cameo

**cámara** (*kah*-mah-rah) *f* camera; ~ **fotográfica** camera

**camarada** (kah-mah-*rah*-dhah) *m* comrade

**camarera** (kah-mah-*ray*-rah) *f* waitress

**camarero** (kah-mah-*ray*-roa) *m* waiter; steward; **jefe de camareros** head-waiter

**camarón** (kah-mah-*roan*) *m* shrimp

**camastro** (kah-*mahss*-troa) *m* bunk

**cambiar** (kahm-*b*<sup>y</sup>*ahr*) *v* alter, change; vary; exchange, switch; ~ **de marcha** change gear

**cambio** (*kahm*-b<sup>y</sup>oa) *m* alteration, change, variation; turn; exchange; exchange rate; **oficina de** ~ money exchange

**camello** (kah-*may*-l<sup>y</sup>oa) *m* camel

**caminar** (kah-mee-*nahr*) *v* \*go; hike

**caminata** (kah-mee-*nah*-tah) *f* walk

**camino** (kah-*mee*-noa) *m* way; road; **a mitad de** ~ halfway; **borde del** ~ roadside; ~ **de** bound for; ~ **en obras** road up; ~ **principal** main road

**camión** (kah-*m*<sup>y</sup>*oan*) *m* lorry; truck *nAm*

**camioneta** (kah-m<sup>y</sup>oa-*nay*-tah) *f* van

**camisa** (kah-*mee*-sah) *f* shirt

**camiseta** (kah-mee-*say*-tah) *f* undershirt; vest

**camisón** (kah-mee-*soan*) *m* nightdress

**campamento** (kahm-pah-*mayn*-toa) *m* camp

**campana** (kahm-*pah*-nah) *f* bell

**campanario** (kahm-pah-*nah*-r<sup>y</sup>oa) *m* steeple

**campaña** (kahm-*pah*-ñah) *f* campaign; **catre de** ~ camp-bed

**campeón** (kahm-pay-*oan*) *m* champion

**campesino** (kahm-pay-*see*-noa) *m* peasant

**camping** (*kahm*-peeng) *m* camping site, camping

**campo** (*kahm*-poa) *m* countryside, country; field; ~ **de aviación** airfield; ~ **de golf** golf-course; ~ **de tenis** tennis-court; **día de** ~ picnic

**Canadá** (kah-nah-*dhah*) *m* Canada

**canadiense** (kah-nah-*dh*<sup>y</sup>*ayn*-say) *adj*

Canadian; *m* Canadian

**canal** (kah-*nahl*) *m* canal; channel;
**Canal de la Mancha** English Channel

**canario** (kah-*nah*-r*Y*oa) *m* canary

**cancelación** (kahn-thay-lah-th*Y*oan) *f*
cancellation

**cancelar** (kahn-thay-*lahr*) *v* cancel

**cáncer** (*kahn*-thayr) *m* cancer

**canción** (kahn-th*Y*oan) *f* song

**cancha** (*kahn*-chah) *f* tennis-court

**candado** (kahn-*dah*-dhoa) *m* padlock

**candela** (kahn-*day*-lah) *f* candle

**candelabro** (kahn-day-*lah*-bhroa) *m*
candelabrum

**candidato** (kahn-dee-*dhah*-toa) *m* candidate

**canela** (kah-*nay*-lah) *f* cinnamon

**cangrejo** (kahng-*gray*-khoa) *m* crab

**canguro** (kahng-*goo*-roa) *m* kangaroo

**canica** (kah-*nee*-kah) *f* marble

**canoa** (kah-*noa*-ah) *f* canoe

**cansancio** (kahn-*sahn*-th*Y*oa) *m* fatigue

**cansar** (kahn-*sahr*) *v* tire; **cansado**
tired, weary

**cantadora** (kahn-tah-*dhoa*-rah) *f* singer

**cantante** (kahn-*tahn*-tay) *m* singer

**cantar** (kahn-*tahr*) *v* \*sing

**cántaro** (*kahn*-tah-roa) *m* pitcher; jug

**cantera** (kahn-*tay*-rah) *f* quarry

**cantidad** (kahn-tee-*dhahdh*) *f* amount,
quantity; number; lot

**cantina** (kahn-*tee*-nah) *f* canteen; *fMe*
saloon

**canto** (*kahn*-toa) *m* singing; edge

**caña** (*kah*-ñah) *f* cane; ~ **de pescar**
fishing rod

**cañada** (kah-*ñah*-dhah) *f* glen

**cáñamo** (*kah*-ñah-moa) *m* hemp

**cañón** (kah-*ñoan*) *m* gun; gorge

**caos** (*kah*-oass) *m* chaos

**caótico** (kah-*oa*-tee-koa) *adj* chaotic

**capa** (*kah*-pah) *f* cloak, cape; layer,
deposit

**capacidad** (kah-pah-thee-*dhahdh*) *f* capacity

**capataz** (kah-pah-*tahth*) *m* foreman

**capaz** (kah-*pahth*) *adj* able; capable;
**\*ser ~ de** \*be able to; qualify

**capellán** (kah-pay-*lYahn*) *m* chaplain

**capilla** (kah-*pee*-lYah) *f* chapel

**capital** (kah-pee-*tahl*) *m* capital; *adj*
capital

**capitalismo** (kah-pee-tah-*leez*-moa) *m*
capitalism

**capitán** (kah-pee-*tahn*) *m* captain

**capitulación** (kah-pee-too-lah-th*Y*oan) *f*
capitulation

**capítulo** (kah-*pee*-too-loa) *m* chapter

**capó** (kah-*poa*) *m* bonnet; hood *nAm*

**capricho** (kah-*pree*-choa) *m* fancy,
whim

**cápsula** (*kahp*-soo-lah) *f* capsule

**captura** (kahp-*too*-rah) *f* capture

**capturar** (kahp-too-*rahr*) *v* capture

**capucha** (kah-*poo*-chah) *f* hood

**capullo** (kah-*poo*-lYoa) *m* bud

**caqui** (*kah*-kee) *m* khaki

**cara** (*kah*-rah) *f* face

**caracol** (kah-rah-*koal*) *m* snail; ~ **marino** winkle

**carácter** (kah-*rahk*-tayr) *m* character

**característica** (kah-rahk-tay-*reess*-tee-kah) *f* characteristic, feature; quality

**característico** (kah-rahk-tay-*reess*-tee-koa) *adj* typical, characteristic

**caracterizar** (kah-rahk-tay-ree-*thahr*) *v*
characterize, mark

**caramelo** (kah-rah-*may*-loa) *m* caramel, toffee, sweet

**caravana** (kah-rah-*bhah*-nah) *f* caravan; trailer *nAm*

**carbón** (kahr-*bhoan*) *m* coal; ~ **de leña** charcoal

**carburador** (kahr-bhoo-rah-*dhoar*) *m*
carburettor

**cárcel** (*kahr*-thayl) *f* jail, gaol

**carcelero** (kahr-thay-*lay*-roa) *m* jailer

**cardenal** (kahr-dhay-*nahl*) *m* cardinal

**cardinal** (kahr-dhee-*nahl*) *adj* cardinal

**cardo** (*kahr*-dhoa) *m* thistle

*\***carecer** (kah-ray-*thayr*) *v* lack

**carencia** (kah-*rayn*-th<sup>y</sup>ah) *f* want, shortage

**carga** (*kahr*-gah) *f* charge; cargo, freight, load; batch

**cargar** (kahr-*gahr*) *v* charge; load

**cargo** (*kahr*-goa) *m* office; freight

**cari** (*kah*-ree) *m* curry

**caridad** (kah-ree-*dhahdh*) *f* charity

**carillón** (kah-ree-l<sup>y</sup>oan) *m* chimes *pl*

**cariño** (kah-*ree*-ñoa) *m* affection; pet

**cariñoso** (kah-ree-*ñoa*-soa) *adj* affectionate

**carmesí** (kahr-may-*see*) *adj* crimson

**carnaval** (kahr-nah-*bhahl*) *m* carnival

**carne** (*kahr*-nay) *f* meat; flesh; ~ **de cerdo** pork; ~ **de gallina** gooseflesh; ~ **de ternera** veal; ~ **de vaca** beef

**carnero** (kahr-*nay*-roa) *m* mutton

**carnicero** (kahr-nee-*thay*-roa) *m* butcher

**caro** (*kah*-roa) *adj* expensive, dear

**carpa** (*kahr*-pah) *f* carp

**carpintero** (kahr-peen-*tay*-roa) *m* carpenter

**carrera** (kah-*rray*-rah) *f* career; race; ~ **de caballos** horserace; **pista para carreras** race-track

**carretera** (kah-rray-*tay*-rah) *f* highway

**carretilla** (kah-rray-*tee*-l<sup>y</sup>ah) *f* wheelbarrow

**carro** (*kah*-rroa) *m* cart; *mMe* car; ~ **de gitanos** caravan

**carrocería** (kah-rroa-thay-*ree*-ah) *f* coachwork

**carroza** (kah-*rroa*-thah) *f* coach

**carta** (*kahr*-tah) *f* map; letter; ~ **certificada** registered letter; ~ **de crédito** letter of credit; ~ **de recomen-** **dación** letter of recommendation; ~ **de vinos** wine-list; ~ **marina** chart

**cartel** (kahr-*tayl*) *m* poster, placard

**cárter** (*kahr*-tayr) *m* crankcase

**cartera** (kahr-*tay*-rah) *f* bag; satchel; wallet

**cartero** (kahr-*tay*-roa) *m* postman

**cartílago** (kahr-*tee*-lah-goa) *m* cartilage

**cartón** (kahr-*toan*) *m* cardboard; carton; **de** ~ cardboard

**cartucho** (kahr-*too*-choa) *m* cartridge

**casa** (*kah*-sah) *f* house; home; **a** ~ home; **ama de** ~ housewife; ~ **de campo** cottage; ~ **de correos** post-office; ~ **del párroco** vicarage; ~ **de pisos** block of flats; apartment house *Am*; ~ **de reposo** rest-home; ~ **flotante** houseboat; ~ **señorial** manor-house; **en** ~ at home; indoors, indoor, home; **gobierno de la** ~ housekeeping

**casarse** (kah-*sahr*-say) *v* marry

**cascada** (kahss-*kah*-dhah) *f* waterfall

**cascanueces** (kahss-kah-*nway*-thayss) *m* nutcrackers *pl*

**cáscara** (*kahss*-kah-rah) *f* shell; skin; ~ **de nuez** nutshell

**casco** (*kahss*-koa) *m* helmet; hoof

**casero** (kah-*say*-roa) *adj* home-made

**casi** (*kah*-see) *adv* almost, nearly

**casimir** (kah-see-*meer*) *m* cashmere

**casino** (kah-*see*-noa) *m* casino

**caso** (*kah*-soa) *m* event; case; instance; ~ **de urgencia** emergency; **en** ~ **de** in case of; **en ningún** ~ by no means; **en tal** ~ then; **en todo** ~ at any rate, anyway

**caspa** (*kahss*-pah) *f* dandruff

**casquillo** (kahss-*kee*-l<sup>y</sup>oa) *m* socket

**castaña** (kahss-*tah*-ñah) *f* chestnut

**castellano** (kahss-tay-*l<sup>y</sup>ah*-noa) *adj* Castilian; *m* Castilian

**castigar** (kahss-tee-*gahr*) *v* punish

**castigo** (kahss-*tee*-goa) *m* penalty, punishment

**castillo** (kahss-*tee*-l<sup>y</sup>oa) *m* castle

**casto** (*kahss*-toa) *adj* chaste; pure

**castor** (kahss-*toar*) *m* beaver

**por casualidad** (poar kah-swah-lee-*dhahdh*) by chance

**catacumba** (kah-tah-*koom*-bah) *f* catacomb

**catálogo** (kah-*tah*-loa-goa) *m* catalogue

**catarro** (kah-*tah*-rroa) *m* catarrh

**catástrofe** (kah-*tahss*-troa-fay) *f* disaster, catastrophe, calamity

**catedral** (kah-tay-*dhrahl*) *f* cathedral

**catedrático** (kah-tay-*dhrah*-tee-koa) *m* professor

**categoría** (kah-tay-goa-*ree*-ah) *f* category

**católico** (kah-*toa*-lee-koa) *adj* catholic, Roman Catholic

**catorce** (kah-*toar*-thay) *num* fourteen

**catorceno** (kah-toar-*thay*-noa) *num* fourteenth

**caucho** (*kou*-choa) *m* rubber

**causa** (*kou*-sah) *f* cause, reason; case; lawsuit; **a ~ de** because of, on account of, for, owing to

**causar** (kou-*sahr*) *v* cause

**cautela** (kou-*tay*-lah) *f* caution

**cautivar** (kou-tee-*bhahr*) *v* fascinate

**cavar** (kah-*bhahr*) *v* *dig

**caviar** (kah-*bh<sup>y</sup>ahr*) *m* caviar

**cavidad** (kah-bhee-*dhahdh*) *f* cavity

**caza** (*kah*-thah) *f* chase, hunt; game; **apeadero de ~** lodge

**cazador** (kah-thah-*dhoar*) *m* hunter

**cazar** (kah-*thahr*) *v* hunt; chase; **~ en vedado** poach

**cebada** (thay-*bhah*-dhah) *f* barley

**cebo** (*thay*-bhoa) *m* bait

**cebolla** (thay-*bhoa*-l<sup>y</sup>ah) *f* onion

**cebollino** (thay-bhoa-*l<sup>y</sup>ee*-noa) *m*

chives *pl*

**cebra** (*thay*-bhrah) *f* zebra

**ceder** (thay-*dhayr*) *v* indulge; *give in

**\*cegar** (thay-*gahr*) *v* blind

**ceja** (*thay*-khah) *f* eyebrow

**celda** (*thayl*-dah) *f* cell

**celebración** (thay-lay-bhrah-th<sup>y</sup>oan) *f* celebration

**celebrar** (thay-lay-*bhrahr*) *v* celebrate

**célebre** (*thay*-lay-bhray) *adj* famous

**celebridad** (thay-lay-bhree-*dhahdh*) *f* celebrity

**celeste** (thay-*layss*-tay) *adj* heavenly

**celibato** (thay-lee-*bhah*-toa) *m* celibacy

**celo** (*thay*-loa) *m* zeal, diligence; **celos** jealousy

**celofán** (thay-loa-*fahn*) *m* cellophane

**celoso** (thay-*loa*-soa) *adj* zealous, diligent; envious, jealous

**célula** (*thay*-loo-lah) *f* cell

**cementerio** (thay-mayn-*tay*-r<sup>y</sup>oa) *m* churchyard, graveyard, cemetery

**cemento** (thay-*mayn*-toa) *m* cement

**cena** (*thay*-nah) *f* dinner, supper

**cenar** (thay-*nahr*) *v* dine, *eat

**cenicero** (thay-nee-*thay*-roa) *m* ashtray

**cenit** (thay-*neet*) *m* zenith

**ceniza** (thay-*nee*-thah) *f* ash

**censura** (thayn-*soo*-rah) *f* censorship

**centelleante** (thayn-tay-l<sup>y</sup>ay-*ahn*-tay) *adj* sparkling

**centígrado** (thayn-*tee*-grah-dhoa) *adj* centigrade

**centímetro** (thayn-*tee*-may-troa) *m* centimetre; tape-measure

**central** (thayn-*trahl*) *adj* central; **central eléctrica** power-station; **central telefónica** telephone exchange

**centralizar** (thayn-trah-lee-*thahr*) *v* centralize

**centro** (*thayn*-troa) *m* centre; **~ comercial** shopping centre; **~ de la ciudad** town centre; **~ de recreo** recreation centre

**cepillar** (thay-pee-*lYahr*) v brush

**cepillo** (thay-*pee*-lYoa) m brush; ~ **de dientes** toothbrush; ~ **de la ropa** clothes-brush; ~ **para el cabello** hairbrush; ~ **para las uñas** nail-brush

**cera** (*thay*-rah) f wax

**cerámica** (thay-*rah*-mee-kah) f ceramics pl; crockery, pottery

**cerca** (*thayr*-kah) f fence

**cerca de** (*thayr*-kah day) near, by; almost

**cercano** (thayr-*kah*-noa) adj close, nearby, near

**cercar** (thayr-*kahr*) v encircle, surround

**cerdo** (*thayr*-dhoa) m pig

**cereales** (thay-ray-*ah*-layss) mpl corn

**cerebro** (thay-*ray*-bhroa) m brain; **conmoción cerebral** concussion

**ceremonia** (thay-ray-*moa*-nYah) f ceremony

**cereza** (thay-*ray*-thah) f cherry

**cerilla** (thay-*ree*-lYah) f match

**cerillo** (thay-*ree*-lYoa) mMe match

**cero** (*thay*-roa) m zero, nought

**cerradura** (thay-rrah-*dhoo*-rah) f lock; **ojo de la ~** keyhole

*****cerrar** (thay-*rrahr*) v close, *shut; fasten; turn off; ~ **con llave** lock

**cerrojo** (thay-*rroa*-khoa) m bolt

**certificación** (thayr-tee-fee-kah-*thYoan*) f certificate

**certificado** (thayr-tee-fee-*kah*-dhoa) m certificate; ~ **de salud** health certificate

**certificar** (thayr-tee-fee-*kahr*) v register

**cervato** (thayr-*bhah*-toa) m fawn

**cervecería** (thayr-bhay-thay-*ree*-ah) f brewery

**cerveza** (thayr-*bhay*-thah) f beer; ale

**cesar** (thay-*sahr*) v cease, quit, stop, discontinue

**césped** (*thayss*-paydh) m lawn; grass

**cesta** (*thayss*-tah) f basket

**cesto** (*thayss*-toa) m hamper; ~ **para papeles** wastepaper-basket

**cicatriz** (thee-kah-*treeth*) f scar

**ciclista** (thee-*kleess*-tah) m cyclist

**ciclo** (*thee*-kloa) m cycle

**ciego** (*thYay*-goa) adj blind

**cielo** (*thYay*-loa) m heaven; sky; ~ **raso** ceiling

**ciencia** (*thYayn*-thYah) f science

**científico** (thYayn-*tee*-fee-koa) adj scientific; m scientist

**ciento** (*thYayn*-toa) num hundred; **por ~** percent

**cierre** (*thYay*-rray) m fastener; ~ **relámpago** zipper

**cierto** (*thYayr*-toa) adj certain; **por ~** indeed

**ciervo** (*thYayr*-bhoa) m deer

**cifra** (*thee*-frah) f number, figure

**cigarrillo** (thee-gah-*rree*-lYoa) m cigarette

**cigüeña** (thee-*gway*-ñah) f stork

**cigüeñal** (thee-gway-*ñahl*) m crankshaft

**cilindro** (thee-*leen*-droa) m cylinder; **culata del ~** cylinder head

**cima** (*thee*-mah) f top, summit; hilltop

**cinc** (theengk) m zinc

**cincel** (theen-*thayl*) m chisel

**cinco** (*theeng*-koa) num five

**cincuenta** (theeng-*kwayn*-tah) num fifty

**cine** (*thee*-nay) m pictures

**cinematógrafo** (thee-nay-mah-*toa*-grah-foa) m cinema

**cinta** (*theen*-tah) f ribbon, tape; ~ **adhesiva** scotch tape, adhesive tape; ~ **de goma** elastic band; ~ **métrica** tape-measure

**cintura** (theen-*too*-rah) f waist

**cinturón** (theen-too-*roan*) m belt; bypass; ~ **de seguridad** seat-belt

**cipo** (*thee*-poa) *m* milepost

**circo** (*theer*-koa) *m* circus

**\*circuir** (theer-*kweer*) *v* encircle

**circulación** (theer-koo-lah-*th<sup>y</sup>oan*) *f* circulation

**circular** (theer-koo-*lahr*) *v* circulate

**círculo** (*theer*-koo-loa) *m* circle, ring; club

**circundante** (theer-koon-*dahn*-tay) *adj* surrounding

**circundar** (theer-koon-*dahr*) *v* circle

**circunstancia** (theer-koons-*tahn*-th<sup>y</sup>ah) *f* circumstance, condition

**ciruela** (thee-*rway*-lah) *f* plum; ~ **pasa** prune

**cirujano** (thee-roo-*khah*-noa) *m* surgeon

**cisne** (*theez*-nay) *m* swan

**cistitis** (theess-*tee*-teess) *f* cystitis

**cita** (*thee*-tah) *f* date, appointment; quotation

**citación** (thee-tah-*th<sup>y</sup>oan*) *f* summons

**citar** (thee-*tahr*) *v* quote

**ciudad** (th<sup>y</sup>oo-*dhahdh*) *f* city, town

**ciudadanía** (th<sup>y</sup>oo-dhah-dhah-*nee*-ah) *f* citizenship

**ciudadano** (th<sup>y</sup>oo-dhah-*dhah*-noa) *m* citizen

**cívico** (*thee*-bhee-koa) *adj* civic

**civil** (thee-*bheel*) *adj* civilian, civil

**civilización** (thee-bhee-lee-thah-*th<sup>y</sup>oan*) *f* civilization

**civilizado** (thee-bhee-lee-*thah*-dhoa) *adj* civilized

**claridad** (klah-ree-*dhahdh*) *f* clarity

**clarificar** (klah-ree-fee-*kahr*) *v* clarify

**claro** (*klah*-roa) *adj* clear; plain, distinct; serene, bright; *m* clearing

**clase** (*klah*-say) *f* class; sort; form; classroom; ~ **media** middle class; ~ **turista** tourist class; **de primera** ~ first-rate; **toda** ~ **de** all sorts of

**clásico** (*klah*-see-koa) *adj* classical

**clasificar** (klah-see-fee-*kahr*) *v* classify, assort, sort, arrange

**cláusula** (*klou*-soo-lah) *f* clause

**clavar** (klah-*bhahr*) *v* pin

**clavicémbalo** (klah-bhee-*thaym*-bah-loa) *m* harpsichord

**clavícula** (klah-*bhee*-koo-lah) *f* collarbone

**clavo** (*klah*-bhoa) *m* nail

**clemencia** (klay-*mayn*-th<sup>y</sup>ah) *f* mercy

**clérigo** (*klay*-ree-goa) *m* clergyman, minister

**cliente** (kl<sup>y</sup>*ayn*-tay) *m* client, customer

**clima** (*klee*-mah) *m* climate

**climatizado** (klee-mah-tee-*thah*-dhoa) *adj* air-conditioned

**clínica** (*klee*-nee-kah) *f* clinic

**cloro** (*kloa*-roa) *m* chlorine

**club de yates** yacht-club

**coagularse** (koa-ah-goo-*lahr*-say) *v* coagulate

**cobarde** (koa-*bhahr*-dhay) *adj* cowardly; *m* coward

**cobertizo** (koa-bhayr-*tee*-thoa) *m* shed

**cobrador** (koa-bhrah-*dhoar*) *m* conductor

**cobrar** (koa-*bhrahr*) *v* cash

**cobre** (*koa*-bhray) *m* copper, brass; **cobres** *mpl* brassware

**cocaína** (koa-kah-*ee*-nah) *f* cocaine

**cocina** (koa-*thee*-nah) *f* kitchen; cooker, stove; ~ **de gas** gas cooker

**cocinar** (koa-thee-*nahr*) *v* cook

**cocinero** (koa-thee-*nay*-roa) *m* cook

**coco** (*koa*-koa) *m* coconut

**cocodrilo** (koa-koa-*dhree*-l<sup>y</sup>oa) *m* crocodile

**cóctel** (*koak*-tayl) *m* cocktail

**coche** (*koa*-chay) *m* car; carriage; ~ **cama** sleeping-car; ~ **comedor** dining-car; ~ **de carreras** sports-car; ~ **Pullman** Pullman

**cochecillo** (koa-chay-*thee*-l<sup>y</sup>oa) *m* pram; baby carriage *Am*

**cochinillo** (koa-chee-*nee*-l<sup>y</sup>oa) *m* piglet

**codicia** (koa-*dhee*-th<sup>y</sup>ah) *f* greed

**codicioso** (koa-dhee-*th<sup>y</sup>oa*-soa) *adj* greedy

**código** (*koa*-dhee-goa) *m* code; ~ **postal** zip code *Am*

**codo** (*koa*-dhoa) *m* elbow

**codorniz** (koa-dhoar-*neeth*) *f* quail

**coger** (koa-*khayr*) *v* *catch; *take; **llegar a** ~ *catch

**coherencia** (koa-ay-*rayn*-th<sup>y</sup>ah) *f* coherence

**cohete** (koa-*ay*-tay) *m* rocket

**coincidencia** (koa-een-thee-*dhayn*-th<sup>y</sup>ah) *f* concurrence

**coincidir** (koa-een-thee-*dheer*) *v* coincide

**cojear** (koa-khay-*ahr*) *v* limp

**cojo** (*koa*-khoa) *adj* lame

**col** (koal) *m* cabbage; ~ **de Bruselas** sprouts *pl*

**cola** (*koa*-lah) *f* queue, file, line; tail; gum, glue; *hacer ~ queue

**colaboración** (koa-lah-bhoa-rah-*th<sup>y</sup>oan*) *f* co-operation

**colcha** (*koal*-chah) *f* counterpane, quilt

**colchón** (koal-*choan*) *m* mattress

**colección** (koa-layk-*th<sup>y</sup>oan*) *f* collection; ~ **de arte** art collection

**coleccionar** (koa-layk-th<sup>y</sup>oa-*nahr*) *v* gather

**coleccionista** (koa-layk-th<sup>y</sup>oa-*neess*-tah) *m* collector

**colectivo** (koa-layk-*tee*-bhoa) *adj* collective

**colector** (koa-layk-*toar*) *m* collector

**colega** (koa-*lay*-gah) *m* colleague

**colegio** (koa-*lay*-kh<sup>y</sup>oa) *m* college

**cólera** (*koa*-lay-rah) *f* anger, passion, temper

**colérico** (koa-*lay*-ree-koa) *adj* hot-tempered

***colgar** (koal-*gahr*) *v* *hang

**coliflor** (koa-lee-*floar*) *f* cauliflower

**colina** (koa-*lee*-nah) *f* hill

**colisión** (koa-lee-s<sup>y</sup>oan) *f* collision

**colmena** (koal-*may*-nah) *f* beehive

**colmo** (*koal*-moa) *m* height

**colocar** (koa-loa-*kahr*) *v* *lay, place, *put

**Colombia** (koa-*loam*-b<sup>y</sup>ah) *f* Colombia

**colombiano** (koa-loam-*b<sup>y</sup>ah*-noa) *adj* Colombian; *m* Colombian

**colonia** (koa-*loa*-n<sup>y</sup>ah) *f* colony; ~ **veraniega** holiday camp

**color** (koa-*loar*) *m* colour; ~ **de agua-da** water-colour; **de ~** coloured

**colorado** (koa-loa-*rah*-dhoa) *adj* colourful

**colorante** (koa-loa-*rahn*-tay) *m* colourant

**colorete** (koa-loa-*ray*-tay) *m* rouge

**columna** (koa-*loom*-nah) *f* column, pillar; ~ **del volante** steering-column

**columpiarse** (koa-loom-*p<sup>y</sup>ahr*-say) *v* *swing

**columpio** (koa-*loom*-p<sup>y</sup>oa) *m* swing; seesaw

**collar** (koa-*l<sup>y</sup>ahr*) *m* beads *pl*, necklace; collar

**coma** (*koa*-mah) *f* comma; *m* coma

**comadrona** (koa-mah-*dhroa*-nah) *f* midwife

**comandante** (koa-mahn-*dahn*-tay) *m* commander; captain

**comarca** (koa-*mahr*-kah) *f* district

**comba** (*koam*-bah) *f* bend

**combate** (koam-*bah*-tay) *m* combat, battle, struggle, fight; ~ **de boxeo** boxing match

**combatir** (koam-bah-*teer*) *v* combat, battle, *fight

**combinación** (koam-bee-nah-*th<sup>y</sup>oan*) *f* combination; slip

**combinar** (koam-bee-*nahr*) *v* combine

**combustible** (koam-booss-*tee*-bhlay) *m* fuel; ~ **líquido** fuel oil

**comedia** (koa-*may*-dh<sup>y</sup>ah) *f* comedy;

~ **musical** musical

**comediante** (koa-may-dh<sup>y</sup>ahn-tay) m comedian

**comedor** (koa-may-dhoar) m dining-room; ~ **de gala** banqueting-hall

**comentar** (koa-mayn-tahr) v comment

**comentario** (koa-mayn-tah-r<sup>y</sup>oa) m comment

*comenzar (koa-mayn-thahr) v commence, *begin

**comer** (koa-mayr) v *eat

**comercial** (koa-mayr-th<sup>y</sup>ahl) adj commercial

**comerciante** (koa-mayr-th<sup>y</sup>ahn-tay) m merchant; trader, dealer; ~ **al por menor** retailer

**comerciar** (koa-mayr-th<sup>y</sup>ahr) v trade

**comercio** (koa-mayr-th<sup>y</sup>oa) m commerce, trade, business; ~ **al por menor** retail trade

**comestible** (koa-mayss-tee-bhlay) adj edible

**comestibles** (koa-mayss-tee-bhlayss) mpl groceries pl; **tienda de** ~ **finos** delicatessen

**cometer** (koa-may-tayr) v commit

**cómico** (koa-mee-koa) adj comic, funny; m comedian; entertainer

**comida** (koa-mee-dhah) f food; meal; ~ **principal** dinner

**comidilla** (koa-mee-dhee-l<sup>y</sup>ah) f hobby-horse

**comienzo** (koa-m<sup>y</sup>ayn-thoa) m beginning, start

**comillas** (koa-mee-l<sup>y</sup>ahss) fpl quotation marks

**comisaría** (koa-mee-sah-ree-ah) f police-station

**comisión** (koa-mee-s<sup>y</sup>oan) f committee, commission

**comité** (koa-mee-tay) m committee

**comitiva** (koa-mee-tee-bhah) f procession

**como** (koa-moa) adv as, like, like; **así**

~ **as well as;** ~ **máximo** at most; ~ **si** as if

**cómo** (koa-moa) adv how

**cómoda** (koa-moa-dhah) f chest of drawers; bureau nAm

**comodidad** (koa-moa-dhee-dhahdh) f comfort, leisure

**cómodo** (koa-moa-dhoa) adj convenient, easy

**compacto** (koam-pahk-toa) adj compact

**compadecerse de** (koam-pah-dhay-thayr-say) pity

**compañero** (koam-pah-ñay-roa) m companion; associate; ~ **de clase** class-mate

**compañía** (koam-pah-ñee-ah) f company; society

**comparación** (koam-pah-rah-th<sup>y</sup>oan) f comparison

**comparar** (koam-pah-rahr) v compare

**compartimento** (koam-pahr-tee-mayn-toa) m compartment; ~ **para fumadores** smoking-compartment

**compartir** (koam-pahr-teer) v share

**compasión** (koam-pah-s<sup>y</sup>oan) f sympathy

**compasivo** (koam-pah-see-bhoa) adj sympathetic

**compatriota** (koam-pah-tr<sup>y</sup>oa-tah) m countryman

**compeler** (koam-pay-layr) v compel

**compensación** (koam-payn-sah-th<sup>y</sup>oan) f compensation

**compensar** (koam-payn-sahr) v compensate; *make good

**competencia** (koam-pay-tayn-th<sup>y</sup>ah) f competition, rivalry; capacity

**competente** (koam-pay-tayn-tay) adj expert, qualified

**competidor** (koam-pay-tee-dhoar) m competitor, rival

*competir (koam-pay-teer) v compete

**compilar** (koam-pee-lahr) v compile

**complacer** (koam-plah-*thayr*) *v* please; *give satisfaction

**complejo** (koam-*play*-khoa) *adj* complex; *m* complex

**completamente** (koam-play-tah-*mayn*-tay) *adv* completely, quite

**completar** (koam-play-*tahr*) *v* complete; fill in; fill out *Am*

**completo** (koam-*play*-toa) *adj* complete; whole, total, utter; full up

**complicado** (koam-plee-*kah*-dhoa) *adj* complicated

**cómplice** (*koam*-plee-thay) *m* accessary

**complot** (koam-*ploat*) *m* plot

**componer** (koam-poa-*nayr*) *v* compose

**comportarse** (koam-poar-*tahr*-say) *v* behave, act

**composición** (koam-poa-see-*th*ⁱ*oan*) *f* composition; essay

**compositor** (koam-poa-see-*toar*) *m* composer

**compra** (*koam*-prah) *f* purchase; *ir de compras** shop

**comprador** (koam-prah-*dhoar*) *m* purchaser, buyer

**comprar** (koam-*prahr*) *v* purchase, *buy

**comprender** (koam-prayn-*dayr*) *v* *understand; *see; *take; comprise, contain

**comprensión** (koam-prayn-*s*ⁱ*oan*) *m* understanding

**comprobante** (koam-proa-*bhahn*-tay) *m* voucher

**comprobar** (koam-proa-*bhahr*) *v* ascertain, diagnose, establish, note; prove

**comprometerse** (koam-proa-may-*tayr*-say) *v* engage

**compromiso** (koam-proa-*mee*-soa) *m* compromise; engagement

**compuerta** (koam-*pwayr*-tah) *f* sluice

**común** (koa-*moon*) *adj* common; ordinary; **en ~** joint

**comuna** (koa-*moo*-nah) *f* commune

**comunicación** (koa-moo-nee-kah-*th*ⁱ*oan*) *f* communication

**comunicado** (koa-moo-nee-*kah*-dhoa) *m* communiqué, information

**comunicar** (koa-moo-nee-*kahr*) *v* communicate, inform

**comunidad** (koa-moo-nee-*dhahdh*) *f* congregation

**comunismo** (koa-moo-*neez*-moa) *m* communism

**comunista** (koa-moo-*neess*-tah) *m* communist

**con** (koan) *prep* with; by

**concebir** (koan-thay-*bheer*) *v* conceive

**conceder** (koan-thay-*dhayr*) *v* extend, grant; award

**concentración** (koan-thayn-trah-*th*ⁱ*oan*) *f* concentration

**concentrarse** (koan-thayn-*trahr*-say) *v* concentrate

**concepción** (koan-thayp-*th*ⁱ*oan*) *f* conception

**concepto** (koan-*thayp*-toa) *m* idea

**concernir** (koan-thayr-*neer*) *v* touch, concern; **concerniente a** concerning

**concesión** (koan-thay-*s*ⁱ*oan*) *f* concession

**conciencia** (koan-*th*ⁱ*ayn*-th*ⁱ*ah) *f* conscience; consciousness

**concierto** (koan-*th*ⁱ*ayr*-toa) *m* concert

**conciso** (koan-*thee*-soa) *adj* concise

**concluir** (koang-*klweer*) *v* conclude

**conclusión** (koang-kloo-*s*ⁱ*oan*) *f* conclusion; issue, ending

**concordar** (koang-koar-*dhahr*) *v* agree

**concreto** (koang-*kray*-toa) *adj* concrete

**concupiscencia** (koang-koo-pee-*thayn*-th*ⁱ*ah) *f* lust

**concurrido** (koang-koo-*rree*-dhoa) *adj*

busy

**concurrir** (koang-koo-*rreer*) v coincide; concur

**concurso** (koang-*koor*-soa) m competition, contest; quiz

**concha** (*koan*-chah) f shell; sea-shell

**condado** (koan-*dah*-dhoa) m county

**conde** (*koan*-day) m count, earl

**condena** (koan-*day*-nah) f conviction

**condenado** (koan-day-*nah*-dhoa) m convict

**condesa** (koan-*day*-sah) f countess

**condición** (koan-dee-th*y*oan) f condition, term

**condicional** (koan-dee-th*y*oa-*nahl*) adj conditional

**condimentado** (koan-dee-mayn-*tah*-dhoa) adj spiced

*****conducir** (koan-doo-*theer*) v *lead, carry, conduct; *drive

**conducta** (koan-*dook*-tah) f behaviour, conduct

**conducto** (koan-*dook*-toa) m pipe

**conductor** (koan-dook-*toar*) m driver; mMe conductor

**conectar** (koa-nayk-*tahr*) v connect

**conejo** (koa-*nay*-khoa) m rabbit; **conejillo de Indias** guinea-pig

**conexión** (koa-nayk-s*y*oan) f connection

**confeccionado** (koan-fayk-th*y*oa-*nah*-dhoa) adj ready-made

**confederación** (koan-fay-day-rah-*th*y*oan*) f union

**conferencia** (koan-fay-*rayn*-th*y*ah) f conference; lecture; ~ **interurbana** trunk-call

*****confesarse** (koan-fay-*sahr*-say) v confess

**confesión** (koan-fay-s*y*oan) f confession

**confiable** (koan-f*y*ah-bhlay) adj trustworthy

**confianza** (koan-f*y*ahn-thah) f faith,

trust, confidence; **indigno de** ~ untrustworthy

**confiar** (koan-f*y*ahr) v commit; ~ **en** trust

**confidencial** (koan-fee-dhayn-th*y*ahl) adj confidential

**confirmación** (koan-feer-mah-th*y*oan) f confirmation

**confirmar** (koan-feer-*mahr*) v confirm, acknowledge

**confiscar** (koan-feess-*kahr*) v confiscate, impound

**confitería** (koan-fee-tay-*ree*-ah) f sweetshop

**confitero** (koan-fee-*tay*-roa) m confectioner

**confitura** (koan-fee-*too*-rah) f marmalade

**conflicto** (koan-*fleek*-toa) m conflict

**conforme** (koan-*foar*-may) adj alike; in agreement; ~ **a** according to, in agreement with

**conformidad** (koan-foar-mee-*dhahdh*) f agreement

**confort** (koan-*foart*) m comfort

**confortable** (koan-foar-*tah*-bhlay) adj comfortable; cosy

**confundir** (koan-foon-*deer*) v *mistake, confuse

**confusión** (koan-foo-s*y*oan) f confusion; disturbance

**confuso** (koan-*foo*-soa) adj confused

**congelado** (koang-khay-*lah*-dhoa) adj frozen; **alimento** ~ frozen food

**congelador** (koang-khay-lah-*dhoar*) m deep-freeze

**congelar** (koang-khay-*lahr*) v *freeze

**congestión** (koang-khayss-t*y*oan) f jam

**congregación** (koang-gray-gah-th*y*oan) f congregation

**congreso** (koang-*gray*-soa) m congress

**conjetura** (koang-khay-*too*-rah) f guess

**conjeturar** (koang-khay-too-*rahr*) v guess

**conjuración** (koang-khoo-rah-*th<sup>y</sup>oan*) *f* plot

**conmemoración** (koan-may-moa-rah-*th<sup>y</sup>oan*) *f* commemoration

**conmovedor** (koan-moa-bhay-*dhoar*) *adj* touching

*****conmover** (koan-moa-*bhayr*) *v* move

**connotación** (koan-noa-tah-*th<sup>y</sup>oan*) *f* connotation

*****conocer** (koa-noa-*thayr*) *v* *know

**conocido** (koa-noa-*thee*-dhoa) *m* acquaintance

**conocimiento** (koa-noa-thee-*m<sup>y</sup>ayn*-toa) *m* knowledge

**conquista** (koang-*keess*-tah) *f* conquest, capture

**conquistador** (koang-keess-tah-*dhoar*) *m* conqueror

**conquistar** (koang-keess-*tahr*) *v* conquer, capture

**consciente** (koan-*th<sup>y</sup>ayn*-tay) *adj* conscious, aware

**consecuencia** (koan-say-*kwayn*-th<sup>y</sup>ah) *f* consequence, result; issue

*****conseguir** (koan-say-*geer*) *v* *get; *make, obtain

**consejero** (koan-say-*khay*-roa) *m* counsellor; councillor

**consejo** (koan-*say*-khoa) *m* advice, counsel; council, board

**consentimiento** (koan-sayn-tee-*m<sup>y</sup>ayn*-toa) *m* consent; approval

*****consentir** (koan-sayn-*teer*) *v* agree, consent

**conserje** (koan-*sayr*-khay) *m* concierge, janitor

**conservación** (koan-sayr-bhah-*th<sup>y</sup>oan*) *f* preservation

**conservador** (koan-sayr-bhah-*dhoar*) *adj* conservative

**conservar** (koan-sayr-*bhahr*) *v* preserve

**conservas** (koan-*sayr*-bhahss) *fpl* tinned food

**conservatorio** (koan-sayr-bhah-toa-r<sup>y</sup>oa) *m* music academy

**considerable** (koan-see-dhay-*rah*-bhlay) *adj* considerable

**consideración** (koan-see-dhay-rah-*th<sup>y</sup>oan*) *f* consideration

**considerado** (koan-see-dhay-*rah*-dhoa) *adj* considerate

**considerando** (koan-see-dhay-*rahn*-doa) *prep* considering

**considerar** (koan-see-dhay-*rahr*) *v* regard, consider; *think over; count, reckon

**consigna** (koan-*seeg*-nah) *f* left luggage office

**por consiguiente** (poar koan-see-*g<sup>y</sup>ayn*-tay) consequently

**consistir en** (koan-seess-*teer*) consist of

*****consolar** (koan-soa-*lahr*) *v* comfort

**consorcio** (koan-*soar*-th<sup>y</sup>oa) *m* concern

**conspirar** (koans-pee-*rahr*) *v* conspire

**constante** (koans-*tahn*-tay) *adj* even, constant; steadfast

**constar de** (koans-*tahr*) consist of

**constitución** (koans-tee-too-*th<sup>y</sup>oan*) *f* constitution

*****constituir** (koans-tee-*tweer*) *v* constitute; represent

**construcción** (koans-trook-*th<sup>y</sup>oan*) *f* construction

*****construir** (koans-*trweer*) *v* construct, *build

**consuelo** (koan-*sway*-loa) *m* comfort

**cónsul** (*koan*-sool) *m* consul

**consulado** (koan-soo-*lah*-dhoa) *m* consulate

**consulta** (koan-*sool*-tah) *f* consultation

**consultar** (koan-sool-*tahr*) *v* consult

**consultorio** (koan-sool-*toa*-r<sup>y</sup>oa) *m* surgery

**consumidor** (koan-soo-mee-*dhoar*) *m* consumer

**consumir** (koan-soo-*meer*) v use up

**contacto** (koan-*tahk*-toa) m contact; touch

**contador** (koan-tah-*dhoar*) m meter

**contagioso** (koan-tah-*kh*ʸoa-soa) *adj* infectious, contagious

**contaminación** (koan-tah-mee-nah-*th*ʸoan) f pollution

*contar* (koan-*tahr*) v count; relate, *tell; ~ con rely on

**contemplar** (koan-taym-*plahr*) v contemplate

**contemporáneo** (koan-taym-poa-*rah*-nay-oa) *adj* contemporary; m contemporary

**contenedor** (koan-tay-nay-*dhoar*) m container

*contener* (koan-tay-*nayr*) v contain; restrain

**contenido** (koan-tay-*nee*-dhoa) m contents *pl*

**contentar** (koan-tayn-*tahr*) v satisfy

**contento** (koan-*tayn*-toa) *adj* happy, glad, content, joyful; pleased

**contestar** (koan-tayss-*tahr*) v answer

**contienda** (koan-t*ʸayn*-dah) f dispute

**contiguo** (koan-*tee*-gwoa) *adj* neighbouring

**continental** (koan-tee-nayn-*tahl*) *adj* continental

**continente** (koan-tee-*nayn*-tay) m continent

**continuación** (koan-tee-nwah-*th*ʸoan) f sequel

**continuamente** (koan-tee-nwah-*mayn*-tay) *adv* all the time, continually

**continuar** (koan-tee-*nwahr*) v *go on, *go ahead; carry on, continue, *keep on; *keep

**continuo** (koan-*tee*-nwoa) *adj* continuous, continual

**contorno** (koan-*toar*-noa) m outline, contour

**contra** (*koan*-trah) *prep* against, versus

**contrabandear** (koan-trah-bhahn-day-*ahr*) v smuggle

*contradecir* (koan-trah-dhay-*theer*) v contradict

**contradictorio** (koan-trah-dheek-*toa*-rʸoa) *adj* contradictory

**contrahecho** (koan-trah-*ay*-choa) *adj* deformed

**contralto** (koan-*trahl*-toa) m alto

**contrario** (koan-*trah*-rʸoa) *adj* opposite, contrary; m contrary, reverse; al ~ on the contrary

**contraste** (koan-*trahss*-tay) m contrast

**contratiempo** (koan-trah-t*ʸaym*-poa) m misfortune

**contratista** (koan-trah-*teess*-tah) m contractor

**contrato** (koan-*trah*-toa) m agreement, contract

**contribución** (koan-tree-bhoo-*th*ʸoan) f contribution

*contribuir* (koan-tree-*bhweer*) v contribute

**contrincante** (koan-treeng-*kahn*-tay) m opponent

**control** (koan-*troal*) m inspection, control

**controlar** (koan-troa-*lahr*) v check, control

**controvertible** (koan-troa-bhayr-*tee*-bhlay) *adj* controversial

**controvertido** (koan-troa-bhayr-*tee*-dhoa) *adj* controversial

**convencer** (koam-bayn-*thayr*) v convince, persuade; convict

**convencimiento** (koam-bayn-thee-m*ʸayn*-toa) m conviction

**conveniente** (koam-bay-n*ʸayn*-tay) *adj* adequate, proper; convenient

**convenio** (koam-*bay*-nʸoa) m settlement

*convenir* (koam-bay-*neer*) v agree; fit, suit

**convento** (koam-*bayn*-toa) m cloister,

convent; nunnery

**conversación** (koam-bayr-sah-*th<sup>Y</sup>oan*) *f* conversation, talk, discussion

\***convertir** (koam-bayr-*teer*) *v* convert; **\*convertirse en** turn into

**convicción** (koam-beek-*th<sup>Y</sup>oan*) *f* persuasion

**convidar** (koam-bee-*dhahr*) *v* invite

**convulsión** (koam-bool-s<sup>Y</sup>oan) *f* convulsion

**cónyuges** (*koan*-<sup>Y</sup>oo-khayss) *mpl* married couple

**coñac** (koa-*ñahk*) *m* cognac

**cooperación** (koa-oa-pay-rah-*th<sup>Y</sup>oan*) *f* co-operation

**cooperador** (koa-oa-pay-rah-*dhoar*) *adj* co-operative

**cooperativa** (koa-oa-pay-rah-*tee*-bhah) *f* co-operative

**cooperativo** (koa-oa-pay-rah-*tee*-bhoa) *adj* co-operative

**coordinación** (koa-oar-dhee-nah-*th<sup>Y</sup>oan*) *f* co-ordination

**coordinar** (koa-oar-dhee-*nahr*) *v* co-ordinate

**copa** (*koa*-pah) *f* cup

**copia** (*koa*-p<sup>Y</sup>ah) *f* copy, carbon copy

**copiar** (koa-*p<sup>Y</sup>ahr*) *v* copy

**coraje** (koa-*rah*-khay) *m* guts

**coral** (koa-*rahl*) *m* coral

**corazón** (koa-rah-*thoan*) *m* heart; core

**corbata** (koar-*bhah*-tah) *f* tie, necktie; **~ de lazo** bow tie

**corbatín** (koar-bhah-*teen*) *m* bow tie

**corcino** (koar-*thee*-noa) *m* fawn

**corcho** (*koar*-choa) *m* cork

**cordel** (koar-*dhayl*) *m* string

**cordero** (koar-*dhay*-roa) *m* lamb

**cordial** (koar-*dh<sup>Y</sup>ahl*) *adj* cordial, hearty, sympathetic

**cordillera** (koar-dhee-*l<sup>Y</sup>ay*-rah) *f* mountain range

**cordón** (koar-*dhoan*) *m* cord, line; lace, shoe-lace; **~ de extensión** ex-

tension cord; **~ flexible** flex

**cornamenta** (koar-nah-*mayn*-tah) *f* antlers *pl*

**corneja** (koar-*nay*-khah) *f* crow

**coro** (*koa*-roa) *m* choir

**corona** (koa-*roa*-nah) *f* crown

**coronar** (koa-roa-*nahr*) *v* crown

**coronel** (koa-roa-*nayl*) *m* colonel

**corpulento** (koar-poo-*layn*-toa) *adj* corpulent, stout

**corral** (koa-*rrahl*) *m* yard; **aves de ~** poultry

**correa** (koa-*rray*-ah) *f* leash, strap; **~ del ventilador** fan belt; **~ de reloj** watch-strap

**corrección** (koa-rrayk-*th<sup>Y</sup>oan*) *f* correction

**correcto** (koa-*rrayk*-toa) *adj* correct; right

**corredor** (koa-rray-*dhoar*) *m* broker; bookmaker; **~ de casas** house agent

\***corregir** (koa-rray-*kheer*) *v* correct

**correo** (koa-*rray*-oa) *m* post, mail; **~ aéreo** airmail; **enviar por ~** mail; **sello de correos** postage stamp

**correr** (koa-*rrayr*) *v* \*run; dash; flow

**correspondencia** (koa-rrayss-poan-*dayn*-th<sup>Y</sup>ah) *f* correspondence

**corresponder** (koa-rrayss-poan-*dayr*) *v* correspond; **corresponderse** *v* correspond

**corresponsal** (koa-rrayss-poan-*sahl*) *m* correspondent

**corrida de toros** (koa-*rree*-dhah day *toa*-roass) bullfight

**corriente** (koa-*rr<sup>Y</sup>ayn*-tay) *adj* current; regular, customary, plain; *f* current; stream; **~ alterna** alternating current; **~ continua** direct current; **~ de aire** draught

**corromper** (koa-rroam-*payr*) *v* corrupt

**corrupción** (koa-rroop-*th<sup>Y</sup>oan*) *f* corruption

**corrupto** (koa-*rroop*-toa) *adj* corrupt
**corsé** (koar-*say*) *m* corset
**cortadura** (koar-tah-*dhoo*-rah) *f* cut
**cortaplumas** (koar-tah-*ploo*-mahss) *m* penknife
**cortar** (koar-*tahr*) *v* *cut; chip, *cut off
**corte** (*koar*-tay) *f* court
**cortés** (koar-*tayss*) *adj* civil, courteous, polite
**corteza** (koar-*tay*-thah) *f* bark; crust
**cortijo** (koar-*tee*-khoa) *m* farmhouse
**cortina** (koar-*tee*-nah) *f* curtain
**corto** (*koar*-toa) *adj* short
**cortocircuito** (koar-toa-theer-*kwee*-toa) *m* short circuit
**cosa** (*koa*-sah) *f* thing; **entre otras cosas** among other things
**cosecha** (koa-*say*-chah) *f* harvest, crop
**coser** (koa-*sayr*) *v* sew
**cosméticos** (koaz-*may*-tee-koass) *mpl* cosmetics *pl*
**cosquillear** (koass-kee-l*Y*ahr) *v* tickle
**costa** (*koass*-tah) *f* coast
**costar** (koass-*tahr*) *v* *cost
**coste** (*koass*-tay) *m* cost
**costilla** (koass-*tee*-l*Y*ah) *f* rib
**costoso** (koass-*toa*-soa) *adj* expensive
**costumbre** (koass-*toom*-bray) *f* custom; **costumbres** morals
**costura** (koass-*too*-rah) *f* seam; **sin ~** seamless
**cotidiano** (koa-tee-*dh*Y*ah*-noa) *adj* everyday
**cotorra** (koa-*toa*-rrah) *f* parakeet
**cráneo** (*krah*-nay-oa) *m* skull
**cráter** (*krah*-tayr) *m* crater
**creación** (kray-ah-*th*Y*oan*) *f* creation
**crear** (kray-*ahr*) *v* create
**crecer** (kray-*thayr*) *v* *grow
**crecimiento** (kray-thee-*m*Y*ayn*-toa) *m* growth
**crédito** (*kray*-dhee-toa) *m* credit
**crédulo** (*kray*-dhoo-loa) *adj* credulous

**creencia** (kray-*ayn*-th*Y*ah) *f* belief
**creer** (kray-*ayr*) *v* believe; guess, reckon
**crema** (*kray*-mah) *f* cream; **~ de afeitar** shaving-cream; **~ de base** foundation cream; **~ de noche** night-cream; **~ facial** face-cream; **~ hidratante** moisturizing cream; **~ para la piel** skin cream; **~ para las manos** hand cream
**cremallera** (kray-mah-*l*Y*ay*-rah) *f* zip
**cremoso** (kray-*moa*-soa) *adj* creamy
**crepúsculo** (kray-*pooss*-koo-loa) *m* twilight, dusk
**crespo** (*krayss*-poa) *adj* curly
**cresta** (*krayss*-tah) *f* ridge
**creta** (*kray*-tah) *f* chalk
**criada** (kr*Y*ah-dhah) *f* housemaid
**criado** (kr*Y*ah-dhoa) *m* servant
**criar** (kr*Y*ahr) *v* rear; raise
**criatura** (kr*Y*ah-*too*-rah) *f* creature; infant
**crimen** (*kree*-mayn) *m* crime
**criminal** (kree-mee-*nahl*) *adj* criminal; *m* criminal
**criminalidad** (kree-mee-nah-lee-*dhahdh*) *f* criminality
**crisis** (*kree*-seess) *f* crisis
**cristal** (kreess-*tahl*) *m* crystal; pane; **de ~** crystal
**cristiano** (kreess-*t*Y*ah*-noa) *adj* Christian; *m* Christian
**Cristo** (*kreess*-toa) Christ
**criterio** (kree-*tay*-r*Y*oa) *m* criterion
**crítica** (*kree*-tee-kah) *f* criticism
**criticar** (kree-tee-*kahr*) *v* criticize
**crítico** (*kree*-tee-koa) *adj* critical; *m* critic
**cromo** (*kroa*-moa) *m* chromium
**crónica** (*kroa*-nee-kah) *f* chronicle
**crónico** (*kroa*-nee-koa) *adj* chronic
**cronológico** (kroa-noa-*loa*-khee-koa) *adj* chronological
**cruce** (*kroo*-thay) *m* crossroads; **~ pa-**

**ra peatones** pedestrian crossing; crosswalk *nAm*

**crucero** (kroo-*thay*-roa) *m* cruise

**crucificar** (kroo-thee-fee-*kahr*) *v* crucify

**crucifijo** (kroo-thee-*fee*-khoa) *m* crucifix

**crucifixión** (kroo-thee-feek-s<sup>y</sup>oan) *f* crucifixion

**crudo** (*kroo*-dhoa) *adj* raw

**cruel** (krwayl) *adj* harsh, cruel

**crujido** (kroo-*khee*-dhoa) *m* crack

**crujiente** (kroo-kh<sup>y</sup>ayn-tay) *adj* crisp

**crujir** (kroo-*kheer*) *v* creak, crack

**cruz** (krooth) *f* cross

**cruzada** (kroo-*thah*-dhah) *f* crusade

**cruzar** (kroo-*thahr*) *v* cross

**cuadrado** (kwah-*dhrah*-dhoa) *adj* square; *m* square

**cuadriculado** (kwah-dhree-koo-*lah*-dhoa) *adj* chequered

**cuadro** (*kwah*-dhroa) *m* cadre; picture; **a cuadros** chequered; ~ **de distribución** switchboard

**cuál** (kwahl) *pron* which

**cualidad** (kwah-lee-*dhahdh*) *f* property

**cualquiera** (kwahl-*k<sup>y</sup>ay*-rah) *pron* anyone, anybody; whichever; **cualquier cosa** anything

**cuando** (*kwahn*-doa) *conj* when; ~ **quiera que** whenever

**cuándo** (*kwahn*-doa) *adv* when

**cuánto** (*kwahn*-toa) *adv* how much; how many; **cuanto más ... más** the ... the; **en cuanto a** as regards

**cuarenta** (kwah-*rayn*-tah) *num* forty

**cuarentena** (kwah-rayn-*tay*-nah) *f* quarantine

**cuartel** (kwahr-*tayl*) *m* barracks *pl*; ~ **general** headquarters *pl*

**cuarterón** (kwahr-tay-*roan*) *m* panel

**cuarto¹** (*kwahr*-toa) *num* fourth; *m* quarter; ~ **de hora** quarter of an hour

**cuarto²** (*kwahr*-toa) *m* chamber; ~ **de aseo** lavatory; washroom *nAm*; ~ **de baño** bathroom; ~ **de niños** nursery; ~ **para huéspedes** spare room

**cuatro** (*kwah*-troa) *num* four

**Cuba** (*koo*-bhah) *f* Cuba

**cubano** (koo-*bhah*-noa) *adj* Cuban; *m* Cuban

**cubierta** (koo-*bh<sup>y</sup>ayr*-tah) *f* cover; deck

**cubierto** (koo-*bh<sup>y</sup>ayr*-toa) *adj* cloudy

**cubiertos** (koo-*bh<sup>y</sup>ayr*-toass) *mpl* cutlery

**cubo** (*koo*-bhoa) *m* cube; ~ **de la basura** dustbin

**cubrir** (koo-*bhreer*) *v* cover

**cuclillo** (koo-*klee*-l<sup>y</sup>oa) *m* cuckoo

**cuchara** (koo-*chah*-rah) *f* spoon; soupspoon, tablespoon

**cucharada** (koo-chah-*rah*-dhah) *f* spoonful

**cucharadita** (koo-chah-rah-*dhee*-tah) *f* teaspoonful

**cucharilla** (koo-chah-*ree*-l<sup>y</sup>ah) *f* teaspoon

**cuchillo** (koo-*chee*-l<sup>y</sup>oa) *m* knife

**cuello** (*kway*-l<sup>y</sup>oa) *m* neck; collar; ~ **de botella** bottleneck

**cuenta** (*kwayn*-tah) *f* account; bill; check *nAm*; bead; ~ **de banco** bank account; \***darse** ~ \*see

**cuento** (*kwayn*-toa) *m* story, tale

**cuerda** (*kwayr*-dhah) *f* cord; string; \***dar** ~ \*wind

**cuerno** (*kwayr*-noa) *m* horn

**cuero** (*kway*-roa) *m* leather; ~ **vacuno** cow-hide

**cuerpo** (*kwayr*-poa) *m* body

**cuervo** (*kwayr*-bhoa) *m* raven

**cuestión** (kwayss-t<sup>y</sup>oan) *f* matter, issue, question

**cueva** (*kway*-bhah) *f* cavern, cave; wine-cellar

**cuidado** (kwee-*dhah*-dhoa) *m* care;
 *tener ~ watch out, look out
**cuidadoso** (kwee-dhah-*dhoa*-soa) *adj*
 careful; diligent
**cuidar de** (kwee-*dhahr*) attend to, look
 after, tend, *take care of
**culebra** (koo-*lay*-bhrah) *f* snake
**culpa** (*kool*-pah) *f* guilt, fault, blame
**culpable** (kool-*pah*-bhlay) *adj* guilty
**culpar** (kool-*pahr*) *v* blame
**cultivar** (kool-tee-*bhahr*) *v* cultivate;
 *grow, raise
**cultivo** (kool-*tee*-bhoa) *m* cultivation
**culto** (*kool*-toa) *adj* cultured; *m* worship
**cultura** (kool-*too*-rah) *f* culture
**cultural** (kool-too-*rahl*) *adj* cultural
**cumbre** (*koom*-bray) *f* peak
**cumpleaños** (koom-play-ah-ñoass) *m*
 birthday
**cumplimentar** (koom-plee-mayn-*tahr*)
 *v* compliment
**cumplimiento** (koom-plee-m<sup>y</sup>ayn-toa)
 *m* compliment
**cumplir** (koom-*pleer*) *v* accomplish
**cuna** (*koo*-nah) *f* cradle; ~ de viaje
 carry-cot
**cuneta** (koo-*nay*-tah) *f* ditch; gutter
**cuña** (*koo*-ñah) *f* wedge
**cuñada** (koo-*ñah*-dhah) *f* sister-in-law
**cuñado** (koo-*ñah*-dhoa) *m* brother-in-
 law
**cuota** (*kwoa*-tah) *f* quota
**cupón** (koo-*poan*) *m* coupon
**cúpula** (*koo*-poo-lah) *f* dome
**cura** (*koo*-rah) *m* priest; *f* cure
**curación** (koo-rah-th<sup>y</sup>oan) *f* cure, recovery
**curandero** (koo-rahn-*day*-roa) *m* quack
**curar** (koo-*rahr*) *v* cure, heal; curarse
 *v* recover
**curato** (koo-*rah*-toa) *m* parsonage
**curiosidad** (koo-r<sup>y</sup>oa-see-*dhahdh*) *f*
 curiosity; sight; curio

**curioso** (koo-r<sup>y</sup>oa-soa) *adj* curious; inquisitive; quaint
**cursiva** (koor-*see*-bhah) *f* italics *pl*
**curso** (*koor*-soa) *m* course; lecture; ~
 intensivo intensive course
**curva** (koor-bhah) *f* turn, curve, bend
**curvado** (koor-*bhah*-dhoa) *adj* curved
**curvo** (*koor*-bhoa) *adj* crooked, bent
**custodia** (kooss-*toa*-dh<sup>y</sup>ah) *f* custody
**cuyo** (*koo*-<sup>y</sup>oa) *pron* whose; of which

# CH

**chabacano** (chah-bhah-*kah*-noa) *mMe*
 apricot
**chal** (chahl) *m* shawl
**chaleco** (chah-*lay*-koa) *m* waistcoat;
 vest *nAm*; ~ salvavidas lifebelt
**chalet** (chah-*layt*) *m* chalet
**champán** (chahm-*pahn*) *m* champagne
**champú** (chahm-*poo*) *m* shampoo
**chantaje** (chahn-*tah*-khay) *m* blackmail; *hacer ~ blackmail
**chapa** (*chah*-pah) *f* plate, sheet
**chaparrón** (chah-pah-*rroan*) *m* cloud-
 burst
**chapucero** (chah-poo-*thay*-roa) *adj*
 sloppy
**chaqueta** (chah-*kay*-tah) *f* jacket; cardigan; ~ ligera blazer
**charanga** (chah-*rahng*-gah) *f* brass
 band
**charco** (*chahr*-koa) *m* puddle
**charla** (*chahr*-lah) *f* chat
**charlar** (chahr-*lahr*) *v* chat
**charlatán** (chahr-lah-*tahn*) *m* chatterbox; quack
**charola** (chah-*roa*-lah) *fMe* tray
**chasis** (chah-*seess*) *m* chassis
**chatarra** (chah-*tah*-rrah) *f* scrap-iron
**checo** (*chay*-koa) *adj* Czech; *m* Czech
**Checoslovaquia** (chay-koaz-loa-*bhah*-

kᵞah) f Czechoslovakia

**cheque** (*chay*-kay) m cheque; check nAm; ~ **de viajero** traveller's cheque

**chicle** (*chee*-klay) m chewing-gum

**chico** (*chee*-koa) m boy; kid

**chichón** (chee-*choan*) m lump

**Chile** (*chee*-lay) m Chile

**chileno** (chee-*lay*-noa) adj Chilean; m Chilean

**chillar** (chee-*lᵞahr*) v scream, shriek

**chillido** (chee-*lᵞee*-dhoa) m scream, shriek

**chimenea** (chee-may-*nay*-ah) f chimney; fireplace

**China** (*chee*-nah) f China

**chinche** (*cheen*-chay) f bug; drawing-pin; thumbtack nAm

**chinchorro** (cheen-*choa*-rroa) m dinghy

**chino** (*chee*-noa) adj Chinese; m Chinese; adjMe curly

**chisguete** (cheez-*gay*-tay) m squirt

**chisme** (*cheez*-may) m gossip; *****contar chismes** gossip

**chispa** (*cheess*-pah) f spark

**chistoso** (cheess-*toa*-soa) adj witty, humorous

**chocante** (choa-*kahn*-tay) adj revolting, shocking

**chocar** (choa-*kahr*) v collide, crash, bump; shock; ~ **contra** knock against

**chocolate** (choa-koa-*lah*-tay) m chocolate

**chófer** (*choa*-fayr) m chauffeur

**choque** (*choa*-kay) m crash; shock

**chorro** (*choa*-rroa) m spout, jet

**chuleta** (choo-*lay*-tah) f chop, cutlet

**chupar** (choo-*pahr*) v suck

# D

**dactilógrafa** (dahk-tee-*loa*-grah-fah) f typist

**dadivoso** (dah-dhee-*bhoa*-soa) adj liberal

**daltoniano** (dahl-toa-*nᵞah*-noa) adj colour-blind

**dama** (*dah*-mah) f lady

**danés** (dah-*nayss*) adj Danish; m Dane

**dañar** (dah-*ñahr*) v damage; *****hurt

**daño** (*dah*-ñoa) m mischief; harm; *****hacer** ~ *****hurt

**dañoso** (dah-*ñoa*-soa) adj harmful

*****dar** (dahr) v *****give; **dado que** supposing that

**dátil** (*dah*-teel) m date

**dato** (*dah*-toa) m data pl

**de** (day) prep of; out of, from, off; with

**debajo** (day-*bhah*-khoa) adv underneath, beneath, below; ~ **de** under, beneath, below

**debate** (day-*bhah*-tay) m debate, discussion

**debatir** (day-bhah-*teer*) v discuss

**debe** (*day*-bhay) m debit

**deber** (day-*bhayr*) m duty; v *****have to, need to, need; owe; ~ **de** *****be bound to

**debido** (day-*bhee*-dhoa) adj due; proper; ~ **a** owing to

**débil** (*day*-bheel) adj faint, weak, feeble

**debilidad** (day-bhee-lee-*dhahdh*) f weakness

**decencia** (day-*thayn*-thᵞah) f decency

**decente** (day-*thayn*-tay) adj decent

**decepcionar** (day-thayp-thᵞoa-*nahr*) v *****let down, disappoint

**decidir** (day-thee-*dheer*) v decide; decidido resolute

**décimo** (*day-thee-moa*) *num* tenth

**decimoctavo** (day-thee-moak-*tah*-bhoa) *num* eighteenth

**decimonono** (day-thee-moa-*noa*-noa) *num* nineteenth

**decimoséptimo** (day-thee-moa-*sayp*-tee-moa) *num* seventeenth

**decimosexto** (day-thee-moa-*sayks*-toa) *num* sixteenth

***decir** (day-*theer*) *v* *say, *tell; **querer** ~ *mean

**decisión** (day-thee-*s*ʸ*oan*) *f* decision

**decisivo** (day-thee-*see*-bhoa) *adj* decisive

**declaración** (day-klah-rah-*th*ʸ*oan*) *f* statement, declaration

**declarar** (day-klah-*rahr*) *v* state, declare

**decoración** (day-koa-rah-*th*ʸ*oan*) *f* decoration

**decorativo** (day-koa-rah-*tee*-bhoa) *adj* decorative

**decreto** (day-*kray*-toa) *m* decree

**dedal** (day-*dhahl*) *m* thimble

**dédalo** (*day*-dhah-loa) *m* muddle

**dedicar** (day-dhee-*kahr*) *v* devote, dedicate

**dedo** (*day*-dhoa) *m* finger; ~ **auricular** little finger; ~ **del pie** toe

***deducir** (day-dhoo-*theer*) *v* infer, deduce; deduct

**defecto** (day-*fayk*-toa) *m* fault

**defectuoso** (day-fayk-*twoa*-soa) *adj* defective, faulty

***defender** (day-fayn-*dayr*) *v* defend

**defensa** (day-*fayn*-sah) *f* defence; plea; *fMe* fender

**defensor** (day-fayn-*soar*) *m* champion

**deficiencia** (day-fee-*th*ʸ*ayn*-th*ʸ*ah) *f* deficiency, shortcoming

**déficit** (*day*-fee-theet) *m* deficit

**definición** (day-fee-nee-*th*ʸ*oan*) *f* definition

**definir** (day-fee-*neer*) *v* define; **definido** definite

**definitivo** (day-fee-nee-*tee*-bhoa) *adj* definitive

**deforme** (day-*foar*-may) *adj* deformed

**dejar** (day-*khahr*) *v* *let, *leave; *leave behind, desert; ~ **de** stop

**delantal** (day-lahn-*tahl*) *m* apron

**delante de** (day-*lahn*-tay day) before, in front of, ahead of

**delegación** (day-lay-gah-*th*ʸ*oan*) *f* delegation

**delegado** (day-lay-*gah*-dhoa) *m* delegate

**deleitable** (day-lay-*tah*-bhlay) *adj* enjoyable

**deleite** (day-*lay*-tay) *m* delight

**deleitoso** (day-lay-*toa*-soa) *adj* delightful

**deletrear** (day-lay-tray-*ahr*) *v* *spell

**deletreo** (day-lay-*tray*-oa) *m* spelling

**delgado** (dayl-*gah*-dhoa) *adj* thin

**deliberación** (day-lee-bhay-rah-*th*ʸ*oan*) *f* deliberation

**deliberar** (day-lee-bhay-*rahr*) *v* deliberate; **deliberado** *adj* deliberate

**delicado** (day-lee-*kah*-dhoa) *adj* delicate, tender

**delicia** (day-*lee*-th*ʸ*ah) *f* joy, delight

**delicioso** (day-lee-*th*ʸ*oa*-soa) *adj* wonderful, delightful, delicious, lovely

**delincuente** (day-leeng-*kwayn*-tay) *m* criminal

**delito** (day-*lee*-toa) *m* crime

**demanda** (day-*mahn*-dah) *f* request; application; demand

**demás** (day-*mahss*) *adj* remaining

**demasiado** (day-mah-*s*ʸ*ah*-dhoa) *adv* too

**democracia** (day-moa-*krah*-th*ʸ*ah) *f* democracy

**democrático** (day-moa-*krah*-tee-koa) *adj* democratic

***demoler** (day-moa-*layr*) *v* demolish

**demolición** (day-moa-lee-*th*ʸ*oan*) *f*
demolition

**demonio** (day-*moa*-nʸoa) *m* devil

**demostración** (day-moass-trah-*th*ʸ*oan*)
*f* demonstration

**\*demostrar** (day-moass-*trahr*) *v* demonstrate, \*show, prove

**\*denegar** (day-nay-*gahr*) *v* deny

**denominación** (day-noa-mee-nah-
*th*ʸ*oan*) *f* denomination

**denso** (*dayn*-soa) *adj* thick, dense

**dentadura postiza** (dayn-tah-*dhoo*-rah
poass-*tee*-thah) false teeth, denture

**dentista** (dayn-*teess*-tah) *m* dentist

**dentro** (*dayn*-troa) *adv* inside; **de ~**
within; **~ de** inside, within; into; in

**departamento** (day-pahr-tah-*mayn*-toa)
*m* department; section, division

**depender de** (day-payn-*dayr*) depend
on

**dependiente** (day-payn-*d*ʸ*ayn*-tay) *adj*
dependant; *m* shop assistant

**deporte** (day-*poar*-tay) *m* sport; **conjunto de ~** sportswear; **chaqueta
de ~** sports-jacket

**deportista** (day-poar-*teess*-tah) *m*
sportsman

**depositar** (day-poa-see-*tahr*) *v* bank

**depósito** (day-*poa*-see-toa) *m* deposit;
**~ de gasolina** petrol tank

**depresión** (day-pray-sʸ*oan*) *f* depression

**deprimente** (day-pree-*mayn*-tay) *adj*
depressing

**deprimir** (day-pree-*meer*) *v* depress;
**deprimido** blue, depressed, low

**derecho** (day-*ray*-choa) *m* right; law,
right, justice, straight; *adj* upright;
right-hand; **~ administrativo** administrative law; **~ civil** civil law;
**~ comercial** commercial law; **~
electoral** franchise, suffrage; **~ penal** criminal law

**derivar de** (day-ree-*bhahr*) \*be derived

from

**derramar** (day-rrah-*mahr*) *v* \*shed

**derribar** (day-rree-*bhahr*) *v* knock
down

**derrochador** (day-rroa-chah-*dhoar*) *adj*
wasteful

**derrota** (day-*rroa*-tah) *f* defeat

**derrotar** (day-rroa-*tahr*) *v* defeat

**derrumbarse** (day-rroom-*bahr*-say) *v*
collapse

**desabotonar** (day-sah-bhoa-toa-*nahr*) *v*
unbutton

**desacelerar** (day-sah-thay-lay-*rahr*) *v*
slow down

**desacostumbrado** (day-sah-koass-
toom-*brah*-dhoa) *adj* unaccustomed

**desacostumbrar** (day-sah-koass-toom-
*brahr*) *v* unlearn

**desafiar** (day-sah-*f*ʸ*ahr*) *v* dare; challenge

**desafilado** (day-sah-fee-*lah*-dhoa) *adj*
blunt

**desafortunado** (day-sah-foar-too-*nah*-
dhoa) *adj* unlucky, unfortunate

**desagradable** (day-sah-grah-*dhah*-
bhlay) *adj* nasty, disagreeable, unpleasant; unkind

**desagradar** (day-sah-grah-*dhahr*) *v* displease

**desagüe** (day-*sah*-gway) *m* sewer,
drain

**desaliñado** (day-sah-lee-*ñah*-doa) *adj*
untidy

**desamueblado** (day-sah-mway-*bhlah*-
dhoa) *adj* unfurnished

**desánimo** (day-*sah*-nee-moa) *m* depression

**\*desaparecer** (day-sah-pah-ray-*thayr*)
*v* disappear; vanish

**desaparecido** (day-sah-pah-ray-*thee*-
dhoa) *adj* lost; *m* missing person

**desapasionado** (day-sah-pah-sʸoa-*nah*-
dhoa) *adj* matter-of-fact

**\*desaprobar** (day-sah-proa-*bhahr*) *v*

disapprove

**desarrollar** (day-sah-rroa-*l*<sup>y</sup>*ahr*) v develop

**desarrollo** (day-sah-*rroa*-l<sup>y</sup>oa) m development

**desasosiego** (day-sah-soa-*s*<sup>y</sup>*ay*-goa) m unrest

**desastre** (day-*sahss*-tray) m disaster, calamity

**desastroso** (day-sahss-*troa*-soa) adj disastrous

**desatar** (day-sah-*tahr*) v *undo, untie, unfasten

**desautorizado** (day-sou-toa-ree-*thah*-dhoa) adj unauthorized

**desayuno** (day-sah-*Yoo*-noa) m breakfast

**descafeinado** (dayss-kah-fay-*nah*-dhoa) adj decaffeinated

**descansar** (dayss-kahn-*sahr*) v rest; relax

**descanso** (dayss-*kahn*-soa) m rest; break; half-time

**descarado** (dayss-kah-*rah*-dhoa) adj bold, impertinent

**descargar** (dayss-kahr-*gahr*) v discharge, unload

**descendencia** (day-thayn-*dayn*-th<sup>y</sup>ah) f origin

*descender* (day-thayn-*dhayr*) v *fall

**descendiente** (day-thayn-*d*<sup>y</sup>*ayn*-tay) m descendant

**descolorido** (dayss-koa-loa-ree-dhoa) adj discoloured

**descompostura** (dayss-koam-poass-*too*-rah) fMe breakdown

*desconcertar* (dayss-koan-thayr-*tahr*) v overwhelm, embarrass

**desconectar** (dayss-koa-nayk-*tahr*) v disconnect

**desconfiado** (dayss-koan-*f*<sup>y</sup>*ah*-dhoa) adj suspicious

**desconfianza** (dayss-koan-*f*<sup>y</sup>*ahn*-thah) f suspicion

**desconfiar de** (dayss-koan-*f*<sup>y</sup>*ahr*) v mistrust

**descongelarse** (dayss-koang-khay-*lahr*-say) v thaw

*desconocer* (dayss-koa-noa-*thayr*) v not to *know, fail to recognize

**desconocido** (dayss-koa-noa-*thee*-dhoa) adj unknown; unfamiliar

**descontento** (dayss-koan-*tayn*-toa) adj discontented

**descorchar** (dayss-koar-*chahr*) v uncork

**descortés** (dayss-koar-*tayss*) adj impolite

**describir** (dayss-kree-*bheer*) v describe

**descripción** (dayss-kreep-*th*<sup>y</sup>*oan*) f description

**descubrimiento** (dayss-koo-bhree-*m*<sup>y</sup>*ayn*-toa) m discovery

**descubrir** (dayss-koo-*bhreer*) v discover, detect

**descuento** (dayss-*kwayn*-toa) m discount; ~ **bancario** bank-rate

**descuidar** (dayss-kwee-*dhahr*) v neglect; **descuidado** slovenly

**descuido** (dayss-*kwee*-dhoa) m oversight

**desde** (*dayz*-dhay) prep from; since; ~ **entonces** since; ~ **que** since

**desdén** (dayz-*dhayn*) m disdain

**desdichado** (dayz-dhee-*chah*-dhoa) adj unhappy

**deseable** (day-say-ah-bhlay) adj desirable

**desear** (day-say-*ahr*) v desire; wish, want

**desecar** (day-say-*kahr*) v drain

**desechable** (day-say-*chah*-bhlay) adj disposable

**desechar** (day-say-*chahr*) v discard

**desecho** (day-*say*-choa) m refuse

**desembarcar** (day-saym-bahr-*kahr*) v disembark; land

**desembocadura** (day-saym-boa-kah-

*dhoo*-rah ) *f* mouth

**desempaquetar** (day-saym-pah-kay-*tahr*) *v* unpack

**desempeñar** (day-saym-pay-*ñahr*) *v* perform

**desempleo** (day-saym-*play*-oa ) *m* unemployment

**desengaño** (day-sayng-*gah*-ñoa ) *m* disappointment

**desenvoltura** (day-saym-boal-*too*-rah ) *f* ease

**\*desenvolver** (day-saym-boal-*bhayr*) *v* unwrap

**deseo** (day-*say*-oa ) *m* wish, desire

**desertar** (day-sayr-*tahr*) *v* desert

**desesperación** (day-sayss-pay-rah-th<sup>y</sup>oan ) *f* despair

**desesperado** (day-sayss-pay-*rah*-dhoa ) *adj* hopeless, desperate; **\*estar ~** despair

**desfavorable** (dayss-fah-bhoa-*rah*-bhlay ) *adj* unfavourable

**desfile** (dayss-*fee*-lay ) *m* parade

**desgarrar** (dayz-gah-*rrahr*) *v* \*tear

**desgracia** (dayz-*grah*-th<sup>y</sup>ah ) *f* misfortune

**desgraciadamente** (dayz-grah-th<sup>y</sup>ah-dhah-*mayn*-tay ) *adv* unfortunately

**\*deshacer** (day-sah-*thayr*) *v* \*undo

**deshielo** (day-s<sup>y</sup>ay-loa ) *m* thaw

**deshilacharse** (day-see-lah-*chahr*-say ) *v* fray

**deshonesto** (day-soa-*nayss*-toa ) *adj* crooked

**deshonor** (day-soa-*noar*) *m* disgrace

**deshonra** (day-*soan*-rah ) *f* shame

**deshuesar** (day-sway-*sahr*) *v* bone

**desierto** (day-s<sup>y</sup>ayr-toa ) *adj* desert; *m* desert

**designar** (day-seeg-*nahr*) *v* designate; appoint

**desigual** (day-see-*gwahl*) *adj* unequal, uneven

**desinclinado** (day-seeng-klee-*nah-*

dhoa ) *adj* unwilling

**desinfectante** (day-seen-fayk-*tahn*-tay ) *m* disinfectant

**desinfectar** (day-seen-fayk-*tahr*) *v* disinfect

**desinteresado** (day-seen-tay-ray-sah-dhoa ) *adj* unselfish

**desliz** (dayz-*leeth*) *m* slide; slip

**deslizarse** (dayz-lee-*thahr*-say ) *v* \*slide; slip

**deslucido** (dayz-loo-*thee*-dhoa ) *adj* dim

**deslumbrador** (dayz-loom-brah-*dhoar*) *adj* glaring

**desmayarse** (dayz-mah-<sup>y</sup>ahr-say ) *v* faint

**desnudarse** (dayz-noo-*dhahr*-say ) *v* undress

**desnudo** (dayz-*noo*-dhoa ) *adj* naked, nude, bare; *m* nude

**desnutrición** (dayz-noo-tree-th<sup>y</sup>oan ) *f* malnutrition

**desocupado** (day-soa-koo-*pah*-dhoa ) *adj* unoccupied; unemployed

**desodorante** (day-soa-dhoa-*rahn*-tay ) *m* deodorant

**desorden** (day-*soar*-dayn ) *m* disorder; mess

**despachar** (dayss-pah-*chahr*) *v* dispatch, despatch, \*send off

**despacho** (dayss-*pah*-choa ) *m* study

**despedida** (dayss-pay-*dhee*-dhah ) *f* parting; departure

**\*despedir** (dayss-pay-*dheer*) *v* dismiss; fire; **\*despedirse** *v* check out

**despegar** (dayss-pay-*gahr*) *v* \*take off

**despegue** (dayss-*pay*-gay ) *m* take-off

**despensa** (dayss-*payn*-sah ) *f* larder

**desperdicio** (dayss-payr-*dhee*-th<sup>y</sup>oa ) *m* litter; waste

**despertador** (dayss-payr-tah-*dhoar*) *m* alarm-clock

**\*despertar** (dayss-payr-*tahr*) *v* \*wake, \*awake; **\*despertarse** *v* wake up

**despierto** (dayss-p<sup>y</sup>ayr-toa ) *adj*

awake; vigilant

* **desplegar** (dayss-play-*gahr*) v unfold; expand

**desplomarse** (dayss-ploa-*mahr*-say) v collapse

**despreciar** (dayss-pray-*th*Yahr) v scorn, despise

**desprecio** (dayss-*pray*-th Yoa) m scorn, contempt

**despreocupado** (dayss-pray-oa-koo-pah-dhoa) adj carefree

**después** (dayss-*pwayss*) adv afterwards; then; ~ **de** after; ~ **de que** after

**destacado** (dayss-tah-*kah*-dhoa) adj outstanding

**destacarse** (dayss-tah-*kahr*-say) v *stand out

**destapar** (dayss-tah-*pahr*) v uncover

**destartalado** (dayss-tahr-tah-*lah*-dhoa) adj ramshackle

**destello** (dayss-*tay*-lYoa) m glare

* **desteñirse** (dayss-tay-*ñeer*-say) v fade, discolour; **no destiñe** fast-dyed

**destinar** (dayss-tee-*nahr*) v destine; address

**destinatario** (dayss-tee-nah-*tah*-rYoa) m addressee

**destino** (dayss-*tee*-noa) m fate, destiny, lot; destination

**destornillador** (dayss-toar-nee-lYah-*dhoar*) m screw-driver

**destornillar** (dayss-toar-nee-*lYahr*) v unscrew

**destrucción** (dayss-trook-*th*Yoan) f destruction

* **destruir** (dayss-*trweer*) v destroy; wreck

**desvalorización** (dayz-bhah-loa-ree-thah-*th*Yoan) f devaluation

**desvalorizar** (dayz-bhah-loa-ree-*thahr*) v devalue

**desvelado** (dayz-bhay-*lah*-dhoa) adj

sleepless

**desventaja** (dayz-bhayn-*tah*-khah) f disadvantage

**desviar** (dayz-*bh*Yahr) v avert; **desviarse** v deviate

**desvío** (dayz-*bhee*-oa) m detour; diversion

**detallado** (day-tah-*l*Yah-dhoa) adj detailed

**detalle** (day-*tah*-lYay) m detail; **vender al** ~ retail

**detective** (day-tayk-*tee*-bhay) m detective

**detención** (day-tayn-*th*Yoan) f custody

* **detener** (day-tay-*nayr*) v detain

**detergente** (day-tayr-*khayn*-tay) m detergent

**determinar** (day-tayr-mee-*nahr*) v define, determine; **determinado** definite

**detestar** (day-tayss-*tahr*) v hate, dislike

**detrás** (day-*trahss*) adv behind; ~ **de** behind, after

**deuda** (*day*oo-dhah) f debt

* **devolver** (day-bhoal-*bhayr*) v *bring back; *send back

**día** (*dee*-ah) m day; **¡buenos días!** hello!; **de** ~ by day; ~ **de trabajo** working day; ~ **laborable** weekday; **el otro** ~ recently

**diabetes** (dYah-*bhay*-tayss) f diabetes

**diabético** (dYah-*bhay*-tee-koa) m diabetic

**diablo** (dYah-bhloa) m devil

**diabluras** (dYah-bhloo-rahss) fpl mischief

**diagnosis** (dYahg-*noa*-seess) m diagnosis

**diagnosticar** (dYahg-noass-tee-*kahr*) v diagnose

**diagonal** (dYah-goa-*nahl*) adj diagonal; f diagonal

**dialecto** (dYah-*layk*-toa) m dialect

**diamante** (dᵞah-*mahn*-tay) *m* diamond

**diapositiva** (dᵞah-poa-see-*tee*-bhah) *f* slide

**diario** (dᵞah-rᵞoa) *adj* daily; *m* daily, newspaper; diary; **a ~** per day; **~ matutino** morning paper

**diarrea** (dᵞah-*rray*-ah) *f* diarrhoea

**dibujar** (dee-bhoo-*khahr*) *v* sketch, *draw

**dibujo** (dee-*bhoo*-khoa) *m* sketch, drawing; **dibujos animados** cartoon

**diccionario** (deek-thᵞoa-*nah*-rᵞoa) *m* dictionary

**diciembre** (dee-*thᵞaym*-bray) December

**dictado** (deek-*tah*-dhoa) *m* dictation

**dictador** (deek-tah-*dhoar*) *m* dictator

**dictadura** (deek-tah-*dhoo*-rah) *f* dictatorship

***dictáfono** (deek-*tah*-foa-noa) *m* dictaphone

**dictar** (deek-*tahr*) *v* dictate

**dichoso** (dee-*choa*-soa) *adj* happy

**diecinueve** (dᵞay-thee-*nway*-bhay) *num* nineteen

**dieciocho** (dᵞay-thᵞoa-choa) *num* eighteen

**dieciséis** (dᵞay-thee-*sayss*) *num* sixteen

**diecisiete** (dᵞay-thee-sᵞay-tay) *num* seventeen

**diente** (dᵞayn-tay) *m* tooth; **~ de león** dandelion

**diesel** (*dee*-sayl) *m* diesel

**diestro** (dᵞayss-troa) *adj* skilful

**diez** (dᵞayth) *num* ten

**diferencia** (dee-fay-*rayn*-thᵞah) *f* difference; contrast, distinction

**diferente** (dee-fay-*rayn*-tay) *adj* different; unlike

***diferir** (dee-fay-*reer*) *v* vary, differ; delay

**difícil** (dee-*fee*-theel) *adj* hard, difficult

**dificultad** (dee-fee-kool-*tahdh*) *f* difficulty

**difteria** (deef-*tay*-rᵞah) *f* diphtheria

**difunto** (dee-*foon*-toa) *adj* dead

**difuso** (dee-*foo*-soa) *adj* dim

**digerible** (dee-khayss-*tee*-bhlay) *adj* digestible

***digerir** (dee-khay-*reer*) *v* digest

**digestión** (dee-khayss-tᵞoan) *f* digestion

**dignidad** (deeg-nee-*dhahdh*) *f* dignity

**digno de** (*dee*-ñoa day) worthy of

**dilación** (dee-lah-*thᵞoan*) *f* delay, respite

**diligencia** (dee-lee-*khayn*-thᵞah) *f* diligence

**diligente** (dee-lee-*khayn*-tay) *adj* industrious

***diluir** (dee-*lweer*) *v* dilute

**dimensión** (dee-mayn-sᵞoan) *f* extent, size

**Dinamarca** (dee-nah-*mahr*-kah) *f* Denmark

**dínamo** (*dee*-nah-moa) *f* dynamo

**dinero** (dee-*nay*-roa) *m* money; **~ contante** cash

**dios** (dᵞoass) *m* god

**diosa** (dᵞoa-sah) *f* goddess

**diploma** (dee-*ploa*-mah) *m* diploma, certificate

**diplomático** (dee-ploa-*mah*-tee-koa) *m* diplomat

**diputado** (dee-poo-*tah*-dhoa) *m* deputy; Member of Parliament

**dique** (*dee*-kay) *m* dike, dam

**dirección** (dee-rayk-thᵞoan) *f* direction; way; address; leadership, lead; **~ de escena** direction; **~ única** one-way traffic

**directamente** (dee-rayk-tah-*mayn*-tay) *adv* straight; straight away

**directo** (dee-*rayk*-toa) *adj* direct

**director** (dee-rayk-*toar*) *m* director,

manager; conductor; ~ **de escuela**
head teacher, headmaster; principal

**directorio telefónico** (dee-rayk-*toa*-r<sup>y</sup>oa tay-lay-*foa*-nee-koa) *Me* telephone directory

**directriz** (dee-rayk-*treeth*) *f* directive

**dirigir** (dee-ree-*kheer*) *v* head; direct; **dirigirse a** address

**disciplina** (dee-thee-*plee*-nah) *f* discipline

**discípulo** (deess-*thee*-poo-loa) *m* pupil

**disco** (*deess*-koa) *m* disc; record

**discreto** (deess-*kray*-toa) *adj* inconspicuous

**disculpa** (deess-*kool*-pah) *f* apology

**disculpar** (deess-kool-*pahr*) *v* excuse; **disculparse** *v* apologize; **¡disculpe!** sorry!

**discurso** (deess-*koor*-soa) *m* speech

**discusión** (deess-koo-s<sup>y</sup>oan) *f* discussion, argument

**discutir** (deess-koo-*teer*) *v* discuss, deliberate, argue

**disentería** (dee-sayn-tay-*ree*-ah) *f* dysentery

**\*disentir** (dee-sayn-*teer*) *v* disagree

**diseñar** (dee-say-*ñahr*) *v* design

**diseño** (dee-*say*-ñoa) *m* design; pattern; **cuaderno de** ~ sketch-book

**disfraz** (deess-*frahth*) *m* disguise

**disfrazarse** (deess-frah-*thahr*-say) *v* disguise

**disfrutar** (deess-froo-*tahr*) *v* enjoy

**disgustar** (deez-gooss-*tahr*) *v* displease

**disimular** (dee-see-moo-*lahr*) *v* conceal

**dislocado** (deez-loa-kah-dhoa) *adj* dislocated

**dislocar** (deez-loa-*kahr*) *v* wrench

**disminución** (deez-mee-noo-th<sup>y</sup>oan) *f* decrease

**\*disminuir** (deez-mee-*nweer*) *v* reduce, lessen, decrease

**\*disolver** (dee-soal-*bhayr*) *v* dissolve

**disparar** (deess-pah-*rahr*) *v* fire

**disparo** (deess-*pah*-roa) *m* shot

**dispensar** (deess-payn-*sahr*) *v* exempt; ~ **de** discharge of; **¡dispense usted!** sorry!

**dispensario** (deess-payn-*sah*-r<sup>y</sup>oa) *m* health centre

**\*disponer** (deess-poa-*nayr*) *v* sort; ~ **de** dispose of

**disponible** (deess-poa-*nee*-bhlay) *adj* available; spare

**disposición** (deess-poa-see-th<sup>y</sup>oan) *f* disposal

**dispuesto** (deess-*pwayss*-toa) *adj* inclined, willing

**disputa** (deess-*poo*-tah) *f* dispute, argument, quarrel

**disputar** (deess-poo-*tahr*) *v* argue, quarrel; dispute

**distancia** (deess-*tahn*-th<sup>y</sup>ah) *f* distance; space, way

**distinción** (deess-teen-th<sup>y</sup>oan) *f* distinction, difference

**distinguido** (deess-teeng-*gee*-dhoa) *adj* distinguished, dignified

**distinguir** (deess-teeng-*geer*) *v* distinguish; **distinguirse** *v* excel

**distinto** (deess-*teen*-toa) *adj* distinct

**distracción** (deess-trahk-th<sup>y</sup>oan) *f* amusement

**\*distraer** (deess-trah-*ayr*) *v* distract

**distribuidor** (deess-tree-bhwee-*dhoar*) *m* distributor

**\*distribuir** (deess-tree-*bhweer*) *v* distribute; issue

**distrito** (deess-*tree*-toa) *m* district; ~ **electoral** constituency

**disturbio** (deess-*toor*-bh<sup>y</sup>oa) *m* disturbance

**disuadir** (dee-swah-*dheer*) *v* dissuade from

**diván** (dee-*bhahn*) *m* couch

**diversión** (dee-bhayr-s<sup>y</sup>oan) *f* pleasure, fun; diversion, entertainment

**diverso** (dee-*bhayr*-soa) *adj* diverse

**divertido** (dee-bhayr-*tee*-dhoa) *adj* amusing, entertaining

*__divertir__ (dee-bhayr-*teer*) *v* amuse, entertain

**dividir** (dee-bhee-*dheer*) *v* divide

**divino** (dee-*bhee*-noa) *adj* divine

**división** (dee-bhee-s<sup>y</sup>*oan*) *f* division; section

**divorciar** (dee-bhoar-th<sup>y</sup>*ahr*) *v* divorce

**divorcio** (dee-*bhoar*-th<sup>y</sup>oa) *m* divorce

**dobladillo** (doa-bhlah-*dhee*-l<sup>y</sup>oa) *m* hem

**doblar** (doa-*bhlahr*) *v* \*bend; fold

**doble** (*doa*-bhlay) *adj* double

**doce** (*doa*-thay) *num* twelve

**docena** (doa-*thay*-nah) *f* dozen

**doctor** (doak-*toar*) *m* doctor

**doctrina** (doak-*tree*-nah) *f* doctrine

**documento** (doa-koo-*mayn*-toa) *m* document

*__doler__ (doa-*layr*) *v* ache

**dolor** (doa-*loar*) *m* ache, pain; grief; **dolores** *mpl* labour; **sin ~** painless

**dolorido** (doa-loa-*ree*-dhoa) *adj* painful

**doloroso** (doa-loa-*roa*-soa) *adj* sore

**domesticado** (doa-mayss-tee-*kah*-dhoa) *adj* tame

**domesticar** (doa-mayss-tee-*kahr*) *v* tame

**doméstico** (doa-*mayss*-tee-koa) *adj* domestic; **faenas domésticas** housework

**domicilio** (doa-mee-*thee*-l<sup>y</sup>oa) *m* domicile

**dominación** (doa-mee-nah-*th<sup>y</sup>oan*) *f* domination

**dominante** (doa-mee-*nahn*-tay) *adj* leading

**dominar** (doa-mee-*nahr*) *v* master

**domingo** (doa-*meeng*-goa) *m* Sunday

**dominio** (doa-*mee*-n<sup>y</sup>oa) *m* dominion, rule

**don** (doan) *m* faculty

**donación** (doa-nah-*th<sup>y</sup>oan*) *f* donation

**donante** (doa-*nahn*-tay) *m* donor

**donar** (doa-*nahr*) *v* donate

**doncella** (doan-*thay*-l<sup>y</sup>ah) *f* chambermaid

**donde** (*doan*-day) *conj* where; **en ~ sea** anywhere

**dónde** (*doan*-day) *adv* where

**dondequiera** (doan-day-k<sup>y</sup>*ay*-rah) *adv* anywhere; **~ que** wherever

**dorado** (doa-*rah*-dhoa) *adj* gilt; golden

**dormido** (doar-*mee*-dhoa) *adj* asleep; **quedarse ~** \*oversleep

*__dormir__ (doar-*meer*) *v* \*sleep

**dormitorio** (doar-mee-*toa*-r<sup>y</sup>oa) *m* bedroom; dormitory

**dos** (doass) *num* two; **~ veces** twice

**dosis** (*doa*-seess) *f* dose

**dotado** (doa-*tah*-dhoa) *adj* talented

**dragón** (drah-*goan*) *m* dragon

**drama** (*drah*-mah) *m* drama

**dramático** (drah-*mah*-tee-koa) *adj* dramatic

**dramaturgo** (drah-mah-*toor*-goa) *m* playwright, dramatist

**drenar** (dray-*nahr*) *v* drain

**droguería** (droa-gay-*ree*-ah) *f* chemist's, pharmacy; drugstore *nAm*

**ducha** (*doo*-chah) *f* shower

**duda** (*doo*-dhah) *f* doubt; *__poner en ~** query; **sin ~** undoubtedly, without doubt

**dudar** (doo-*dhahr*) *v* doubt

**dudoso** (doo-*dhoa*-soa) *adj* doubtful

**duelo** (*dway*-loa) *m* duel; grief

**duende** (*dwayn*-dhay) *m* elf

**dueña** (*dway*-ñah) *f* mistress

**dueño** (*dway*-ñoa) *m* landlord

**dulce** (*dool*-thay) *adj* sweet; smooth; *m* sweet; **dulces** cake; sweets; candy *nAm*

**duna** (*doo*-nah) *f* dune

**duodécimo** (dwoa-*day*-thee-moa) *num* twelfth

**duque** (*doo*-kay) *m* duke

**duquesa** (doo-*kay*-sah) *f* duchess
**duración** (doo-rah-*th*ʸ*oan*) *f* duration
**duradero** (doo-rah-*dhay*-roa) *adj* permanent, lasting
**durante** (doo-*rahn*-tay) *prep* for, during
**durar** (doo-*rahr*) *v* last; continue
**duro** (*doo*-roa) *adj* hard; tough

# E

**ébano** (*ay*-bhah-noa) *m* ebony
**eclipse** (ay-*kleep*-say) *m* eclipse
**eco** (*ay*-koa) *m* echo
**economía** (ay-koa-noa-*mee*-ah) *f* economy
**económico** (ay-koa-*noa*-mee-koa) *adj* economic; thrifty, economical; cheap
**economista** (ay-koa-noa-*meess*-tah) *m* economist
**economizar** (ay-koa-noa-mee-*thahr*) *v* economize
**Ecuador** (ay-kwah-*dhoar*) *m* Ecuador
**ecuador** (ay-kwah-*dhoar*) *m* equator
**ecuatoriano** (ay-kwah-toa-*r*ʸ*ah*-noa) *m* Ecuadorian
**eczema** (ayk-*thay*-mah) *m* eczema
**echada** (ay-*chah*-dhah) *f* cast
**echar** (ay-*chahr*) *v* toss; ~ **al correo** post; ~ **a perder** *spoil; ~ **la culpa** blame
**edad** (ay-*dhahdh*) *f* age; **mayor de** ~ of age; **menor de** ~ under age
**Edad Media** (ay-*dhahdh* may-dh*ʸ*ah) Middle Ages
**edición** (ay-dhee-*th*ʸ*oan*) *f* issue, edition; ~ **de mañana** morning edition
**edificar** (ay-dhee-fee-*kahr*) *v* construct
**edificio** (ay-dhee-*fee*-th*ʸ*oa) *m* construction, building

**editor** (ay-dhee-*toar*) *m* publisher
**edredón** (ay-dhray-*dhoan*) *m* eiderdown
**educación** (ay-dhoo-kah-*th*ʸ*oan*) *f* education
**educar** (ay-dhoo-*kahr*) *v* educate, *bring up, raise
**efectivamente** (ay-fayk-tee-bhah-*mayn*-tay) *adv* as a matter of fact, in fact
**efectivo** (ay-fayk-*tee*-bhoa) *m* cash; *hacer ~ cash
**efecto** (ay-*fayk*-toa) *m* effect
**efectuar** (ay-fayk-*twahr*) *v* effect; implement
**efervescencia** (ay-fayr-bhay-*thayn*-th*ʸ*ah) *f* fizz
**eficacia** (ay-fee-*kah*-th*ʸ*ah) *f* efficacy
**eficaz** (ay-fee-*kahth*) *adj* effective
**eficiente** (ay-fee-*th*ʸ*ayn*-tay) *adj* efficient
**egipcio** (ay-*kheep*-th*ʸ*oa) *adj* Egyptian; *m* Egyptian
**Egipto** (ay-*kheep*-toa) *m* Egypt
**egocéntrico** (ay-goa-*thayn*-tree-koa) *adj* self-centred
**egoísmo** (ay-goa-*eez*-moa) *m* selfishness
**egoísta** (ay-goa-*eess*-tah) *adj* egoistic, selfish
**eje** (*ay*-khay) *m* axle
**ejecución** (ay-khay-koo-*th*ʸ*oan*) *f* execution
**ejecutar** (ay-khay-koo-*tahr*) *v* perform, execute
**ejecutivo** (ay-khay-koo-*tee*-bhoa) *adj* executive; *m* executive
**ejemplar** (ay-khaym-*plahr*) *m* copy
**ejemplo** (ay-*khaym*-ploa) *m* instance, example; **por** ~ for instance, for example
**ejercer** (ay-khayr-*thayr*) *v* exercise
**ejercicio** (ay-khayr-*thee*-th*ʸ*oa) *m* exercise
**ejercitar** (ay-khayr-thee-*tahr*) *v* exercise

**ejército** (ay-*khayr*-thee-toa) *m* army

**ejote** (ay-*khoa*-tay) *mMe* bean

**el** (ayl) *art* (f la; pl los, las) the *art*

**él** (ayl) *pron* he

**elaborar** (ay-lah-boa-*rahr*) *v* elaborate

**elasticidad** (ay-lahss-tee-thee-*dhahdh*) *f* elasticity

**elástico** (ay-*lahss*-tee-koa) *adj* elastic; *m* rubber band

**elección** (ay-layk-*th<sup>y</sup>oan*) *f* choice, pick, selection; election

**electricidad** (ay-layk-tree-thee-*dhahdh*) *f* electricity

**electricista** (ay-layk-tree-*theess*-tah) *m* electrician

**eléctrico** (ay-*layk*-tree-koa) *adj* electric

**electrónico** (ay-layk-*troa*-nee-koa) *adj* electronic

**elefante** (ay-lay-*fahn*-tay) *m* elephant

**elegancia** (ay-lay-*gahn*-th<sup>y</sup>ah) *f* elegance

**elegante** (ay-lay-*gahn*-tay) *adj* smart, elegant

*****elegir** (ay-lay-*kheer*) *v* elect, select

**elemental** (ay-lay-mayn-*tahl*) *adj* primary

**elemento** (ay-lay-*mayn*-toa) *m* element

**elevador** (ay-lay-bhah-*dhoar*) *mMe* lift; elevator *nAm*

**elevar** (ay-lay-*bhahr*) *v* elevate

**eliminar** (ay-lee-mee-*nahr*) *v* eliminate

**elogio** (ay-*loa*-kh<sup>y</sup>oa) *m* praise, glory

**elucidar** (ay-loo-thee-*dhahr*) *v* elucidate

**ella** (*ay*-l<sup>y</sup>ah) *pron* she

**ello** (*ay*-l<sup>y</sup>oa) *pron* it

**ellos** (*ay*-l<sup>y</sup>oass) *pron* they

**emancipación** (ay-mahn-thee-pah-*th<sup>y</sup>oan*) *f* emancipation

**embajada** (aym-bah-*khah*-dhah) *f* embassy

**embajador** (aym-bah-khah-*dhoar*) *m* ambassador

**embalaje** (aym-bah-*lah*-khay) *m* packing

**embalar** (aym-bah-*lahr*) *v* pack

**embalse** (aym-*bahl*-say) *m* reservoir

**embarazada** (aym-bah-rah-*thah*-dhah) *adj* pregnant

**embarazoso** (aym-bah-rah-*thoa*-soa) *adj* embarrassing, awkward; puzzling

**embarcación** (aym-bahr-kah-*th<sup>y</sup>oan*) *f* vessel; embarkation

**embarcar** (aym-bahr-*kahr*) *v* embark

**embargar** (aym-bahr-*gahr*) *v* confiscate

**embargo** (aym-*bahr*-goa) *m* embargo; **sin ~** yet, however, though, still

**emblema** (aym-*blay*-mah) *m* emblem

**emboscada** (aym-boass-*kah*-dhah) *f* ambush

**embotado** (aym-boa-*tah*-dhoa) *adj* dull

**embotellamiento** (aym-boa-tay-l<sup>y</sup>ah-m<sup>y</sup>ayn-toa) *m* traffic jam

**embrague** (aym-*brah*-gay) *m* clutch

**embriagado** (aym-br<sup>y</sup>ah-*gah*-dhoa) *adj* intoxicated

**embrollar** (aym-broa-*l<sup>y</sup>ahr*) *v* muddle

**embrollo** (aym-*broa*-l<sup>y</sup>oa) *m* muddle

**embromar** (aym-broa-*mahr*) *v* kid

**embudo** (aym-*boo*-dhoa) *m* funnel

**emergencia** (ay-mayr-*khayn*-th<sup>y</sup>ah) *f* emergency

**emigración** (ay-mee-grah-*th<sup>y</sup>oan*) *f* emigration

**emigrante** (ay-mee-*grahn*-tay) *m* emigrant

**emigrar** (ay-mee-*grahr*) *v* emigrate

**eminente** (ay-mee-*nayn*-tay) *adj* outstanding

**emisión** (ay-mee-*s<sup>y</sup>oan*) *f* issue

**emisor** (ay-mee-*soar*) *m* transmitter

**emitir** (ay-mee-*teer*) *v* *broadcast; utter

**emoción** (ay-moa-*th<sup>y</sup>oan*) *f* emotion

**empalme** (aym-*pahl*-may) *m* junction

**empapar** (aym-pah-*pahr*) *v* soak

**empaquetar** (aym-pah-kay-*tahr*) *v* pack up

**emparedado** (aym-pah-ray-*dhah*-dhoa) *m* sandwich

**emparentado** (aym-pah-rayn-*tah*-dhoa) *adj* related

**empaste** (aym-*pahss*-tay) *m* filling

**empeñar** (aym-pay-*ñahr*) *v* pawn

**empeño** (aym-*pay*-ño) *m* pawn; determination

**emperador** (aym-pay-rah-*dhoar*) *m* emperor

**emperatriz** (aym-pay-rah-*treeth*) *f* empress

*****empezar** (aym-pay-*thahr*) *v* *begin, start

**empleado** (aym-play-*ah*-dhoa) *m* employee; ~ **de oficina** clerk

**emplear** (aym-play-*ahr*) *v* employ; engage

**empleo** (aym-*play*-oa) *m* job, employment

**emprender** (aym-prayn-*dayr*) *v* *undertake

**empresa** (aym-*pray*-sah) *f* undertaking, enterprise; concern, business

**empujar** (aym-poo-*khahr*) *v* push; press

**empujón** (aym-poo-*khoan*) *m* push

**en** (ayn) *prep* at, in; inside, to

**enamorado** (ay-nah-moa-*rah*-dhoa) *adj* in love

**enamorarse** (aynah-moa-*rahr*-say) *v* *fall in love

**enano** (ay-*nah*-noa) *m* dwarf

**encantado** (ayng-kahn-*tah*-dhoa) *adj* delighted

**encantador** (ayng-kahn-tah-*dhoar*) *adj* glamorous; charming, enchanting

**encantar** (ayng-kahn-*tahr*) *v* delight; bewitch

**encanto** (ayng-*kahn*-toa) *m* glamour, charm; spell

**encarcelamiento** (ayng-kahr-thay-lah-*m*ᵛ*ayn*-toa) *m* imprisonment

**encarcelar** (ayng-kahr-thay-*lahr*) *v* imprison

**encargarse de** (ayng-kahr-*gahr*-say) *take over, *take charge of

**encargo** (ayng-*kahr*-goa) *m* assignment

**encariñado con** (ayng-kah-ree-*ñah*-dhoa koan) attached to

**encendedor** (ayn-thayn-day-*dhoar*) *m* cigarette-lighter

*****encender** (ayn-thayn-*dayr*) *v* *light; turn on, switch on

**encendido** (ayn-thayn-*dee*-dhoa) *m* ignition

*****encerrar** (ayn-thay-*rrahr*) *v* *shut in; encircle

**encía** (ayn-*thee*-ah) *f* gum

**enciclopedia** (ayn-thee-kloa-*pay*-dhᵛah) *f* encyclopaedia

**encima** (ayn-*thee*-mah) *adv* above; over; ~ **de** over, above, on top of

**encinta** (ayn-*theen*-tah) *adj* pregnant

**encogerse** (ayng-koa-*khayr*-say) *v* *shrink; **no encoge** shrinkproof

*****encontrar** (ayng-koan-*trahr*) *v* *come across, *find; *****encontrarse con** *meet, encounter, run into

**encorvado** (ayng-koar-*bhah*-dhoa) *adj* curved

**encrucijada** (ayng-kroo-thee-*khah*-dhah) *f* crossing, junction

**encuentro** (ayng-*kwayn*-troa) *m* meeting, encounter

**encuesta** (ayng-*kwayss*-tah) *f* inquiry; enquiry

**encurtidos** (ayng-koor-*tee*-dhoass) *mpl* pickles *pl*

**enchufar** (ayn-choo-*fahr*) *v* plug in

**enchufe** (ayn-*choo*-fay) *m* plug

**endosar** (ayn-doa-*sahr*) *v* endorse

**endulzar** (ayn-dool-*thahr*) *v* sweeten

**enemigo** (ay-nay-*mee*-goa) *m* enemy

**energía** (ay-nayr-*khee*-ah) *f* energy;

power; zest; ~ **nuclear** nuclear energy

**enérgico** (ay-*nayr*-khee-koa) *adj* energetic

**enero** (ay-*nay*-roa) January

**enfadado** (ayn-fah-*dhah*-dhoa) *adj* angry, cross

**énfasis** (*ayn*-fah-seess) *m* stress

**enfatizar** (ayn-fah-tee-*thahr*) *v* emphasize

**enfermedad** (ayn-fayr-may-*dhahdh*) *f* disease; ailment, sickness, illness; ~ **venérea** venereal disease

**enfermera** (ayn-fayr-*may*-rah) *f* nurse

**enfermería** (ayn-fayr-may-*ree*-ah) *f* infirmary

**enfermizo** (ayn-fayr-*mee*-thoa) *adj* unsound

**enfermo** (ayn-*fayr*-moa) *adj* sick, ill

**enfoque** (ayn-*foa*-kay) *m* approach

**enfrentarse con** (ayn-frayn-*tahr*-say) face

**enfrente de** (ayn-*frayn*-tay day) facing, opposite

**engañar** (ayng-gah-*ñahr*) *v* cheat, deceive; fool

**engaño** (ayng-*gah*-ñoa) *m* deceit

**engrasar** (ayng-grah-*sahr*) *v* grease

**enhebrar** (ay-nay-*bhrahr*) *v* thread

**enigma** (ay-*neeg*-mah) *m* mystery, enigma, puzzle

**enjuagar** (ayng-khwah-*gahr*) *v* rinse

**enjuague** (ayng-*khwah*-gay) *m* rinse; ~ **bucal** mouthwash

**enjugar** (ayng-khoo-*gahr*) *v* wipe

**enlace** (ayn-*lah*-thay) *m* connection, link

**enlazar** (ayn-lah-*thahr*) *v* link

**enmaderado** (ayn-mah-dhay-*rah*-dhoa) *m* panelling

**enmohecido** (ayn-moa-ay-*thee*-dhoa) *adj* mouldy

**enojado** (ay-noa-*khah*-doa) *adj* angry, cross

**enojo** (ay-*noa*-khoa) *m* anger

**enorme** (ay-*noar*-may) *adj* huge, enormous, immense

**enrollar** (ayn-roa-*lʸahr*) *v* \*wind

**ensalada** (ayn-sah-*lah*-dhah) *f* salad

**ensamblar** (ayn-sahm-*blahr*) *v* join

**ensanchar** (ayn-sahn-*chahr*) *v* widen

**ensayar** (ayn-sah-*ʸahr*) *v* test; rehearse; **ensayarse** *v* practise

**ensayo** (ayn-*sah*-ʸoa) *m* test; rehearsal; essay

**ensenada** (ayn-say-*nah*-dhah) *f* inlet, creek

**enseñanza** (ayn-say-*ñahn*-thah) *f* tuition; teachings *pl*

**enseñar** (ayn-say-*ñahr*) *v* \*teach; \*show

**ensueño** (ayn-*sway*-ñoa) *m* day-dream

**entallar** (ayn-tah-*lʸahr*) *v* carve

**\*entender** (ayn-tayn-*dayr*) *v* conceive; \*take

**entendimiento** (ayn-tayn-dee-*mʸayn*-toa) *m* insight; conception

**enteramente** (ayn-tay-rah-*mayn*-tay) *adv* completely, entirely, quite

**enterar** (ayn-tay-*rahr*) *v* inform

**entero** (ayn-*tay*-roa) *adj* whole, entire

**\*enterrar** (ayn-tay-*rrahr*) *v* bury

**entierro** (ayn-*tʸay*-rroa) *m* burial

**entonces** (ayn-*toan*-thayss) *adv* then; **de** ~ contemporary

**entrada** (ayn-*trah*-dhah) *f* entry, entrance, way in; admission; appearance; entrance-fee; **prohibida la** ~ no admittance

**entrañas** (ayn-*trah*-ñahss) *fpl* insides

**entrar** (ayn-*trahr*) *v* \*go in, enter

**entre** (*ayn*-tray) *prep* among, amid; between

**entreacto** (ayn-tray-*ahk*-toa) *m* intermission

**entrega** (ayn-*tray*-gah) *f* delivery

**entregar** (ayn-tray-*gahr*) *v* \*give; deliver; commit; extradite

**entremeses** (ayn-tray-*may*-sayss ) *mpl* hors-d'œuvre

**entrenador** (ayn-tray-nah-*dhoar*) *m* coach

**entrenamiento** (ayn-tray-nah-*m*ᵞ*ayn*-toa) *m* training

**entrenar** (ayn-tray-*nahr*) *v* train, drill

**entresuelo** (ayn-tray-*sway*-loa) *m* mezzanine

**entretanto** (ayn-tray-*tahn*-toa) *adv* meanwhile, in the meantime

*****entretener** (ayn-tray-tay-*nayr*) *v* amuse, entertain

**entretenido** (ayn-tray-tay-*nee*-dhoa) *adj* entertaining

**entretenimiento** (ayn-tray-tay-nee-*m*ᵞ*ayn*-toa) *m* amusement, entertainment

**entrevista** (ayn-tray-*bheess*-tah) *f* interview

**entumecido** (ayn-too-may-*thee*-dhoa) *adj* numb

**entusiasmo** (ayn-too-*s*ᵞ*ahz*-moa) *m* enthusiasm

**entusiasta** (ayn-too-*s*ᵞ*ahss*-tah) *adj* enthusiastic, keen

**envenenar** (aym-bay-nay-*nahr*) *v* poison

**enviado** (aym-*b*ᵞ*ah*-dhoa) *m* envoy

**enviar** (aym-*b*ᵞ*ahr*) *v* dispatch, *send

**envidia** (aym-*bee*-dhᵞah) *f* envy

**envidiar** (aym-bee-*dh*ᵞ*ahr*) *v* grudge, envy

**envidioso** (aym-bee-*dh*ᵞ*oa*-soa) *adj* envious

**envío** (aym-*bee*-oa) *m* expedition, consignment

*****envolver** (aym-boal-*bhayr*) *v* wrap; involve

**épico** (*ay*-pee-koa) *adj* epic

**epidemia** (ay-pee-*dhay*-mᵞah) *f* epidemic

**epilepsia** (ay-pee-*layp*-sᵞah) *f* epilepsy

**epílogo** (ay-*pee*-loa-goa) *m* epilogue

**episodio** (ay-pee-*soa*-dheeoa) *m* episode

**época** (*ay*-poa-kah) *f* period

**equilibrio** (ay-kee-*lee*-bhrᵞoa) *m* balance

**equipaje** (ay-kee-*pah*-khay) *m* baggage, luggage; ~ **de mano** hand luggage; hand baggage *Am*; **furgón de equipajes** luggage van

**equipar** (ay-kee-*pahr*) *v* equip

**equipo** (ay-*kee*-poa) *m* outfit, equipment; gang; team; crew; soccer team

**equitación** (ay-kee-tah-*th*ᵞ*oan*) *f* riding

**equivalente** (ay-kee-bhah-*layn*-tay) *adj* equivalent

**equivocación** (ay-kee-bhoa-kah-*th*ᵞ*oan*) *f* misunderstanding, mistake

**equivocado** (ay-kee-bhoa-*kah*-dhoa) *adj* mistaken

**equivocarse** (ay-kee-bhoa-*kahr*-say) *v* *be mistaken

**equívoco** (ay-*kee*-bhoa-koa) *adj* ambiguous

**era** (*ay*-rah) *f* era

**erguido** (ayr-*gee*-dhoa) *adj* erect

**erigir** (ay-ree-*kheer*) *v* erect

**erizo** (ay-*ree*-thoa) *m* hedgehog; ~ **de mar** sea-urchin

*****errar** (ay-*rrahr*) *v* err; wander

**erróneo** (ay-*rroa*-nay-oa) *adj* wrong

**error** (ay-*rroar*) *m* mistake, error

**erudito** (ay-roo-*dhee*-toa) *m* scholar

**esbelto** (ayz-*bhayl*-toa) *adj* slim, slender

**escala** (ayss-*kah*-lah) *f* scale; ~ **de incendios** fire-escape; ~ **musical** scale

**escalar** (ayss-kah-*lahr*) *v* ascend

**escalera** (ayss-kah-*lay*-rah) *f* stairs *pl*, staircase; ~ **de mano** ladder; ~ **móvil** escalator

**escalofrío** (ayss-kah-loa-*free*-oa) *m* chill, shiver

**escama** (ayss-*kah*-mah) *f* scale

**escándalo** (ayss-*kahn*-dah-loa) *m* scandal; offence

**Escandinavia** (ayss-kahn-dee-*nah*-bh<sup>y</sup>ah) *f* Scandinavia

**escandinavo** (ayss-kahn-dee-*nah*-bhoa) *adj* Scandinavian; *m* Scandinavian

**escapar** (ayss-kah-*pahr*) *v* escape

**escaparate** (ayss-kah-pah-*rah*-tay) *m* shop-window

**escape** (ayss-*kah*-pay) *m* exhaust; **gases de ~** exhaust gases

**escaque** (ayss-*kah*-kay) *m* check

**escarabajo** (ayss-kah-rah-*bhah*-khoa) *m* beetle, bug

**escarcha** (ayss-*kahr*-chah) *f* frost

**escarcho** (ayss-*kahr*-choa) *m* roach

**escarlata** (ayss-kahr-*lah*-tah) *adj* scarlet

**escarnio** (ayss-*kahr*-n<sup>y</sup>oa) *m* scorn

**escasez** (ayss-kah-*sayth*) *f* scarcity, shortage

**escaso** (ayss-*kah*-soa) *adj* scarce; minor

**escena** (ay-*thay*-nah) *f* scene; setting

**escenario** (ayss-thay-*nah*-r<sup>y</sup>oa) *m* stage

**esclavo** (ayss-*klah*-bhoa) *m* slave

**esclusa** (ayss-*kloo*-sah) *f* lock

**escoba** (ayss-*koa*-bhah) *f* broom

**escocés** (ayss-koa-*thayss*) *adj* Scottish, Scotch; *m* Scot

**Escocia** (ayss-*koa*-th<sup>y</sup>ah) *f* Scotland

**escoger** (ayss-koa-*khayr*) *v* \*choose, pick

**escolta** (ayss-*koal*-tah) *f* escort

**escoltar** (ayss-koal-*tahr*) *v* escort

**escombro** (ayss-*koam*-broa) *m* mackerel

**esconder** (ayss-koan-*dayr*) *v* \*hide

**escribano** (ayss-kree-*bhah*-noa) *m* clerk

**escribir** (ayss-kree-*bheer*) *v* \*write; ~ a máquina type; papel de ~ notepaper; por escrito written, in writ-

ing

**escrito** (ayss-*kree*-toa) *m* writing

**escritor** (ayss-kree-*toar*) *m* writer

**escritorio** (ayss-kree-toa-*r<sup>y</sup>oa*) *m* desk, bureau

**escritura** (ayss-kree-*too*-rah) *f* handwriting

**escrupuloso** (ayss-kroo-poo-*loa*-soa) *adj* careful

**escuadrilla** (ayss-kwah-*dhree*-l<sup>y</sup>ah) *f* squadron

**escuchar** (ayss-koo-*chahr*) *v* listen; eavesdrop

**escuela** (ayss-*kway*-lah) *f* school; **director de ~** head teacher, headmaster; **~ secundaria** secondary school

**escultor** (ayss-kool-*toar*) *m* sculptor

**escultura** (ayss-kool-*too*-rah) *f* sculpture

**escupir** (ayss-koo-*peer*) *v* \*spit

**escurridor** (ayss-koo-rree-*dhoar*) *m* strainer

**ese** (*ay*-say) *adj* that; **ése** *pron* that

**esencia** (ay-*sayn*-th<sup>y</sup>ah) *f* essence

**esencial** (ay-sayn-*th<sup>y</sup>ahl*) *adj* essential; vital

**esfera** (ayss-*fay*-rah) *f* sphere; atmosphere

**\*esforzarse** (ayss-foar-*thahr*-say) *v* try, bother

**esfuerzo** (ayss-*fwayr*-thoa) *m* effort; strain; stress

**esgrimir** (ayz-gree-*meer*) *v* fence

**eslabón** (ayz-lah-*bhoan*) *m* link

**esmaltado** (ayz-mahl-*tah*-dhoa) *adj* enamelled

**esmaltar** (ayz-mahl-*tahr*) *v* glaze

**esmalte** (ayz-*mahl*-tay) *m* enamel

**esmeralda** (ayz-may-*rahl*-dah) *f* emerald

**esnórquel** (ayz-*noar*-kayl) *m* snorkel

**eso** (*ay*-soa) *pron* that

**espaciar** (ayss-pah-*th<sup>y</sup>ahr*) *v* space

**espacio** (ayss-*pah*-th<sup>y</sup>oa) *m* room;

space

**espacioso** (ayss-pah-*th<sup>y</sup>oa*-soa ) *adj* spacious, roomy, large

**espada** (ayss-*pah*-dhah ) *f* sword

**espalda** (ayss-*pahl*-dah ) *f* back; **dolor de ~** backache

**espantado** (ayss-pahn-*tah*-dhoa ) *adj* frightened

**espantar** (ayss-pahn-*tahr*) *v* frighten

**espanto** (ayss-*pahn*-toa ) *m* fright; horror

**espantoso** (ayss-pahn-*toa*-soa ) *adj* dreadful

**España** (ayss-*pah*-ñah ) *f* Spain

**español** (ayss-pah-*ñoal*) *adj* Spanish; *m* Spaniard

**esparadrapo** (ayss-pah-rah-*dhrah*-poa ) *m* adhesive tape, plaster

**esparcir** (ayss-pahr-*theer*) *v* scatter, *shed

**espárrago** (ayss-*pah*-rrah-goa ) *m* asparagus

**especia** (ayss-*pay*-th<sup>y</sup>ah ) *f* spice

**especial** (ayss-pay-*th<sup>y</sup>ahl*) *adj* special; peculiar, particular

**especialidad** (ayss-pay-th<sup>y</sup>ah-lee-*dhahdh*) *f* speciality

**especialista** (ayss-pay-th<sup>y</sup>ah-*leess*-tah ) *m* specialist

**especializarse** (ayss-pay-th<sup>y</sup>ah-lee-*thahr*-say) *v* specialize; **especializado** skilled

**especialmente** (ayss-pay-th<sup>y</sup>ahl-*mayn*-tay) *adv* especially

**especie** (ayss-*payth<sup>y</sup>ay*) *f* species, breed

**específico** (ayss-pay-*thee*-fee-koa) *adj* specific

**espécimen** (ayss-*pay*-thee-mayn ) *m* specimen

**espectáculo** (ayss-payk-*tah*-koo-loa ) *m* spectacle, show; **~ de variedades** floor show

**espectador** (ayss-payk-tah-*dhoar*) *m* spectator

**espectro** (ayss-*payk*-troa ) *m* ghost; spectrum

**especular** (ayss-pay-koo-*lahr*) *v* speculate

**espejo** (ayss-*pay*-khoa ) *m* mirror, looking-glass

**espeluznante** (ayss-pay-looth-*nahn*-tay) *adj* creepy

**espera** (ayss-*pay*-rah ) *f* waiting

**esperanza** (ayss-pay-*rahn*-thah ) *f* hope; expectation

**esperanzado** (ayss-pay-rahn-*thah*-dhoa ) *adj* hopeful

**esperar** (ayss-pay-*rahr*) *v* hope; wait; expect, await

**espesar** (ayss-pay-*sahr*) *v* thicken

**espeso** (ayss-*pay*-soa ) *adj* thick

**espesor** (ayss-pay-*soar*) *m* thickness

**espetón** (ayss-pay-*toan*) *m* spit

**espía** (ayss-*pee*-ah ) *m* spy

**espiar** (ayss-*p<sup>y</sup>ahr*) *v* peep

**espina** (ayss-*pee*-nah ) *f* thorn; fishbone; **~ dorsal** backbone

**espinacas** (ayss-pee-*nah*-kahss ) *fpl* spinach

**espinazo** (ayss-pee-*nah*-thoa ) *m* spine

**espirar** (ayss-pee-*rahr*) *v* expire

**espíritu** (ayss-*pee*-ree-too ) *m* spirit; ghost

**espiritual** (ayss-pee-ree-*twahl*) *adj* spiritual

**espléndido** (ayss-*playn*-dee-dhoa ) *adj* splendid; glorious, enchanting, magnificent

**esplendor** (ayss-playn-*doar*) *m* splendour

**esponja** (ayss-*poang*-khah ) *f* sponge

**esposa** (ayss-*poa*-sah ) *f* wife; **esposas** *fpl* handcuffs *pl*

**esposo** (ayss-*poa*-soa ) *m* husband

**espuma** (ayss-*poo*-mah ) *f* froth, foam, lather

**espumante** (ayss-poo-*mahn*-tay ) *adj*

sparkling

**espumar** (ayss-poo-*mahr*) v foam

**esputo** (ayss-*poo*-toa) m spit

**esquela** (ayss-*kay*-lah) f note

**esqueleto** (ayss-kay-*lay*-toa) m skeleton

**esquema** (ayss-*kay*-mah) m diagram; scheme

**esquí** (ayss-*kee*) m ski; skiing; ~ **acuático** water ski; **salto de** ~ ski-jump

**esquiador** (ayss-k<sup>y</sup>ah-*dhoar*) m skier

**esquiar** (ayss-k<sup>y</sup>*ahr*) v ski

**esquina** (ayss-*kee*-nah) f corner

**esquivo** (ayss-*kee*-bhoa) adj shy

**estable** (ayss-*tah*-bhlay) adj permanent, stable

*** establecer** (ayss-tah-bhlay-*thayr*) v establish

**establo** (ayss-*tah*-bhloa) m stable

**estación** (ayss-tah-th<sup>y</sup>*oan*) f season; station; depot nAm; ~ **central** central station; ~ **de servicio** filling station; ~ **terminal** terminal

**estacionamiento** (ayss-tah-th<sup>y</sup>oa-nah-*m<sup>y</sup>ayn*-toa) m parking lot Am; **derechos de** ~ parking fee

**estacionar** (ayss-tah-th<sup>y</sup>oa-*nahr*) v park; **prohibido estacionarse** no parking

**estacionario** (ayss-tah-th<sup>y</sup>oa-*nah*-r<sup>y</sup>oa) adj stationary

**estadio** (ayss-*tah*-dh<sup>y</sup>oa) m stadium

**estadista** (ayss-tah-*dheess*-tah) m statesman

**estadística** (ayss-tah-*dheess*-tee-kah) f statistics pl

**Estado** (ayss-*tah*-doa) m state

**estado** (ayss-*tah*-dhoa) m state, condition

**Estados Unidos** (ayss-*tah*-dhoass oo-*nee*-dhoass) the States, United States

**estafa** (ayss-*tah*-fah) f swindle

**estafador** (ayss-tah-fah-*dhoar*) m swindler

**estafar** (ayss-tah-*fahr*) v cheat, swindle

**estallar** (ayss-tah-*l<sup>y</sup>ahr*) v explode

**estambre** (ayss-*tahm*-bray) m/f worsted

**estampa** (ayss-*tahm*-pah) f engraving

**estampilla** (ayss-tahm-*pee*-l<sup>y</sup>ah) fMe stamp

**estancia** (ayss-*tahn*-th<sup>y</sup>ah) f stay

**estanco** (ayss-*tahng*-koa) m cigar shop, tobacconist's

**estanque** (ayss-*tahng*-kay) m pond

**estanquero** (ayss-tahng-*kay*-roa) m tobacconist

**estante** (ayss-*tahn*-tay) m shelf

**estaño** (ayss-*tah*-ñoa) m tin; pewter

*** estar** (ayss-*tahr*) v *be

**estatua** (ayss-*tah*-twah) f statue

**estatura** (ayss-tah-*too*-rah) f figure

**este**[1] (*ayss*-tay) m east

**este**[2] (*ayss*-tay) adj this; **éste** pron this

**estera** (ayss-*tay*-rah) f mat

**estercolero** (ayss-tayr-koa-*lay*-roa) m dunghill

**estéril** (ayss-*tay*-reel) adj sterile

**esterilizar** (ayss-tay-ree-lee-*thahr*) v sterilize

**estético** (ayss-*tay*-tee-koa) adj aesthetic

**estilo** (ayss-*tee*-loa) m style

**estilográfica** (ayss-tee-loa-*grah*-fee-kah) f fountain-pen

**estima** (ayss-*tee*-mah) f esteem

**estimación** (ayss-tee-mah-th<sup>y</sup>*oan*) f respect; estimate

**estimar** (ayss-teĕ-*mahr*) v esteem; estimate

**estimulante** (ayss-tee-moo-*lahn*-tay) m stimulant

**estimular** (ayss-tee-moo-*lahr*) v stimulate; urge

**estímulo** (ayss-*tee*-moo-loa) m impulse

**estipulación** (ayss-tee-poo-lah-th<sup>y</sup>*oan*)

*f* stipulation

**estipular** (ayss-tee-poo-*lahr*) *v* stipulate

**estirar** (ayss-tee-*rahr*) *v* stretch

**estirón** (ayss-tee-*roan*) *m* tug

**esto** (*ayss*-toa) *adj* this

**estola** (ayss-*toa*-lah) *f* stole

**estómago** (ayss-*toa*-mah-goa) *m* stomach; **dolor de ~** stomach-ache

**estorbar** (ayss-toar-*bhahr*) *v* disturb, embarrass

**estornino** (ayss-toar-*nee*-noa) *m* starling

**estornudar** (ayss-toar-noo-*dhahr*) *v* sneeze

**estrangular** (ayss-trahng-goo-*lahr*) *v* choke, strangle

**estrato** (ayss-*trah*-toa) *m* layer

**estrechar** (ayss-tray-*chahr*) *v* tighten

**estrecho** (ayss-*tray*-choa) *adj* narrow; tight

**estrella** (ayss-*tray*-lᵞah) *f* star

**estremecido** (ayss-tray-may-*thee*-dhoa) *adj* shivery

**estremecimiento** (ayss-tray-may-thee-mᵞayn-toa) *m* shudder

**estreñido** (ayss-tray-*ñee*-dhoa) *adj* constipated

**estreñimiento** (ayss-tray-ñee-mᵞayn-toa) *m* constipation

**estribo** (ayss-*tree*-bhoa) *m* stirrup

**estribor** (ayss-*tree*-bhoar) *m* starboard

**estricto** (ayss-*treek*-toa) *adj* strict

**estrofa** (ayss-*troa*-fah) *f* stanza

**estropeado** (ayss-troa-pay-ah-dhoa) *adj* broken; crippled

**estropear** (ayss-troa-pay-*ahr*) *v* mess up

**estructura** (ayss-trook-*too*-rah) *f* structure; fabric

**estuario** (ayss-*twah*-rᵞoa) *m* estuary

**estuco** (ayss-*too*-koa) *m* plaster

**estuche** (ayss-*too*-chay) *m* case

**estudiante** (ayss-too-dhᵞ*ahn*-tay) *m* student

**estudiar** (ayss-too-dhᵞ*ahr*) *v* study

**estudio** (ayss-*too*-dhᵞoa) *m* study

**estufa** (ayss-*too*-fah) *f* stove; **~ de gas** gas stove

**estupefaciente** (ayss-too-pay-fah-thᵞ*ayn*-tay) *m* drug

**estupendo** (ayss-too-*payn*-doa) *adj* wonderful

**estúpido** (ayss-*too*-pee-dhoa) *adj* stupid; dumb

**etapa** (ay-*tah*-pah) *f* stage

**etcétera** (ayt-*thay*-tay-rah) and so on, etcetera

**éter** (*ay*-tayr) *m* ether

**eternidad** (ay-tayr-nee-*dhahdh*) *f* eternity

**eterno** (ay-*tayr*-noa) *adj* eternal

**etíope** (ay-*tee*-oa-pay) *adj* Ethiopian; *m* Ethiopian

**Etiopía** (ay-tᵞ*oa*-pᵞah) *f* Ethiopia

**etiqueta** (ay-tee-*kay*-tah) *f* tag

**Europa** (ayᵒᵒ-*roa*-pah) *f* Europe

**europeo** (ayᵒᵒ-roa-*pay*-oa) *adj* European; *m* European

**evacuar** (ay-bhah-*kwahr*) *v* evacuate

**evaluar** (ay-bhah-*lwahr*) *v* evaluate, estimate

**evangelio** (ay-bhahng-*khay*-lᵞoa) *m* gospel

**evaporar** (ay-bhah-poa-*rahr*) *v* evaporate

**evasión** (ay-bhah-*sᵞoan*) *f* escape

**eventual** (ay-bhayn-*twahl*) *adj* eventual; possible

**evidente** (ay-bhee-*dhayn*-tay) *adj* evident; self-evident

**evidentemente** (ay-bhee-dhayn-tay-*mayn*-tay) *adv* apparently

**evitar** (ay-bhee-*tahr*) *v* avoid

**evolución** (ay-bhoa-loo-*thᵞoan*) *f* evolution

**exactamente** (ayk-sahk-tah-*mayn*-tay) *adv* exactly

**exactitud** (ayk-sahk-tee-*toodh*) *f* correctness

**exacto** (ayk-*sahk*-toa) *adj* precise, exact, accurate

**exagerar** (ayk-sah-khay-*rahr*) *v* exaggerate

**examen** (ayk-*sah*-mayn) *m* examination

**examinar** (ayk-sah-mee-*nahr*) *v* examine

**excavación** (ayks-kah-bhah-th<sup>y</sup>oan) *f* excavation

**exceder** (ayk-thay-*dhayr*) *v* exceed

**excelencia** (ayk-thay-*layn*-th<sup>y</sup>ah) *f* excellence

**excelente** (ayk-thay-*layn*-tay) *adj* excellent, fine

**excéntrico** (ayk-*thayn*-tree-koa) *adj* eccentric

**excepción** (ayk-thayp-*th<sup>y</sup>oan*) *f* exception

**excepcional** (ayk-thayp-th<sup>y</sup>oa-*nahl*) *adj* exceptional

**excepto** (ayk-*thayp*-toa) *prep* except

**excesivo** (ayk-thay-*see*-bhoa) *adj* excessive

**exceso** (ayk-*thay*-soa) *m* excess; ~ **de velocidad** speeding

**excitación** (ayk-thee-tah-*th<sup>y</sup>oan*) *f* excitement

**excitante** (ayk-thee-*tahn*-tay) *adj* exciting

**excitar** (ayk-thee-*tahr*) *v* excite

**exclamación** (ayks-klah-mah-*th<sup>y</sup>oan*) *f* exclamation

**exclamar** (ayks-klah-*mahr*) *v* exclaim

*excluir** (ayks-*klweer*) *v* exclude

**exclusivamente** (ayks-kloo-see-bhah-*mayn*-tay) *adv* exclusively, solely

**exclusivo** (ayks-kloo-*see*-bhoa) *adj* exclusive

**excursión** (ayks-koor-s<sup>y</sup>oan) *f* trip, excursion

**excusa** (ayks-*koo*-sah) *f* apology, excuse

**excusar** (ayks-koo-*sahr*) *v* excuse

**exención** (ayk-sayn-*th<sup>y</sup>oan*) *f* exemption

**exento** (ayk-*sayn*-toa) *adj* exempt; ~ **de impuestos** duty-free

**exhalar** (ayk-sah-*lahr*) *v* exhale

**exhausto** (ayk-*souss*-toa) *adj* overtired

**exhibir** (ayk-see-*bheer*) *v* exhibit, display

**exigencia** (ayk-see-*khayn*-th<sup>y</sup>ah) *f* demand

**exigente** (ayk-see-*khayn*-tay) *adj* particular

**exigir** (ayk-see-*kheer*) *v* demand

**exiliado** (ayk-see-*l<sup>y</sup>ah*-dhoa) *m* exile

**exilio** (ayk-*see*-l<sup>y</sup>oa) *m* exile

**eximir** (ayk-see-*meer*) *v* exempt

**existencia** (ayk-seess-*tayn*-th<sup>y</sup>ah) *f* existence; **existencias** *fpl* supply, stock; *tener en ~** stock

**existir** (ayk-seess-*teer*) *v* exist

**éxito** (*ayk*-see-toa) *m* success, luck; hit; **de ~** successful; *tener ~** manage, succeed

**exorbitante** (ayk-soar-bhee-*tahn*-tay) *adj* prohibitive

**exótico** (ayk-*soa*-tee-koa) *adj* exotic

**expansión** (ayks-pahn-s<sup>y</sup>oan) *f* expansion

**expedición** (ayks-pay-dhee-*th<sup>y</sup>oan*) *f* expedition

**expediente** (ayks-pay-*dh<sup>y</sup>ayn*-tay) *m* file

**experiencia** (ayks-pay-r<sup>y</sup>ayn-th<sup>y</sup>ah) *f* experience

**experimentar** (ayks-pay-ree-mayn-*tahr*) *v* experiment; experience; **experimentado** experienced

**experimento** (ayks-pay-ree-*mayn*-toa) *m* experiment

**experto** (ayks-*payr*-toa) *m* expert

**expirar** (ayks-pee-*rahr*) *v* expire

**explanada** (ayks-plah-*nah*-dhah) *f* esplanade

**explicable** (ayks-plee-*kah*-bhlay) *adj* accountable

**explicación** (ayks-plee-kah-*th<sup>Y</sup>oan*) *f* explanation

**explicar** (ayks-plee-*kahr*) *v* explain; account for

**explícito** (ayks-*plee*-thee-toa) *adj* express, explicit

**explorador** (ayks-ploa-rah-*dhoar*) *m* scout, boy scout

**exploradora** (ayks-ploa-rah-*dhoa*-rah) *f* girl guide

**explorar** (ayks-ploa-*rahr*) *v* explore

**explosión** (ayks-ploa-*s<sup>Y</sup>oan*) *f* explosion, blast; outbreak

**explosivo** (ayks-ploa-*see*-bhoa) *adj* explosive; *m* explosive

**explotar** (ayks-ploa-*tahr*) *v* exploit

*****exponer** (ayks-poa-*nayr*) *v* exhibit

**exportación** (ayks-poar-tah-*th<sup>Y</sup>oan*) *f* exportation, export

**exportar** (ayks-poar-*tahr*) *v* export

**exposición** (ayks-poa-see-*th<sup>Y</sup>oan*) *f* exposition, exhibition, display, show; exposure; ~ **de arte** art exhibition

**exposímetro** (ayks-poa-*see*-may-troa) *m* exposure meter

**expresar** (ayks-pray-*sahr*) *v* express

**expresión** (ayks-pray-*s<sup>Y</sup>oan*) *f* expression

**expresivo** (ayks-pray-*see*-bhoa) *adj* expressive

**expreso** (ayks-*pray*-soa) *adj* explicit; express; **por** ~ special delivery

**expulsar** (ayks-pool-*sahr*) *v* chase; expel

**exquisito** (ayks-kee-*see*-toa) *adj* exquisite; delicious

**éxtasis** (*ayks*-tah-seess) *m* ecstasy

*****extender** (ayks-tayn-*dayr*) *v* *spread, expand

**extenso** (ayks-*tayn*-soa) *adj* comprehensive, extensive

**extenuar** (ayks-tay-*nwahr*) *v* exhaust

**exterior** (ayks-tay-*r<sup>Y</sup>oar*) *adj* external, exterior; *m* exterior, outside

**externo** (ayks-*tayr*-noa) *adj* outward

**extinguir** (ayks-teeng-*geer*) *v* extinguish

**extintor** (ayks-teen-*toar*) *m* fire-extinguisher

**extorsión** (ayks-toar-*s<sup>Y</sup>oan*) *f* extortion

**extorsionar** (ayks-toar-s<sup>Y</sup>oa-*nahr*) *v* extort

**extra** (*ayks*-trah) *adj* extra

**extracto** (ayks-*trahk*-toa) *m* excerpt

*****extraer** (ayks-trah-*ayr*) *v* extract

**extranjero** (ayks-trahng-*khay*-roa) *adj* alien, foreign; *m* alien, foreigner; stranger; **en el** ~ abroad

**extrañar** (ayks-trah-*ñahr*) *v* amaze, surprise; banish

**extraño** (ayks-*trah*-ñoa) *adj* foreign, strange; peculiar, queer, funny

**extraoficial** (ayks-trah-oa-fee-*th<sup>Y</sup>ahl*) *adj* unofficial

**extraordinario** (ayks-trah-oar-dhee-*nah-r<sup>Y</sup>oa*) *adj* extraordinary, exceptional

**extravagante** (ayks-trah-bhah-*gahn*-tay) *adj* extravagant

**extraviar** (ayks-trah-*bh<sup>Y</sup>ahr*) *v* *mislay

**extremo** (ayks-*tray*-moa) *adj* extreme; very, utmost; *m* extreme; end

**exuberante** (ayk-soo-bhay-*rahn*-tay) *adj* exuberant

# F

**fábrica** (*fah*-bhree-kah) *f* factory; works *pl*, mill; ~ **de gas** gasworks

**fabricante** (fah-bhree-*kahn*-tay) *m* manufacturer

**fabricar** (fah-bhree-*kahr*) *v* manufacture

**fábula** (*fah*-bhoo-lah) *f* fable

**fácil** (*fah*-theel) *adj* easy

**facilidad** (fah-thee-lee-*dhahdh*) *f* ease; facility

**facilitar** (fah-thee-lee-*tahr*) *v* facilitate

**factible** (fahk-*tee*-bhlay) *adj* attainable

**factor** (fahk-*toar*) *m* factor

**factura** (fahk-*too*-rah) *f* invoice

**facturar** (fahk-too-*rahr*) *v* bill

**facultad** (fah-kool-*tahdh*) *f* faculty

**fachada** (fah-*chah*-dhah) *f* façade

**faisán** (figh-*sahn*) *m* pheasant

**faja** (*fah*-khah) *f* strip; girdle

**falda** (*fahl*-dah) *f* skirt

**faldón** (fahl-*doan*) *m* gable

**falsificación** (fahl-see-fee-kah-*th*ʸ*oan*) *f* fake

**falsificar** (fahl-see-fee-*kahr*) *v* forge, counterfeit

**falso** (*fahl*-soa) *adj* false; untrue

**falta** (*fahl*-tah) *f* error; want, lack; offence; **sin ~** without fail

**faltar** (fahl-*tahr*) *v* fail

**fallar** (fah-*l*ʸ*ahr*) *v* fail

*****fallecer** (fah-lʸay-*thayr*) *v* depart

**fama** (*fah*-mah) *f* fame; **de ~ mundial** world-famous; **de mala ~** notorious

**familia** (fah-*mee*-lʸah) *f* family

**familiar** (fah-mee-*l*ʸ*ahr*) *adj* familiar

**famoso** (fah-*moa*-soa) *adj* famous

**fanal** (fah-*nahl*) *m* headlamp

**fanático** (fah-*nah*-tee-koa) *adj* fanatical

**fantasía** (fahn-tah-*see*-ah) *f* fantasy

**fantasma** (fahn-*tahz*-mah) *m* spook, phantom, ghost

**fantástico** (fahn-*tahss*-tee-koa) *adj* fantastic

**farallón** (fah-rah-*l*ʸ*oan*) *m* cliff

**fardo** (*fahr*-dhoa) *m* load

**farmacéutico** (fahr-mah-*thay*ᵒᵒ-tee-koa) *m* chemist

**farmacia** (fahr-*mah*-thʸah) *f* chemist's;

pharmacy; drugstore *nAm*

**farmacología** (fahr-mah-koa-loa-*khee*-ah) *f* pharmacology

**faro** (*fah*-roa) *m* headlight; lighthouse

**farol trasero** (fah-*roal* trah-*say*-roa) taillight

**farsa** (*fahr*-sah) *f* farce

**fascismo** (fah-*theez*-moa) *m* fascism

**fascista** (fah-*theess*-tah) *adj* fascist; *m* fascist

**fase** (*fah*-say) *f* stage, phase

**fastidiar** (fahss-tee-*dh*ʸ*ahr*) *v* annoy, bother

**fastidioso** (fahss-tee-*dh*ʸ*oa*-soa) *adj* difficult

**fatal** (fah-*tahl*) *adj* fatal; mortal

**favor** (fah-*bhoar*) *m* favour; **a ~ de** on behalf of; **por ~** please

**favorable** (fah-bhoa-*rah*-bhlay) *adj* favourable

*****favorecer** (fah-bhoa-ray-*thayr*) *v* favour

**favorecido** (fah-bhoa-ray-*thee*-dhoa) *m* payee

**favorito** (fah-bhoa-*ree*-toa) *adj* pet; *m* favourite

**fe** (fay) *f* faith

**febrero** (fay-*bhray*-roa) February

**febril** (fay-*bhreel*) *adj* feverish

**fecundo** (fay-*koon*-doa) *adj* fertile

**fecha** (*fay*-chah) *f* date

**federación** (fay-dhay-rah-*th*ʸ*oan*) *f* federation

**federal** (fay-dhay-*rahl*) *adj* federal

**felicidad** (fay-lee-thee-*dhahdh*) *f* happiness

**felicitación** (fay-lee-thee-tah-*th*ʸ*oan*) *f* congratulation

**felicitar** (fay-lee-thee-*tahr*) *v* congratulate

**feliz** (fay-*leeth*) *adj* happy

**femenino** (fay-may-*nee*-noa) *adj* feminine; female

**fenómeno** (fay-*noa*-may-noa) *m* phenomenon

**feo** (fay-oa) adj ugly

**feria** (fay-rʸah) f fair

**fermentar** (fayr-mayn-tahr) v ferment

**feroz** (fay-roath) adj wild

**ferretería** (fay-rray-tay-ree-ah) f hardware store

**ferrocarril** (fay-rroa-kah-rreel) m railway; railroad nAm

**fértil** (fayr-teel) adj fertile

**fertilidad** (fayr-tee-lee-dhahdh) f fertility

**festival** (fayss-tee-bhahl) m festival

**festivo** (fayss-tee-bhoa) adj festive

**feudal** (fayºº-dhahl) adj feudal

**fiable** (fʸah-bhlay) adj reliable

**fianza** (fʸahn-thah) f security; bail; deposit

**fiasco** (fʸahss-koa) m failure

**fibra** (fee-bhrah) f fibre

**ficción** (feek-thʸoan) f fiction

**ficha** (fee-chah) f chip, token

**fiebre** (fʸay-bhray) f fever; ~ **del heno** hay fever

**fiel** (fʸayl) adj faithful, true

**fieltro** (fʸayl-troa) m felt

**fiero** (fʸay-roa) adj fierce

**fiesta** (fʸayss-tah) f feast; party; holiday

**figura** (fee-goo-rah) f figure

**figurarse** (fee-goo-rahr-say) v imagine

**fijador** (fee-khah-dhoar) m setting lotion

**fijar** (fee-khahr) v attach; **fijarse en** mind

**fijo** (fee-khoa) adj fixed; permanent

**fila** (fee-lah) f row, rank

**Filipinas** (fee-lee-pee-nahss) fpl Philippines pl

**filipino** (fee-lee-pee-noa) adj Philippine; m Filipino

**filmar** (feel-mahr) v film

**filme** (feel-may) m movie

**filosofía** (fee-loa-soa-fee-ah) f philos-

ophy

**filosófico** (fee-loa-soa-fee-koa) adj philosophical

**filósofo** (fee-loa-soa-foa) m philosopher

**filtrar** (feel-trahr) v strain

**filtro** (feel-troa) m filter; ~ **de aire** air-filter; ~ **del aceite** oil filter

**fin** (feen) m end; aim, purpose; **a** ~ **de** so that; **al** ~ at last

**final** (fee-nahl) adj eventual, final; m end; **al** ~ at last

**financiar** (fee-nahn-thʸahr) v finance

**financiero** (fee-nahn-thʸay-roa) adj financial

**finanzas** (fee-nahn-thahss) fpl finances pl

**finca** (feeng-kah) f premises pl

**fingir** (feeng-kheer) v pretend

**finlandés** (feen-lahn-dayss) adj Finnish; m Finn

**Finlandia** (feen-lahn-dʸah) f Finland

**fino** (fee-noa) adj delicate, fine; sheer

**firma** (feer-mah) f signature; firm

**firmar** (feer-mahr) v sign

**firme** (feer-may) adj steady, firm; secure

**física** (fee-see-kah) f physics

**físico** (fee-see-koa) adj physical; m physicist

**fisiología** (fee-sʸoa-loa-khee-ah) f physiology

**flaco** (flah-koa) adj thin

**flamenco** (flah-mayng-koa) m flamingo

**flauta** (flou-tah) f flute

**flecha** (flay-chah) f arrow

**flexible** (flayk-see-bhlay) adj flexible; supple, elastic

**flojel** (floa-khayl) m down

**flojo** (floa-khoa) adj weak

**flor** (floar) f flower

**florista** (floa-reess-tah) m florist

**floristería** (floa-reess-tay-ree-ah) f

flower-shop

**flota** (*floa*-tah ) *f* fleet

**flotador** (floa-tah-*dhoar*) *m* float

**flotar** (floa-*tahr*) *v* float

**fluido** (*floo*-ee-dhoa) *adj* fluid; *m* fluid

**\*fluir** (flweer ) *v* flow, stream

**foca** (*foa*-kah) *f* seal

**foco** (*foa*-koa) *m* focus; *mMe* light bulb

**folklore** (foal-*kloa*-ray) *m* folklore

**folleto** (foa-*lʸay*-toa) *m* brochure

**fondo** (*foan*-doa) *m* background; ground, bottom; *mMe* slip; **fondos** *mpl* fund

**fonético** (foa-*nay*-tee-koa) *adj* phonetic

**foque** (*foa*-kay ) *m* foresail

**forastero** (foa-rahss-*tay*-roa ) *m* foreigner; stranger

**forma** (*foar*-mah ) *f* form, shape

**formación** (foar-mah-*thʸoan*) *f* formation

**formal** (foar-*mahl*) *adj* formal

**formalidad** (foar-mah-lee-*dhahdh*) *f* formality

**formar** (foar-*mahr*) *v* form, shape; educate

**formato** (foar-*mah*-toa) *m* size

**formidable** (foar-mee-*dhah*-bhlay) *adj* huge

**fórmula** (*foar*-moo-lah) *f* formula

**formulario** (foar-moo-*lah*-rʸoa) *m* form; ~ **de matriculación** registration form

**forro** (*foa*-rroa) *m* lining

**fortaleza** (foar-tah-*lay*-thah) *f* fortress, fort

**fortuna** (foar-*too*-nah) *f* fortune

**forúnculo** (foa-*roong*-koo-loa) *m* boil

**\*forzar** (foar-*thahr*) *v* force; strain

**forzosamente** (foar-thoa-sah-*mayn*-tay) *adv* by force

**foso** (*foa*-soa) *m* moat

**foto** (*foa*-toa) *f* photo

**fotocopia** (foa-toa-*koa*-pʸah) *f* photostat

**fotografía** (foa-toa-grah-*fee*-ah) *f* photograph; photography; ~ **de pasaporte** passport photograph

**fotografiar** (foa-toa-grah-*fʸahr*) *v* photograph

**fotógrafo** (foa-*toa*-grah-foa) *m* photographer

**fracasado** (frah-kah-*sah*-dhoa) *adj* unsuccessful

**fracaso** (frah-*kah*-soa) *m* failure

**fracción** (frahk-*thʸoan*) *f* fraction

**fractura** (frahk-*too*-rah) *f* fracture, break

**fracturar** (frahk-too-*rahr*) *v* fracture

**frágil** (*frah*-kheel) *adj* fragile

**fragmento** (frahg-*mayn*-toa) *m* fragment, piece; extract

**frambuesa** (frahm-*bway*-sah) *f* raspberry

**francés** (frahn-*thayss*) *adj* French; *m* Frenchman

**Francia** (*frahn*-thʸah) *f* France

**franco** (*frahng*-koa) *adj* postage paid, post-paid

**francotirador** (frahng-koa-tee-rah-*dhoar*) *m* sniper

**franela** (frah-*nay*-lah) *f* flannel

**franja** (*frahng*-khah) *f* fringe

**franqueo** (frahng-*kay*-oa) *m* postage

**frasco** (*frahss*-koa) *m* flask

**frase** (*frah*-say) *f* sentence; phrase

**fraternidad** (frah-tayr-nee-*dhahdh*) *f* fraternity

**fraude** (*frou*-dhay) *m* fraud

**frecuencia** (fray-*kwayn*-thʸah) *f* frequency

**frecuentar** (fray-kwayn-*tahr*) *v* associate with

**frecuente** (fray-*kwayn*-tay) *adj* frequent

**frecuentemente** (fray-kwayn-tay-*mayn*-tay) *adv* frequently, often

**\*fregar** (fray-*gahr*) *v* wash up; scrub

**\*freír** (fray-*eer*) *v* fry

**frenar** (fray-*nahr*) *v* slow down

**freno** (*fray*-noa) *m* brake; ~ **de mano** hand-brake; ~ **de pie** foot-brake

**frente** (*frayn*-tay) *f* forehead; *m* front

**fresa** (*fray*-sah) *f* strawberry

**fresco** (*frayss*-koa) *adj* fresh; chilly, cool

**fricción** (freek-*th*<sup>y</sup>*oan*) *f* friction

**frigorífico** (free-goa-*ree*-fee-koa) *m* fridge

**frío** (*free*-oa) *adj* cold; *m* cold

**frontera** (froan-*tay*-rah) *f* frontier, border; boundary, bound

**frotar** (froa-*tahr*) *v* rub

**fruta** (*froo*-tah) *f* fruit

**fruto** (*froo*-toa) *m* fruit

**fuego** (*fway*-goa) *m* fire

**fuente** (*fwayn*-tay) *f* source, fountain; dish

**fuera** (*fway*-rah) *adv* out; off, away; ~ **de** outside, out of; ~ **de lugar** misplaced; ~ **de temporada** off season

**fuerte** (*fwayr*-tay) *adj* powerful, strong; mighty; loud

**fuerza** (*fwayr*-thah) *f* force; power, might, energy; strength; ~ **de voluntad** will-power; ~ **motriz** driving force; **fuerzas armadas** military force, armed forces

**fugitivo** (foo-khee-*tee*-bhoa) *m* runaway

**fumador** (foo-mah-*dhoar*) *m* smoker; **compartimento para fumadores** smoker

**fumar** (foo-*mahr*) *v* smoke; **prohibido** ~ no smoking

**función** (foon-*th*<sup>y</sup>*oan*) *f* function

**funcionamiento** (foon-th<sup>y</sup>oa-nah-m<sup>y</sup>ayn-toa) *m* working, operation

**funcionar** (foon-th<sup>y</sup>oa-*nahr*) *v* work, operate

**funcionario** (foon-th<sup>y</sup>oa-nah-r<sup>y</sup>oa) *m* civil servant

**funda** (*foon*-dah) *f* sleeve; ~ **de almohada** pillow-case

**fundación** (foon-dah-*th*<sup>y</sup>*oan*) *f* foundation

**fundamentado** (foon-dah-mayn-*tah*-dhoa) *adj* well-founded

**fundamental** (foon-dah-mayn-*tahl*) *adj* fundamental, basic

**fundamento** (foon-dah-*mayn*-toa) *m* basis, base

**fundar** (foon-*dahr*) *v* found

**fundir** (foon-*deer*) *v* melt

**funerales** (foo-nay-*rah*-layss) *mpl* funeral

**furgoneta** (foor-goa-*nay*-tah) *f* delivery van

**furioso** (foo-r<sup>y</sup>oa-soa) *adj* furious

**furor** (foo-*roar*) *m* anger, rage

**fusible** (foo-*see*-bhlay) *m* fuse

**fusil** (foo-*seel*) *m* gun

**fusión** (foo-s<sup>y</sup>*oan*) *f* merger

**fútbol** (*foot*-bhoal) *m* soccer; football

**fútil** (*foo*-teel) *adj* petty

**futuro** (foo-*too*-roa) *adj* future

# G

**gabinete** (gah-bhee-*nay*-tay) *m* cabinet

**gafas** (*gah*-fahss) *fpl* goggles *pl*; ~ **de sol** sun-glasses *pl*

**gaitero** (gigh-*tay*-roa) *adj* gay

**galería** (gah-lay-*ree*-ah) *f* gallery; ~ **de arte** art gallery

**galgo** (*gahl*-goa) *m* greyhound

**galope** (gah-*loa*-pay) *m* gallop

**galleta** (gah-*l*<sup>y</sup>*ay*-tah) *f* biscuit

**gallina** (gah-*l*<sup>y</sup>*ee*-nah) *f* hen

**gallo** (*gah*-l<sup>y</sup>oa) *m* cock; ~ **de bosque** grouse

**gamba** (*gahm*-bah) *f* prawn

**gamuza** (gah-*moo*-thah) f suede
**gana** (*gah*-nah) f fancy; appetite
**ganado** (gah-*nah*-dhoa) m cattle pl
**ganador** (gah-nah-*dhoar*) adj winning
**ganancia** (gah-*nahn*-th ͭ ah) f gain, profit
**ganar** (gah-*nahr*) v gain; *make, earn
**ganas** (*gah*-nahss) fpl desire
**gancho** (*gahn*-choa) m hook
**ganga** (*gahng*-gah) f bargain
**garaje** (gah-*rah*-khay) m garage; **dejar en ~** garage
**garante** (gah-*rahn*-tay) m guarantor
**garantía** (gah-rahn-*tee*-ah) f guarantee
**garantizar** (gah-rahn-tee-*thahr*) v guarantee
**garganta** (gahr-*gahn*-tah) f throat; **dolor de ~** sore throat
**garra** (*gah*-rrah) f claw
**garrafa** (gah-*rrah*-fah) f carafe
**garrote** (gah-*rroa*-tay) m club, cudgel
**garza** (*gahr*-thah) f heron
**gas** (gahss) m gas; **cocina de ~** gas cooker
**gasa** (*gah*-sah) f gauze
**gasolina** (gah-soa-*lee*-nah) f petrol; gasoline nAm; gas nAm; **puesto de ~** petrol station
**gastado** (gahss-*tah*-dhoa) adj worn-out, worn, threadbare
**gastar** (gahss-*tahr*) v *spend; wear out
**gasto** (*gahss*-toa) m expense, expenditure; **gastos de viaje** fare, travelling expenses
**gástrico** (*gahss*-tree-koa) adj gastric
**gastrónomo** (gahss-*troa*-noa-moa) m gourmet
**gatear** (gah-tay-*ahr*) v *creep
**gatillo** (gah-*tee*-l ͭ oa) m trigger
**gato** (*gah*-toa) m cat; jack
**gaviota** (gah-*bh ͭ oa*-tah) f gull, seagull
**gema** (*khay*-mah) f gem
**gemelos** (khay-*may*-loass) mpl twins

pl; binoculars pl; cuff-links pl; ~ **de campaña** field glasses
***gemir** (khay-*meer*) v groan, moan
**generación** (khay-nay-rah-th ͭ oan) f generation
**generador** (khay-nay-rah-*dhoar*) m generator
**general** (khay-nay-*rahl*) adj general; universal, public, broad; m general; **en ~** in general
**generalmente** (khay-nay-rahl-*mayn*-tay) adv mostly, as a rule
**generar** (khay-nay-*rahr*) v generate
**género** (*khay*-nay-roa) m gender; kind
**generosidad** (khay-nay-roa-see-*dhahdh*) f generosity
**generoso** (khay-nay-*roa*-soa) adj generous, liberal
**genial** (khay-*n ͭ ahl*) adj genial
**genio** (*khay*-n ͭ oa) m genius
**genital** (khay-nee-*tahl*) adj genital
**gente** (*khayn*-tay) f folk; people pl
**gentil** (khayn-*teel*) adj gentle
**genuino** (khay-*nwee*-noa) adj genuine
**geografía** (khay-oa-grah-*fee*-ah) f geography
**geográfico** (khay-oa-*grah*-fee-koa) adj geographical
**geología** (khay-oa-loa-*khee*-ah) f geology
**geometría** (khay-oa-may-*tree*-ah) f geometry
**gerencial** (khay-rayn-*th ͭ ahl*) adj administrative
**germen** (*khayr*-mayn) m germ
**gesticular** (khayss-tee-koo-*lahr*) v gesticulate
**gestión** (khayss-*t ͭ oan*) f administration, management
**gesto** (*khayss*-toa) m sign
**gigante** (khee-*gahn*-tay) m giant
**gigantesco** (khee-gahn-*tayss*-koa) adj enormous, gigantic
**gimnasia** (kheem-*nah*-s ͭ ah) f gymnas-

tics *pl*

**gimnasio** (kheem-*nah*-s<sup>y</sup>oa ) *m* gymnasium

**gimnasta** (kheem-*nahss*-tah ) *m* gymnast

**ginecólogo** (khee-nay-*koa*-loa-goa ) *m* gynaecologist

**girar** (khee-*rahr*) *v* turn

**giro** (*khee*-roa) *m* draft; ~ **postal** postal order

**gitano** (khee-*tah*-noa) *m* gipsy

**glaciar** (glah-th<sup>y</sup>ahr) *m* glacier

**glándula** (*glahn*-doo-lah ) *f* gland

**globo** (*gloa*-bhoa) *m* globe; balloon

**gloria** (*gloa*-r<sup>y</sup>ah) *f* glory

**glorieta** (gloa-*r<sup>y</sup>ay*-tah ) *f* roundabout

**glosario** (gloa-*sah*-r<sup>y</sup>oa ) *m* vocabulary

**glotón** (gloa-*toan*) *adj* greedy

**gobernador** (goa-bhayr-nah-*dhoar*) *m* governor

**gobernante** (goa-bhayr-*nahn*-tay) *m* ruler

**\*gobernar** (goa-bhayr-*nahr*) *v* reign, rule

**gobierno** (goa-*bh<sup>y</sup>ayr*-noa) *m* government, rule; ~ **de la casa** housekeeping

**goce** (*goa*-thay) *m* enjoyment

**gol** (goal ) *m* goal

**golf** (goalf) *m* golf; **campo de** ~ golflinks

**golfo** (*goal*-foa) *m* gulf

**golondrina** (goa-loan-*dree*-nah) *f* swallow

**golosina** (goa-loa-*see*-nah) *f* delicacy; **golosinas** sweets; candy *nAm*

**golpe** (*goal*-pay) *m* blow; knock, bump; **\*dar golpes** bump

**golpear** (goal-pay-*ahr*) *v* \*beat, knock, \*strike; thump, tap

**golpecito** (goal-pay-*thee*-toa) *m* tap

**gollerías** (goa-l<sup>y</sup>ay-*ree*-ahss) *fpl* delicatessen

**goma** (*goa*-mah) *f* gum; ~ **de borrar** eraser, rubber; ~ **de mascar** chewing-gum; ~ **espumada** foam-rubber

**góndola** (*goan*-doa-lah) *f* gondola

**gordo** (*goar*-dhoa) *adj* big; fat, stout

**gorra** (*goa*-rrah) *f* cap

**gorrión** (goa-rr<sup>y</sup>oan) *m* sparrow

**gorro** (*goa*-rroa) *m* cap; ~ **de baño** bathing-cap

**gota** (*goa*-tah) *f* drop; gout

**gotear** (goa-tay-*ahr*) *v* leak

**goteo** (goa-*tay*-oa) *m* leak

**gozar** (goa-*thahr*) *v* enjoy

**grabación** (grah-bhah-*th<sup>y</sup>oan*) *f* recording

**grabado** (grah-*bhah*-dhoa) *m* engraving; picture, print

**grabador** (grah-bhah-*dhoar*) *m* engraver

**grabar** (grah-*bhahr*) *v* engrave

**gracia** (*grah*-th<sup>y</sup>ah) *f* grace

**gracias** (*grah*-th<sup>y</sup>ahss) thank you

**gracioso** (grah-*th<sup>y</sup>oa*-soa) *adj* funny, humorous; graceful

**grado** (*grah*-dhoa) *m* degree; grade; **a tal** ~ so

**gradual** (grah-*dhwahl*) *adj* gradual

**graduar** (grah-*dhwahr*) *v* grade; **graduarse** *v* graduate

**gráfico** (*grah*-fee-koa) *adj* graphic; *m* graph, chart, diagram

**gramática** (grah-*mah*-tee-kah ) *f* grammar

**gramatical** (grah-mah-tee-*kahl*) *adj* grammatical

**gramo** (*grah*-moa) *m* gram

**gramófono** (grah-*moa*-foa-noa) *m* gramophone

**Gran Bretaña** (grahn bray-*tah*-ñah ) Great Britain

**grande** (*grahn*-day) *adj* big; great, large, major

**grandeza** (grahn-*day*-thah ) *f* greatness; grandness

**grandioso** (grahn-d$^y$oa-soa) adj superb, magnificent

**granero** (grah-nay-roa) m barn

**granito** (grah-nee-toa) m granite

**granizo** (grah-nee-thoa) m hail

**granja** (grahng-khah) f farm

**granjera** (grahng-khay-rah) f farmer's wife

**granjero** (grahng-khay-roa) m farmer

**grano** (grah-noa) m grain; corn; pimple

**grapa** (grah-pah) f clamp; staple

**grasa** (grah-sah) f fat, grease; fMe shoe polish

**grasiento** (grah-s$^y$ayn-toa) adj fatty, greasy

**graso** (grah-soa) adj fat

**grasoso** (grah-soa-soa) adj greasy

**gratis** (grah-teess) adv free of charge

**gratitud** (grah-tee-toodh) f gratitude

**grato** (grah-toa) adj enjoyable

**gratuito** (grah-twee-toa) adj gratis, free of charge, free

**grava** (grah-bhah) f gravel

**grave** (grah-bhay) adj grave; bad

**gravedad** (grah-bhay-dhahdh) f gravity

**Grecia** (gray-th$^y$ah) f Greece

**griego** (gr$^y$ay-goa) adj Greek; m Greek

**grieta** (gr$^y$ay-tah) f cleft, chasm; cave

**grifo** (gree-foa) m tap; faucet nAm

**grillo** (gree-l$^y$oa) m cricket

**gripe** (gree-pay) f influenza, flu

**gris** (greess) adj grey

**gritar** (gree-tahr) v cry; yell, scream, shout

**grito** (gree-toa) m cry; yell, scream, shout

**grosella** (groa-say-l$^y$ah) f currant; ~ espinosa gooseberry; ~ negra black-currant

**grosero** (groa-say-roa) adj gross; coarse, rude, impertinent

**grotesco** (groa-tayss-koa) adj ludicrous

**grúa** (groo-ah) f crane

**gruesa** (grway-sah) f gross

**grueso** (grway-soa) adj corpulent

**grumo** (groo-moa) m lump

\***gruñir** (groo-ñeer) v growl

**grupo** (groo-poa) m group; party, set, bunch

**gruta** (groo-tah) f grotto

**guante** (gwahn-tay) m glove

**guapo** (gwah-poa) adj handsome

**guarda** (gwahr-dhah) m custodian

**guardabarros** (gwahr-dhah-bhah-rroass) m mud-guard

**guardabosques** (gwahr-dhah-bhoass-kayss) m forester

**guardar** (gwahr-dhahr) v \*keep, \*put away; guard; ~ con llave lock up; **guardarse** v beware

**guardarropa** (gwahr-dhah-rroa-pah) m wardrobe; cloakroom; checkroom nAm

**guardería** (gwahr-dhay-ree-ah) f nursery

**guardia** (gwahr-dh$^y$ah) f guard; m policeman; ~ personal bodyguard

**guardián** (gwahr-dh$^y$ahn) m attendant, warden; caretaker

**guateque** (gwah-tay-kay) m party

**guerra** (gay-rrah) f war; ~ mundial world war

**guía** (gee-ah) m guide; f guidebook; ~ telefónica telephone directory; telephone book Am

**guiar** (g$^y$ahr) v guide

**guijarro** (gee-khah-rroa) m pebble

**guión** (g$^y$oan) m dash; hyphen

**guisante** (gee-sahn-tay) m pea

**guisar** (gee-sahr) v cook

**guiso** (gee-soa) m dish

**guitarra** (gee-tah-rrah) f guitar

**gusano** (goo-sah-noa) m worm

**gustar** (gooss-tahr) v care for, like; fancy

**gusto** (*gooss*-toa) *m* taste; **con mucho ~** gladly

**gustosamente** (gooss-toa-sah-*mayn*-tay) *adv* willingly, gladly

# H

**\*haber** (ah-*bhayr*) *v* \*have

**hábil** (*ah*-bheel) *adj* able, skilful, skilled

**habilidad** (ah-bhee-lee-*dhahdh*) *f* ability; skill, art

**habitable** (ah-bhee-*tah*-bhlay) *adj* inhabitable, habitable

**habitación** (ah-bhee-tah-*th<sup>y</sup>oan*) *f* room; **~ para huéspedes** guestroom

**habitante** (ah-bhee-*tahn*-tay) *m* inhabitant

**habitar** (ah-bhee-*tahr*) *v* inhabit

**hábito** (*ah*-bhee-toa) *m* habit

**habitual** (ah-bhee-*twahl*) *adj* habitual

**habitualmente** (ah-bhee-twahl-*mayn*-tay) *adv* usually

**habla** (*ah*-bhlah) *f* speech

**habladuría** (ah-bhlah-dhoo-*ree*-ah) *f* rubbish

**hablar** (ah-*bhlahr*) *v* \*speak, talk

**\*hacer** (ah-*thayr*) *v* act; \*do; \*have, cause to, \*make; **hace** ago; **\*hacerse** *v* \*become; \*grow, \*go, \*get

**hacia** (*ah*-th<sup>y</sup>ah) *prep* at, towards, to; about; **~ abajo** down; **~ adelante** forward; **~ arriba** upwards, up; **~ atrás** backwards

**hacienda** (ah-*th<sup>y</sup>ayn*-dah) *f* estate

**hacha** (*ah*-chah) *f* axe

**hada** (*ah*-dhah) *f* fairy; **cuento de hadas** fairytale

**halcón** (ahl-*koan*) *m* hawk

**halibut** (ah-lee-*bhoot*) *m* halibut

**hallar** (ah-*l<sup>y</sup>ahr*) *v* \*come across

**hallazgo** (ah-*l<sup>y</sup>ahdh*-goa) *m* finding

**hamaca** (ah-*mah*-kah) *f* hammock

**hambre** (*ahm*-bray) *f* hunger

**hambriento** (ahm-*br<sup>y</sup>ayn*-toa) *adj* hungry

**harina** (ah-*ree*-nah) *f* flour

**harto de** (*ahr*-toa day) fed up with, tired of

**hasta** (*ahss*-tah) *prep* to, till, until; **~ ahora** so far; **~ que** till

**haya** (*ah*-<sup>y</sup>ah) *f* beech

**hebilla** (ay-*bhee*-l<sup>y</sup>ah) *f* buckle

**hebreo** (ay-*bhray*-oa) *m* Hebrew

**hechizar** (ay-chee-*thahr*) *v* bewitch

**hecho** (*ay*-choa) *m* fact

**\*heder** (ay-*dhayr*) *v* \*smell

**hediondo** (ay-*dh<sup>y</sup>oan*-doa) *adj* smelly

**helado** (ay-*lah*-dhoa) *adj* freezing; *m* ice-cream

**\*helar** (ay-*lahr*) *v* \*freeze

**hélice** (*ay*-lee-thay) *f* propeller

**hemorragia** (ay-moa-*rrah*-kh<sup>y</sup>ah) *f* haemorrhage; **~ nasal** nosebleed

**hemorroides** (ay-moa-*rroi*-dhayss) *fpl* haemorrhoids *pl*, piles *pl*

**\*hender** (ayn-*dayr*) *v* \*split

**hendidura** (ayn-dee-*dhoo*-rah) *f* chink, crack

**heno** (*ay*-noa) *m* hay

**heredar** (ay-ray-*dhahr*) *v* inherit

**hereditario** (ay-ray-dhee-*tah*-r<sup>y</sup>oa) *adj* hereditary

**herencia** (ay-*rayn*-th<sup>y</sup>ah) *f* inheritance, legacy

**herida** (ay-*ree*-dhah) *f* injury, wound

**\*herir** (ay-*reer*) *v* injure, wound

**hermana** (ayr-*mah*-nah) *f* sister

**hermano** (ayr-*mah*-noa) *m* brother

**hermético** (ayr-*may*-tee-koa) *adj* airtight

**hermoso** (ayr-*moa*-soa) *adj* beautiful

**hernia** (*ayr*-n<sup>y</sup>ah) *f* hernia; **~ intervertebral** slipped disc

**héroe** (*ay*-roa-ay) *m* hero

**heroico** (ay-*roi*-koa) *adj* heroic

**heroísmo** (ay-roa-*eez*-moa) *m* heroism

**herradura** (ay-rrah-*dhoo*-rah) *f* horse-shoe

**herramienta** (ay-rrah-*m<sup>y</sup>ayn*-tah) *f* tool, utensil, implement; **bolsa de herramientas** tool kit

**herrería** (ay-rray-*ree*-ah) *f* ironworks

**herrero** (ay-*rray*-roa) *m* smith, blacksmith

**herrumbre** (ay-*rroom*-bray) *f* rust

*****hervir** (ayr-*bheer*) *v* boil

**heterosexual** (ay-tay-roa-sayk-*swahl*) *adj* heterosexual

**hidalgo** (ee-*dhahl*-goa) *m* nobleman

**hidrógeno** (ee-*dhroa*-khay-noa) *m* hydrogen

**hiedra** (*<sup>y</sup>ay*-dhrah) *f* ivy

**hielo** (*<sup>y</sup>ay*-loa) *m* ice

**hierba** (*<sup>y</sup>ayr*-bhah) *f* herb; **brizna de ~** blade of grass; **mala ~** weed

**hierro** (*<sup>y</sup>ay*-rroa) *m* iron; **de ~** iron; **~ fundido** cast iron

**hígado** (*ee*-gah-dhoa) *m* liver

**higiene** (ee-*kh<sup>y</sup>ay*-nay) *f* hygiene

**higiénico** (ee-*kh<sup>y</sup>ay*-nee-koa) *adj* hygienic; **papel ~** toilet-paper

**higo** (*ee*-goa) *m* fig

**hija** (*ee*-khah) *f* daughter

**hijastro** (ee-*khahss*-troa) *m* stepchild

**hijo** (*ee*-khoa) *m* son

**hilar** (ee-*lahr*) *v* *spin

**hilo** (*ee*-loa) *m* yarn, thread; **~ de zurcir** darning wool

**himno** (*eem*-noa) *m* hymn; **~ nacional** national anthem

**hinchar** (een-*chahr*) *v* inflate; **hincharse** *v* *swell

**hinchazón** (een-chah-*thoan*) *f* swelling

**hipo** (*ee*-poa) *m* hiccup

**hipocresía** (ee-poa-kray-*see*-ah) *f* hypocrisy

**hipócrita** (ee-*poa*-kree-tah) *adj* hypocritical; *m* hypocrite

**hipódromo** (ee-*poa*-dhroa-moa) *m* race-course

**hipoteca** (ee-poa-*tay*-kah) *f* mortgage

**hispanoamericano** (eess-pah-noa-ah-may-ree-*kah*-noa) *adj* Spanish-American

**histérico** (eess-*tay*-ree-koa) *adj* hysterical

**historia** (eess-*toa*-r<sup>y</sup>ah) *f* history; **~ de amor** love-story; **~ del arte** art history

**historiador** (eess-toa-r<sup>y</sup>ah-*dhoar*) *m* historian

**histórico** (eess-*toa*-ree-koa) *adj* historical, historic

**hocico** (oa-*thee*-koa) *m* mouth, snout

**hogar** (oa-*gahr*) *m* hearth

**hoja** (*oa*-khah) *f* leaf; sheet; blade; **~ de afeitar** razor-blade; **~ de pedido** order-form; **hojas de oro** gold leaf

**¡hola!** (*oa*-lah) hello!

**Holanda** (oa-*lahn*-dah) *f* Holland

**holandés** (oa-lahn-*dayss*) *adj* Dutch; *m* Dutchman

**hombre** (*oam*-bray) *m* man

**hombro** (*oam*-broa) *m* shoulder

**homenaje** (oa-may-*nah*-khay) *m* tribute, homage

**homosexual** (oa-moa-sayk-*swahl*) *adj* homosexual

**hondo** (*oan*-doa) *adj* deep

**honesto** (oa-*nayss*-toa) *adj* honest; honourable, straight

**hongo** (*oang*-goa) *m* mushroom; toadstool

**honor** (oa-*noar*) *m* honour; glory

**honorable** (oa-noa-*rah*-bhlay) *adj* honourable

**honorarios** (oa-noa-*rah*-r<sup>y</sup>oass) *mpl* fee

**honra** (*oan*-rrah) *f* honour

**honradez** (oan-rah-*dhayth*) *f* honesty

**honrado** (oan-*rrah*-dhoa) *adj* honest

**honrar** (oan-*rahr*) *v* honour

**hora** (*oa*-rah) *f* hour; ~ **de afluencia** rush-hour; ~ **de llegada** time of arrival; ~ **de salida** time of departure; ~ **punta** peak hour; **horas de consulta** consultation hours; **horas de oficina** office hours, business hours; **horas de visita** visiting hours; **horas hábiles** business hours

**horario** (oa-*rah*-r<sup>y</sup>oa) *m* schedule; timetable; ~ **de verano** summer time

**horca** (*oar*-kah) *f* gallows *pl*

**horizontal** (oa-ree-thoan-*tahl*) *adj* horizontal

**horizonte** (oa-ree-*thoan*-tay) *m* horizon

**hormiga** (oar-*mee*-gah) *f* ant

**hormigón** (oar-mee-*goan*) *m* concrete

**hornear** (oar-nay-*ahr*) *v* bake

**horno** (*oar*-noa) *m* oven; furnace

**horquilla** (oar-*kee*-l<sup>y</sup>ah) *f* hairpin, hair-grip; bobby pin *Am*

**horrible** (oa-*rree*-bhlay) *adj* horrible; hideous

**horror** (oa-*rroar*) *m* horror

**horticultura** (oar-tee-kool-*too*-rah) *f* horticulture

**hospedar** (oass-pay-*dhahr*) *v* entertain; **hospedarse** *v* stay

**hospedería** (oass-pay-dhay-*ree*-ah) *f* hostel

**hospicio** (oass-*pee*-th<sup>y</sup>oa) *m* home

**hospital** (oass-pee-*tahl*) *m* hospital

**hospitalario** (oass-pee-tah-*lah*-r<sup>y</sup>oa) *adj* hospitable

**hospitalidad** (oass-pee-tah-lee-*dhahdh*) *f* hospitality

**hostil** (oass-*teel*) *adj* hostile

**hotel** (oa-*tayl*) *m* hotel

**hoy** (oi) *adv* today; ~ **en día** nowadays

**hoyo** (*oa*-<sup>y</sup>oa) *m* pit

**hueco** (*way*-koa) *adj* hollow; *m* gap

**huelga** (*wayl*-gah) *f* strike; \***estar en** ~ \*strike

**huella** (*way*-l<sup>y</sup>ah) *f* trace

**huérfano** (*wayr*-fah-noa) *m* orphan

**huerto** (*wayr*-toa) *m* kitchen garden

**hueso** (*way*-soa) *m* bone; stone

**huésped** (*wayss*-paydh) *m* guest; lodger, boarder

**hueva** (*way*-bhah) *f* roe

**huevera** (way-*bhay*-rah) *f* egg-cup

**huevo** (*way*-bhoa) *m* egg; **yema de** ~ egg-yolk

\***huir** (weer) *v* escape

**hule** (*oo*-lay) *mMe* rubber

**humanidad** (oo-mah-nee-*dhahdh*) *f* humanity, mankind

**humano** (oo-*mah*-noa) *adj* human

**humedad** (oo-may-*dhahdh*) *f* moisture, humidity, damp

\***humedecer** (oo-may-dhay-*thayr*) *v* moisten, damp

**húmedo** (*oo*-may-dhoa) *adj* moist, humid, damp; wet

**humilde** (oo-*meel*-day) *adj* humble

**humo** (*oo*-moa) *m* smoke

**humor** (oo-*moar*) *m* spirit, mood; humour; **de buen** ~ good-tempered, good-humoured

**humorístico** (oo-moa-*reess*-tee-koa) *adj* humorous

**hundimiento** (oon-dee-*m<sup>y</sup>ayn*-toa) *m* ruination

**hundirse** (oon-*deer*-say) *v* \*sink

**húngaro** (*oong*-gah-roa) *adj* Hungarian; *m* Hungarian

**Hungría** (oong-*gree*-ah) *m* Hungary

**huracán** (oo-rah-*kahn*) *m* hurricane

**hurtar** (oor-*tahr*) *v* \*steal

**hurto** (*oor*-toa) *m* theft

**husmear** (oos-may-*ahr*) *v* scent, \*get wind of

# I

**ibérico** (ee-*bhay*-ree-koa) *adj* Iberian
**icono** (ee-*koa*-noa) *m* icon
**ictericia** (eek-tay-*ree*-th<sup>y</sup>ah) *f* jaundice
**idea** (ee-*dhay*-ah) *f* idea
**ideal** (ee-dhay-*ahl*) *adj* ideal; *m* ideal
**idear** (ee-dhay-*ahr*) *v* devise
**idéntico** (ee-*dhayn*-tee-koa) *adj* identical
**identidad** (ee-dhayn-tee-*dhahdh*) *f* identity; **carnet de ~** identity card
**identificación** (ee-dhayn-tee-fee-kah-th<sup>y</sup>oan) *f* identification
**identificar** (ee-dhayn-tee-fee-*kahr*) *v* identify
**idioma** (ee-*dh<sup>y</sup>oa*-mah) *m* language
**idiomático** (ee-dh<sup>y</sup>oa-*mah*-tee-koa) *adj* idiomatic
**idiota** (ee-*dh<sup>y</sup>oa*-tah) *adj* idiotic; *m* idiot, fool
**ídolo** (*ee*-dhoa-loa) *m* idol
**iglesia** (ee-*glay*-s<sup>y</sup>ah) *f* chapel, church
**ignorancia** (eeg-noa-*rahn*-th<sup>y</sup>ah) *f* ignorance
**ignorante** (eeg-noa-*rahn*-tay) *adj* ignorant
**ignorar** (eeg-noa-*rahr*) *v* ignore
**igual** (ee-*gwahl*) *adj* equal, alike; level, even; **sin ~** unsurpassed
**igualar** (ee-gwah-*lahr*) *v* level, equalize; equal
**igualdad** (ee-gwahl-*dahdh*) *f* equality
**igualmente** (ee-gwahl-*mayn*-tay) *adv* alike; equally
**ilegal** (ee-lay-*gahl*) *adj* illegal, unlawful
**ilegible** (ee-lay-*khee*-bhlay) *adj* illegible
**ileso** (ee-*lay*-soa) *adj* unhurt
**ilimitado** (ee-lee-mee-*tah*-dhoa) *adj* unlimited

**iluminación** (ee-loo-mee-nah-th<sup>y</sup>oan) *f* illumination
**iluminar** (ee-loo-mee-*nahr*) *v* illuminate
**ilusión** (ee-loo-s<sup>y</sup>oan) *f* illusion
**ilustración** (ee-looss-trah-th<sup>y</sup>oan) *f* illustration; picture
**ilustrar** (ee-looss-*trahr*) *v* illustrate
**ilustre** (ee-*looss*-tray) *adj* illustrious
**imagen** (ee-*mah*-khayn) *f* image, picture; **~ reflejada** reflection
**imaginación** (ee-mah-khee-nah-th<sup>y</sup>oan) *f* fancy, imagination
**imaginar** (ee-mah-khee-*nahr*) *v* conceive; **imaginarse** *v* fancy, imagine
**imaginario** (ee-mah-khee-*nah*-r<sup>y</sup>oa) *adj* imaginary
**imitación** (ee-mee-tah-th<sup>y</sup>oan) *f* imitation
**imitar** (ee-mee-*tahr*) *v* imitate, copy
**impaciente** (eem-pah-th<sup>y</sup>ayn-tay) *adj* eager, impatient
**impar** (eem-*pahr*) *adj* odd
**imparcial** (eem-pahr-th<sup>y</sup>*ahl*) *adj* impartial
**impecable** (eem-pay-*kah*-bhlay) *adj* faultless
**impedimento** (eem-pay-dhee-*mayn*-toa) *m* impediment
***impedir** (eem-pay-*dheer*) *v* hinder, impede; restrain, prevent
**impeler** (eem-pay-*layr*) *v* propel
**imperdible** (eem-payr-*dhee*-bhlay) *m* safety-pin
**imperfección** (eem-payr-fayk-th<sup>y</sup>oan) *f* fault
**imperfecto** (eem-payr-*fayk*-toa) *adj* imperfect
**imperial** (eem-pay-r<sup>y</sup>*ahl*) *adj* imperial
**imperio** (eem-*pay*-r<sup>y</sup>oa) *m* empire
**impermeable** (eem-payr-may-*ah*-bhlay) *adj* waterproof, rainproof; *m* raincoat, mackintosh
**impersonal** (eem-payr-soa-*nahl*) *adj*

impersonal

**impertinencia** (eem-payr-tee-*nayn*-th<sup>y</sup>ah) *f* impertinence

**impertinente** (eem-payr-tee-*nayn*-tay) *adj* bold, impertinent

**impetuoso** (eem-pay-*twoa*-soa) *adj* violent

**implicar** (eem-plee-*kahr*) *v* imply; **implicado** involved

**imponente** (eem-poa-*nayn*-tay) *adj* grand, imposing

**imponible** (eem-poa-*nee*-bhlay) *adj* dutiable

**impopular** (eem-poa-poo-*lahr*) *adj* unpopular

**importación** (eem-poar-tah-th<sup>y</sup>oan) *f* import

**importador** (eem-poar-tah-*dhoar*) *m* importer

**importancia** (eem-poar-*tahn*-th<sup>y</sup>ah) *f* importance; *tener ~ matter

**importante** (eem-poar-*tahn*-tay) *adj* important; considerable, capital, big

**importar** (eem-poar-*tahr*) *v* import

**importuno** (eem-poar-*too*-noa) *adj* annoying

**imposible** (eem-poa-*see*-bhlay) *adj* impossible

**impotencia** (eem-poa-*tayn*-th<sup>y</sup>ah) *f* impotence

**impotente** (eem-poa-*tayn*-tay) *adj* powerless; impotent

**impresión** (eem-pray-s<sup>y</sup>oan) *f* impression; ~ **digital** fingerprint

**impresionante** (eem-pray-s<sup>y</sup>oa-*nahn*-tay) *adj* impressive; striking

**impresionar** (eem-pray-s<sup>y</sup>oa-*nahr*) *v* *strike, impress

**impreso** (eem-*pray*-soa) *m* printed matter

**imprevisto** (eem-pray-*bheess*-toa) *adj* unexpected, incidental

**\*imprimir** (eem-pree-*meer*) *v* print

**improbable** (eem-proa-*bhah*-bhlay) *adj* unlikely, improbable

**ímprobo** (*eem*-proa-bhoa) *adj* unfair, dishonest

**impropio** (eem-*proa*-p<sup>y</sup>oa) *adj* improper; wrong

**improvisar** (eem-proa-bhee-*sahr*) *v* improvise

**imprudente** (eem-proo-*dhayn*-tay) *adj* unwise

**impudente** (eem-poo-*dhayn*-tay) *adj* impudent

**impuesto** (eem-*pwayss*-toa) *m* taxation, tax; Customs duty; ~ **de aduana** Customs duty; **impuestos de importación** import duty; **libre de impuestos** tax-free

**impulsivo** (eem-pool-*see*-bhoa) *adj* impulsive

**impulso** (eem-*pool*-soa) *m* urge, impulse

**inaccesible** (ee-nahk-thay-*see*-bhlay) *adj* inaccessible

**inaceptable** (ee-nah-thayp-*tah*-bhlay) *adj* unacceptable

**inadecuado** (ee-nah-dhay-*kwah*-dhoa) *adj* inadequate; unfit, unsuitable

**inapreciable** (ee-nah-pray-th<sup>y</sup>ah-bhlay) *adj* priceless

**incapaz** (eeng-kah-*pahth*) *adj* unable, incapable

**incendio** (een-*thayn*-d<sup>y</sup>oa) *m* fire

**incidente** (een-thee-*dhayn*-tay) *m* incident

**incienso** (een-th<sup>y</sup>ayn-soa) *m* incense

**incierto** (een-th<sup>y</sup>ayr-toa) *adj* uncertain

**incineración** (een-thee-nay-rah-th<sup>y</sup>oan) *f* cremation

**incinerar** (een-thee-nay-*rahr*) *v* cremate

**incisión** (een-thee-s<sup>y</sup>oan) *f* cut

**incitar** (een-thee-*tahr*) *v* incite

**inclinación** (eeng-klee-nah-th<sup>y</sup>oan) *f* tendency, inclination; incline

**inclinar** (eeng-klee-*nahr*) v bow; **inclinado** inclined; sloping, slanting; **inclinarse** v *be inclined to; slope, slant

***incluir** (eeng-*klweer*) v include; enclose; count; **todo incluido** all in

**incluso** (eeng-*kloo*-soa) adj inclusive, included

**incombustible** (eeng-koam-booss-*tee*-bhlay) adj fireproof

**incomible** (eeng-koa-*mee*-bhlay) adj inedible

**incomodidad** (eeng-koa-moa-dhee-*dhahdh*) f inconvenience

**incómodo** (eeng-*koa*-moa-dhoa) adj uncomfortable

**incompetente** (eeng-koam-pay-*tayn*-tay) adj incompetent; unqualified

**incompleto** (eeng-koam-*play*-toa) adj incomplete

**inconcebible** (eeng-koan-thay-*bhee*-bhlay) adj inconceivable

**incondicional** (eeng-koan-dee-th⁀oa-*nahl*) adj unconditional

**inconsciente** (eeng-koan-*th⁀ayn*-tay) adj unaware; unconscious

**inconveniencia** (eeng-koam-bay-n⁀ayn-th⁀ah) f inconvenience

**incorrecto** (eeng-koa-*rrayk*-toa) adj incorrect

**increíble** (eeng-kray-*ee*-bhlay) adj incredible

**incrementar** (eeng-kray-mayn-*tahr*) v increase

**inculto** (eeng-*kool*-toa) adj uncultivated; uneducated

**incurable** (eeng-koo-*rah*-bhlay) adj incurable

**indagación** (een-dah-gah-*th⁀oan*) f inquiry

**indagar** (een-dah-*gahr*) v query

**indecente** (een-day-*thayn*-tay) adj indecent

**indefenso** (een-day-*fayn*-soa) adj un-

protected

**indefinido** (een-day-fee-*nee*-dhoa) adj indefinite

**indemnización** (een-daym-nee-thah-*th⁀oan*) f compensation, indemnity

**independencia** (een-day-payn-*dayn*-th⁀ah) f independence

**independiente** (een-day-payn-*d⁀ayn*-tay) adj self-employed, independent

**indeseable** (een-day-say-*ah*-bhlay) adj undesirable

**India** (*een*-d⁀ah) f India

**indicación** (een-dee-kah-*th⁀oan*) f indication

**indicador** (een-dee-kah-*dhoar*) m trafficator, indicator

**indicar** (een-dee-*kahr*) v indicate; declare

**indicativo** (een-dee-kah-*tee*-bhoa) m area code

**índice** (*een*-dee-thay) m index, table of contents; index finger

**indiferencia** (een-dee-fay-*rayn*-th⁀ah) f indifference

**indiferente** (een-dee-fay-*rayn*-tay) adj indifferent; careless

**indígena** (een-*dee*-khay-nah) m native

**indigestión** (een-dee-khayss-*t⁀oan*) f indigestion

**indignación** (een-deeg-nah-*th⁀oan*) f indignation

**indio** (*een*-d⁀oa) adj Indian; m Indian

**indirecto** (een-dee-*rayk*-toa) adj indirect

**indispensable** (een-deess-payn-*sah*-bhlay) adj essential

**indispuesto** (een-deess-*pwayss*-toa) adj unwell

**individual** (een-dee-bhee-*dhwahl*) adj individual

**individuo** (een-dee-*bhee*-dhwoa) m individual

**Indonesia** (een-doa-*nay*-s⁀ah) f Indonesia

**indonesio** (een-doa-*nay*-s<sup>y</sup>oa) *adj* Indonesian; *m* Indonesian

**indudable** (een-doo-*dhah*-bhlay) *adj* undoubted

**indulto** (een-*dool*-toa) *m* pardon

**industria** (een-*dooss*-tr<sup>y</sup>ah) *f* industry; ingenuity

**ineficiente** (ee-nay-fee-*th<sup>y</sup>ayn*-tay) *adj* inefficient

**inerte** (ee-*nayr*-tay) *adj* limp

**inesperado** (ee-nayss-pay-*rah*-dhoa) *adj* unexpected

**inestable** (ee-nayss-*tah*-bhlay) *adj* unsteady, unstable

**inevitable** (ee-nay-bhee-*tah*-bhlay) *adj* unavoidable, inevitable

**inexacto** (ee-nayk-*sahk*-toa) *adj* incorrect, inaccurate; false

**inexperto** (ee-nayks-*payr*-toa) *adj* inexperienced

**inexplicable** (ee-nayks-plee-*kah*-bhlay) *adj* unaccountable

**infancia** (een-*fahn*-th<sup>y</sup>ah) *f* infancy

**infantería** (een-fahn-tay-*ree*-ah) *f* infantry

**infantil** (een-fahn-*teel*) *adj* childlike

**infección** (een-fayk-*th<sup>y</sup>oan*) *f* infection

**infectar** (een-fayk-*tahr*) *v* infect; **infectarse** *v* \*become septic

**inferior** (een-fay-r<sup>y</sup>oar) *adj* inferior; bottom

**infiel** (een-*f<sup>y</sup>ayl*) *adj* unfaithful

**infierno** (een-*f<sup>y</sup>ayr*-noa) *m* hell

**infinidad** (een-fee-nee-*dhahdh*) *f* infinity

**infinitivo** (een-fee-nee-*tee*-bhoa) *m* infinitive

**infinito** (een-fee-*nee*-toa) *adj* endless, infinite

**inflable** (een-*flah*-bhlay) *adj* inflatable

**inflación** (een-flah-*th<sup>y</sup>oan*) *f* inflation

**inflamable** (een-flah-*mah*-bhlay) *adj* inflammable

**inflamación** (een-flah-mah-*th<sup>y</sup>oan*) *f* inflammation

**influencia** (een-*flwayn*-th<sup>y</sup>ah) *f* influence

\***influir** (een-*flweer*) *v* influence

**influjo** (een-*floo*-khoa) *m* influence

**influyente** (een-floo-*<sup>y</sup>ayn*-tay) *adj* influential

**información** (een-foar-mah-*th<sup>y</sup>oan*) *f* enquiry, information; **oficina de informaciones** inquiry office

**informal** (een-foar-*mahl*) *adj* informal; casual

**informar** (een-foar-*mahr*) *v* report, inform; plead; **informarse** *v* inquire

**informe** (een-*foar*-may) *m* report; **informes** *mpl* information; \***pedir informes** inquire

**infortunio** (een-foar-*too*-n<sup>y</sup>oa) *m* misfortune

**infrarrojo** (een-frah-*rroa*-khoa) *adj* infra-red

**infrecuente** (een-fray-*kwayn*-tay) *adj* infrequent

**infringir** (een-freeng-*kheer*) *v* trespass

**ingeniero** (eeng-khay-n<sup>y</sup>ay-roa) *m* engineer

**ingenioso** (eeng-khay-n<sup>y</sup>oa-soa) *adj* ingenious

**ingenuo** (eeng-*khay*-nwoa) *adj* naïve; simple

**Inglaterra** (eeng-glah-*tay*-rrah) *f* England; Britain

**ingle** (*eeng*-glay) *f* groin

**inglés** (eeng-*glayss*) *adj* English; *m* Englishman; Briton

**ingrato** (eeng-*grah*-toa) *adj* ungrateful

**ingrediente** (eeng-gray-dh<sup>y</sup>ayn-tay) *m* ingredient

**ingresar** (eeng-gray-*sahr*) *v* deposit

**ingreso** (eenggray-soa) *m* entry

**ingresos** (eeng-*gray*-soass) *mpl* revenue, earnings *pl*, income; **impuesto sobre los ~** income-tax

**inhabitable** (ee-nah-bhee-*tah*-bhlay) *adj* uninhabitable

**inhabitado** (ee-nah-bhee-*tah*-dhoa) *adj* uninhabited

**inhalar** (ee-nah-*lahr*) *v* inhale

**inicial** (ee-nee-*th<sup>y</sup>ahl*) *adj* initial; *f* initial

**iniciar** (ee-nee-*th<sup>y</sup>ahr*) *v* initiate

**iniciativa** (ee-nee-th<sup>y</sup>ah-*tee*-bhah) *f* initiative

**ininterrumpido** (ee-neen-tay-rroom-*pee*-dhoa) *adj* continuous

**injusticia** (eeng-khooss-*tee*-th<sup>y</sup>ah) *f* injustice

**injusto** (eeng-*khooss*-toa) *adj* unfair, unjust

**inmaculado** (een-mah-koo-*lah*-dhoa) *adj* stainless, spotless

**inmediatamente** (een-may-dh<sup>y</sup>ah-tah-*mayn*-tay) *adv* instantly, immediately

**inmediato** (een-may-*dh<sup>y</sup>ah*-toa) *adj* immediate, prompt; **de ~** immediately

**inmenso** (een-*mayn*-soa) *adj* immense

**inmerecido** (een-may-ray-*thee*-dhoa) *adj* unearned

**inmigración** (een-mee-grah-*th<sup>y</sup>oan*) *f* immigration

**inmigrante** (een-mee-*grahn*-tay) *m* immigrant

**inmigrar** (een-mee-*grahr*) *v* immigrate

**inmodesto** (een-moa-*dhayss*-toa) *adj* immodest

**inmueble** (een-*mway*-bhlay) *m* house

**inmundo** (een-*moon*-doa) *adj* filthy

**inmunidad** (een-moo-nee-*dhahdh*) *f* immunity

**inmunizar** (een-moo-nee-*thahr*) *v* immunize

**innato** (een-*nah*-toa) *adj* natural

**innecesario** (een-nay-thay-sah-*r<sup>y</sup>oa*) *adj* unnecessary

**innumerable** (een-noo-may-*rah*-bhlay) *adj* innumerable

**inocencia** (ee-noa-*thayn*-th<sup>y</sup>ah) *f* innocence

**inocente** (ee-noa-*thayn*-tay) *adj* innocent

**inoculación** (ee-noa-koo-lah-*th<sup>y</sup>oan*) *f* inoculation

**inocuo** (ee-*noa*-kwoa) *adj* harmless

**inoportuno** (ee-noa-poar-*too*-noa) *adj* inconvenient; misplaced

**inquietarse** (eeng-k<sup>y</sup>ay-*tahr*-say) *v* worry

**inquieto** (een-*k<sup>y</sup>ay*-toa) *adj* restless; uneasy, worried

**inquietud** (eeng-k<sup>y</sup>ay-*toodh*) *f* unrest; worry

**inquilino** (eeng-kee-*lee*-noa) *m* tenant

**insalubre** (een-sah-*loo*-bhray) *adj* unhealthy

**insatisfecho** (een-sah-teess-*fay*-choa) *adj* dissatisfied

**inscribir** (eens-kree-*bheer*) *v* enter, book, list; **inscribirse** *v* register, check in

**inscripción** (eens-kreep-*th<sup>y</sup>oan*) *f* inscription; registration

**insecticida** (een-sayk-tee-*thee*-dhah) *m* insecticide

**insectífugo** (een-sayk-*tee*-foo-goa) *m* insect repellent

**insecto** (een-*sayk*-toa) *m* insect; bug *nAm*

**inseguro** (een-say-*goo*-roa) *adj* unsafe; doubtful

**insensato** (een-sayn-*sah*-toa) *adj* senseless

**insensible** (een-sayn-*see*-bhlay) *adj* insensitive; heartless

**insertar** (een-sayr-*tahr*) *v* insert

**insignificante** (een-seeg-nee-fee-*kahn*-tay) *adj* unimportant, petty, insignificant

**insípido** (een-*see*-pee-dhoa) *adj* tasteless

**insistir** (een-seess-*teer*) *v* insist

**insolación** (een-soa-lah-*th<sup>y</sup>oan*) *f* sunstroke

**insolencia** (een-soa-*layn*-th<sup>y</sup>ah) *f* insolence

**insolente** (een-soa-*layn*-tay) *adj* insolent

**insólito** (een-*soa*-lee-toa) *adj* uncommon, unusual

**insomnio** (een-*soam*-n<sup>y</sup>oa) *m* insomnia

**insonorizado** (een-soa-noa-ree-*thah*-dhoa) *adj* soundproof

**insoportable** (een-soa-poar-*tah*-bhlay) *adj* intolerable

**inspección** (eens-payk-*th<sup>y</sup>oan*) *f* inspection; ~ **de pasaportes** passport control

**inspeccionar** (eens-payk-th<sup>y</sup>oa-*nahr*) *v* inspect

**inspector** (eens-payk-*toar*) *m* inspector

**inspirar** (een-spee-*rahr*) *v* inspire

**instalación** (eens-tah-lah-*th<sup>y</sup>oan*) *f* installation; plant

**instalar** (eens-tah-*lahr*) *v* install; furnish

**instantánea** (eens-tahn-*tah*-nay-ah) *f* snapshot

**instantáneamente** (eens-tahn-tah-nay-ah-*mayn*-tay) *adv* instantly

**instante** (eens-*tahn*-tay) *m* instant; second; **al** ~ instantly

**instinto** (een-*steen*-toa) *m* instinct

**institución** (eens-tee-too-*th<sup>y</sup>oan*) *f* institution, institute

*****instituir** (eens-tee-*tweer*) *v* institute

**instituto** (eens-tee-*too*-toa) *m* institution, institute

**institutor** (eens-tee-too-*toar*) *m* teacher

**instrucción** (eens-trook-*th<sup>y</sup>oan*) *f* instruction; direction

**instructivo** (eens-trook-*tee*-bhoa) *adj* instructive

**instructor** (eens-trook-*toar*) *m* instructor

*****instruir** (eens-*trweer*) *v* instruct

**instrumento** (eens-troo-*mayn*-toa) *m* instrument; ~ **músico** musical instrument

**insuficiente** (een-soo-fee-*th<sup>y</sup>ayn*-tay) *adj* insufficient

**insufrible** (een-soo-*free*-bhlay) *adj* unbearable

**insultante** (een-sool-*tahn*-tay) *adj* offensive

**insultar** (een-sool-*tahr*) *v* insult; scold, call names

**insulto** (een-*sool*-toa) *m* insult

**intacto** (een-*tahk*-toa) *adj* intact; unbroken, whole

**integral** (een-tay-*grahl*) *adj* integral

**integrar** (een-tay-*grahr*) *v* integrate

**intelecto** (een-tay-*layk*-toa) *m* intellect

**intelectual** (een-tay-layk-*twahl*) *adj* intellectual

**inteligencia** (een-tay-lee-*khayn*-th<sup>y</sup>ah) *f* intelligence, brain

**inteligente** (een-tay-lee-*khayn*-tay) *adj* intelligent; clever, smart

**intención** (een-tayn-*th<sup>y</sup>oan*) *f* intention, purpose; *****tener la** ~ **de** intend

**intencionado** (een-tayn-th<sup>y</sup>oa-*nah*-dhoa) *adj* on purpose

**intencional** (een-tayn-th<sup>y</sup>oa-*nahl*) *adj* intentional

**intensidad** (een-tayn-see-*dhahdh*) *f* intensity

**intenso** (een-*tayn*-soa) *adj* intense

**intentar** (een-tayn-*tahr*) *v* attempt, try; intend

**intercambiar** (een-tayr-kahm-*b<sup>y</sup>ahr*) *v* exchange

**interés** (een-tay-*rayss*) *m* interest

**interesado** (een-tay-ray-*sah*-dhoa) *adj* interested; concerned; *m* candidate

**interesante** (een-tay-ray-*sahn*-tay) *adj*

interesting
**interesar** (een-tay-ray-*sahr*) v interest
**interferencia** (een-tayr-fay-*rayn*-th<sup>y</sup>ah ) f interference
**interferir** (een-tayr-fay-*reer*) v interfere
**ínterin** (*een*-tay-reen ) m interim
**interior** (een-tay-r<sup>y</sup>oar) adj inside, inner; domestic; m interior, inside
**intermediario** (een-tayr-may-dh<sup>y</sup>ah-r<sup>y</sup>oa ) m intermediary
**intermedio** (een-tayr-*may*-dh<sup>y</sup>oa ) m interlude
**internacional** (een-tayr-nah-th<sup>y</sup>oa-*nahl*) adj international
**internado** (een-tayr-*nah*-dhoa ) m boarding-school
**interno** (een-*tayr*-noa ) adj internal; resident
**interpretar** (een-tayr-pray-*tahr*) v interpret
**intérprete** (een-*tayr*-pray-tay) m interpreter
**interrogar** (een-tay-rroa-*gahr*) v interrogate
**interrogativo** (een-tay-rroa-gah-*tee*-bhoa ) adj interrogative
**interrogatorio** (een-tay-rroa-gah-*toa*-r<sup>y</sup>oa ) m interrogation, examination
**interrumpir** (een-tay-rroom-*peer*) v interrupt
**interrupción** (een-tay-rroop-*th<sup>y</sup>oan*) f interruption
**interruptor** (een-tay-rroop-*toar*) m switch
**intersección** (een-tayr-sayk-*th<sup>y</sup>oan*) f intersection
**intervalo** (een-tayr-*bhah*-loa ) m interval
**intervención** (een-tayr-bhayn-*th<sup>y</sup>oan*) f intervention
***intervenir** (een-tayr-bhay-*neer*) v intervene
**intestino** (een-tayss-*tee*-noa ) m intestine, gut; ~ **recto** rectum; **intesti-**

**nos** intestines pl, bowels pl
**intimidad** (een-tee-mee-*dhahdh*) f privacy
**íntimo** (*een*-tee-moa ) adj intimate; cosy
**intoxicación alimentaria** (een-toak-see-kah-*th<sup>y</sup>oan* ah-lee-mayn-*tah*-r<sup>y</sup>ah ) food poisoning
**intransitable** (een-trahn-see-*tah*-bhlay) adj impassable
**intriga** (een-*tree*-gah) f intrigue
**introducción** (een-troa-dhook-*th<sup>y</sup>oan*) f introduction
***introducir** (een-troa-dhoo-*theer*) v introduce; *bring up
**intruso** (een-*troo*-soa) m trespasser
**inundación** (ee-noon-dah-*th<sup>y</sup>oan*) f flood
**inusitado** (ee-noo-see-*tah*-dhoa ) adj unusual
**inútil** (ee-*noo*-teel ) adj useless
**inútilmente** (ee-noo-teel-*mayn*-tay ) adv in vain
**invadir** (eem-bah-*dheer*) v invade
**inválido** (eem-*bah*-lee-dhoa ) adj invalid, disabled; m invalid
**invasión** (eem-bah-*s<sup>y</sup>oan*) f invasion
**invención** (eem-bayn-*th<sup>y</sup>oan*) f invention
**inventar** (eem-bayn-*tahr*) v invent
**inventario** (eem-bayn-*tah*-r<sup>y</sup>oa ) m inventory
**inventivo** (eem-bayn-*tee*-bhoa ) adj inventive
**inventor** (eem-bayn-*toar*) m inventor
**invernáculo** (eem-bayr-*nah*-koo-loa ) m greenhouse
**invernadero** (eem-bayr-nah-*dhay*-roa ) m greenhouse
**inversión** (eem-bayr-*s<sup>y</sup>oan*) f investment
**inversionista** (eem-bayr-s<sup>y</sup>oa-*neess*-tah ) m investor
**inverso** (eem-*bayr*-soa ) adj reverse

**\*invertir** (eem-bayr-*teer*) *v* invert; invest

**investigación** (eem-bayss-tee-gah-*th*ʸoan) *f* research; investigation, enquiry

**investigador** (eem-bhayss-tee-gah-*dhoar*) *m* research worker

**investigar** (eem-bayss-tee-*gahr*) *v* investigate, enquire

**invierno** (eem-*b*ʸayr-noa) *m* winter; **deportes de ~** winter sports

**invisible** (eem-bee-*see*-bhlay) *adj* invisible

**invitación** (eem-bee-tah-*th*ʸoan) *f* invitation

**invitado** (eem-bee-*tah*-dhoa) *m* guest

**invitar** (eem-bee-*tahr*) *v* invite; ask

**inyección** (een-ʸayk-*th*ʸoan) *f* shot, injection

**inyectar** (een-ʸayk-*tahr*) *v* inject

**\*ir** (eer) *v* \*go; **~ por** fetch; **\*irse** *v* \*go away

**Irak** (ee-*rahk*) *m* Iraq

**Irán** (ee-*rahn*) *m* Iran

**iraní** (ee-rah-*nee*) *adj* Iranian; *m* Iranian

**iraquí** (ee-rah-*kee*) *adj* Iraqi; *m* Iraqi

**irascible** (ee-rahss-*thee*-bhlay) *adj* irascible, quick-tempered

**Irlanda** (eer-*lahn*-dah) *f* Ireland

**irlandés** (eer-lahn-*dayss*) *adj* Irish; *m* Irishman

**ironía** (ee-roa-*nee*-ah) *f* irony

**irónico** (ee-*roa*-nee-koa) *adj* ironical

**irrazonable** (ee-rrah-thoa-*nah*-bhlay) *adj* unreasonable

**irreal** (ee-rray-*ahl*) *adj* unreal

**irreflexivo** (ee-rray-flayk-*see*-bhoa) *adj* rash

**irregular** (ee-rray-goo-*lahr*) *adj* irregular; uneven

**irrelevante** (ee-rray-lay-*bhahn*-tay) *adj* insignificant

**irreparable** (ee-rray-pah-*rah*-bhlay) *adj* irreparable

**irrevocable** (ee-rray-bhoa-*kah*-bhlay) *adj* irrevocable

**irritable** (ee-rree-*tah*-bhlay) *adj* irritable

**irritante** (ee-rree-*tahn*-tay) *adj* annoying

**irritar** (ee-rree-*tahr*) *v* annoy, irritate

**irrompible** (ee-rroam-*pee*-bhlay) *adj* unbreakable

**irrupción** (ee-rroop-*th*ʸoan) *f* invasion, raid

**isla** (*eez*-lah) *f* island

**islandés** (eez-lahn-*dayss*) *adj* Icelandic; *m* Icelander

**Islandia** (eez-*lahn*-dʸah) *f* Iceland

**Israel** (eess-rah-*ayl*) *m* Israel

**israelí** (eess-rah-ay-*lee*) *adj* Israeli; *m* Israeli

**istmo** (*eest*-moa) *m* isthmus

**Italia** (ee-tah-*l*ʸah) *f* Italy

**italiano** (ee-tah-*l*ʸah-noa) *adj* Italian; *m* Italian

**ítem** (*ee*-taym) *m* item

**itinerario** (ee-tee-nay-*rah*-rʸoa) *m* itinerary

**izar** (ee-*thahr*) *v* hoist

**izquierdo** (eeth-*k*ʸayr-dhoa) *adj* left; left-hand

# J

**jabón** (khah-*bhoan*) *m* soap; **~ de afeitar** shaving-soap; **~ en polvo** soap powder, washing-powder

**jade** (*khah*-dhay) *m* jade

**jadear** (khah-dhay-*ahr*) *v* pant

**jalar** (khah-*lahr*) *vMe* \*draw

**jalea** (khah-*lay*-ah) *f* jelly

**jamás** (khah-*mahss*) *adv* ever

**jamón** (khah-*moan*) *m* ham

**Japón** (khah-*poan*) *m* Japan

**japonés** (khah-poa-*nayss*) *adj* Japanese; *m* Japanese

**¡jaque!** (*khah*-kay) check!

**jarabe** (khah-*rah*-bhay) *m* syrup

**jardín** (khahr-*dheen*) *m* garden; ~ **de infancia** kindergarten; ~ **público** public garden; ~ **zoológico** zoological gardens, zoo

**jardinero** (khahr-dhee-*nay*-roa) *m* gardener

**jarra** (*khah*-rrah) *f* jar

**jaula** (*khou*-lah) *f* cage

**jefe** (*khay*-fay) *m* chief, manager, boss; leader; chieftain; ~ **de cocina** chef; ~ **de estación** stationmaster; ~ **de Estado** head of state; ~ **de gobierno** premier

**jengibre** (khayng-*khee*-bhray) *m* ginger

**jerarquía** (khay-rahr-*kee*-ah) *f* hierarchy

**jeringa** (khay-*reeng*-gah) *f* syringe

**jersey** (khayr-*say*) *m* jersey; jumper

**jinete** (khee-*nay*-tay) *m* horseman, rider

**jitomate** (khee-toa-*mah*-tay) *mMe* tomato

**Jordania** (khoar-*dhah*-nᵞah) *f* Jordan

**jordano** (khoar-*dhah*-noa) *adj* Jordanian; *m* Jordanian

**jornada** (khoar-*nah*-dhah) *f* day trip

**joven** (*khoa*-bhayn) *adj* young; *m* lad

**jovencito** (khoa-bhayn-*thee*-toa) *m* teenager

**jovial** (khoa-*bhᵞahl*) *adj* jolly

**joya** (*khoa*-ᵞah) *f* jewel, gem

**joyería** (khoa-ᵞay-*ree*-ah) *f* jewellery

**joyero** (khoa-*ᵞay*-roa) *m* jeweller

**jubilado** (khoo-bhee-*lah*-dhoa) *adj* retired

**judía** (khoo-*dhee*-ah) *f* bean

**judío** (khoo-*dhee*-oa) *adj* Jewish; *m* Jew

**juego** (*khway*-goa) *m* game, play; set; *hacer ~ con match; ~ **de bolos**

bowling; ~ **de damas** draughts; ~ **de té** tea-set

**jueves** (*khway*-bhayss) *m* Thursday

**juez** (khwayth) *m* judge

**jugada** (khoo-*gah*-dhah) *f* move

**jugador** (khoo-gah-*dhoar*) *m* player

*****jugar** (khoo-*gahr*) *v* play

**juguete** (khoo-*gay*-tay) *m* toy

**juguetería** (khoo-gay-tay-*ree*-ah) *f* toyshop

**juicio** (*khwee*-thᵞoa) *m* sense; judgment

**julio** (*khoo*-lᵞoa) July

**junco** (*khoong*-koa) *m* rush

**jungla** (*khoong*-glah) *f* jungle

**junio** (*khoo*-nᵞoa) June

**junquillo** (khoong-*kee*-lᵞoa) *m* reed

**junta** (*khoon*-tah) *f* meeting

**juntamente** (khoon-tah-*mayn*-tay) *adv* jointly

**juntar** (khoon-*tahr*) *v* attach; collect; join; **juntarse** *v* gather

**junto a** (*khoon*-toa ah) beside; next to

**juntos** (*khoon*-toass) *adv* together

**jurado** (khoo-*rah*-dhoa) *m* jury

**juramento** (khoo-rah-*mayn*-toa) *m* vow, oath; **prestar ~** vow

**jurar** (khoo-*rahr*) *v* *swear

**jurídico** (khoo-*ree*-dhee-koa) *adj* legal

**jurista** (khoo-*reess*-tah) *m* lawyer

**justamente** (khooss-tah-*mayn*-tay) *adv* rightly; just

**justicia** (khooss-*tee*-thᵞah) *f* justice

**justificar** (khooss-tee-fee-*kahr*) *v* justify

**justo** (*khooss*-toa) *adj* fair, just, righteous, right; correct, appropriate, proper

**juvenil** (khoo-bhay-*neel*) *adj* juvenile

**juventud** (khoo-bhayn-*toodh*) *f* youth

**juzgar** (khoodh-*gahr*) *v* judge

# K

**Kenya** (*kay*-nᵛah) *m* Kenya
**kilogramo** (kee-loa-*grah*-moa) *m* kilogram
**kilometraje** (kee-loa-may-*trah*-khay) *m* distance in kilometres
**kilómetro** (kee-*loa*-may-troa) *m* kilometre

# L

**la** (lah) *pron* her
**laberinto** (lah-bhay-*reen*-toa) *m* maze, labyrinth
**labio** (*lah*-bhᵛoa) *m* lip
**labor** (lah-*bhoar*) *f* labour
**laboratorio** (lah-bhoa-rah-*toa*-rᵛoa) *m* laboratory; ~ **de lenguas** language laboratory
**laca** (*lah*-kah) *f* lacquer; ~ **para el cabello** hair-spray
**ladera** (lah-*dhay*-rah) *f* hillside
**lado** (*lah*-dhoa) *m* side; way; **al** ~ next-door; **al otro** ~ across; **al otro** ~ **de** across
**ladrar** (lah-*dhrahr*) *v* bay, bark
**ladrillo** (lah-*dhree*-lᵛoa) *m* brick
**ladrón** (lah-*dhroan*) *m* thief, robber; burglar
**lago** (*lah*-goa) *m* lake
**lágrima** (*lah*-gree-mah) *f* tear
**laguna** (lah-*goo*-nah) *f* lagoon
**lamentable** (lah-mayn-*tah*-bhlay) *adj* lamentable
**lamentar** (lah-mayn-*tahr*) *v* lament; grieve
**lamer** (lah-*mayr*) *v* lick
**lámpara** (*lahm*-pah-rah) *f* lamp; ~ **para lectura** reading-lamp; ~ **sorda**

hurricane lamp
**lana** (*lah*-nah) *f* wool; **de** ~ woollen
**landa** (*lahn*-dhah) *f* heath
**langosta** (lahng-*goass*-tah) *f* lobster
**lanza** (*lahn*-thah) *f* spear
**lanzamiento** (lahn-thah-*mᵛayn*-toa) *m* throw
**lanzar** (lahn-*thahr*) *v* *cast; launch
**lápida** (*lah*-pee-dhah) *f* gravestone, tombstone
**lápiz** (*lah*-peeth) *m* pencil; ~ **labial** lipstick; ~ **para las cejas** eye-pencil
**largo** (*lahr*-goa) *adj* long; **a lo** ~ **de** along, past; **pasar de** ~ pass by
**laringitis** (lah-reeng-*khee*-teess) *f* laryngitis
**¡qué lástima!** (kay *lahss*-tee-mah) what a pity!
**lata** (*lah*-tah) *f* tin, canister, can
**lateralmente** (lah-tay-rahl-*mayn*-tay) *adv* sideways
**latín** (lah-*teen*) *m* Latin
**latinoamericano** (lah-tee-noa-ah-may-ree-*kah*-noa) *adj* Latin-American
**latitud** (lah-tee-*toodh*) *f* latitude
**latón** (lah-*toan*) *m* brass
**lavable** (lah-*bhah*-bhlay) *adj* washable; fast-dyed
**lavabo** (lah-*bhah*-bhoa) *m* wash-stand
**lavabos** (lah-*bhah*-bhoass) *mpl* bathroom; ~ **para caballeros** men's room; ~ **para señoras** ladies' room
**lavado** (lah-*bhah*-dhoa) *m* washing
**lavandería** (lah-bhahn-day-*ree*-ah) *f* laundry; ~ **de autoservicio** launderette
**lavar** (lah-*bhahr*) *v* wash
**laxante** (lahk-*sahn*-tay) *m* laxative
**le** (lay) *pron* him; her
**leal** (lay-*ahl*) *adj* true, loyal
**lección** (layk-*thᵛoan*) *f* lesson
**lectura** (layk-*too*-rah) *f* reading
**leche** (*lay*-chay) *f* milk; **batido de** ~ milk-shake

**lechería** (lay-chay-*ree*-ah) *f* dairy

**lechero** (lay-*chay*-roa) *m* milkman

**lechigada** (lay-chee-*gah*-dhah) *f* litter

**lechoso** (lay-*choa*-soa) *adj* milky

**lechuga** (lay-*choo*-gah) *f* lettuce

**\*leer** (lay-ayr) *v* \*read

**legación** (lay-gah-th<sup>y</sup>oan) *f* legation

**legal** (lay-*gahl*) *adj* legal

**legalización** (lay-gah-lee-thah-th<sup>y</sup>oan) *f* legalization

**legible** (lay-*khee*-bhlay) *adj* legible

**legítimo** (lay-*khee*-tee-moa) *adj* legitimate, legal

**legumbre** (lay-*goom*-bray) *f* vegetable

**lejano** (lay-*khah*-noa) *adj* remote, far, distant

**lejos** (*lay*-khoass) *adv* far

**lema** (*lay*-mah) *f* motto, slogan

**lengua** (*layng*-gwah) *f* tongue; language; ~ **materna** native language, mother tongue

**lenguado** (layng-*gwah*-dhoa) *m* sole

**lenguaje** (layng-*gwah*-khay) *m* speech

**lente** (*layn*-tay) *m/f* lens; ~ **de aumento** magnifying glass; **lentillas** *fpl* contact lenses

**lento** (*layn*-toa) *adj* slow; slack

**león** (lay-*oan*) *m* lion

**lepra** (*lay*-prah) *f* leprosy

**lerdo** (*layr*-dhoa) *adj* slow

**les** (layss) *pron* them

**lesión** (lay-s<sup>y</sup>oan) *f* injury

**letra** (*lay*-trah) *f* letter

**levadura** (lay-bhah-*dhoo*-rah) *f* yeast

**levantamiento** (lay-bhahn-tah-m<sup>y</sup>ayn-toa) *m* rise; rising

**levantar** (lay-bhahn-*tahr*) *v* lift; \*bring up; **levantarse** *v* \*rise, \*get up

**leve** (*lay*-bhay) *adj* slight

**ley** (lay) *f* law

**leyenda** (lay-*y*ayn-dah) *f* legend

**liar** (l<sup>y</sup>ahr) *v* bundle

**libanés** (lee-bhah-*nayss*) *adj* Lebanese; *m* Lebanese

**Líbano** (*lee*-bhah-noa) *m* Lebanon

**liberación** (lee-bhay-rah-th<sup>y</sup>oan) *f* liberation; delivery

**liberal** (lee-bhay-*rahl*) *adj* liberal

**liberalismo** (lee-bhay-rah-*leez*-moa) *m* liberalism

**Liberia** (lee-*bhay*-r<sup>y</sup>ah) *f* Liberia

**liberiano** (lee-bhay-*r<sup>y</sup>ah*-noa) *adj* Liberian; *m* Liberian

**libertad** (lee-bhayr-*tahdh*) *f* liberty, freedom

**libra** (*lee*-bhrah) *f* pound

**libranza** (lee-*bhrahn*-thah) *f* money order

**librar** (lee-*bhrahr*) *v* deliver

**libre** (*lee*-bhray) *adj* free

**librería** (lee-bhray-*ree*-ah) *f* bookstore

**librero** (lee-*bhray*-roa) *m* bookseller

**libro** (*lee*-bhroa) *m* book; ~ **de bolsillo** paperback; ~ **de cocina** cookery-book; ~ **de reclamaciones** complaints book; ~ **de texto** textbook

**licencia** (lee-*thayn*-th<sup>y</sup>ah) *f* permission, licence; leave

**lícito** (*lee*-thee-toa) *adj* lawful

**licor** (lee-*koar*) *m* liqueur

**líder** (*lee*-dhayr) *m* leader

**liebre** (*l<sup>y</sup>ay*-bhray) *f* hare

**liga** (*lee*-gah) *f* union, league

**ligero** (lee-*khay*-roa) *adj* light; slight

**lima** (*lee*-mah) *f* file; lime; ~ **para las uñas** nail-file

**limitar** (lee-mee-*tahr*) *v* limit

**límite** (*lee*-mee-tay) *m* boundary, limit; ~ **de velocidad** speed limit

**limón** (lee-*moan*) *m* lemon

**limonada** (lee-moa-*nah*-dhah) *f* lemonade

**limpiaparabrisas** (leem-p<sup>y</sup>ah-pah-rah-*bhree*-sahss) *m* windscreen wiper

**limpiapipas** (leem-p<sup>y</sup>ah-*pee*-pahss) *m* pipe cleaner

**limpiar** (leem-*p<sup>y</sup>ahr*) *v* clean; ~ **en se-**

co dry-clean

**limpieza** (leem-*p*ʸay-thah) f cleaning

**limpio** (*leem*-pʸoa) adj clean

**lindo** (*leen*-doa) adj sweet

**línea** (*lee*-nay-ah) f line; ~ **de navegación** shipping line; ~ **de pesca** fishing line; ~ **principal** main line

**lino** (*lee*-noa) m linen

**linterna** (leen-*tayr*-nah) f lantern; torch, flash-light

**liquidación** (lee-kee-dhah-*th*ʸoan) f clearance sale

**líquido** (*lee*-kee-dhoa) adj liquid

**liso** (*lee*-soa) adj smooth

**lista** (*leess*-tah) f list; ~ **de correos** poste restante; ~ **de espera** waiting-list; ~ **de precios** price-list

**listín telefónico** (leess-*teen* tay-lay-foa-nee-koa) telephone directory; telephone book *Am*

**listo** (*leess*-toa) adj bright; clever; smart; ready

**litera** (lee-*tay*-rah) f berth

**literario** (lee-tay-*rah*-rʸoa) adj literary

**literatura** (lee-tay-rah-*too*-rah) f literature

**litoral** (lee-toa-*rahl*) m sea-coast

**litro** (*lee*-troa) m litre

**lo** (loa) pron it; ~ **que** what

**lobo** (*loa*-bhoa) m wolf

**local** (loa-*kahl*) adj local

**localidad** (loa-kah-lee-*dhahdh*) f locality; seat

**localizar** (loa-kah-lee-*thahr*) v locate

**loción** (loa-*th*ʸoan) f lotion

**loco** (*loa*-koa) adj crazy; mad

**locomotora** (loa-koa-moa-*toa*-rah) f engine, locomotive

**locuaz** (loa-*kwahth*) adj talkative

**locura** (loa-*koo*-rah) f madness, lunacy

**lodo** (*loa*-dhoa) m mud

**lodoso** (loa-*dhoa*-soa) adj muddy

**lógica** (*loa*-khee-kah) f logic

**lógico** (*loa*-khee-koa) adj logical

**lograr** (loa-*grahr*) v achieve; secure

**lona** (*loa*-nah) f canvas; ~ **impermeable** tarpaulin

**longitud** (loang-khee-*toodh*) f length; longitude; ~ **de onda** wave-length

**longitudinalmente** (loang-khee-too-dhee-nahl-*mayn*-tay) adv lengthways

**loro** (*loa*-roa) m parrot

**lotería** (loa-tay-*ree*-ah) f lottery

**loza** (*loa*-thah) f earthenware; pottery, faience, crockery

**lubricación** (loo-bhree-kah-*th*ʸoan) f lubrication

**lubricar** (loo-bhree-*kahr*) v lubricate

**lubrificar** (loo-bhree-fee-*kahr*) v lubricate

**lucio** (*loo*-thʸoa) m pike

\***lucir** (loo-*theer*) v \*shine

**lucha** (*loo*-chah) f combat, fight; contest, strife; struggle

**luchar** (loo-*chahr*) v struggle, \*fight

**luego** (*lway*-goa) adv later; ¡**hasta luego**! so long!

**lugar** (loo-*gahr*) m place; spot; **en** ~ **de** instead of; ~ **de camping** camping site; ~ **de descanso** holiday resort; ~ **de nacimiento** place of birth; ~ **de reunión** meeting-place; \***tener** ~ \*take place

**lúgubre** (*loo*-goo-bhray) adj creepy

**lujo** (*loo*-khoa) m luxury

**lujoso** (loo-*khoa*-soa) adj luxurious

**lumbago** (loom-*bah*-goa) m lumbago

**luminoso** (loo-mee-*noa*-soa) adj luminous

**luna** (*loo*-nah) f moon; ~ **de miel** honeymoon

**lunático** (loo-*nah*-tee-koa) adj insane, lunatic

**lunes** (*loo*-nayss) m Monday

**lúpulo** (*loo*-poo-loa) m hop

**lustroso** (looss-*troa*-soa) adj glossy

**luto** (*loo*-toa) m mourning

**luz** (looth) f light; **luces de freno**

brake lights; ~ **de estacionamiento** parking light; ~ **de la luna** moonlight; ~ **del día** daylight; ~ **del sol** sunlight; ~ **lateral** sidelight; ~ **trasera** rear-light

# LL

**llaga** (lᵞah-gah) f sore
**llama** (lᵞah-mah) f flame
**llamada** (lᵞah-mah-dhah) f call; ~ **local** local call; ~ **telefónica** telephone call
**llamar** (lᵞah-mahr) v cry, call; **así llamado** so-called; ~ **por teléfono** phone; **llamarse** v *be called
**llano** (lᵞah-noa) adj flat; level, even, smooth; m plain
**llanta** (lᵞahn-tah) f rim; fMe tire
**llave** (lᵞah-bhay) f key; **ama de llaves** housekeeper; **guardar con** ~ lock up; ~ **de la casa** latchkey; ~ **inglesa** spanner
**llegada** (lᵞay-gah-dhah) f arrival; coming
**llegar** (lᵞay-gahr) v arrive; ~ **a** attain
**llenar** (lᵞay-nahr) v fill; fill in; fill out Am; fill up
**lleno** (lᵞay-noa) adj full
**llevar** (lᵞay-bhahr) v *take; *bear, carry; *wear; **llevarse** v *take away
**llorar** (lᵞoa-rahr) v cry, *weep
***llover** (lᵞoa-bhayr) v rain
**llovizna** (lᵞoa-bheeth-nah) f drizzle
**lluvia** (lᵞoo-bhᵞah) f rain
**lluvioso** (lᵞoo-bhᵞoa-soa) adj rainy

# M

**macizo** (mah-thee-thoa) adj solid, massive
**machacar** (mah-chah-kahr) v mash
**macho** (mah-choa) adj male
**madera** (mah-dhay-rah) f wood; **de** ~ wooden; ~ **de construcción** timber
**madero** (mah-dhay-roa) m log
**madrastra** (mah-dhrahss-trah) f stepmother
**madre** (mah-dhray) f mother
**madriguera** (mah-dhree-gay-rah) f den
**madrugada** (mah-dhroo-gah-dhah) f daybreak
**madrugar** (mah-dhroo-gahr) v *rise early
**madurez** (mah-dhoo-rayth) f maturity
**maduro** (mah-dhoo-roa) adj mature, ripe
**maestro** (mah-ayss-troa) m master; schoolteacher, schoolmaster, teacher; ~ **particular** tutor
**magia** (mah-khᵞah) f magic
**mágico** (mah-khee-koa) adj magic
**magistrado** (mah-kheess-trah-dhoa) m magistrate
**magnético** (mahg-nay-tee-koa) adj magnetic
**magneto** (mahg-nay-toa) m magneto
**magnetófono** (mahg-nay-toa-foa-noa) m tape-recorder
**magnífico** (mahg-nee-fee-koa) adj splendid, gorgeous, magnificent, swell
**magro** (mah-groa) adj lean
**magulladura** (mah-goo-lᵞah-dhoo-rah) f bruise
**magullar** (mah-goo-lᵞahr) v bruise
**maíz** (mah-eeth) m maize; ~ **en la mazorca** corn on the cob
**majestad** (mah-khayss-tahdh) f majes-

ty

**mal** (mahl) *m* harm, evil; wrong; mischief

**malaria** (mah-*lah*-rʸah) *f* malaria

**Malasia** (mah-*lah*-sʸah) *f* Malaysia

**malayo** (mah-*lah*-ʸoa) *adj* Malaysian; *m* Malay

\***maldecir** (mahl-day-*theer*) *v* curse

**maldición** (mahl-dee-*th*ʸoan) *f* curse

**maleta** (mah-*lay*-tah) *f* suitcase, bag

**maletín** (mah-lay-*teen*) *m* grip *nAm*

**malévolo** (mah-*lay*-bhoa-loa) *adj* spiteful

**malicia** (mah-*lee*-thʸah) *f* mischief

**malicioso** (mah-lee-*th*ʸoa-soa) *adj* malicious

**maligno** (mah-*leeg*-noa) *adj* malignant; ill

**malo** (*mah*-loa) *adj* bad; evil, ill

**malva** (*mahl*-bhah) *adj* mauve

**malvado** (mahl-*bhah*-dhoa) *adj* wicked, evil

**malla** (*mah*-lʸah) *f* mesh

**mamífero** (mah-*mee*-fay-roa) *m* mammal

**mampara** (mahm-*pah*-rah) *f* screen

**mampostear** (mahm-poass-tay-*ahr*) *v* \*lay bricks

**mamut** (mah-*moot*) *m* mammoth

**manada** (mah-*nah*-dhah) *f* herd

**manantial** (mah-nahn-*t*ʸahl) *m* spring

**mancuernillas** (mahn-kwayr-*nee*-lʸahss) *fplMe* cuff-links *pl*

**mancha** (*mahn*-chah) *f* stain, spot, speck; blot

**manchado** (mahn-*chah*-dhoa) *adj* soiled

**manchar** (mahn-*chahr*) *v* stain

**mandar** (mahn-*dahr*) *v* command; \*send; ~ **a buscar** \*send for

**mandarina** (mahn-dah-*ree*-nah) *f* mandarin, tangerine

**mandato** (mahn-*dah*-toa) *m* mandate; order

**mandíbula** (mahn-*dee*-bhoo-lah) *f* jaw

**mando** (*mahn*-doa) *m* command

**manejable** (mah-nay-*khah*-bhlay) *adj* handy; manageable

**manejar** (mah-nay-*khahr*) *v* handle

**manejo** (mah-*nay*-khoa) *m* management

**manera** (mah-*nay*-rah) *f* way, manner; **de otra ~** otherwise

**manga** (*mahng*-gah) *f* sleeve

**mango** (*mahng*-goa) *m* handle

**manía** (mah-*nee*-ah) *f* craze

**manicura** (mah-nee-*koo*-rah) *f* manicure; \***hacer la ~** manicure

**manifestación** (mah-nee-fayss-tah-*th*ʸoan) *f* demonstration; \***hacer una ~** demonstrate

\***manifestar** (mah-nee-fayss-*tahr*) *v* reveal

**maniquí** (mah-nee-*kee*) *m* model, mannequin

**mano** (*mah*-noa) *f* hand; **de segunda ~** second-hand; **hecho a ~** handmade

**mansión** (mahn-*s*ʸoan) *f* mansion

**manso** (*mahn*-soa) *adj* tame

**manta** (*mahn*-tah) *f* blanket

**mantel** (mahn-*tayl*) *m* table-cloth

\***mantener** (mahn-tay-*nayr*) *v* maintain

**mantenimiento** (mahn-tay-nee-*m*ʸayn-toa) *m* maintenance

**mantequilla** (mahn-tay-*kee*-lʸah) *f* butter

**manual** (mah-*nwahl*) *adj* manual; *m* handbook; ~ **de conversación** phrase-book

**manuscrito** (mah-nooss-*kree*-toa) *m* manuscript

**manutención** (mah-noo-tayn-*th*ʸoan) *f* upkeep

**manzana** (mahn-*thah*-nah) *f* apple; ~ **de casas** house block *Am*

**mañana** (mah-*ñah*-nah) *f* morning;

*adv* tomorrow; **esta** ~ this morning

**mapa** (*mah*-pah) *m* map; ~ **de carreteras** road map

**maquillaje** (mah-kee-*lᵞah*-khay) *m* make-up

**máquina** (*mah*-kee-nah) *f* engine, machine; ~ **de afeitar** razor; ~ **de billetes** ticket machine; ~ **de coser** sewing-machine; ~ **de escribir** typewriter; ~ **de lavar** washing-machine; ~ **tragamonedas** slot-machine

**maquinaria** (mah-kee-*nah*-rᵞah) *f* machinery

**mar** (mahr) *m* sea; **orilla del** ~ seaside, seashore

**maravilla** (mah-rah-*bhee*-lᵞah) *f* marvel

**maravillarse** (mah-rah-bhee-*lᵞahr*-say) *v* marvel

**maravilloso** (mah-rah-bhee-*lᵞoa*-soa) *adj* wonderful, marvellous, fine

**marca** (*mahr*-kah) *f* brand; mark; ~ **de fábrica** trademark

**marcar** (mahr-*kahr*) *v* mark; score

**marco** (*mahr*-koa) *m* frame

**marcha** (*mahr*-chah) *f* march; *dar ~ **atrás** reverse; ~ **atrás** reverse

**marchar** (mahr-*chahr*) *v* march

**marea** (mah-*ray*-ah) *f* tide

**mareado** (mah-ray-*ah*-dhoa) *adj* dizzy, giddy; seasick

**mareo** (mah-*ray*-oa) *m* giddiness; seasickness

**marfil** (mahr-*feel*) *m* ivory

**margarina** (mahr-gah-*ree*-nah) *f* margarine

**margen** (*mahr*-khayn) *m* margin

**marido** (mah-*ree*-dhoa) *m* husband

**marina** (mah-*ree*-nah) *f* navy; seascape

**marinero** (mah-ree-*nay*-roa) *m* sailor

**marino** (mah-*ree*-noa) *m* seaman

**mariposa** (mah-ree-*poa*-sah) *f* butterfly

**marisco** (mah-*reess*-koa) *m* shellfish

**marisma** (mah-*reez*-mah) *f* swamp

**marítimo** (mah-*ree*-tee-moa) *adj* maritime

**mármol** (*mahr*-moal) *m* marble

**marqués** (mahr-*kayss*) *m* marquis

**marroquí** (mah-rroa-*kee*) *adj* Moroccan; *m* Moroccan

**Marruecos** (mah-*rway*-koass) *m* Morocco

**martes** (*mahr*-tayss) *m* Tuesday

**martillo** (mahr-*tee*-lᵞoa) *m* hammer

**mártir** (*mahr*-teer) *m* martyr

**marzo** (*mahr*-thoa) March

**mas** (mahss) *conj* but

**más** (mahss) *adv* more; plus; **algo** ~ some more; **el** ~ most; ~ **de** over

**masa** (*mah*-sah) *f* mass; crowd, lot; dough, batter

**masaje** (mah-*sah*-khay) *m* massage; *dar ~ massage; ~ **facial** face massage

**masajista** (mah-sah-*kheess*-tah) *m* masseur

**máscara** (*mahss*-kah-rah) *f* mask; ~ **facial** face-pack

**masculino** (mahss-koo-*lee*-noa) *adj* masculine

**masticar** (mahss-tee-*kahr*) *v* chew

**mástil** (*mahss*-teel) *m* mast

**matar** (mah-*tahr*) *v* kill

**mate** (*mah*-tay) *adj* mat, dim, dull

**matemáticas** (mah-tay-*mah*-tee-kahss) *fpl* mathematics

**matemático** (mah-tay-*mah*-tee-koa) *adj* mathematical

**materia** (mah-*tay*-rᵞah) *f* matter; ~ **prima** raw material

**material** (mah-tay-*rᵞahl*) *adj* material, substantial; *m* material

**matiz** (mah-*teeth*) *m* nuance

**matorral** (mah-toa-*rrahl*) *m* scrub, bush

**matrícula** (mah-*tree*-koo-lah ) *f* registration number

**matrimonial** (mah-tree-moa-*n*ʸ*ahl*) *adj* matrimonial

**matrimonio** (mah-tree-*moa*-nʸoa ) *m* wedding, marriage; matrimony

**matriz** (mah-*treeth*) *f* womb

**mausoleo** (mou-soa-*lay*-oa ) *m* mausoleum

**máximo** (*mahk*-see-moa ) *m* maximum

**mayo** (*mah*-ʸoa ) May

**mayor** (mah-ʸ*oar*) *adj* superior, major; main, eldest; *m* major

**mayoría** (mah-ʸoa-*ree*-ah ) *f* majority; bulk

**mayorista** (mah-ʸoa-*reess*-tah ) *m* wholesale dealer

**mayúscula** (mah-ʸ*ooss*-koo-lah ) *f* capital letter

**mazo** (*mah*-thoa ) *m* mallet

**me** (may ) *pron* me; myself

**mecánico** (may-*kah*-nee-koa ) *adj* mechanical; *m* mechanic

**mecanismo** (may-kah-*neez*-moa ) *m* mechanism, machinery

**mecanografiar** (may-kah-noa-grah-fʸ*ahr*) *v* type

**mecer** (may-*thayr*) *v* rock

**mecha** (*may*-chah ) *f* fuse

**medalla** (may-*dhah*-lʸah ) *f* medal

**media** (*may*-dhʸah ) *f* stocking; ~ **pantalón** panty-hose; **medias elásticas** support hose

**mediador** (may-dhʸah-*dhoar*) *m* mediator

**medianamente** (may-dhʸah-nah-*mayn*-tay) *adv* fairly

**mediano** (may-*dhʸah*-noa ) *adj* medium

**medianoche** (may-dhʸah-*noa*-chay ) *f* midnight

**mediante** (may-*dhʸahn*-tay) *adv* by means of

**mediar** (may-*dhʸahr*) *v* mediate

**medicamento** (may-dhee-kah-*mayn*-toa ) *m* medicine, drug

**medicina** (may-dhee-*thee*-nah ) *f* medicine

**médico** (*may*-dhee-koa ) *adj* medical; *m* doctor, physician; ~ **de cabecera** general practitioner

**medida** (may-*dhee*-dhah ) *f* measure; **hecho a la** ~ made to order, tailor-made

**medidor** (may-dhee-*dhoar*) *m* gauge

**medieval** (may-dhʸay-*bhahl*) *adj* mediaeval

**medio** (*may*-dhʸoa ) *adj* half; medium; middle; *m* midst, middle; means; **en** ~ **de** amid; ~ **ambiente** milieu, environment

**mediocre** (may-*dhʸoa*-kray) *adj* moderate, poor

**mediodía** (may-dhʸoa-*dhee*-ah ) *m* midday, noon

* **medir** (may-*dheer*) *v* measure

**meditación** (may-dhee-tah-*th*ʸ*oan*) *f* meditation

**meditar** (may-dhee-*tahr*) *v* meditate

**Mediterráneo** (may-dhee-tay-*rrah*-nay-oa ) Mediterranean

**médula** (*may*-dhoo-lah ) *f* marrow

**medusa** (may-*dhoo*-sah ) *f* jelly-fish

**mejicano** (may-khee-*kah*-noa ) *adj* Mexican; *m* Mexican

**Méjico** (*may*-khee-koa ) *m* Mexico

**mejilla** (may-*khee*-lʸah ) *f* cheek

**mejillón** (may-khee-*l*ʸ*oan*) *m* mussel

**mejor** (may-*khoar*) *adj* better; superior

**mejora** (may-*khoa*-rah ) *f* improvement

**mejorar** (may-khoa-*rahr*) *v* improve

**melancolía** (may-lahng-koa-*lee*-ah ) *f* melancholy

**melancólico** (may-lahng-*koa*-lee-koa ) *adj* sad

**melocotón** (may-loa-koa-*toan*) *m* peach

**melodía** (may-loa-*dhee*-ah ) *f* melody

**melodioso** (may-loa-*dh*ʸoa-soa ) *adj* tuneful

**melodrama** (may-loa-*drah*-mah ) *m* melodrama

**melón** (may-*loan*) *m* melon

**membrana** (maym-*brah*-nah ) *f* diaphragm

**memorable** (may-moa-*rah*-bhlay) *adj* memorable

**memoria** (may-*moa*-rʸah ) *f* memory; **de ~** by heart

**menaje** (may-*nah*-khay ) *m* household

**mención** (mayn-*th*ʸoan ) *f* mention

**mencionar** (mayn-thʸoa-*nahr*) *v* mention

**mendigar** (mayn-dee-*gahr*) *v* beg

**mendigo** (mayn-*dee*-goa ) *m* beggar

**menor** (may-*noar*) *adj* minor; junior

**menos** (*may*-noass) *adv* less; minus; but; **a ~ que** unless; **por lo ~** at least

**menosprecio** (may-noass-*pray*-thʸoa ) *m* contempt

**mensaje** (mayn-*sah*-khay ) *m* message

**mensajero** (mayn-sah-*khay*-roa ) *m* messenger

**menstruación** (mayns-trwah-*th*ʸoan ) *f* menstruation

**mensual** (mayn-*swahl*) *adj* monthly

**menta** (*mayn*-tah ) *f* mint; peppermint

**mental** (mayn-*tahl*) *adj* mental

**mente** (*mayn*-tay ) *f* mind

**\*mentir** (mayn-*teer*) *v* lie

**mentira** (mayn-*tee*-rah ) *f* lie

**menú** (may-*noo*) *m* menu

**menudo** (may-*noo*-dhoa ) *adj* minute, small, tiny; **a ~** often

**mercado** (mayr-*kah*-dhoa ) *m* market; **~ negro** black market

**mercancía** (mayr-kahn-*thee*-ah ) *f* merchandise

**mercería** (mayr-thay-*ree*-ah ) *f* haberdashery

**mercurio** (mayr-*koo*-rʸoa ) *m* mercury

**\*merecer** (may-ray-*thayr*) *v* merit, deserve

**meridional** (may-ree-dhʸoa-*nahl*) *adj* southern, southerly

**merienda** (may-*r*ʸayn-dah ) *f* tea

**mérito** (*may*-ree-toa ) *m* merit

**merluza** (mayr-*loo*-thah ) *f* whiting

**mermelada** (mayr-may-*lah*-dhah ) *f* jam

**mes** (mayss ) *m* month

**mesa** (*may*-sah ) *f* table

**mesera** (may-*say*-rah ) *fMe* waitress

**mesero** (may-*say*-roa ) *mMe* waiter

**meseta** (may-*say*-tah ) *f* plateau

**meta** (*may*-tah ) *f* goal; finish

**metal** (may-*tahl*) *m* metal

**metálico** (may-*tah*-lee-koa ) *adj* metal

**meter** (may-*tayr* ) *v* \*put

**meticuloso** (may-tee-koo-*loa*-soa ) *adj* precise

**metódico** (may-*toa*-dhee-koa ) *adj* methodical

**método** (*may*-toa-dhoa ) *m* method

**métrico** (*may*-tree-koa ) *adj* metric

**metro** (*may*-troa ) *m* metre; underground; subway *Am*

**mezcla** (*mayth*-klah ) *f* mixture

**mezclar** (mayth-*klahr*) *v* mix; **mezclarse en** interfere with

**mezquino** (mayth-*kee*-noa ) *adj* narrow-minded, stingy; mean

**mezquita** (mayth-*kee*-tah ) *f* mosque

**mi** (mee ) *adj* my

**micrófono** (mee-*kroa*-foa-noa ) *m* microphone

**microscopio** (mee-kroass-*koa*-pʸoa ) *m* microscope

**microsurco** (mee-kroa-*soor*-koa ) *m* long-playing record

**miedo** (*m*ʸay-dhoa ) *m* fear, fright; **\*tener ~** \*be afraid

**miel** (mʸayl ) *f* honey

**miembro** (*m*ʸaym-broa ) *m* limb; member

**mientras** (*m<sup>y</sup>ayn*-trahss) *conj* whilst, while

**miércoles** (*m<sup>y</sup>ayr*-koa-layss) *m* Wednesday

**migaja** (mee-*gah*-khah) *f* crumb

**migraña** (mee-*grah*-ñah) *f* migraine

**mil** (meel) *num* thousand

**milagro** (mee-*lah*-groa) *m* wonder, miracle

**milagroso** (mee-lah-*groa*-soa) *adj* miraculous

**militar** (mee-lee-*tahr*) *adj* military; *m* soldier

**milla** (*mee*-l<sup>y</sup>ah) *f* mile

**millaje** (mee-*l<sup>y</sup>ah*-khay) *m* mileage

**millón** (mee-*l<sup>y</sup>oan*) *m* million

**millonario** (mee-l<sup>y</sup>oa-nah-r<sup>y</sup>oa) *m* millionaire

**mimar** (mee-*mahr*) *v* *spoil

**mina** (*mee*-nah) *f* mine; pit; ~ **de oro** goldmine

**mineral** (mee-nay-*rahl*) *m* mineral; ore

**minería** (mee-nay-*ree*-ah) *f* mining

**minero** (mee-*nay*-roa) *m* miner

**miniatura** (mee-n<sup>y</sup>ah-*too*-rah) *f* miniature

**mínimo** (*mee*-nee-moa) *adj* least

**mínimum** (*mee*-nee-moom) *m* minimum

**ministerio** (mee-neess-*tay*-r<sup>y</sup>oa) *m* ministry

**ministro** (mee-*neess*-troa) *m* minister

**minoría** (mee-noa-*ree*-ah) *f* minority

**minorista** (mee-noa-*reess*-tah) *m* retailer

**minucioso** (mee-noo-*th<sup>y</sup>oa*-soa) *adj* thorough

**minusválido** (mee-nooz-*bhah*-lee-dhoa) *adj* disabled

**minuto** (mee-*noo*-toa) *m* minute

**mío** (*mee*-oa) *pron* mine

**miope** (*m<sup>y</sup>oa*-pay) *adj* short-sighted

**mirada** (mee-*rah*-dhah) *f* look

**mirar** (mee-*rahr*) *v* look; watch, view, look at; stare, gaze

**mirlo** (*meer*-loa) *m* blackbird

**misa** (*mee*-sah) *f* Mass

**misceláneo** (mee-thay-*lah*-nay-oa) *adj* miscellaneous

**miserable** (mee-say-*rah*-bhlay) *adj* miserable

**miseria** (mee-*say*-r<sup>y</sup>ah) *f* misery

**misericordia** (mee-say-ree-*koar*-d<sup>y</sup>ah) *f* mercy

**misericordioso** (mee-say-ree-koar-*d<sup>y</sup>oa*-soa) *adj* merciful

**misión** (mee-*s<sup>y</sup>oan*) *f* mission

**mismo** (*meez*-moa) *adj* same

**misterio** (meess-*tay*-r<sup>y</sup>oa) *m* mystery

**misterioso** (meess-tay-*r<sup>y</sup>oa*-soa) *adj* mysterious; obscure

**mitad** (mee-*tahdh*) *f* half; **partir por la ~** halve

**mito** (*mee*-toa) *m* myth

**moción** (moa-*th<sup>y</sup>oan*) *f* motion

**mochila** (moa-*chee*-lah) *f* rucksack, knapsack

**moda** (*moa*-dhah) *f* fashion; **a la ~** fashionable

**modales** (moa-*dhah*-layss) *mpl* manners *pl*

**modelar** (moa-dhay-*lahr*) *v* model

**modelo** (moa-*dhay*-loa) *m* model

**moderado** (moa-dhay-*rah*-dhoa) *adj* moderate

**moderno** (moa-*dhayr*-noa) *adj* modern

**modestia** (moa-*dhayss*-t<sup>y</sup>ah) *f* modesty

**modesto** (moa-*dhayss*-toa) *adj* modest

**modificación** (moa-dhee-fee-kah-*th<sup>y</sup>oan*) *f* change

**modificar** (moa-dhee-fee-*kahr*) *v* change, modify

**modismo** (moa-*dheez*-moa) *m* idiom

**modista** (moa-*dheess*-tah) *f* dressmaker

**modo** (*moa*-dhoa) *m* fashion, manner; **de cualquier ~** anyhow; **de ningún ~** by no means; **de todos modos**

any way; at any rate; **en ~ alguno** at all; **~ de empleo** directions for use

**mohair** (moa-*ayr*) *m* mohair

**moho** (*moa*-oa) *m* mildew

**mojado** (moa-*khah*-dhoa) *adj* wet; moist, damp

**mojigato** (moa-khee-*gah*-toa) *adj* hypocritical

**mojón** (moa-*khoan*) *m* landmark

*****moler** (moa-*layr*) *v* *grind

**molestar** (moa-layss-*tahr*) *v* disturb, trouble, bother

**molestia** (moa-*layss*-tʸah) *f* trouble, nuisance, bother

**molesto** (moa-*layss*-toa) *adj* troublesome, inconvenient

**molinero** (moa-lee-*nay*-roa) *m* miller

**molino** (moa-*lee*-noa) *m* mill; **~ de viento** windmill

**momentáneo** (moa-mayn-*tah*-nay-oa) *adj* momentary

**momento** (moa-*mayn*-toa) *m* moment

**monarca** (moa-*nahr*-kah) *m* monarch, ruler

**monarquía** (moa-nahr-*kee*-ah) *f* monarchy

**monasterio** (moa-nahss-*tay*-rʸoa) *m* monastery

**moneda** (moa-*nay*-dhah) *f* currency; coin; change; **~ extranjera** foreign currency

**monedero** (moa-nay-*dhay*-roa) *m* purse

**monetario** (moa-nay-*tah*-rʸoa) *adj* monetary; **unidad monetaria** monetary unit

**monja** (*moang*-khah) *f* nun

**monje** (*moang*-khay) *m* monk

**mono** (*moa*-noa) *m* monkey; overalls *pl*

**monólogo** (moa-*noa*-loa-goa) *m* monologue

**monopolio** (moa-noa-*poa*-lʸoa) *m*

monopoly

**monótono** (moa-*noa*-toa-noa) *adj* monotonous

**monstruo** (*moans*-trwoa) *m* monster

**montaña** (moan-*tah*-ñah) *f* mountain

**montañismo** (moan-tah-*ñeez*-moa) *m* mountaineering

**montañoso** (moan-tah-*ñoa*-soa) *adj* mountainous

**montar** (moan-*tahr*) *v* mount, *get on; assemble; *ride

**monte** (*moan*-tay) *m* mount

**montículo** (moan-*tee*-koo-loa) *m* mound

**montón** (moan-*toan*) *m* heap, stack, pile

**montuoso** (moan-*twoa*-soa) *adj* hilly

**monumento** (moa-noo-*mayn*-toa) *m* monument; memorial

**mora** (*moa*-rah) *f* mulberry; blackberry

**morado** (moa-*rah*-dhoa) *adj* violet

**moral** (moa-*rahl*) *adj* moral; *f* moral; spirits

**moralidad** (moa-rah-lee-*dhahdh*) *f* morality

**mordaza** (moar-*dhah*-thah) *f* clamp

**mordedura** (moar-dhay-*dhoo*-rah) *f* bite

*****morder** (moar-*dhayr*) *v* *bite

**morena** (moa-*ray*-nah) *f* brunette

**moreno** (moa-*ray*-noa) *adj* brown

**moretón** (moa-ray-*toan*) *m* bruise

**morfina** (moar-*fee*-nah) *f* morphine, morphia

*****morir** (moa-*reer*) *v* die

**moro** (*moa*-roa) *m* Moor

**morral** (moa-*rrahl*) *m* haversack

**morro** (*moa*-rroa) *m* pussy-cat

**mortal** (moar-*tahl*) *adj* mortal; fatal

**mosaico** (moa-*sigh*-koa) *m* mosaic

**mosca** (*moass*-kah) *f* fly

**mosquitero** (moass-kee-*tay*-roa) *m* mosquito-net

**mosquito** (moass-*kee*-toa ) *m* mosquito

**mostaza** (moass-*tah*-thah ) *f* mustard

**mostrador** (moass-trah-*dhoar*) *m* counter

***mostrar** (moass-*trahr*) *v* display, *show

**mote** (*moa*-tay) *m* nickname

**moteado** (moa-tay-*ah*-dhoa) *adj* spotted

**motel** (moa-*tayl*) *m* motel

**motín** (moa-*teen*) *m* riot

**motivo** (moa-*tee*-bhoa) *m* motive; cause, occasion

**motocicleta** (moa-toa-thee-*klay*-tah) *f* motor-cycle; motorbike *nAm*

**motoneta** (moa-toa-*nay*-tah) *f* scooter

**motor** (moa-*toar*) *m* motor, engine; ~ **de arranque** starter motor

***mover** (moa-*bhayr*) *v* move; stir

**movible** (moa-*bhee*-bhlay) *adj* movable

**móvil** (*moa*-bheel) *adj* mobile

**movimiento** (moa-bhee-*m*ʸ*ayn*-toa) *m* movement, motion

**mozo** (*moa*-thoa) *m* boy; porter

**muchacha** (moo-*chah*-chah) *f* girl; maid

**muchacho** (moo-*chah*-choa) *m* boy; lad

**muchedumbre** (moo-chay-*dhoom*-bray) *f* crowd

**mucho** (*moo*-choa) *adv* much; far, very; *adj* much; **con** ~ by far; **muchos** *adj* many

**mudanza** (moo-*dhahn*-thah) *f* move

**mudarse** (moo-*dhahr*-say) *v* move; change

**mudo** (*moo*-dhoa) *adj* mute, dumb

**muebles** (*mway*-bhlayss) *mpl* furniture

**muela** (*mway*-lah) *f* molar; **dolor de muelas** toothache

**muelle** (*mway*-lʸay) *m* dock, wharf, quay; pier, jetty; spring

**muerte** (*mwayr*-tay) *f* death

**muerto** (*mwayr*-toa) *adj* dead

**muestra** (*mwayss*-trah) *f* sample

**mugir** (moo-*kheer*) *v* roar

**mujer** (moo-*khayr*) *f* woman; wife

**mújol** (*moo*-khoal) *m* mullet

**muleta** (moo-*lay*-tah) *f* crutch

**mulo** (*moo*-loa) *m* mule

**multa** (*mool*-tah) *f* fine; ticket

**multiplicación** (mool-tee-plee-kah-*th*ʸ*oan*) *f* multiplication

**multiplicar** (mool-tee-plee-*kahr*) *v* multiply

**multitud** (mool-tee-*toodh*) *f* crowd

**mundial** (moon-*d*ʸ*ahl*) *adj* world-wide, global

**mundo** (*moon*-doa) *m* world; **todo el** ~ everyone

**municipal** (moo-nee-thee-*pahl*) *adj* municipal

**municipalidad** (moo-nee-thee-pah-lee-*dhahdh*) *f* municipality

**muñeca** (moo-*ñay*-kah) *f* doll; wrist

**muralla** (moo-*rah*-lʸah) *f* wall

**muro** (*moo*-roa) *m* wall

**músculo** (*mooss*-koo-loa) *m* muscle

**musculoso** (mooss-koo-*loa*-soa) *adj* muscular

**muselina** (moo-say-*lee*-nah) *f* muslin

**museo** (moo-*say*-oa) *m* museum; ~ **de figuras de cera** waxworks *pl*

**musgo** (*mooz*-goa) *m* moss

**música** (*moo*-see-kah) *f* music

**musical** (moo-see-*kahl*) *adj* musical; **comedia** ~ musical comedy

**músico** (*moo*-see-koa) *m* musician

**muslo** (*mooz*-loa) *m* thigh

**musulmán** (moo-sool-*mahn*) *m* Muslim

**mutuo** (*moo*-twoa) *adj* mutual

**muy** (moo ᵉᵉ) *adv* very, quite

# N

**nácar** (*nah*-kahr) *m* mother-of-pearl

***nacer** (nah-*thayr*) *v* *be born

**nacido** (nah-*thee*-dhoa) *adj* born

**nacimiento** (nah-thee-*mᵞayn*-toa) *m* birth; rise

**nación** (nah-*thᵞoan*) *f* nation

**nacional** (nah-thᵞoa-*nahl*) *adj* national

**nacionalidad** (nah-thᵞoa-nah-lee-*dhahdh*) *f* nationality

**nacionalizar** (nah-thᵞoa-nah-lee-*thahr*) *v* nationalize

**nada** (*nah*-dhah) nothing; nil

**nadador** (nah-dhah-*dhoar*) *m* swimmer

**nadar** (nah-*dhahr*) *v* *swim

**nadie** (*nah*-dhᵞay) *pron* nobody, no one

**naipe** (*nigh*-pay) *m* playing-card

**nalga** (*nahl*-gah) *m* buttock

**naranja** (nah-*rahng*-khah) *f* orange

**narciso** (nahr-*thee*-soa) *m* daffodil

**narcosis** (nahr-*koa*-seess) *f* narcosis

**narcótico** (nahr-*koa*-tee-koa) *m* narcotic

**nariz** (nah-*reeth*) *f* nose

**narración** (nah-rrah-*thᵞoan*) *f* account

**nata** (*nah*-tah) *f* cream

**natación** (nah-tah-*thᵞoan*) *f* swimming

**nativo** (nah-*tee*-bhoa) *adj* native

**natural** (nah-too-*rahl*) *adj* natural; *m* nature

**naturaleza** (nah-too-rah-*lay*-thah) *f* nature

**naturalmente** (nah-too-rahl-*mayn*-tay) *adv* naturally

**náusea** (*nou*-say-ah) *f* nausea, sickness

**navaja** (nah-*bhah*-khah) *f* pocket-knife

**naval** (nah-*bhahl*) *adj* naval

**navegable** (nah-bhay-*gah*-bhlay) *adj* navigable

**navegación** (nah-bhay-gah-*thᵞoan*) *f* navigation

**navegar** (nah-bhay-*gahr*) *v* sail; navigate

**Navidad** (nah-bhee-*dhahdh*) *f* Xmas, Christmas

**nebuloso** (nay-bhoo-*loa*-soa) *adj* misty

**necesario** (nay-thay-*sah*-rᵞoa) *adj* necessary; requisite

**neceser** (nay-thay-*sayr*) *m* toilet case

**necesidad** (nay-thay-see-*dhahdh*) *f* need, necessity; want; misery

**necesitar** (nay-thay-see-*tahr*) *v* need

**necio** (*nay*-thᵞoa) *adj* foolish, silly

***negar** (nay-*gahr*) *v* deny

**negativa** (nay-gah-*tee*-bhah) *f* refusal

**negativo** (nay-gah-*tee*-bhoa) *adj* negative; *m* negative

**negligencia** (nay-glee-*khayn*-thᵞah) *f* neglect

**negligente** (nay-glee-*khayn*-tay) *adj* neglectful, careless

**negociación** (nay-goa-thᵞah-*thᵞoan*) *f* negotiation

**negociante** (nay-goa-*thᵞahn*-tay) *m* dealer

**negociar** (nay-goa-*thᵞahr*) *v* negotiate

**negocio** (nay-*goa*-thᵞoa) *m* business; ***hacer negocios con** *deal with; **hombre de negocios** businessman; ~ **fotográfico** camera shop; **viaje de negocios** business trip

**negro** (*nay*-groa) *adj* black; *m* Negro

**neón** (nay-*oan*) *m* neon

**nervio** (*nayr*-bhᵞoa) *m* nerve

**nervioso** (nayr-*bhᵞoa*-soa) *adj* nervous

**neto** (*nay*-toa) *adj* net

**neumático** (nayᵒᵒ-*mah*-tee-koa) *adj* pneumatic; *m* tyre, tire; ~ **de repuesto** spare tyre; ~ **desinflado** flat tyre

**neumonía** (nayᵒᵒ-moa-*nee*-ah) *f* pneumonia

**neuralgia** (nayᵒᵒ-*rahl*-khᵞah) *f* neuralgia

**neurosis** (nay⁰⁰-*roa*-seess ) *f* neurosis

**neutral** (nay⁰⁰-*trahl*) *adj* neutral

**neutro** (nay⁰⁰-troa) *adj* neuter

**\*nevar** (nay-*bhahr*) *v* snow

**nevasca** (nay-*bhahss*-kah) *f* snowstorm

**nevoso** (nay-*bhoa*-soa) *adj* snowy

**ni … ni** (nee) neither … nor

**nicotina** (nee-koa-*tee*-nah) *f* nicotine

**nido** (*nee*-dhoa) *m* nest

**niebla** (*nʸay*-bhlah) *f* mist, fog; haze; **faro de ~** foglamp

**nieta** (*nʸay*-tah) *f* granddaughter

**nieto** (*nʸay*-toa) *m* grandson

**nieve** (*nʸay*-bhay) *f* snow

**Nigeria** (nee-*khay*-rʸah) *f* Nigeria

**nigeriano** (nee-khay-*rʸah*-noa) *adj* Nigerian; *m* Nigerian

**ninguno** (neeng-*goo*-noa) *adj* no; *pron* none; **~ de los dos** neither

**niñera** (nee-*ñay*-rah) *f* nurse

**niño** (*nee*-ñoa) *m* child; kid

**níquel** (*nee*-kayl) *m* nickel

**nitrógeno** (nee-*troa*-khay-noa) *m* nitrogen

**nivel** (nee-*bhayl*) *m* level; **~ de vida** standard of living; **paso a ~** level crossing

**nivelar** (nee-bhay-*lahr*) *v* level

**no** (noa) not; no; **si ~** otherwise, else

**noble** (*noa*-bhlay) *adj* noble

**nobleza** (noa-*bhlay*-thah) *f* nobility

**noción** (noa-*thʸoan*) *f* notion; idea

**nocturno** (noak-*toor*-noa) *adj* nightly

**noche** (*noa*-chay) *f* night; **de ~** overnight, by night; **esta ~** tonight

**nogal** (noa-*gahl*) *m* walnut

**nombramiento** (noam-brah-*mʸayn*-toa) *m* appointment, nomination

**nombrar** (noam-*brahr*) *v* name, mention; appoint, nominate

**nombre** (*noam*-bray) *m* noun; name; denomination; **en ~ de** on behalf of, in the name of; **~ de pila** Chris-

tian name, first name

**nominación** (noa-mee-nah-*thʸoan*) *f* nomination

**nominal** (noa-mee-*nahl*) *adj* nominal

**nordeste** (noar-*dhayss*-tay) *m* northeast

**norma** (*noar*-mah) *f* standard

**normal** (noar-*mahl*) *adj* normal; regular, standard

**noroeste** (noa-roa-*ayss*-tay) *m* northwest

**norte** (*noar*-tay) *m* north; **del ~** northerly; **polo ~** North Pole

**norteño** (noar-*tay*-ñoa) *adj* northern

**Noruega** (noa-*rway*-gah) *f* Norway

**noruego** (noa-*rway*-goa) *adj* Norwegian; *m* Norwegian

**nos** (noass) *pron* ourselves

**nosotros** (noa-*soa*-troass) *pron* we; us

**nostalgia** (noass-*tahl*-khʸah) *f* homesickness

**nota** (*noa*-tah) *f* ticket; note; mark

**notable** (noa-*tah*-bhlay) *adj* considerable; remarkable, striking, noticeable

**notar** (noa-*tahr*) *v* notice; note

**notario** (noa-tah-*rʸoa*) *m* notary

**noticia** (noa-*tee*-thʸah) *f* news, notice; **noticias** *fpl* news, tidings *pl*

**noticiario** (noa-tee-*thʸah*-rʸoa) *m* news; newsreel

**notificar** (noa-tee-fee-*kahr*) *v* notify

**notorio** (noa-*toa*-rʸoa) *adj* well-known

**novedad** (noa-bhay-*dhahdh*) *f* novelty

**novela** (noa-*bhay*-lah) *f* novel; **~ policíaca** detective story; **~ por entregas** serial

**novelista** (noa-bhay-*leess*-tah) *m* novelist

**noveno** (noa-*bhay*-noa) *num* ninth

**noventa** (noa-*bhayn*-tah) *num* ninety

**novia** (*noa*-bhʸah) *f* fiancée; bride

**noviazgo** (noa-*bhʸahth*-goa) *m* engagement

**noviembre** (noa-*bhᵞaym*-bray) November

**\*hacer novillos** (ah-*thayr* noa-*bhee*-lᵞoass) play truant

**novio** (*noa*-bhᵞoa) *m* fiancé; bridegroom

**nube** (*noo*-bhay) *f* cloud

**nublado** (noo-*bhlah*-dhoa) *adj* cloudy, overcast

**nuca** (*noo*-kah) *f* nape of the neck

**nuclear** (noo-klay-*ahr*) *adj* nuclear

**núcleo** (*noo*-klay-oa) *m* nucleus; heart, essence, core

**nudillo** (noo-*dhee*-lᵞoa) *m* knuckle

**nudo** (*noo*-dhoa) *m* knot; lump; ~ **corredizo** loop

**nuestro** (*nwayss*-troa) *adj* our

**Nueva Zelanda** (*nway*-bhah thay-*lahn*-dah) New Zealand

**nueve** (*nway*-bhay) *num* nine

**nuevo** (*nway*-bhoa) *adj* new; **de** ~ again

**nuez** (nwayth) *f* nut; ~ **moscada** nutmeg

**nulo** (*noo*-loa) *adj* invalid, void

**numeral** (noo-may-*rahl*) *m* numeral

**número** (*noo*-may-roa) *m* number; digit; quantity; size; act

**numeroso** (noo-may-*roa*-soa) *adj* numerous

**nunca** (*noong*-kah) *adv* never

**nutritivo** (noo-tree-*tee*-bhoa) *adj* nutritious, nourishing

**nylon** (*nigh*-loan) *m* nylon

# O

**o** (oa) *conj* or; **o ... o** either ... or

**oasis** (oa-*ah*-seess) *f* oasis

**\*obedecer** (oa-bhay-dhay-*thayr*) *v* obey

**obediencia** (oa-bhay-*dhᵞayn*-thᵞah) *f* obedience

**obediente** (oa-bhay-*dhᵞayn*-tay) *adj* obedient

**obertura** (oa-bhayr-*too*-rah) *f* overture

**obesidad** (oa-bhay-see-*dhahdh*) *f* fatness

**obeso** (oa-*bhay*-soa) *adj* corpulent

**obispo** (oa-*bheess*-poa) *m* bishop

**objeción** (oabh-khay-*thᵞoan*) *f* objection; **\*hacer** ~ **a** mind

**objetar** (oabh-khay-*tahr*) *v* object

**objetivo** (oabh-khay-*tee*-bhoa) *adj* objective; *m* design, objective, target

**objeto** (oabh-*khay*-toa) *m* object; **objetos de valor** valuables *pl*; **objetos perdidos** lost and found

**oblea** (oa-*bhlay*-ah) *f* wafer

**oblicuo** (oa-*bhlee*-kwoa) *adj* slanting

**obligar** (oa-bhlee-*gahr*) *v* oblige; force

**obligatorio** (oa-bhlee-gah-*toa*-rᵞoa) *adj* compulsory, obligatory

**oblongo** (oa-*bhloang*-goa) *adj* oblong

**obra** (*oa*-bhrah) *f* work; ~ **de arte** work of art; ~ **de teatro** play; ~ **hecha a mano** handwork; ~ **maestra** masterpiece

**obrar** (oa-*bhrahr*) *v* work; perform

**obrero** (oa-*bhray*-roa) *m* workman, worker, labourer; ~ **portuario** docker

**obsceno** (oabh-*thay*-noa) *adj* obscene

**obscuridad** (oabhs-koo-ree-*dhahdh*) *f* gloom

**obscuro** (oabhs-*koo*-roa) *adj* dark, obscure

**observación** (oabh-sayr-bhah-*thᵞoan*) *f* observation; remark; **\*hacer una** ~ remark

**observar** (oabh-sayr-*bhahr*) *v* watch, observe, notice, note

**observatorio** (oabh-sayr-bhah-*toa*-rᵞoa) *m* observatory

**obsesión** (oabh-say-*sᵞoan*) *f* obsession

**obstáculo** (oabhs-*tah*-koo-loa) *m* obstacle

**no obstante** (noa oabhs-*tahn*-tay )
nevertheless

**obstinado** (oabhs-tee-*nah*-dhoa ) *adj*
dogged, obstinate

\* **obstruir** (oabhs-*trweer*) *v* block

\* **obtener** (oabh-tay-*nayr*) *v* obtain

**obtenible** (oabh-tay-*nee*-bhlay ) *adj*
available

**obtuso** (oabh-*too*-soa) *adj* blunt

**obvio** (*oabh*-bhᵛoa ) *adj* apparent, obvious

**oca** (*oa*-kah) *f* goose

**ocasión** (oa-kah-sᵛoan) *f* occasion;
chance

**ocasionalmente** (oa-kah-sᵛoa-nahl-
*mayn*-tay ) *adv* occasionally

**ocaso** (oa-*kah*-soa ) *m* sunset

**occidental** (oak-thee-dhayn-*tahl*) *adj*
westerly; western

**occidente** (oak-thee-*dhayn*-tay ) *m* west

**océano** (oa-*thay*-ah-noa ) *m* ocean;
**Océano Pacífico** Pacific Ocean

**ocio** (*oa*-thᵛoa) *m* leisure

**ocioso** (oa-*thᵛoa*-soa ) *adj* idle

**octavo** (oak-*tah*-bhoa ) *num* eighth

**octubre** (oak-*too*-bhray) October

**oculista** (oa-koo-*leess*-tah ) *m* oculist

**ocultar** (oa-kool-*tahr*) *v* \*hide

**ocupación** (oa-koo-pah-*thᵛoan*) *f* occupation; business

**ocupante** (oa-koo-*pahn*-tay ) *m* occupant

**ocupar** (oa-koo-*pahr*) *v* occupy; \*take
up; **ocupado** *adj* engaged, busy;
occupied; **ocuparse de** look after

**ocurrencia** (oa-koo-*rrayn*-thᵛah ) *f* idea

**ocurrir** (oa-koo-*rreer*) *v* occur

**ochenta** (oa-*chayn*-tah ) *num* eighty

**ocho** (*oa*-choa ) *num* eight

**odiar** (oa-*dhᵛahr*) *v* hate

**odio** (*oa*-dhᵛoa ) *m* hatred, hate

**oeste** (oa-*ayss*-tay) *m* west

**ofender** (oa-fayn-*dayr*) *v* wound,
\*hurt, offend, injure

**ofensa** (oa-*fayn*-sah) *f* offence

**ofensivo** (oa-fayn-*see*-bhoa ) *adj* offensive; *m* offensive

**oferta** (oa-*fayr*-tah ) *f* offer, supply

**oficial** (oa-fee-*thᵛahl*) *adj* official; *m*
officer; ~ **de aduanas** Customs officer

**oficina** (oa-fee-*thee*-nah) *f* office; ~ **de
cambio** exchange office; ~ **de colocación** employment exchange; ~
**de informaciones** information
bureau; ~ **de objetos perdidos** lost
property office

**oficinista** (oa-fee-thee-*neess*-tah ) *m*
clerk

**oficio** (oa-*fee*-thᵛoa ) *m* trade

\* **ofrecer** (oa-fray-*thayr*) *v* offer

**oído** (oa-*ee*-dhoa ) *m* hearing; **dolor
de oídos** earache

\* **oír** (oa-*eer*) *v* \*hear

**ojal** (oa-*khahl*) *m* buttonhole

**ojeada** (oa-khay-*ah*-dhah ) *f* glimpse,
glance; look

**ojear** (oa-khay-*ahr*) *v* glance

**ojo** (*oa*-khoa ) *m* eye

**ola** (*oa*-lah) *f* wave

\* **oler** (oa-*layr*) *v* \*smell

**olmo** (*oal*-moa ) *m* elm

**olor** (oa-*loar*) *m* smell, odour

**olvidadizo** (oal-bhee-dhah-*dhee*-thoa )
*adj* forgetful

**olvidar** (oal-bhee-*dhahr*) *v* \*forget

**olla** (*oa*-lᵛah) *f* pot; kettle; ~ **a presión** pressure-cooker

**ombligo** (oam-*blee*-goa ) *m* navel

**omitir** (oa-mee-*teer*) *v* \*leave out,
omit; fail

**omnipotente** (oam-nee-poa-*tayn*-tay )
*adj* omnipotent

**once** (*oan*-thay) *num* eleven

**onceno** (oan-*thay*-noa ) *num* eleventh

**onda** (*oan*-dah ) *f* wave

**ondulación** (oan-doo-lah-*thᵛoan*) *f*

wave; ~ **permanente** permanent wave

**ondulado** (oan-doo-*lah*-dhoa) *adj* wavy

**ondulante** (oan-doo-*lahn*-tay) *adj* undulating

**ónix** (*oa*-neeks) *m* onyx

**ópalo** (*oa*-pah-loa) *m* opal

**opcional** (oap-th<sup>Y</sup>oa-*nahl*) *adj* optional

**ópera** (*oa*-pay-rah) *f* opera

**operación** (oa-pay-rah-*th<sup>Y</sup>oan*) *f* operation, surgery

**operar** (oa-pay-*rahr*) *v* operate

**opereta** (oa-pay-*ray*-tah) *f* operetta

**opinar** (oa-pee-*nahr*) *v* consider

**opinión** (oa-pee-*n<sup>Y</sup>oan*) *f* view, opinion

*\***oponerse** (oa-poa-*nayr*-say) *v* oppose; ~ **a** object to

**oportunidad** (oa-poar-too-nee-*dhahdh*) *f* chance, opportunity

**oportuno** (oa-poar-*too*-noa) *adj* convenient

**oposición** (oa-poa-see-*th<sup>Y</sup>oan*) *f* opposition

**oprimir** (oa-pree-*meer*) *v* oppress

**óptico** (*oap*-tee-koa) *m* optician

**optimismo** (oap-tee-*meez*-moa) *m* optimism

**optimista** (oap-tee-*meess*-tah) *adj* optimistic; *m* optimist

**óptimo** (*oap*-tee-moa) *adj* best

**opuesto** (oa-*pwayss*-toa) *adj* opposite; averse

**oración** (oa-rah-*th<sup>Y</sup>oan*) *f* prayer

**oral** (oa-*rahl*) *adj* oral

**orar** (oa-*rahr*) *v* pray

**orden** (*oar*-dhayn) *f* command; order; *m* method; **de primer** ~ first-rate; ~ **del día** agenda

**ordenar** (oar-dhay-*nahr*) *v* arrange; order

**ordinario** (oar-dhee-*nah*-r<sup>Y</sup>oa) *adj* simple, ordinary; common, vulgar

**oreja** (oa-*ray*-khah) *f* ear

**orfebre** (oar-*fay*-bhray) *m* goldsmith

**orgánico** (oar-*gah*-nee-koa) *adj* organic

**organillo** (oar-gah-*nee*-l<sup>Y</sup>oa) *m* street-organ

**organismo** (oar-gah-*neez*-moa) *m* organism

**organización** (oar-gah-nee-thah-*th<sup>Y</sup>oan*) *f* organization

**organizar** (oar-gah-nee-*thahr*) *v* organize; arrange

**órgano** (*oar*-gah-noa) *m* organ

**orgullo** (oar-*goo*-l<sup>Y</sup>oa) *m* pride

**orgulloso** (oar-goo-*l<sup>Y</sup>oa*-soa) *adj* proud

**orientación** (oa-r<sup>Y</sup>ayn-tah-*th<sup>Y</sup>oan*) *f* orientation

**oriental** (oa-r<sup>Y</sup>ayn-*tahl*) *adj* eastern, easterly; oriental

**orientarse** (oa-r<sup>Y</sup>ayn-*tahr*-say) *v* orientate

**oriente** (oa-r<sup>Y</sup>*ayn*-tay) *m* Orient

**origen** (oa-*ree*-khayn) *m* origin

**original** (oa-ree-khee-*nahl*) *adj* original

**originalmente** (oa-ree-khee-nahl-*mayn*-tay) *adv* originally

**originar** (oa-ree-khee-*nahr*) *v* originate

**orilla** (oa-*ree*-l<sup>Y</sup>ah) *f* bank; shore

**orina** (oa-*ree*-nah) *f* urine

**orlón** (oar-*loan*) *m* orlon

**ornamental** (oar-nah-mayn-*tahl*) *adj* ornamental

**oro** (*oa*-roa) *m* gold

**orquesta** (oar-*kayss*-tah) *f* orchestra; band

**ortodoxo** (oar-toa-*dhoak*-soa) *adj* orthodox

**os** (oass) *pron* you

**osar** (oa-*sahr*) *v* dare

**oscilar** (oa-thee-*lahr*) *v* \*swing

**oscuridad** (oass-koo-ree-*dhahdh*) *f* dark

**oscuro** (oass-*koo*-roa) *adj* dark, dim, obscure

**oso** (*oa*-soa) *m* bear

**ostentación** (oass-tayn-tah-*th<sup>y</sup>oan*) *f* fuss

**ostra** (*oass*-trah) *f* oyster

**otoño** (oa-*toa*-ñoa) *m* autumn; fall *nAm*

**otro** (*oa*-troa) *adj* other, different; another; ~ **más** another

**ovalado** (oa-bhah-*lah*-dhoa) *adj* oval

**oveja** (oa-*bhay*-khah) *f* sheep

**overol** (oa-bhay-*roal*) *mMe* overalls *pl*

**oxidado** (oak-see-*dhah*-dhoa) *adj* rusty

**oxígeno** (oak-*see*-khay-noa) *m* oxygen

**oyente** (oa-*<sup>y</sup>ayn*-tay) *m* auditor, listener

# P

**pabellón** (pah-bhay-*l<sup>y</sup>oan*) *m* pavilion

\***pacer** (pah-*thayr*) *v* graze

**paciencia** (pah-*th<sup>y</sup>ayn*-th<sup>y</sup>ah) *f* patience

**paciente** (pah-*th<sup>y</sup>ayn*-tay) *adj* patient; *m* patient

**pacifismo** (pah-thee-*feez*-moa) *m* pacifism

**pacifista** (pah-thee-*feess*-tah) *adj* pacifist; *m* pacifist

\***padecer** (pah-dhay-*thayr*) *v* suffer

**padrastro** (pah-*dhrahss*-troa) *m* stepfather

**padre** (*pah*-dhray) *m* father

**padres** (*pah*-dhrayss) *mpl* parents *pl*; ~ **adoptivos** foster-parents *pl*; ~ **políticos** parents-in-law *pl*

**padrino** (pah-*dhree*-noa) *m* godfather

**paga** (*pah*-gah) *f* wages *pl*

**pagano** (pah-*gah*-noa) *adj* heathen, pagan; *m* heathen, pagan

**pagar** (pah-*gahr*) *v* \*pay; **pagado por adelantado** prepaid; ~ **a plazos** \*pay on account

**página** (*pah*-khee-nah) *f* page

**pago** (*pah*-goa) *m* payment; **primer** ~ down payment

**painel** (pigh-*nayl*) *m* panel

**país** (pah-*eess*) *m* country, land; ~ **natal** native country

**paisaje** (pigh-*sah*-khay) *m* scenery, landscape

**paisano** (pigh-*sah*-noa) *m* civilian

**Países Bajos** (pah-*ee*-sayss -*bah*-khoass) *mpl* the Netherlands

**paja** (*pah*-khah) *f* straw

**pájaro** (*pah*-khah-roa) *m* bird

**paje** (*pah*-khay) *m* page-boy

**pala** (*pah*-lah) *f* spade, shovel

**palabra** (pah-*lah*-bhrah) *f* word

**palacio** (pah-*lah*-th<sup>y</sup>oa) *m* palace

**palanca** (pah-*lahng*-kah) *f* lever; ~ **de cambios** gear lever

**palangana** (pah-lahng-*gah*-nah) *f* basin; wash-basin

**pálido** (*pah*-lee-dhoa) *adj* pale; dull; light

**palillo** (pah-*lee*-l<sup>y</sup>oa) *m* toothpick

**palma** (*pahl*-mah) *f* palm

**palo** (*pah*-loa) *m* stick; ~ **de golf** golf-club

**paloma** (pah-*loa*-mah) *f* pigeon

**palpable** (pahl-*pah*-bhlay) *adj* palpable

**palpar** (pahl-*pahr*) *v* \*feel

**palpitación** (pahl-pee-tah-*th<sup>y</sup>oan*) *f* palpitation

**pan** (pahn) *m* bread, loaf; ~ **integral** wholemeal bread; ~ **tostado** toast

**pana** (*pah*-nah) *f* corduroy, velveteen

**panadería** (pah-nah-dhay-*ree*-ah) *f* bakery

**panadero** (pah-nah-*dhay*-roa) *m* baker

**panecillo** (pah-nay-*thee*-l<sup>y</sup>oa) *m* roll

**pánico** (*pah*-nee-koa) *m* panic

**pantalones** (pahn-tah-*loa*-nayss) *mpl* trousers *pl*; slacks *pl*; pants *plAm*; ~ **cortos** shorts *pl*; ~ **de esquí** ski pants; ~ **de gimnasia** trunks *pl*

**pantalla** (pahn-*tah*-l<sup>y</sup>ah) *f* lampshade;

screen

**pantano** (pahn-*tah*-noa) *m* marsh, bog

**pantanoso** (pahn-tah-*noa*-soa) *adj* marshy

**pantorrilla** (pahn-toa-*rree*-lᵞah) *f* calf

**pañal** (pah-*ñahl*) *m* nappy; diaper *nAm*

**pañería** (pah-ñay-*ree*-ah) *f* drapery

**pañero** (pah-*ñay*-roa) *m* draper

**paño** (*pah*-ñoa) *m* cloth; ~ **higiénico** sanitary towel

**pañuelo** (pah-*ñway*-loa) *m* handkerchief; ~ **de papel** tissue, Kleenex®

**Papa** (*pah*-pah) *m* pope

**papa** (*pah*-pah) *fMe* potato

**papá** (pah-*pah*) *m* dad

**papaíto** (pah-pah-*ee*-toa) *m* daddy

**papel** (pah-*payl*) *m* paper; **de** ~ paper; ~ **carbón** carbon paper; ~ **de envolver** wrapping paper; ~ **de escribir** writing-paper; ~ **de estaño** tinfoil; ~ **de lija** sandpaper; ~ **higiénico** toilet-paper; ~ **para cartas** notepaper; ~ **para mecanografiar** typing paper; ~ **pintado** wallpaper; ~ **secante** blotting paper

**papelería** (pah-pay-lay-*ree*-ah) *f* stationery; stationer's

**paperas** (pah-*pay*-rahss) *fpl* mumps

**paquete** (pah-*kay*-tay) *m* packet, package, parcel; bundle

**Paquistán** (pah-keess-*tahn*) *m* Pakistan

**paquistaní** (pah-keess-tah-*nee*) *adj* Pakistani; *m* Pakistani

**par** (pahr) *adj* even; *m* pair

**para** (*pah*-rah) *prep* to, for; to, in order to; ~ **con** towards; ~ **que** what for

**parabrisas** (pah-rah-*bhree*-sahss) *m* windscreen; windshield *nAm*

**parachoques** (pah-rah-*choa*-kayss) *m* fender, bumper

**parada** (pah-*rah*-dhah) *f* parade; stop;

~ **de taxis** taxi rank; taxi stand *Am*

**parado** (pah-*rah*-dhoa) *adjMe* erect

**parador** (pah-rah-*dhoar*) *m* roadhouse

**parafina** (pah-rah-*fee*-nah) *f* paraffin

**paraguas** (pah-*rah*-gwahss) *m* umbrella

**paraíso** (pah-rah-*ee*-soa) *m* paradise

**paralelo** (pah-rah-*lay*-loa) *adj* parallel; *m* parallel

**paralítico** (pah-rah-*lee*-tee-koa) *adj* lame

**paralizar** (pah-rah-lee-*thahr*) *v* paralise

**pararse** (pah-*rahr*-say) *v* halt; pull up

**parcela** (pahr-*thay*-lah) *f* plot

**parcial** (pahr-*thᵞahl*) *adj* partial

**parecer** (pah-ray-*thayr*) *m* view, opinion

*\***parecer** (pah-ray-*thayr*) *v* appear, seem, look

**parecido** (pah-ray-*thee*-dhoa) *adj* alike; **bien** ~ good-looking

**pared** (pah-*raydh*) *f* wall

**pareja** (pah-*ray*-khah) *f* couple; partner

**pariente** (pah-rᵞ*ayn*-tay) *m* relative, relation

**parlamentario** (pahr-lah-mayn-*tah*-rᵞoa) *adj* parliamentary

**parlamento** (pahr-lah-*mayn*-toa) *m* parliament

**párpado** (*pahr*-pah-dhoa) *m* eyelid

**parque** (*pahr*-kay) *m* park; ~ **de estacionamiento** car park; ~ **de reserva zoológica** game reserve; ~ **nacional** national park

**parquímetro** (pahr-*kee*-may-troa) *m* parking meter

**párrafo** (*pahr*-rrah-foa) *m* paragraph

**parrilla** (pah-*rree*-lᵞah) *f* grill; grillroom; **asar en** ~ grill

**parroquia** (pah-*rroa*-kᵞah) *f* parish

**parsimonioso** (pahr-see-moa-*nᵞoa*-soa) *adj* economical

**parte** (*pahr*-tay) *f* part; share; **en al-**

**guna** ~ somewhere; **en ninguna** ~ nowhere; **en** ~ partly; **otra** ~ elsewhere; ~ **posterior** rear; ~ **superior** top, top side; **por otra** ~ besides; **por todas partes** everywhere, throughout

**participante** (pahr-tee-thee-*pahn*-tay) *m* participant

**participar** (pahr-tee-thee-*pahr*) *v* participate

**particular** (pahr-tee-koo-*lahr*) *adj* private; particular; **en** ~ specially, in particular

**particularidad** (pahr-tee-koo-lah-ree-*dhahdh*) *f* detail; peculiarity

**partida** (pahr-*tee*-dhah) *f* departure

**partido** (pahr-*tee*-dhoa) *m* side, party; match; ~ **de fútbol** football match

**partir** (pahr-*teer*) *v* *leave, depart, pull out; *set out; **a** ~ **de** as from; from

**parto** (*pahr*-toa) *m* childbirth, delivery

**párvulo** (*pahr*-bhoo-loa) *m* toddler; **escuela de párvulos** kindergarten

**pasa** (*pah*-sah) *f* raisin; ~ **de Corinto** currant

**pasado** (pah-*sah*-dhoa) *adj* past; *m* past

**pasaje** (pah-*sah*-khay) *m* passage

**pasajero** (pah-sah-*khay*-roa) *m* passenger

**pasaporte** (pah-sah-*poar*-tay) *m* passport

**pasar** (pah-*sahr*) *v* happen; *go through; pass; *spend; ~ **por alto** overlook; **pasarse sin** spare

**pasarela** (pah-sah-*ray*-lah) *f* gangway

**Pascua** (*pahss*-kwah) Easter

**paseante** (pah-say-*ahn*-tay) *m* walker

**pasear** (pah-say-*ahr*) *v* walk, stroll

**paseo** (pah-*say*-oa) *m* stroll; ride; promenade

**pasillo** (pah-*see*-lʸoa) *m* corridor; aisle

**pasión** (pah-sʸoan) *f* passion

**pasivo** (pah-*see*-bhoa) *adj* passive

**paso** (*pah*-soa) *m* step, pace; move, gait; crossing; mountain pass; **de** ~ **casual**; ~ **a nivel** crossing; **prioridad de** ~ right of way; **prohibido el** ~ no entry

**pasta** (*pahss*-tah) *f* paste; ~ **dentífrica** toothpaste

**pastel** (pahss-*tayl*) *m* cake

**pastelería** (pahss-tay-lay-*ree*-ah) *f* pastry, cake; pastry shop

**pastilla** (pahss-*tee*-lʸah) *f* tablet

**pastor** (pahss-*toar*) *m* shepherd; clergyman, parson, rector

**pata** (*pah*-tah) *f* paw; leg

**patada** (pah-*tah*-dhah) *f* kick

**patata** (pah-*tah*-tah) *f* potato; **patatas fritas** chips

**patear** (pah-tay-*ahr*) *v* kick; stamp

**patente** (pah-*tayn*-tay) *f* patent

**patillas** (pah-*tee*-lʸahss) *fpl* whiskers *pl*, sideburns *pl*

**patín** (pah-*teen*) *m* skate; scooter

**patinaje** (pah-tee-*nah*-khay) *m* skating

**patinar** (pah-tee-*nahr*) *v* skate; skid

**pato** (*pah*-toa) *m* duck

**patria** (*pah*-trʸah) *f* native country, fatherland

**patriota** (pah-trʸoa-tah) *m* patriot

**patrón** (pah-*troan*) *m* boss, master; employer; landlord

**patrona** (pah-*troa*-nah) *f* landlady

**patrulla** (pah-*troo*-lʸah) *f* patrol

**patrullar** (pah-troo-*lʸahr*) *v* patrol

**paulatinamente** (pou-lah-tee-nah-*mayn*-tay) *adv* gradually

**pausa** (*pou*-sah) *f* pause; *hacer una ~ pause

**pavimentar** (pah-bhee-mayn-*tahr*) *v* pave

**pavimento** (pah-bhee-*mayn*-toa) *m* pavement

**pavo** (*pah*-bhoa) *m* peacock; turkey

**payaso** (pah-ʸah-soa) *m* clown

**paz** (pahth) *f* peace; quiet

**peaje** (pay-*ah*-khay) *m* toll

**peatón** (pay-ah-*toan*) *m* pedestrian; **prohibido para los peatones** no pedestrians

**pecado** (pay-*kah*-dhoa) *m* sin

**pecio** (pay-th<sup>y</sup>oa) *m* wreck

**peculiar** (pay-koo-l<sup>y</sup>*ahr*) *adj* peculiar

**pecho** (*pay*-choa) *m* chest; bosom

**pedal** (pay-*dhahl*) *m* pedal

**pedazo** (pay-*dhah*-thoa) *m* piece; scrap

**pedernal** (pay-dhayr-*nahl*) *m* flint

**pedicuro** (pay-dhee-*koo*-roa) *m* chiropodist, pedicure

**pedido** (pay-*dhee*-dhoa) *m* order

**\*pedir** (pay-*dheer*) *v* beg; order; charge

**pegajoso** (pay-gah-*khoa*-soa) *adj* sticky

**pegar** (pay-*gahr*) *v* smack, slap, \*hit; \*stick, paste; **pegarse** *v* \*burn

**peinado** (pay-*nah*-dhoa) *m* hair-do

**peinar** (pay-*nahr*) *v* comb

**peine** (*pay*-nay) *m* comb; ~ **de bolsillo** pocket-comb

**pelar** (pay-*lahr*) *v* peel

**peldaño** (payl-*dah*-ño) *m* step

**pelea** (pay-*lay*-ah) *f* battle

**peletero** (pay-lay-*tay*-roa) *m* furrier

**pelícano** (pay-*lee*-kah-noa) *m* pelican

**película** (pay-*lee*-koo-lah) *f* film; ~ **en colores** colour film

**peligro** (pay-*lee*-groa) *m* danger; peril, risk; distress

**peligroso** (pay-lee-*groa*-soa) *adj* dangerous; perilous

**pelmazo** (payl-*mah*-thoa) *m* bore

**pelota** (pay-*loa*-tah) *f* ball

**peluca** (pay-*loo*-kah) *f* wig

**peluquero** (pay-loo-*kay*-roa) *m* hairdresser

**pelvis** (*payl*-bheess) *m* pelvis

**pellizcar** (pay-l<sup>y</sup>eeth-*kahr*) *v* pinch

**pena** (*pay*-nah) *f* sorrow; pains; penalty; ~ **de muerte** death penalty

**pendiente** (payn-d<sup>y</sup>*ayn*-tay) *adj* slanting; *m* earring, pendant; *f* gradient, slope

**penetrar** (pay-nay-*trahr*) *v* penetrate

**penicilina** (pay-nee-thee-*lee*-nah) *f* penicillin

**península** (pay-*neen*-soo-lah) *f* peninsula

**pensador** (payn-sah-*dhoar*) *m* thinker

**pensamiento** (payn-sah-m<sup>y</sup>*ayn*-toa) *m* idea, thought

**\*pensar** (payn-*sahr*) *v* \*think; ~ **en** \*think of

**pensativo** (payn-sah-*tee*-bhoa) *adj* thoughtful

**pensión** (payn-s<sup>y</sup>*oan*) *f* guest-house, pension, boarding-house; board; ~ **alimenticia** alimony; ~ **completa** full board, board and lodging

**Pentecostés** (payn-tay-koass-*tayss*) *m* Whitsun

**peña** (*pay*-ña) *f* boulder

**peón** (pay-*oan*) *m* pawn

**peor** (pay-*oar*) *adj* worse; *adv* worse

**pepino** (pay-*pee*-noa) *m* cucumber

**pepita** (pay-*pee*-tah) *f* pip

**pequeño** (pay-*kay*-ño) *adj* small, little; petty, minor

**pera** (*pay*-rah) *f* pear

**perca** (*payr*-kah) *f* perch, bass

**percepción** (payr-thayp-th<sup>y</sup>*oan*) *f* perception

**perceptible** (payr-thayp-*tee*-bhlay) *adj* perceptible, noticeable

**percibir** (payr-thee-*bheer*) *v* perceive

**percha** (*payr*-chah) *f* hanger, coathanger, peg; hat rack

**\*perder** (payr-*dhayr*) *v* \*lose; miss; waste

**pérdida** (*payr*-dhee-dhah) *f* loss

**perdiz** (payr-*dheeth*) *f* partridge

**perdón** (payr-*dhoan*) *m* pardon;

grace; ¡perdón! sorry!

**perdonar** (payr-dhoa-*nahr*) *v* \*forgive

**perecedero** (pay-ray-thay-*dhay*-roa) *adj* perishable

\***perecer** (pay-ray-*thayr*) *v* perish

**peregrinación** (pay-ray-gree-nah-*th*ʸoan) *f* pilgrimage

**peregrino** (pay-ray-*gree*-noa) *m* pilgrim

**perejil** (pay-ray-*kheel*) *m* parsley

**perezoso** (pay-ray-*thoa*-soa) *adj* lazy

**perfección** (payr-fayk-*th*ʸoan) *f* perfection

**perfecto** (payr-*fayk*-toa) *adj* perfect; faultless

**perfil** (payr-*feel*) *m* profile

**perfume** (payr-*foo*-may) *m* perfume; scent

**periódico** (pay-rʸoa-dhee-koa) *adj* periodical; *m* periodical, paper; **vendedor de periódicos** newsagent

**periodismo** (pay-rʸoa-*deez*-moa) *m* journalism

**periodista** (pay-rʸoa-*dheess*-tah) *m* journalist

**período** (pay-*ree*-oa-dhoa) *m* period, term

**perito** (pay-*ree*-toa) *m* expert, connoisseur

**perjudicar** (payr-khoo-dhee-*kahr*) *v* harm

**perjudicial** (payr-khoo-dhee-*th*ʸahl) *adj* harmful, hurtful

**perjuicio** (payr-*khwee*-thʸoa) *m* harm, damage

**perjurio** (payr-*khoo*-rʸoa) *m* perjury

**perla** (*payr*-lah) *f* pearl

\***permanecer** (payr-mah-nay-*thayr*) *v* remain

**permanente** (payr-mah-*nayn*-tay) *adj* permanent; **planchado ~** permanent press

**permiso** (payr-*mee*-soa) *m* permission, authorization; permit, licence; **~ de**

**conducir** driving licence; **~ de pesca** fishing licence; **~ de residencia** residence permit; **~ de trabajo** work permit; labor permit *Am*

**permitir** (payr-mee-*teer*) *v* permit, allow; enable; **permitirse** *v* afford

**perno** (*payr*-noa) *m* bolt

**pero** (*pay*-roa) *conj* yet, only, but

**peróxido** (pay-*roak*-see-dhoa) *m* peroxide

**perpendicular** (payr-payn-dee-koo-*lahr*) *adj* perpendicular

**perpetuo** (payr-*pay*-twoa) *adj* perpetual

**perra** (*pay*-rrah) *f* bitch

**perrera** (pay-*rray*-rah) *f* kennel

**perro** (*pay*-rroa) *m* dog; **~ lazarillo** guide-dog

**persa** (*payr*-sah) *adj* Persian; *m* Persian

\***perseguir** (payr-say-*geer*) *v* pursue

**perseverar** (payr-say-bhay-*rahr*) *v* \*keep up

**Persia** (*payr*-sʸah) *f* Persia

**persiana** (payr-sʸah-nah) *f* shutter, blind

**persistir** (payr-seess-*teer*) *v* insist

**persona** (payr-*soa*-nah) *f* person; **por ~** per person

**personal** (payr-soa-*nahl*) *adj* personal, private; *m* personnel, staff

**personalidad** (payr-soa-nah-lee-*dhahdh*) *f* personality

**perspectiva** (payrs-payk-*tee*-bhah) *f* perspective; prospect

**persuadir** (payr-swah-*dheer*) *v* persuade

\***pertenecer** (payr-tay-nay-*thayr*) *v* belong

**pertenencias** (payr-tay-*nayn*-thʸahss) *fpl* belongings *pl*

**pertinaz** (payr-tee-*nahth*) *adj* obstinate

**pesado** (pay-*sah*-dhoa) *adj* heavy

**pesadumbre** (pay-sah-*dhoom*-bray) *f*

grief

**pesar** (pay-*sahr*) v weigh; **a ~ de** despite, in spite of

**pesca** (*payss*-kah) f fishing; fishing industry

**pescadería** (payss-kah-dhay-*ree*-ah) f fish shop

**pescador** (payss-kah-*dhoar*) m fisherman

**pescar** (payss-*kahr*) v fish; **~ con caña** angle

**pesebre** (pay-*say*-bhray) m manger

**pesimismo** (pay-see-*meez*-moa) m pessimism

**pesimista** (pay-see-*meess*-tah) adj pessimistic; m pessimist

**pésimo** (*pay*-see-moa) adj worst; terrible

**peso** (*pay*-soa) m weight; burden

**pestaña** (payss-*tah*-ñah) f eyelash

**petaca** (pay-*tah*-kah) f pouch; tobacco pouch

**pétalo** (*pay*-tah-loa) m petal

**petición** (pay-tee-*thᵞoan*) f petition

**petirrojo** (pay-tee-*rroa*-khoa) m robin

**petróleo** (pay-*troa*-lay-oa) m petroleum, oil; **~ lampante** kerosene; **pozo de ~** oil-well; **refinería de ~** oil-refinery

**pez** (payth) m fish

**piadoso** (pᵞah-*dhoa*-soa) adj pious

**pianista** (pᵞah-*neess*-tah) m pianist

**piano** (*pᵞah*-noa) m piano; **~ de cola** grand piano

**picadero** (pee-kah-*dhay*-roa) m riding-school

**picadura** (pee-kah-*dhoo*-rah) f sting, bite; cigarette tobacco

**picante** (pee-*kahn*-tay) adj spicy, savoury

**picar** (pee-*kahr*) v itch; mince; *sting

**pícaro** (*pee*-kah-roa) m rascal

**picazón** (pee-kah-*thoan*) f itch

**pico** (*pee*-koa) m beak; peak; pick-

axe

**pie** (pᵞay) m foot; **a ~** on foot; walking; **de ~** upright; *estar de ~ *stand; **~ de cabra** crowbar

**piedad** (pᵞay-*dhahdh*) f pity; *tener ~ de pity

**piedra** (*pᵞay*-dhrah) f stone; **de ~** stone; **~ miliar** milestone; **~ pómez** pumice stone; **~ preciosa** stone

**piel** (pᵞayl) f skin; fur, hide; peel; **de ~** leather; **~ de cerdo** pigskin

**pierna** (*pᵞayr*-nah) f leg

**pieza** (*pᵞay*-thah) f part; **de dos piezas** two-piece; **~ de repuesto** spare part; **~ en un acto** one-act play

**pijama** (pee-*khah*-mah) m pyjamas pl

**pilar** (pee-*lahr*) m pillar

**píldora** (*peel*-doa-rah) f pill

**pileta** (pee-*lay*-tah) f sink

**piloto** (pee-*loa*-toa) m pilot

**pillo** (*pee*-lᵞoa) m rascal

**pimienta** (pee-mᵞ*ayn*-tah) f pepper

**pincel** (peen-*thayl*) m paint-brush

**pinchado** (peen-*chah*-dhoa) adj punctured

**pinchar** (peen-*chahr*) v prick

**pinchazo** (peen-*chah*-thoa) m puncture

**pingüino** (peeng-*gwee*-noa) m penguin

**pino** (*pee*-noa) m fir-tree

**pintar** (peen-*tahr*) v paint

**pintor** (peen-*toar*) m painter

**pintoresco** (peen-toa-*rayss*-koa) adj picturesque, scenic

**pintura** (peen-*too*-rah) f paint; painting; **~ al óleo** oil-painting

**pinzas** (*peen*-thahss) fpl tweezers pl

**pinzón** (peen-*thoan*) m finch

**piña** (*pee*-ñah) f pineapple

**pío** (*pee*-oa) adj pious

**piojo** (*pᵞoa*-khoa) m louse

**pionero** (pᵞoa-*nay*-roa) m pioneer

**pipa** (*pee*-pah) f pipe

**pirata** (pee-*rah*-tah) m pirate

**pisar** (pee-*sahr*) *v* step

**piscina** (pee-*thee*-nah) *f* swimming pool

**piso** (*pee*-soa) *m* storey, floor; flat; apartment *nAm*; ~ **bajo** ground floor

**pista** (*peess*-tah) *f* ring; track; lane; ~ **de aterrizaje** runway; ~ **de patinaje** skating-rink; ~ **para carreras** race-course

**pistola** (peess-*toa*-lah) *f* pistol

**pistón** (peess-*toan*) *m* piston

**pitillera** (pee-tee-*l*ᵛ*ay*-rah) *f* cigarette-case

**pizarra** (pee-*thah*-rrah) *f* slate; blackboard

**placa** (*plah*-kah) *f* registration plate

**placer** (plah-*thayr*) *m* pleasure

**\*placer** (plah-*thayr*) *v* please

**plaga** (*plah*-gah) *f* plague

**plan** (plahn) *m* plan, project

**plancha** (*plahn*-chah) *f* iron; **no precisa** ~ wash and wear, drip-dry

**planchar** (plahn-*chahr*) *v* iron; press

**planeador** (plah-nay-ah-*dhoar*) *m* glider

**planear** (plah-nay-*ahr*) *v* plan

**planeta** (plah-*nay*-tah) *m* planet

**planetario** (plah-nay-*tah*-rᵛoa) *m* planetarium

**plano** (*plah*-noa) *adj* level, even, plane; *m* plan, map; **primer** ~ foreground

**planta** (*plahn*-tah) *f* plant

**plantación** (plahn-tah-*th*ᵛ*oan*) *f* plantation

**plantar** (plahn-*tahr*) *v* plant

**plantear** (plahn-tay-*ahr*) *v* \*put

**plástico** (*plahss*-tee-koa) *m* plastic; **de** ~ plastic

**plata** (*plah*-tah) *f* silver; **de** ~ silver; ~ **labrada** silverware

**plátano** (*plah*-tah-noa) *m* banana

**platero** (plah-*tay*-roa) *m* silversmith

**platija** (plah-*tee*-khah) *f* plaice

**platillo** (plah-*tee*-lᵛoa) *m* saucer

**platino** (plah-*tee*-noa) *m* platinum

**plato** (*plah*-toa) *m* dish, plate; course; ~ **para sopa** soup-plate

**playa** (*plah*-ᵛah) *f* beach; ~ **de veraneo** seaside resort; ~ **para nudistas** nudist beach

**plaza** (*plah*-thah) *f* square; ~ **de mercado** market-place; ~ **de toros** bullring; ~ **fuerte** stronghold

**plazo** (*plah*-thoa) *m* term; instalment; **compra a plazos** hire-purchase

**pleamar** (play-ah-*mahr*) *f* high tide

**\*plegar** (play-*gahr*) *v* crease

**pliegue** (*pl*ᵛ*ay*-gay) *m* crease, fold

**plomero** (ploa-*may*-roa) *m* plumber

**plomo** (*ploa*-moa) *m* lead

**pluma** (*ploo*-mah) *f* feather; pen

**plural** (ploo-*rahl*) *m* plural

**población** (poa-bhlah-*th*ᵛ*oan*) *f* population

**pobre** (*poa*-bhray) *adj* poor

**pobreza** (poa-*bhray*-thah) *f* poverty

**poco** (*poa*-koa) *adj* little; *m* bit; **dentro de** ~ presently; **pocos** *adj* few; **un** ~ some

**poder** (poa-*dhayr*) *m* power; authority

**\*poder** (poa-*dhayr*) *v* \*be able to, \*can; \*might, \*may

**poderoso** (poa-dhay-*roa*-soa) *adj* powerful

**podrido** (poa-*dhree*-dhoa) *adj* rotten

**poema** (poa-*ay*-mah) *m* poem; ~ **épico** epic

**poesía** (poa-ay-*see*-ah) *f* poetry

**poeta** (poa-*ay*-tah) *m* poet

**poético** (poa-*ay*-tee-koa) *adj* poetic

**polaco** (poa-*lah*-koa) *adj* Polish; *m* Pole

**polea** (poa-*lay*-aᵸ) *f* pulley

**policía** (poa-lee-*thee*-ah) *f* police *pl*

**polifacético** (poa-lee-fah-*thay*-tee-koa) *adj* all-round

**polilla** (poa-*lee*-l<sup>y</sup>ah) *f* moth
**polio** (*poa*-l<sup>y</sup>oa) *f* polio
**poliomielitis** (poa-l<sup>y</sup>oa-m<sup>y</sup>ay-*lee*-teess) *f* polio
**política** (poa-*lee*-tee-kah) *f* policy; politics
**político** (poa-*lee*-tee-koa) *adj* political; *m* politician
**póliza** (*poa*-lee-thah) *f* policy
**Polonia** (poa-*loa*-n<sup>y</sup>ah) *f* Poland
**polución** (poa-loo-*th<sup>y</sup>oan*) *f* pollution
**polvera** (poal-*bhay*-rah) *f* powder compact
**polvo** (*poal*-bhoa) *m* dust; powder; grit; ~ **facial** face-powder; ~ **para los dientes** toothpowder; ~ **para los pies** foot powder
**pólvora** (*poal*-bhoa-rah) *f* gunpowder
**polvoriento** (poal-bhoa-r<sup>y</sup>ayn-toa) *adj* dusty
**pollero** (poa-*l<sup>y</sup>ay*-roa) *m* poulterer
**pollo** (*poa*-l<sup>y</sup>oa) *m* chicken
**pomelo** (poa-*may*-loa) *m* grapefruit
**pómulo** (*poa*-moo-loa) *m* cheek-bone
**ponderado** (poan-day-*rah*-dhoa) *adj* sober
* **poner** (poa-*nayr*) *v* place, *lay, *put, *set; * **ponerse** *v* *put on
**pony** (*poa*-nee) *m* pony
**popelín** (poa-pay-*leen*) *m* poplin
**popular** (poa-poo-*lahr*) *adj* popular; vulgar; **canción** ~ folk song; **danza** ~ folk-dance
**populoso** (poa-poo-*loa*-soa) *adj* populous
**por** (poar) *prep* by; for; via; times
**porcelana** (poar-thay-*lah*-nah) *f* china, porcelain
**porcentaje** (poar-thayn-*tah*-khay) *m* percentage
**porción** (poar-*th<sup>y</sup>oan*) *f* portion, helping
**porque** (*poar*-kay) *conj* because, for, as; **por qué** why

**porra** (*poa*-rrah) *f* club
**portabagajes** (poar-tah-bah-*khah*-gayss) *m* luggage rack
**portador** (poar-tah-*dhoar*) *m* bearer
**portaequipajes** (poar-tah-ay-kee-*pah*-khayss) *m* boot; trunk *nAm*
**portafolio** (poar-tah-*foa*-l<sup>y</sup>oa) *m* attaché case, briefcase
**portaligas** (poar-tah-*lee*-gahss) *m* suspender belt
**portátil** (poar-*tah*-teel) *adj* portable
**portero** (poar-*tay*-roa) *m* doorman, door-keeper, porter; goalkeeper
**pórtico** (*poar*-tee-koa) *m* arcade
**portilla** (poar-*tee*-l<sup>y</sup>ah) *f* porthole
**portón** (poar-*toan*) *m* gate
**Portugal** (poar-too-*gahl*) *m* Portugal
**portugués** (poar-too-*gayss*) *adj* Portuguese; *m* Portuguese
**porvenir** (poar-bhay-*neer*) *m* future
**posada** (poa-*sah*-dhah) *f* inn
**posadero** (poa-sah-*dhay*-roa) *m* innkeeper
* **poseer** (poa-say-*ayr*) *v* own, possess
**posesión** (poa-say-*s<sup>y</sup>oan*) *f* possession
**posibilidad** (poa-see-bhee-lee-*dhahdh*) *f* possibility
**posible** (poa-*see*-bhlay) *adj* possible
**posición** (poa-see-*th<sup>y</sup>oan*) *f* position
**positiva** (poa-see-*tee*-bhah) *f* positive, print
**positivo** (poa-see-*tee*-bhoa) *adj* positive
**postal ilustrada** (poass-*tahl* ee-looss-*trah*-dhah) picture postcard
**poste** (*poass*-tay) *m* post, pole; ~ **de farol** lamp-post; ~ **de indicador** signpost
**posterior** (poass-tay-r<sup>y</sup>*oar*) *adj* subsequent
**postizo** (poass-*tee*-thoa) *m* hair piece
**postre** (*poass*-tray) *m* dessert
**potable** (poa-*tah*-bhlay) *adj* for drinking

**potencia** (poa-*tayn*-th<sup>y</sup>ah) *f* capacity; power

**pozo** (*poa*-thoa) *m* well; ~ **de petróleo** oil-well

**práctica** (*prahk*-tee-kah) *f* practice

**prácticamente** (*prahk*-tee-kah-mayn-tay) *adv* practically

**practicar** (prahk-tee-*kahr*) *v* practise

**práctico** (*prahk*-tee-koa) *adj* practical; business-like; *m* pilot

**prado** (*prah*-dhoa) *m* meadow, pasture

**precario** (pray-*kah*-r<sup>y</sup>oa) *adj* critical, precarious

**precaución** (pray-kou-*th<sup>y</sup>oan*) *f* precaution

**precaverse** (pray-kah-*bhayr*-say) *v* beware

**precedente** (pray-thay-*dhayn*-tay) *adj* previous, preceding, last

**preceder** (pray-thay-*dhayr*) *v* precede

**precio** (*pray*-th<sup>y</sup>oa) *m* price; charge, cost, rate; ~ **de compra** purchase price; ~ **del billete** fare

**precioso** (pray-*th<sup>y</sup>oa*-soa) *adj* precious; lovely

**precipicio** (pray-thee-*pee*-th<sup>y</sup>oa) *m* precipice

**precipitación** (pray-thee-pee-tah-*th<sup>y</sup>oan*) *f* precipitation

**precipitarse** (pray-thee-pee-*tahr*-say) *v* rush; crash; **precipitado** *adj* rash

**preciso** (pray-*thee*-soa) *adj* precise; very

**predecesor** (pray-dhay-thay-*soar*) *m* predecessor

**\*predecir** (pray-dhay-*theer*) *v* predict

**predicar** (pray-dhee-*kahr*) *v* preach

**preferencia** (pray-fay-*rayn*-th<sup>y</sup>ah) *f* preference

**preferible** (pray-fay-*ree*-bhlay) *adj* preferable

**\*preferir** (pray-fay-*reer*) *v* prefer; **preferido** *adj* favourite

**prefijo** (pray-*fee*-khoa) *m* prefix

**pregunta** (pray-*goon*-tah) *f* question; query, inquiry

**preguntar** (pray-goon-*tahr*) *v* ask; enquire; **preguntarse** *v* wonder

**prejuicio** (pray-*khwee*-th<sup>y</sup>oa) *m* prejudice

**preliminar** (pray-lee-mee-*nahr*) *adj* preliminary

**prematuro** (pray-mah-*too*-roa) *adj* premature

**premio** (*pray*-m<sup>y</sup>oa) *m* award, prize; ~ **de consolación** consolation prize

**prender** (prayn-*dayr*) *v* attach

**prensa** (*prayn*-sah) *f* press; **conferencia de** ~ press conference

**preocupación** (pray-oa-koo-pah-*th<sup>y</sup>oan*) *f* concern, anxiety, worry; trouble

**preocupado** (pray-oa-koo-*pah*-dhoa) *adj* concerned, anxious

**preocuparse de** (pray-oa-koo-*pahr*-say) care about

**preparación** (pray-pah-rah-*th<sup>y</sup>oan*) *f* preparation

**preparado** (pray-pah-*rah*-dhoa) *adj* prepared, ready

**preparar** (pray-pah-*rahr*) *v* prepare; cook

**preposición** (pray-poa-see-*th<sup>y</sup>oan*) *f* preposition

**presa** (*pray*-sah) *f* dam

**prescindir** (pray-theen-*deer*) *v* omit; disregard; **prescindiendo de** apart from

**prescribir** (prayss-kree-*bheer*) *v* prescribe

**prescripción** (prayss-kreep-*th<sup>y</sup>oan*) *f* prescription

**presencia** (pray-*sayn*-th<sup>y</sup>ah) *f* presence

**presenciar** (pray-sayn-*th<sup>y</sup>ahr*) *v* witness

**presentación** (pray-sayn-tah-*th<sup>y</sup>oan*) *f* introduction

**presentar** (pray-sayn-*tahr*) *v* introduce,

present; offer; **presentarse** v report

**presente** (pray-*sayn*-tay) adj present; m present

**preservar** (pray-sayr-*bahr*) v preserve

**presidente** (pray-see-*dhayn*-tay) m president, chairman

**presidir** (pray-see-*dheer*) v preside at

**presión** (pray-s<sup>y</sup>oan) f pressure; ~ **atmosférica** atmospheric pressure; ~ **del aceite** oil pressure; ~ **del neumático** tyre pressure

**preso** (*pray*-soa) m prisoner; **coger** ~ capture

**prestamista** (prayss-tah-*meess*-tah) m pawnbroker

**préstamo** (*prayss*-tah-moa) m loan

**prestar** (prayss-*tahr*) v \*lend; ~ **atención a** attend to, \*pay attention to; **tomar prestado** borrow

**prestidigitador** (prayss-tee-dhee-khee-tah-*dhoar*) m magician

**prestigio** (prayss-*tee*-kh<sup>y</sup>oa) m prestige

**presumible** (pray-soo-*mee*-bhlay) adj presumable

**presumido** (pray-soo-*mee*-dhoa) adj presumptuous

**presumir** (pray-soo-*meer*) v assume; boast

**presuntuoso** (pray-soon-*twoa*-soa) adj conceited; presumptuous

**presupuesto** (pray-soo-*pwayss*-toa) m budget

**pretender** (pray-tayn-*dayr*) v claim

**pretensión** (pray-tayn-s<sup>y</sup>oan) f claim

**pretexto** (pray-*tayks*-toa) m pretext, pretence

**\*prevenir** (pray-bhay-*neer*) v anticipate, prevent

**preventivo** (pray-bhayn-*tee*-bhoa) adj preventive

**\*prever** (pray-*bhayr*) v anticipate

**previo** (*pray*-bh<sup>y</sup>oa) adj previous

**previsión** (pray-bhee-s<sup>y</sup>oan) f outlook, forecast

**prima** (*pree*-mah) f cousin; premium

**primario** (pree-*mah*-r<sup>y</sup>oa) adj primary

**primavera** (pree-mah-*bhay*-rah) f springtime, spring

**primero** (pree-*may*-roa) num first; adj foremost; primary

**primitivo** (pree-mee-*tee*-bhoa) adj primitive

**primo** (*pree*-moa) m cousin

**primordial** (pree-moar-*dh<sup>y</sup>ahl*) adj primary

**princesa** (preen-*thay*-sah) f princess

**principal** (preen-thee-*pahl*) adj principal; chief, main, cardinal; m principal

**principalmente** (preen-thee-pahl-*mayn*-tay) adv mainly

**príncipe** (*preen*-thee-pay) m prince

**principiante** (preen-thee-p<sup>y</sup>ahn-tay) m beginner, learner

**principio** (preen-*thee*-p<sup>y</sup>oa) m principle; **al** ~ at first

**prioridad** (pr<sup>y</sup>oa-ree-*dhahdh*) f priority

**prisa** (*pree*-sah) f haste, speed, hurry; **\*dar** ~ \*speed; **\*darse** ~ hurry; **de** ~ in a hurry

**prisión** (pree-s<sup>y</sup>oan) f prison

**prisionero** (pree-s<sup>y</sup>oa-*nay*-roa) m prisoner; ~ **de guerra** prisoner of war

**prismáticos** (preez-*mah*-tee-koass) mpl binoculars pl

**privado** (pree-*bhah*-dhoa) adj private

**privar de** (pree-*bhahr*) deprive of

**privilegio** (pree-bhee-*lay*-kh<sup>y</sup>oa) m privilege

**probable** (proa-*bhah*-bhlay) adj probable; likely

**probablemente** (proa-bhah-bhlay-*mayn*-tay) adv probably

**probador** (proa-bhah-*dhoar*) m fitting room

**\*probar** (proa-*bhahr*) v attempt; test; taste; **\*probarse** v try on

**problema** (proa-*bhlay*-mah ) *m* problem, question

**procedencia** (proa-thay-*dhayn*-th<sup>y</sup>ah ) *f* origin

**proceder** (proa-thay-*dhayr*) *v* proceed

**procedimiento** (proa-thay-dhee-*m<sup>y</sup>ayn*-toa) *m* procedure; process

**procesión** (proa-thay-*s<sup>y</sup>oan*) *f* procession

**proceso** (proa-*thay*-soa ) *m* process, trial, lawsuit

**proclamar** (proa-klah-*mahr*) *v* proclaim

**procurador** (proa-koo-rah-*dhoar*) *m* solicitor

**procurar** (proa-koo-*rahr*) *v* furnish

**pródigo** (*proa*-dhee-goa) *adj* lavish

**producción** (proa-dhook-*th<sup>y</sup>oan*) *f* production, output; ~ **en serie** mass production

**\*producir** (proa-dhoo-*theer*) *v* produce

**producto** (proa-*dhook*-toa) *m* product, produce

**productor** (proa-dhook-*toar*) *m* producer

**profano** (proa-*fah*-noa) *m* layman

**profesar** (proa-fay-*sahr*) *v* confess

**profesión** (proa-fay-*s<sup>y</sup>oan*) *f* profession

**profesional** (proa-fay-s<sup>y</sup>oa-*nahl*) *adj* professional

**profesor** (proa-fay-*soar*) *m* master, teacher; professor

**profesora** (proa-fay-*soa*-rah) *f* teacher

**profeta** (proa-*fay*-tah) *m* prophet

**profundidad** (proa-foon-dee-*dhahdh*) *f* depth

**profundo** (proa-*foon*-doa) *adj* low; profound

**programa** (proa-*grah*-mah) *m* programme

**progresista** (proa-gray-*seess*-tah) *adj* progressive

**progresivo** (proa-gray-*see*-bhoa) *adj* progressive

**progreso** (proa-*gray*-soa) *m* progress

**prohibición** (proa-ee-bhee-*th<sup>y</sup>oan*) *f* prohibition

**prohibido** (proa-ee-*bhee*-dhoa) *adj* prohibited

**prohibir** (proa-ee-*bheer*) *v* prohibit, \*forbid

**prolongación** (proa-loang-gah-*th<sup>y</sup>oan*) *f* prolongation

**prolongar** (proa-loang-*gahr*) *v* extend

**promedio** (proa-*may*-dh<sup>y</sup>oa) *adj* average; *m* average, mean; **en** ~ on the average

**promesa** (proa-*may*-sah) *f* promise

**prometer** (proa-may-*tayr*) *v* promise

**prometido** (proa-may-*tee*-dhoa) *adj* engaged

**promoción** (proa-moa-*th<sup>y</sup>oan*) *f* promotion

**promontorio** (proa-moan-*toa*-r<sup>y</sup>oa) *m* headland

**\*promover** (proa-moa-*bhayr*) *v* promote

**pronombre** (proa-*noam*-bray) *m* pronoun

**pronosticar** (proa-noass-tee-*kahr*) *v* forecast

**pronto** (*proan*-toa) *adj* prompt; *adv* soon, shortly; **tan** ~ **como** as soon as

**pronunciación** (proa-noon-th<sup>y</sup>ah-*th<sup>y</sup>oan*) *f* pronunciation

**pronunciar** (proa-noon-*th<sup>y</sup>ahr*) *v* pronounce

**propaganda** (proa-pah-*gahn*-dah) *f* propaganda

**propicio** (proa-*pee*-th<sup>y</sup>oa) *adj* favourable; well-disposed

**propiedad** (proa-p<sup>y</sup>ay-*dhahdh*) *f* property; estate

**propietario** (proa-p<sup>y</sup>ay-*tah*-r<sup>y</sup>oa) *m* owner, proprietor; landlord

**propina** (proa-*pee*-nah) *f* gratuity, tip

**propio** (*proa*-p<sup>y</sup>oa) *adj* own

**\* proponer** (proa-poa-*nayr*) *v* propose

**proporción** (proa-poar-*th*ᵉ*oan*) *f* proportion

**proporcional** (proa-poar-th*ᵉ*oa-*nahl*) *adj* proportional

**proporcionar** (proa-poar-th*ᵉ*oa-*nahr*) *v* adjust; procure

**propósito** (proa-*poa*-see-toa) *m* purpose; **a ~** by the way

**propuesta** (proa-*pwayss*-tah) *f* proposition, proposal

**prórroga** (*proa*-rroa-gah) *f* extension

**prosa** (*proa*-sah) *f* prose

**\* proseguir** (proa-say-*geer*) *v* proceed, continue, carry on

**prospecto** (proass-*payk*-toa) *m* prospectus

**prosperidad** (proass-pay-ree-*dhahdh*) *f* prosperity

**próspero** (*proass*-pay-roa) *adj* prosperous

**prostituta** (proass-tee-*too*-tah) *f* prostitute

**protección** (proa-tayk-*th*ᵉ*oan*) *f* protection

**proteger** (proa-tay-*khayr*) *v* protect

**proteína** (proa-tay-*ee*-nah) *f* protein

**protesta** (proa-*tayss*-tah) *f* protest

**protestante** (proa-tayss-*tahn*-tay) *adj* Protestant

**protestar** (proa-tayss-*tahr*) *v* protest

**provechoso** (proa-bhay-*choa*-soa) *adj* profitable

**\* proveer** (proa-bhay-*ayr*) *v* provide; **~ de** furnish with

**proverbio** (proa-*bhayr*-bh*ᵉ*oa) *m* proverb

**provincia** (proa-*bheen*-th*ᵉ*ah) *f* province

**provincial** (proa-bheen-*th*ᵉ*ahl*) *adj* provincial

**provisional** (proa-bhee-s*ᵉ*oa-*nahl*) *adj* provisional, temporary

**provisiones** (proa-bhee-s*ᵉ*oa-nayss) *fpl* provisions *pl*

**provocar** (proa-bhoa-*kahr*) *v* cause

**próximamente** (*proak*-see-mah-mayn-tay) *adv* shortly

**próximo** (*proak*-see-moa) *adj* next

**proyectar** (proa-*y*ayk-*tahr*) *v* project

**proyecto** (proa-*y*ayk-toa) *m* project, scheme

**proyector** (proa-*y*ayk-*toar*) *m* spotlight

**prudente** (proo-*dhayn*-tay) *adj* cautious, wary, gentle

**prueba** (*prway*-bhah) *f* experiment, trial, test; proof, token, evidence; **a ~** on approval

**prurito** (proo-*ree*-toa) *m* itch

**psicoanalista** (see-koa-ah-nah-*leess*-tah) *m* analyst, psychoanalyst

**psicología** (see-koa-loa-*khee*-ah) *f* psychology

**psicológico** (see-koa-*loa*-khee-koa) *adj* psychological

**psicólogo** (see-*koa*-loa-goa) *m* psychologist

**psiquiatra** (see-k*ᵉ*ah-trah) *m* psychiatrist

**psíquico** (*see*-kee-koa) *adj* psychic

**publicación** (poo-bhlee-kah-*th*ᵉ*oan*) *f* publication

**publicar** (poo-bhlee-*kahr*) *v* publish

**publicidad** (poo-bhlee-thee-*dhahdh*) *f* advertising, publicity

**público** (*poo*-bhlee-koa) *adj* public; *m* public

**pueblo** (*pway*-bhloa) *m* nation, people; village

**puente** (*pwayn*-tay) *m* bridge; **~ colgante** suspension bridge; **~ levadizo** drawbridge; **~ superior** main deck

**puerta** (*pwayr*-tah) *f* door; **~ corrediza** sliding door; **~ giratoria** revolving door

**puerto** (*pwayr*-toa) *m* harbour, port; **~ de mar** seaport

**pues** (pwayss) *conj* since
**puesta** (*pwayss*-tah) *f* bet
**puesto** (loo-*gahr*) *m* spot; job, post, position; stand, stall, booth; **~ de gasolina** service station; gas station *Am*; **~ de libros** bookstand
**puesto que** (*pwayss*-toa kay) because, since
**pulcro** (*pool*-kroa) *adj* neat
**pulgar** (pool-*gahr*) *m* thumb
**pulir** (poo-*leer*) *v* polish
**pulmón** (pool-*moan*) *m* lung
**pulóver** (pool-*loa*-bhayr) *m* pullover
**púlpito** (*pool*-pee-toa) *m* pulpit
**pulpo** (*pool*-poa) *m* octopus
**pulsera** (pool-*say*-rah) *f* bracelet, bangle
**pulso** (*pool*-soa) *m* pulse
**pulverizador** (pool-bhay-ree-thah-*dhoar*) *m* atomizer
**punta** (*poon*-tah) *f* tip, point
**puntiagudo** (poon-tʸah-*goo*-dhoa) *adj* pointed
**puntilla** (poon-*tee*-lʸah) *f* lace
**punto** (*poon*-toa) *m* point; item, issue; period, full stop; stitch; **géneros de ~** hosiery; **\*hacer ~** \*knit; **~ de congelación** freezing-point; **~ de partida** starting-point; **~ de vista** point of view; **~ y coma** semicolon
**puntual** (poon-*twahl*) *adj* punctual
**punzada** (poon-*thah*-dhah) *f* stitch
**punzar** (poon-*thahr*) *v* pierce
**puñado** (poo-*ñah*-dhoa) *m* handful
**puñetazo** (poo-ñay-*tah*-thoa) *m* punch; **\*dar puñetazos** punch
**puño** (*poo*-ñoa) *m* fist; cuff
**pupitre** (poo-*pee*-tray) *m* desk
**purasangre** (poo-rah-*sahng*-gray) *adj* thoroughbred
**puro** (*poo*-roa) *adj* pure; clean, neat, sheer; *m* cigar
**purpúreo** (poor-*poo*-ray-oa) *adj* purple

**pus** (pooss) *f* pus

# Q

**que** (kay) *pron* who, which, that; *conj* that; as, than
**qué** (kay) *pron* what; *adv* how
**quebradizo** (kay-bhrah-*dhee*-thoa) *adj* crisp
**quebrantar** (kay-bhrahn-*tahr*) *v* \*break
**\*quebrar** (kay-*bhrahr*) *v* crack, \*break, \*burst
**quedar** (kay-*dhahr*) *v* remain; **quedarse** *v* remain, stay
**queja** (*kay*-khah) *f* complaint
**quejarse** (kay-*khahr*-say) *v* complain
**quemadura** (kay-mah-*dhoo*-rah) *f* burn; **~ del sol** sunburn
**quemar** (kay-*mahr*) *v* \*burn
**\*querer** (kay-*rayr*) *v* \*will, want; like, \*be fond of
**querida** (kay-*ree*-dhah) *f* sweetheart; mistress
**querido** (kay-*ree*-dhoa) *adj* beloved, dear; precious; *m* darling
**queso** (*kay*-soa) *m* cheese
**quien** (kʸayn) *pron* who; **a ~** whom
**quienquiera** (kʸayng-*kʸay*-rah) *pron* whoever
**quieto** (*kʸay*-toa) *adj* still, quiet; **\*estarse ~** \*keep quiet
**quilate** (kee-*lah*-tay) *m* carat
**quilla** (*kee*-lʸah) *f* keel
**química** (*kee*-mee-kah) *f* chemistry
**químico** (*kee*-mee-koa) *adj* chemical
**quincalla** (keeng-*kah*-lʸah) *f* hardware
**quince** (*keen*-thay) *num* fifteen
**quincena** (keen-*thay*-nah) *f* fortnight
**quinceno** (keen-*thay*-noa) *num* fifteenth
**quinina** (kee-*nee*-nah) *f* quinine
**quinta** (*keen*-tah) *f* country house

**quinto**[1] (*keen*-toa) *num* fifth

**quinto**[2] (*keen*-toa) *m* conscript

**quiosco** (*kʸoass*-koa) *m* kiosk; ~ **de periódicos** newsstand

**quitamanchas** (kee-tah-*mahn*-chahss) *m* cleaning fluid, stain remover

**quitar** (kee-*tahr*) *v* *take away

**quitasol** (kee-tah-*soal*) *m* sunshade

**quizás** (kee-*thahss*) *adv* maybe, perhaps

# R

**rábano** (*rah*-bhah-noa) *m* radish; ~ **picante** horseradish

**rabia** (*rah*-bhʸah) *f* rage; rabies

**rabiar** (rah-*bhʸahr*) *v* rage

**rabioso** (rah-*bhʸoa*-soa) *adj* mad

**racial** (rah-*thʸahl*) *adj* racial

**ración** (rah-*thʸoan*) *f* ration

**radiador** (rah-dhʸah-*dhoar*) *m* radiator

**radical** (rah-dhee-*kahl*) *adj* radical

**radio** (*rah*-dhʸoa) *m* radius; spoke; *f* wireless, radio

**radiografía** (rah-dhʸoa-grah-*fee*-ah) *f* X-ray

**radiografiar** (rah-dhʸoa-grah-*fʸahr*) *v* X-ray

**raedura** (rah-ay-*dhoo*-rah) *f* scratch; *hacer raeduras scratch

**ráfaga** (*rah*-fah-gah) *f* gust, blow

**raíz** (rah-*eeth*) *f* root

**rallar** (rah-*lʸahr*) *v* grate

**rama** (*rah*-mah) *f* branch, bough

**ramita** (rah-*mee*-tah) *f* twig

**ramo** (*rah*-moa) *m* bouquet, bunch

**rampa** (*rahm*-pah) *f* ramp

**rana** (*rah*-nah) *f* frog

**rancio** (*rahn*-thʸoa) *adj* rancid

**rancho** (*rahn*-choa) *mMe* farmhouse

**rango** (*rahng*-goa) *m* rank

**ranura** (rah-*noo*-rah) *f* slot

**rápidamente** (rah-pee-dah-*mayn*-tay) *adv* soon

**rapidez** (rah-pee-*dhayth*) *f* speed

**rápido** (*rah*-pee-dhoa) *adj* fast, rapid, quick; **rápidos de río** rapids *pl*

**raqueta** (rah-*kay*-tah) *f* racquet

**raro** (*rah*-roa) *adj* uncommon, rare; strange, odd; **raras veces** rarely

**rascacielos** (rahss-kah-*thʸay*-loass) *m* skyscraper

**rascar** (rahss-*kahr*) *v* scratch

**rasgar** (rahz-*gahr*) *v* rip

**rasgo** (*rahz*-goa) *m* trait; feature; ~ **característico** characteristic

**rasgón** (rahz-*goan*) *m* tear

**rasguño** (rahz-*goo*-ño̱a) *m* scratch

**raso** (*rah*-soa) *adj* bare; *m* satin

**raspar** (rahss-*pahr*) *v* scrape

**rastrear** (rahss-tray-*ahr*) *v* trace

**rastrillo** (rahss-*tree*-lʸoa) *m* rake

**rastro** (*rahss*-troa) *m* trail

**rasurarse** (rah-soo-*rahr*-say) *v* shave

**rata** (*rah*-tah) *f* rat

**rato** (*rah*-toa) *m* while

**ratón** (rah-*toan*) *m* mouse

**raya** (*rah*-ʸah) *f* line, stripe; crease; parting

**rayado** (rah-*ʸah*-dhoa) *adj* striped

**rayador** (rah-ʸah-*dhoar*) *m* grater

**rayo** (*rah*-ʸoa) *m* beam, ray

**rayón** (rah-*ʸoan*) *m* rayon

**raza** (*rah*-thah) *f* race; breed

**razón** (rah-*thoan*) *f* wits *pl*, sense, reason; **no *tener ~** *be wrong; *tener ~ ** be right

**razonable** (rah-thoa-*nah*-bhlay) *adj* reasonable

**razonar** (rah-thoa-*nahr*) *v* reason

**reacción** (ray-ahk-*thʸoan*) *f* reaction

**reaccionar** (ray-ahk-thʸoa-*nahr*) *v* react

**real** (ray-*ahl*) *adj* factual, true, substantial; royal

**realidad** (ray-ah-lee-*dhahdh*) *f* reality;

**en** ~ actually, as a matter of fact, really, in effect

**realizable** (ray-ah-lee-*thah*-bhlay) *adj* feasible, realizable

**realización** (ray-ah-lee-thah-*th%oan*) *f* achievement

**realizar** (ray-ah-lee-*thahr*) *v* realize; carry out

**rebaja** (ray-*bhah*-khah) *f* reduction, rebate; **rebajas** *fpl* sales

**rebajar** (ray-bhah-*khahr*) *v* lower, reduce

**rebaño** (ray-*bhah*-ñoa) *m* flock

**rebelde** (ray-*bhayl*-day) *m* rebel

**rebelión** (ray-bhay-*l%oan*) *f* revolt, rebellion

**recado** (ray-*kah*-dhoa) *m* errand

**recambio** (ray-*kahm*-b%oa) *m* spare part

**recaudar** (ray-kou-*dhahr*) *v* raise

**recepción** (ray-thayp-*th%oan*) *f* reception

**recepcionista** (ray-thayp-th%oa-*neess*-tah) *f* receptionist

**receptáculo** (ray-thayp-*tah*-koo-loa) *m* container

**receptor** (ray-thayp-*toar*) *m* receiver

**receta** (ray-*thay*-tah) *f* recipe

**recibir** (ray-thee-*bheer*) *v* receive

**recibo** (ray-*thee*-bhoa) *m* voucher, receipt; **oficina de** ~ reception office

**recién** (ray-*th%ayn*) *adv* recently

**reciente** (ray-*th%ayn*-tay) *adj* recent

**recientemente** (ray-th%ayn-tay-*mayn*-tay) *adv* lately, recently

**recio** (*ray*-th%oa) *adj* strong

**recíproco** (ray-*thee*-proa-koa) *adj* mutual

**recital** (ray-thee-*tahl*) *m* recital

**reclamar** (ray-klah-*mahr*) *v* claim

**recluta** (ray-*kloo*-tah) *m* recruit

**recoger** (ray-koa-*khayr*) *v* pick up, pick; collect, gather; *overtake

**recogida** (ray-koa-*khee*-dhah) *f* collec-

tion

**recomendación** (ray-koa-mayn-dah-*th%oan*) *f* recommendation

*****recomendar** (ray-koa-mayn-*dahr*) *v* recommend

*****recomenzar** (ray-koa-mayn-*thahr*) *v* recommence

**recompensa** (ray-koam-*payn*-sah) *f* prize, reward

**recompensar** (ray-koam-payn-*sahr*) *v* reward

**reconciliación** (ray-koan-thee-l%ah-*th%oan*) *f* reconciliation

*****reconocer** (ray-koa-noa-*thayr*) *v* recognize; admit, confess, acknowledge; realize

**reconocimiento** (ray-koa-noa-thee-*m%ayn*-toa) *m* recognition; check-up

**récord** (*ray*-koardh) *m* record

*****recordar** (ray-koar-*dhahr*) *v* remind; *think of

**recorrer** (ray-koa-*rrayr*) *v* cross

**recortar** (ray-koar-*tahr*) *v* trim

**recreación** (ray-kray-ah-*th%oan*) *f* recreation

**recreo** (ray-*kray*-oa) *m* recreation; **patio de** ~ playground

**recriar** (ray-kr%*ahr*) *v* *breed

**rectangular** (rayk-tahng-goo-*lahr*) *adj* rectangular

**rectángulo** (rayk-*tahng*-goo-loa) *m* oblong, rectangle

**rectificación** (rayk-tee-fee-kah-*th%oan*) *f* correction

**recto** (*rayk*-toa) *adj* erect

**rector** (rayk-*toar*) *m* rector

**rectoría** (rayk-toa-*ree*-ah) *f* rectory

**recuerdo** (ray-*kwayr*-dhoa) *m* remembrance, memory; souvenir

**recuperación** (ray-koo-pay-rah-*th%oan*) *f* revival

**recuperar** (ray-koo-pay-*rahr*) *v* recover

**rechazar** (ray-chah-*thahr*) *v* reject, turn down

**red** (raydh) f net; network; ~ **de ca-rreteras** road system; ~ **de pescar** fishing net

**redacción** (ray-dhahk-th<sup>y</sup>oan) f wording; editorial staff

**redactar** (ray-dhahk-tahr) v *make up; *draw up

**redactor** (ray-dhahk-toar) m editor

**redecilla** (ray-dhay-thee-l<sup>y</sup>ah) f hairnet

**redimir** (ray-dhee-meer) v redeem

**rédito** (ray-dhee-toa) m interest

**redondeado** (ray-dhoan-day-ah-dhoa) adj rounded

**redondo** (ray-dhoan-doa) adj round

**reducción** (ray-dhook-th<sup>y</sup>oan) f reduction, rebate

* **reducir** (ray-dhoo-theer) v *cut, decrease, reduce

**reembolsar** (ray-aym-boal-sahr) v reimburse

**reemplazar** (ray-aym-plah-thahr) v replace

**reemprender** (ray-aym-prayn-dayr) v resume

**reexpedir** (ray-ayks-pay-dheer) v forward

**referencia** (ray-fay-rayn-th<sup>y</sup>ah) f reference; **punto de** ~ landmark

* **referir** (ray-fay-reer) v refer; narrate

**refinería** (ray-fee-nay-ree-ah) f refinery

**reflector** (ray-flayk-toar) m reflector; searchlight

**reflejar** (ray-flay-khahr) v reflect

**reflejo** (ray-flay-khoa) m reflection

**reflexionar** (ray-flayk-s<sup>y</sup>oa-nahr) v *think

**Reforma** (ray-foar-mah) f reformation

**refractario** (ray-frahk-tah-r<sup>y</sup>oa) adj fireproof

**refrenar** (ray-fray-nahr) v curb

**refrescar** (ray-frayss-kahr) v refresh

**refresco** (ray-frayss-koa) m refreshment

**refrigerador** (ray-free-khay-rah-dhoar) m fridge, refrigerator

**refugio** (ray-foo-kh<sup>y</sup>oa) m cover, shelter

**refunfuñar** (ray-foon-foo-ñahr) v grumble

**regalar** (ray-gah-lahr) v present

**regaliz** (ray-gah-leeth) m liquorice

**regalo** (ray-gah-loa) m present, gift

**regata** (ray-gah-tah) f regatta

**regatear** (ray-gah-tay-ahr) v bargain

**régimen** (ray-khee-mayn) m (pl regímenes) régime; government, rule; diet

**regimiento** (ray-khee-m<sup>y</sup>ayn-toa) m regiment

**región** (ray-kh<sup>y</sup>oan) f region; zone, country, area

**regional** (ray-kh<sup>y</sup>oa-nahl) adj regional

* **regir** (ray-kheer) v govern, rule

**registrar** (ray-kheess-trahr) v book, record

**registro** (ray-kheess-troa) m record

**regla** (ray-glah) f rule; regulation; ruler; **en** ~ in order; **por** ~ **general** as a rule

**reglamento** (ray-glah-mayn-toa) m regulation

**regocijo** (ray-goa-thee-khoa) m joy

**regordete** (ray-goar-dhay-tay) adj plump

**regresar** (ray-gray-sahr) v *go back, *get back

**regreso** (ray-gray-soa) m return; **viaje de** ~ return journey; **vuelo de** ~ return flight

**regulación** (ray-goo-lah-th<sup>y</sup>oan) f regulation

**regular** (ray-goo-lahr) v regulate; adj regular

**rehabilitación** (ray-ah-bhee-lee-tah-th<sup>y</sup>oan) f rehabilitation

**rehén** (ray-ayn) m hostage

**rehusar** (ray<sup>oo</sup>-sahr) v refuse; reject

**reina** ( *ray*-nah ) *f* queen
**reinado** (ray-*nah*-dhoa ) *m* reign
**reino** ( *ray*-noa) *m* kingdom
**reintegrar** (rayn-tay-*grahr*) *v* \*repay, refund
**reintegro** (rayn-*tay*-groa) *m* repayment, refund
\***reír** (ray-*eer*) *v* laugh
**reivindicación** (ray-bheen-dee-kah-*th*ᵞ*oan*) *f* claim
**reivindicar** (ray-bheen-dee-*kahr*) *v* claim
**reja** ( *ray*-khah ) *f* grate; fence, gate
**rejilla** (ray-*khee*-lᵞah ) *f* luggage rack
**relación** (ray-lah-*th*ᵞ*oan*) *f* connection, relation; reference; report
**relacionar** (ray-lah-th*ᵞ*oa-*nahr*) *v* relate
**relajación** (ray-lah-khah-*th*ᵞ*oan*) *f* relaxation
**relajado** (ray-lah-*khah*-dhoa) *adj* easygoing
**relámpago** (ray-*lahm*-pah-goa ) *m* lightning; flash
**relatar** (ray-lah-*tahr*) *v* report
**relativo** (ray-lah-*tee*-bhoa) *adj* comparative, relative; ~ **a** regarding
**relato** (ray-*lah*-toa) *m* tale
**relevar** (ray-lay-*bhahr*) *v* relieve
**relieve** (ray-*l*ᵞ*ay*-bhay) *m* relief
**religión** (ray-lee-*kh*ᵞ*oan*) *f* religion
**religioso** (ray-lee-*kh*ᵞ*oa*-soa) *adj* religious
**reliquia** (ray-*lee*-kᵞah ) *f* relic
**reloj** (ray-*loakh*) *m* clock; watch; ~ **de bolsillo** pocket-watch; ~ **de pulsera** wrist-watch
**relojero** (ray-loa-*khay*-roa ) *m* watchmaker
**reluciente** (ray-loo-*th*ᵞ*ayn*-tay) *adj* bright
\***relucir** (ray-loo-*theer*) *v* \*shine
**rellenado** (ray-lᵞay-*nah*-doa) *adj* stuffed

**relleno** (ray-*l*ᵞ*ay*-noa) *m* stuffing; filling
**remanente** (ray-mah-*nayn*-tay) *m* remnant
**remar** (ray-*mahr*) *v* row
**remedio** (ray-*may*-dh*ᵞ*oa) *m* remedy
\***remendar** (ray-mayn-*dahr*) *v* mend; patch
**remesa** (ray-*may*-sah) *f* remittance
**remitir** (ray-mee-*teer*) *v* remit; ~ **a** refer to
**remo** ( *ray*-moa) *m* paddle, oar
**remoción** (ray-moa-*th*ᵞ*oan*) *f* removal
**remojar** (ray-moa-*khahr*) *v* soak
**remolacha** (ray-moa-*lah*-chah) *f* beetroot, beet
**remolcador** (ray-moal-kah-*dhoar*) *m* tug
**remolcar** (ray-moal-*kahr*) *v* tug, tow
**remolque** (ray-*moal*-kay) *m* trailer
**remoto** (ray-*moa*-toa) *adj* remote, faraway, far-off
\***remover** (ray-moa-*bhayr*) *v* remove
**remuneración** (ray-moo-nay-rah-*th*ᵞ*oan*) *f* remuneration
**remunerar** (ray-moo-nay-*rahr*) *v* remunerate
**Renacimiento** (ray-nah-thee-*m*ᵞ*ayn*-toa ) *m* Renaissance
**rendición** (rayn-dee-*th*ᵞ*oan*) *f* surrender
\***rendir** (rayn-*deer*) *v* \*pay; ~ **homenaje** honour; \***rendirse** *v* surrender
**renglón** (rayng-*gloan*) *m* line
**reno** ( *ray*-noa) *m* reindeer
**renombre** (ray-*noam*-bray) *m* reputation
\***renovar** (ray-noa-*bhahr*) *v* renew
**renta** ( *rayn*-tah) *f* revenue
**rentable** (rayn-*tah*-bhlay) *adj* paying
**renunciar** (ray-noon-*th*ᵞ*ahr*) *v* \*give up
\***reñir** (ray-*ñeer*) *v* dispute, quarrel
**reparación** (ray-pah-rah-*th*ᵞ*oan*) *f* reparation; repair

**reparar** (ray-pah-*rahr*) *v* repair, mend

**repartir** (ray-pahr-*teer*) *v* divide, *deal

**reparto** (ray-*pahr*-toa) *m* delivery; **camioneta de** ~ pick-up van

**repelente** (ray-pay-*layn*-tay) *adj* repellent, revolting

**repentinamente** (ray-payn-tee-nah-*mayn*-tay) *adv* suddenly

**repertorio** (ray-payr-*toa*-rᵞoa) *m* repertory

**repetición** (ray-pay-tee-*thᵞoan*) *f* repetition

**repetidamente** (ray-pay-tee-dhah-*mayn*-tay) *adv* again and again

*repetir (ray-pay-*teer*) *v* repeat

**repleto** (ray-*play*-toa) *adj* chock-full, crowded

**reportero** (ray-poar-*tay*-roa) *m* reporter

**reposado** (ray-poa-*sah*-dhoa) *adj* restful

**reposo** (ray-*poa*-soa) *m* rest

**reprender** (ray-prayn-*dayr*) *v* reprimand, scold

**representación** (ray-pray-sayn-tah-*thᵞoan*) *f* representation; show, performance

**representante** (ray-pray-sayn-*tahn*-tay) *m* agent

**representar** (ray-pray-sayn-*tahr*) *v* represent

**representativo** (ray-pray-sayn-tah-*tee*-bhoa) *adj* representative

**reprimir** (ray-pree-*meer*) *v* suppress

*reprobar (ray-proa-*bhahr*) *v* reject

**reprochar** (ray-proa-*chahr*) *v* reproach

**reproche** (ray-*proa*-chay) *m* reproach, blame

**reproducción** (ray-proa-dhook-*thᵞoan*) *f* reproduction

*reproducir (ray-proa-dhoo-*theer*) *v* reproduce

**reptil** (rayp-*teel*) *m* reptile

**república** (ray-*poo*-bhlee-kah) *f* republic

**republicano** (ray-poo-bhlee-*kah*-noa) *adj* republican

**repuesto** (ray-*pwayss*-toa) *m* store; refill

**repugnancia** (ray-poog-*nahn*-thᵞah) *f* dislike

**repugnante** (ray-poog-*nahn*-tay) *adj* repellent, disgusting, revolting

**repulsivo** (ray-pool-*see*-bhoa) *adj* repulsive

**reputación** (ray-poo-tah-*thᵞoan*) *f* reputation, fame

**requerimiento** (ray-kay-ree-*mᵞayn*-toa) *m* requirement

*requerir (ray-kay-*reer*) *v* require, demand

**resaca** (ray-*sah*-kah) *f* undercurrent; hangover

**resbaladizo** (rayz-bhah-lah-*dhee*-thoa) *adj* slippery

**resbalar** (rayz-bhah-*lahr*) *v* slip, glide

**rescatar** (rayss-kah-*tahr*) *v* rescue

**rescate** (rayss-*kah*-tay) *m* rescue; ransom

*resentirse por (ray-sayn-*teer*-say) resent

**reseña** (ray-*say*-ñah) *f* review

**reserva** (ray-*sayr*-bhah) *f* qualification; reserve; booking; **de** ~ spare

**reservación** (ray-sayr-bhah-*thᵞoan*) *f* reservation, booking

**reservar** (ray-sayr-*bhahr*) *v* engage; reserve, book

**resfriado** (rayss-*frᵞah*-dhoa) *m* cold

**resfriarse** (rayss-*frᵞahr*-say) *v* catch a cold

**residencia** (ray-see-*dhayn*-thᵞah) *f* residence

**residente** (ray-see-*dhayn*-tay) *adj* resident; *m* resident

**residir** (ray-see-*dheer*) *v* reside

**residuo** (ray-*see*-dhwoa) *m* remnant

**resignación** (ray-seeg-nah-*thᵞoan*) *f* resignation

**resignar** (ray-seeg-*nahr*) v resign

**resina** (ray-*see*-nah) f resin

**resistencia** (ray-seess-*tayn*-th<sup>y</sup>ah) f resistance

**resistir** (ray-seess-*teer*) v resist

**resolución** (ray-soa-loo-*th<sup>y</sup>oan*) f resolution

\* **resolver** (ray-soal-*bhayr*) v solve

\* **resonar** (ray-soa-*nahr*) v sound

**respectivo** (rayss-payk-*tee*-bhoa) adj respective

**respecto a** (rayss-*payk*-toa ah) about, regarding

**respetable** (rayss-pay-*tah*-bhlay) adj respectable

**respetar** (rayss-pay-*tahr*) v respect

**respeto** (rayss-*pay*-toa) m respect, esteem, regard

**respetuoso** (rayss-pay-*twoa*-soa) adj respectful

**respiración** (rayss-pee-rah-*th<sup>y</sup>oan*) f respiration, breathing

**respirar** (rayss-pee-*rahr*) v breathe

\* **resplandecer** (rayss-plahn-day-*thayr*) v \*shine

**resplandor** (rayss-plahn-*doar*) m glare

**responder** (rayss-poan-*dayr*) v reply, answer

**responsabilidad** (rayss-poan-sah-bhee-lee-*dhahdh*) f responsibility; liability

**responsable** (rayss-poan-*sah*-bhlay) adj responsible; liable

**respuesta** (rayss-*pwayss*-tah) f reply, answer

\* **restablecerse** (rayss-tah-bhlay-*thayr*-say) v recover

**restablecimiento** (rayss-tah-bhlay-thee-m<sup>y</sup>*ayn*-toa) m recovery

**restante** (rayss-*tahn*-tay) adj remaining

**restar** (rayss-*tahr*) v subtract

**restaurante** (rayss-tou-*rahn*-tay) m restaurant; ~ **de autoservicio** self-service restaurant

**resto** (*rayss*-toa) m rest; remnant, remainder

**restricción** (rayss-treek-*th<sup>y</sup>oan*) f restriction; qualification

**resuelto** (ray-*swayl*-toa) adj resolute, determined

**resultado** (ray-sool-*tah*-dhoa) m result; issue, outcome, effect

**resultar** (ray-sool-*tahr*) v result; prove

**resumen** (ray-*soo*-mayn) m résumé, survey, summary

**retardar** (ray-tahr-*dhahr*) v delay

\* **retener** (ray-tay-*nayr*) v \*hold

**retina** (ray-*tee*-nah) f retina

**retirar** (ray-tee-*rahr*) v \*withdraw

**reto** (*ray*-toa) m challenge

**retrasado** (ray-trah-*sah*-dhoa) adj late

**retraso** (ray-*trah*-soa) m delay

**retrato** (ray-*trah*-toa) m portrait

**retrete** (ray-*tray*-tay) m toilet

**retroceso** (ray-troa-*thay*-soa) m recession

**retumbo** (ray-*toom*-boa) m roar

**reumatismo** (ray<sup>oo</sup>-mah-*teez*-moa) m rheumatism

**reunión** (ray<sup>oo</sup>-*n<sup>y</sup>oan*) f meeting, assembly, rally

**reunir** (ray<sup>oo</sup>-*neer*) v join, assemble; reunite

**revelación** (ray-bhay-lah-*th<sup>y</sup>oan*) f revelation

**revelar** (ray-bhay-*lahr*) v reveal; \*give away; develop

**revendedor** (ray-bhayn-day-*dhoar*) m retailer

\* **reventar** (ray-bhayn-*tahr*) v crack, \*burst

**reventón** (ray-bhayn-*toan*) m blow-out

**reverencia** (ray-bhay-*rayn*-th<sup>y</sup>ah) f respect

**reverso** (ray-*bhayr*-soa) m reverse

**revés** (ray-*bhayss*) m reverse; **al** ~ the other way round; upside-down; inside out

**revisar** (ray-bhee-*sahr*) v revise, overhaul

**revisión** (ray-bhee-s<sup>y</sup>oan) f revision

**revisor** (ray-bhee-*soar*) m ticket collector

**revista** (ray-*bheess*-tah) f journal; review, magazine; revue; ~ **mensual** monthly magazine

**revocar** (ray-bhoa-*kahr*) v recall

**revolución** (ray-bhoa-loo-th<sup>y</sup>oan) f revolution

**revolucionar** (ray-bhoa-loo-th<sup>y</sup>oa-*nahr*) v revolutionize

**revolucionario** (ray-bhoa-loo-th<sup>y</sup>oa-nah-r<sup>y</sup>oa) adj revolutionary

*****revolver** (ray-bhoal-*bhayr*) v stir

**revólver** (ray-*bhoal*-bhayr) m revolver, gun

**revuelta** (ray-*bhwayl*-tah) f revolt

**rey** (ray) m king

**rezar** (ray-*thahr*) v pray

**riada** (r<sup>y</sup>ah-dhah) f flood

**ribera** (ree-*bhay*-rah) f riverside, river bank, shore

**rico** (*ree*-koa) adj rich; wealthy; nice, enjoyable, tasty

**ridiculizar** (ree-dhee-koo-lee-*thahr*) v ridicule

**ridículo** (ree-*dhee*-koo-loa) adj ridiculous, ludicrous

**riesgo** (r<sup>y</sup>ayz-goa) m hazard, chance, risk

**rigoroso** (ree-goa-*roa*-soa) adj severe

**riguroso** (ree-goo-*roa*-soa) adj bleak

**rima** (*ree*-mah) f rhyme

**rímel** (*ree*-mayl) m mascara

**rincón** (reeng-*koan*) m angle

**rinoceronte** (ree-noa-thay-*roan*-tay) m rhinoceros

**riña** (*ree*-ñah) f dispute

**riñón** (ree-*ñoan*) m kidney

**río** (*ree*-oa) m river; ~ **abajo** downstream; ~ **arriba** upstream

**riqueza** (ree-*kay*-thah) f riches pl, wealth

**risa** (*ree*-sah) f laughter, laugh

**ritmo** (*reet*-moa) m rhythm; pace

**rival** (ree-*bhahl*) m rival

**rivalidad** (ree-bhah-lee-*dhahdh*) f rivalry

**rivalizar** (ree-bhah-lee-*thahr*) v rival

**rizador** (ree-thah-*dhoar*) m curling-tongs pl; **rizadores** mpl hair rollers

**rizar** (ree-*thahr*) v curl

**rizo** (*ree*-thoa) m curl

**robar** (roa-*bhahr*) v rob; burgle

**roble** (*roa*-bhlay) m oak

**robo** (*roa*-bhoa) m robbery, theft

**robusto** (roa-*bhooss*-toa) adj solid, robust

**roca** (*roa*-kah) f rock

**rocío** (roa-*thee*-oa) m dew

**rocoso** (roa-*koa*-soa) adj rocky

**rodaballo** (roa-dhah-*bhah*-l<sup>y</sup>oa) m brill

*****rodar** (roa-*dhahr*) v roll

**rodear** (roa-dhay-*ahr*) v circle, surround; by-pass

**rodilla** (roa-*dhee*-l<sup>y</sup>ah) f knee

*****rogar** (roa-*gahr*) v ask

**rojo** (*roa*-khoa) adj red

**rollo** (*roa*-l<sup>y</sup>oa) m roll

**romano** (roa-*mah*-noa) adj Roman

**Romanticismo** (roa-mahn-tee-*theez*-moa) m Romanticism

**romántico** (roa-*mahn*-tee-koa) adj romantic

**rompecabezas** (roam-pay-kah-*bhay*-thahss) m puzzle; jigsaw puzzle

**romper** (roam-*payr*) v *break

**roncar** (roang-*kahr*) v snore

**ronco** (*roang*-koa) adj hoarse

**ropa** (*roa*-pah) f clothes pl; ~ **blanca** linen; ~ **de cama** bedding; ~ **interior** underwear; ~ **interior de mujer** lingerie; ~ **sucia** washing, laundry

**rosa** (*roa*-sah) f rose; adj rose

**rosado** (roa-*sah*-dhoa) adj pink

**rosario** (roa-*sah*-r<sup>y</sup>oa ) *m* beads *pl*, rosary

**rostro** (*roas*-troa ) *m* face

**rota** (*roa*-tah ) *f* rattan

**roto** (*roa*-toa ) *adj* broken

**rótula** (*roa*-too-lah ) *f* kneecap

**rotular** (roa-too-*lahr* ) *v* label

**rótulo** (*roa*-too-loa ) *m* label

**rozadura** (roa-thah-*dhoo*-rah ) *f* graze

**rubí** (roo-*bhee* ) *m* ruby

**rubia** (*roo*-bh<sup>y</sup>ah ) *f* blonde

**rubio** (*roo*-bh<sup>y</sup>oa ) *adj* fair

**ruborizarse** (roo-bhoa-ree-*thahr*-say )
blush

**rubricar** (roo-bhree-*kahr* ) *v* initial

**rueda** (*rway*-dhah ) *f* wheel; **patinaje
de ruedas** roller-skating; ~ **de repuesto** spare wheel

**ruego** (*rway*-goa ) *m* request

**rugido** (roo-*khee*-dhoa ) *m* roar

**rugir** (roo-*kheer* ) *v* roar

**ruibarbo** (rwee-*bhahr*-bhoa ) *m* rhubarb

**ruido** (*rwee*-dhoa ) *m* noise

**ruidoso** (rwee-*dhoa*-soa ) *adj* noisy

**ruina** (*rwee*-nah ) *f* ruins; ruin, destruction

**ruinoso** (rwee-*noa*-soa ) *adj* dilapidated

**ruiseñor** (rwee-say-*ñoar* ) *m* nightingale

**ruleta** (roo-*lay*-tah ) *f* roulette

**rulo** (*roo*-loa ) *m* curler

**Rumania** (roo-*mah*-n<sup>y</sup>ah ) *f* Rumania

**rumano** (roo-*mah*-noa ) *adj* Rumanian; *m* Rumanian

**rumbo** (*room*-boa ) *m* course

**rumor** (roo-*moar* ) *m* rumour

**rural** (roo-*rahl* ) *adj* rural

**Rusia** (*roo*-s<sup>y</sup>ah ) *f* Russia

**ruso** (*roo*-soa ) *adj* Russian; *m* Russian

**rústico** (*rooss*-tee-koa ) *adj* rustic

**ruta** (*roo*-tah ) *f* route; ~ **principal**
thoroughfare

**rutina** (roo-*tee*-nah ) *f* routine

# S

**sábado** (*sah*-bhah-dhoa ) *m* Saturday

**sábana** (*sah*-bhah-nah ) *f* sheet

**sabañón** (sah-bhah-*ñoan* ) *m* chilblain

***saber** (sah-*bhayr* ) *v* *know; *be able
to; **a** ~ namely; ~ **a** taste

**sabiduría** (sah-bhee-dhoo-*ree*-ah ) *f* wisdom

**sabio** (*sah*-bh<sup>y</sup>oa ) *adj* wise

**sabor** (sah-*bhoar* ) *m* flavour

**sabroso** (sah-*bhroa*-soa ) *adj* savoury,
tasty

**sacacorchos** (sah-kah-*koar*-choass )
*mpl* corkscrew

**sacapuntas** (sah-kah-*poon*-tahss ) *m*
pencil-sharpener

**sacar** (sah-*kahr* ) *v* *take out; *draw;
~ **brillo** brush

**sacarina** (sah-kah-*ree*-nah ) *f* saccharin

**sacerdote** (sah-thayr-*dhoa*-tay ) *m*
priest

**saco** (*sah*-koa ) *m* sack; *mMe* jacket;
~ **de compras** shopping bag; ~ **de
dormir** sleeping-bag

**sacrificar** (sah-kree-fee-*kahr* ) *v* sacrifice

**sacrificio** (sah-kree-*fee*-th<sup>y</sup>oa ) *m* sacrifice

**sacrilegio** (sah-kree-*lay*-kh<sup>y</sup>oa ) *m* sacrilege

**sacristán** (sah-kreess-*tahn* ) *m* sexton

**sacudir** (sah-koo-*dheer* ) *v* *shake

**sagrado** (sah-*grah*-dhoa ) *adj* sacred

**sainete** (sigh-*nay*-tay ) *m* farce

**sal** (sahl ) *f* salt; **sales de baño** bath
salts

**sala** (*sah*-lah ) *f* hall; ~ **de conciertos**
concert hall; ~ **de espera** waiting-
room; ~ **de estar** sitting-room, liv-

ing-room; ~ **de lectura** reading-room; ~ **para fumar** smoking-room

**salado** (sah-*lah*-dhoa) *adj* salty

**salario** (sah-*lah*-r<sup>y</sup>oa) *m* pay

**salchicha** (sahl-*chee*-chah) *f* sausage

**saldo** (*sahl*-doa) *m* balance

**salero** (sah-*lay*-roa) *m* salt-cellar

**salida** (sah-*lee*-dhah) *f* issue, exit, way out; ~ **de emergencia** emergency exit

*__salir__ (sah-*leer*) *v* *go out; appear

**saliva** (sah-*lee*-bhah) *f* spit

**salmón** (sahl-*moan*) *m* salmon

**salón** (sah-*loan*) *m* salon, lounge, drawing-room; ~ **de baile** ball-room; ~ **de belleza** beauty parlour; ~ **de demostraciones** showroom; ~ **de té** tea-shop

**salpicadera** (sahl-pee-kah-*dhay*-rah) *fMe* mud-guard

**salpicar** (sahl-pee-*kahr*) *v* splash

**salsa** (*sahl*-sah) *f* sauce; gravy

**saltamontes** (sahl-tah-*moan*-tayss) *m* grasshopper

**saltar** (sahl-*tahr*) *v* jump, *leap; skip

**salto** (*sahl*-toa) *m* jump, leap, hop

**salud** (sah-*loodh*) *f* health

**saludable** (sah-loo-*dhah*-bhlay) *adj* wholesome

**saludar** (sah-loo-*dhahr*) *v* greet; salute

**saludo** (sah-*loo*-dhoa) *m* greeting

**salvador** (sahl-bhah-*dhoar*) *m* saviour

**salvaje** (sahl-*bhah*-khay) *adj* wild, savage; fierce, desert

**salvar** (sahl-*bhahr*) *v* save

**sanatorio** (sah-nah-*toa*-r<sup>y</sup>oa) *m* sanatorium

**sandalia** (sahn-*dah*-l<sup>y</sup>ah) *f* sandal; **sandalias de gimnasia** gym shoes

**sandía** (sahn-*dee*-ah) *f* watermelon

**sangrar** (sahng-*grahr*) *v* *bleed

**sangre** (*sahng*-gray) *f* blood

**sangriento** (sahng-gr<sup>y</sup>ayn-toa) *adj* bloody

**sanitario** (sah-nee-*tah*-r<sup>y</sup>oa) *adj* sanitary

**sano** (*sah*-noa) *adj* healthy, well

**santo** (*sahn*-toa) *adj* holy; *m* saint; ~ **y seña** password

**santuario** (sahn-*twah*-r<sup>y</sup>oa) *m* shrine

**sapo** (*sah*-poa) *m* toad

**sarampión** (sah-rahm-*p<sup>y</sup>oan*) *m* measles

**sardina** (sahr-*dhee*-nah) *f* sardine

**sartén** (sahr-*tayn*) *f* pan; frying-pan

**sastre** (*sahss*-tray) *m* tailor

**satélite** (sah-*tay*-lee-tay) *m* satellite

**satisfacción** (sah-teess-fahk-*th<sup>y</sup>oan*) *f* satisfaction

*__satisfacer__ (sah-teess-fah-*thayr*) *v* satisfy; **satisfecho** satisfied

**saudí** (sou-*dhee*) *adj* Saudi Arabian

**sauna** (*sou*-nah) *f* sauna

**sazonar** (sah-thoa-*nahr*) *v* flavour

**se** (*say*) *pron* himself; herself; yourselves; themselves

**secadora** (say-kah-dhoa-rah) *f* dryer

**secar** (say-*kahr*) *v* dry

**sección** (sayk-*th<sup>y</sup>oan*) *f* section; agency

**seco** (*say*-koa) *adj* dry

**secretaria** (say-kray-*tah*-r<sup>y</sup>ah) *f* secretary

**secretario** (say-kray-*tah*-r<sup>y</sup>oa) *m* secretary; clerk

**secreto** (say-*kray*-toa) *adj* secret; *m* secret

**sector** (sayk-*toar*) *m* sector

**secuencia** (say-*kwayn*-th<sup>y</sup>ah) *f* shot

**secuestrador** (say-kwayss-trah-*dhoar*) *m* hijacker

**secundario** (say-koon-*dah*-r<sup>y</sup>oa) *adj* secondary; minor

**sed** (*saydh*) *f* thirst

**seda** (*say*-dhah) *f* silk

**sede** (*say*-dhay) *f* seat

**sediento** (say-*dh<sup>y</sup>ayn*-toa) *adj* thirsty

**sedoso** (say-*dhoa*-soa) *adj* silken

**\* seducir** (say-dhoo-*theer*) v seduce

**en seguida** (ayn say-*gee*-dhah) straight away, at once, presently

**\* seguir** (say-*geer*) v follow; **~ el paso** \*keep up with; **todo seguido** straight on, straight ahead

**según** (say-*goon*) prep according to

**segundo** (say-*goon*-doa) num second; m second

**seguramente** (say-goo-rah-*mayn*-tay) adv surely

**seguridad** (say-goo-ree-*dhahdh*) f security, safety; **cinturón de ~** safety-belt

**seguro** (say-*goo*-roa) adj safe; sure; m insurance; **póliza de ~** insurance policy; **~ de viaje** travel insurance; **~ de vida** life insurance

**seis** (sayss) num six

**selección** (say-layk-th<sup>y</sup>oan) f selection; choice

**seleccionado** (say-layk-th<sup>y</sup>oa-nah-dhoa) adj select

**seleccionar** (say-layk-th<sup>y</sup>oa-nahr) v select

**selecto** (say-*layk*-toa) adj select

**selva** (*sayl*-bhah) f jungle, forest

**selvoso** (sayl-*bhoa*-soa) adj wooded

**sellar** (say-*l<sup>y</sup>ahr*) v stamp

**sello** (say-*l<sup>y</sup>oa*) m stamp; seal

**semáforo** (say-*mah*-foa-roa) m traffic light

**semana** (say-*mah*-nah) f week; **fin de ~** weekend

**semanal** (say-mah-*nahl*) adj weekly

**\* sembrar** (saym-*brahr*) v \*sow

**semejante** (say-may-*khahn*-tay) adj like

**semejanza** (say-may-*khahn*-thah) f resemblance, similarity

**semi-** (*say*-mee) semi-

**semicírculo** (say-mee-*theer*-koo-loa) m semicircle

**semilla** (say-*mee*-l<sup>y</sup>ah) f seed

**senado** (say-*nah*-dhoa) m senate

**senador** (say-nah-*dhoar*) m senator

**sencillo** (sayn-*thee*-l<sup>y</sup>oa) adj plain

**senda** (*sayn*-dah) f footpath

**sendero** (sayn-*day*-roa) m trail

**senil** (say-*neel*) adj senile

**seno** (*say*-noa) m bosom; breast

**sensación** (sayn-sah-th<sup>y</sup>oan) f sensation; feeling

**sensacional** (sayn-sah-th<sup>y</sup>oa-*nahl*) adj sensational

**sensato** (sayn-*sah*-toa) adj sensible; down-to-earth

**sensibilidad** (sayn-see-bhee-lee-*dhahdh*) f sensibility

**sensible** (sayn-*see*-bhlay) adj sensitive; perceptible

**sensitivo** (sayn-see-*tee*-bhoa) adj sensitive

**\* sentarse** (sayn-*tahr*-say) v \*sit down; **\* estar sentado** \*sit; **\* sentar bien** \*become

**sentencia** (sayn-*tayn*-th<sup>y</sup>ah) f sentence, verdict

**sentenciar** (sayn-tayn-th<sup>y</sup>ahr) v sentence

**sentido** (sayn-*tee*-dhoa) m sense; reason; **~ del honor** sense of honour; **sin ~** meaningless

**sentimental** (sayn-tee-mayn-*tahl*) adj sentimental

**sentimiento** (sayn-tee-*m<sup>y</sup>ayn*-toa) m sentiment

**\* sentir** (sayn-*teer*) v \*feel, sense; regret

**seña** (*say*-ñah) f sign; **señas personales** description

**señal** (say-*ñahl*) f signal, sign, indication; m token, tick; **\* hacer señales** signal; wave; **~ de alarma** distress signal

**señalar** (say-ñah-*lahr*) v tick off, indicate

**señor** (say-*ñoar*) m mister; sir

**señora** (say-ñoa-rah) *f* lady; mistress; madam

**señorita** (say-ñoa-*ree*-tah) *f* miss

**separación** (say-pah-rah-th<sup>y</sup>oan) *f* division

**separadamente** (say-pah-rah-dhah-*mayn*-tay) *adv* apart

**separado** (say-pah-*rah*-dhoa) *adj* separate; **por** ~ apart, separately

**separar** (say-pah-*rahr*) *v* separate, part; divide; detach

**septentrional** (sayp-tayn-tr<sup>y</sup>oa-*nahl*) *adj* north

**septicemia** (sayp-tee-*thay*-m<sup>y</sup>ah) *f* blood-poisoning

**séptico** (*sayp*-tee-koa) *adj* septic

**septiembre** (sayp-*t<sup>y</sup>aym*-bray) September

**séptimo** (*sayp*-tee-moa) *num* seventh

**sepulcro** (say-*pool*-kroa) *m* sepulchre

**sepultura** (say-pool-*too*-rah) *f* grave

**sequía** (say-*kee*-ah) *f* drought

**ser** (sayr) *m* being, creature; ~ **humano** human being

\***ser** (sayr) *v* \*be

**sereno** (say-*ray*-noa) *adj* serene

**serie** (*say*-r<sup>y</sup>ay) *f* series; sequence

**seriedad** (say-r<sup>y</sup>ay-*dhahdh*) *f* seriousness, gravity

**serio** (*say*-r<sup>y</sup>oa) *adj* serious

**sermón** (sayr-*moan*) *m* sermon

**serpentear** (sayr-payn-tay-*ahr*) *v* \*wind

**serrín** (say-*rreen*) *m* sawdust

**servicial** (sayr-bhee-*th<sup>y</sup>ahl*) *adj* helpful

**servicio** (sayr-bhee-th<sup>y</sup>oa) *m* service; service charge; ~ **de habitación** room service; ~ **de mesa** dinner-service; ~ **postal** postal service

**servilleta** (sayr-bhee-*l<sup>y</sup>ay*-tah) *f* napkin, serviette; ~ **de papel** paper napkin

\***servir** (sayr-*bheer*) *v* serve; attend on, wait on; \*be of use

**sesenta** (say-*sayn*-tah) *num* sixty

**sesión** (say-*s<sup>y</sup>oan*) *f* session

**seta** (*say*-tah) *f* mushroom

**setenta** (say-*tayn*-tah) *num* seventy

**seto** (*say*-toa) *m* hedge

**severo** (say-*bhay*-roa) *adj* harsh, strict, severe

**sexo** (*sayk*-soa) *m* sex

**sexto** (*sayks*-toa) *num* sixth

**sexual** (sayk-*swahl*) *adj* sexual

**sexualidad** (sayk-swah-lee-*dhahdh*) *f* sexuality; sex

**si** (see) *conj* if; in case; whether; **si ... o** whether ... or; ~ **bien** though

**sí** (see) yes

**Siam** (s<sup>y</sup>ahm) *m* Siam

**siamés** (s<sup>y</sup>ah-*mayss*) *adj* Siamese; *m* Siamese

**siempre** (*s<sup>y</sup>aym*-pray) *adv* ever, always

**sien** (s<sup>y</sup>ayn) *f* temple

**sierra** (*s<sup>y</sup>ay*-rrah) *f* saw

**siesta** (*s<sup>y</sup>ayss*-tah) *f* nap

**siete** (*s<sup>y</sup>ay*-tay) *num* seven

**sifón** (see-*foan*) *m* siphon, syphon

**siglo** (*see*-gloa) *m* century

**significado** (seeg-nee-fee-*kah*-dhoa) *m* meaning

**significar** (seeg-nee-fee-*kahr*) *v* \*mean

**significativo** (seeg-nee-fee-kah-*tee*-bhoa) *adj* significant

**signo** (*seeg*-noa) *m* sign; ~ **de interrogación** question mark

**siguiente** (see-*g<sup>y</sup>ayn*-tay) *adj* following

**sílaba** (*see*-lah-bhah) *f* syllable

**silbar** (seel-*bhahr*) *v* whistle

**silbato** (seel-*bhah*-toa) *m* whistle

**silenciador** (see-layn-th<sup>y</sup>ah-*dhoar*) *m* silencer

**silencio** (see-*layn*-th<sup>y</sup>oa) *m* stillness, quiet, silence

**silencioso** (see-layn-*th<sup>y</sup>oa*-soa) *adj* silent

**silla** (*see*-l<sup>y</sup>ah) *f* chair; saddle; ~ **de ruedas** wheelchair; ~ **de tijera**

deck chair

**sillón** (see-*l*Yoan) *m* armchair

**simbólico** (seem-*boa*-lee-koa) *adj* symbolic

**símbolo** (*seem*-boa-loa) *m* symbol

**similar** (see-mee-*lahr*) *adj* similar

**simpatía** (seem-pah-*tee*-ah) *f* sympathy

**simpático** (seem-*pah*-tee-koa) *adj* nice, pleasant; obliging

**simple** (*seem*-play) *adj* simple

**simular** (see-moo-*lahr*) *v* simulate

**simultáneo** (see-mool-*tah*-nay-oa) *adj* simultaneous

**sin** (seen) *prep* without

**sinagoga** (see-nah-*goa*-gah) *f* synagogue

**sincero** (seen-*thay*-roa) *adj* sincere; open, honest

**sindicato** (seen-dee-*kah*-toa) *m* trade-union

**sinfonía** (seen-foa-*nee*-ah) *f* symphony

**singular** (seeng-goo-*lahr*) *adj* singular, queer; *m* singular

**siniestro** (see-n*Y*ayss-troa) *adj* ominous, sinister

**sino** (*see*-noa) *conj* but

**sinónimo** (see-*noa*-nee-moa) *m* synonym

**sintético** (seen-*tay*-tee-koa) *adj* synthetic

**síntoma** (*seen*-toa-mah) *m* symptom

**sintonizar** (seen-toa-nee-*thahr*) *v* tune in

**siquiera** (see-k*Y*ay-rah) *adv* at least; *conj* even though

**sirena** (see-*ray*-nah) *f* siren; mermaid

**Siria** (*see*-r*Y*ah) *f* Syria

**sirio** (*see*-r*Y*oa) *adj* Syrian; *m* Syrian

**sirviente** (seer-*bh*Yayn-tay) *m* domestic; boy

**sistema** (seess-*tay*-mah) *m* system; ~ **decimal** decimal system; ~ **de lubricación** lubrication system; ~ **de**

**refrigeración** cooling system

**sistemático** (seess-tay-*mah*-tee-koa) *adj* systematic

**sitio** (*see*-tYoa) *m* site; seat, room; siege

**situación** (see-twah-*th*Yoan) *f* situation

**situado** (see-*twah*-dhoa) *adj* situated

**situar** (see-*twahr*) *v* locate

**slogan** (*sloa*-gahn) *m* slogan

**smoking** (*smoa*-keeng) *m* dinner-jacket; tuxedo *nAm*

**soberano** (soa-bhay-*rah*-noa) *m* sovereign

**soberbio** (soa-*bhayr*-bhYoa) *adj* superb

**sobornar** (soa-bhoar-*nahr*) *v* bribe

**soborno** (soa-*bhoar*-noa) *m* bribery

**sobra** (soa-*bhrah*) *f* surplus

**sobrar** (soa-*bhrahr*) *v* *be left over; *be in plenty

**sobre** (soa-*bhray*) *prep* on, upon; *m* envelope

**sobrecubierta** (soa-bhray-koo-*bh*Yayr-tah) *f* jacket

**sobreexcitado** (soa-bhray-ayk-thee-*tah*-dhoa) *adj* overstrung

**sobrepeso** (soa-bhray-*pay*-soa) *m* overweight

**sobretasa** (soa-bhray-*tah*-sah) *f* surcharge

**sobretodo** (soa-bhray-*toa*-dhoa) *m* coat, topcoat

**sobrevivir** (soa-bhray-bhee-*bheer*) *v* survive

**sobrina** (soa-*bhree*-nah) *f* niece

**sobrino** (soa-*bhree*-noa) *m* nephew

**sobrio** (*soa*-bhrYoa) *adj* sober

**social** (soa-*th*Yahl) *adj* social

**socialismo** (soa-thYah-*leez*-moa) *m* socialism

**socialista** (soa-thYah-*leess*-tah) *adj* socialist; *m* socialist

**sociedad** (soa-thYay-*dhahdh*) *f* community, society; company

**socio** (*soa*-thYoa) *m* associate; partner

**socorro** (soa-*koa*-rroa) *m* aid; **puesto de ~** first-aid post

**soda** (*soa*-dhah) *f* soda-water

**sofá** (soa-*fah*) *m* sofa

**sofocante** (soa-foa-*kahn*-tay) *adj* stuffy

**sofocarse** (soa-foa-*kahr*-say) *v* choke

**soga** (*soa*-gah) *f* rope

**sol** (soal) *m* sun; **tomar el ~** sunbathe

**solamente** (soa-lah-*mayn*-tay) *adv* merely, only

**solapa** (soa-*lah*-pah) *f* lapel

**soldado** (soal-*dah*-dhoa) *m* soldier

**soldador** (soal-dah-*dhoar*) *m* soldering-iron

**soldadura** (soal-dah-*dhoo*-rah) *f* joint

\***soldar** (soal-*dahr*) *v* solder; weld

**soleado** (soa-lay-ah-dhoa) *adj* sunny

**soledad** (soa-lay-*dhahdh*) *f* solitude

**solemne** (soa-*laym*-nay) *adj* solemn

\***soler** (soa-*layr*) *v* would

**solicitar** (soa-lee-thee-*tahr*) *v* request; **~ un puesto** apply

**solicitud** (soa-lee-thee-*toodh*) *f* application

**sólido** (*soa*-lee-dhoa) *adj* solid, firm; *m* solid

**solitario** (soa-lee-tah-r<sup>y</sup>oa) *adj* lonely

**solo** (*soa*-loa) *adj* only, single

**sólo** (*soa*-loa) *adv* alone; only

\***soltar** (soal-*tahr*) *v* loosen

**soltero** (soal-*tay*-roa) *adj* single; *m* bachelor

**solterona** (soal-tay-*roa*-nah) *f* spinster

**soluble** (soa-*loo*-bhlay) *adj* soluble

**solución** (soa-loo-th<sup>y</sup>oan) *f* solution

**sombra** (*soam*-brah) *f* shade; shadow; **~ para los ojos** eye-shadow

**sombreado** (soam-bray-*ah*-dhoa) *adj* shady

**sombrerera** (soam-bray-*ray*-rah) *f* milliner

**sombrero** (soam-*bray*-roa) *m* hat

**sombrío** (soam-*bree*-oa) *adj* sombre, gloomy

**someter** (soa-may-*tayr*) *v* subject; **someterse** *v* submit

**somnífero** (soam-*nee*-fay-roa) *m* sleeping-pill

\***sonar** (soa-*nahr*) *v* sound; \*ring

**sonido** (soa-*nee*-dhoa) *m* sound

**sonreír** (soan-ray-*eer*) *v* smile

**sonrisa** (soan-*ree*-sah) *f* smile

\***soñar** (soa-*ñahr*) *v* \*dream

**soñoliento** (soa-ñoa-l<sup>y</sup>ayn-toa) *adj* sleepy

**sopa** (*soa*-pah) *f* soup

**soplar** (soa-*plahr*) *v* \*blow

**soportar** (soa-poar-*tahr*) *v* \*bear, endure, sustain; support

**sóquet** (*soa*-kayt) *mMe* socket

**sorbo** (*soar*-bhoa) *m* sip

**sórdido** (*soar*-dhee-dhoa) *adj* filthy

**sordo** (*soar*-dhoa) *adj* deaf

**sorprender** (soar-prayn-*dayr*) *v* surprise; \*catch

**sorpresa** (soar-*pray*-sah) *f* surprise; astonishment

**sorteo** (soar-*tay*-oa) *m* draw

**sosegado** (soa-say-*gah*-dhoa) *adj* sedate

**sospecha** (soass-*pay*-chah) *f* suspicion

**sospechar** (soass-pay-*chahr*) *v* suspect

**sospechoso** (soass-pay-*choa*-soa) *adj* suspicious; **persona sospechosa** suspect

**sostén** (soass-*tayn*) *m* brassiere, bra

\***sostener** (soass-tay-*nayr*) *v* support, \*hold up

**sota** (*soa*-tah) *f* knave

**sótano** (*soa*-tah-noa) *m* basement; cellar

**soto** (*soa*-toa) *m* grove

**soviético** (soa-bh<sup>y</sup>ay-tee-koa) *adj* Soviet

**starter** (*stahr*-tayr) *m* choke

**su** (soo) *adj* his; her; their

**suahili** (swah-*ee*-lee) *m* Swahili

**suave** (*swah*-bhay) *adj* mild, mellow; gentle

**subacuático** (soo-bhah-*kwah*-tee-koa) *adj* underwater

**subalterno** (soo-bhahl-*tayr*-noa) *adj* subordinate

**subasta** (soo-*bhahss*-tah) *f* auction

**súbdito** (*soobh*-dhee-toa) *m* subject

**subestimar** (soo-bhayss-tee-*mahr*) *v* underestimate

**subida** (soo-*bhee*-dhah) *f* climb, rise, ascent

**subir** (soo-*bheer*) *v* *rise, ascend; *get on

**súbito** (*soo*-bhee-toa) *adj* sudden

**sublevación** (soo-bhlay-bhah-*th<sup>y</sup>oan*) *f* rebellion

**sublevarse** (soo-bhlay-*bhahr*-say) *v* revolt

**subordinado** (soo-bhoar-dhee-*nah*-dhoa) *adj* subordinate

**subrayar** (soobh-rah-*<sup>y</sup>ahr*) *v* underline

**subsidio** (soobh-*see*-dh<sup>y</sup>oa) *m* subsidy

**substancia** (soobhs-*tahn*-th<sup>y</sup>ah) *f* substance

**substantivo** (soobh-stahn-*tee*-bhoa) *m* noun

***substituir** (soobhs-tee-*tweer*) *v* replace

**subterráneo** (soobh-tay-*rrah*-nay-oa) *adj* underground

**subtítulo** (soobh-*tee*-too-loa) *m* subtitle

**suburbano** (soo-bhoor-*bhah*-noa) *adj* suburban; *m* commuter

**suburbio** (soo-*bhoor*-bh<sup>y</sup>oa) *m* suburb

**subvención** (soobh-bhayn-*th<sup>y</sup>oan*) *f* grant

**subyugar** (soobh-<sup>y</sup>oo-*gahr*) *v* overwhelm

**suceder** (soo-thay-*dhayr*) *v* happen, occur; succeed

**sucesión** (soo-thay-*s<sup>y</sup>oan*) *f* sequence

**suceso** (soo-*thay*-soa) *m* event

**suciedad** (soo-th<sup>y</sup>ay-*dhahdh*) *f* dirt; muck

**sucio** (*soo*-th<sup>y</sup>oa) *adj* dirty; unclean, foul

**sucumbir** (soo-koom-*beer*) *v* succumb

**sucursal** (soo-koor-*sahl*) *f* branch

**sudar** (soo-*dhahr*) *v* perspire, sweat

**sudeste** (soo-*dhayss*-tay) *m* south-east

**sudoeste** (soo-dhoa-*ayss*-tay) *m* south-west

**sudor** (soo-*dhoar*) *m* perspiration, sweat

**Suecia** (*sway*-th<sup>y</sup>ah) *f* Sweden

**sueco** (*sway*-koa) *adj* Swedish; *m* Swede

**suegra** (*sway*-grah) *f* mother-in-law

**suegro** (*sway*-groa) *m* father-in-law

**suela** (*sway*-lah) *f* sole

**sueldo** (*swayl*-doa) *m* salary, pay; **aumento de** ~ rise; raise *nAm*

**suelo** (*sway*-loa) *m* soil, earth; floor

**suelto** (*swayl*-toa) *adj* loose

**sueño** (*sway*-ñoa) *m* sleep; dream

**suero** (*sway*-roa) *m* serum

**suerte** (*swayr*-tay) *f* luck; fortune, lot; chance; **mala** ~ bad luck

**suéter** (*sway*-tayr) *m* sweater

**suficiente** (soo-fee-*th<sup>y</sup>ayn*-tay) *adj* enough, sufficient; *ser ~ *do

**sufragio** (soo-*frah*-kh<sup>y</sup>oa) *m* suffrage

**sufrimiento** (soo-free-*m<sup>y</sup>ayn*-toa) *m* affliction, sorrow, suffering

**sufrir** (soo-*freer*) *v* suffer

***sugerir** (soo-khay-*reer*) *v* suggest

**sugestión** (soo-khayss-*t<sup>y</sup>oan*) *f* suggestion

**suicidio** (swee-*thee*-dh<sup>y</sup>oa) *m* suicide

**Suiza** (*swee*-thah) *f* Switzerland

**suizo** (*swee*-thoa) *adj* Swiss; *m* Swiss

**sujetador** (soo-khay-tah-*dhoar*) *m* brassiere, bra

**sujeto** (soo-*khay*-toa) *m* subject; theme

**sujeto a** (soo-*khay*-toa ah) liable to,

subject to

**suma** (*soo-mah*) *f* amount, sum

**sumar** (soo-*mahr*) *v* add; amount to

**sumario** (soo-*mah*-r<sup>y</sup>oa) *m* summary

**suministrar** (soo-mee-neess-*trahr*) *v* furnish, supply

**suministro** (soo-mee-*neess*-troa) *m* supply

**a lo sumo** (*soo*-moa) at most

**superar** (soo-pay-*rahr*) *v* exceed, \*outdo

**superficial** (soo-payr-fee-th<sup>y</sup>*ahl*) *adj* superficial

**superficie** (soo-payr-*fee*-th<sup>y</sup>ay) *f* surface; area

**superfluo** (soo-*payr*-flwoa) *adj* superfluous, redundant

**superior** (soo-pay-r<sup>y</sup>*oar*) *adj* superior, upper; top

**superlativo** (soo-payr-lah-*tee*-bhoa) *adj* superlative; *m* superlative

**supermercado** (soo-payr-mayr-*kah*-dhoa) *m* supermarket

**superstición** (soo-payrs-tee-th<sup>y</sup>*oan*) *f* superstition

**supervisar** (soo-payr-bhee-*sahr*) *v* supervise

**supervisión** (soo-payr-bhee-s<sup>y</sup>*oan*) *f* supervision

**supervisor** (soo-payr-bhee-*soar*) *m* supervisor

**supervivencia** (soo-payr-bhee-*bhayn*-th<sup>y</sup>ah) *f* survival

**suplemento** (soo-play-*mayn*-toa) *m* supplement

**suplicar** (soo-plee-*kahr*) *v* beg

\***suponer** (soo-poa-*nayr*) *v* assume, suppose

**supositorio** (soo-poa-see-*toa*-r<sup>y</sup>oa) *m* suppository

**supremo** (soo-*pray*-moa) *adj* supreme

**suprimir** (soo-pree-*meer*) *v* discontinue

**por supuesto** (poar soo-*pwayss*-toa)

naturally, of course

**sur** (soor) *m* south; **polo ~** South Pole

**surco** (*soor*-koa) *m* groove

**surgir** (soor-*kheer*) *v* \*arise

**surtido** (soor-*tee*-dhoa) *m* assortment

**suscribir** (sooss-kree-*bheer*) *v* sign

**suscripción** (sooss-kreep-th<sup>y</sup>*oan*) *f* subscription

**suscrito** (sooss-*kree*-toa) *m* undersigned

**suspender** (sooss-payn-*dayr*) *v* suspend; \***ser suspendido** fail

**suspensión** (sooss-payn-s<sup>y</sup>*oan*) *f* suspension

**suspicacia** (sooss-pee-*kah*-th<sup>y</sup>ah) *f* suspicion

**suspicaz** (sooss-pee-*kahth*) *adj* suspicious

**sustancia** (sooss-*tahn*-th<sup>y</sup>ah) *f* substance

**sustancial** (sooss-tahn-*th<sup>y</sup>ahl*) *adj* substantial

**sustento** (sooss-*tayn*-toa) *m* livelihood

\***sustituir** (sooss-tee-*tweer*) *v* substitute

**sustituto** (sooss-tee-*too*-toa) *m* deputy, substitute

**susto** (*sooss*-toa) *m* scare

**susurrar** (soo-soo-*rrahr*) *v* whisper

**susurro** (soo-*soo*-rroa) *m* whisper

**sutil** (soo-*teel*) *adj* subtle

**sutura** (soo-*too*-rah) *f* stitch; \***hacer una ~** sew up

**suyo** (*soo*-<sup>y</sup>oa) *pron* his

# T

**tabaco** (tah-*bhah*-koa) *m* tobacco; **~ de pipa** pipe tobacco

**taberna** (tah-*bhayr*-nah) *f* public house, pub; tavern; **moza de ~**

barmaid

**tabique** (tah-*bhee*-kay) m partition

**tabla** (*tah*-bhlah) f board; chart, table; ~ **de conversión** conversion chart; ~ **para surf** surf-board

**tablero** (tah-*bhlay*-roa) m board; ~ **de ajedrez** checkerboard nAm; ~ **de damas** draught-board; ~ **de instrumentos** dashboard

**tablón** (tah-*bhloan*) m plank

**tabú** (tah-*bhoo*) m taboo

**tacón** (tah-*koan*) m heel

**táctica** (*tahk*-tee-kah) f tactics pl

**tacto** (*tahk*-toa) m touch

**tailandés** (tigh-lahn-*dayss*) adj Thai; m Thai

**Tailandia** (tigh-*lahn*-dYah) f Thailand

**tajada** (tah-*khah*-dhah) f slice

**tajar** (tah-*khahr*) v chop

**tal** (tahl) adj such; **con ~ que** provided that; ~ **como** such as

**taladrar** (tah-lah-*dhrahr*) v drill, bore

**taladro** (tah-*lah*-dhroa) m drill

**talco** (*tahl*-koa) m talc powder

**talento** (tah-*layn*-toa) m gift, talent

**talentoso** (tah-layn-*toa*-soa) adj gifted

**talismán** (tah-leez-*mahn*) m lucky charm

**talón** (tah-*loan*) m heel; counterfoil, stub

**talonario** (tah-loa-*nah*-rYoa) m chequebook; check-book nAm

**talla** (*tah*-lYah) f wood-carving, carving

**tallar** (tah-*lYahr*) v carve

**taller** (tah-*lYayr*) m workshop

**tallo** (*tah*-lYoa) m stem

**tamaño** (tah-*mah*-ñoa) m size; ~ **extraordinario** outsize

**también** (tahm-*bYayn*) adv too, also, as well; **así ~** likewise

**tambor** (tahm-*boar*) m drum; ~ **del freno** brake drum

**tamiz** (tah-*meeth*) m sieve

**tamizar** (tah-mee-*thahr*) v sift, sieve

**tampoco** (tahm-*poa*-koa) adv not … either

**tan** (tahn) adv so, such

**tangible** (tahng-*khee*-bhlay) adj tangible

**tanque** (*tahng*-kay) m tank

**tanteo** (tahn-*tay*-oa) m score

**tanto** (*tahn*-toa) adv as much; as; **por lo ~** therefore; **por ~** so; **tanto … como** both … and

**tapa** (*tah*-pah) f lid, top, cover; appetizer

**tapiz** (tah-*peeth*) m tapestry

**tapizar** (tah-pee-*thahr*) v upholster

**tapón** (tah-*poan*) m stopper, cork; tampon

**taquigrafía** (tah-kee-grah-*fee*-ah) f shorthand

**taquígrafo** (tah-*kee*-grah-foa) m stenographer

**taquilla** (tah-*kee*-lYah) f box-office

**tararear** (tah-rah-ray-*ahr*) v hum

**tardanza** (tahr-*dhahn*-thah) f delay

**tarde** (*tahr*-dhay) f afternoon; evening

**tardío** (tahr-*dhee*-oa) adj late

**tarea** (tah-*ray*-ah) f duty, task; job

**tarifa** (tah-*ree*-fah) f rate; ~ **nocturna** night rate

**tarjeta** (tahr-*khay*-tah) f card; ~ **de crédito** credit card; charge plate Am; ~ **de temporada** season-ticket; ~ **de visita** visiting-card; ~ **postal** postcard, card; ~ **postal ilustrada** picture postcard; ~ **verde** green card

**tarta** (*tahr*-tah) f cake

**taxi** (*tahk*-see) m cab, taxi

**taxímetro** (tahk-*see*-may-troa) m taximeter

**taxista** (tahk-*seess*-tah) m cab-driver, taxi-driver

**taza** (*tah*-thah) f cup; mug; ~ **de té** teacup

**tazón** (tah-*thoan*) m bowl, basin

**te** (tay) *pron* yourself

**té** (tay) m tea

**teatro** (tay-ah-troa) m drama; theatre; ~ **de la ópera** opera house; ~ **de variedades** music-hall, variety theatre; ~ **guiñol** puppet-show

**tebeo** (tay-*bhay*-oa) m comics pl

**técnica** (*tayk*-nee-kah) f technique

**técnico** (*tayk*-nee-koa) adj technical; m technician

**tecnología** (tayk-noa-loa-*khee*-ah) f technology

**techo** (*tay*-choa) m roof; ~ **de paja** thatched roof

**teja** (*tay*-khah) f tile

**tejedor** (tay-khay-*dhoar*) m weaver

**tejer** (tay-*khayr*) v *weave

**tejido** (tay-*khee*-dhoa) m fabric, tissue, material

**tela** (*tay*-lah) f cloth; ~ **para toallas** towelling

**telaraña** (tay-lah-*rah*-ñah) f spider's web

**telefonear** (tay-lay-foa-nay-*ahr*) v phone; call up Am

**telefonista** (tay-lay-foa-*neess*-tah) f telephonist, telephone operator

**teléfono** (tay-*lay*-foa-noa) m phone, telephone; **llamar por** ~ ring up

**telegrafiar** (tay-lay-grah-*fYahr*) v telegraph

**telegrama** (tay-lay-*grah*-mah) m telegram

**telémetro** (tay-*lay*-may-troa) m range-finder

**teleobjetivo** (tay-lay-oabh-khay-*tee*-bhoa) m telephoto lens

**telepatía** (tay-lay-pah-*tee*-ah) f telepathy

**telesilla** (tay-lay-*see*-lYah) m ski-lift

**televisión** (tay-lay-bhee-*sYoan*) f television

**televisor** (tay-lay-bhee-*soar*) m television set

**télex** (*tay*-layks) m telex

**telón** (tay-*loan*) m curtain

**tema** (*tay*-mah) m theme

***temblar** (taym-*bhlahr*) v tremble, shiver

**temer** (tay-*mayr*) v fear, dread

**temor** (tay-*moar*) m fear, dread

**temperamento** (taym-pay-rah-*mayn*-toa) m temperament

**temperatura** (taym-pay-rah-*too*-rah) f temperature; ~ **ambiente** room temperature

**tempestad** (taym-payss-*tahdh*) f tempest

**tempestuoso** (taym-payss-*twoa*-soa) adj stormy

**templo** (*taym*-ploa) m temple

**temporada** (taym-poa-*rah*-dhah) f season; **apogeo de la** ~ high season; ~ **baja** low season

**temporal** (taym-poa-*rahl*) adj temporary

**temprano** (taym-*prah*-noa) adj early

**tenazas** (tay-*nah*-thahss) f tongs pl, pincers pl

**tendencia** (tayn-*dayn*-thYah) f tendency

***tender a** (tayn-*dayr*) tend; ***tenderse** v *lie down

**tendero** (tayn-*day*-roa) m shopkeeper; tradesman

**tendón** (tayn-*doan*) m sinew, tendon

**tenedor** (tay-nay-*dhoar*) m fork

***tener** (tay-*nayr*) v *have; *keep, *hold; ~ **que** *must; *ought to, *should, *shall; *be obliged to; **tenga usted** here you are

**teniente** (tay-*nYayn*-tay) m lieutenant

**tenis** (*tay*-neess) m tennis; ~ **de mesa** ping-pong, table tennis

**tensión** (tayn-*sYoan*) f strain, pressure, tension; ~ **arterial** blood pressure

**tenso** (*tayn*-soa) adj tense

**tentación** (tayn-tah-*th*Yoan) *f* temptation

\*__tentar__ (tayn-*tahr*) *v* tempt

**tentativa** (tayn-tah-*tee*-bhah) *f* attempt, try

**tentempié** (tayn-taym-*p*Yay) *m* snack

\*__teñir__ (tay-*ñeer*) *v* dye

**teología** (tay-oa-loa-*khee*-ah) *f* theology

**teoría** (tay-oa-*ree*-ah) *f* theory

**teórico** (tay-*oa*-ree-koa) *adj* theoretical

**terapia** (tay-*rah*-pYah) *f* therapy

**tercero** (tayr-*thay*-roa) *num* third

**terciopelo** (tayr-thYoa-*pay*-loa) *m* velvet

**terilene** (tay-ree-*lay*-nay) *m* terylene

**terminación** (tayr-mee-nah-*th*Yoan) *f* finish

**terminar** (tayr-mee-*nahr*) *v* end, finish; accomplish; **terminarse** *v* expire, end

**término** (*tayr*-mee-noa) *m* term; issue

**termo** (*tayr*-moa) *m* vacuum flask, thermos flask

**termómetro** (tayr-*moa*-may-troa) *m* thermometer

**termostato** (tayr-moass-*tah*-toa) *m* thermostat

**ternero** (tayr-*nay*-roa) *m* calf

**ternura** (tayr-*noo*-rah) *f* tenderness

**terraplén** (tay-rrah-*playn*) *m* embankment

**terraza** (tay-*rrah*-thah) *f* terrace

**terremoto** (tay-rray-*moa*-toa) *m* earthquake

**terreno** (tay-*rray*-noa) *m* terrain; field, grounds

**terrible** (tay-*rree*-bhlay) *adj* frightful; awful, horrible, terrible, dreadful

**territorio** (tay-rree-*toa*-rYoa) *m* territory

**terrón** (tay-*rroan*) *m* lump

**terror** (tay-*rroar*) *m* terror; terrorism

**terrorismo** (tay-rroa-*reez*-moa) *m* terrorism

**terrorista** (tay-rroa-*reess*-tah) *m* terrorist

**tesis** (*tay*-seess) *f* thesis

**Tesorería** (tay-soa-ray-*ree*-ah) *f* treasury

**tesorero** (tay-soa-*ray*-roa) *m* treasurer

**tesoro** (tay-*soa*-roa) *m* treasure

**testamento** (tayss-tah-*mayn*-toa) *m* will

**testarudo** (tayss-tah-*roo*-dhoa) *adj* pigheaded, stubborn

**testigo** (tayss-*tee*-goa) *m* witness; ~ **de vista** eye-witness

**testimoniar** (tayss-tee-moa-*n*Yahr) *v* testify

**testimonio** (tayss-tee-*moa*-nYoa) *m* testimony

**tetera** (tay-*tay*-rah) *f* teapot

**textil** (tayks-*teel*) *m* textile

**texto** (*tayks*-toa) *m* text

**textura** (tayks-*too*-rah) *f* texture

**tez** (tayth) *f* complexion

**ti** (tee) *pron* you

**tía** (*tee*-ah) *f* aunt

**tibio** (*tee*-bhYoa) *adj* tepid, lukewarm

**tiburón** (tee-bhoo-*roan*) *m* shark

**tiempo** (*t*Yaym-poa) *m* time; weather; **a** ~ in time; ~ **libre** spare time

**tienda** (*t*Yayn-dah) *f* shop; tent

**tierno** (*t*Yayr-noa) *adj* gentle, tender

**tierra** (*t*Yay-rrah) *f* earth; ground, soil; land; **en** ~ ashore; ~ **baja** lowlands *pl*; ~ **firme** mainland

**tieso** (*t*Yay-soa) *adj* stiff

**tifus** (*tee*-fooss) *m* typhoid

**tigre** (*tee*-gray) *m* tiger

**tijeras** (tee-*khay*-rahss) *fpl* scissors *pl*; ~ **para las uñas** nail-scissors *pl*

**tilo** (*tee*-loa) *m* limetree, lime

**timbre** (*teem*-bray) *m* tone; bell; doorbell; *mMe* postage stamp

**timidez** (tee-mee-*dhayth*) *f* timidity, shyness

**tímido** (tee-mee-dhoa) *adj* timid, embarrassed, shy

**timón** (tee-*moan*) *m* helm, rudder

**timonel** (tee-moa-*nayl*) *m* steersman

**timonero** (tee-moa-*nay*-roa) *m* helmsman

**tímpano** (*teem*-pah-noa) *m* ear-drum

**tinta** (*teen*-tah) *f* ink

**tintorería** (teen-toa-ray-*ree*-ah) *f* dry-cleaner's

**tintura** (teen-*too*-rah) *f* dye

**tío** (*tee*-oa) *m* uncle

**típico** (*tee*-pee-koa) *adj* typical, characteristic

**tipo** (*tee*-poa) *m* type; fellow, guy

**tirada** (tee-*rah*-dhah) *f* issue

**tirano** (tee-*rah*-noa) *m* tyrant

**tirantes** (tee-*rahn*-tayss) *mpl* braces *pl*; suspenders *plAm*

**tirar** (tee-*rahr*) *v* pull; \*throw; \*shoot

**tiritar** (tee-ree-*tahr*) *v* shiver

**tiro** (*tee*-roa) *m* shot

**tirón** (tee-*roan*) *m* wrench

**titular** (tee-too-*lahr*) *m* headline

**título** (*tee*-too-loa) *m* heading, title; degree

**toalla** (toa-ah-l<sup>y</sup>ah) *f* towel; ~ **de baño** bath towel

**tobera** (toa-*bhay*-rah) *f* nozzle

**tobillo** (toa-*bhee*-l<sup>y</sup>oa) *m* ankle

**tobogán** (toa-bhoa-*gahn*) *m* slide

**tocadiscos** (toa-kah-*deess*-koass) *m* record-player

**tocador** (toa-kah-*dhoar*) *m* dressing-table; powder-room; **artículos de** ~ toiletry

**tocante a** (toa-*kahn*-tay ah) regarding

**tocar** (toa-*kahr*) *v* touch; \*hit; play; **no** ~ \*keep off

**tocino** (toa-*thee*-noa) *m* bacon

**todavía** (toa-dhah-*bhee*-ah) *adv* still, however

**todo** (*toa*-dhoa) *adj* all; entire; *pron* everything; **sobre** ~ most of all, essentially, especially; **todos** *pron* everybody

**toldo** (*toal*-doa) *m* awning

**tolerable** (toa-lay-*rah*-bhlay) *adj* tolerable

**tomar** (toa-*mahr*) *v* \*catch; \*take; ~ **el pelo** tease

**tomate** (toa-*mah*-tay) *m* tomato

**tomillo** (toa-*mee*-l<sup>y</sup>oa) *m* thyme

**tomo** (*toa*-moa) *m* volume

**tonada** (toa-*nah*-dhah) *f* tune

**tonel** (toa-*nayl*) *m* barrel, cask

**tonelada** (toa-nay-*lah*-dhah) *f* ton

**tónico** (*toa*-nee-koa) *m* tonic; ~ **para el cabello** hair tonic

**tono** (*toa*-noa) *m* tone; note; shade

**tontería** (toan-tay-*ree*-ah) *f* nonsense, rubbish; \***decir tonterías** talk rubbish

**tonto** (*toan*-toa) *adj* foolish; *m* fool

**topetar** (toa-pay-*tahr*) *v* bump

**topetón** (toa-pay-*toan*) *m* bump

**toque** (*toa*-kay) *m* touch

**torcedura** (toar-thay-*dhoo*-rah) *f* sprain

\***torcer** (toar-*thayr*) *v* twist; \***torcerse** *v* sprain

**tordo** (*toar*-dhoa) *m* thrush

**tormenta** (toar-*mayn*-tah) *f* storm

**tormento** (toar-*mayn*-toa) *m* torment

**tormentoso** (toar-mayn-*toa*-soa) *adj* thundery

**tornar** (toar-*nahr*) *v* return

**torneo** (toar-*nay*-oa) *m* tournament

**tornillo** (toar-*nee*-l<sup>y</sup>oa) *m* screw

**en torno** (ayn *toar*-noa) about, around

**en torno de** (ayn *toar*-noa day) round, around

**toro** (*toa*-roa) *m* bull

**toronja** (toa-*roan*-khah) *fMe* grapefruit

**torpe** (*toar*-pay) *adj* clumsy, awkward

**torre** (*toa*-rray) *f* tower

**torsión** (toar-s<sup>y</sup>oan) *f* twist

**tortilla** (toar-*tee*-l<sup>y</sup>ah) *f* omelette

**tortuga** (toar-*too*-gah) *f* turtle

**tortuoso** (toar-*twoa*-soa) *adj* winding

**tortura** (toar-*too*-rah) *f* torture

**torturar** (toar-too-*rahr*) *v* torture

**tos** (toass) *f* cough

**toser** (toa-*sayr*) *v* cough

**tostado** (toass-*tah*-dhoa) *adj* tanned

**total** (toa-*tahl*) *adj* total; overall, utter; *m* total; whole; **en ~** altogether

**totalitario** (toa-tah-lee-*tah*-rʸoa) *adj* totalitarian

**totalizador** (toa-tah-lee-thah-*dhoar*) *m* totalizator

**totalmente** (toa-tahl-*mayn*-tay) *adv* completely, altogether, wholly

**tóxico** (*toak*-see-koa) *adj* toxic

**trabajar** (trah-bhah-*khahr*) *v* work

**trabajo** (trah-*bhah*-khoa) *m* work, labour; difficulty; **~ manual** handicraft

**tractor** (trahk-*toar*) *m* tractor

**tradición** (trah-dhee-*thʸoan*) *f* tradition

**tradicional** (trah-dhee-thʸoa-*nahl*) *adj* traditional

**traducción** (trah-dhook-*thʸoan*) *f* translation

\***traducir** (trah-dhoo-*theer*) *v* translate

**traductor** (trah-dhook-*toar*) *m* translator

\***traer** (trah-*ayr*) *v* \*bring

**tragar** (trah-*gahr*) *v* swallow

**tragedia** (trah-*khay*-dhʸah) *f* drama, tragedy

**trágico** (*trah*-khee-koa) *adj* tragic

**traición** (trigh-*thʸoan*) *f* treason

**traicionar** (trigh-thʸoa-*nahr*) *v* betray

**traidor** (trigh-*dhoar*) *m* traitor

**traílla** (trah-ee-lʸah) *f* lead

**traje** (*trah*-khay) *m* suit; gown; robe; **~ de baño** bathing-suit; **~ de eti-queta** evening dress; **~ del país** national dress; **~ de malla** tights *pl*; **~ pantalón** pant-suit

**trama** (*trah*-mah) *f* plot

**trampa** (*trahm*-pah) *f* trap; hatch

**tranquilidad** (trahng-kee-lee-*dhahdh*) *f* tranquillity

**tranquilizar** (trahng-kee-lee-*thahr*) *v* reassure

**tranquilo** (trahng-*kee*-loa) *adj* tranquil, quiet, calm; peaceful

**transacción** (trahn-sahk-*thʸoan*) *f* transaction, deal; **volumen de transacciones** turnover

**transatlántico** (trahn-saht-*lahn*-tee-koa) *adj* transatlantic

**transbordador** (trahnz-bhoar-dhah-*dhoar*) *m* ferry-boat; **~ de trenes** train ferry

**transcurrir** (trahns-koo-*rreer*) *v* pass

**transeúnte** (trahn-say-*oon*-tay) *m* passer-by

\***transferir** (trahns-fay-*reer*) *v* transfer

**transformador** (trahns-foar-mah-*dhoar*) *m* transformer

**transformar** (trahns-foar-*mahr*) *v* transform

**transgredir** (trahnz-gray-*deer*) *v* offend

**transición** (trahn-see-*thʸoan*) *f* transition

**tránsito** (*trahn*-see-toa) *m* traffic

**transmisión** (trahnz-mee-*sʸoan*) *f* transmission, broadcast

**transmitir** (trahnz-mee-*teer*) *v* transmit

**transparente** (trahns-pah-*rayn*-tay) *adj* transparent

**transpiración** (trahns-pee-rah-*thʸoan*) *f* perspiration

**transpirar** (trahns-pee-*rahr*) *v* perspire

**transportar** (trahns-poar-*tahr*) *v* transport; ship

**transporte** (trahns-*poar*-tay) *m* transportation, transport

**tranvía** (trahm-*bee*-ah) *m* tram; streetcar *nAm*

**trapo** (*trah*-poa) *m* rag; **~ de cocina** tea-cloth

**tras** (trahss) *prep* behind

**\*hacer trasbordo** (ah-*thayr* trahz-*bhoar*-dhoa) change

**trasero** (trah-*say*-roa) *m* bottom

**trasladar** (trahz-lah-*dhahr*) *v* move

**traslúcido** (trahz-*loo*-thee-dhoa) *adj* sheer

**trastornado** (trahss-toar-*nah*-dhoa) *adj* upset

**trastornar** (trahss-toar-*nahr*) *v* upset

**trastos** (*trahss*-toass) *mpl* litter

**tratado** (trah-*tah*-dhoa) *m* essay; treaty

**tratamiento** (trah-tah-*mᵛayn*-toa) *m* treatment; ~ **de belleza** beauty treatment

**tratar** (trah-*tahr*) *v* handle, treat; ~ **con** \*deal with

**trato** (*trah*-toa) *m* intercourse

**a través de** (ah trah-*bhayss* day) across, through

**travesía** (trah-bhay-*see*-ah) *f* crossing, passage

**travieso** (trah-*bhᵛay*-soa) *adj* naughty, bad; mischievous

**trazar** (trah-*thahr*) *v* sketch

**trébol** (*tray*-bhoal) *m* clover, shamrock

**trece** (*tray*-thay) *num* thirteen

**treceno** (tray-*thay*-noa) *num* thirteenth

**trecho** (*tray*-choa) *m* stretch

**treinta** (*trayn*-tah) *num* thirty

**treintavo** (trayn-*tah*-bhoa) *num* thirtieth

**tremendo** (tray-*mayn*-doa) *adj* awful, terrible; tremendous, terrific

**trementina** (tray-mayn-*tee*-nah) *f* turpentine

**tren** (trayn) *m* train; ~ **de cercanías** stopping train; ~ **de mercancías** goods train; ~ **de pasajeros** passenger train; ~ **directo** through train; ~ **expreso** express train; ~ **nocturno** night train; ~ **ómnibus** local train

**trenza** (*trayn*-thah) *f* twine

**trepar** (tray-*pahr*) *v* climb

**tres** (trayss) *num* three

**triangular** (trᵛahng-goo-*lahr*) *adj* triangular

**triángulo** (*trᵛahng*-goo-loa) *m* triangle

**tribu** (*tree*-bhoo) *m* tribe

**tribuna** (tree-*bhoo*-nah) *f* stand

**tribunal** (tree-bhoo-*nahl*) *m* court, law court

**trigal** (tree-*gahl*) *m* cornfield

**trigo** (*tree*-goa) *m* grain, corn; wheat

**trimestral** (tree-mayss-*trahl*) *adj* quarterly

**trimestre** (tree-*mayss*-tray) *m* quarter

**trinchar** (treen-*chahr*) *v* carve

**trineo** (tree-*nay*-oa) *m* sleigh, sledge

**triste** (*treess*-tay) *adj* sad

**tristeza** (treess-*tay*-thah) *f* sorrow, sadness

**triturar** (tree-too-*rahr*) *v* \*grind

**triunfante** (trᵛoon-*fahn*-tay) *adj* triumphant

**triunfar** (trᵛoon-*fahr*) *v* triumph

**triunfo** (trᵛoon-foa) *m* triumph

**\*trocar** (troa-*kahr*) *v* swap

**trolebús** (troa-lay-*bhooss*) *m* trolleybus

**trompeta** (troam-*pay*-tah) *f* trumpet

**tronada** (troa-*nah*-dhah) *f* thunderstorm

**\*tronar** (troa-*nahr*) *v* thunder

**tronco** (*troang*-koa) *m* trunk

**trono** (*troanoa*) *m* throne

**tropas** (troa-pahss) *fpl* troops *pl*

**\*tropezarse** (troa-pay-*thahr*-say) *v* stumble

**tropical** (troa-pee-*kahl*) *adj* tropical

**trópicos** (*troa*-pee-koass) *mpl* tropics *pl*

**trozo** (*troa*-thoa) *m* chunk, morsel, bit; fragment, passage

**truco** (*troo*-koa) *m* trick

**trucha** (*troo*-chah) *f* trout

**trueno** (*trway*-noa) *m* thunder

**tu** (too) *adj* your

**tú** (too) *pron* you

**tuberculosis** (too-bhayr-koo-*loa*-seess) *f* tuberculosis

**tubo** (*too*-bhoa) *m* tube

**tuerca** (*twayr*-kah) *f* nut

**tulipán** (too-lee-*pahn*) *m* tulip

**tumba** (*toom*-bah) *f* tomb

**tumor** (too-*moar*) *m* growth, tumour

**tunecino** (too-nay-*thee*-noa) *adj* Tunisian; *m* Tunisian

**túnel** (*too*-nayl) *m* tunnel

**Túnez** (*too*-nayth) *m* Tunisia

**túnica** (*too*-nee-kah) *f* tunic

**turbar** (toor-*bhahr*) *v* embarrass

**turbera** (toor-*bhay*-rah) *f* moor

**turbina** (toor-*bhee*-nah) *f* turbine

**turco** (*toor*-koa) *adj* Turkish; *m* Turk

**turismo** (too-*reez*-moa) *m* tourism

**turista** (too-*reess*-tah) *m* tourist; **oficina para turistas** tourist office

**turno** (*toor*-noa) *m* turn; shift

**Turquía** (toor-*kee*-ah) *f* Turkey

**turrón** (too-*rroan*) *m* nougat

**tutela** (too-*tay*-lah) *f* custody

**tutor** (too-*toar*) *m* tutor; guardian

**tuyos** (*too*-Yoass) *adj* your

# U

**ubicación** (oo-bhee-kah-*th*Yoan) *f* situation, location

**ujier** (oo-*kh*Yayr) *m* bailiff

**úlcera** (*ool*-thay-rah) *f* ulcer, sore; ~ **gástrica** gastric ulcer

**ulterior** (ool-tay-*r*Yoar) *adj* further

**últimamente** (*ool*-tee-mah-mayn-tay) *adv* lately

**último** (*ool*-tee-moa) *adj* ultimate; last

**ultraje** (ool-*trah*-khay) *m* outrage

**ultramar** (ool-trah-*mahr*) *adv* overseas

**ultravioleta** (ool-trah-bh Yoa-*lay*-tah) *adj* ultraviolet

**umbral** (oom-*brahl*) *m* threshold

**un** (oon) *art* a art

**unánime** (oo-*nah*-nee-may) *adj* likeminded, unanimous

**ungüento** (oong-*gwayn*-toa) *m* ointment, salve

**únicamente** (oo-nee-kah-mayn-tay) *adv* exclusively

**único** (oo-*nee*-koa) *adj* unique, sole

**unidad** (oo-nee-*dhahdh*) *f* unity; unit

**unido** (oo-*nee*-dhoa) *adj* joint

**uniforme** (oo-nee-*foar*-may) *adj* uniform; *m* uniform

**unilateral** (oo-nee-lah-tay-*rahl*) *adj* one-sided

**unión** (oo-*n*Yoan) *f* union

**Unión Soviética** (oo-*n*Yoan soa-bh Yay-tee-kah) Soviet Union

**unir** (oo-*neer*) *v* unite; combine; **unirse** *a* join

**universal** (oo-nee-bhayr-*sahl*) *adj* universal

**universidad** (oo-nee-bhayr-see-*dhahdh*) *f* university

**universo** (oo-nee-*bhayr*-soa) *m* universe

**uno** (*oo*-noa) *num* one; *pron* one; **unos** *adj* some; *pron* some

**uña** (*oo*-ñah) *f* nail

**urbano** (oor-*bhah*-noa) *adj* urban

**urgencia** (oor-*khayn*-th Yah) *f* urgency; emergency; **botiquín de** ~ first-aid kit

**urgente** (oor-*khayn*-tay) *adj* pressing, urgent

**urraca** (oo-*rrah*-kah) *f* magpie

**Uruguay** (oo-roo-*gwigh*) *m* Uruguay

**uruguayo** (oo-roo-*gwah*-Yoa) *adj* Uruguayan; *m* Uruguayan

**usar** (oo-*sahr*) *v* use

**uso** (*oo*-soa) *m* use, usage

**usted** (ooss-*taydh*) *pron* you; **a** ~

you; **de ~** your

**usual** (oo-*swahl*) *adj* common, customary, usual

**usuario** (oo-*swah*-rʸoa) *m* user

**utensilio** (oo-tayn-*see*-lʸoa) *m* utensil

**útil** (*oo*-teel) *adj* useful

**utilidad** (oo-tee-lee-*dhahdh*) *f* utility, use

**utilizable** (oo-tee-lee-*thah*-bhlay) *adj* usable

**utilizar** (oo-tee-lee-*thahr*) *v* utilize

**uvas** (*oo*-bhahss) *fpl* grapes *pl*

# V

**vaca** (*bah*-kah) *f* cow

**vacaciones** (bah-kah-*thʸoa*-nayss) *fpl* holiday, vacation; **de ~** on holiday

**vacante** (bah-*kahn*-tay) *adj* vacant; *f* vacancy

**vaciar** (bah-*thʸahr*) *v* empty; vacate

**vacilante** (bah-thee-lahn-tay) *adj* unsteady, shaky

**vacilar** (bah-thee-*lahr*) *v* hesitate; falter

**vacío** (bah-*thee*-oa) *adj* empty; *m* vacuum

**vacunación** (bah-koo-nah-*thʸoan*) *f* vaccination

**vacunar** (bah-koo-*nahr*) *v* vaccinate, inoculate

**vadear** (bah-dhay-*ahr*) *v* wade

**vado** (*bah*-dhoa) *m* ford

**vagabundear** (bah-gah-bhoon-day-*ahr*) *v* tramp, roam

**vagabundo** (bah-gah-*bhoon*-doa) *m* tramp

**vagancia** (bah-*gahn*-thʸah) *f* vagrancy

**vagar** (bah-*gahr*) *v* wander

**vago** (*bah*-goa) *adj* vague; faint, dim; idle

**vagón** (bah-*goan*) *m* waggon, car-

riage; coach

**vainilla** (bigh-*nee*-lʸah) *f* vanilla

**vale** (*bah*-lay) *m* banknote

*****valer** (bah-*layr*) *v* *be worth; **~ la pena** *be worth-while

**valiente** (bah-*lʸayn*-tay) *adj* courageous, plucky, brave

**valija** (bah-*lee*-khah) *f* case

**valioso** (bah-*lʸoa*-soa) *adj* valuable

**valor** (bah-*loar*) *m* worth, value; courage; **bolsa de valores** stock exchange; **sin ~** worthless

**vals** (bahls) *m* waltz

**valuar** (bah-*lwahr*) *v* value; appreciate

**válvula** (*bahl*-bhoo-lah) *f* valve

**valle** (*bah*-lʸay) *m* valley

**vanidoso** (bah-nee-*dhoa*-soa) *adj* vain

**vano** (*bah*-noa) *adj* idle, vain; **en ~** in vain

**vapor** (bah-*poar*) *m* steam, vapour; steamer; **~ de línea** liner

**vaporizador** (bah-poa-ree-thah-*dhoar*) *m* atomizer

**vaqueros** (bah-*kay*-roass) *mpl* jeans *pl*

**variable** (bah-*rʸah*-bhlay) *adj* variable

**variación** (bah-rʸah-*thʸoan*) *f* variation

**variado** (bah-*rʸah*-dhoa) *adj* varied

**variar** (bah-*rʸahr*) *v* vary

**varice** (*bah*-ree-thay) *f* varicose vein

**varicela** (bah-ree-*thay*-lah) *f* chickenpox

**variedad** (bah-*rʸay*-dhahdh) *f* variety; **espectáculo de variedades** variety show

**varios** (*bah*-rʸoass) *adj* various, several

**vaselina** (bah-say-*lee*-nah) *f* vaseline

**vasija** (bah-*see*-khah) *f* vessel

**vaso** (*bah*-soa) *m* glass; mug, tumbler; vase; **~ sanguíneo** blood-vessel

**vasto** (*bahss*-toa) *adj* wide, vast; extensive

**vatio** (*bah*-tʸoa) *m* watt

**vecindad** (bay-theen-*dahdh*) f neighbourhood, vicinity

**vecindario** (bay-theen-*dah*-rʸoa) m community

**vecino** (bay-*thee*-noa) adj neighbouring; m neighbour

**vegetación** (bay-khay-tah-*th*ʸoan) f vegetation

**vegetariano** (bay-khay-tah-*r*ʸah-noa) m vegetarian

**vehículo** (bay-*ee*-koo-loa) m vehicle

**veinte** (*bayn*-tay) num twenty

**vejez** (bay-*khayth*) f old age

**vejiga** (bay-*khee*-gah) f bladder

**vela** (*bay*-lah) f sail; **deporte de ~** yachting

**velo** (*bay*-loa) m veil

**velocidad** (bay-loa-thee-*dhahdh*) f speed; rate; gear; **límite de ~** speed limit; **~ de cruce** cruising speed

**velocímetro** (bay-loa-*thee*-may-troa) m speedometer

**veloz** (bay-*loath*) adj swift

**vena** (*bay*-nah) f vein

**vencedor** (bayn-thay-*dhoar*) m winner

**vencer** (bayn-*thayr*) v *overcome, conquer; *win

**vencimiento** (bayn-thee-*m*ʸayn-toa) m expiry

**vendaje** (bayn-*dah*-khay) m bandage

**vendar** (bayn-*dahr*) v dress

**vendedor** (bayn-day-*dhoar*) m salesman

**vendedora** (bayn-day-*dhoa*-rah) f salesgirl

**vender** (bayn-*dayr*) v *sell; **~ al detalle** retail

**vendible** (bayn-*dee*-bhlay) adj saleable

**vendimia** (bayn-*dee*-mʸah) f vintage

**veneno** (bay-*nay*-noa) m poison

**venenoso** (bay-nay-*noa*-soa) adj poisonous

**venerable** (bay-nay-*rah*-bhlay) adj venerable

**venerar** (bay-nay-*rahr*) v worship

**venezolano** (bay-nay-thoa-*lah*-noa) adj Venezuelan; m Venezuelan

**Venezuela** (bay-nay-*thway*-lah) f Venezuela

**venganza** (bayng-*gahn*-thah) f revenge

**venidero** (bay-nee-*dhay*-roa) adj oncoming

***venir** (bay-*neer*) v *come

**venta** (*bayn*-tah) f sale; **de ~** for sale; **~ al por mayor** wholesale

**ventaja** (bayn-*tah*-khah) f benefit, advantage; profit; lead

**ventajoso** (bayn-tah-*khoa*-soa) adj advantageous

**ventana** (bayn-*tah*-nah) f window; **~ de la nariz** nostril

**ventarrón** (bayn-tah-*rroan*) m gale

**ventilación** (bayn-tee-lah-*th*ʸoan) f ventilation

**ventilador** (bayn-tee-lah-*dhoar*) m fan, ventilator

**ventilar** (bayn-tee-*lahr*) v ventilate

**ventisca** (bhayn-*teess*-kah) f blizzard

**ventoso** (bayn-*toa*-soa) adj windy

***ver** (bayr) v *see, notice

**veranda** (bay-*rahn*-dah) f veranda

**verano** (bay-*rah*-noa) m summer; **pleno ~** midsummer

**verbal** (bayr-*bhahl*) adj verbal

**verbo** (*bayr*-bhoa) m verb

**verdad** (bayr-*dhahdh*) f truth

**verdaderamente** (bayr-dhah-dhay-rah-*mayn*-tay) adv really

**verdadero** (bayr-dhah-*dhay*-roa) adj true; real, very; actual

**verde** (*bayr*-dhay) adj green

**verdulero** (bayr-dhoo-*lay*-roa) m greengrocer

**veredicto** (bay-ray-*dheek*-toa) m verdict

**vergel** (*bayr*-gayl) m orchard

**vergüenza** (bayr-*gwayn*-thah) f shame;

**¡qué vergüenza!** shame!

**verídico** (bay-*ree*-dhee-koa) *adj* truthful

**verificar** (bay-ree-fee-*kahr*) *v* check, verify

**verosímil** (bay-roa-*see*-meel) *adj* credible

**versión** (bayr-s*y*oan) *f* version

**verso** (bayr-soa) *m* verse

*****verter** (bayr-*tayr*) *v* pour; *spill

**vertical** (bayr-tee-*kahl*) *adj* vertical

**vértigo** (*bayr*-tee-goa) *m* dizziness, vertigo

**vestíbulo** (bayss-*tee*-bhoo-loa) *m* hall, lobby; foyer

**vestido** (bayss-*tee*-dhoa) *m* frock, dress; **vestidos** *mpl* clothes *pl*

*****vestir** (bayss-*teer*) *v* dress; *vestirse *v* dress

**vestuario** (bayss-*twah*-r*y*oa) *m* wardrobe; dressing-room

**veterinario** (bay-tay-ree-*nah*-r*y*oa) *m* veterinary surgeon

**vez** (bayth) *f* time; **alguna ~** some time; **a veces** sometimes; **de ~ en cuando** occasionally, now and then; **otra ~** again, once more; **pocas veces** seldom; **una ~** once

**vía** (*bee*-ah) *f* track; **~ del tren** railroad *nAm*; **~ navegable** waterway

**viaducto** (b*y*ah-*dhook*-toa) *m* viaduct

**viajar** (b*y*ah-*khahr*) *v* travel

**viaje** (b*y*ah-khay) *m* journey; trip, voyage

**viajero** (b*y*ah-*khay*-roa) *m* traveller

**vibración** (bee-bhrah-th*y*oan) *f* vibration

**vibrar** (bee-*bhrahr*) *v* tremble, vibrate

**vicario** (bee-*kah*-r*y*oa) *m* vicar

**vicepresidente** (bee-thay-pray-see-*dhayn*-tay) *m* vice-president

**vicioso** (bee-th*y*oa-soa) *adj* vicious

**víctima** (*beek*-tee-mah) *f* casualty, victim

**victoria** (beek-*toa*-r*y*ah) *f* victory

**vid** (beedh) *f* vine

**vida** (*bee*-dhah) *f* life; lifetime; **en ~** alive; **~ privada** privacy

**vidrio** (bee-dhr*y*oa) *m* glass; **de ~** glass; **~ de color** stained glass

**viejo** (b*y*ay-khoa) *adj* old; ancient, aged; stale

**viento** (b*y*ayn-toa) *m* wind

**vientre** (b*y*ayn-tray) *m* belly

**viernes** (b*y*ayr-nayss) *m* Friday

**viga** (*bee*-gah) *f* beam

**vigente** (bee-*khayn*-tay) *adj* valid

**vigésimo** (bee-*khay*-see-moa) *num* twentieth

**vigilar** (bee-khee-*lahr*) *v* watch, patrol

**vigor** (bee-*goar*) *m* strength; stamina

**vil** (beel) *adj* foul

**villa** (*bee*-l*y*ah) *f* villa

**villano** (bee-*l*Y*ah*-noa) *m* villain

**vinagre** (bee-*nah*-gray) *m* vinegar

**vinatero** (bee-nah-*tay*-roa) *m* wine-merchant

**vino** (*bee*-noa) *m* wine

**viña** (*bee*-ñah) *f* vineyard

**violación** (b*y*oa-lah-th*y*oan) *f* violation

**violar** (b*y*oa-*lahr*) *v* assault, rape

**violencia** (b*y*oa-*layn*-th*y*ah) *f* violence

**violento** (b*y*oa-*layn*-toa) *adj* violent; fierce, severe

**violeta** (b*y*oa-*lay*-tah) *f* violet

**violín** (b*y*oa-*leen*) *m* violin

**virgen** (*beer*-khayn) *f* virgin

**virtud** (beer-*toodh*) *f* virtue

**viruelas** (bee-*rway*-lahss) *fpl* smallpox

**visado** (bee-*sah*-dhoa) *m* visa

**visar** (bee-*sahr*) *v* endorse

**visibilidad** (bee-see-bhee-lee-*dhahdh*) *f* visibility

**visible** (bee-*see*-bhlay) *adj* visible

**visión** (bee-s*y*oan) *f* vision

**visita** (bee-*see*-tah) *f* visit, call

**visitante** (bee-see-*tahn*-tay) *m* visitor

**visitar** (bee-see-*tahr*) *v* visit, call on

**vislumbrar** (beez-loom-*brahr*) *v* glimpse

**vislumbre** (beez-*loom*-bray) *m* glimpse

**visón** (bee-*soan*) *m* mink

**visor** (bee-*soar*) *m* view-finder

**vista** (*beess*-tah) *f* sight; view; **punto de ~** outlook

**vistoso** (beess-*toa*-soa) *adj* striking

**vital** (bee-*tahl*) *adj* vital

**vitamina** (bee-tah-*mee*-nah) *f* vitamin

**vitrina** (bee-*tree*-nah) *f* show-case

**viuda** (b<sup>y</sup>oo-dhah) *f* widow

**viudo** (b<sup>y</sup>oo-dhoa) *m* widower

**vivaz** (bee-*bhahth*) *adj* active

**vivero** (bee-*bhay*-roa) *m* nursery

**vivienda** (bee-bh<sup>y</sup>ayn-dah) *f* house

**vivir** (bee-*bheer*) *v* live; experience

**vivo** (*bee*-bhoa) *adj* alive, live; brisk, vivid, lively

**vocabulario** (boa-kah-bhoo-*lah*-r<sup>y</sup>oa) *m* vocabulary

**vocación** (boa-kah-th<sup>y</sup>oan) *f* vocation

**vocal** (boa-*kahl*) *f* vowel; *adj* vocal

**vocalista** (boa-kah-*leess*-tah) *m* vocalist

**volante** (boa-*lahn*-tay) *m* steering-wheel

*****volar** (boa-*lahr*) *v* *fly

**volatería** (boa-lah-tay-*ree*-ah) *f* fowl

**volcán** (boal-*kahn*) *m* volcano

**voltaje** (boal-*tah*-khay) *m* voltage

**voltio** (*boal*-t<sup>y</sup>oa) *m* volt

**volumen** (boa-*loo*-mayn) *m* volume

**voluminoso** (boa-loo-mee-*noa*-soa) *adj* bulky, big

**voluntad** (boa-loon-*tahdh*) *f* will; **buena ~** goodwill

**voluntario** (boa-loon-*tah*-r<sup>y</sup>oa) *adj* voluntary; *m* volunteer

*****volver** (boal-*bhayr*) *v* return, turn back; turn over, turn, turn round; **~ a casa** *go home; *****volverse** *v* turn round

**vomitar** (boa-mee-*tahr*) *v* vomit

**vosotros** (boa-*soa*-troass) *pron* you

**votación** (boa-tah-*th<sup>y</sup>oan*) *f* vote

**votar** (boa-*tahr*) *v* vote

**voto** (*boa*-toa) *m* vote; vow

**voz** (boath) *f* voice; cry; **en ~ alta** aloud

**vuelo** (*bway*-loa) *m* flight; **~ fletado** charter flight; **~ nocturno** night flight

**vuelta** (*bwayl*-tah) *f* return journey, way back; tour; turning, turn; round; **ida y ~** round trip *Am*

**vuestro** (*bwayss*-troa) *adj* your

**vulgar** (bool-*gahr*) *adj* vulgar

**vulnerable** (bool-nay-*rah*-bhlay) *adj* vulnerable

# Y

**y** (ee) *conj* and

**ya** (<sup>y</sup>ah) *adv* already; **~ no** no longer; **~ que** as

*****yacer** (<sup>y</sup>ah-*thayr*) *v* *lie

**yacimiento** (<sup>y</sup>ah-thee-*m<sup>y</sup>ayn*-toa) *m* deposit

**yate** (<sup>y</sup>*ah*-tay) *m* yacht

**yegua** (<sup>y</sup>*ay*-gwah) *f* mare

**yema** (<sup>y</sup>*ay*-mah) *f* yolk

**yerno** (<sup>y</sup>*ayr*-noa) *m* son-in-law

**yeso** (<sup>y</sup>*ay*-soa) *m* plaster

**yo** (<sup>y</sup>oa) *pron* I

**yodo** (<sup>y</sup>*oa*-dhoa) *m* iodine

**yugo** (<sup>y</sup>*oo*-goa) *m* yoke

**Yugoslavia** (<sup>y</sup>oo-goaz-*lah*-bh<sup>y</sup>ah) *f* Yugoslavia, Jugoslavia

**yugoslavo** (<sup>y</sup>oo-goaz-*lah*-bhoa) *adj* Jugoslav; *m* Yugoslav, Jugoslav

# Z

**zafiro** (thah-*fee*-roa ) *m* sapphire

**zanahoria** (thah-nah-*oa*-r<sup>y</sup>ah ) *f* carrot

**zanja** ( *thahng*-khah ) *f* ditch

**zapatería** (thah-pah-tay-*ree*-ah ) *f* shoe-shop

**zapatero** (thah-pah-*tay*-roa ) *m* shoe-maker

**zapatilla** (thah-pah-*tee*-l<sup>y</sup>ah ) *f* slipper

**zapato** (thah-*pah*-toa ) *m* shoe; **zapatos de gimnasia** plimsolls *pl*; sneakers *plAm*; **zapatos de tenis** tennis shoes

**zatara** (thah-*tah*-rah ) *f* raft

**zodíaco** (thoa-*dhee*-ah-koa ) *m* zodiac

**zona** ( *thoa*-nah ) *f* zone; area; ~ **industrial** industrial area

**zoología** (thoa-oa-loa-*khee*-ah ) *f* zoology

**zorro** ( *thoa*-rroa ) *m* fox

**zueco** ( *thway*-koa ) *m* wooden shoe

**zumo** ( *thoo*-moa ) *m* juice; squash

**zumoso** (thoo-*moa*-soa ) *adj* juicy

**zurcir** (thoor-*theer*) *v* darn

**zurdo** ( *thoor*-dhoa ) *adj* left-handed

**zurra** ( *thoo*-rrah ) *f* spanking

# Menu Reader

## Food

**a caballo** steak topped with two eggs
**acedera** sorrel
**aceite** oil
**aceituna** olive
**achicoria** endive (US chicory)
**(al) adobo** marinated
**aguacate** avocado (pear)
**ahumado** smoked
**ajiaceite** garlic mayonnaise
**ajiaco bogotano** chicken soup with potatoes
**(al) ajillo** cooked in garlic and oil
**ajo** garlic
**al, a la** in the style of, with
**albahaca** basil
**albaricoque** apricot
**albóndiga** spiced meat- or fishball
**alcachofa** artichoke
**alcaparra** caper
**aliñado** seasoned
**alioli** garlic mayonnaise
**almeja** clam, cockle
**almejas a la marinera** cooked in hot, pimento sauce
**almendra** almond
  ~ **garrapiñada** sugared almond
**almíbar** syrup
**almuerzo** lunch
**alubia** bean

**anchoa** anchovy
**anguila** eel
**angula** baby eel
**anticucho** beef heart grilled on a skewer with green peppers
**apio** celery
**a punto** medium (done)
**arenque** herring
  ~ **en escabeche** marinated, pickled herring
**arepa** flapjack made of maize (corn)
**arroz** rice
  ~ **blanco** boiled, steamed
  ~ **escarlata** with tomatoes and prawns
  ~ **a la española** with chicken liver, pork, tomatoes, fish stock
  ~ **con leche** rice pudding
  ~ **primavera** with spring vegetables
  ~ **a la valenciana** with vegetables, chicken, shellfish (and sometimes eel)
**asado** roast
  ~ **antiguo a la venezolana mechado** roast beef stuffed with capers
**asturias** a strong, fermented cheese with a sharp flavour

**atún** tunny (US tuna)

**avellana** hazelnut

**azafrán** saffron

**azúcar** sugar

**bacalao** cod

~ **a la vizcaína** with green peppers, potatoes, tomato sauce

**barbo** barbel (fish)

**batata** sweet potato, yam

**becada** woodcock

**berberecho** cockle

**berenjena** aubergine (US eggplant)

**berraza** parsnip

**berro** cress

**berza** cabbage

**besugo** sea bream

**bien hecho** well-done

**biftec, bistec** beef steak

**bizcocho** sponge cake, sponge finger (US ladyfinger)

~ **borracho** cake steeped in rum (or wine) and syrup

**bizcotela** glazed biscuit (US cookie)

**blando** soft

**bocadillo** 1) sandwich 2) sweet (Colombia)

**bollito, bollo** roll, bun

**bonito** a kind of tunny (US tuna)

**boquerón** 1) anchovy 2) whitebait

**(en) brocheta** (on a) skewer

**budín** blancmange, custard

**buey** ox

**buñuelo** 1) doughnut 2) fritter with ham, mussels and prawns (sometimes flavoured with brandy)

**burgos** a popular soft, creamy cheese named after the Spanish province of its origin

**butifarra** spiced sausage

**caballa** fish of the mackerel family

**cabeza de ternera** calf's head

**cabra** goat

**cabrales** blue-veined goat's-milk cheese

**cabrito** kid

**cacahuete** peanut

**cachelos** diced potatoes boiled with cabbage, paprika, garlic, bacon, *chorizo* sausage

**calabacín** vegetable marrow, courgette (US zucchini)

**calabaza** pumpkin

**calamar** squid

**calamares a la romana** squids fried in batter

**caldereta de cabrito** kid stew (often cooked in red wine)

**caldillo de congrio** conger-eel soup with tomatoes and potatoes

**caldo** consommé

~ **gallego** meat and vegetable broth

**callos** tripe (often served in pimento sauce)

~ **a la madrileña** in piquant sauce with *chorizo* sausage and tomatoes

**camarón** shrimp

**canela** cinnamon

**cangrejo de mar** crab

**cangrejo de río** crayfish

**cantarela** chanterelle mushroom

**caracol** snail

**carbonada criolla** baked pumpkin stuffed with diced beef

**carne** meat

~ **asada al horno** roast meat

~ **molida** minced meat

~ **a la parrilla** charcoal-grilled steak

~ **picada** minced beef

**carnero** mutton

**carpa** carp

**casero** home made

**castaña** chestnut
**castañola** sea perch
**(a la) catalana** with onions, parsley, tomatoes and herbs
**caza** game
**(a la) cazadora** with mushrooms, spring onions, herbs in wine
**cazuela de cordero** lamb stew with vegetables
**cebolla** onion
**cebolleta** chive
**cebrero** blue-veined cheese of creamy texture with a pale, yellow rind; sharp taste
**cena** dinner, supper
**centolla** spider-crab, served cold
**cerdo** pork
**cereza** cherry
**ceviche** fish marinated in lemon and lime juice
**cigala** Dublin Bay prawn
**cincho** a hard cheese made from sheep's milk
**ciruela** plum
~ **pasa** prune
**cocido** 1) cooked, boiled 2) stew of beef with ham, fowl, chick peas, potatoes and vegetables (the broth is eaten first)
**cochifrito de cordero** highly seasoned stew of lamb or kid
**codorniz** quail
**col** cabbage
~ **de Bruselas** brussels sprout
**coliflor** cauliflower
**comida** meal
**compota** stewed fruit
**conejo** rabbit
**confitura** jam
**congrio** conger eel
**consomé al jerez** chicken broth with sherry
**copa nuria** egg-yolk and egg-white, whipped and served with

jam
**corazón de alcachofa** artichoke heart
**corazonada** heart stewed in sauce
**cordero** lamb
~ **recental** spring lamb
**cortadillo** small pancake with lemon
**corzo** deer
**costilla** chop
**crema** 1) cream or mousse
~ **batida** whipped cream
~ **española** dessert of milk, eggs, fruit jelly
~ **nieve** frothy egg-yolk, sugar, rum (or wine)
**crema** 2) soup
**criadillas (de toro)** glands (of bull)
**(a la) criolla** with green peppers, spices and tomatoes
**croqueta** croquette, fish or meat dumpling
**crudo** raw
**cubierto** cover charge
**cuenta** bill (US check)
**curanto** dish consisting of seafood, vegetables and suck(l)ing pig, all cooked in an earthen well, lined with charcoal
**chabacano** apricot
**chalote** shallot
**champiñón** mushroom
**chancho adobado** pork braised with sweet potatoes, orange and lemon juice
**chanfaina** goat's liver and kidney stew, served in a thick sauce
**chanquete** whitebait
**chile** chili pepper
**chiles en nogada** green peppers stuffed with whipped cream and nut sauce
**chimichurri** hot parsley sauce
**chipirón** small squid

**chopa** a kind of sea bream

**chorizo** pork sausage, highly seasoned with garlic and paprika

**chuleta** cutlet

**chupe de mariscos** scallops served with a creamy sauce and gratinéed with cheese

**churro** sugared tubular fritter

**damasco** variety of apricot

**dátil** date

**desayuno** breakfast

**dorada** gilt-head

**dulce** sweet

  ~ **de naranja** marmalade

**durazno** peach

**embuchado** stuffed with meat

**embutido** spicy sausage

**empanada** pie or tart with meat or fish filling

  ~ **de horno** dough filled with minced meat, similar to ravioli

**empanadilla** small patty stuffed with seasoned meat or fish

**empanado** breaded

**emperador** swordfish

**encurtido** pickle

**enchilada** a maizeflour (US cornmeal) pancake *(tortilla)* stuffed and usually served with vegetable garnish and sauce

  ~ **roja** sausage-filled maizeflour pancake dipped into a red sweet-pepper sauce

  ~ **verde** maizeflour pancake stuffed with meat or fowl and braised in a green-tomato sauce

**endibia** chicory (US endive)

**eneldo** dill

**ensalada** salad

  ~ **común** green

  ~ **de frutas** fruit salad

  ~ **(a la) primavera** spring

  ~ **valenciana** with green peppers, lettuce and oranges

**ensaladilla rusa** diced cold vegetables with mayonnaise

**entremés** appetizer, hors-d'oeuvre

**erizo de mar** sea urchin

**(en) escabeche** marinated, pickled

  ~ **de gallina** chicken marinated in vinegar

**escarcho** red gurnard (fish)

**escarola** endive (US chicory)

**espalda** shoulder

**(a la) española** with tomatoes

**espárrago** asparagus

**especia** spice

**especialidad de la casa** chef's speciality

**espinaca** spinach

**esqueixada** mixed fish salad

**(al) estilo de** in the style of

**estofado** stew(ed)

**estragón** tarragon

**fabada (asturiana)** stew of pork, beans, bacon and sausage

**faisán** pheasant

**fiambres** cold meat (US cold cuts)

**fideo** thin noodle

**filete** steak

  ~ **de lomo** fillet steak (US tenderloin)

  ~ **de res** beef steak

  ~ **de lenguado empanado** breaded fillet of sole

**(a la) flamenca** with onions, peas, green peppers, tomatoes and spiced sausage

**flan** caramel mould, custard

**frambuesa** raspberry

**(a la) francesa** sautéed in butter

**fresa** strawberry

  ~ **de bosque** wild

**fresco** fresh, chilled

**fresón** large strawberry

**fricandó** veal bird, thin slice of meat rolled in bacon and braised

**frijol** bean

**frijoles refritos** fried mashed beans

**frío** cold

**frito** 1) fried 2) fry

  ~ **de patata** deep-fried potato croquette

**fritura** fry

  ~ **mixta** meat, fish or vegetables deep-fried in batter

**fruta** fruit

  ~ **escarchada** crystallized (US candied) fruit

**galleta** salted or sweet biscuit (US cracker or cookie)

  ~ **de nata** cream biscuit (US sandwich cookie)

**gallina** hen

  ~ **de Guinea** guinea fowl

**gallo** cockerel

**gamba** shrimp

  ~ **grande** prawn

**gambas con mayonesa** shrimp cocktail

**ganso** goose

**garbanzo** chick pea

**gazpacho** seasoned broth made of raw onions, garlic, tomatoes, cucumber and green pepper; served chilled

**(a la) gitanilla** with garlic

**gordo** fatty, rich (of food)

**granada** pomegranate

**grande** large

**(al) gratín** gratinéed

**gratinado** gratinéed

**grelo** turnip greens

**grosella** currant

  ~ **espinosa** gooseberry

  ~ **negra** blackcurrant

  ~ **roja** redcurrant

**guacamole** a purée of avocado and spices used as a dip, in a salad, for a *tortilla* filling or as a garnish

**guarnición** garnish, trimming

**guayaba** guava (fruit)

**guinda** sour cherry

**guindilla** chili pepper

**guisado** stew(ed)

**guisante** green pea

**haba** broad bean

**habichuela verde** French bean (US green bean)

**hamburguesa** hamburger

**hayaca central** maizeflour (US cornmeal) pancake, usually with a minced-meat filling

**helado** ice-cream, ice

**hervido** 1) boiled 2) stew of beef and vegetables (Latin America)

**hielo** ice

**hierba** herb

**hierbas finas** finely chopped mixture of herbs

**hígado** liver

**higo** fig

**hinojo** fennel

**hongo** mushroom

**(al) horno** baked

**hortaliza** greens

**hueso** bone

**huevo** egg

  ~ **cocido** boiled

  ~ **duro** hard-boiled

  ~ **escalfado** poached

  ~ **a la española** stuffed with tomatoes and served with cheese sauce

  ~ **a la flamenca** baked with asparagus, peas, peppers, onions, tomatoes and sausage

  ~ **frito** fried

  ~ **al nido** egg-yolk placed into small, soft roll, fried, then covered with egg-white

  ~ **pasado por agua** soft-boiled

  ~ **revuelto** scrambled

~ **con tocino** bacon and egg

**humita** boiled maize (US corn) with tomatoes, green peppers, onions and cheese

**(a la) inglesa** 1) underdone (of meat) 2) boiled 3) served with boiled vegetables

**jabalí** wild boar

**jalea** jelly

**jamón** ham

~ **cocido** boiled (often referred to as *jamón de York*)

~ **en dulce** boiled and served cold

~ **gallego** smoked and cut thinly

~ **serrano** cured and cut thinly

**(a la) jardinera** with carrots, peas and other vegetables

**jengibre** ginger

**(al) jerez** braised in sherry

**judía** bean

~ **verde** French bean (US green bean)

**jugo** gravy, meat juice

**en su** ~ in its own juice

**juliana** with shredded vegetables

**jurel** variety of mackerel

**lacón** shoulder of pork

~ **curado** salted pork

**lamprea** lamprey

**langosta** spiny lobster

**langostino** Norway lobster, Dublin Bay prawn

**laurel** bay leaf

**lechón** suck(l)ing pig

**lechuga** lettuce

**legumbre** vegetable

**lengua** tongue

**lenguado** sole, flounder

~ **frito** fried fillet of sole on bed of vegetables

**lenteja** lentil

**liebre** hare

~ **estofada** jugged hare

**lima** 1) lime 2) sweet lime (Latin America)

**limón** lemon

**lista de platos** menu

**lista de vinos** wine list

**lobarro** a variety of bass

**lombarda** red cabbage

**lomo** loin

**longaniza** long, highly seasoned sausage

**lonja** slice of meat

**lubina** bass

**macarrones** macaroni

**(a la) madrileña** with *chorizo* sausage, tomatoes and paprika

**magras al estilo de Aragón** cured ham in tomato sauce

**maíz** maize (US corn)

**(a la) mallorquina** usually refers to highly seasoned fish and shellfish

**manchego** hard cheese from La Mancha, made from sheep's milk, white or golden-yellow in colour

**maní** peanut

**mantecado** 1) small butter cake 2) custard ice-cream

**mantequilla** butter

**manzana** apple

~ **en dulce** in honey

**(a la) marinera** usually with mussels, onions, tomatoes, herbs and wine

**marisco** seafood

**matambre** rolled beef stuffed with vegetables

**mayonesa** mayonnaise

**mazapán** marzipan, almond paste

**mejillón** mussel

**mejorana** marjoram

**melaza** treacle, molasses

**melocotón** peach

**membrillo** quince

**menestra** boiled green vegetable soup

~ **de pollo** chicken and vegetable soup

**menta** mint

**menú** menu

~ **del día** set menu

~ **turístico** tourist menu

**menudillos** giblets

**merengue** meringue

**merienda** snack

**merluza** hake

**mermelada** jam

**mezclado** mixed

**miel** honey

**(a la) milanesa** with cheese, generally baked

**minuta** menu

**mixto** mixed

**mole poblano** chicken served with a sauce of chili peppers, spices and chocolate

**molusco** mollusc (snail, mussel, clam)

**molleja** sweetbread

**mora** mulberry

**morcilla** black pudding (US blood sausage)

**morilla** morel mushroom

**moros y cristianos** rice and black beans with diced ham, garlic, green peppers and herbs

**mostaza** mustard

**mújol** mullet

**nabo** turnip

**naranja** orange

**nata** cream

~ **batida** whipped cream

**natillas** custard

~ **al limón** lemon cream

**níspola** medlar (fruit)

**nopalito** young cactus leaf served with salad dressing

**nuez** nut

~ **moscada** nutmeg

**olla** stew

~ **gitana** vegetable stew

~ **podrida** stew made of vegetables, meat, fowl and ham

**ostra** oyster

**oveja** ewe

**pabellón criollo** beef in tomato sauce garnished with beans, rice and bananas

**paella** consists basically of saffron rice with assorted seafood and sometimes meat

~ **alicantina** with green peppers, onions, tomatoes, artichokes and fish

~ **catalana** with sausages, pork, squid, tomatoes, red sweet peppers and peas

~ **marinera** with fish, shellfish and meat

~ **(a la) valenciana** with chicken, shrimps, peas, tomatoes, mussels and garlic

**palmito** palm heart

**palta** avocado (pear)

**pan** bread

**panecillo** roll

**papa** potato

**papas a Ja huancaína** with cheese and green peppers

**(a la) parrilla** grilled

**parrillada mixta** mixed grill

**pasado** done, cooked

**bien** ~ well-done

**poco** ~ underdone (US rare)

**pastas** noodles, macaroni, spaghetti

**pastel** cake, pie

~ **de choclo** maize with minced beef, chicken, raisins and olives

**pastelillo** small tart

**pata** trotter (US foot)

**patatas** potatoes
  ~ **fritas** fried; usually chips (US french fries)
  ~ **(a la) leonesa** with onions
  ~ **nuevas** new
**pato** duck, duckling
**pavo** turkey
**pechuga** breast (of fowl)
**pepinillo** gherkin (US pickle)
**pepino** cucumber
**(en) pepitoria** stewed with onions, green peppers and tomatoes
**pera** pear
**perca** perch
**percebe** barnacle (shellfish)
**perdiz** partridge
  ~ **en escabeche** cooked in oil with vinegar, onions, parsley, carrots and green pepper; served cold
  ~ **estofada** stewed and served with a white-wine sauce
**perejil** parsley
**perifollo** chervil
**perilla** a firm, bland cheese
**pescadilla** whiting
**pescado** fish
**pez espada** swordfish
**picadillo** minced meat, hash
**picado** minced
**picante** sharp, spicy, highly seasoned
**picatoste** deep-fried slice of bread
**pichoncillo** young pigeon (US squab)
**pierna** leg
**pimentón** chili pepper
**pimienta** pepper
**pimiento** sweet pepper
  ~ **morrón** red (sweet) pepper
**pincho moruno** grilled meat (often kidneys) on a skewer, sometimes served with spicy sauces
**pintada** guinea fowl

**piña** pineapple
**pisto** diced and sautéed vegetables: mainly aubergines, green peppers and tomatoes; served cold
**(a la) plancha** grilled on a girdle
**plátano** banana
**plato** plate, dish, portion
  ~ **típico de la región** regional speciality
**pollito** spring chicken
**pollo** chicken
  ~ **pibil** simmered in fruit juice and spices
**polvorón** hazelnut biscuit (US cookie)
**pomelo** grapefruit
**porción** portion
**porotos granados** shelled beans served with pumpkin and maize (US corn)
**postre** dessert, sweet
**potaje** vegetable soup
**puchero** stew
**puerro** leek
**pulpo** octopus
**punta de espárrago** asparagus tip
**punto de nieve** dessert of whipped cream with beaten egg-whites
**puré de patatas** mashed potatoes
**queso** cheese
**quisquilla** shrimp
**rábano** radish
  ~ **picante** horse-radish
**raja** slice or portion
**rallado** grated
**rape** angler fish
**ravioles** ravioli
**raya** skate, ray
**rebanada** slice
**rebozado** breaded or fried in batter
**recargo** extra charge
**rehogada** sautéed

**relleno** stuffed
**remolacha** beetroot
**repollo** cabbage
**requesón** a fresh-curd cheese
**riñón** kidney
**róbalo** haddock
**rodaballo** turbot, flounder
**(a la) romana** dipped in batter and fried
**romero** rosemary
**roncal** cheese made from sheep's milk; close grained and hard in texture with a few small holes; piquant flavour
**ropa vieja** cooked, left-over meat and vegetables, covered with tomatoes and green peppers
**rosbif** roast beef
**rosquilla** doughnut
**rubio** red mullet
**ruibarbo** rhubarb
**sal** salt
**salado** salted, salty
**salchicha** small pork sausage for frying
**salchichón** salami
**salmón** salmon
**salmonete** red mullet
**salsa** sauce
  ~ **blanca** white
  ~ **española** brown sauce with herbs, spices and wine
  ~ **mayordoma** butter and parsley
  ~ **picante** hot pepper
  ~ **romana** bacon or ham, egg, cream (sometimes flavoured with nutmeg)
  ~ **tártara** tartar
  ~ **verde** parsley
**salsifí** salsify
**salteado** sauté(ed)
**salvia** sage
**san simón** a firm, bland cheese

resembling *perilla*; shiny yellow rind
**sandía** watermelon
**sardina** sardine, pilchard
**sémola** semolina
**sencillo** plain
**sepia** cuttlefish
**servicio** service
  ~ **(no) incluido** (not) included
**sesos** brains
**seta** mushroom
**sobrasada** salami
**solomillo** fillet steak (US tenderloin)
**sopa** soup
  ~ **(de) cola de buey** oxtail
  ~ **sevillana** a highly spiced fish soup
**suave** soft
**suflé** soufflé
**suizo** bun
**surtido** assorted
**taco** wheat or maizeflour (US cornmeal) pancake usually with a meat filling and garnished with a spicy sauce
**tajada** slice
**tallarín** noodle
**tamal** a pastry dough of coarsely ground maizeflour with meat or fruit filling, steamed in maizehusks (US corn husks)
**tapa** appetizer, snack
**tarta** cake, tart
  ~ **helada** ice-cream tart
**ternera** veal
**tocino** bacon
  ~ **de cielo** 1) caramel mould 2) custard-filled cake
**tomate** tomato
**tomillo** thyme
**tordo** thrush
**toronja** variety of grapefruit
**tortilla** 1) omelet 2) a type of

pancake made with maizeflour (US cornmeal)

~ **de chorizo** with pieces of a spicy sausage

~ **a la española** with onions, potatoes and seasoning

~ **a la francesa** plain

~ **gallega** potatoes with ham, red sweet peppers and peas

~ **a la jardinera** with mixed, diced vegetables

~ **al ron** rum

**tortita** waffle

**tortuga** turtle

**tostada** toast

**tripas** tripe

**trucha** trout

~ **frita a la asturiana** floured and fried in butter, garnished with lemon

**trufa** truffle

**turrón** nougat

**ulloa** a soft cheese from Galicia, rather like a mature camembert

**uva** grape

~ **pasa** raisin

**vaca salada** corned beef

**vainilla** vanilla

**(a la) valenciana** with rice, tomatoes and garlic

**variado** varied, assorted

**varios** sundries

**venado** venison

**venera** scallop, coquille St. Jacques

**verdura** greens

**vieira** scallop

**villalón** a cheese from sheep's milk

**vinagre** vinegar

**vinagreta** a piquant vinegar dressing (vinaigrette) to accompany salads

**(a la)** ~ marinated in oil and vinegar or lemon juice with mixed herbs

**(a la) vizcaína** with green peppers, tomatoes, garlic and paprika

**yema** egg-yolk

**yemas** a dessert of whipped egg-yolks and sugar

**zanahoria** carrot

**zarzamora** blackberry

**zarzuela** savoury stew of assorted fish and shellfish

~ **de mariscos** seafood stew

~ **de pescado** selection of fish served with a highly seasoned sauce

~ **de verduras** vegetable stew

# Drinks

**abocado** sherry made from a blend of sweet and dry wines

**agua** water

**aguardiente** spirits

**Alicante** this region to the south of Valencia produces a large quantity of red table wine and some good rosé, particularly from Yecla

**Amontillado** medium-dry sherry,

light amber in colour, with a
nutty flavour

**Andalucía** a drink of dry sherry
and orange juice

**Angélica** a Basque herb liqueur
similar to yellow Chartreuse

**anís** aniseed liqueur

**Anís del Mono** a Calatonian aniseed liqueur

**anís seco** aniseed brandy

**anisado** an aniseed-based soft
drink which may be slightly
alcoholic

**batido** milk shake

**bebida** drink

**Bobadilla Gran Reserva** a wine-
distilled brandy

**botella** bottle

**media ~** half bottle

**café** coffee

**~ cortado** small cup of strong
coffee with a dash of milk or
cream

**~ descafeinado** coffeine-free

**~ exprés** espresso

**~ granizado** iced (white)

**~ con leche** white

**~ negro/solo** black

**Calisay** a quinine-flavoured liqueur

**Carlos I** a wine-distilled brandy

**Cataluña** Catalonia; this region
southwest of Barcelona is
known for its *xampañ*, bearing
little resemblance to the famed
French sparkling wine

**Cazalla** an aniseed liqueur

**cerveza** beer

**~ de barril** draught (US draft)

**~ dorada** light

**~ negra** dark

**cola de mono** a blend of coffee,
milk, rum and *pisco*

**coñac** 1) French Cognac 2) term

applied to any Spanish wine-
distilled brandy

**Cordoníu** a brand-name of Catalonian sparkling wine locally referred to as *xampañ* (champagne)

**cosecha** harvest; indicates the
vintage of wine

**crema de cacao** cocoa liqueur,
crème de cacao

**Cuarenta y Tres** an egg liqueur

**Cuba libre** rum and Coke

**champán, champaña** 1) French
Champagne 2) term applied to
any Spanish sparkling wine

**chicha de manzana** apple brandy

**Chinchón** an aniseed liqueur

**chocolate** chocolate drink

**~ con leche** hot chocolate with
milk

**Dulce** dessert wine

**Fino** dry sherry wine, very pale
and straw-coloured

**Fundador** a wine-distilled brandy

**Galicia** this Atlantic coastal region
has good table wines

**gaseosa** fizzy (US carbonated)
water

**ginebra** gin

**gran vino** term found on Chilean
wine labels to indicate a wine of
exceptional quality

**granadina** pomegranate syrup
mixed with wine or brandy

**horchata de almendra** (or **de chu-
fa**) drink made from ground al-
monds (or Jerusalem artichoke)

**Jerez** 1) sherry 2) the Spanish
region near the Portuguese border, internationally renowned
for its *Jerez*

**jugo** fruit juice

**leche** milk

**limonada** lemonade, lemon

squash

**Málaga** 1) dessert wine 2) the region in the south of Spain, is particularly noted for its dessert wine

**Manzanilla** dry sherry, very pale and straw-coloured

**margarita** *tequila* with lime juice

**Montilla** a dessert wine from near Cordoba, often drunk as an aperitif

**Moscatel** fruity dessert wine

**naranjada** orangeade

**Oloroso** sweet, dark sherry, drunk as dessert wine, resembles brown cream sherry

**Oporto** port (wine)

**pisco** grape brandy

**ponche crema** egg-nog liquor

**Priorato** the region south of Barcelona produces good quality red and white wine but also a dessert wine, usually called *Priorato* but renamed *Tarragona* when it is exported

**refresco** a soft drink

**reservado** term found on Chilean wine labels to indicate a wine of exceptional quality

**Rioja** the northern region near the French border is considered to produce Spain's best wines—especially red; some of the finest Rioja wines resemble good Bordeaux wines

**ron** rum

**sangría** a mixture of red wine, ice, orange, lemon, brandy and sugar

**sangrita** *tequila* with tomato, orange and lime juices

**sidra** cider

**sol y sombra** a blend of wine-distilled brandy and aniseed liqueur

**sorbete** (iced) fruit drink

**té** tea

**tequila** brandy made from agave (US aloe)

**tinto** 1) red wine 2) black coffee with sugar (Colombia)

**Tío Pepe** a brand-name sherry

**Triple Seco** an orange liqueur

**Valdepeñas** the region south of Madrid is an important wine-producing area

**vermú** vermouth

**Veterano Osborne** a wine-distilled brandy

**vino** wine

  ~ **blanco** white

  ~ **clarete** rosé

  ~ **común** table wine

  ~ **dulce** dessert

  ~ **espumoso** sparkling

  ~ **de mesa** table wine

  ~ **del país** local wine

  ~ **rosado** rosé

  ~ **seco** dry

  ~ **suave** sweet

  ~ **tinto** red

**xampañ** Catalonian sparkling wine

**Yerba mate** South American holly tea

**zumo** juice

# Spanish Verbs

Below are some examples of Spanish verbs in the three regular conjugations, grouped by families according to their infinitive endings, *-ar*, *-er* and *-ir*. Verbs which do not follow the conjugations below are considered irregular (see irregular verb list). Note that there are some verbs which follow the regular conjugation of the category they belong to, but present some minor changes in spelling. Examples: *tocar, toque; cargar, cargue*. The personal pronoun is not generally expressed, since the verb endings clearly indicate the person.

| | | 1st conj. | 2nd conj. | 3rd conj. |
|---|---|---|---|---|
| | | **am ar** | **tem er** | **viv ir** |
| Infinitive | | *(to love)* | *(to fear)* | *(to live)* |
| Present | (yo) | am **o** | tem **o** | viv **o** |
| | (tú) | am **as** | tem **es** | viv **es** |
| | (él) | am **a** | tem **e** | viv **e** |
| | (nosotros) | am **amos** | tem **emos** | viv **imos** |
| | (vosotros) | am **áis** | tem **éis** | viv **ís** |
| | (ellos) | am **an** | tem **en** | viv **en** |
| Imperfect | (yo) | am **aba** | tem **ía** | viv **ía** |
| | (tú) | am **abas** | tem **ías** | viv **ías** |
| | (él) | am **aba** | tem **ía** | viv **ía** |
| | (nosotros) | am **ábamos** | tem **íamos** | viv **íamos** |
| | (vosotros) | am **abais** | tem **íais** | viv **íais** |
| | (ellos) | am **aban** | tem **ían** | viv **ían** |
| Past. def. | (yo) | am **é** | tem **í** | viv **í** |
| | (tú) | am **aste** | tem **iste** | viv **iste** |
| | (él) | am **ó** | tem **ió** | viv **ió** |
| | (nosotros) | am **amos** | tem **imos** | viv **imos** |
| | (vosotros) | am **asteis** | tem **isteis** | viv **isteis** |
| | (ellos) | am **aron** | tem **ieron** | viv **ieron** |
| Future | (yo) | am **aré** | tem **eré** | viv **iré** |
| | (tú) | am **arás** | tem **erás** | viv **irás** |
| | (él) | am **ará** | tem **erá** | viv **irá** |
| | (nosotros) | am **aremos** | tem **eremos** | viv **iremos** |
| | (vosotros) | am **aréis** | tem **eréis** | viv **iréis** |
| | (ellos) | am **arán** | tem **erán** | viv **irán** |
| Conditional | (yo) | am **aría** | tem **ería** | viv **iría** |
| | (tú) | am **arías** | tem **erías** | viv **irías** |
| | (él) | am **aría** | tem **ería** | viv **iría** |
| | (nosotros) | am **aríamos** | tem **eríamos** | viv **iríamos** |
| | (vosotros) | am **aríais** | tem **eríais** | viv **iríais** |
| | (ellos) | am **arían** | tem **erían** | viv **irían** |
| Subj. Pres. | (yo) | am **e** | tem **a** | viv **a** |
| | (tú) | am **es** | tem **as** | viv **as** |
| | (él) | am **e** | tem **a** | viv **a** |
| | (nosotros) | am **emos** | tem **amos** | viv **amos** |
| | (vosotros) | am **éis** | tem **áis** | viv **áis** |
| | (ellos) | am **en** | tem **an** | viv **an** |

| Pres. Part./Gerund | am **ando** | tem **iendo** | viv **iendo** |
| Past. Part. | am **ado** | tem **ido** | viv **ido** |

## Auxiliary verbs

The verb **to have** is translated either by *haber* or by *tener*. *Haber* is the auxiliary (e.g. he has gone) and *tener* (see list of irregular verbs) is a transitive verb, which conveys the idea of possession (e.g. she has a house).

The verb **to be** is translated either by *ser* or *estar*. *Ser* is used as an auxiliary verb to form the passive (e.g. they are understood) and to express an intrinsic quality of a fundamental characteristic (e.g. man is mortal). *Estar* (see list of irregular verbs) expresses a state or an attitude, whether lasting or not, of a thing or a person (e.g. she is hungry).

|  | **haber** *(to have)* |  | **ser** *(to be)* |  |
|---|---|---|---|---|
|  | *Present* | *Imperfect* | *Present* | *Imperfect* |
| (yo) | he | había | soy | era |
| (tú) | has | habías | eres | eras |
| (él) | ha | había | es | era |
| (nosotros) | hemos | habíamos | somos | éramos |
| (vosotros) | habéis | habíais | sois | erais |
| (ellos) | han | habían | son | eran |
|  | *Future* | *Conditional* | *Future* | *Conditional* |
| (yo) | habré | habría | seré | sería |
| (tú) | habrás | habrías | serás | serías |
| (él) | habrá | habría | será | sería |
| (nosotros) | habremos | habríamos | seremos | seríamos |
| (vosotros) | habréis | habríais | seréis | seríais |
| (ellos) | habrán | habrían | serán | serían |
|  | *Present subjunctive* | *Present perfect* | *Present subjunctive* | *Present perfect* |
| (yo) | haya | he habido | sea | he sido |
| (tú) | hayas | has habido | seas | has sido |
| (él) | haya | ha habido | sea | ha sido |
| (nosotros) | hayamos | hemos habido | seamos | hemos sido |
| (vosotros) | hayáis | habéis habido | seáis | habéis sido |
| (ellos) | hayan | han habido | sean | han sido |
|  | *Present participle* | *Past participle* | *Present participle* | *Past participle* |
|  | habiendo | habido | siendo | sido |

## Irregular verbs

Below is a list of the verbs and tenses commonly used in spoken Spanish. In the listing, a) stands for the present tense, b) for the imperfect, c) for the past def., d) for the future, e) for the present participle and f) for the past participle. The only forms given below are the irregular ones commonly used. There can be other irregular forms, but they are considered rare. In tenses other than present, all persons can be regularly formed from the first person. Unless otherwise indicated, verbs with prefixes (*ad-, ante-, com-, con-, de-, des-, dis-, en-, ex-, im-, pos-, pre-, pro-, re-, sobre-, sub-, tras-,* etc.) are conjugated like the stem verb.

**abstenerse**
*refrain*
→tener

**acertar**
*guess*
→cerrar

**acontecer**
*happen*
→agradecer

**acordar**
*agree ; decide*
→contar

**acostarse**
*lie down*
→contar

**acrecentar**
*increase ; advance*
→cerrar

**adormecer**
*put to sleep*
→agradecer

**adquirir**
*acquire*
a) adquiero, adquieres, adquiere, adquirimos, adquirís, adquieren; b) adquiría; c) adquirí; d) adquiriré; e) adquiriendo; f) adquirido

**advertir**
*notice*
→sentir

**agradecer**
*thank*
a) agradezco, agradeces, agradece, agradecemos, agradecéis, agradecen; b) agradecía; c) agradecí; d) agradeceré; e) agradeciendo; f) agradecido

**alentar**
*encourage*
→cerrar

**almorzar**
*have lunch*
→contar

**amanecer**
*dawn*
→agradecer

**andar**
*walk*
a) ando, andas, anda, andamos, andáis, andan; b) andaba; c) anduve; d) andaré; e) andando; f) andado

**anochecer**
*begin to get dark*
→agradecer

**apetecer**
*want*
→agradecer

**apostar**
*bet*
→contar

**apretar**
*tighten, squeeze*
→cerrar

**arrendar** →cerrar
*let, lease, rent*

**arrepentirse** →sentir
*repent, regret*

**ascender** →perder
*climb, reach*

**atenerse** →tener
*obey; rely on*

**atravesar** →cerrar
*cross, pierce*

**atribuir** →instruir
*attribute*

**aventar** →cerrar
*fan, air*

**avergonzar** →contar
*put to shame,*
*embarrass*

**bendecir** →decir
*bless*

**caber** a) quepo, cabes, cabe, cabemos, cabéis, caben;
*contain; fit* b) cabía; c) cupe; d) cabré; e) cabiendo; f) cabido

**caer** a) caigo, caes, cae, caemos, caéis, caen; b) caía;
*fall* c) caí; d) caeré; e) cayendo; f) caído

**calentar** →cerrar
*heat*

**carecer** →agradecer
*lack*

**cegar** →cerrar
*blind*

**cerrar** a) cierro, cierras, cierra, cerramos, cerráis, cierran;
*close* b) cerraba; c) cerré; d) cerraré; e) cerrando; f) cerrado

**cocer** a) cuezo, cueces, cuece, cocemos, cocéis, cuecen;
*boil* b) cocía; c) cocí; d) coceré; e) cociendo; f) cocido

**colar** →contar
*strain; filter*

**colgar** →contar
*hang*

**comenzar** →cerrar
*begin*

**competir** →pedir
*compete*

**concebir** →pedir
*conceive*

**concernir**
*concern* →sentir

**concluir**
*conclude, finish* →instruir

**concordar**
*agree, reconcile* →contar

**conducir**
*drive* →traducir

**conferir**
*confer* →sentir

**confesar**
*confess* →cerrar

**conocer**
*know*
a) conozco, conoces, conoce, conocemos, conocéis, conocen; b) conocía; c) conocí; d) conoceré; e) conociendo; f) conocido

**consolar**
*console, comfort* →contar

**constituir**
*constitute, be* →instruir

**construir**
*build, erect* →instruir

**contar**
*count, bear in mind*
a) cuento, cuentas, cuenta, contamos, contáis, cuentan; b) contaba; c) conté; d) contaré; e) contando; f) contado

**contribuir**
*contribute* →instruir

**convertir**
*convert* →sentir

**corregir**
*correct* →pedir

**costar**
*cost* →contar

**crecer**
*grow, rise* →agradecer

**dar**
*give*
a) doy, das, da, damos, dais, dan; b) daba; c) di; d) daré; e) dando; f) dado

**decir**
*say*
a) digo, dices, dice, decimos, decís, dicen; b) decía; c) dije; d) diré e) diciendo; f) dicho

**deducir**
*deduce* →traducir

**defender**
*defend* →perder

**derretir**
*melt* →pedir

**descender** →perder
*descend, let down*

**descollar** →contar
*be outstanding*

**desconcertar** →cerrar
*damage; upset*

**despertar** →cerrar
*awaken, revive*

**desterrar** →cerrar
*banish*

**destituir** →instruir
*deprive, dismiss*

**destruir** →instruir
*destroy*

**desvanecer** →agradecer
*make disappear,*
*take out*

**diferir** →sentir
*defer*

**digerir** →sentir
*digest*

**diluir** →instruir
*dilute*

**discernir** →sentir
*discern*

**disminuir** →instruir
*diminish*

**disolver** →morder
*dissolve*

**distribuir** →instruir
*distribute*

**divertir** →sentir
*entertain, distract*

**doler** →morder
*hurt*

**dormir** a) duermo, duermes, duerme, dormimos, dormís
*sleep* duermen; b) dormía; c) dormí; d) dormiré;
e) durmiendo; f) dormido

**elegir** →pedir
*elect, choose*

**embestir** →pedir
*assault*

**empezar** →cerrar
*begin, start*

**enaltecer** →agradecer
*exalt, praise*

**enardecer** →agradecer
*excite; inflame*

**encender** →perder
*light, ignite*

**encomendar** →cerrar
*entrust*

**encontrar** →contar
*find*

**engrandecer** →agradecer
*enlarge, exaggerate*

**enloquecer** →agradecer
*madden*

**enmendar** →cerrar
*emend, correct*

**enmudecer** →agradecer
*silence*

**enorgullecer** →agradecer
*fill with pride*

**enriquecer** →agradecer
*enrich*

**ensangrentar** →cerrar
*stain with blood*

**ensoberbecer** →agradecer
*make proud*

**ensordecer** →agradecer
*deafen*

**enternecer** →agradecer
*soften; affect*

**enterrar** →cerrar
*bury*

**entristecer** →agradecer
*sadden*

**envejecer** →agradecer
*age*

**errar** →cerrar
*miss; wander*

**escarmentar** →cerrar
*chastise, punish*

**escarnecer** →agradecer
*scoff*

**establecer** →agradecer
*establish*

| | |
|---|---|
| **estar** | a) estoy, estás, está, estamos, estáis, están; b) estaba; |
| *be* | c) estuve; d) estaré; e) estando; f) estado |
| **estremecer** | →agradecer |
| *shake* | |
| **excluir** | →instruir |
| *exclude* | |
| **fallecer** | →agradecer |
| *die* | |
| **favorecer** | →agradecer |
| *favour* | |
| **florecer** | →agradecer |
| *blossom* | |
| **fluir** | →instruir |
| *flow* | |
| **fortalecer** | →agradecer |
| *strengthen* | |
| **forzar** | →contar |
| *compel, force* | |
| **fregar** | →cerrar |
| *wash up; scrub* | |
| **freír** | →reír |
| *fry* | |
| **gemir** | →pedir |
| *groan* | |
| **gobernar** | →cerrar |
| *govern* | |
| **gruñir** | a) gruño, gruñes, gruñe, gruñimos, gruñís, gruñen; |
| *grunt* | b) gruñía; c) gruñí; d) gruñiré; e) gruñiendo; f) gruñido |
| **haber** | a) he, has, ha, hemos, habéis, han; b) había; c) hube; |
| *have* | d) habré; e) habiendo; f) habido |
| **hacer** | a) hago, haces, hace, hacemos, hacéis, hacen; b) hacía; |
| *make* | c) hice; d) haré; e) haciendo; f) hecho |
| **heder** | →perder |
| *stink* | |
| **helar** | →cerrar |
| *freeze* | |
| **hender** | →perder |
| *crack* | |
| **herir** | →sentir |
| *injure* | |
| **hervir** | →sentir |
| *boil* | |
| **huir** | →instruir |
| *escape* | |

**humedecer** →agradecer
*humidify*

**incluir** →instruir
*include*

**inducir** →traducir
*induce*

**ingerir** →sentir
*swallow ; consume*

**instituir** →instruir
*institute*

**instruir** a) instruyo, instruyes, instruye, instruimos, instruís,
*instruct* instruyen; b) instruía; c) instruí; d) instruiré;
e) instruyendo; f) instruido

**introducir** →traducir
*introduce*

**invertir** →sentir
*invest*

**ir** a) voy, vas, va, vamos, vais, van; b) iba; c) fui; d) iré;
*go* e) yendo; f) ido

**jugar** a) juego, juegas, juega, jugamos, jugáis, juegan;
*play* b) jugaba; c) jugué; d) jugaré; e) jugando; f) jugado

**lucir** a) luzco, luces, luce, lucimos, lucís, lucen; b) lucía;
*shine* c) lucí; d) luciré; e) luciendo; f) lucido

**llover** a) llueve; b) llovía; c) llovió; d) lloverá; e) lloviendo;
*rain* f) llovido

**manifestar** →cerrar
*manifest*

**mantener** →tener
*maintain*

**medir** →pedir
*measure*

**mentir** →sentir
*tell a lie*

**merecer** →agradecer
*deserve*

**merendar** →cerrar
*have tea, snack*

**moler** →morder
*grind*

**morder** a) muerdo, muerdes, muerde, mordemos, mordéis,
*bite* muerden; b) mordía; c) mordí; d) morderé;
e) mordiendo; f) mordido

**morir** →dormir
*die*

| | |
|---|---|
| **mostrar**<br>*show* | →contar |
| **mover**<br>*move* | →morder |
| **nacer**<br>*be born* | a) nazco, naces, nace, nacemos, nacéis, nacen; b) nacía;<br>c) nací; d) naceré; e) naciendo; f) nacido |
| **negar**<br>*deny* | →cerrar |
| **nevar**<br>*snow* | a) nieva; b) nevaba; c) nevó; d) nevará; e) nevando;<br>f) nevado |
| **obedecer**<br>*obey* | →agradecer |
| **obscurecer**<br>*darken* | →agradecer |
| **obstruir**<br>*obstruct* | →instruir |
| **obtener**<br>*obtain* | →tener |
| **ofrecer,**<br>*offer* | →agradecer |
| **oír**<br>*hear, listen* | a) oigo, oyes, oye, oímos, oís, oyen; b) oía; c) oí; d) oiré;<br>e) oyendo; f) oído |
| **oler**<br>*smell* | →morder |
| **pacer**<br>*graze* | →nacer |
| **padecer**<br>*suffer* | →agradecer |
| **parecer**<br>*seem* | →agradecer |
| **pedir**<br>*ask for, request* | a) pido, pides, pide, pedimos, pedís, piden; b) pedía;<br>c) pedí; d) pediré; e) pidiendo; f) pedido |
| **pensar**<br>*think* | →cerrar |
| **perder**<br>*lose* | a) pierdo, pierdes, pierde, perdemos, perdéis, pierden;<br>b) perdía; c) perdí; d) perderé; e) perdiendo; f) perdido |
| **perecer**<br>*perish* | →agradecer |
| **permanecer**<br>*stay* | →agradecer |
| **pertenecer**<br>*belong to* | →agradecer |
| **pervertir**<br>*pervert* | →sentir |

| | |
|---|---|
| **placer** *please* | a) plazco, places, place, placemos, placéis, placen; b) placía; c) plací; d) placeré; e) placiendo; f) placido |
| **plegar** *fold* | →cerrar |
| **poblar** *populate* | →contar |
| **poder** *can, be able* | a) puedo, puedes, puede, podemos, podéis, pueden; b) podía; c) pude; d) podré; e) pudiendo; f) podido |
| **poner** *put* | a) pongo, pones, pone, ponemos, ponéis, ponen; b) ponía; c) puse; d) pondré; e) poniendo; f) puesto |
| **preferir** *prefer* | →sentir |
| **probar** *try* | →contar |
| **producir** *produce* | →traducir |
| **proferir** *utter* | →sentir |
| **quebrar** *break* | →cerrar |
| **querer** *want, wish* | a) quiero, quieres, quiere, queremos, queréis, quieren; b) quería; c) quise; d) querré; e) queriendo; f) querido |
| **recomendar** *recommend* | →cerrar |
| **recordar** *remember* | →contar |
| **reducir** *reduce* | →traducir |
| **referir** *refer, relate* | →sentir |
| **regar** *water* | →cerrar |
| **regir** *govern* | →pedir |
| **reír** *laugh* | a) río, ríes, ríe, reímos, reís, ríen; b) reía; c) rei; d) reiré; e) riendo; f) reído |
| **remendar** *mend* | →cerrar |
| **rendir** *produce; overcome* | →pedir |
| **renovar** *renew* | →contar |
| **reñir** *scold; quarrel* | →teñir |

| | |
|---|---|
| **repetir**<br>*repeat* | →pedir |
| **requerir**<br>*request* | →sentir |
| **resolver**<br>*resolve* | →morder |
| **resplandecer**<br>*shine* | →agradecer |
| **restituir**<br>*restore, return* | →instruir |
| **retribuir**<br>*pay; reward* | →instruir |
| **reventar**<br>*burst* | →cerrar |
| **robustecer**<br>*strengthen* | →agradecer |
| **rodar**<br>*drive; roll* | →contar |
| **rogar**<br>*beg, plead* | →contar |
| **saber**<br>*know* | a) sé, sabes, sabe, sabemos, sabéis, saben; )b sabía; c) supe; d) sabré; e) sabiendo; f) sabido |
| **salir**<br>*go out* | a) salgo, sales, sale, salimos, salís, salen; b) salía; c) salí; d) saldré; e) saliendo; f) salido |
| **satisfacer**<br>*satisfy* | →hacer |
| **seducir**<br>*seduce* | →traducir |
| **seguir**<br>*follow* | →pedir |
| **sembrar**<br>*sow* | →cerrar |
| **sentar**<br>*sit, seat* | →cerrar |
| **sentir**<br>*feel* | a) siento, sientes, siente, sentimos, sentís, sienten; b) sentía; c) sentí; d) sentiré; e) sintiendo; f) sentido |
| **ser**.<br>*be* | a) soy, eres, es, somos, sois, son; b) era c) fui; d) seré; e) siendo; f) sido |
| **servir**<br>*serve* | →pedir |
| **soldar**<br>*solder; join* | →contar |
| **soler**<br>*be used to* | a) suelo, sueles, suele, solemos, soléis, suelen; b) solía; c) solí; e) soliendo; f) solido |

**soltar** →contar
*release ; loosen*

**sonar** →contar
*ring, sound*

**soñar** →contar
*dream*

**sugerir** →sentir
*suggest*

**sustituir** →instruir
*substitute*

**temblar** →cerrar
*tremble*

**tender** →perder
*stretch, extend*

**tener** a) tengo, tienes, tiene, tenemos, tenéis, tienen; b) tenía;
*have (got)* c) tuve; d) tendré; e) teniendo; f) tenido

**tentar** →cerrar
*touch ; try*

**teñir** a) tiño, tiñes, tiñe, teñimos, teñís, tiñen; b) teñía;
*dye* c) teñí; d) teñiré; e) tiñiendo; f) teñido

**torcer** →cocer
*twist*

**tostar** →contar
*roast*

**traducir** a) traduzco, traduces, traduce, traducimos, traducís,
*translate* traducen; b) traducía; c) traduje; d) traduciré;
e) traduciendo; f) traducido

**traer** a) traigo, traes, trae, traemos, traéis, traen; b) traía;
*bring* c) traje; d) traeré; e) trayendo; f) traído

**transferir** →sentir
*transfer*

**trocar** →contar
*(ex)change*

**tronar** a) trueno, truenas, truena, tronamos, tronáis, truenan;
*thunder* b) tronaba; c) troné; d) tronaré; e) tronando; f) tronado

**tropezar** →cerrar
*stumble*

**valer** a) valgo, vales, vale, valemos, valéis, valen; b) valía;
*protect ; be worth* c) valí; d) valdré; e) valiendo; f) valido

**venir** a) vengo, vienes, viene, venimos, venís, vienen; b) venía;
*come* c) vine; d) vendré; e) viniendo; f) venido

**ver** a) veo, ves, ve, vemos, veis, ven; b) veía; c) vi; d) veré;
*see* e) viendo; f) visto

| | |
|---|---|
| **verter**<br>*pour; spill* | →perder |
| **vestir**<br>*dress* | →pedir |
| **volar**<br>*fly* | →contar |
| **volcar**<br>*tip over* | →contar |
| **volver**<br>*(re)turn* | →morder |
| **yacer**<br>*lie, rest* | →nacer |
| **zambullir**<br>*plunge* | a) zambullo, zambulles, zambulle, zambullimos, zambullís, zambullen; b) zambullía; c) zambullí; d) zambulliré; e) zambullendo; f) zambullido |

# Spanish Abbreviations

| | | |
|---|---|---|
| **a.C.** | *antes de Cristo* | B.C. |
| **A.C.** | *año de Cristo* | A.D. |
| **admón.** | *administración* | administration |
| **A.L.A.L.C.** | *Asociación Latino-Americana de Libre Comercio* | Latin American Free Trade Association |
| **apdo.** | *apartado de correos* | P.O. Box |
| **Av./Avda.** | *Avenida* | avenue |
| **Barna.** | *Barcelona* | Barcelona |
| **C/** | *Calle* | street, road |
| **c/c.** | *cuenta corriente* | current account |
| **Cía.** | *Compañía* | company |
| **ct(s).** | *céntimo(s)* | 1/100 of a peseta |
| **cta.** | *cuenta* | account; bill |
| **cte.** | *corriente* | inst., of this month |
| **CV.** | *caballos de vapor* | horsepower |
| **D.** | *Don* | courtesy title for gentlemen, only used together with the Christian name |
| **D.ª** | *Doña* | courtesy title for ladies, only used together with the Christian name |
| **dcha.** | *derecha* | right (direction) |
| **D.N.I.** | *Documento Nacional de Identidad* | identity card |
| **d.v.** | *días de visita* | open days |
| **EE.UU.** | *Estados Unidos* | USA |
| **Exc.ª** | *Excelencia* | Your Excellency |
| **f.c.** | *ferrocarril* | railway |
| **G.C.** | *Guardia Civil* | Spanish police force |
| **gral.** | *general* | general |
| **h.** | *hora* | hour |
| **hab.** | *habitantes* | inhabitants, population |
| **hnos.** | *hermanos* | brothers (in firms) |
| **íd.** | *idem* | ditto |
| **igla.** | *iglesia* | church |
| **izq./izqda.** | *izquierda* | left (direction) |
| **lic.** | *licenciado* | licentiate; lawyer |
| **M.I.T.** | *Ministerio de Información y Turismo* | Spanish Ministry of Information and Tourism |
| **Mons.** | *Monseñor* | Roman Catholic title (approx. Your Grace) |

| | | |
|---|---|---|
| **N.ª S.ª** | *Nuestra Señora* | Our Lady, Virgin Mary |
| **n.º/núm.** | *número* | number |
| **O.E.A.** | *Organización de Estados Americanos* | Organization of American States |
| **P.** | *Padre* | Father (ecclesiastical title) |
| **pág.** | *página* | page |
| **P.D.** | *posdata* | P.S. |
| **p.ej.** | *por ejemplo* | e.g. |
| **P.P.** | *porte pagado* | postage paid |
| **pta(s).** | *peseta(s)* | peseta(s) |
| **P.V.P.** | *precio de venta al público* | retail price |
| **R.A.C.E.** | *Real Automóvil Club de España* | Royal Automobile Association of Spain |
| **R.A.E.** | *Real Academia Española* | Royal Academy of the Spanish Language |
| **R.C.** | *Real Club…* | Royal… Association |
| **RENFE** | *Red Nacional de los Ferrocarriles Españoles* | Spanish National Railways |
| **R.M.** | *Reverenda Madre* | Mother Superior, abbess |
| **R.P.** | *Reverendo Padre* | Reverend Father (title for Catholic priests and abbots) |
| **Rte.** | *Remite, Remitente* | sender (of a letter) |
| **RTVE** | *Radio Televisión Española* | Spanish Radio and Television Corporation |
| **S./Sto./ Sta.** | *San/Santo/Santa* | saint |
| **S.A.** | *Sociedad Anónima* | Ltd., Inc. |
| **S.A.R.** | *Su Alteza Real* | His/Her Royal Highness |
| **s.a.s.s.** | *su atento y seguro servidor* | approx. Yours faithfully |
| **S.E.** | *Su Excelencia* | His Excellency |
| **sgte.** | *siguiente* | following |
| **S.M.** | *Su Majestad* | His/Her Majesty |
| **Sr.** | *Señor* | Mr. |
| **Sra.** | *Señora* | Mrs. |
| **S.R.C.** | *se ruega contestación* | please reply |
| **Sres./Srs.** | *Señores* | Sirs, Gentlemen |
| **Srta.** | *Señorita* | Miss |
| **S.S.** | *Su Santidad* | His Holiness |
| **Ud./Vd.** | *Usted* | you (singular) |
| **Uds./Vds.** | *Ustedes* | you (plural) |
| **Vda.** | *viuda* | widow |
| **v.g./v.gr.** | *verbigracia* | e.g. |

# Numerals

| Cardinal numbers | | Ordinal numbers | |
|---|---|---|---|
| 0 | cero | 1.° | primero |
| 1 | uno | 2.° | segundo |
| 2 | dos | 3.° | tercero |
| 3 | tres | 4.° | cuarto |
| 4 | cuatro | 5.° | quinto |
| 5 | cinco | 6.° | sexto |
| 6 | seis | 7.° | séptimo |
| 7 | siete | 8.° | octavo |
| 8 | ocho | 9.° | noveno (nono) |
| 9 | nueve | 10.° | décimo |
| 10 | diez | 11.° | undécimo |
| 11 | once | 12.° | duodécimo |
| 12 | doce | 13.° | decimotercero |
| 13 | trece | 14.° | decimocuarto |
| 14 | catorce | 15.° | decimoquinto |
| 15 | quince | 16.° | decimosexto |
| 16 | dieciséis | 17.° | decimoséptimo |
| 17 | diecisiete | 18.° | decimoctavo |
| 18 | dieciocho | 19.° | decimonoveno |
| 19 | diecinueve | 20.° | vigésimo |
| 20 | veinte | 21.° | vigésimo primero |
| 21 | veintiuno | 22.° | vigésimo segundo |
| 30 | treinta | 30.° | trigésimo |
| 31 | treinta y uno | 40.° | cuadragésimo |
| 40 | cuarenta | 50.° | quincuagésimo |
| 50 | cincuenta | 60.° | sexagésimo |
| 60 | sesenta | 70.° | septuagésimo |
| 70 | setenta | 80.° | octogésimo |
| 80 | ochenta | 90.° | nonagésimo |
| 90 | noventa | 100.° | centésimo |
| 100 | ciento (cien) | 230.° | ducentésimo trigésimo |
| 101 | ciento uno | 300.° | tricentésimo |
| 230 | doscientos treinta | 400.° | cuadringentésimo |
| 500 | quinientos | 500.° | quingentésimo |
| 700 | setecientos | 600.° | sexcentésimo |
| 900 | novecientos | 700.° | septingentésimo |
| 1.000 | mil | 800.° | octingentésimo |
| 100.000 | cien mil | 900.° | noningentésimo |
| 1.000.000 | un millón | 1.000.° | milésimo |

# Time

Although official time in Spain is based on the 24-hour clock, the 12-hour system is used in conversation.

In some Latin American countries you can specify *a.m.* or *p.m.* as in English, but it is far more common to add *de la mañana, de la tarde* or *de la noche* as in Spain.

Thus:

| | |
|---|---|
| *las ocho de la mañana* | 8 a.m. |
| *la una de la tarde* | 1 p.m. |
| *las ocho de la noche* | 8 p.m. |

## Days of the Week

| | | | |
|---|---|---|---|
| *domingo* | Sunday | *jueves* | Thursday |
| *lunes* | Monday | *viernes* | Friday |
| *martes* | Tuesday | *sábado* | Saturday |
| *miércoles* | Wednesday | | |

| C° | F° |
|---|---|
| **100** | **212** |
| 40 | 105 |
| **36,9** | **98,6** |
| 35 | |
| 30 | 90 |
| | 80 |
| 25 | |
| 20 | 70 |
| 15 | 60 |
| 10 | 50 |
| 5 | |
| | 40 |
| **0** | **32** |
| | 30 |
| −5 | |
| | 20 |
| −10 | |
| | 10 |
| −15 | |
| | 0 |
| −20 | |

# Conversion tables/
# Tablas de conversión

**Metres and feet**
The figure in the middle stands for both metres and feet, e.g. 1 metre = 3.281 ft. and 1 foot = 0.30 m.

**Metros y pies**
La columna del centro corresponde a metros y pies, por ejemplo 1 metro = 3,281 pies y 1 pie = 0,30 metros.

| Metres/Metros | | Feet/Pies |
|---|---|---|
| 0.30 | **1** | 3.281 |
| 0.61 | **2** | 6.563 |
| 0.91 | **3** | 9.843 |
| 1.22 | **4** | 13.124 |
| 1.52 | **5** | 16.403 |
| 1.83 | **6** | 19.686 |
| 2.13 | **7** | 22.967 |
| 2.44 | **8** | 26.248 |
| 2.74 | **9** | 29.529 |
| 3.05 | **10** | 32.810 |
| 3.66 | **12** | 39.372 |
| 4.27 | **14** | 45.934 |
| · 6.10 | **20** | 65.620 |
| 7.62 | **25** | 82.023 |
| 15.24 | **50** | 164.046 |
| 22.86 | **75** | 246.069 |
| 30.48 | **100** | 328.092 |

**Temperature**
To convert Centigrade to Fahrenheit, multiply by 1.8 and add 32.
To convert Fahrenheit to Centigrade, subtract 32 from Fahrenheit and divide by 1.8.

**Temperatura**
Para convertir grados centígrados en Fahrenheit multiplique los centígrados por 1,8 y sume 32 al resultado.
Para convertir grados Fahrenheit en centígrados reste 32 de los Fahrenheit y divida el resultado entre 1,8.

| **Some Basic Phrases** | **Algunas expresiones útiles** |
|---|---|
| Please. | Por favor. |
| Thank you very much. | Muchas gracias. |
| Don't mention it. | No hay de qué. |
| Good morning. | Buenos días. |
| Good afternoon. | Buenas tardes. |
| Good evening. | Buenas noches. |
| Good night. | Buenas noches (despedida). |
| Good-bye. | Adiós. |
| See you later. | Hasta luego. |
| Where is/Where are...? | ¿Dónde está/Dónde están...? |
| What do you call this? | ¿Cómo se llama esto? |
| What does that mean? | ¿Qué quiere decir eso? |
| Do you speak English? | ¿Habla usted inglés? |
| Do you speak German? | ¿Habla usted alemán? |
| Do you speak French? | ¿Habla usted francés? |
| Do you speak Spanish? | ¿Habla usted español? |
| Do you speak Italian? | ¿Habla usted italiano? |
| Could you speak more slowly, please? | ¿Puede usted hablar más despacio, por favor? |
| I don't understand. | No comprendo. |
| Can I have...? | ¿Puede darme...? |
| Can you show me...? | ¿Puede usted enseñarme...? |
| Can you tell me...? | ¿Puede usted decirme...? |
| Can you help me, please? | ¿Puede usted ayudarme, por favor? |
| I'd like... | Quisiera... |
| We'd like... | Quisiéramos... |
| Please give me... | Por favor, déme... |
| Please bring me... | Por favor, tráigame... |
| I'm hungry. | Tengo hambre. |
| I'm thirsty. | Tengo sed. |
| I'm lost. | Me he perdido. |
| Hurry up! | ¡Dése prisa! |

There is/There are…                 Hay…
There isn't/There aren't…           No hay…

## Arrival

## Llegada

Your passport, please.              Su pasaporte, por favor.

Have you anything to declare?       ¿Tiene usted algo que declarar?

No, nothing at all.                 No, nada en absoluto.

Can you help me with my luggage,    ¿Puede usted ayudarme con mi
please?                             equipaje, por favor?

Where's the bus to the centre of    ¿Dónde está el autobús que va al
town, please?                       centro, por favor?

This way, please.                   Por aquí, por favor.

Where can I get a taxi?             ¿Dónde puedo coger un taxi?

What's the fare to…?                ¿Cuánto es la tarifa a…?

Take me to this address, please.    Lléveme a esta dirección, por
                                    favor.

I'm in a hurry.                     Tengo mucha prisa.

## Hotel

## Hotel

My name is…                         Me llamo…

Have you a reservation?             ¿Ha hecho usted una reserva?

I'd like a room with a bath.        Quisiera una habitación con
                                    baño.

What's the price per night?         ¿Cuánto cuesta por noche?

May I see the room?                 ¿Puedo ver la habitación?

What's my room number, please?      ¿Cuál es el número de mi habita-
                                    ción, por favor?

There's no hot water.               No hay agua caliente.

May I see the manager, please?      ¿Puedo ver al director, por favor?

Did anyone telephone me?            ¿Me ha llamado alguien?

Is there any mail for me?           ¿Hay correo para mí?

May I have my bill (check),         ¿Puede darme mi cuenta,
please?                             por favor?

| **Eating out** | **Restaurante** |
|---|---|
| Do you have a fixed-price menu? | ¿Tiene usted un menú de precio fijo? |
| May I see the menu? | ¿Puedo ver la carta? |
| May we have an ashtray, please? | ¿Nos puede traer un cenicero, por favor? |
| Where's the toilet, please? | ¿Dónde están los servicios, por favor? |
| I'd like an hors d'œuvre (starter). | Quisiera un entremés. |
| Have you any soup? | ¿Tiene usted sopa? |
| I'd like some fish. | Quisiera pescado. |
| What kind of fish do you have? | ¿Qué clases de pescado tiene usted? |
| I'd like a steak. | Quisiera un bistec. |
| What vegetables have you got? | ¿Qué verduras tiene usted? |
| Nothing more, thanks. | Nada más, gracias. |
| What would you like to drink? | ¿Qué le gustaría beber? |
| I'll have a beer, please. | Tomaré una cerveza, por favor. |
| I'd like a bottle of wine. | Quisiera una botella de vino. |
| May I have the bill (check), please? | ¿Podría darme la cuenta, por favor? |
| Is service included? | ¿Está incluido el servicio? |
| Thank you, that was a very good meal. | Gracias. Ha sido una comida muy buena. |

| **Travelling** | **Viajes** |
|---|---|
| Where's the railway station, please? | ¿Dónde está la estación de ferro-carril, por favor? |
| Where's the ticket office, please? | ¿Dónde está la taquilla, por favor? |
| I'd like a ticket to... | Quisiera un billete para... |
| First or second class? | ¿Primera o segunda clase? |
| First class, please. | Primera clase, por favor. |
| Single or return (one way or roundtrip)? | ¿Ida, o ida y vuelta? |

| | |
|---|---|
| Do I have to change trains? | ¿Tengo que transbordar? |
| What platform does the train for... leave from? | ¿De qué andén sale el tren para...? |
| Where's the nearest underground (subway) station? | ¿Dónde está la próxima estación de Metro? |
| Where's the bus station, please? | ¿Dónde está la estación de autobuses, por favor? |
| When's the first bus to...? | ¿Cuándo sale el primer autobús para...? |
| Please let me off at the next stop. | Por favor, deténgase en la próxima parada. |

## Relaxing / Diversiones

| | |
|---|---|
| What's on at the cinema (movies)? | ¿Qué dan en el cine? |
| What time does the film begin? | ¿A qué hora empieza la película? |
| Are there any tickets for tonight? | ¿Quedan entradas para esta noche? |
| Where can we go dancing? | ¿Dónde se puede ir a bailar? |

## Meeting people / Presentaciones – Citas

| | |
|---|---|
| How do you do. | Buenos días Señora/Señorita/Señor. |
| How are you? | ¿Cómo está usted? |
| Very well, thank you. And you? | Muy bien, gracias. ¿Y usted? |
| May I introduce...? | ¿Me permite presentarle a...? |
| My name is... | Me llamo... |
| I'm very pleased to meet you. | Tanto gusto (en conocerle). |
| How long have you been here? | ¿Cuánto tiempo lleva usted aquí? |
| It was nice meeting you. | Ha sido un placer conocerle. |
| Do you mind if I smoke? | ¿Le molesta si fumo? |
| Do you have a light, please? | ¿Tiene usted fuego, por favor? |
| May I get you a drink? | ¿Me permite invitarle a una bebida (una copa)? |
| May I invite you for dinner tonight? | ¿Me permite invitarle a cenar esta noche? |
| Where shall we meet? | ¿Dónde quedamos citados? |

## Shops, stores and services

Where's the nearest bank, please?

Where can I cash some travellers' cheques?

Can you give me some small change, please?

Where's the nearest chemist's (pharmacy)?

How do I get there?

Is it within walking distance?

Can you help me, please?

How much is this? And that?

It's not quite what I want.

I like it.

Can you recommend something for sunburn?

I'd like a haircut, please.

I'd like a manicure, please.

## Comercios y servicios

Dónde está el banco más cercano, por favor?

¿Dónde puedo cambiar unos cheques de viaje?

¿Puede usted darme algún dinero suelto, por favor?

¿Dónde está la farmacia más cercana?

¿Cómo podría ir hasta allí?

¿Se puede ir andando?

¿Puede usted atenderme, por favor?

¿Cuánto cuesta éste? ¿Y ése?

No es exactamente lo que quiero.

Me gusta.

¿Podría recomendarme algo para las quemaduras del sol?

Quisiera cortarme el pelo, por favor.

Quisiera una manicura, por favor.

## Street directions

Can you show me on the map where I am?

You are on the wrong road.

Go/Walk straight ahead.

It's on the left/on the right.

## Direcciones

¿Puede enseñarme en el mapa dónde estoy?

Está usted equivocado de camino.

Siga todo derecho.

Está a la izquierda/a la derecha.

## Emergencies

Call a doctor quickly.

Call an ambulance.

Please call the police.

## Urgencias

Llame a un médico rápidamente.

Llame a una ambulancia.

Llame a la policía, por favor.

inglés-español

english-spanish

# Abreviaturas

| | | | |
|---|---|---|---|
| *adj* | adjetivo | *n* | nombre |
| *adv* | adverbio | | (sustantivo) |
| *Am* | inglés americano | *nAm* | nombre |
| *art* | artículo | | (inglés americano) |
| *conj* | conjunción | *num* | numeral |
| *f* | femenino | *p* | tiempo pasado |
| *fMe* | femenino (mexicano) | *pl* | plural |
| *fpl* | femenino plural | *plAm* | plural (inglés americano) |
| *fplMe* | femenino plural | *pp* | participio pasado |
| | (mexicano) | *pr* | tiempo presente |
| *m* | masculino | *pref* | prefijo |
| *Me* | mexicano | *prep* | preposición |
| *mMe* | masculino (mexicano) | *pron* | pronombre |
| *mpl* | masculino plural | *v* | verbo |
| *mplMe* | masculino plural | *vAm* | verbo (inglés americano) |
| | (mexicano) | *vMe* | verbo (mexicano) |

# Introducción

Este diccionario ha sido concebido para resolver de la mejor manera posible sus problemas prácticos de lenguaje. Se han suprimido las informaciones lingüísticas innecesarias. Los vocablos se suceden en un estricto orden alfabético, sin tener en cuenta si la palabra es simple o compuesta, o si se trata de una expresión formada por dos o más términos separados. Como única excepción, algunas expresiones idiomáticas están colocadas en orden alfabético, considerando para ello la palabra más característica. Cuando un término principal va seguido de otras palabras, expresiones o locuciones, éstas se hallan anotadas también en orden alfabético.

Cada palabra va seguida de una transcripción fonética (véase la guía de pronunciación). Después de la transcripción fonética se encuentra una indicación de la parte de la oración a la que pertenece el vocablo. Cuando una palabra puede desempeñar distintos oficios en la oración, las diferentes traducciones se dan una a continuación de la otra, precedidas de la indicación correspondiente.

Se indica el plural de los nombres cuando son irregulares y en algunos otros casos dudosos.

Cuando haya que repetir una palabra para formar el plural irregular o en las series de palabras se usa la tilde (~) para representar el vocablo principal.

En los plurales irregulares de las palabras compuestas sólo se escribe la parte que cambia, mientras que la parte invariable se representa por un guión (-).

Un asterisco (*) colocado antes de un verbo indica que dicho verbo es irregular. Para más detalles puede consultar la lista de los verbos irregulares.

Las palabras de este diccionario están escritas en su forma inglesa. La forma y significado americanos están señalados como tales (véase la lista de abreviaturas empleadas en el texto).

# Guía de pronunciación

Cada vocablo principal de esta parte del diccionario va acompañado de una transcripción fonética destinada a indicar la pronunciación. Esta representación fonética debe leerse como si se tratara del idioma español hablado en Castilla. A continuación figuran tan solo las letras y los símbolos ambiguos o particularmente difíciles de comprender.

Cada sílaba está separada por un guión y la que lleva el acento está impresa en letra *bastardilla*.

Por supuesto, los sonidos de dos lenguas rara vez coinciden exactamente, pero siguiendo con atención nuestras explicaciones, el lector de habla española llegará a pronunciar las palabras extranjeras de manera que pueda ser comprendido. A fin de facilitar su tarea, algunas veces nuestras transcripciones simplifican ligeramente el sistema fonético del idioma, sin dejar por ello de reflejar·las diferencias de sonido esenciales.

## Consonantes

| | |
|---|---|
| b | como en **b**ueno |
| d | como en **d**ía |
| ð | como **d** en rui**d**o |
| dȝ | como la **ll** argentina, precedida por una **d** |
| gh | como **g** en **g**ato |
| h | sonido que es una espiración suave |
| ng | como **n** en bla**n**co |
| r | ponga la lengua en la misma posición que para pronunciar ȝ (véase más abajo), luego abra ligeramente la boca y baje la lengua |
| s | sonido siempre suave y sonoro como en mi**s**mo |
| ʃ | como **ch** en mu**ch**o, pero sin la **t** inicial que compone el sonido |
| v | más o menos como en la**v**a; sonido que se obtiene colocando los dientes incisivos superiores sobre el labio inferior y expulsando suavemente el aire |
| ȝ | como la **ll** argentina |

## Vocales y diptongos

| æ | sonido que combina el de la **a** en c**a**so con el de la **e** en sab**e**r |
|---|---|
| ê | como **e** en sab**e**r |
| o | como **o** en p**o**r |
| ö | vocal neutra; sonido parecido al de la **a** española, pero con los labios extendidos |

1) Las vocales largas están impresas a doble.

2) Las letras situadas más arriba que las otras (por ej.: **ᵘi, uö**) deben pronunciarse con menor intensidad y rápidamente.

3) Algunas palabras inglesas toman del francés las vocales nasales, que están indicadas con un símbolo de vocal mas **ng** (por ej.: **ang**). Este signo **ng** *no* se debe pronunciar y sólo sirve para indicar la nasalidad de la vocal precedente. Las vocales nasales se pronuncian con la boca y la nariz simultáneamente.

## Pronunciación americana

Nuestra transcripción representa la pronunciación de Gran Bretaña. Aunque existen notables variaciones regionales en la lengua americana, ésta presenta en general algunas diferencias importantes respecto al inglés de Gran Bretaña.

He aquí algunos ejemplos:

1) La **r**, delante de una consonante o al final de una palabra, siempre se pronuncia, lo cual es contrario a la costumbre inglesa.

2) En muchas palabras (por ej.: *ask, castle, laugh,* etc.) la **aa** se transforma en **ææ**.

3) El sonido inglés **o** se pronuncia **a** o también **oo**.

4) En palabras como *duty, tune, new,* etc., el sonido **y** se omite a menudo antes de **uu**.

5) Por último, el acento tónico de algunas palabras puede variar considerablemente.

# A

**a** (ei,ö) *art* (an) un *art*

**abbey** (æ-bi) *n* abadía *f*

**abbreviation** (ö-brii-vi-*ei*-ʃön) *n* abreviatura *f*

**aberration** (æ-bö-*rei*-ʃön) *n* anomalía *f*

**ability** (ö-*bi*-lö-ti) *n* habilidad *f*

**able** (*ei*-böl) *adj* capaz; hábil; **\*be ~ to** \*ser capaz de; \*saber, \*poder

**abnormal** (æb-*noo*-möl) *adj* anormal

**aboard** (ö-*bood*) *adv* a bordo

**abolish** (ö-*bo*-liʃ) *v* abolir

**abortion** (ö-*boo*-ʃön) *n* aborto *m*

**about** (ö-*baut*) *prep* acerca de; respecto a; alrededor de; *adv* hacia, aproximadamente; en torno

**above** (ö-*bav*) *prep* encima de; *adv* encima

**abroad** (ö-*brood*) *adv* en el extranjero

**abscess** (æb-ssèss) *n* absceso *m*

**absence** (æb-ssönss) *n* ausencia *f*

**absent** (æb-ssönt) *adj* ausente

**absolutely** (æb-ssö-luut-li) *adv* absolutamente

**abstain from** (öb-*sstein*) \*abstenerse de

**abstract** (æb-sstrækt) *adj* abstracto

**absurd** (öb-*ssööd*) *adj* absurdo

**abundance** (ö-*ban*-dönss) *n* abundancia *f*

**abundant** (ö-*ban*-dönt) *adj* abundante

**abuse** (ö-*byuuss*) *n* abuso *m*

**abyss** (ö-*biss*) *n* abismo *m*

**academy** (ö-*kæ*-dö-mi) *n* academia *f*

**accelerate** (ök-*ssê*-lö-reit) *v* acelerar

**accelerator** (ök-*ssê*-lö-rei-tö) *n* acelerador *m*

**accent** (æk-ssönt) *n* acento *m*

**accept** (ök-*ssêpt*) *v* aceptar

**access** (æk-ssèss) *n* acceso *m*

**accessary** (ök-*ssê*-ssö-ri) *n* cómplice *m*

**accessible** (ök-*ssê*-ssö-böl) *adj* accesible

**accessories** (ök-*ssê*-ssö-ris) *pl* accesorios *mpl*

**accident** (æk-ssi-dönt) *n* accidente *m*

**accidental** (æk-ssi-*dên*-töl) *adj* accidental

**accommodate** (ö-*ko*-mö-deit) *v* acomodar

**accommodation** (ö-ko-mö-*dei*-ʃön) *n* acomodación *f*, alojamiento *m*

**accompany** (ö-*kam*-pö-ni) *v* acompañar

**accomplish** (ö-*kam*-pliʃ) *v* terminar; cumplir

**in accordance with** (in ö-*koo*-dönss ᵘið) con arreglo a

**according to** (ö-*koo*-ding tuu) según; conforme a

**account** (ö-*kaunt*) *n* cuenta *f*; narración f; ~ for explicar; on ~ of a causa de

**accountable** (ö-*kaun*-tö-böl) *adj* explicable

**accurate** (æ-kyu-röt) *adj* exacto

**accuse** (ö-*kyuus*) *v* acusar

**accused** (ö-*kyuusd*) *n* acusado *m*

**accustom** (ö-*ka*-sstöm) *v* acostumbrar; **accustomed** acostumbrado

**ache** (eik) *v* *doler; *n* dolor *m*

**achieve** (ö-*chiiv*) *v* alcanzar; lograr

**achievement** (ö-*chiiv*-mönt) *n* realización *f*

**acid** (æ-ssid) *n* ácido *m*

**acknowledge** (ök-*no*-lidʒ) *v* *reconocer; admitir; confirmar

**acne** (æk-ni) *n* acné *m*

**acorn** (*ei*-koon) *n* bellota *f*

**acquaintance** (ö-*k*ʷ*ein*-tönss) *n* conocido *m*

**acquire** (ö-*k*ʷ*ai*ᵒ) *v* *adquirir

**acquisition** (æ-k*ʷ*i-si-*ʃ*ön) *n* adquisición *f*

**acquittal** (ö-*k*ʷ*i*-töl) *n* absolución *f*

**across** (ö-*kross*) *prep* a través de; al otro lado de; *adv* al otro lado

**act** (ækt) *n* acto *m*; número *m*; *v* actuar, *hacer; comportarse

**action** (æk-ʃön) *n* acción *f*

**active** (æk-tiv) *adj* activo; vivaz

**activity** (æk-*ti*-vö-ti) *n* actividad *f*

**actor** (æk-tö) *n* actor *m*

**actress** (æk-triss) *n* actriz *f*

**actual** (æk-chu-öl) *adj* verdadero

**actually** (æk-chu-ö-li) *adv* en realidad

**acute** (ö-*kyuut*) *adj* agudo

**adapt** (ö-*dæpt*) *v* adaptar

**add** (æd) *v* sumar, adicionar; añadir

**adding-machine** (æ-ding-mö-ʃiin) *n* calculadora *f*

**addition** (ö-*di*-ʃön) *n* adición *f*

**additional** (ö-*di*-ʃö-nöl) *adj* adicional; accesorio

**address** (ö-*drêss*) *n* dirección *f*; *v*

destinar; dirigirse a

**addressee** (æ-drê-*ssii*) *n* destinatario *m*

**adequate** (æ-di-k*ʷ*öt) *adj* adecuado; conveniente

**adjective** (æ-dʒik-tiv) *n* adjetivo *m*

**adjourn** (ö-*dʒöön*) *v* aplazar

**adjust** (ö-*dʒasst*) *v* ajustar

**administer** (öd-*mi*-ni-sstö) *v* administrar

**administration** (öd-mi-ni-*sstrei*-ʃön) *n* administración *f*; gestión *f*

**administrative** (öd-*mi*-ni-sströ-tiv) *adj* gerencial; administrativo; ~ **law** derecho administrativo

**admiral** (æd-mö-röl) *n* almirante *m*

**admiration** (æd-mö-*rei*-ʃön) *n* admiración *f*

**admire** (öd-*mai*ᵒ) *v* admirar

**admission** (öd-*mi*-ʃön) *n* entrada *f*; admisión *f*

**admit** (öd-*mit*) *v* admitir; *reconocer

**admittance** (öd-*mi*-tönss) *n* admisión *f*; **no** ~ prohibida la entrada

**adopt** (ö-*dopt*) *v* adoptar

**adorable** (ö-*doo*-rö-böl) *adj* adorable

**adult** (æ-dalt) *n* adulto *m*; *adj* adulto

**advance** (öd-*vaanss*) *n* adelanto *m*; anticipo *m*; *v* avanzar; anticipar; **in** ~ por adelantado

**advanced** (öd-*vaansst*) *adj* avanzado

**advantage** (öd-*vaan*-tidʒ) *n* ventaja *f*

**advantageous** (æd-vön-*tei*-dʒöss) *adj* ventajoso

**adventure** (öd-*vên*-chö) *n* aventura *f*

**adverb** (æd-vööb) *n* adverbio *m*

**advertisement** (öd-*vöö*-tiss-mönt) *n* anuncio *m*

**advertising** (æd-vö-tai-sing) *n* publicidad *f*

**advice** (öd-*vaiss*) *n* consejo *m*

**advise** (öd-*vais*) *v* aconsejar

**advocate** (æd-vö-köt) *n* abogado *m*

**aerial** (*ê*ᵒ-ri-öl) *n* antena *f*

**aeroplane** (êᵒ-rö-plein) n avión m

**affair** (ö-fêᵒ) n asunto m; amorío m

**affect** (ö-fêkt) v afectar

**affected** (ö-fêk-tid) adj afectado

**affection** (ö-fêk-ʃön) n afección f; cariño m

**affectionate** (ö-fêk-ʃö-nit) adj cariñoso

**affiliated** (ö-fi-li-ei-tid) adj afiliado

**affirmative** (ö-föö-mö-tiv) adj afirmativo

**affliction** (ö-flik-ʃön) n sufrimiento m

**afford** (ö-food) v permitirse

**afraid** (ö-freid) adj angustioso, asustado; *be ~ *tener miedo

**Africa** (æ-fri-kö) África f

**African** (æ-fri-kön) adj africano

**after** (aaf-tö) prep después de; detrás de; conj después de que

**afternoon** (aaf-tö-nuun) n tarde f

**afterwards** (aaf-tö-ᵘöds) adv después

**again** (ö-ghên) adv otra vez; de nuevo; ~ and again repetidamente

**against** (ö-ghênsst) prep contra

**age** (eidʒ) n edad f; vejez f; of ~ mayor de edad; under ~ menor de edad

**aged** (ei-dʒid) adj viejo; anciano

**agency** (ei-dʒön-ssi) n agencia f; sección f

**agenda** (ö-dʒên-dö) n orden del día m

**agent** (ei-dʒönt) n agente m, representante m

**aggressive** (ö-ghrê-ssiv) adj agresivo

**ago** (ö-ghou) adv hace

**agrarian** (ö-ghrêᵒ-ri-ön) adj agrario, agrícola

**agree** (ö-ghrii) v *convenir, *concordar; *consentir; *acordar

**agreeable** (ö-ghrii-ö-böl) adj agradable

**agreement** (ö-ghrii-mönt) n contrato m; acuerdo m; conformidad f

**agriculture** (æ-ghri-kal-chö) n agricultura f

**ahead** (ö-hêd) adv adelante; ~ of delante de; *go ~ continuar; straight ~ todo seguido

**aid** (eid) n socorro m; v asistir, ayudar

**ailment** (eil-mönt) n enfermedad f

**aim** (eim) n fin m; ~ at apuntar; aspirar a

**air** (êᵒ) n aire m; v airear

**air-conditioning** (êᵒ-kön-di-ʃö-ning) n aire acondicionado; **air-conditioned** adj climatizado

**aircraft** (êᵒ-kraaft) n (pl ~) avión m

**airfield** (êᵒ-fiild) n campo de aviación

**air-filter** (êᵒ-fil-tö) n filtro de aire

**airline** (êᵒ-lain) n aerolínea f

**airmail** (êᵒ-meil) n correo aéreo

**airplane** (êᵒ-plein) nAm avión m

**airport** (êᵒ-poot) n aeropuerto m

**air-sickness** (êᵒ-ssik-nöss) n mal de las alturas

**airtight** (êᵒ-tait) adj hermético

**airy** (êᵒ-ri) adj airoso

**aisle** (ail) n nave lateral; pasillo m

**alarm** (ö-laam) n alarma f; v alarmar

**alarm-clock** (ö-laam-klok) n despertador m

**album** (æl-böm) n álbum m

**alcohol** (æl-kö-hol) n alcohol m

**alcoholic** (æl-kö-ho-lik) adj alcohólico

**ale** (eil) n cerveza f

**algebra** (æl-dʒi-brö) n álgebra f

**Algeria** (æl-dʒiᵒ-ri-ö) Argelia f

**Algerian** (æl-dʒiᵒ-ri-ön) adj argelino

**alien** (ei-li-ön) n extranjero m; adj extranjero

**alike** (ö-laik) adj igual, parecido; adv igualmente

**alimony** (æ-li-mö-ni) n pensión alimenticia

**alive** (ö-laiv) adj en vida, vivo

**all** (ool) adj todo; ~ in todo incluido; ~ right! ¡bien!; at ~ en modo alguno

**allergy** (æ-lö-dʒi ) *n* alergia *f*

**alley** (æ-li ) *n* callejón *m*

**alliance** (ö-*lai*-önss ) *n* alianza *f*

**Allies** (æ-lais ) *pl* Aliados *mpl*

**allot** (ö-*lot*) *v* asignar

**allow** (ö-*lau*) *v* permitir, autorizar; ~ **to** autorizar a ; *be allowed *estar autorizado

**allowance** (ö-*lau*-önss ) *n* asignación *f*

**all-round** (ool-*raund*) *adj* polifacético

**almanac** (*ool*-mö-næk ) *n* almanaque *m*

**almond** (*aa*-mönd ) *n* almendra *f*

**almost** (*ool*-moust) *adv* casi ; cerca de

**alone** (ö-*loun*) *adv* sólo

**along** (ö-*long*) *prep* a lo largo de

**aloud** (ö-*laud*) *adv* en voz alta

**alphabet** (*æl*-fö-bêt ) *n* abecedario *m*

**already** (ool-*rê*-di ) *adv* ya

**also** (*ool*-ssou ) *adv* también; asimismo

**altar** (*ool*-tö ) *n* altar *m*

**alter** (*ool*-tö ) *v* cambiar, alterar

**alteration** (ool-tö-*rei*-jön ) *n* cambio *m*, alteración *f*

**alternate** (ool-*töö*-nöt ) *adj* alternativo

**alternative** (ool-*töö*-nö-tiv ) *n* alternativa *f*

**although** (ool-*ðou* ) *conj* aunque

**altitude** (*æl*-ti-tyuud ) *n* altitud *f*

**alto** (*æl*-tou ) *n* (pl ~s) contralto *m*

**altogether** (ool-tö-*ghê*-ðö ) *adv* totalmente; en total

**always** (*ool*-ueis ) *adv* siempre

**am** (æm ) *v* (pr be)

**amaze** (ö-*meis*) *v* extrañar, asombrar

**amazement** (ö-*meis*-mönt ) *n* asombro *m*

**ambassador** (æm-*bæ*-ssö-dö ) *n* embajador *m*

**amber** (*æm*-bö ) *n* ámbar *m*

**ambiguous** (æm-*bi*-ghyu-öss ) *adj* ambiguo; equívoco

**ambitious** (æm-*bi*-ʃöss ) *adj* ambicioso

**ambulance** (*æm*-byu-lönss ) *n* ambulancia *f*

**ambush** (*æm*-buʃ ) *n* emboscada *f*

**America** (ö-*mê*-ri-kö ) América *f*

**American** (ö-*mê*-ri-kön ) *adj* americano

**amethyst** (*æ*-mi-zisst ) *n* amatista *f*

**amid** (ö-*mid*) *prep* entre; en medio de

**ammonia** (ö-*mou*-ni-ö ) *n* amoníaco *m*

**amnesty** (*æm*-ni-ssti ) *n* amnistía *f*

**among** (ö-*mang*) *prep* entre; ~ **other things** entre otras cosas

**amount** (ö-*maunt*) *n* cantidad *f*; suma *f*; ~ **to** sumar

**amuse** (ö-*myuus*) *v* *divertir, *entretener

**amusement** (ö-*myuus*-mönt ) *n* distracción *f*, entretenimiento *m*

**amusing** (ö-*myuu*-sing ) *adj* divertido

**anaemia** (ö-*nii*-mi-ö ) *n* anemia *f*

**anaesthesia** (æ-niss-*zii*-si-ö ) *n* anestesia *f*

**anaesthetic** (æ-niss-*zê*-tik ) *n* anestésico *m*

**analyse** (*æ*-nö-lais ) *v* analizar

**analysis** (ö-*næ*-lö-ssiss ) *n* (pl -ses) análisis *f*

**analyst** (*æ*-nö-lisst ) *n* analista *m*; psicoanalista *m*

**anarchy** (*æ*-nö-ki ) *n* anarquía *f*

**anatomy** (ö-*næ*-tö-mi ) *n* anatomía *f*

**ancestor** (*æn*-ssê-sstö ) *n* antepasado *m*

**anchor** (*æng*-kö ) *n* ancla *f*

**anchovy** (*æn*-chö-vi ) *n* anchoa *f*

**ancient** (*ein*-ʃönt ) *adj* viejo, antiguo; anticuado

**and** (ænd, önd ) *conj* y

**angel** (*ein*-dʒöl ) *n* ángel *m*

**anger** (*æng*-ghö ) *n* cólera *f*, enojo *m*; furor *m*

**angle** (*æng*-ghöl ) *v* pescar con caña; *n* ángulo *m*

**angry** (*æng*-ghri) *adj* enfadado, enojado

**animal** (*æ*-ni-möl) *n* animal *m*

**ankle** (*æng*-köl) *n* tobillo *m*

**annex¹** (*æ*-nêkss) *n* anexo *m*

**annex²** (ö-*nêkss*) *v* anexar

**anniversary** (æ-ni-*vöö*-ssö-ri) *n* aniversario *m*

**announce** (ö-*naunss*) *v* anunciar

**announcement** (ö-*naunss*-mönt) *n* anuncio *m*

**annoy** (ö-*noi*) *v* irritar, fastidiar; aburrir

**annoyance** (ö-*noi*-önss) *n* aburrimiento *m*

**annoying** (ö-*noi*-ing) *adj* irritante, importuno

**annual** (*æ*-nyu-öl) *adj* anual; *n* anuario *m*

**per annum** (pör *æ*-nöm) al año

**anonymous** (ö-*no*-ni-möss) *adj* anónimo

**another** (ö-*na*-ðö) *adj* otro más; otro

**answer** (*aan*-ssö) *v* responder a; *n* respuesta *f*

**ant** (ænt) *n* hormiga *f*

**anthology** (æn-*zo*-lö-dʒi) *n* antología *f*

**antibiotic** (æn-ti-bai-*o*-tik) *n* antibiótico *m*

**anticipate** (æn-*ti*-ssi-peit) *v* *prever; *prevenir

**antifreeze** (*æn*-ti-friis) *n* anticongelante *m*

**antipathy** (æn-*ti*-pö-zi) *n* antipatía *f*

**antique** (æn-*tiik*) *adj* antiguo; *n* antigualla *f*; ~ **dealer** anticuario *m*

**antiquity** (æn-*ti*-kᵘö-ti) *n* Antigüedad *f*; **antiquities** *pl* antigüedades *fpl*

**antiseptic** (æn-ti-*ssêp*-tik) *n* antiséptico *m*

**antlers** (*ænt*-lös) *pl* cornamenta *f*

**anxiety** (æng-*sai*-ö-ti) *n* preocupación *f*

**anxious** (*ængk*-föss) *adj* ansioso; preocupado

**any** (*ê*-ni) *adj* alguno

**anybody** (*ê*-ni-bo-di) *pron* cualquiera

**anyhow** (*ê*-ni-hau) *adv* de cualquier modo

**anyone** (*ê*-ni-ᵘan) *pron* cualquiera

**anything** (*ê*-ni-zing) *pron* cualquier cosa

**anyway** (*ê*-ni-ᵘei) *adv* en todo caso

**anywhere** (*ê*-ni-ᵘêᵒ) *adv* en donde sea; dondequiera

**apart** (ö-*paat*) *adv* por separado, separadamente; ~ **from** prescindiendo de

**apartment** (ö-*paat*-mönt) *nAm* apartamento *m*; piso *m*; ~ **house** *Am* casa de pisos

**aperitif** (ö-*pê*-rö-tiv) *n* aperitivo *m*

**apologize** (ö-*po*-lö-dʒais) *v* disculparse

**apology** (ö-*po*-lö-dʒi) *n* excusa *f*, disculpa *f*

**apparatus** (æ-pö-*rei*-töss) *n* aparato *m*

**apparent** (ö-*pæ*-rönt) *adj* aparente; obvio

**apparently** (ö-*pæ*-rönt-li) *adv* por lo visto; evidentemente

**apparition** (æ-pö-*ri*-fön) *n* aparición *f*

**appeal** (ö-*piil*) *n* apelación *f*

**appear** (ö-*pi*ᵒ) *v* *parecer; *salir; *aparecer

**appearance** (ö-*pi*ᵒ-rönss) *n* apariencia *f*; aspecto *m*; entrada *f*

**appendicitis** (ö-pên-di-*ssai*-tiss) *n* apendicitis *f*

**appendix** (ö-*pên*-dikss) *n* (pl -dices, -dixes) apéndice *m*

**appetite** (*æ*-pö-tait) *n* apetito *m*

**appetizer** (*æ*-pö-tai-sö) *n* tapa *f*

**appetizing** (*æ*-pö-tai-sing) *adj* apetitoso

**applause** (ö-*ploos*) *n* aplauso *m*

**apple** (*æ*-pöl) *n* manzana *f*

**appliance** (ö-*plai*-önss) *n* aparato *m*

**application** (æ-pli-*kei*-ſön) *n* aplicación *f*; demanda *f*; solicitud *f*

**apply** (ö-*plai*) *v* aplicar; solicitar un puesto; aplicarse a

**appoint** (ö-*point*) *v* designar, nombrar

**appointment** (ö-*point*-mönt) *n* cita *f*; nombramiento *m*

**appreciate** (ö-*prii*-ſi-eit) *v* valuar; apreciar

**appreciation** (ö-prii-ſi-*ei*-ſön) *n* aprecio *m*

**approach** (ö-*prouch*) *v* acercarse; *n* enfoque *m*; acceso *m*

**appropriate** (ö-*prou*-pri-öt) *adj* justo, apropiado, adecuado

**approval** (ö-*pruu*-völ) *n* aprobación *f*; consentimiento *m*, acuerdo *m*; **on ~** a prueba

**approve** (ö-*pruuv*) *v* *aprobar; **~ of** *estar de acuerdo con

**approximate** (ö-*prok*-ssi-möt) *adj* aproximado

**approximately** (ö-*prok*-ssi-möt-li) *adv* aproximadamente

**apricot** (*ei*-pri-kot) *n* albaricoque *m*; chabacano *mMe*

**April** (*ei*-pröl) abril

**apron** (*ei*-prön) *n* delantal *m*

**Arab** (æ-röb) *adj* árabe

**arbitrary** (*aa*-bi-trö-ri) *adj* arbitrario

**arcade** (aa-*keid*) *n* pórtico *m*, arcada *f*

**arch** (aach) *n* arco *m*; bóveda *f*

**archaeologist** (aa-ki-*o*-lö-dʒisst) *n* arqueólogo *m*

**archaeology** (aa-ki-*o*-lö-dʒi) *n* arqueología *f*

**archbishop** (aach-*bi*-ſöp) *n* arzobispo *m*

**arched** (aacht) *adj* arqueado

**architect** (*aa*-ki-têkt) *n* arquitecto *m*

**architecture** (*aa*-ki-têk-chö) *n* arquitectura *f*

**archives** (*aa*-kaivs) *pl* archivo *m*

**are** (aa) *v* (pr be)

**area** (*ê*[o]-ri-ö) *n* región *f*; zona *f*; superficie *f*; **~ code** indicativo *m*

**Argentina** (aa-dʒön-*tii*-nö) Argentina *f*

**Argentinian** (aa-dʒön-*ti*-ni-ön) *adj* argentino

**argue** (*aa*-ghyuu) *v* argumentar, discutir; disputar

**argument** (*aa*-ghyu-mönt) *n* argumento *m*; discusión *f*; disputa *f*

**arid** (æ-rid) *adj* árido

***arise** (ö-*rais*) *v* surgir

**arithmetic** (ö-*riz*-mö-tik) *n* aritmética *f*

**arm** (aam) *n* brazo *m*; arma *f*; *v* armar

**armchair** (*aam*-chê[o]) *n* butaca *f*, sillón *m*

**armed** (aamd) *adj* armado; **~ forces** fuerzas armadas

**armour** (*aa*-mö) *n* armadura *f*

**army** (*aa*-mi) *n* ejército *m*

**aroma** (ö-*rou*-mö) *n* aroma *m*

**around** (ö-*raund*) *prep* alrededor de, en torno de; *adv* en torno

**arrange** (ö-*reindʒ*) *v* clasificar, ordenar; organizar

**arrangement** (ö-*reindʒ*-mönt) *n* arreglo *m*

**arrest** (ö-*rêsst*) *v* arrestar; *n* arresto *m*

**arrival** (ö-*rai*-völ) *n* llegada *f*

**arrive** (ö-*raiv*) *v* llegar

**arrow** (æ-rou) *n* flecha *f*

**art** (aat) *n* arte *m/f*; habilidad *f*; **~ collection** colección de arte; **~ exhibition** exposición de arte; **~ gallery** galería de arte; **~ history** historia del arte; **arts and crafts** artes industriales; **~ school** academia de bellas artes

**artery** (*aa*-tö-ri) *n* arteria *f*

**artichoke** (*aa*-ti-chouk) *n* alcachofa *f*

**article** (*aa*-ti-köl) *n* artículo *m*

**artifice** (*aa*-ti-fiss) *n* artificio *m*

**artificial** (aa-ti-*fi*-föl) *adj* artificial

**artist** (*aa*-tisst) *n* artista *m/f*

**artistic** (aa-*ti*-sstik) *adj* artístico

**as** (æs) *conj* como; tanto; que; ya que, porque; ~ **from** a partir de; ~ **if** como si

**asbestos** (æs-*bé*-sstoss) *n* asbesto *m*

**ascend** (ö-*ssênd*) *v* subir; escalar

**ascent** (ö-*ssênt*) *n* subida *f*

**ascertain** (æ-ssö-*tein*) *v* \*comprobar; asegurarse de

**ash** (æ∫) *n* ceniza *f*

**ashamed** (ö-*feimd*) *adj* avergonzado; \***be** ~ \*avergonzarse

**ashore** (ö-*foo*) *adv* en tierra

**ashtray** (*æf*-trei) *n* cenicero *m*

**Asia** (*ei*-∫ö) Asia *f*

**Asian** (*ei*-∫ön) *adj* asiático

**aside** (ö-*ssaid*) *adv* aparte

**ask** (aassk) *v* preguntar; \*rogar; invitar

**asleep** (ö-*ssliip*) *adj* dormido

**asparagus** (ö-*sspæ*-rö-ghöss) *n* espárrago *m*

**aspect** (*æ*-sspêkt) *n* aspecto *m*

**asphalt** (*æss*-fælt) *n* asfalto *m*

**aspire** (ö-*sspaiⁿ*) *v* aspirar

**aspirin** (*æ*-sspö-rin) *n* aspirina *f*

**ass** (æss) *n* burro *m*

**assassination** (ö-ssæ-ssi-*nei*-∫ön) *n* asesinato *m*

**assault** (ö-*ssoolt*) *v* atacar; violar

**assemble** (ö-*ssêm*-böl) *v* reunir; montar

**assembly** (ö-*ssêm*-bli) *n* reunión *f*, asamblea *f*

**assignment** (ö-*ssain*-mönt) *n* encargo *m*

**assign to** (ö-*ssain*) asignar a; \*atribuir a

**assist** (ö-*ssisst*) *v* asistir

**assistance** (ö-*ssi*-sstönss) *n* auxilio *m*; apoyo *m*, asistencia *f*

**assistant** (ö-*ssi*-sstönt) *n* asistente *m*

**associate¹** (ö-*ssou*-∫i-öt) *n* compañero *m*, asociado *m*; aliado *m*; socio *m*

**associate²** (ö-*ssou*-∫i-eit) *v* asociar; ~ **with** frecuentar

**association** (ö-ssou-ssi-*ei*-∫ön) *n* asociación *f*

**assort** (ö-*ssoot*) *v* clasificar

**assortment** (ö-*ssoot*-mönt) *n* surtido *m*

**assume** (ö-*ssyuum*) *v* \*suponer, presumir

**assure** (ö-*fuⁿ*) *v* asegurar

**asthma** (*æss*-mö) *n* asma *f*

**astonish** (ö-*ssto*-ni∫) *v* asombrar

**astonishing** (ö-*ssto*-ni-∫ing) *adj* asombroso

**astonishment** (ö-*ssto*-ni∫-mönt) *n* sorpresa *f*

**astronomy** (ö-*sstro*-nö-mi) *n* astronomía *f*

**asylum** (ö-*ssai*-löm) *n* asilo *m*

**at** (æt) *prep* en, a; hacia

**ate** (êt) *v* (p eat)

**atheist** (*ei*-zi-isst) *n* ateo *m*

**athlete** (*æz*-liit) *n* atleta *m*

**athletics** (æz-*lê*-tikss) *pl* atletismo *m*

**Atlantic** (öt-*læn*-tik) Atlántico *m*

**atmosphere** (*æt*-möss-fiⁿ) *n* atmósfera *f*; esfera *f*, ambiente *m*

**atom** (*æ*-töm) *n* átomo *m*

**atomic** (ö-*to*-mik) *adj* atómico

**atomizer** (*æ*-tö-mai-sö) *n* vaporizador *m*; aerosol *m*, pulverizador *m*

**attach** (ö-*tæch*) *v* prender; fijar; juntar; **attached to** encariñado con

**attack** (ö-*tæk*) *v* atacar; *n* ataque *m*

**attain** (ö-*tein*) *v* llegar a

**attainable** (ö-*tei*-nö-böl) *adj* factible; alcanzable

**attempt** (ö-*têmpt*) *v* intentar; \*probar; *n* tentativa *f*

**attend** (ö-*tênd*) *v* asistir a; ~ **on** \*servir; ~ **to** cuidar de, \*atender a;

prestar atención a
**attendance** (ö-*tên*-dönss) *n* asistencia *f*
**attendant** (ö-*tên*-dönt) *n* guardián *m*
**attention** (ö-*tên*-∫ön) *n* atención *f*;
   *\*pay ~ prestar atención
**attentive** (ö-*tên*-tiv) *adj* atento
**attic** (æ-tik) *n* buhardilla *f*
**attitude** (æ-ti-tyuud) *n* actitud *f*
**attorney** (ö-*töö*-ni) *n* abogado *m*
**attract** (ö-*trækt*) *v* \*atraer
**attraction** (ö-*træk*-∫ön) *n* atracción *f*
**attractive** (ö-*træk*-tiv) *adj* atractivo
**auburn** (*oo*-bön) *adj* castaño
**auction** (*ook*-∫ön) *n* subasta *f*
**audible** (*oo*-di-böl) *adj* audible
**audience** (*oo*-di-önss) *n* auditorio *m*
**auditor** (*oo*-di-tö) *n* oyente *m*
**auditorium** (oo-di-*too*-ri-öm) *n* aula *f*
**August** (*oo*-ghösst) agosto
**aunt** (aant) *n* tía *f*
**Australia** (o-*sstrei*-li-ö) Australia *f*
**Australian** (o-*sstrei*-li-ön) *adj* australiano
**Austria** (o-*sstri*-ö) Austria *f*
**Austrian** (o-*sstri*-ön) *adj* austríaco
**authentic** (oo-*zên*-tik) *adj* auténtico
**author** (*oo*-zö) *n* autor *m*
**authoritarian** (oo-zo-ri-*tê°*-ri-ön) *adj* autoritario
**authority** (oo-*zo*-rö-ti) *n* autoridad *f*; poder *m*
**authorization** (oo-zö-rai-*sei*-∫ön) *n* autorización *f*; permiso *m*
**automatic** (oo-tö-*mæ*-tik) *adj* automático
**automation** (oo-tö-*mei*-∫ön) *n* automatización *f*
**automobile** (*oo*-tö-mö-biil) *n* automóvil *m*; ~ **club** automóvil club
**autonomous** (oo-*to*-nö-möss) *adj* autónomo
**autopsy** (*oo*-to-pssi) *n* autopsia *f*
**autumn** (*oo*-töm) *n* otoño *m*

**available** (ö-*vei*-lö-böl) *adj* adquirible, obtenible, disponible
**avalanche** (æ-vö-laan∫) *n* avalancha *f*
**avaricious** (æ-vö-*ri*-∫öss) *adj* avaro
**avenue** (æ-vö-nyuu) *n* avenida *f*
**average** (æ-vö-rid3) *adj* promedio; *n* promedio *m*; **on the ~** en promedio
**averse** (ö-*vööss*) *adj* opuesto
**aversion** (ö-*vöö*-∫ön) *n* aversión *f*
**avert** (ö-*vööt*) *v* desviar
**avoid** (ö-*void*) *v* evitar
**await** (ö-*ᵘeit*) *v* esperar
**awake** (ö-*ᵘeik*) *adj* despierto
**\*awake** (ö-*ᵘeik*) *v* \*despertar
**award** (ö-*ᵘood*) *n* premio *m*; *v* conceder
**aware** (ö-*ᵘê°*) *adj* consciente
**away** (ö-*ᵘei*) *adv* fuera; **\*go ~** \*irse
**awful** (*oo*-föl) *adj* terrible, tremendo
**awkward** (*oo*-kᵘöd) *adj* embarazoso; torpe
**awning** (*oo*-ning) *n* toldo *m*
**axe** (ækss) *n* hacha *f*
**axle** (æk-ssöl) *n* eje *m*

# B

**baby** (*bei*-bi) *n* bebé *m*; ~ **carriage** *Am* cochecillo *m*
**babysitter** (*bei*-bi-ssi-tö) *n* babysitter *m*
**bachelor** (bæ-chö-lö) *n* soltero *m*
**back** (bæk) *n* espalda *f*; *adv* atrás; **\*go ~** regresar
**backache** (bæ-keik) *n* dolor de espalda
**backbone** (bæk-boun) *n* espina dorsal
**background** (bæk-ghraund) *n* fondo *m*; antecedentes *mpl*
**backwards** (bæk-ᵘöds) *adv* hacia atrás

**bacon** (*bei*-kön) *n* tocino *m*

**bacterium** (bæk-*tii*-ri-öm) *n* (pl -ria) bacteria *f*

**bad** (bæd) *adj* malo; grave; travieso

**bag** (bægh) *n* bolsa *f*; bolso *m*, cartera *f*; maleta *f*

**baggage** (*bæ*-ghidʒ) *n* equipaje *m*; **hand ~** *Am* equipaje de mano

**bail** (beil) *n* fianza *f*

**bailiff** (*bei*-lif) *n* ujier *m*

**bait** (beit) *n* cebo *m*

**bake** (beik) *v* hornear

**baker** (*bei*-kö) *n* panadero *m*

**bakery** (*bei*-kö-ri) *n* panadería *f*

**balance** (*bæ*-lönss) *n* equilibrio *m*; balance *m*; saldo *m*

**balcony** (*bæl*-kö-ni) *n* balcón *m*

**bald** (boold) *adj* calvo

**ball** (bool) *n* pelota *f*; baile *m*

**ballet** (*bæ*-lei) *n* ballet *m*

**balloon** (bö-*luun*) *n* globo *m*

**ballpoint-pen** (*bool*-point-pên) *n* bolígrafo *m*

**ballroom** (*bool*-ruum) *n* salón de baile

**bamboo** (bæm-*buu*) *n* (pl ~s) bambú *m*

**banana** (bö-*naa*-nö) *n* plátano *m*

**band** (bænd) *n* orquesta *f*; banda *f*

**bandage** (*bæn*-didʒ) *n* vendaje *m*

**bandit** (*bæn*-dit) *n* bandido *m*

**bangle** (*bæng*-ghöl) *n* pulsera *f*

**banisters** (*bæ*-ni-sstöss) *pl* baranda *f*

**bank** (bængk) *n* orilla *f*; banco *m*; *v* depositar; **~ account** cuenta de banco

**banknote** (*bængk*-nout) *n* vale *m*, billete de banco

**bank-rate** (*bængk*-reit) *n* descuento bancario

**bankrupt** (*bængk*-rapt) *adj* en quiebra

**banner** (*bæ*-nö) *n* bandera *f*

**banquet** (*bæng*-kᵘit) *n* banquete *m*

**banqueting-hall** (*bæng*-kᵘi-ting-hool) *n* comedor de gala

**baptism** (*bæp*-ti-söm) *n* bautismo *m*, bautizo *m*

**baptize** (bæp-*taiss*) *v* bautizar

**bar** (baa) *n* bar *m*; barra *f*; barrote *m*

**barber** (*baa*-bö) *n* barbero *m*

**bare** (bêᵒ) *adj* desnudo; raso

**barely** (*bêᵒ*-li) *adv* apenas

**bargain** (*baa*-ghin) *n* ganga *f*; *v* regatear

**baritone** (*bæ*-ri-toun) *n* barítono *m*

**bark** (baak) *n* corteza *f*; *v* ladrar

**barley** (*baa*-li) *n* cebada *f*

**barmaid** (*baa*-meid) *n* moza de taberna

**barman** (*baa*-mön) *n* (pl -men) barman *m*

**barn** (baan) *n* granero *m*

**barometer** (bö-*ro*-mi-tö) *n* barómetro *m*

**baroque** (bö-*rok*) *adj* barroco

**barracks** (*bæ*-rökss) *pl* cuartel *m*

**barrel** (*bæ*-röl) *n* tonel *m*, barril *m*

**barrier** (*bæ*-ri-ö) *n* barrera *f*

**barrister** (*bæ*-ri-sstö) *n* abogado *m*

**bartender** (*baa*-tên-dö) *n* barman *m*

**base** (beiss) *n* base *f*; fundamento *m*; *v* basar

**baseball** (*beiss*-bool) *n* béisbol *m*

**basement** (*beiss*-mönt) *n* sótano *m*

**basic** (*bei*-ssik) *adj* fundamental

**basilica** (bö-*si*-li-kö) *n* basílica *f*

**basin** (*bei*-ssön) *n* tazón *m*, palangana *f*

**basis** (*bei*-ssiss) *n* (pl bases) fundamento *m*, base *f*

**basket** (*baa*-sskit) *n* cesta *f*

**bass**[1] (beiss) *n* bajo *m*

**bass**[2] (bæss) *n* (pl ~) perca *f*

**bastard** (*baa*-sstöd) *n* bastardo *m*; descarado *m*

**batch** (bæch) *n* carga *f*

**bath** (baaz) *n* baño *m*; **~ salts** sales de baño; **~ towel** toalla de baño bathe (beið) v bañarse

bathing-cap (*bei*-ðing-kæp) n gorro de baño

bathing-suit (*bei*-ðing-ssuut) n traje de baño

bathing-trunks (*bei*-ðing-trangkss) n bañador m

bathrobe (*baaz*-roub) n bata de baño

bathroom (*baaz*-ruum) n cuarto de baño; lavabos mpl; baño mMe

batter (*bæ*-tö) n masa f

battery (*bæ*-tö-ri) n batería f; acumulador m

battle (*bæ*-töl) n batalla f; pelea f, combate m; v combatir

bay (bei) n bahía f; v ladrar

*be (bii) v *estar, *ser

beach (biich) n playa f; nudist ~ playa para nudistas

bead (biid) n cuenta f; beads pl collar m; rosario m

beak (biik) n pico m

beam (biim) n rayo m; viga f

bean (biin) n judía f; ejote mMe

bear (beô) n oso m

*bear (beô) v llevar; aguantar; soportar

beard (bið) n barba f

bearer (*beô*-rö) n portador m

beast (biisst) n animal m; ~ of prey animal de presa

*beat (biit) v batir, golpear

beautiful (*byuu*-ti-föl) adj hermoso

beauty (*byuu*-ti) n belleza f; ~ parlour salón de belleza; ~ salon salón de belleza; ~ treatment tratamiento de belleza

beaver (*bii*-vö) n castor m

because (bi-*kos*) conj porque; puesto que; ~ of a causa de

*become (bi-*kam*) v *hacerse; *sentar bien

bed (bêd) n cama f; ~ and board pensión completa; ~ and breakfast cama y desayuno

bedding (*bê*-ding) n ropa de cama

bedroom (*bêd*-ruum) n dormitorio m

bee (bii) n abeja f

beech (bii-ch) n haya f

beef (biif) n carne de vaca

beehive (*bii*-haiv) n colmena f

been (biin) v (pp be)

beer (biô) n cerveza f

beet (biit) n remolacha f

beetle (*bii*-töl) n escarabajo m

beetroot (*biit*-ruut) n remolacha f

before (bi-*foo*) prep antes de; delante de; conj antes de que; adv antes

beg (bêgh) v mendigar; suplicar; *pedir

beggar (*bê*-ghö) n mendigo m

*begin (bi-*ghin*) v *empezar; *comenzar

beginner (bi-*ghi*-nö) n principiante m

beginning (bi-*ghi*-ning) n comienzo m

on behalf of (on bi-*haaf* ov) en nombre de; a favor de

behave (bi-*heiv*) v comportarse

behaviour (bi-*hei*-vyö) n conducta f

behind (bi-*haind*) prep detrás de; adv detrás

beige (beiʒ) adj beige

being (*bii*-ing) n ser m

Belgian (*bêl*-dʒön) adj belga

Belgium (*bêl*-dʒöm) Bélgica f

belief (bi-*liif*) n creencia f

believe (bi-*liiv*) v *creer

bell (bêl) n campana f; timbre m

bellboy (*bêl*-boi) n botones mpl

belly (*bê*-li) n vientre m

belong (bi-*long*) v *pertenecer

belongings (bi-*long*-ings) pl pertenencias fpl

beloved (bi-*lavd*) adj querido

below (bi-*lou*) prep debajo de; bajo; adv debajo

belt (bêlt) n cinturón m

bench (bênch) n banco m

**bend** (bênd) *n* comba *f*, curva *f*

**\*bend** (bênd) *v* doblar; ~ **down** bajarse

**beneath** (bi-*niiz*) *prep* debajo de; *adv* debajo

**benefit** (*bê*-ni-fit) *n* beneficio *m*; ventaja *f*; *v* aprovechar

**bent** (bênt) *adj* (pp bend) curvo

**beret** (*bê*-rei) *n* boina *f*

**berry** (*bê*-ri) *n* baya *f*

**berth** (bööz) *n* litera *f*

**beside** (bi-*ssaid*) *prep* junto a

**besides** (bi-*ssaids*) *adv* además; por otra parte; *prep* además de

**best** (bêsst) *adj* óptimo

**bet** (bêt) *n* apuesta *f*; puesta *f*

**\*bet** (bêt) *v* \*apostar

**betray** (bi-*trei*) *v* traicionar

**better** (*bê*-tö) *adj* mejor

**between** (bi-*tᵘiin*) *prep* entre

**beverage** (*bê*-vö-ridʒ) *n* bebida *f*

**beware** (bi-ᵘêᵒ) *v* precaverse, guardarse

**bewitch** (bi-ᵘ*ich*) *v* hechizar, encantar

**beyond** (bi-*yond*) *prep* más allá de; además de; *adv* más allá

**bible** (*bai*-böl) *n* biblia *f*

**bicycle** (*bai*-ssi-köl) *n* bicicleta *f*; biciclo *m*

**big** (bigh) *adj* grande; voluminoso; gordo; importante

**bile** (bail) *n* bilis *f*

**bilingual** (bai-*ling*-ghᵘöl) *adj* bilingüe

**bill** (bil) *n* cuenta *f*; *v* facturar

**billiards** (*bil*-yöds) *pl* billar *m*

**\*bind** (baind) *v* atar

**binding** (*bain*-ding) *n* atadura *f*

**binoculars** (bi-*no*-kyö-lös) *pl* prismáticos *mpl*; gemelos *mpl*

**biology** (bai-*o*-lö-dʒi) *n* biología *f*

**birch** (bööch) *n* abedul *m*

**bird** (bööd) *n* pájaro *m*

**Biro** (*bai*-rou) *n* bolígrafo *m*

**birth** (bööz) *n* nacimiento *m*

**birthday** (*bööz*-dei) *n* cumpleaños *m*

**biscuit** (*biss*-kit) *n* galleta *f*

**bishop** (*bi*-ʃöp) *n* obispo *m*

**bit** (bit) *n* trozo *m*; poco *m*

**bitch** (bich) *n* perra *f*

**bite** (bait) *n* bocado *m*; mordedura *f*; picadura *f*

**\*bite** (bait) *v* \*morder

**bitter** (*bi*-tö) *adj* amargo

**black** (blæk) *adj* negro; ~ **market** mercado negro

**blackberry** (*blæk*-bö-ri) *n* mora *f*

**blackbird** (*blæk*-bööd) *n* mirlo *m*

**blackboard** (*blæk*-bood) *n* pizarra *f*

**black-currant** (blæk-*ka*-rönt) *n* grosella negra

**blackmail** (*blæk*-meil) *n* chantaje *m*; *v* \*hacer chantaje

**blacksmith** (*blæk*-ssmiz) *n* herrero *m*

**bladder** (*blæ*-dö) *n* vejiga *f*

**blade** (bleid) *n* hoja *f*; ~ **of grass** brizna de hierba

**blame** (bleim) *n* culpa *f*; reproche *m*; *v* echar la culpa, culpar

**blank** (blængk) *adj* blanco

**blanket** (*blæng*-kit) *n* manta *f*

**blast** (blaasst) *n* explosión *f*

**blazer** (*blei*-sö) *n* chaqueta de sport, chaqueta ligera

**bleach** (bliich) *v* blanquear

**bleak** (bliik) *adj* riguroso

**\*bleed** (bliid) *v* sangrar; chupar la sangre

**bless** (blêss) *v* \*bendecir

**blessing** (*blê*-ssing) *n* bendición *f*

**blind** (blaind) *n* persiana *f*; *adj* ciego; *v* \*cegar

**blister** (*bli*-sstö) *n* ampolla *f*

**blizzard** (*bli*-söd) *n* ventisca *f*

**block** (blok) *v* \*obstruir, bloquear; *n* bloque *m*; ~ **of flats** casa de pisos

**blonde** (blond) *n* rubia *f*

**blood** (blad) *n* sangre *f*; ~ **pressure** tensión arterial

**blood-poisoning** (*blad*-poi-sö-ning) *n*
septicemia *f*

**blood-vessel** (*blad*-vê-ssöl) *n* vaso
sanguíneo

**blot** (blot) *n* borrón *m*; mancha *f*;
**blotting paper** papel secante

**blouse** (blaus) *n* blusa *f*

**blow** (blou) *n* golpe *m*; ráfaga *f*

***blow** (blou) *v* soplar

**blow-out** (*blou*-aut) *n* reventón *m*

**blue** (bluu) *adj* azul; deprimido

**blunt** (blant) *adj* desafilado; obtuso

**blush** (blaʃ) *v* ruborizarse

**board** (bood) *n* tabla *f*; tablero *m*;
pensión *f*; consejo *m*; ~ **and lodging** pensión completa

**boarder** (*boo*-dö) *n* huésped *m*

**boarding-house** (*boo*-ding-hauss) *n*
pensión *f*

**boarding-school** (*boo*-ding-sskuul) *n*
internado *m*

**boast** (bousst) *v* presumir

**boat** (bout) *n* barco *m*, barca *f*

**body** (*bo*-di) *n* cuerpo *m*

**bodyguard** (*bo*-di-ghaad) *n* guardia
personal

**bog** (bogh) *n* pantano *m*

**boil** (boil) *v* *hervir; *n* forúnculo *m*

**bold** (bould) *adj* audaz; impertinente,
descarado

**Bolivia** (bö-*li*-vi-ö) Bolivia *f*

**Bolivian** (bö-*li*-vi-ön) *adj* boliviano

**bolt** (boult) *n* cerrojo *m*; perno *m*

**bomb** (bom) *n* bomba *f*; *v* bombardear

**bond** (bond) *n* obligación *f*

**bone** (boun) *n* hueso *m*; espina *f*; *v*
deshuesar

**bonnet** (*bo*-nit) *n* capó *m*

**book** (buk) *n* libro *m*; *v* reservar; inscribir, registrar

**booking** (*bu*-king) *n* reservación *f*, reserva *f*

**bookmaker** (*buk*-mei-kö) *n* corredor
*m*

**bookseller** (*buk*-ssê-lö) *n* librero *m*

**bookstand** (*buk*-sstænd) *n* puesto de
libros

**bookstore** (*buk*-sstoo) *n* librería *f*

**boot** (buut) *n* bota *f*; portaequipajes
*m*

**booth** (buuð) *n* puesto *m*; cabina *f*

**border** (*boo*-dö) *n* frontera *f*; borde
*m*

**bore¹** (boo) *v* aburrir; taladrar; *n*
pelmazo *m*

**bore²** (boo) *v* (p bear)

**boring** (*boo*-ring) *adj* aburrido

**born** (boon) *adj* nacido

**borrow** (*bo*-rou) *v* tomar prestado;
tomar

**bosom** (*bu*-söm) *n* pecho *m*; seno *m*

**boss** (boss) *n* jefe *m*, patrón *m*

**botany** (*bo*-tö-ni) *n* botánica *f*

**both** (bouz) *adj* ambos; **both ... and**
tanto ... como

**bother** (*bo*-ðö) *v* fastidiar, molestar;
*esforzarse; *n* molestia *f*

**bottle** (*bo*-töl) *n* botella *f*; ~ **opener**
destapador de botellas; **hot-water**
~ calorífero *m*

**bottleneck** (*bo*-töl-nêk) *n* cuello de
botella

**bottom** (*bo*-töm) *n* fondo *m*; trasero
*m*; *adj* inferior

**bough** (bau) *n* rama *f*

**bought** (boot) *v* (p, pp buy)

**boulder** (*boul*-dö) *n* peña *f*

**bound** (baund) *n* frontera *f*; ***be** ~ **to**
deber de; ~ **for** camino de

**boundary** (*baun*-dö-ri) *n* límite *m*;
frontera *f*

**bouquet** (bu-*kei*) *n* ramo *m*

**bourgeois** (*buᵒ*-ȝ*ᵘ*aa) *adj* burgués

**boutique** (bu-*tiik*) *n* boutique *f*

**bow¹** (bau) *v* inclinar

**bow²** (bou) *n* arco *m*; ~ **tie** corbata
de lazo, corbatín *m*

**bowels** (bau⁰ls) *pl* intestinos *mpl*

**bowl** (boul) *n* tazón *m*

**bowling** (*bou*-ling) *n* bowling *m*, juego de bolos; ~ **alley** bolera *f*

**box¹** (bokss) *v* boxear; **boxing match** combate de boxeo

**box²** (bokss) *n* caja *f*

**box-office** (*bokss*-o-fiss) *n* taquilla *f*

**boy** (boi) *n* muchacho *m*; chico *m*, mozo *m*; sirviente *m*; ~ **scout** explorador *m*

**bra** (braa) *n* sujetador *m*, sostén *m*

**bracelet** (*breiss*-lit) *n* pulsera *f*

**braces** (*brei*-ssis) *pl* tirantes *mpl*

**brain** (brein) *n* cerebro *m*; inteligencia *f*

**brain-wave** (*brein*-ᵘeiv) *n* ocurrencia *f*

**brake** (breik) *n* freno *m*; ~ **drum** tambor del freno; ~ **lights** luces de freno

**branch** (braanch) *n* rama *f*; sucursal *f*

**brand** (brænd) *n* marca *f*

**brand-new** (brænd-*nyuu*) *adj* flamante

**brass** (braass) *n* latón *m*; cobre *m*, cobre amarillo; ~ **band** *n* charanga *f*

**brassiere** (*bræ*-si⁰) *n* sujetador *m*, sostén *m*

**brassware** (*braass*-ᵘê̂⁰) *n* cobres *mpl*

**brave** (breiv) *adj* valiente

**Brazil** (brö-*sil*) Brasil *m*

**Brazilian** (brö-*sil*-yön) *adj* brasileño

**breach** (briich) *n* brecha *f*

**bread** (brêd) *n* pan *m*; **wholemeal** ~ pan integral

**breadth** (brêdz) *n* ancho *m*

**break** (breik) *n* fractura *f*; descanso *m*

*****break** (breik) *v* *quebrar, quebrantar; ~ **down** averiarse; analizar

**breakdown** (*breik*-daun) *n* avería *f*; descompostura *fMe*

**breakfast** (*brêk*-fösst) *n* desayuno *m*

**bream** (briim) *n* (pl ~) brema *f*

**breast** (brêsst) *n* seno *m*

**breaststroke** (*brêsst*-sstrouk) *n* braza *f*

**breath** (brêz) *n* aliento *m*; aire *m*

**breathe** (briið) *v* respirar

**breathing** (*brii*-ðing) *n* respiración *f*

**breed** (briid) *n* raza *f*; especie *f*

*****breed** (briid) *v* recriar

**breeze** (briis) *n* brisa *f*

**brew** (bruu) *v* fabricar cerveza

**brewery** (*bruu*-ö-ri) *n* cervecería *f*

**bribe** (braib) *v* sobornar

**bribery** (*brai*-bö-ri) *n* soborno *m*

**brick** (brik) *n* ladrillo *m*

**bricklayer** (*brik*-lei⁰) *n* albañil *m*

**bride** (braid) *n* novia *f*

**bridegroom** (*braid*-ghruum) *n* novio *m*

**bridge** (briʤ) *n* puente *m*; bridge *m*

**brief** (briif) *adj* breve

**briefcase** (*briif*-keiss) *n* portafolio *m*

**briefs** (briifss) *pl* braga *f*, calzoncillos *mpl*

**bright** (brait) *adj* claro; reluciente; listo

**brill** (bril) *n* rodaballo *m*

**brilliant** (*bril*-yönt) *adj* brillante

**brim** (brim) *n* borde *m*

*****bring** (bring) *v* *traer; ~ **back** *devolver; ~ **up** educar; *introducir, levantar

**brisk** (brissk) *adj* vivo

**Britain** (*bri*-tön) Inglaterra *f*

**British** (*bri*-tiʃ) *adj* británico

**Briton** (*bri*-tön) *n* británico *m*; inglés *m*

**broad** (brood) *adj* ancho; amplio; general

**broadcast** (*brood*-kaasst) *n* transmisión *f*

*****broadcast** (*brood*-kaasst) *v* emitir

**brochure** (*brou*-ʃu⁰) *n* folleto *m*

**broke¹** (brouk) *v* (p break)

**broke²** (brouk) *adj* arruinado

**broken** (*brou*-kön) *adj* (pp break) estropeado, roto

**broker** ( *brou*-kö ) *n* corredor *m*

**bronchitis** (brong-*kai*-tiss ) *n* bronquitis *f*

**bronze** (brons ) *n* bronce *m*; *adj* de bronce

**brooch** (brouch ) *n* broche *m*

**brook** (bruk ) *n* arroyo *m*

**broom** (bruum ) *n* escoba *f*

**brothel** ( *bro*-zöl ) *n* burdel *m*

**brother** ( *bra*-ðö ) *n* hermano *m*

**brother-in-law** ( *bra*-ðö-rin-loo ) *n* (pl brothers-) cuñado *m*

**brought** (broot ) *v* (p, pp bring)

**brown** (braun ) *adj* moreno

**bruise** (bruus ) *n* moretón *m*, magulladura *f*; *v* magullar

**brunette** (bruu-*nêt* ) *n* morena *f*

**brush** (braʃ ) *n* cepillo *m*; brocha *f*; *v* sacar brillo, cepillar

**brutal** ( *bruu*-töl ) *adj* brutal

**bubble** ( *ba*-böl ) *n* burbuja *f*

**bucket** ( *ba*-kit ) *n* balde *m*

**buckle** ( *ba*-köl ) *n* hebilla *f*

**bud** (bad ) *n* capullo *m*

**budget** ( *ba*-dʒit ) *n* presupuesto *m*

**buffet** ( *bu*-fei ) *n* buffet *m*

**bug** (bagh ) *n* chinche *f*; escarabajo *m*; *nAm* insecto *m*

**\*build** (bild ) *v* \*construir

**building** ( *bil*-ding ) *n* edificio *m*

**bulb** (balb ) *n* bulbo *m*; **light ~** bombilla *f*; foco *mMe*

**Bulgaria** (bal-*ghê*ᵒ-ri-ö ) Bulgaria *f*

**Bulgarian** (bal-*ghê*ᵒ-ri-ön ) *adj* búlgaro

**bulk** (balk ) *n* bulto *m*; mayoría *f*

**bulky** ( *bal*-ki ) *adj* voluminoso

**bull** (bul ) *n* toro *m*

**bullet** ( *bu*-lit ) *n* bala *f*

**bullfight** ( *bul*-fait ) *n* corrida de toros *f*

**bullring** ( *bul*-ring ) *n* plaza de toros *f*

**bump** (bamp ) *v* topetar; chocar; \*dar golpes; *n* golpe *m*, topetón *m*

**bumper** ( *bam*-pö ) *n* parachoques *m*

**bumpy** ( *bam*-pi ) *adj* lleno de baches

**bun** (ban ) *n* bollo *m*

**bunch** (banch ) *n* ramo *m*; grupo *m*

**bundle** ( *ban*-döl ) *n* paquete *m*; *v* atar, liar

**bunk** (bangk ) *n* camastro *m*

**buoy** (boi ) *n* boya *f*

**burden** ( *böö*-dön ) *n* peso *m*

**bureau** ( *byu*ᵒ-rou ) *n* (pl ~x, ~s) escritorio *m*; *nAm* cómoda *f*

**bureaucracy** (byu-ᵒ-*ro*-krö-ssi ) *n* burocracia *f*

**burglar** ( *böö*-ghlö ) *n* ladrón *m*

**burgle** ( *böö*-ghöl ) *v* robar

**burial** ( *bê*-ri-öl ) *n* entierro *m*

**burn** (böön ) *n* quemadura *f*

**\*burn** (böön ) *v* quemar; pegarse

**\*burst** (böösst ) *v* \*reventar; \*quebrar

**bury** ( *bê*-ri ) *v* \*enterrar

**bus** (bass ) *n* autobús *m*

**bush** (buʃ ) *n* matorral *m*

**business** ( *bis*-nöss ) *n* negocios *mpl*, comercio *m*; empresa *f*, negocio *m*; ocupación *f*; asunto *m*; **~ hours** horas hábiles, horas de oficina; **~ trip** viaje de negocios; **on ~** por asuntos de negocio

**business-like** ( *bis*-niss-laik ) *adj* práctico

**businessman** ( *bis*-nöss-mön ) *n* (pl -men) hombre de negocios

**bust** (basst ) *n* busto *m*

**bustle** ( *ba*-ssöl ) *n* agitación *f*

**busy** ( *bi*-si ) *adj* ocupado; concurrido, atareado

**but** (bat ) *conj* mas; pero; *prep* menos

**butcher** ( *bu*-chö ) *n* carnicero *m*

**butter** ( *ba*-tö ) *n* mantequilla *f*

**butterfly** ( *ba*-tö-flai ) *n* mariposa *f*; **~ stroke** braza de mariposa

**buttock** ( *ba*-tök ) *n* nalga *m*

**button** ( *ba*-tön ) *n* botón *m*; *v* abrochar

**buttonhole** ( *ba*-tön-houl ) *n* ojal *m*

**\*buy** (bai ) *v* comprar; \*adquirir

**buyer** (*bai*-ö) *n* comprador *m*
**by** (bai) *prep* por; con; cerca de
**by-pass** (*bai*-paass) *n* cinturón *m*; *v* rodear

# C

**cab** (kæb) *n* taxi *m*
**cabaret** (*kæ*-bö-rei) *n* cabaret *m*
**cabbage** (*kæ*-bidʒ) *n* col *m*
**cab-driver** (*kæb*-drai-vö) *n* taxista *m*
**cabin** (*kæ*-bin) *n* cabina *f*; cabaña *f*
**cabinet** (*kæ*-bi-nöt) *n* gabinete *m*
**cable** (*kei*-böl) *n* cable *m*; cablegrama *m*; *v* cablegrafiar
**cadre** (*kaa*-dö) *n* cuadro *m*
**café** (*kæ*-fei) *n* bar *m*
**cafeteria** (kæ-fö-*tiô*-ri-ö) *n* cafetería *f*
**caffeine** (*kæ*-fiin) *n* cafeína *f*
**cage** (keidʒ) *n* jaula *f*
**cake** (keik) *n* pastel *m*; pastelería *f*, tarta *f*, dulces
**calamity** (kö-*læ*-mö-ti) *n* desastre *m*, catástrofe *f*
**calcium** (*kæl*-ssi-öm) *n* calcio *m*
**calculate** (*kæl*-kyu-leit) *v* calcular
**calculation** (kæl-kyu-*lei*-fön) *n* cálculo *m*
**calendar** (*kæ*-lön-dö) *n* calendario *m*
**calf** (kaaf) *n* (pl calves) ternero *m*; pantorrilla *f*; ~ **skin** becerro *m*
**call** (kool) *v* llamar; *n* llamada *f*; visita *f*; \***be called** llamarse; ~ **names** insultar; ~ **on** visitar; ~ **up** *Am* telefonear
**callus** (*kæ*-löss) *n* callo *m*
**calm** (kaam) *adj* tranquilo; ~ **down** calmar
**calorie** (*kæ*-lö-ri) *n* caloría *f*
**Calvinism** (*kæl*-vi-ni-söm) *n* calvinismo *m*
**came** (keim) *v* (p come)

**camel** (*kæ*-möl) *n* camello *m*
**cameo** (*kæ*-mi-ou) *n* (pl ~s) camafeo *m*
**camera** (*kæ*-mö-rö) *n* cámara fotográfica; cámara *f*; ~ **shop** negocio fotográfico
**camp** (kæmp) *n* campamento *m*; *v* acampar
**campaign** (kæm-*pein*) *n* campaña *f*
**camp-bed** (kæmp-*bêd*) *n* catre de campaña, cama de tijera
**camper** (*kæm*-pö) *n* acampador *m*
**camping** (*kæm*-ping) *n* camping *m*; ~ **site** camping *m*, lugar de camping
**camshaft** (*kæm*-ʃaaft) *n* árbol de levas
**can** (kæn) *n* lata *f*; ~ **opener** abrelatas *m*
\***can** (kæn) *v* \*poder
**Canada** (*kæ*-nö-dö) Canadá *m*
**Canadian** (kö-*nei*-di-ön) *adj* canadiense
**canal** (kö-*næl*) *n* canal *m*
**canary** (kö-*nê*^*ô*-ri) *n* canario *m*
**cancel** (*kæn*-ssöl) *v* cancelar; anular
**cancellation** (kæn-ssö-*lei*-fön) *n* cancelación *f*
**cancer** (*kæn*-ssö) *n* cáncer *m*
**candelabrum** (kæn-dö-*laa*-bröm) *n* (pl -bra) candelabro *m*
**candidate** (*kæn*-di-döt) *n* candidato *m*, interesado *m*
**candle** (*kæn*-döl) *n* candela *f*
**candy** (*kæn*-di) *nAm* bombón *m*; dulces, golosinas
**cane** (kein) *n* caña *f*; bastón *m*
**canister** (*kæ*-ni-sstö) *n* caja metálica, lata *f*
**canoe** (kö-*nuu*) *n* canoa *f*
**canteen** (kæn-*tiin*) *n* cantina *f*
**canvas** (*kæn*-vöss) *n* lona *f*
**cap** (kæp) *n* gorra *f*, gorro *m*
**capable** (*kei*-pö-böl) *adj* capaz
**capacity** (kö-*pæ*-ssö-ti) *n* capacidad

*f*; potencia *f*; competencia *f*

**cape** (keip) *n* capa *f*; cabo *m*

**capital** (*kæ*-pi-töl) *n* capital *f*; capital *m*; *adj* importante, capital; ~ **letter** mayúscula *f*

**capitalism** (*kæ*-pi-tö-li-ssöm) *n* capitalismo *m*

**capitulation** (kö-pi-tyu-*lei*-ʃön) *n* capitulación *f*

**capsule** (*kæp*-ssyuul) *n* cápsula *f*

**captain** (*kæp*-tin) *n* capitán *m*; comandante *m*

**capture** (*kæp*-chö) *v* coger preso, capturar; conquistar; *n* captura *f*; conquista *f*

**car** (kaa) *n* coche *m*; carro *mMe*; ~ **hire** alquiler de coches; ~ **park** parque de estacionamiento

**carafe** (kö-*ræf*) *n* garrafa *f*

**caramel** (*kæ*-rö-möl) *n* caramelo *m*

**carat** (*kæ*-röt) *n* quilate *m*

**caravan** (*kæ*-rö-væn) *n* caravana *f*; carro de gitanos

**carburettor** (kaa-byu-*rê*-tö) *n* carburador *m*

**card** (kaad) *n* tarjeta *f*; tarjeta postal

**cardboard** (*kaad*-bood) *n* cartón *m*; *adj* de cartón

**cardigan** (*kaa*-di-ghön) *n* chaqueta *f*

**cardinal** (*kaa*-di-nöl) *n* cardenal *m*; *adj* cardinal, principal

**care** (kêᵒ) *n* cuidado *m*; ~ **about** preocuparse de; ~ **for** gustar; *take ~ of cuidar de

**career** (kö-*riᵒ*) *n* carrera *f*

**carefree** (*kêᵒ*-frii) *adj* despreocupado

**careful** (*kêᵒ*-föl) *adj* cuidadoso; escrupuloso

**careless** (*kêᵒ*-löss) *adj* indiferente, negligente

**caretaker** (*kêᵒ*-tei-kö) *n* guardián *m*

**cargo** (*kaa*-ghou) *n* (pl ~es) carga *f*

**carnival** (*kaa*-ni-völ) *n* carnaval *m*

**carp** (kaap) *n* (pl ~) carpa *f*

**carpenter** (*kaa*-pin-tö) *n* carpintero *m*

**carpet** (*kaa*-pit) *n* alfombra *f*

**carriage** (*kæ*-ridʒ) *n* vagón *m*; coche *m*, carruaje *m*

**carriageway** (*kæ*-ridʒ-ᵘei) *n* calzada *f*

**carrot** (*kæ*-röt) *n* zanahoria *f*

**carry** (*kæ*-ri) *v* llevar; *conducir; ~ **on** continuar; *proseguir; ~ **out** realizar

**carry-cot** (*kæ*-ri-kot) *n* cuna de viaje

**cart** (kaat) *n* carro *m*

**cartilage** (*kaa*-ti-lidʒ) *n* cartílago *m*

**carton** (*kaa*-tön) *n* caja de cartón; cartón *m*

**cartoon** (kaa-*tuun*) *n* dibujos animados

**cartridge** (*kaa*-tridʒ) *n* cartucho *m*

**carve** (kaav) *v* trinchar; entallar, tallar

**carving** (*kaa*-ving) *n* talla *f*

**case** (keiss) *n* caso *m*; causa *f*; valija *f*; estuche *m*; **attaché** ~ portafolio *m*; **in** ~ si; **in** ~ **of** en caso de

**cash** (kæʃ) *n* dinero contante, efectivo *m*; *v* cobrar, *hacer efectivo

**cashier** (kæ-*ʃiᵒ*) *n* cajero *m*; cajera *f*

**cashmere** (*kæʃ*-miᵒ) *n* casimir *m*

**casino** (kö-*ssii*-nou) *n* (pl ~s) casino *m*

**cask** (kaassk) *n* barril *m*, tonel *m*

**cast** (kaasst) *n* echada *f*

***cast** (kaasst) *v* lanzar; **cast iron** hierro fundido

**castle** (*kaa*-ssöl) *n* castillo *m*

**casual** (*kæ*-ʒu-öl) *adj* informal; de paso, por casualidad

**casualty** (*kæ*-ʒu-öl-ti) *n* víctima *f*

**cat** (kæt) *n* gato *m*

**catacomb** (*kæ*-tö-koum) *n* catacumba *f*

**catalogue** (*kæ*-tö-logh) *n* catálogo *m*

**catarrh** (kö-*taa*) *n* catarro *m*

**catastrophe** (kö-*tæ*-ssströ-fi) *n* catástrofe *f*

\*catch (kæch) v coger; sorprender

category (kæ-ti-ghö-ri) n categoría f

cathedral (kö-zii-dröl) n catedral f

catholic (kæ-zö-lik) adj católico

cattle (kæ-töl) pl ganado m

caught (koot) v (p, pp catch)

cauliflower (ko-li-flau⁶) n coliflor f

cause (koos) v causar; provocar; n causa f; motivo m; ~ to \*hacer

causeway (koos-ᵁei) n calzada f

caution (koo-ʃön) n cautela f; v \*advertir

cautious (koo-ʃöss) adj prudente

cave (keiv) n cueva f; grieta f

cavern (kæ-vön) n cueva f

caviar (kæ-vi-aa) n caviar m

cavity (kæ-vö-ti) n cavidad f

cease (ssiiss) v cesar

ceiling (ssii-ling) n cielo raso

celebrate (ssè-li-breit) v celebrar

celebration (ssè-li-brei-ʃön) n celebración f

celebrity (ssi-lê-brö-ti) n celebridad f

celery (ssè-lö-ri) n apio m

celibacy (ssê-li-bö-ssi) n celibato m

cell (ssèl) n celda f

cellar (ssê-lö) n sótano m

cellophane (ssê-lö-fein) n celofán m

cement (ssi-mênt) n cemento m

cemetery (ssê-mi-tri) n cementerio m

censorship (ssên-ssö-ʃip) n censura f

centigrade (ssên-ti-ghreid) adj centigrado

centimetre (ssên-ti-mii-tö) n centímetro m

central (ssên-tröl) adj central; ~ heating calefacción central; ~ station estación central

centralize (ssên-trö-lais) v centralizar

centre (ssên-tö) n centro m

century (ssên-chö-ri) n siglo m

ceramics (ssi-ræ-mikss) pl cerámica f

ceremony (ssê-rö-mö-ni) n ceremonia f

certain (ssöö-tön) adj cierto

certificate (ssö-ti-fi-köt) n certificado m; certificación f, acta f, diploma m

chain (chein) n cadena f

chair (chê⁶) n silla f

chairman (chê⁶-mön) n (pl -men) presidente m

chalet (ʃæ-lei) n chalet m

chalk (chook) n creta f

challenge (chæ-löndʒ) v desafiar; n reto m

chamber (cheim-bö) n cuarto m

chambermaid (cheim-bö-meid) n doncella f

champagne (ʃæm-pein) n champán m

champion (chæm-pyön) n campeón m; defensor m

chance (chaanss) n azar m; oportunidad f, ocasión f; riesgo m; suerte f; by ~ por casualidad

change (cheindʒ) v modificar, cambiar; mudarse; \*hacer trasbordo; n modificación f, cambio m; moneda f

channel (chæ-nöl) n canal m; English Channel Canal de la Mancha

chaos (kei-oss) n caos m

chaotic (kei-o-tik) adj caótico

chap (chæp) n hombre m

chapel (chæ-pöl) n iglesia f, capilla f

chaplain (chæ-plin) n capellán m

character (kæ-rök-tö) n carácter m

characteristic (kæ-rök-tö-ri-sstik) adj típico, característico; n característica f; rasgo característico

characterize (kæ-rök-tö-rais) v caracterizar

charcoal (chaa-koul) n carbón de leña

charge (chaadʒ) v \*pedir; cargar; acusar; n precio m; carga f; acusación f; ~ plate Am tarjeta de crédito; free of ~ gratuito; in ~ of encargado de; \*take ~ of encargarse de

**charity** ( *chæ*-rö-ti ) *n* caridad *f*

**charm** (chaam ) *n* encanto *m* ; amuleto *m*

**charming** (chaa-ming) *adj* encantador

**chart** (chaat ) *n* tabla *f* ; gráfico *m* ; carta marina ; **conversion** ~ tabla de conversión

**chase** (cheiss) *v* cazar; expulsar, ahuyentar ; *n* caza *f*

**chasm** ( *kæ*-söm ) *n* grieta *f*

**chassis** ( /*æ*-ssi ) *n* (pl ~) chasis *m*

**chaste** (cheisst ) *adj* casto

**chat** (chæt ) *v* charlar; *n* charla *f*

**chatterbox** ( *chæ*-tö-bokss ) *n* charlatán *m*

**chauffeur** ( /ou-fö ) *n* chófer *m*

**cheap** (chiip ) *adj* barato ; económico

**cheat** (chiit ) *v* engañar; estafar

**check** (chêk ) *v* controlar, verificar; *n* escaque *m* ; *nAm* cuenta *f* ; cheque *m* ; **check!** ¡jaque! ; ~ **in** inscribirse ; ~ **out** *despedirse

**check-book** ( *chêk*-buk) *nAm* talonario *m*

**checkerboard** ( *chê*-kö-bood) *nAm* tablero de ajedrez

**checkroom** ( *chêk*-ruum) *nAm* guardarropa *m*

**check-up** ( *chê*-kap) *n* reconocimiento *m*

**cheek** (chiik ) *n* mejilla *f*

**cheek-bone** ( *chiik*-boun) *n* pómulo *m*

**cheer** (chi⁰ ) *v* aclamar; ~ **up** alegrar

**cheerful** ( *chi⁰*-föl ) *adj* alegre

**cheese** (chiis ) *n* queso *m*

**chef** (/êf ) *n* jefe de cocina

**chemical** ( *kê*-mi-köl) *adj* químico

**chemist** ( *kê*-misst ) *n* farmacéutico *m* ; **chemist's** farmacia *f* ; droguería *f*

**chemistry** ( *kê*-mi-sstri ) *n* química *f*

**cheque** (chêk ) *n* cheque *m*

**cheque-book** ( *chêk*-buk) *n* talonario *m*

**chequered** ( *chê*-köd) *adj* a cuadros, cuadriculado

**cherry** ( *chê*-ri ) *n* cereza *f*

**chess** (chêss ) *n* ajedrez *m*

**chest** (chêsst ) *n* pecho *m* ; arca *f* ; ~ **of drawers** cómoda *f*

**chestnut** ( *chêss*-nat) *n* castaña *f*

**chew** (chuu ) *v* masticar

**chewing-gum** ( *chuu*-ing-gham ) *n* goma de mascar, chicle *m*

**chicken** ( *chi*-kin) *n* pollo *m*

**chickenpox** ( *chi*-kin-pokss) *n* varicela *f*

**chief** (chiif ) *n* jefe *m* ; *adj* principal

**chieftain** ( *chiif*-tön ) *n* jefe *m*

**chilblain** ( *chil*-blein) *n* sabañón *m*

**child** (chaild ) *n* (pl **children**) niño *m*

**childbirth** ( *chaild*-bööz ) *n* parto *m*

**childhood** ( *chaild*-hud ) *n* infancia *f*

**Chile** ( *chi*-li ) Chile *m*

**Chilean** ( *chi*-li-ön ) *adj* chileno

**chill** (chil ) *n* escalofrío *m*

**chilly** ( *chi*-li ) *adj* fresco

**chimes** (chaims ) *pl* carillón *m*

**chimney** ( *chim*-ni ) *n* chimenea *f*

**chin** (chin ) *n* barbilla *f*

**China** ( *chai*-nö ) China *f*

**china** ( *chai*-nö ) *n* porcelana *f*

**Chinese** (chai-*niis*) *adj* chino

**chink** (chingk) *n* hendidura *f*

**chip** (chip ) *n* astilla *f* ; ficha *f* ; *v* cortar, astillar; **chips** patatas fritas

**chiropodist** (ki-*ro*-pö-disst ) *n* pedicuro *m*

**chisel** ( *chi*-söl ) *n* cincel *m*

**chives** (chaivs ) *pl* cebollino *m*

**chlorine** ( *kloo*-riin ) *n* cloro *m*

**chock-full** (chok-*ful*) *adj* de bote en bote, repleto

**chocolate** ( *cho*-klöt ) *n* chocolate *m* ; bombón *m*

**choice** (choiss ) *n* elección *f* ; selección *f*

**choir** (k⁰ai⁰ ) *n* coro *m*

**choke** (chouk) *v* sofocarse; estrangular; *n* starter *m*

*** choose** (chuus) *v* escoger

**chop** (chop) *n* chuleta *f*; *v* tajar

**Christ** (kraisst) Cristo

**christen** (*kri*-ssön) *v* bautizar

**christening** (*kri*-ssö-ning) *n* bautizo *m*

**Christian** (*kriss*-chön) *adj* cristiano; ~ **name** nombre de pila

**Christmas** (*kriss*-möss) Navidad *f*

**chromium** (*krou*-mi-öm) *n* cromo *m*

**chronic** (*kro*-nik) *adj* crónico

**chronological** (kro-nö-*lo*-dʒi-köl) *adj* cronológico

**chuckle** (*cha*-köl) *v* *reírse entre dientes

**chunk** (changk) *n* trozo *m*

**church** (chööch) *n* iglesia *f*

**churchyard** (*chööch*-yaad) *n* cementerio *m*

**cigar** (ssi-*ghaa*) *n* puro *m*; ~ **shop** estanco *m*

**cigarette** (ssi-ghö-*rêt*) *n* cigarrillo *m*; ~ **tobacco** picadura *f*

**cigarette-case** (ssi-ghö-*rêt*-keiss) *n* pitillera *f*

**cigarette-holder** (ssi-ghö-*rêt*-houl-dö) *n* boquilla *f*

**cigarette-lighter** (ssi-ghö-*rêt*-lai-tö) *n* encendedor *m*

**cinema** (*ssi*-nö-mö) *n* cinematógrafo *m*

**cinnamon** (*ssi*-nö-mön) *n* canela *f*

**circle** (*ssöö*-köl) *n* círculo *m*; balcón *m*; *v* rodear, circundar

**circulation** (ssöö-kyu-*lei*-ʃön) *n* circulación *f*; circulación de la sangre

**circumstance** (*ssöö*-köm-sstænss) *n* circunstancia *f*

**circus** (*ssöö*-köss) *n* circo *m*

**citizen** (*ssi*-ti-sön) *n* ciudadano *m*

**citizenship** (*ssi*-ti-sön-ʃip) *n* ciudadanía *f*

**city** (*ssi*-ti) *n* ciudad *f*

**civic** (*ssi*-vik) *adj* cívico

**civil** (*ssi*-völ) *adj* civil; cortés; ~ **law** derecho civil; ~ **servant** funcionario *m*

**civilian** (ssi-*vil*-yön) *adj* civil; *n* paisano *m*

**civilization** (ssi-vö-lai-*sei*-ʃön) *n* civilización *f*

**civilized** (*ssi*-vö-laisd) *adj* civilizado

**claim** (kleim) *v* reivindicar, reclamar; afirmar; *n* reivindicación *f*, pretensión *f*

**clamp** (klæmp) *n* mordaza *f*; grapa *f*

**clap** (klæp) *v* aplaudir

**clarify** (*klæ*-ri-fai) *v* aclarar, clarificar

**class** (klaass) *n* clase *f*

**classical** (*klæ*-ssi-köl) *adj* clásico

**classify** (*klæ*-ssi-fai) *v* clasificar

**class-mate** (*klaass*-meit) *n* compañero de clase

**classroom** (*klaass*-ruum) *n* clase *f*

**clause** (kloos) *n* cláusula *f*

**claw** (kloo) *n* garra *f*

**clay** (klei) *n* arcilla *f*

**clean** (kliin) *adj* puro, limpio; *v* limpiar

**cleaning** (*klii*-ning) *n* limpieza *f*; ~ **fluid** quitamanchas *m*

**clear** (kliö) *adj* claro; *v* limpiar

**clearing** (*kliö*-ring) *n* claro *m*

**cleft** (klêft) *n* grieta *f*

**clergyman** (*klöö*-dʒi-mön) *n* (pl -men) pastor *m*; clérigo *m*

**clerk** (klaak) *n* empleado de oficina, oficinista *m*; escribano *m*; secretario *m*

**clever** (*klê*-vö) *adj* inteligente; astuto, listo

**client** (*klai*-önt) *n* cliente *m*

**cliff** (klif) *n* acantilado *m*, farallón *m*

**climate** (*klai*-mit) *n* clima *m*

**climb** (klaim) *v* trepar; *n* subida *f*

**clinic** (*kli*-nik) *n* clínica *f*

**cloak** (klouk) *n* capa *f*

**cloakroom** (*klouk*-ruum) *n* guardarropa *m*

**clock** (klok) *n* reloj *m*; **at ... o'clock** a las ...

**cloister** (*kloi*-sstö) *n* convento *m*

**close**[1] (klous) *v* *cerrar

**close**[2] (klouss) *adj* cercano

**closet** (*klo*-sit) *n* armario *m*

**cloth** (kloz) *n* tela *f*; paño *m*

**clothes** (klouðs) *pl* ropa *f*, vestidos *mpl*

**clothes-brush** (*klouðs*-braʃ) *n* cepillo de la ropa

**clothing** (*klou*-ðing) *n* vestido *m*

**cloud** (klaud) *n* nube *f*

**cloud-burst** (*klaud*-böösst) *n* chaparrón *m*

**cloudy** (*klau*-di) *adj* cubierto, nublado

**clover** (*klou*-vö) *n* trébol *m*

**clown** (klaun) *n* payaso *m*

**club** (klab) *n* club *m*; círculo *m*, asociación *f*; porra *f*, garrote *m*

**clumsy** (*klam*-si) *adj* torpe

**clutch** (klach) *n* embrague *m*; apretón *m*

**coach** (kouch) *n* autobús *m*; vagón *m*; carroza *f*; entrenador *m*

**coachwork** (*kouch*-ᵘöök) *n* carrocería *f*

**coagulate** (kou-æ-ghyu-leit) *v* coagularse

**coal** (koul) *n* carbón *m*

**coarse** (kooss) *adj* burdo; grosero

**coast** (kousst) *n* costa *f*

**coat** (kout) *n* sobretodo *m*, abrigo *m*

**coat-hanger** (*kout*-hæng-ö) *n* percha *f*

**cobweb** (*kob*-ᵘêb) *n* tela de araña

**cocaine** (kou-*kein*) *n* cocaína *f*

**cock** (kok) *n* gallo *m*

**cocktail** (*kok*-teil) *n* cóctel *m*

**coconut** (*kou*-kö-nat) *n* coco *m*

**cod** (kod) *n* (pl ~) bacalao *m*

**code** (koud) *n* código *m*

**coffee** (*ko*-fi) *n* café *m*

**cognac** (*ko*-nyæk) *n* coñac *m*

**coherence** (kou-*hi*ᵈ-rönss) *n* coherencia *f*

**coin** (koin) *n* moneda *f*

**coincide** (kou-in-*ssaid*) *v* coincidir

**cold** (kould) *adj* frío; *n* frío *m*; resfriado *m*; **catch a ~** resfriarse

**collapse** (kö-*læpss*) *v* desplomarse, derrumbarse

**collar** (*ko*-lö) *n* collar *m*; cuello *m*; ~ **stud** botón del cuello

**collarbone** (*ko*-lö-boun) *n* clavícula *f*

**colleague** (*ko*-liigh) *n* colega *m*

**collect** (kö-*lêkt*) *v* juntar; recoger; *hacer una colecta

**collection** (kö-*lêk*-ʃön) *n* colección *f*; recogida *f*

**collective** (kö-*lêk*-tiv) *adj* colectivo

**collector** (kö-*lêk*-tö) *n* coleccionista *m*; colector *m*

**college** (*ko*-lidʒ) *n* colegio *m*

**collide** (kö-*laid*) *v* chocar

**collision** (kö-*li*-ʒön) *n* colisión *f*

**Colombia** (kö-*lom*-bi-ö) Colombia *f*

**Colombian** (kö-*lom*-bi-ön) *adj* colombiano

**colonel** (*köö*-nöl) *n* coronel *m*

**colony** (*ko*-lö-ni) *n* colonia *f*

**colour** (*ka*-lö) *n* color *m*; *v* colorear; ~ **film** película en colores

**colourant** (*ka*-lö-rönt) *n* colorante *m*

**colour-blind** (*ka*-lö-blaind) *adj* daltoniano

**coloured** (*ka*-löd) *adj* de color

**colourful** (*ka*-lö-föl) *adj* colorado, lleno de color

**column** (*ko*-löm) *n* columna *f*

**coma** (*kou*-mö) *n* coma *m*

**comb** (koum) *v* peinar; *n* peine *m*

**combat** (*kom*-bæt) *n* lucha *f*, combate *m*; *v* combatir

**combination** (kom-bi-*nei*-ʃön) *n* combinación *f*

**combine** (köm-*bain*) *v* combinar; unir

\*come (kam) v \*venir; ~ across \*encontrar; hallar

comedian (kö-mii-di-ön) n comediante m; cómico m

comedy (ko-mö-di) n comedia f; musical ~ comedia musical

comfort (kam-föt) n comodidad f, confort m; consuelo m; v \*consolar

comfortable (kam-fö-tö-böl) adj confortable

comic (ko-mik) adj cómico

comics (ko-mikss) pl tebeo m

coming (ka-ming) n llegada f

comma (ko-mö) n coma f

command (kö-maand) v mandar; n orden f

commander (kö-maan-dö) n comandante m

commemoration (kö-mê-mö-rei-ʃön) n conmemoración f

commence (kö-mênss) v \*comenzar

comment (ko-mênt) n comentario m; v comentar

commerce (ko-mööss) n comercio m

commercial (kö-möö-ʃöl) adj comercial; n anuncio publicitario; ~ law derecho comercial

commission (kö-mi-ʃön) n comisión f

commit (kö-mit) v confiar, entregar; cometer

committee (kö-mi-ti) n comisión f, comité m

common (ko-mön) adj común; usual; ordinario

commune (ko-myuun) n comuna f

communicate (kö-myuu-ni-keit) v comunicar

communication (kö-myuu-ni-kei-ʃön) n comunicación f

communiqué (kö-myuu-ni-kei) n comunicado m

communism (ko-myu-ni-söm) n comunismo m

communist (ko-myu-nisst) n comunista m

community (kö-myuu-nö-ti) n sociedad f, vecindario m

commuter (kö-myuu-tö) n suburbano m

compact (kom-pækt) adj compacto

companion (köm-pæ-nyön) n compañero m

company (kam-pö-ni) n compañía f; sociedad f

comparative (köm-pæ-rö-tiv) adj relativo

compare (köm-pêö) v comparar

comparison (köm-pæ-ri-ssön) n comparación f

compartment (köm-paat-mönt) n compartimento m

compass (kam-pöss) n brújula f

compel (köm-pêl) v compeler

compensate (kom-pön-sseit) v compensar

compensation (kom-pön-ssei-ʃön) n compensación f; indemnización f

compete (köm-piit) v \*competir

competition (kom-pö-ti-ʃön) n concurso m; competencia f

competitor (köm-pê-ti-tör) n competidor m

compile (köm-pail) v compilar

complain (köm-plein) v quejarse

complaint (köm-pleint) n queja f; complaints book libro de reclamaciones

complete (köm-pliit) adj completo; v completar

completely (köm-pliit-li) adv enteramente, totalmente, completamente

complex (kom-plêkss) n complejo m; adj complejo

complexion (köm-plêk-ʃön) n tez f

complicated (kom-pli-kei-tid) adj complicado

compliment (kom-pli-mönt) n cumplimiento *m*; *v* cumplimentar

**compose** (köm-*pous*) *v* *componer

**composer** (köm-*pou*-sö) *n* compositor *m*

**composition** (kom-pö-*si*-∫ön) *n* composición *f*

**comprehensive** (kom-pri-*hên*-ssiv) *adj* extenso

**comprise** (köm-*prais*) *v* comprender

**compromise** (*kom*-prö-mais) *n* compromiso *m*

**compulsory** (köm-*pal*-ssö-ri) *adj* obligatorio

**comrade** (*kom*-reid) *n* camarada *m*

**conceal** (kön-*ssiil*) *v* disimular

**conceited** (kön-*ssii*-tid) *adj* presuntuoso

**conceive** (kön-*ssiiv*) *v* *concebir, *entender; imaginar

**concentrate** (*kon*-ssön-treit) *v* concentrarse

**concentration** (kon-ssön-*trei*-∫ön) *n* concentración *f*

**conception** (kön-*ssêp*-∫ön) *n* entendimiento *m*; concepción *f*

**concern** (kön-*ssöön*) *v* *concernir, atañer; *n* preocupación *f*; asunto *m*; empresa *f*, consorcio *m*

**concerned** (kön-*ssöönd*) *adj* preocupado; interesado

**concerning** (kön-*ssöö*-ning) *prep* en lo que se refiere a, concerniente a

**concert** (*kon*-ssöt) *n* concierto *m*; ~ **hall** sala de conciertos

**concession** (kön-*ssê*-∫ön) *n* concesión *f*

**concierge** (kong-ssi-ê^ö ʒ) *n* conserje *m*

**concise** (kön-*ssaiss*) *adj* conciso

**conclusion** (köng-*kluu*-ʒön) *n* conclusión *f*

**concrete** (*kong*-kriit) *adj* concreto; *n* hormigón *m*

**concurrence** (köng-*ka*-rönss) *n* coincidencia *f*

**concussion** (köng-*ka*-∫ön) *n* conmoción cerebral

**condition** (kön-*di*-∫ön) *n* condición *f*; estado *m*; circunstancia *f*

**conditional** (kön-*di*-∫ö-nöl) *adj* condicional

**conduct**[1] (*kon*-dakt) *n* conducta *f*

**conduct**[2] (kön-*dakt*) *v* *conducir; acompañar

**conductor** (kön-*dak*-tö) *n* cobrador *m*; director *m*; conductor *m*Me

**confectioner** (kön-*fêk*-∫ö-nö) *n* confitero *m*

**conference** (*kon*-fö-rönss) *n* conferencia *f*

**confess** (kön-*fêss*) *v* *reconocer; *confesarse; profesar

**confession** (kön-*fê*-∫ön) *n* confesión *f*

**confidence** (*kon*-fi-dönss) *n* confianza *f*

**confident** (*kon*-fi-dönt) *adj* lleno de confianza

**confidential** (kon-fi-*dên*-∫öl) *adj* confidencial

**confirm** (kön-*fööm*) *v* confirmar

**confirmation** (kon-fö-*mei*-∫ön) *n* confirmación *f*

**confiscate** (*kon*-fi-sskeit) *v* embargar, confiscar

**conflict** (*kon*-flikt) *n* conflicto *m*

**confuse** (kön-*fyuus*) *v* confundir; **confused** *adj* confuso

**confusion** (kön-*fyuu*-ʒön) *n* confusión *f*

**congratulate** (köng-*ghræ*-chu-leit) *v* felicitar

**congratulation** (köng-ghræ-chu-*lei*-∫ön) *n* felicitación *f*

**congregation** (kong-ghri-*ghei*-∫ön) *n* comunidad *f*, congregación *f*

**congress** (*kong*-ghrêss) *n* congreso *m*

**connect** (kö-*nêkt*) *v* conectar

**connection** (kö-*nêk*-∫ön) *n* relación *f*; conexión *f*; enlace *m* connoisseur (ko-nö-*ssöö*) *n* perito *m*

connotation (ko-nö-*tei*-ʃön) *n* connotación *f*

conquer (*kong*-kö) *v* conquistar; vencer

conqueror (*kong*-kö-rö) *n* conquistador *m*

conquest (*kong*-kʷêsst) *n* conquista *f*

conscience (kon-ʃönss) *n* conciencia *f*

conscious (*kon*-ʃöss) *adj* consciente

consciousness (*kon*-ʃöss-nöss) *n* conciencia *f*

conscript (*kon*-sskript) *n* quinto *m*

consent (kön-*ssênt*) *v* *consentir; *n* consentimiento *m*

consequence (*kon*-ssi-kʷönss) *n* consecuencia *f*

consequently (*kon*-ssi-kʷönt-li) *adv* por consiguiente

conservative (kön-*ssöö*-vö-tiv) *adj* conservador

consider (kön-*ssi*-dö) *v* considerar; opinar

considerable (kön-*ssi*-dö-rö-böl) *adj* considerable; importante, notable

considerate (kön-*ssi*-dö-röt) *adj* considerado

consideration (kön-ssi-dö-*rei*-ʃön) *n* consideración *f*; atención *f*

considering (kön-*ssi*-dö-ring) *prep* considerando

consignment (kön-*ssain*-mönt) *n* envío *m*

consist of (kön-*ssisst*) constar de

conspire (kön-*sspaiº*) *v* conspirar

constant (*kon*-sstönt) *adj* constante

constipated (*kon*-ssti-pei-tid) *adj* estreñido

constipation (kon-ssti-*pei*-ʃön) *n* estreñimiento *m*

constituency (kön-*ssti*-chu-ön-ssi) *n* distrito electoral

constitution (kön-ssti-*tyuu*-ʃön) *n* constitución *f*

construct (kön-*sstrakt*) *v* *construir; edificar

construction (kön-*sstrak*-ʃön) *n* construcción *f*; edificio *m*

consul (*kon*-ssöl) *n* cónsul *m*

consulate (*kon*-ssyu-löt) *n* consulado *m*

consult (kön-*ssalt*) *v* consultar

consultation (kon-ssöl-*tei*-ʃön) *n* consulta *f*; ~ hours *n* horas de consulta

consumer (kön-*ssyuu*-mö) *n* consumidor *m*

contact (*kon*-tækt) *n* contacto *m*; *v* *ponerse en contacto con; ~ lenses lentillas *fpl*

contagious (kön-*tei*-dʒöss) *adj* contagioso

contain (kön-*tein*) *v* *contener; comprender

container (kön-*tei*-nö) *n* receptáculo *m*; contenedor *m*

contemporary (kön-*têm*-pö-rö-ri) *adj* contemporáneo; de entonces; *n* contemporáneo *m*

contempt (kön-*têmpt*) *n* desprecio *m*, menosprecio *m*

content (kön-*tênt*) *adj* contento

contents (*kon*-têntss) *pl* contenido *m*

contest (*kon*-têsst) *n* lucha *f*; concurso *m*

continent (*kon*-ti-nönt) *n* continente *m*

continental (kon-ti-*nên*-töl) *adj* continental

continual (kön-*ti*-nyu-öl) *adj* continuo

continue (kön-*ti*-nyuu) *v* continuar; *proseguir, durar

continuous (kön-*ti*-nyu-öss) *adj* continuo, ininterrumpido

contour (*kon*-tuº) *n* contorno *m*

contraceptive (kon-trö-*ssêp*-tiv) *n* anticonceptivo *m*

contract¹ (*kon*-trækt) *n* contrato *m*

**contract²** (kön-*trækt*) v atrapar

**contractor** (kön-*træk*-tö) n contratista m

**contradict** (kon-trö-*dikt*) v *contradecir

**contradictory** (kon-trö-*dik*-tö-ri) adj contradictorio

**contrary** (*kon*-trö-ri) n contrario m; adj contrario; **on the ~** al contrario

**contrast** (*kon*-traasst) n contraste m; diferencia f

**contribution** (kon-tri-*byuu*-ʃön) n contribución f

**control** (kön-*troul*) n control m; v controlar

**controversial** (kon-trö-*vöö*-ʃöl) adj controvertido, controvertible

**convenience** (kön-*vii*-nyönss) n comodidad f

**convenient** (kön-*vii*-nyönt) adj cómodo; adecuado, conveniente

**convent** (*kon*-vönt) n convento m

**conversation** (kon-vö-*ssei*-ʃön) n conversación f

**convert** (kön-*vööt*) v *convertir

**convict¹** (kön-*vikt*) v convencer

**convict²** (*kon*-vikt) n condenado m

**conviction** (kön-*vik*-ʃön) n convencimiento m; condena f

**convince** (kön-*vinss*) v convencer

**convulsion** (kön-*val*-ʃön) n convulsión f

**cook** (kuk) n cocinero m; v cocinar; guisar, preparar

**cooker** (*ku*-kö) n cocina f; **gas ~** cocina de gas

**cookery-book** (*ku*-kö-ri-buk) n libro de cocina

**cookie** (*ku*-ki) nAm bizcocho m

**cool** (kuul) adj fresco; **cooling system** sistema de refrigeración

**co-operation** (kou-o-pö-*rei*-ʃön) n cooperación f; colaboración f

**co-operative** (kou-o-pö-rö-tiv) adj

cooperativo; cooperador; n cooperativa f

**co-ordinate** (kou-*oo*-di-neit) v coordinar

**co-ordination** (kou-oo-di-*nei*-ʃön) n coordinación f

**copper** (*ko*-pö) n cobre m

**copy** (*ko*-pi) n copia f; ejemplar m; v copiar; imitar; **carbon ~** copia f

**coral** (*ko*-röl) n coral m

**cord** (kood) n cuerda f; cordón m

**cordial** (*koo*-di-öl) adj cordial

**corduroy** (*koo*-dö-roi) n pana f

**core** (koo) n núcleo m; corazón m

**cork** (kook) n corcho m; tapón m

**corkscrew** (*kook*-sskruu) n sacacorchos mpl

**corn** (koon) n grano m; cereales mpl, trigo m; callo m; **~ on the cob** maíz en la mazorca

**corner** (*koo*-nö) n esquina f

**cornfield** (*koon*-fiild) n trigal m

**corpse** (koopss) n cadáver m

**corpulent** (*koo*-pyu-lönt) adj corpulento; grueso, obeso

**correct** (kö-*rêkt*) adj correcto, justo; v *corregir

**correction** (kö-*rêk*-ʃön) n corrección f; rectificación f

**correctness** (kö-*rêkt*-nöss) n exactitud f

**correspond** (ko-ri-*sspond*) v corresponderse; corresponder

**correspondence** (ko-ri-*sspon*-dönss) n correspondencia f

**correspondent** (ko-ri-*sspon*-dönt) n corresponsal m

**corridor** (*ko*-ri-doo) n pasillo m

**corrupt** (kö-*rapt*) adj corrupto; v corromper

**corruption** (kö-*rap*-ʃön) n corrupción f

**corset** (*koo*-ssit) n corsé m

**cosmetics** (kos-*mê*-tikss) pl productos

cosméticos, cosméticos *mpl*

**cost** (kosst) *n* coste *m*; precio *m*

**\*cost** (kosst) *v* \*costar

**cosy** (*kou*-si) *adj* íntimo, confortable

**cot** (kot) *nAm* cama de tijera

**cottage** (*ko*-tidʒ) *n* casa de campo

**cotton** (*ko*-tön) *n* algodón *m*; de algodón

**cotton-wool** (*ko*-tön-ᵘul) *n* algodón *m*

**couch** (kauch) *n* diván *m*

**cough** (kof) *n* tos *f*; *v* toser

**could** (kud) *v* (p can)

**council** (*kaun*-ssöl) *n* consejo *m*

**councillor** (*kaun*-ssö-lö) *n* consejero *m*

**counsel** (*kaun*-ssöl) *n* consejo *m*

**counsellor** (*kaun*-ssö-lö) *n* consejero *m*

**count** (kaunt) *v* \*contar; adicionar; \*incluir; considerar; *n* conde *m*

**counter** (*kaun*-tö) *n* mostrador *m*; barra *f*

**counterfeit** (*kaun*-tö-fiit) *v* falsificar

**counterfoil** (*kaun*-tö-foil) *n* talón *m*

**counterpane** (*kaun*-tö-pein) *n* colcha *f*

**countess** (*kaun*-tiss) *n* condesa *f*

**country** (*kan*-tri) *n* país *m*; campo *m*; región *f*; ~ **house** quinta *f*

**countryman** (*kan*-tri-mön) *n* (pl -men) compatriota *m*

**countryside** (*kan*-tri-ssaid) *n* campo *m*

**county** (*kaun*-ti) *n* condado *m*

**couple** (*ka*-pöl) *n* pareja *f*

**coupon** (*kuu*-pon) *n* cupón *m*

**courage** (*ka*-ridʒ) *n* valor *m*

**courageous** (kö-*rei*-dʒöss) *adj* valiente

**course** (kooss) *n* rumbo *m*; plato *m*; curso *m*; **intensive** ~ curso intensivo; **of** ~ por supuesto

**court** (koot) *n* tribunal *m*; corte *f*

**courteous** (*köö*-ti-öss) *adj* cortés

**cousin** (*ka*-sön) *n* prima *f*, primo *m*

**cover** (*ka*-vö) *v* cubrir; *n* refugio *m*; tapa *f*; cubierta *f*; ~ **charge** precio del cubierto

**cow** (kau) *n* vaca *f*

**coward** (*kau*-öd) *n* cobarde *m*

**cowardly** (*kau*-öd-li) *adj* cobarde

**cow-hide** (*kau*-haid) *n* cuero vacuno

**crab** (kræb) *n* cangrejo *m*

**crack** (kræk) *n* crujido *m*; hendidura *f*; *v* crujir; \*quebrar, \*reventar

**cradle** (*krei*-döl) *n* cuna *f*

**cramp** (kræmp) *n* calambre *m*

**crane** (krein) *n* grúa *f*

**crankcase** (*krængk*-keiss) *n* cárter *m*

**crankshaft** (*krængk*-ʃaaft) *n* cigüeñal *m*

**crash** (kræʃ) *n* choque *m*; *v* chocar; precipitarse; ~ **barrier** barrera de protección

**crate** (kreit) *n* caja *f*

**crater** (*krei*-tö) *n* cráter *m*

**crawl** (krool) *v* arrastrarse; *n* crawl *m*

**craze** (kreis) *n* manía *f*

**crazy** (*krei*-si) *adj* loco

**creak** (kriik) *v* crujir

**cream** (kriim) *n* crema *f*; nata *f*; *adj* de color crema

**creamy** (*krii*-mi) *adj* cremoso

**crease** (kriiss) *v* \*plegar; *n* raya *f*; pliegue *m*

**create** (kri-*eit*) *v* crear

**creature** (*krii*-chö) *n* criatura *f*; ser *m*

**credible** (*krê*-di-böl) *adj* verosímil

**credit** (*krê*-dit) *n* crédito *m*; *v* acreditar; ~ **card** tarjeta de crédito

**creditor** (*krê*-di-tö) *n* acreedor *m*

**credulous** (*krê*-dyu-löss) *adj* crédulo

**creek** (kriik) *n* ensenada *f*

**\*creep** (kriip) *v* gatear

**creepy** (*krii*-pi) *adj* lúgubre, espeluznante

**cremate** (kri-*meit*) *v* incinerar

**cremation** (kri-*mei*-ʃön) *n* incineración *f*

**crew** (kruu) *n* equipo *m*

**cricket** (*kri*-kit) *n* cricquet *m*; grillo *m*

**crime** (kraim) *n* crimen *m*

**criminal** (*kri*-mi-nöl) *n* delincuente *m*, criminal *m*; *adj* criminal; ~ **law** derecho penal

**criminality** (kri-mi-*næ*-lö-ti) *n* criminalidad *f*

**crimson** (*krim*-sön) *adj* carmesí

**crippled** (*kri*-pöld) *adj* estropeado

**crisis** (*krai*-ssiss) *n* (pl crises) crisis *f*

**crisp** (krissp) *adj* crujiente, quebradizo

**critic** (*kri*-tik) *n* crítico *m*

**critical** (*kri*-ti-köl) *adj* crítico; precario

**criticism** (*kri*-ti-ssi-söm) *n* crítica *f*

**criticize** (*kri*-ti-ssais) *v* criticar

**crochet** (*krou*-fei) *v* *hacer croché

**crockery** (*kro*-kö-ri) *n* cerámica *f*, loza *f*

**crocodile** (*kro*-kö-dail) *n* cocodrilo *m*

**crooked** (*kru*-kid) *adj* torcido, curvo; deshonesto

**crop** (krop) *n* cosecha *f*

**cross** (kross) *v* *atravesar; *adj* enojado, enfadado; *n* cruz *f*

**cross-eyed** (*kross*-aid) *adj* bizco

**crossing** (*kro*-ssing) *n* travesía *f*; encrucijada *f*; paso *m*; paso a nivel

**crossroads** (*kross*-rouds) *n* cruce *m*

**crosswalk** (*kross*-ᵁook) *nAm* cruce para peatones

**crow** (krou) *n* corneja *f*

**crowbar** (*krou*-baa) *n* pie de cabra

**crowd** (kraud) *n* masa *f*, muchedumbre *f*

**crowded** (*krau*-did) *adj* animado; repleto

**crown** (kraun) *n* corona *f*; *v* coronar

**crucifix** (*kruu*-ssi-fikss) *n* crucifijo *m*

**crucifixion** (kruu-ssi-*fik*-fön) *n* crucifixión *f*

**crucify** (*kruu*-ssi-fai) *v* crucificar

**cruel** (kru*ö*l) *adj* cruel

**cruise** (kruus) *n* crucero *m*

**crumb** (kram) *n* migaja *f*

**crusade** (kruu-*sseid*) *n* cruzada *f*

**crust** (krasst) *n* corteza *f*

**crutch** (krach) *n* muleta *f*

**cry** (krai) *v* llorar; gritar; llamar; *n* grito *m*; voz *f*

**crystal** (*kri*-sstöl) *n* cristal *m*; *adj* de cristal

**Cuba** (*kyuu*-bö) Cuba *f*

**Cuban** (*kyuu*-bön) *adj* cubano

**cube** (kyuub) *n* cubo *m*

**cuckoo** (*ku*-kuu) *n* cuclillo *m*

**cucumber** (*kyuu*-köm-bö) *n* pepino *m*

**cuddle** (*ka*-döl) *v* acariciar

**cudgel** (*ka*-dʒöl) *n* garrote *m*

**cuff** (kaf) *n* puño *m*

**cuff-links** (*kaf*-lingkss) *pl* gemelos *mpl*; mancuernillas *fplMe*

**cul-de-sac** (*kal*-dö-ssæk) *n* callejon sin salida

**cultivate** (*kal*-ti-veit) *v* cultivar

**culture** (*kal*-chö) *n* cultura *f*

**cultured** (*kal*-chöd) *adj* culto

**cunning** (*ka*-ning) *adj* astuto

**cup** (kap) *n* taza *f*; copa *f*

**cupboard** (*ka*-böd) *n* armario *m*

**curb** (köb) *n* bordillo *m*; *v* refrenar

**cure** (kyu*ö*) *v* curar; *n* cura *f*; curación *f*

**curio** (*kyu*ö-ri-ou) *n* (pl ~s) curiosidad *f*

**curiosity** (kyuö-ri-*o*-ssö-ti) *n* curiosidad *f*

**curious** (*kyu*ö-ri-öss) *adj* curioso

**curl** (köl) *v* rizar; *n* rizo *m*

**curler** (*köö*-lö) *n* rulo *m*

**curling-tongs** (*köö*-ling-tongs) *pl* rizador *m*

**curly** (*köö*-li) *adj* crespo; chino *adjMe*

**currant** (*ka*-rönt) *n* pasa de Corinto; grosella *f*

**currency** (*ka*-rön-ssi) *n* moneda *f*; **foreign** ~ moneda extranjera

**current** (*ka*-rönt) *n* corriente *f*; *adj* corriente; **alternating** ~ corriente alterna; **direct** ~ corriente continua

**curry** (*ka*-ri) *n* cari *m*

**curse** (kööss) *v* *maldecir; *n* maldición *f*

**curtain** (*köö*-tön) *n* cortina *f*; telón *m*

**curve** (kööv) *n* curva *f*

**curved** (köövd) *adj* curvado, encorvado

**cushion** (*ku*-∫ön) *n* almohadón *m*

**custodian** (ka-*sstou*-di-ön) *n* guarda *m*

**custody** (*ka*-sstö-di) *n* detención *f*; custodia *f*; tutela *f*

**custom** (*ka*-sstöm) *n* costumbre *f*

**customary** (*ka*-sstö-mö-ri) *adj* usual, corriente, acostumbrado

**customer** (*ka*-sstö-mö) *n* cliente *m*

**Customs** (*ka*-sstöms) *pl* aduana *f*; ~ **duty** impuesto *m*; ~ **officer** oficial de aduanas

**cut** (kat) *n* incisión *f*; cortadura *f*

*****cut** (kat) *v* cortar; *reducir; ~ **off** cortar

**cutlery** (*kat*-lö-ri) *n* cubiertos *mpl*

**cutlet** (*kat*-löt) *n* chuleta *f*

**cycle** (*ssai*-köl) *n* biciclo *m*; bicicleta *f*; ciclo *m*

**cyclist** (*ssai*-klisst) *n* ciclista *m*

**cylinder** (*ssi*-lin-dö) *n* cilindro *m*; ~ **head** culata del cilindro

**cystitis** (ssi-*sstai*-tiss) *n* cistitis *f*

**Czech** (chêk) *adj* checo

**Czechoslovakia** (chê-kö-sslö-*vaa*-ki-ö) Checoslovaquia *f*

# D

**dad** (dæd) *n* papá *m*

**daddy** (*dæ*-di) *n* papaíto *m*

**daffodil** (*dæ*-fö-dil) *n* narciso *m*

**daily** (*dei*-li) *adj* diario; *n* diario *m*

**dairy** (*dêô*-ri) *n* lechería *f*

**dam** (dæm) *n* presa *f*; dique *m*

**damage** (*dæ*-mid3) *n* perjuicio *m*; *v* dañar

**damp** (dæmp) *adj* húmedo; mojado; *n* humedad *f*; *v* *humedecer

**dance** (daanss) *v* bailar; *n* baile *m*

**dandelion** (*dæn*-di-lai-ön) *n* diente de león

**dandruff** (*dæn*-dröf) *n* caspa *f*

**Dane** (dein) *n* danés *m*

**danger** (*dein*-d3ö) *n* peligro *m*

**dangerous** (*dein*-d3ö-röss) *adj* peligroso

**Danish** (*dei*-ni∫) *adj* danés

**dare** (dêô) *v* atreverse, osar; desafiar

**daring** (*dêô*-ring) *adj* atrevido

**dark** (daak) *adj* oscuro, obscuro; *n* oscuridad *f*

**darling** (*daa*-ling) *n* amor *m*, querido *m*

**darn** (daan) *v* zurcir

**dash** (dæ∫) *v* correr; *n* guión *m*

**dashboard** (*dæf*-bood) *n* tablero de instrumentos

**data** (*dei*-tö) *pl* dato *m*

**date**[1] (deit) *n* fecha *f*; cita *f*; *v* datar; **out of** ~ anticuado

**date**[2] (deit) *n* dátil *m*

**daughter** (*doo*-tö) *n* hija *f*

**dawn** (doon) *n* alba *f*; aurora *f*

**day** (dei) *n* día *m*; **by** ~ de día; ~ **trip** jornada *f*; **per** ~ a diario; **the** ~ **before yesterday** anteayer

**daybreak** (*dei*-breik) *n* amanecer *m*

**daylight** (*dei*-lait) *n* luz del día

**dead** (dêd) *adj* muerto; difunto

**deaf** (dêf) *adj* sordo

**deal** (diil) *n* transacción *f*

*****deal** (diil) *v* repartir; ~ **with** *v* tratar con; *hacer negocios con

**dealer** (*dii*-lö) *n* negociante *m*, comerciante *m*

**dear** (diô) *adj* querido; caro; amado

**death** (dèz) *n* muerte *f*; ~ **penalty** pena de muerte

**debate** (di-*beit*) *n* debate *m*

**debit** (*dê*-bit) *n* debe *m*

**debt** (dêt) *n* deuda *f*

**decaffeinated** (dii-*kæ*-fi-nei-tid) *adj* descafeinado

**deceit** (di-*ssiit*) *n* engaño *m*

**deceive** (di-*ssiiv*) *v* engañar

**December** (di-*ssêm*-bö) diciembre

**decency** (*dii*-ssön-ssi) *n* decencia *f*

**decent** (*dii*-ssönt) *adj* decente

**decide** (di-*ssaid*) *v* decidir

**decision** (di-*ssi*-ȝön) *n* decisión *f*

**deck** (dêk) *n* cubierta *f*; ~ **cabin** camarote en cubierta; ~ **chair** silla de tijera

**declaration** (dê-klö-*rei*-ʃön) *n* declaración *f*

**declare** (di-*klê*ᵒ) *v* declarar; indicar

**decoration** (dê-kö-*rei*-ʃön) *n* decoración *f*

**decrease** (dii-*kriiss*) *v* *reducir; *disminuir; *n* disminución *f*

**dedicate** (*dê*-di-keit) *v* dedicar

**deduce** (di-*dyuuss*) *v* *deducir

**deduct** (di-*dakt*) *v* *deducir

**deed** (diid) *n* acción *f*, acto *m*

**deep** (diip) *adj* hondo

**deep-freeze** (diip-*friis*) *n* congelador *m*

**deer** (diᵒ) *n* (pl ~) ciervo *m*

**defeat** (di-*fiit*) *v* derrotar; *n* derrota *f*

**defective** (di-*fêk*-tiv) *adj* defectuoso

**defence** (di-*fênss*) *n* defensa *f*

**defend** (di-*fênd*) *v* *defender

**deficiency** (di-*fi*-ʃön-ssi) *n* deficiencia *f*

**deficit** (*dê*-fi-ssit) *n* déficit *m*

**define** (di-*fain*) *v* definir, determinar

**definite** (*dê*-fi-nit) *adj* determinado; definido

**definition** (dê-fi-*ni*-ʃön) *n* definición *f*

**deformed** (di-*foomd*) *adj* contrahecho,

deforme

**degree** (di-*ghrii*) *n* grado *m*; título *m*

**delay** (di-*lei*) *v* retardar; *diferir; *n* retraso *m*, tardanza *f*; dilación *f*

**delegate** (*dê*-li-ghöt) *n* delegado *m*

**delegation** (dê-li-*ghei*-ʃön) *n* delegación *f*

**deliberate**¹ (di-*li*-bö-reit) *v* discutir, deliberar

**deliberate**² (di-*li*-bö-röt) *adj* deliberado

**deliberation** (di-li-bö-*rei*-ʃön) *n* deliberación *f*

**delicacy** (*dê*-li-kö-ssi) *n* golosina *f*

**delicate** (*dê*-li-köt) *adj* delicado; fino

**delicatessen** (dê-li-kö-*tê*-ssön) *n* gollerías *fpl*; tienda de comestibles finos

**delicious** (di-*li*-föss) *adj* exquisito, delicioso

**delight** (di-*lait*) *n* delicia *f*, deleite *m*; *v* encantar

**delightful** (di-*lait*-föl) *adj* delicioso, deleitoso

**deliver** (di-*li*-vö) *v* entregar; librar

**delivery** (di-*li*-vö-ri) *n* entrega *f*, reparto *m*; parto *m*; liberación *f*; ~ **van** furgoneta *f*

**demand** (di-*maand*) *v* *requerir, exigir; *n* exigencia *f*; demanda *f*

**democracy** (di-*mo*-krö-ssi) *n* democracia *f*

**democratic** (dê-mö-*kræ*-tik) *adj* democrático

**demolish** (di-*mo*-liʃ) *v* *demoler

**demolition** (dê-mö-*li*-ʃön) *n* demolición *f*

**demonstrate** (*dê*-mön-sstreit) *v* *demostrar; *hacer una manifestación

**demonstration** (dê-mön-*sstrei*-ʃön) *n* manifestación *f*; demostración *f*

**den** (dên) *n* madriguera *f*

**Denmark** (*dên*-maak) Dinamarca *f*

**denomination** (di-no-mi-*nei*-ʃön) *n* denominación *f*

**dense** (dênss) *adj* denso

**dent** (dênt) *n* abolladura *f*

**dentist** (dên-tisst) *n* dentista *m*

**denture** (dên-chö) *n* dentadura postiza

**deny** (di-*nai*) *v* *negar; *denegar

**deodorant** (dii-*ou*-dö-rönt) *n* desodorante *m*

**depart** (di-*paat*) *v* partir; *fallecer

**department** (di-*paat*-mönt) *n* departamento *m*; ~ **store** grandes almacenes

**departure** (di-*paa*-chö) *n* despedida *f*, partida *f*

**dependant** (di-*pên*-dönt) *adj* dependiente

**depend on** (di-*pênd*) depender de

**deposit** (di-*po*-sit) *n* depósito *m*; fianza *f*; capa *f*, yacimiento *m*; *v* ingresar

**depository** (di-*po*-si-tö-ri) *n* almacén *m*

**depot** (*dé*-pou) *n* almacén *m*; *nAm* estación *f*

**depress** (di-*préss*) *v* deprimir

**depression** (di-*prê*-fön) *n* desánimo *m*; depresión *f*

**deprive of** (di-*praiv*) privar de

**depth** (dêpz) *n* profundidad *f*

**deputy** (*dé*-pyu-ti) *n* diputado *m*; sustituto *m*

**descend** (di-*ssênd*) *v* *descender

**descendant** (di-*ssên*-dönt) *n* descendiente *m*

**descent** (di-*ssênt*) *n* bajada *f*

**describe** (di-*sskraib*) *v* describir

**description** (di-*sskrip*-fön) *n* descripción *f*; señas personales

**desert**[1] (*dé*-söt) *n* desierto *m*; *adj* salvaje, desierto

**desert**[2] (di-*sööt*) *v* desertar; dejar

**deserve** (di-*sööv*) *v* *merecer

**design** (di-*sain*) *v* diseñar; *n* diseño *m*; objetivo *m*

**designate** (*dé*-sigh-neit) *v* designar

**desirable** (di-*sai*[ö]-rö-böl) *adj* deseable

**desire** (di-*sai*[ö]) *n* deseo *m*; ganas *fpl*; *v* anhelar, desear

**desk** (dêssk) *n* escritorio *m*; pupitre *m*

**despair** (di-*sspê*[ö]) *n* desesperación *f*; *v* *estar desesperado

**despatch** (di-*sspæch*) *v* despachar

**desperate** (*dé*-sspö-röt) *adj* desesperado

**despise** (di-*sspais*) *v* despreciar

**despite** (di-*sspait*) *prep* a pesar de

**dessert** (di-*sööt*) *n* postre *m*

**destination** (dê-ssti-*nei*-fön) *n* destino *m*

**destine** (*dé*-sstin) *v* destinar

**destiny** (*dé*-ssti-ni) *n* destino *m*

**destroy** (di-*sstroi*) *v* *destruir

**destruction** (di-*sstrak*-fön) *n* destrucción *f*; ruina *f*

**detach** (di-*tæch*) *v* separar

**detail** (*dii*-teil) *n* particularidad *f*, detalle *m*

**detailed** (*dii*-teild) *adj* detallado

**detect** (di-*têkt*) *v* descubrir

**detective** (di-*têk*-tiv) *n* detective *m*; ~ **story** novela policíaca

**detergent** (di-*töö*-dʒönt) *n* detergente *m*

**determine** (di-*töö*-min) *v* determinar

**determined** (di-*töö*-mind) *adj* resuelto

**detour** (*dii*-tu[ö]) *n* desvío *m*

**devaluation** (dii-væl-yu-ei-fön) *n* desvalorización *f*

**devalue** (dii-*væl*-yuu) *v* desvalorizar

**develop** (di-*vê*-löp) *v* desarrollar; revelar

**development** (di-*vê*-löp-mönt) *n* desarrollo *m*

**deviate** (*dii*-vi-eit) *v* desviarse

**devil** (*dé*-völ) *n* diablo *m*

**devise** (di-*vais*) *v* idear

**devote** (di-*vout*) *v* dedicar

**dew** (dyuu) *n* rocío *m*

**diabetes** (dai-ö-*bii*-tiis) *n* diabetes *f*

**diabetic** (dai-ö-*bê*-tik) *n* diabético *m*

**diagnose** (dai-ögh-*nous*) *v* diagnosticar; *comprobar

**diagnosis** (dai-ögh-*nou*-ssiss) *n* (pl -ses) diagnosis *m*

**diagonal** (dai-æ-ghö-nöl) *n* diagonal *f*; *adj* diagonal

**diagram** (*dai*-ö-ghræm) *n* esquema *m*; gráfico *m*

**dialect** (*dai*-ö-lêkt) *n* dialecto *m*

**diamond** (*dai*-ö-mönd) *n* diamante *m*

**diaper** (*dai*-ö-pö) *nAm* pañal *m*

**diaphragm** (*dai*-ö-fræm) *n* membrana *f*

**diarrhoea** (dai-ö-*ri*-ö) *n* diarrea *f*

**diary** (*dai*-ö-ri) *n* agenda *f*; diario *m*

**dictaphone** (*dik*-tö-foun) *n* dictáfono *m*

**dictate** (dik-*teit*) *v* dictar

**dictation** (dik-*tei*-fön) *n* dictado *m*

**dictator** (dik-*tei*-tö) *n* dictador *m*

**dictionary** (*dik*-fö-nö-ri) *n* diccionario *m*

**did** (did) *v* (p do)

**die** (dai) *v* *morir

**diesel** (*dii*-söl) *n* diesel *m*

**diet** (*dai*-öt) *n* régimen *m*

**differ** (*di*-fö) *v* *diferir

**difference** (*di*-fö-rönss) *n* diferencia *f*; distinción *f*

**different** (*di*-fö-rönt) *adj* diferente; otro

**difficult** (*di*-fi-költ) *adj* difícil; fastidioso

**difficulty** (*di*-fi-köl-ti) *n* dificultad *f*; trabajo *m*

***dig** (digh) *v* cavar

**digest** (di-*dʒêsst*) *v* *digerir

**digestible** (di-*dʒê*-sstö-böl) *adj* digerible

**digestion** (di-*dʒêss*-chön) *n* digestión *f*

**digit** (*di*-dʒit) *n* número *m*

**dignified** (*digh*-ni-faid) *adj* distinguido

**dike** (daik) *n* dique *m*

**dilapidated** (di-*læ*-pi-dei-tid) *adj* ruinoso

**diligence** (*di*-li-dʒönss) *n* celo *m*, diligencia *f*

**diligent** (*di*-li-dʒönt) *adj* celoso, cuidadoso

**dilute** (dai-*lyuut*) *v* *diluir

**dim** (dim) *adj* deslucido, mate; oscuro, vago, difuso

**dine** (dain) *v* cenar

**dinghy** (*ding*-ghi) *n* chinchorro *m*

**dining-car** (*dai*-ning-kaa) *n* coche comedor

**dining-room** (*dai*-ning-ruum) *n* comedor *m*

**dinner** (*di*-nö) *n* comida principal; cena *f*

**dinner-jacket** (*di*-nö-dʒæ-kit) *n* smoking *m*

**dinner-service** (*di*-nö-ssöö-viss) *n* servicio de mesa

**diphtheria** (dif-*ziˀö*-ri-ö) *n* difteria *f*

**diploma** (di-*plou*-mö) *n* diploma *m*

**diplomat** (*di*-plö-mæt) *n* diplomático *m*

**direct** (di-*rêkt*) *adj* directo; *v* dirigir; administrar

**direction** (di-*rêk*-fön) *n* dirección *f*; instrucción *f*; dirección de escena; administración *f*; **directions for use** modo de empleo

**directive** (di-*rêk*-tiv) *n* directriz *f*

**director** (di-*rêk*-tö) *n* director *m*; director de escena

**dirt** (dööt) *n* suciedad *f*

**dirty** (*döö*-ti) *adj* sucio

**disabled** (di-*ssei*-böld) *adj* minusválido, inválido

**disadvantage** (di-ssöd-*vaan*-tidʒ) *n* desventaja *f*

**disagree** (di-ssö-*ghrii*) *v* no *estar de

acuerdo, *disentir

**disagreeable** (di-ssö-*ghrii*-ö-böl) *adj*
desagradable

**disappear** (di-ssö-*piº*) *v* *desaparecer

**disappoint** (di-ssö-*point*) *v* decepcionar

**disappointment** (di-ssö-*point*-mönt) *n*
desengaño *m*

**disapprove** (di-ssö-*pruuv*) *v* *desaprobar

**disaster** (di-*saa*-sstö) *n* desastre *m*;
catástrofe *f*, calamidad *f*

**disastrous** (di-*saa*-sströss) *adj* desastroso

**disc** (dissk) *n* disco *m*; **slipped ~** hernia intervertebral

**discard** (di-*sskaad*) *v* desechar

**discharge** (diss-*chaadʒ*) *v* descargar;
**~ of** dispensar de

**discipline** (*di*-ssi-plin) *n* disciplina *f*

**discolour** (di-*sska*-lö) *v* *desteñirse*;
**discoloured** descolorido

**disconnect** (di-sskö-*nêkt*) *v* desconectar

**discontented** (di-sskön-*tên*-tid) *adj*
descontento

**discontinue** (di-sskön-*ti*-nyuu) *v* suprimir, cesar

**discount** (*di*-sskaunt) *n* descuento *m*

**discover** (di-*sska*-vö) *v* descubrir

**discovery** (di-*sska*-vö-ri) *n* descubrimiento *m*

**discuss** (di-*sskass*) *v* discutir; debatir

**discussion** (di-*sska*-ʃön) *n* discusión
*f*; conversación *f*, debate *m*

**disease** (di-*siis*) *n* enfermedad *f*

**disembark** (di-ssim-*baak*) *v* desembarcar

**disgrace** (diss-*ghreiss*) *n* deshonor *m*

**disguise** (diss-*ghais*) *v* disfrazarse; *n*
disfraz *m*

**disgusting** (diss-*gha*-ssting) *adj* repugnante, asqueroso

**dish** (diʃ) *n* plato *m*; fuente *f*; guiso
*m*

**dishonest** (di-*sso*-nisst) *adj* ímprobo

**disinfect** (di-ssin-*fêkt*) *v* desinfectar

**disinfectant** (di-ssin-*fêk*-tönt) *n* desinfectante *m*

**dislike** (di-*sslaik*) *v* detestar, no gustar; *n* repugnancia *f*, aversión *f*, antipatía *f*

**dislocated** (*di*-sslö-kei-tid) *adj* dislocado

**dismiss** (diss-*miss*) *v* *despedir

**disorder** (di-*ssoo*-dö) *n* desorden *m*

**dispatch** (di-*sspæch*) *v* enviar, despachar

**display** (di-*ssplei*) *v* exhibir; *mostrar; *n* exposición *f*

**displease** (di-*sspliis*) *v* disgustar, desagradar

**disposable** (di-*sspou*-sö-böl) *adj* desechable

**disposal** (di-*sspou*-söl) *n* disposición *f*

**dispose of** (di-*sspous*) *disponer de

**dispute** (di-*sspyuut*) *n* disputa *f*; riña
*f*, contienda *f*; *v* *reñir, disputar

**dissatisfied** (di-*ssæ*-tiss-faid) *adj* insatisfecho

**dissolve** (di-*solv*) *v* *disolver

**dissuade from** (di-ssᵘeid) disuadir

**distance** (*di*-sstönss) *n* distancia *f*; **~
in kilometres** kilometraje *m*

**distant** (*di*-sstönt) *adj* lejano

**distinct** (di-*sstingkt*) *adj* claro; distinto

**distinction** (di-*sstingk*-ʃön) *n* distinción *f*, diferencia *f*

**distinguish** (di-*ssting*-ghᵘiʃ) *v* distinguir

**distinguished** (di-*ssting*-ghᵘiʃt) *adj*
distinguido

**distress** (di-*sstrêss*) *n* peligro *m*; **~
signal** señal de alarma

**distribute** (di-*sstri*-byuut) *v* *distribuir

**distributor** (di-*sstri*-byu-tö) *n* distribuidor *m*

**district** (*di*-sstrikt) *n* distrito *m*; comarca *f*; barrio *m*

**disturb** (di-*sstöób*) *v* estorbar, molestar

**disturbance** (di-*sstöö*-bönss) *n* disturbio *m*; confusión *f*

**ditch** (dich) *n* zanja *f*, cuneta *f*

**dive** (daiv) *v* bucear

**diversion** (dai-*vöö*-fön) *n* desvío *m*; diversión *f*

**divide** (di-*vaid*) *v* dividir; repartir; separar

**divine** (di-*vain*) *adj* divino

**division** (di-*vi*-3ön) *n* división *f*; separación *f*; departamento *m*

**divorce** (di-*vooss*) *n* divorcio *m*; *v* divorciar

**dizziness** (*di*-si-nöss) *n* vértigo *m*

**dizzy** (*di*-si) *adj* mareado

**\*do** (duu) *v* \*hacer; \*ser suficiente

**dock** (dok) *n* dock *m*; muelle *m*; *v* atracar

**docker** (*do*-kö) *n* obrero portuario

**doctor** (*dok*-tö) *n* médico *m*; doctor *m*

**document** (*do*-kyu-mönt) *n* documento *m*

**dog** (dogh) *n* perro *m*

**dogged** (*do*-ghid) *adj* obstinado

**doll** (dol) *n* muñeca *f*

**dome** (doum) *n* cúpula *f*

**domestic** (dö-*mê*-sstik) *adj* doméstico; interior; *n* sirviente *m*

**domicile** (*do*-mi-ssail) *n* domicilio *m*

**domination** (do-mi-*nei*-fön) *n* dominación *f*

**dominion** (dö-*mi*-nyön) *n* dominio *m*

**donate** (dou-*neit*) *v* donar

**donation** (dou-*nei*-fön) *n* donación *f*

**done** (dan) *v* (pp do)

**donkey** (*dong*-ki) *n* burro *m*

**donor** (*dou*-nö) *n* donante *m*

**door** (doo) *n* puerta *f*; **revolving ~** puerta giratoria; **sliding ~** puerta corrediza

**doorbell** (*doo*-bêl) *n* timbre *m*

**door-keeper** (*doo*-kii-pö) *n* portero *m*

**doorman** (*doo*-mön) *n* (pl -men) portero *m*

**dormitory** (*doo*-mi-tri) *n* dormitorio *m*

**dose** (douss) *n* dosis *f*

**dot** (dot) *n* punto *m*

**double** (*da*-böl) *adj* doble

**doubt** (daut) *v* dudar; *n* duda *f*; **without ~** sin duda

**doubtful** (*daut*-föl) *adj* dudoso; inseguro

**dough** (dou) *n* masa *f*

**down¹** (daun) *adv* abajo; hacia abajo; *adj* abatido; *prep* a lo largo de, debajo de; **~ payment** primer pago

**down²** (daun) *n* flojel *m*

**downpour** (*daun*-poo) *n* aguacero *m*

**downstairs** (daun-*sstê⁰*s) *adv* abajo

**downstream** (daun-*sstriim*) *adv* río abajo

**down-to-earth** (daun-tu-*ööz*) *adj* sensato

**downwards** (*daun*-ᵁöds) *adv* hacia abajo

**dozen** (*da*-sön) *n* (pl ~, ~s) docena *f*

**draft** (draaft) *n* giro *m*

**drag** (drægh) *v* arrastrar

**dragon** (*dræ*-ghön) *n* dragón *m*

**drain** (drein) *v* desecar; drenar; *n* desagüe *m*

**drama** (*draa*-mö) *n* drama *m*; tragedia *f*; teatro *m*

**dramatic** (drö-*mæ*-tik) *adj* dramático

**dramatist** (*dræ*-mö-tisst) *n* dramaturgo *m*

**drank** (drængk) *v* (p drink)

**draper** (*drei*-pö) *n* pañero *m*

**drapery** (*drei*-pö-ri) *n* pañería *f*

**draught** (draaft) *n* corriente de aire; **draughts** juego de damas

**draught-board** (*draaft*-bood) *n* tablero

de damas

**draw** (droo) *n* sorteo *m*

**\*draw** (droo) *v* dibujar; arrastrar; sacar; jalar *vMe*; ~ **up** redactar

**drawbridge** (*droo*-bridӡ) *n* puente levadizo

**drawer** (*droo*-ö) *n* cajón *m*; **drawers** calzoncillos *mpl*

**drawing** (*droo*-ing) *n* dibujo *m*

**drawing-pin** (*droo*-ing-pin) *n* chinche *f*

**drawing-room** (*droo*-ing-ruum) *n* salón *m*

**dread** (drêd) *v* temer; *n* temor *m*

**dreadful** (*drêd*-föl) *adj* terrible, espantoso

**dream** (driim) *n* sueño *m*

**\*dream** (driim) *v* \*soñar

**dress** (drêss) *v* \*vestir; \*vestirse; vendar; *n* vestido *m*

**dressing-gown** (*drê*-ssing-ghaun) *n* bata *f*

**dressing-room** (*drê*-ssing-ruum) *n* vestuario *m*

**dressing-table** (*drê*-ssing-tei-böl) *n* tocador *m*

**dressmaker** (*drêss*-mei-kö) *n* modista *f*

**drill** (dril) *v* taladrar; entrenar; *n* taladro *m*

**drink** (dringk) *n* aperitivo *m*, bebida *f*

**\*drink** (dringk) *v* beber

**drinking-water** (*dring*-king-ᵘoo-tö) *n* agua potable

**drip-dry** (drip-*drai*) *adj* no precisa plancha

**drive** (draiv) *n* calzada *f*; paseo en coche

**\*drive** (draiv) *v* \*conducir

**driver** (*drai*-vö) *n* conductor *m*

**drizzle** (*dri*-söl) *n* llovizna *f*

**drop** (drop) *v* dejar caer; *n* gota *f*

**drought** (draut) *n* sequía *f*

**drown** (draun) *v* ahogar; **\*be**

**drowned** ahogarse

**drug** (dragh) *n* estupefaciente *m*; medicamento *m*

**drugstore** (*dragh*-sstoo) *nAm* droguería *f*, farmacia *f*; almacén *m*

**drum** (dram) *n* tambor *m*

**drunk** (drangk) *adj* (pp drink) borracho

**dry** (drai) *adj* seco; *v* secar

**dry-clean** (drai-*kliin*) *v* limpiar en seco

**dry-cleaner's** (drai-*klii*-nös) *n* tintorería *f*

**dryer** (*drai*-ö) *n* secadora *f*

**duchess** (da-chiss) *n* duquesa *f*

**duck** (dak) *n* pato *m*

**due** (dyuu) *adj* aguardado; adeudado; debido

**dues** (dyuus) *pl* derechos *mpl*

**dug** (dagh) *v* (p, pp dig)

**duke** (dyuuk) *n* duque *m*

**dull** (dal) *adj* aburrido; pálido, mate; embotado

**dumb** (dam) *adj* mudo; atontado, estúpido

**dune** (dyuun) *n* duna *f*

**dung** (dang) *n* abono *m*

**dunghill** (*dang*-hil) *n* estercolero *m*

**duration** (dyu-*rei*-ʃön) *n* duración *f*

**during** (*dyu*ᵟ-ring) *prep* durante

**dusk** (dassk) *n* crepúsculo *m*

**dust** (dasst) *n* polvo *m*

**dustbin** (*dasst*-bin) *n* cubo de la basura

**dusty** (*da*-ssti) *adj* polvoriento

**Dutch** (dach) *adj* holandés

**Dutchman** (*dach*-mön) *n* (pl -men) holandés *m*

**dutiable** (*dyuu*-ti-ö-böl) *adj* imponible

**duty** (*dyuu*-ti) *n* deber *m*; tarea *f*; arancel *m*; **Customs** ~ impuesto de aduana

**duty-free** (dyuu-ti-*frii*) *adj* exento de impuestos

**dwarf** (dᵘoof) *n* enano *m*

**dye** (dai) v *teñir; n tintura f
**dynamo** (dai-nö-mou) n (pl ~s) dínamo f
**dysentery** (di-ssön-tri) n disentería f

# E

**each** (iich) adj cada; ~ **other** el uno al otro
**eager** (ii-ghö) adj ansioso, impaciente
**eagle** (ii-ghöl) n águila m
**ear** (i⁰) n oreja f
**earache** (i⁰-reik) n dolor de oídos
**ear-drum** (i⁰-dram) n tímpano m
**earl** (ööl) n conde m
**early** (öö-li) adj temprano
**earn** (öön) v ganar
**earnest** (öö-nisst) n seriedad f
**earnings** (öö-nings) pl ingresos mpl, ganancias fpl
**earring** (i⁰-ring) n pendiente m
**earth** (ööz) n tierra f; suelo m
**earthenware** (öö-zön-ᵘê⁰) n loza f
**earthquake** (ööz-kᵘeik) n terremoto m
**ease** (iis) n desenvoltura f, facilidad f; bienestar m
**east** (iisst) n este m
**Easter** (ii-sstö) Pascua
**easterly** (ii-sstö-li) adj oriental
**eastern** (ii-sstön) adj oriental
**easy** (ii-si) adj fácil; cómodo; ~ **chair** butaca f
**easy-going** (ii-si-ghou-ing) adj relajado
***eat** (iit) v comer; cenar
**eavesdrop** (iivs-drop) v escuchar
**ebony** (ê-bö-ni) n ébano m
**eccentric** (ik-ssên-trik) adj excéntrico
**echo** (ê-kou) n (pl ~es) eco m
**eclipse** (i-klipss) n eclipse m
**economic** (ii-kö-no-mik) adj económi-

co
**economical** (ii-kö-no-mi-köl) adj parsimonioso, económico
**economist** (i-ko-nö-misst) n economista m
**economize** (i-ko-nö-mais) v economizar
**economy** (i-ko-nö-mi) n economía f
**ecstasy** (êk-sstö-si) n éxtasis m
**Ecuador** (ê-kᵘö-doo) Ecuador m
**Ecuadorian** (ê-kᵘö-doo-ri-ön) n ecuatoriano m
**eczema** (êk-ssö-mö) n eczema m
**edge** (êdʒ) n borde m
**edible** (ê-di-böl) adj comestible
**edition** (i-di-fön) n edición f; **morning ~** edición de mañana
**editor** (ê-di-tö) n redactor m
**educate** (ê-dʒu-keit) v formar, educar
**education** (ê-dʒu-kei-fön) n educación f
**eel** (iil) n anguila f
**effect** (i-fêkt) n resultado m, efecto m; v efectuar; **in ~** en realidad
**effective** (i-fêk-tiv) adj eficaz
**efficient** (i-fi-fönt) adj eficiente
**effort** (ê-föt) n esfuerzo m
**egg** (êgh) n huevo m
**egg-cup** (êgh-kap) n huevera f
**eggplant** (êgh-plaant) n berenjena f
**egg-yolk** (êgh-youk) n yema de huevo
**egoistic** (ê-ghou-i-sstik) adj egoísta
**Egypt** (ii-dʒipt) Egipto m
**Egyptian** (i-dʒip-fön) adj egipcio
**eiderdown** (ai-dö-daun) n edredón m
**eight** (eit) num ocho
**eighteen** (ei-tiin) num dieciocho
**eighteenth** (ei-tiinz) num decimoctavo
**eighth** (eitz) num octavo
**eighty** (ei-ti) num ochenta
**either** (ai-ðö) pron cualquiera de los dos; **either ... or** o ... o, bien ... bien

**elaborate** (i-*læ*-bö-reit) *v* elaborar

**elastic** (i-*læ*-sstik) *adj* elástico; flexible; ~ **band** cinta de goma

**elasticity** (ê-læ-*ssti*-ssö-ti) *n* elasticidad *f*

**elbow** (*él*-bou) *n* codo *m*

**elder** (*él*-dö) *adj* mayor

**elderly** (*él*-dö-li) *adj* anciano

**eldest** (*él*-disst) *adj* mayor

**elect** (i-*lêkt*) *v* *elegir

**election** (i-*lêk*-ʃön) *n* elección *f*

**electric** (i-*lêk*-trik) *adj* eléctrico; ~ **razor** afeitadora eléctrica

**electrician** (i-lêk-*tri*-ʃön) *n* electricista *m*

**electricity** (i-lêk-*tri*-ssö-ti) *n* electricidad *f*

**electronic** (i-lêk-*tro*-nik) *adj* electrónico

**elegance** (*é*-li-ghönss) *n* elegancia *f*

**elegant** (*é*-li-ghönt) *adj* elegante

**element** (*é*-li-mönt) *n* elemento *m*

**elephant** (*é*-li-fönt) *n* elefante *m*

**elevator** (*é*-li-vei-tö) *n Am* ascensor *m*; elevador *m Me*

**eleven** (i-*lê*-vön) *num* once

**eleventh** (i-*lê*-vönz) *num* onceno

**elf** (êlf) *n* (pl elves) duende *m*

**eliminate** (i-*li*-mi-neit) *v* eliminar

**elm** (êlm) *n* olmo *m*

**else** (êlss) *adv* si no

**elsewhere** (êl-ss*u*ê*ᵒ*) *adv* otra parte

**elucidate** (i-*luu*-ssi-deit) *v* elucidar

**emancipation** (i-mæn-ssi-*pei*-ʃön) *n* emancipación *f*

**embankment** (im-*bængk*-mönt) *n* terraplén *m*

**embargo** (êm-*baa*-ghou) *n* (pl ~es) embargo *m*

**embark** (im-*baak*) *v* embarcar

**embarkation** (êm-baa-*kei*-ʃön) *n* embarcación *f*

**embarrass** (im-*bæ*-röss) *v* turbar; *desconcertar; estorbar; **embar-**

rassed tímido

**embassy** (*êm*-bö-ssi) *n* embajada *f*

**emblem** (*êm*-blöm) *n* emblema *m*

**embrace** (im-*breiss*) *v* abrazar; *n* abrazo *m*

**embroider** (im-*broi*-dö) *v* bordar

**embroidery** (im-*broi*-dö-ri) *n* bordado *m*

**emerald** (*ê*-mö-röld) *n* esmeralda *f*

**emergency** (i-*möö*-dʒön-ssi) *n* caso de urgencia, urgencia *f*; emergencia *f*; ~ **exit** salida de emergencia

**emigrant** (*ê*-mi-ghrönt) *n* emigrante *m*

**emigrate** (*ê*-mi-ghreit) *v* emigrar

**emigration** (ê-mi-*ghrei*-ʃön) *n* emigración *f*

**emotion** (i-*mou*-ʃön) *n* emoción *f*

**emperor** (*êm*-pö-rö) *n* emperador *m*

**emphasize** (*êm*-fö-ssais) *v* enfatizar, acentuar

**empire** (*êm*-paiᵒ) *n* imperio *m*

**employ** (im-*ploi*) *v* emplear

**employee** (êm-ploi-*ii*) *n* empleado *m*

**employer** (im-*ploi*-ö) *n* patrón *m*

**employment** (im-*ploi*-mönt) *n* empleo *m*; ~ **exchange** oficina de colocación

**empress** (*êm*-priss) *n* emperatriz *f*

**empty** (*êm*p-ti) *adj* vacío; *v* vaciar

**enable** (i-*nei*-böl) *v* permitir

**enamel** (i-*næ*-möl) *n* esmalte *m*

**enamelled** (i-*næ*-möld) *adj* esmaltado

**enchanting** (in-*chaan*-ting) *adj* espléndido, encantador

**encircle** (in-*ssöö*-köl) *v* *circuir, cercar; *encerrar

**enclose** (ing-*klous*) *v* *incluir

**enclosure** (ing-*klou*-ʒö) *n* anexo *m*

**encounter** (ing-*kaun*-tö) *v* *encontrarse con; *n* encuentro *m*

**encourage** (ing-*ka*-ridʒ) *v* *alentar

**encyclopaedia** (ên-ssai-klö-*pii*-di-ö) *n* enciclopedia *f*

**end** (énd) *n* fin *m*, extremo *m*; final *m*; *v* terminar, acabar; terminarse

**ending** (*én*-ding) *n* conclusión *f*

**endless** (*énd*-löss) *adj* infinito

**endorse** (in-*dooss*) *v* visar, endosar

**endure** (in-*dyu*ᵒ) *v* soportar

**enemy** (*é*-nö-mi) *n* enemigo *m*

**energetic** (é-nö-*dʒé*-tik) *adj* enérgico

**energy** (*é*-nö-dʒi) *n* energía *f*; fuerza *f*

**engage** (ing-*gheidʒ*) *v* emplear; reservar; comprometerse; **engaged** prometido; ocupado

**engagement** (ing-*gheidʒ*-mönt) *n* noviazgo *m*; compromiso *m*; ~ **ring** anillo de esponsales

**engine** (*én*-dʒin) *n* máquina *f*, motor *m*; locomotora *f*

**engineer** (én-dʒi-*ni*ᵒ) *n* ingeniero *m*

**England** (*ing*-ghlönd) Inglaterra *f*

**English** (*ing*-ghliʃ) *adj* inglés

**Englishman** (*ing*-ghliʃ-mön) *n* (pl - men) inglés *m*

**engrave** (ing-*ghreiv*) *v* grabar

**engraver** (ing-*ghrei*-vö) *n* grabador *m*

**engraving** (ing-*ghrei*-ving) *n* estampa *f*; grabado *m*

**enigma** (i-*nigh*-mö) *n* enigma *m*

**enjoy** (in-*dʒoi*) *v* disfrutar, gozar

**enjoyable** (in-*dʒoi*-ö-böl) *adj* agradable, grato, deleitable; rico

**enjoyment** (in-*dʒoi*-mönt) *n* goce *m*

**enlarge** (in-*laadʒ*) *v* ampliar

**enlargement** (in-*laadʒ*-mönt) *n* ampliación *f*

**enormous** (i-*noo*-möss) *adj* gigantesco, enorme

**enough** (i-*naf*) *adv* bastante; *adj* suficiente

**enquire** (ing-*k*ᵘ*ai*ᵒ) *v* preguntar; investigar

**enquiry** (ing-*k*ᵘ*ai*-ri) *n* información *f*; investigación *f*; encuesta *f*

**enter** (*én*-tö) *v* entrar; inscribir

**enterprise** (*én*-tö-prais) *n* empresa *f*

**entertain** (én-tö-*tein*) *v* \*divertir, \*entretener; hospedar

**entertainer** (én-tö-*tei*-nö) *n* cómico *m*

**entertaining** (én-tö-*tei*-ning) *adj* divertido, entretenido

**entertainment** (én-tö-*tein*-mönt) *n* diversión *f*, entretenimiento *m*

**enthusiasm** (in-*zyuu*-si-æ-söm) *n* entusiasmo *m*

**enthusiastic** (in-zyuu-si-æ-*sstik*) *adj* entusiasta

**entire** (in-*tai*ᵒ) *adj* todo, entero

**entirely** (in-*tai*ᵒ-li) *adv* enteramente

**entrance** (*én*-trönss) *n* entrada *f*; acceso *m*

**entrance-fee** (*én*-trönss-fii) *n* entrada *f*

**entry** (*én*-tri) *n* entrada *f*, ingreso *m*; anotación *f*; **no** ~ prohibido el paso

**envelope** (*én*-vö-loup) *n* sobre *m*

**envious** (*én*-vi-öss) *adj* envidioso, celoso

**environment** (in-*vai*ᵒ-rön-mönt) *n* medio ambiente; alrededores *mpl*

**envoy** (*én*-voi) *n* enviado *m*

**envy** (*én*-vi) *n* envidia *f*; *v* envidiar

**epic** (*é*-pik) *n* poema épico; *adj* épico

**epidemic** (ê-pi-*dé*-mik) *n* epidemia *f*

**epilepsy** (*é*-pi-lêp-ssi) *n* epilepsia *f*

**epilogue** (*é*-pi-logh) *n* epílogo *m*

**episode** (*é*-pi-ssoud) *n* episodio *m*

**equal** (*ii*-kᵘöl) *adj* igual; *v* igualar

**equality** (i-kᵘo-lö-ti) *n* igualdad *f*

**equalize** (*ii*-kᵘö-lais) *v* igualar

**equally** (*ii*-kᵘö-li) *adv* igualmente

**equator** (i-kᵘei-tö) *n* ecuador *m*

**equip** (i-kᵘip) *v* equipar

**equipment** (i-kᵘip-mönt) *n* equipo *m*

**equivalent** (i-kᵘi-vö-lönt) *adj* equivalente

**eraser** (i-*rei*-sö) *n* goma de borrar

**erect** (i-*rêkt*) *v* erigir; *adj* erguido, recto; parado *adjMe*

**err** (öö) *v* \*errar

**errand** (ê-rönd) *n* recado *m*

**error** (ê-rö) *n* falta *f*, error *m*

**escalator** (ê-sskö-lei-tö) *n* escalera móvil

**escape** (i-sskeip) *v* escaparse; \*huir, escapar; *n* evasión *f*

**escort**[1] (ê-sskoot) *n* escolta *f*

**escort**[2] (i-sskoot) *v* escoltar

**especially** (i-sspê-jö-li) *adv* sobre todo, especialmente

**esplanade** (ê-ssplö-neid) *n* explanada *f*

**essay** (ê-ssei) *n* ensayo *m*; tratado *m*, composición *f*

**essence** (ê-ssönss) *n* esencia *f*; núcleo *m*

**essential** (i-ssên-jöl) *adj* indispensable; esencial

**essentially** (i-ssên-jö-li) *adv* sobre todo

**establish** (i-sstæ-blij) *v* \*establecer; \*comprobar

**estate** (i-ssteit) *n* propiedad *f*

**esteem** (i-sstiim) *n* respeto *m*, estima *f*; *v* estimar

**estimate**[1] (ê-ssti-meit) *v* evaluar, estimar

**estimate**[2] (ê-ssti-möt) *n* estimación *f*

**estuary** (êss-chu-ö-ri) *n* estuario *m*

**etcetera** (êt-ssê-tö-rö) etcétera

**etching** (ê-ching) *n* aguafuerte *f*

**eternal** (i-töö-nöl) *adj* eterno

**eternity** (i-töö-nö-ti) *n* eternidad *f*

**ether** (ii-zö) *n* éter *m*

**Ethiopia** (i-zi-ou-pi-ö) Etiopía *f*

**Ethiopian** (i-zi-ou-pi-ön) *adj* etíope

**Europe** (yuö-röp) Europa *f*

**European** (yuö-rö-pii-ön) *adj* europeo

**evacuate** (i-væ-kyu-eit) *v* evacuar

**evaluate** (i-væl-yu-eit) *v* evaluar

**evaporate** (i-væ-pö-reit) *v* evaporar

**even** (ii-vön) *adj* llano, plano, igual; constante; par; *adv* aun

**evening** (iiv-ning) *n* tarde *f*; ~ **dress** traje de etiqueta

**event** (i-vênt) *n* acontecimiento *m*; caso *m*

**eventual** (i-vên-chu-öl) *adj* eventual; final

**ever** (ê-vö) *adv* jamás; siempre

**every** (êv-ri) *adj* cada

**everybody** (êv-ri-bo-di) *pron* todos

**everyday** (êv-ri-dei) *adj* cotidiano

**everyone** (êv-ri-ʉan) *pron* cada uno, todo el mundo

**everything** (êv-ri-zing) *pron* todo

**everywhere** (êv-ri-ʉêô) *adv* por todas partes

**evidence** (ê-vi-dönss) *n* prueba *f*

**evident** (ê-vi-dönt) *adj* evidente

**evil** (ii-völ) *n* mal *m*; *adj* malo, malvado

**evolution** (ii-vö-luu-jön) *n* evolución *f*

**exact** (igh-sækt) *adj* exacto

**exactly** (igh-sækt-li) *adv* exactamente

**exaggerate** (igh-sæ-dzö-reit) *v* exagerar

**examination** (igh-sæ-mi-nei-jön) *n* examen *m*; interrogatorio *m*

**examine** (igh-sæ-min) *v* examinar

**example** (igh-saam-pöl) *n* ejemplo *m*; **for ~** por ejemplo

**excavation** (êkss-kö-vei-jön) *n* excavación *f*

**exceed** (ik-ssiid) *v* exceder; superar

**excel** (ik-ssêl) *v* distinguirse

**excellent** (êk-ssö-lönt) *adj* excelente

**except** (ik-ssêpt) *prep* excepto

**exception** (ik-ssêp-jön) *n* excepción *f*

**exceptional** (ik-ssêp-jö-nöl) *adj* extraordinario, excepcional

**excerpt** (êk-ssööpt) *n* extracto *m*

**excess** (ik-ssêss) *n* exceso *m*

**excessive** (ik-ssê-ssiv) *adj* excesivo

**exchange** (ikss-cheindʒ) *v* intercambiar, cambiar; *n* cambio *m*; bolsa *f*; ~ **office** oficina de cambio; ~

rate cambio *m*

**excite** (ik-*ssait*) *v* excitar

**excitement** (ik-*ssait*-mönt) *n* agitación *f*, excitación *f*

**exciting** (ik-*ssai*-ting) *adj* excitante

**exclaim** (ik-*sskleim*) *v* exclamar

**exclamation** (êk-ssklö-*mei*-ſön) *n* exclamación *f*

**exclude** (ik-*sskluud*) *v* *excluir

**exclusive** (ik-*sskluu*-ssiv) *adj* exclusivo

**exclusively** (ik-*sskluu*-ssiv-li) *adv* exclusivamente, únicamente

**excursion** (ik-*ssköö*-ſön) *n* excursión *f*

**excuse¹** (ik-*sskyuuss*) *n* excusa *f*

**excuse²** (ik-*sskyuus*) *v* excusar, disculpar

**execute** (*êk*-ssi-kyuut) *v* ejecutar

**execution** (êk-ssi-*kyuu*-ſön) *n* ejecución *f*

**executioner** (êk-ssi-*kyuu*-ſö-nö) *n* verdugo *m*

**executive** (igh-*sê*-kyu-tiv) *adj* ejecutivo; *n* poder ejecutivo; ejecutivo *m*

**exempt** (igh-*ʒêmpt*) *v* dispensar, eximir; *adj* exento

**exemption** (igh-*sêmp*-ſön) *n* exención *f*

**exercise** (*êk*-ssö-ssais) *n* ejercicio *m*; *v* ejercitar; ejercer

**exhale** (êkss-*heil*) *v* exhalar

**exhaust** (ig-*soosst*) *n* tubo de escape, escape *m*; *v* extenuar; ~ **gases** gases de escape

**exhibit** (igh-*si*-bit) *v* *exponer; exhibir

**exhibition** (êk-ssi-*bi*-ſön) *n* exposición *f*

**exile** (*êk*-ssail) *n* exilio *m*; exiliado *m*

**exist** (igh-*sisst*) *v* existir

**existence** (igh-*si*-sstönss) *n* existencia *f*

**exit** (*êk*-ssit) *n* salida *f*

**exotic** (ig-*so*-tik) *adj* exótico

**expand** (ik-*sspænd*) *v* *extender;

*desplegar

**expect** (ik-*sspêkt*) *v* aguardar, esperar

**expectation** (êk-sspêk-*tei*-ſön) *n* esperanza *f*

**expedition** (êk-sspö-*di*-ſön) *n* envío *m*; expedición *f*

**expel** (ik-*sspêl*) *v* expulsar

**expenditure** (ik-*sspên*-di-chö) *n* gasto *m*

**expense** (ik-*sspênss*) *n* gasto *m*

**expensive** (ik-*sspên*-ssiv) *adj* caro; costoso

**experience** (ik-*sspi*⁰-ri-önss) *n* experiencia *f*; *v* experimentar, vivir; **experienced** experimentado

**experiment** (ik-*sspê*-ri-mönt) *n* prueba *f*, experimento *m*; *v* experimentar

**expert** (êk-sspööt) *n* perito *m*, experto *m*; *adj* competente

**expire** (ik-*sspai*⁰) *v* expirar, terminarse; espirar; **expired** caducado

**expiry** (ik-*sspai*⁰-ri) *n* vencimiento *m*

**explain** (ik-*ssplein*) *v* explicar

**explanation** (êk-ssplö-*nei*-ſön) *n* aclaración *f*, explicación *f*

**explicit** (ik-*sspli*-ssit) *adj* expreso, explícito

**explode** (ik-*ssploud*) *v* estallar

**exploit** (ik-*ssploit*) *v* abusar de, explotar

**explore** (ik-*ssploo*) *v* explorar

**explosion** (ik-*ssplou*-ʒön) *n* explosión *f*

**explosive** (ik-*ssplou*-ssiv) *adj* explosivo; *n* explosivo *m*

**export¹** (ik-*sspoot*) *v* exportar

**export²** (*êk*-sspoot) *n* exportación *f*

**exportation** (êk-sspoo-*tei*-ſön) *n* exportación *f*

**exports** (*êk*-sspootss) *pl* exportación *f*

**exposition** (êk-sspö-*si*-ſön) *n* exposición *f*

**exposure** (ik-*sspou*-ʒö) *n* exposición *f*; ~ **meter** exposímetro *m*

**express** (ik-*ssprêss*) *v* expresar; *adj*
expreso; explícito; ~ **train** tren expreso

**expression** (ik-*ssprê*-ʃön) *n* expresión
*f*

**exquisite** (ik-*ssk*ᵘ*i*-sit) *adj* exquisito

**extend** (ik-*sstênd*) *v* prolongar; ampliar; conceder

**extension** (ik-*sstên*-ʃön) *n* prórroga *f*;
ampliación *f*; extensión *f*; ~ **cord**
cordón de extensión

**extensive** (ik-*sstên*-ssiv) *adj* extenso;
vasto

**extent** (ik-*sstênt*) *n* dimensión *f*

**exterior** (êk-*ssti*ᵒ-ri-ö) *adj* exterior; *n*
exterior *m*

**external** (êk-*sstöö*-nöl) *adj* exterior

**extinguish** (ik-*ssting*-gh°uiʃ) *v* extinguir, apagar

**extort** (ik-*sstoot*) *v* extorsionar

**extortion** (ik-*sstoo*-ʃön) *n* extorsión *f*

**extra** (*êk*-sströ) *adj* extra

**extract**¹ (ik-*sstrækt*) *v* *extraer

**extract**² (*êk*-sstrækt) *n* fragmento *m*

**extradite** (*êk*-sströ-dait) *v* entregar

**extraordinary** (ik-*sstroo*-dön-ri) *adj* extraordinario

**extravagant** (ik-*sstræ*-vö-ghönt) *adj*
exagerado, extravagante

**extreme** (ik-*sstriim*) *adj* extremo; *n*
extremo *m*

**exuberant** (igh-*syuu*-bö-rönt) *adj* exuberante

**eye** (ai) *n* ojo *m*

**eyebrow** (*ai*-brau) *n* ceja *f*

**eyelash** (*ai*-læʃ) *n* pestaña *f*

**eyelid** (*ai*-lid) *n* párpado *m*

**eye-pencil** (*ai*-pên-ssöl) *n* lápiz para
las cejas

**eye-shadow** (*ai*-ʃæ-dou) *n* sombra para los ojos

**eye-witness** (*ai*-ᵘit-nöss) *n* testigo de
vista

# F

**fable** (*fei*-böl) *n* fábula *f*

**fabric** (*fæ*-brik) *n* tejido *m*; estructura
*f*

**façade** (fö-*ssaad*) *n* fachada *f*

**face** (feiss) *n* cara *f*; *v* enfrentarse
con; ~ **massage** masaje facial;
**facing** enfrente de

**face-cream** (*feiss*-kriim) *n* crema facial

**face-pack** (*feiss*-pæk) *n* máscara facial

**face-powder** (*feiss*-pau-dö) *n* polvo
facial

**facility** (fö-*ssi*-lö-ti) *n* facilidad *f*

**fact** (fækt) *n* hecho *m*; **in** ~ efectivamente

**factor** (*fæk*-tö) *n* factor *m*

**factory** (*fæk*-tö-ri) *n* fábrica *f*

**factual** (*fæk*-chu-öl) *adj* real

**faculty** (*fæ*-köl-ti) *n* facultad *f*; don
*m*, aptitud *f*

**fad** (fæd) *n* antojo *m*

**fade** (feid) *v* *desteñirse

**faience** (fai-*angss*) *n* loza *f*

**fail** (feil) *v* fallar; faltar; omitir; *ser
suspendido; **without** ~ sin falta

**failure** (*feil*-yö) *n* fracaso *m*; fiasco *m*

**faint** (feint) *v* desmayarse; *adj* débil,
vago

**fair** (fêᵒ) *n* feria *f*; *adj* justo; rubio;
bonito

**fairly** (*fêᵒ*-li) *adv* bastante, medianamente

**fairy** (*fêᵒ*-ri) *n* hada *f*

**fairytale** (*fêᵒ*-ri-teil) *n* cuento de hadas

**faith** (feiz) *n* fe *f*; confianza *f*

**faithful** (*feiz*-ful) *adj* fiel

**fake** (feik) *n* falsificación *f*

**fall** (fool) *n* caída *f*; *nAm* otoño *m*

***fall** (fool) *v* *caer

**false** (foolss) *adj* falso; inexacto; ~

**teeth** dentadura postiza
**falter** (*fool*-tö) *v* vacilar; balbucear
**fame** (feim) *n* fama *f*; reputación *f*
**familiar** (fö-*mil*-yö) *adj* familiar
**family** (*fæ*-mö-li) *n* familia *f*; ~ **name** apellido *m*
**famous** (*fei*-möss) *adj* famoso
**fan** (fæn) *n* ventilador *m*; abanico *m*; admirador *m*; ~ **belt** correa del ventilador
**fanatical** (fö-*næ*-ti-köl) *adj* fanático
**fancy** (*fæn*-ssi) *v* gustar, antojarse; imaginarse; *n* capricho *m*; imaginación *f*
**fantastic** (fæn-*tæ*-sstik) *adj* fantástico
**fantasy** (*fæn*-tö-si) *n* fantasía *f*
**far** (faa) *adj* lejano; *adv* mucho; **by** ~ con mucho; **so** ~ hasta ahora
**far-away** (*faa*-rö-<sup>u</sup>ei) *adj* remoto
**farce** (faass) *n* sainete *m*, farsa *f*
**fare** (fê<sup>ö</sup>) *n* gastos de viaje, precio del billete; alimento *m*
**farm** (faam) *n* granja *f*
**farmer** (*faa*-mö) *n* granjero *m*; **farmer's wife** granjera *f*
**farmhouse** (*faam*-hauss) *n* cortijo *m*; rancho *mMe*
**far-off** (*faa*-rof) *adj* remoto
**fascinate** (*fæ*-ssi-neit) *v* cautivar
**fascism** (*fæ*-ʃi-söm) *n* fascismo *m*
**fascist** (*fæ*-ʃisst) *adj* fascista
**fashion** (*fæ*-ʃön) *n* moda *f*; modo *m*
**fashionable** (*fæ*-ʃö-nö-böl) *adj* a la moda
**fast** (faasst) *adj* rápido; firme
**fast-dyed** (faasst-*daid*) *adj* lavable, no destiñe
**fasten** (*faa*-ssön) *v* atar; *cerrar
**fastener** (*faa*-ssö-nö) *n* cierre *m*
**fat** (fæt) *adj* graso, gordo; *n* grasa *f*
**fatal** (*fei*-töl) *adj* fatal, mortal
**fate** (feit) *n* destino *m*
**father** (*faa*-ðö) *n* padre *m*
**father-in-law** (*faa*-ðö-rin-loo) *n* (pl fa-

thers-) suegro *m*
**fatherland** (*faa*-ðö-lönd) *n* patria *f*
**fatness** (*fæt*-nöss) *n* obesidad *f*
**fatty** (*fæ*-ti) *adj* grasiento
**faucet** (*foo*-ssit) *nAm* grifo *m*
**fault** (foolt) *n* culpa *f*; imperfección *f*, defecto *m*
**faultless** (*foolt*-löss) *adj* impecable; perfecto
**faulty** (*fool*-ti) *adj* defectuoso
**favour** (*fei*-vö) *n* favor *m*; *v* *favorecer
**favourable** (*fei*-vö-rö-böl) *adj* favorable
**favourite** (*fei*-vö-rit) *n* favorito *m*; *adj* preferido
**fawn** (foon) *adj* marrón claro; *n* cervato *m*, corcino *m*
**fear** (fi<sup>ö</sup>) *n* temor *m*, miedo *m*; *v* temer
**feasible** (*fii*-sö-böl) *adj* realizable
**feast** (fiisst) *n* fiesta *f*
**feat** (fiit) *n* gran trabajo
**feather** (*fê*-ðö) *n* pluma *f*
**feature** (*fii*-chö) *n* característica *f*; rasgo *m*
**February** (*fê*-bru-ö-ri) febrero
**federal** (*fê*-dö-röl) *adj* federal
**federation** (fê-dö-*rei*-ʃön) *n* federación *f*
**fee** (fii) *n* honorarios *mpl*
**feeble** (*fii*-böl) *adj* débil
***feed** (fiid) *v* alimentar; **fed up with** harto de
***feel** (fiil) *v* *sentir; palpar; ~ **like** antojarse
**feeling** (*fii*-ling) *n* sensación *f*
**fell** (fêl) *v* (p fall)
**fellow** (*fê*-lou) *n* tipo *m*
**felt**[1] (fêlt) *n* fieltro *m*
**felt**[2] (fêlt) *v* (p, pp feel)
**female** (*fii*-meil) *adj* femenino
**feminine** (*fê*-mi-nin) *adj* femenino
**fence** (fênss) *n* cerca *f*; reja *f*; *v* es-

grimir

**fender** (*fên*-dö) n parachoques m; defensa fMe

**ferment** (föö-*mênt*) v fermentar

**ferry-boat** (*fê*-ri-bout) n transbordador m

**fertile** (*föö*-tail) adj fértil

**festival** (*fê*-ssti-völ) n festival m

**festive** (*fê*-sstiv) adj festivo

**fetch** (fêch) v *ir por; *ir a buscar

**feudal** (*fyuu*-döl) adj feudal

**fever** (*fii*-vö) n fiebre f

**feverish** (*fii*-vö-ri∫) adj febril

**few** (fyuu) adj pocos

**fiancé** (fi-*ang*-ssei) n novio m

**fiancée** (fi-*ang*-ssei) n novia f

**fibre** (*fai*-bö) n fibra f

**fiction** (*fik*-∫ön) n ficción f

**field** (fiild) n campo m; terreno m; ~ **glasses** gemelos de campaña

**fierce** (fi°ss) adj fiero; salvaje, violento

**fifteen** (fif-*tiin*) num quince

**fifteenth** (fif-*tiinz*) num quinceno

**fifth** (fifz) num quinto

**fifty** (*fif*-ti) num cincuenta

**fig** (figh) n higo m

**fight** (fait) n combate m, lucha f

**\*fight** (fait) v combatir, luchar

**figure** (*fi*-ghö) n estatura f, figura f; cifra f

**file** (fail) n lima f; expediente m; cola f

**Filipino** (fi-li-*pii*-nou) n filipino m

**fill** (fil) v llenar; ~ **in** completar, llenar; **filling station** estación de servicio; ~ **out** Am completar, llenar; ~ **up** llenar

**filling** (*fi*-ling) n empaste m; relleno m

**film** (film) n película f; v filmar

**filter** (*fil*-tö) n filtro m

**filthy** (*fil*-zi) adj sórdido, inmundo

**final** (*fai*-nöl) adj final

**finance** (fai-*nænss*) v financiar

**finances** (fai-*næn*-ssis) pl finanzas fpl

**financial** (fai-*næn*-∫öl) adj financiero

**finch** (finch) n pinzón m

**\*find** (faind) v *encontrar

**fine** (fain) n multa f; adj fino; bello; excelente, maravilloso; ~ **arts** bellas artes

**finger** (*fing*-ghö) n dedo m; **little** ~ dedo auricular

**fingerprint** (*fing*-ghö-print) n impresión digital

**finish** (*fi*-ni∫) v terminar; n terminación f; meta f; **finished** acabado

**Finland** (*fin*-lönd) Finlandia f

**Finn** (fin) n finlandés m

**Finnish** (*fi*-ni∫) adj finlandés

**fire** (fai°) n fuego m; incendio m; v disparar; *despedir

**fire-alarm** (*fai°*-rö-laam) n alarma de incendio

**fire-brigade** (*fai°*-bri-gheid) n bomberos mpl

**fire-escape** (*fai°*-ri-sskeip) n escala de incendios

**fire-extinguisher** (*fai°*-rik-ssting-gh°i-∫ö) n extintor m

**fireplace** (*fai°*-pleiss) n chimenea f

**fireproof** (*fai°*-pruuf) adj incombustible; refractario

**firm** (fööm) adj firme; sólido; n firma f

**first** (föösst) num primero; **at** ~ antes; al principio; ~ **name** nombre de pila

**first-aid** (föösst-*eid*) n primeros auxilios; ~ **kit** botiquín de urgencia; ~ **post** puesto de socorro

**first-class** (föösst-*klaass*) adj de primera calidad

**first-rate** (föösst-*reit*) adj de primer orden, de primera clase

**fir-tree** (*föö*-trii) n pino m

**fish¹** (fi∫) n (pl ~, ~es) pez m; ~

shop pescadería f

**fish²** (fiʃ) v pescar; **fishing gear** avíos de pesca; **fishing fly** mosca artificial; **fishing hook** anzuelo m; **fishing licence** permiso de pesca; **fishing line** línea de pesca; **fishing net** red de pescar; **fishing rod** caña de pescar; **fishing tackle** aparejo de pesca

**fishbone** (fiʃ-boun) n espina f

**fisherman** (fi-ʃö-mön) n (pl -men) pescador m

**fist** (fisst) n puño m

**fit** (fit) adj apropiado; n ataque m; v *convenir; **fitting room** probador m

**five** (faiv) num cinco

**fix** (fikss) v arreglar

**fixed** (fiksst) adj fijo

**fizz** (fis) n efervescencia f

**fjord** (fyood) n fiordo m

**flag** (flægh) n bandera f

**flame** (fleim) n llama f

**flamingo** (flö-ming-ghou) n (pl ~s, ~es) flamenco m

**flannel** (flæ-nöl) n franela f

**flash** (flæʃ) n relámpago m

**flash-bulb** (flæʃ-balb) n bombilla de flash

**flash-light** (flæʃ-lait) n linterna f

**flask** (flaassk) n frasco m; **thermos ~** termo m

**flat** (flæt) adj llano; n piso m; ~ **tyre** neumático desinflado

**flavour** (flei-vö) n sabor m; v sazonar

**fleet** (fliit) n flota f

**flesh** (fleʃ) n carne f

**flew** (fluu) v (p fly)

**flex** (flékss) n cordón flexible

**flexible** (flék-ssi-böl) adj flexible

**flight** (flait) n vuelo m; **charter ~** vuelo fletado

**flint** (flint) n pedernal m

**float** (flout) v flotar; n flotador m

**flock** (flok) n rebaño m

**flood** (flad) n inundación f; riada f

**floor** (floo) n suelo m; piso m; ~ **show** espectáculo de variedades

**florist** (flo-risst) n florista m

**flour** (flauᵒ) n harina f

**flow** (flou) v correr, *fluir

**flower** (flauᵒ) n flor f

**flowerbed** (flauᵒ-bêd) n arriate m

**flower-shop** (flauᵒ-ʃop) n floristería f

**flown** (floun) v (pp fly)

**flu** (fluu) n gripe f

**fluent** (fluu-önt) adj con soltura

**fluid** (fluu-id) adj fluido; n fluido m

**flute** (fluut) n flauta f

**fly** (flai) n mosca f; bragueta f

***fly** (flai) v *volar

**foam** (foum) n espuma f; v espumar

**foam-rubber** (foum-ra-bö) n goma espumada

**focus** (fou-köss) n foco m

**fog** (fogh) n niebla f

**foggy** (fo-ghi) adj brumoso

**foglamp** (fogh-læmp) n faro de niebla

**fold** (fould) v doblar; n pliegue m

**folk** (fouk) n gente f; ~ **song** canción popular

**folk-dance** (fouk-daanss) n danza popular

**folklore** (fouk-loo) n folklore m

**follow** (fo-lou) v *seguir; **following** adj siguiente

***be fond of** (bii fond ov) *querer

**food** (fuud) n comida f; alimento m; ~ **poisoning** intoxicación alimentaria

**foodstuffs** (fuud-sstafss) pl artículos alimenticios

**fool** (fuul) n idiota m, tonto m; v engañar

**foolish** (fuu-liʃ) adj necio, tonto; absurdo

**foot** (fut) n (pl feet) pie m; ~ **powder** polvo para los pies; **on ~** a pie

**football** (*fut*-bool) *n* fútbol *m*; ~ **match** partido de fútbol

**foot-brake** (*fut*-breik) *n* freno de pie

**footpath** (*fut*-paaz) *n* senda *f*

**footwear** (*fut*-ᵘê°) *n* calzado *m*

**for** (foo, fö) *prep* para; durante; a causa de, por; *conj* porque

*__forbid__ (fö-*bid*) *v* prohibir

**force** (fooss) *v* obligar, *forzar; *n* fuerza *f*; **by** ~ forzosamente; **driving** ~ fuerza motriz

**ford** (food) *n* vado *m*

**forecast** (*foo*-kaasst) *n* previsión *f*; *v* pronosticar

**foreground** (*foo*-ghraund) *n* primer plano

**forehead** (*fo*-rêd) *n* frente *f*

**foreign** (*fo*-rin) *adj* extranjero; extraño

**foreigner** (*fo*-ri-nö) *n* extranjero *m*; forastero *m*

**foreman** (*foo*-mön) *n* (pl -men) capataz *m*

**foremost** (*foo*-mousst) *adj* primero

**foresail** (*foo*-sseil) *n* foque *m*

**forest** (*fo*-risst) *n* selva *f*, bosque *m*

**forester** (*fo*-ri-sstö) *n* guardabosques *m*

**forge** (foodʒ) *v* falsificar

*__forget__ (fö-*ghêt*) *v* olvidar

**forgetful** (fö-*ghêt*-föl) *adj* olvidadizo

*__forgive__ (fö-*ghiv*) *v* perdonar

**fork** (fook) *n* tenedor *m*; bifurcación *f*; *v* bifurcarse

**form** (foom) *n* forma *f*; formulario *m*; clase *f*; *v* formar

**formal** (*foo*-möl) *adj* formal

**formality** (foo-*mæ*-lö-ti) *n* formalidad *f*

**former** (*foo*-mö) *adj* antiguo; anterior; **formerly** antes

**formula** (*foo*-myu-lö) *n* (pl ~e, ~s) fórmula *f*

**fort** (foot) *n* fortaleza *f*

**fortnight** (*foot*-nait) *n* quincena *f*

**fortress** (*foo*-triss) *n* fortaleza *f*

**fortunate** (*foo*-chö-nöt) *adj* afortunado

**fortune** (*foo*-chuun) *n* fortuna *f*; suerte *f*

**forty** (*foo*-ti) *num* cuarenta

**forward** (*foo*-ᵘöd) *adv* hacia adelante, adelante; *v* reexpedir

**foster-parents** (fo-sstö-pê°-röntss) *pl* padres adoptivos

**fought** (foot) *v* (p, pp fight)

**foul** (faul) *adj* sucio; vil

**found¹** (faund) *v* (p, pp find)

**found²** (faund) *v* fundar

**foundation** (faun-*dei*-jön) *n* fundación *f*; ~ **cream** crema de base

**fountain** (*faun*-tin) *n* fuente *f*

**fountain-pen** (*faun*-tin-pên) *n* estilográfica *f*

**four** (foo) *num* cuatro

**fourteen** (foo-*tiin*) *num* catorce

**fourteenth** (foo-*tiinz*) *num* catorceno

**fourth** (fooz) *num* cuarto

**fowl** (faul) *n* (pl ~s, ~) volatería *f*

**fox** (fokss) *n* zorro *m*

**foyer** (*foi*-ei) *n* vestíbulo *m*

**fraction** (*fræk*-jön) *n* fracción *f*

**fracture** (*fræk*-chö) *v* fracturar; fractura *f*

**fragile** (*fræ*-dʒail) *adj* frágil

**fragment** (*frægh*-mönt) *n* fragmento *m*; trozo *m*

**frame** (freim) *n* marco *m*; armadura *f*

**France** (fraanss) Francia *f*

**franchise** (*fræn*-chais) *n* derecho electoral

**fraternity** (frö-*töö*-nö-ti) *n* fraternidad *f*

**fraud** (frood) *n* fraude *m*

**fray** (frei) *v* deshilacharse

**free** (frii) *adj* libre; gratuito; ~ **of charge** gratis; ~ **ticket** billete gratuito

**freedom** (*frii*-döm) *n* libertad *f*

*****freeze** (friis) *v* *helar; congelar

**freezing** (*frii*-sing) *adj* helado

**freezing-point** (*frii*-sing-point) *n* punto de congelación

**freight** (freit) *n* carga *f*, cargo *m*

**French** (frênch) *adj* francés

**Frenchman** (*frênch*-mön) *n* (pl -men) francés *m*

**frequency** (*frii*-kᵘön-ssi) *n* frecuencia *f*

**frequent** (*frii*-kᵘönt) *adj* frecuente

**fresh** (frêʃ) *adj* fresco; ~ **water** agua dulce

**friction** (*frik*-ʃön) *n* fricción *f*

**Friday** (*frai*-di) viernes *m*

**fridge** (fridʒ) *n* frigorífico *m*, refrigerador *m*

**friend** (frênd) *n* amigo *m*; amiga *f*

**friendly** (*frênd*-li) *adj* amable; amistoso

**friendship** (*frênd*-ʃip) *n* amistad *f*

**fright** (frait) *n* miedo *m*, espanto *m*

**frighten** (*frai*-tön) *v* espantar

**frightened** (*frai*-tönd) *adj* espantado; ***be** ~ asustarse

**frightful** (*frait*-föl) *adj* terrible

**fringe** (frindʒ) *n* franja *f*

**frock** (frok) *n* vestido *m*

**frog** (frogh) *n* rana *f*

**from** (from) *prep* desde; de; a partir de

**front** (frant) *n* frente *m*; **in ~ of** delante de

**frontier** (*fran*-tiᵒ) *n* frontera *f*

**frost** (frosst) *n* escarcha *f*

**froth** (froz) *n* espuma *f*

**frozen** (*frou*-sön) *adj* congelado; ~ **food** alimento congelado

**fruit** (fruut) *n* fruta *f*; fruto *m*

**fry** (frai) *v* *freír

**frying-pan** (*frai*-ing-pæn) *n* sartén *f*

**fuel** (*fyuu*-öl) *n* combustible *m*; ~ **pump** *Am* bomba de gasolina

**full** (ful) *adj* lleno; ~ **board** pensión completa; ~ **stop** punto *m*; ~ **up** completo

**fun** (fan) *n* diversión *f*

**function** (*fangk*-ʃön) *n* función *f*

**fund** (fand) *n* fondos *mpl*

**fundamental** (fan-dö-*mên*-töl) *adj* fundamental

**funeral** (*fyuu*-nö-röl) *n* funerales *mpl*

**funnel** (*fa*-nöl) *n* embudo *m*

**funny** (*fa*-ni) *adj* gracioso, cómico; extraño

**fur** (föö) *n* piel *f*; ~ **coat** abrigo de pieles; **furs** piel *f*

**furious** (*fyuᵒ*-ri-öss) *adj* furioso

**furnace** (*föö*-niss) *n* horno *m*

**furnish** (*föö*-niʃ) *v* suministrar, procurar; instalar, amueblar; ~ **with** *proveer de

**furniture** (*föö*-ni-chö) *n* muebles *mpl*

**furrier** (*fa*-ri-ö) *n* peletero *m*

**further** (*föö*-ðö) *adj* más lejos; ulterior

**furthermore** (*föö*-ðö-moo) *adv* además

**furthest** (*föö*-ðisst) *adj* el más alejado

**fuse** (fyuus) *n* fusible *m*; mecha *f*

**fuss** (fass) *n* bulla *f*; ostentación *f*, alharaca *f*

**future** (*fyuu*-chö) *n* porvenir *m*; *adj* futuro

# G

**gable** (*ghei*-böl) *n* faldón *m*

**gadget** (*ghæ*-dʒit) *n* accesorio *m*

**gaiety** (*ghei*-ö-ti) *n* alegría *f*

**gain** (ghein) *v* ganar; *n* ganancia *f*

**gait** (gheit) *n* paso *m*

**gale** (gheil) *n* ventarrón *m*

**gall** (ghool) *n* bilis *f*; ~ **bladder** vesícula biliar

**gallery** (*ghæ*-lö-ri) *n* galería *f*
**gallop** (*ghæ*-löp) *n* galope *m*
**gallows** (*ghæ*-lous) *pl* horca *f*
**gallstone** (*ghool*-sstoun) *n* cálculo biliar
**game** (gheim) *n* juego *m*; caza *f*; ~ **reserve** parque de reserva zoológica
**gang** (ghæng) *n* banda *f*; equipo *m*
**gangway** (*ghæng*-ᵘei) *n* pasarela *f*
**gaol** (dʒeil) *n* cárcel *f*
**gap** (ghæp) *n* hueco *m*
**garage** (*ghæ*-raaʒ) *n* garaje *m*; *v* dejar en garaje
**garbage** (*ghaa*-bidʒ) *n* basura *f*
**garden** (*ghaa*-dön) *n* jardín *m*; **public** ~ jardín público; **zoological gardens** jardín zoológico
**gardener** (*ghaa*-dö-nö) *n* jardinero *m*
**gargle** (*ghaa*-ghöl) *v* *hacer gárgaras
**garlic** (*ghaa*-lik) *n* ajo *m*
**gas** (ghæss) *n* gas *m*; *nAm* gasolina *f*; ~ **cooker** cocina de gas; ~ **station** *Am* puesto de gasolina; ~ **stove** estufa de gas
**gasoline** (*ghæ*-ssö-liin) *nAm* gasolina *f*
**gastric** (*ghæ*-sstrik) *adj* gástrico; ~ **ulcer** úlcera gástrica
**gasworks** (*ghæss*-ᵘöökss) *n* fábrica de gas
**gate** (gheit) *n* portón *m*; reja *f*
**gather** (*ghæ*-ðö) *v* coleccionar; juntarse; recoger
**gauge** (gheidʒ) *n* medidor *m*
**gauze** (ghoos) *n* gasa *f*
**gave** (gheiv) *v* (p give)
**gay** (ghei) *adj* alegre; gaitero
**gaze** (gheis) *v* mirar
**gazetteer** (ghæ-sö-*ti*ᵒ) *n* diccionario geográfico
**gear** (ghiᵒ) *n* velocidad *f*; aparejo *m*; **change** ~ cambiar de marcha; ~ **lever** palanca de cambios
**gear-box** (*ghi*ᵒ-bokss) *n* caja de veloci-

dades
**gem** (dʒêm) *n* joya *f*, gema *f*; alhaja *f*
**gender** (*dʒên*-dö) *n* género *m*
**general** (*dʒê*-nö-röl) *adj* general; *n* general *m*; ~ **practitioner** médico de cabecera; **in** ~ en general
**generate** (*dʒê*-nö-reit) *v* generar
**generation** (dʒê-nö-*rei*-ʃön) *n* generación *f*
**generator** (*dʒê*-nö-rei-tör) *n* generador *m*
**generosity** (dʒê-nö-*ro*-ssö-ti) *n* generosidad *f*
**generous** (*dʒê*-nö-röss) *adj* generoso
**genital** (*dʒê*-ni-töl) *adj* genital
**genius** (*dʒii*-ni-öss) *n* genio *m*
**gentle** (*dʒên*-töl) *adj* gentil; tierno, suave; prudente
**gentleman** (*dʒên*-töl-mön) *n* (pl -men) caballero *m*
**genuine** (*dʒê*-nyu-in) *adj* genuino
**geography** (dʒi-*o*-ghrö-fi) *n* geografía *f*
**geology** (dʒi-*o*-lö-dʒi) *n* geología *f*
**geometry** (dʒi-*o*-mö-tri) *n* geometría *f*
**germ** (dʒööm) *n* germen *m*
**German** (*dʒöö*-mön) *adj* alemán
**Germany** (*dʒöö*-mö-ni) Alemania *f*
**gesticulate** (dʒi-*ssti*-kyu-leit) *v* gesticular
*get** (ghêt) *v* *conseguir; *ir a buscar; *hacerse; ~ **back** regresar; ~ **off** apearse; ~ **on** subir, montar; adelantar; ~ **up** levantarse
**ghost** (ghousst) *n* fantasma *m*; espíritu *m*
**giant** (*dʒai*-önt) *n* gigante *m*
**giddiness** (*ghi*-di-nöss) *n* mareo *m*
**giddy** (*ghi*-di) *adj* mareado
**gift** (ghift) *n* regalo *m*; talento *m*
**gifted** (*ghif*-tid) *adj* talentoso
**gigantic** (dʒai-*ghæn*-tik) *adj* gigantesco
**giggle** (*ghi*-ghöl) *v* *soltar risitas

gill (ghil) n branquia f
gilt (ghilt) adj dorado
ginger (dʒin-dʒö) n jengibre m
gipsy (dʒip-ssi) n gitano m
girdle (ghöö-döl) n faja f
girl (ghööl) n muchacha f; ~ guide
exploradora f
*give (ghiv) v *dar; entregar; ~
away revelar; ~ in ceder; ~ up renunciar
glacier (ghlæ-ssi-ö) n glaciar m
glad (ghlæd) adj alegre, contento;
gladly con mucho gusto, gustosamente
gladness (ghlæd-nöss) n alegría f
glamorous (ghlæ-mö-röss) adj encantador
glamour (ghlæ-mö) n encanto m
glance (ghlaanss) n ojeada f; v ojear
gland (ghlænd) n glándula f
glare (ghlêᵒ) n destello m; resplandor m
glaring (ghlêᵒ-ring) adj deslumbrador
glass (ghlaass) n vaso m; vidrio m;
de vidrio; glasses anteojos mpl;
magnifying ~ lente de aumento
glaze (ghleis) v esmaltar
glen (ghlên) n cañada f
glide (ghlaid) v resbalar
glider (ghlai-dö) n planeador m
glimpse (ghlimpss) n vislumbre m;
ojeada f; v vislumbrar
global (ghlou-böl) adj mundial
globe (ghloub) n globo m
gloom (ghluum) n obscuridad f
gloomy (ghluu-mi) adj sombrío
glorious (ghloo-ri-öss) adj espléndido
glory (ghloo-ri) n gloria f; honor m,
elogio m
gloss (ghloss) n brillo m
glossy (ghlo-ssi) adj lustroso
glove (ghlav) n guante m
glow (ghlou) v brillar; n brillo m
glue (ghluu) n cola f

*go (ghou) v *ir; caminar; *hacerse;
~ ahead continuar; ~ away *irse;
~ back regresar; ~ home *volver a
casa; ~ in entrar; ~ on continuar;
~ out *salir; ~ through pasar
goal (ghoul) n meta f; gol m
goalkeeper (ghoul-kii-pö) n portero m
goat (ghout) n cabrón m, cabra f
god (ghod) n dios m
goddess (gho-diss) n diosa f
godfather (ghod-faa-ðö) n padrino m
goggles (gho-ghöls) pl gafas fpl
gold (ghould) n oro m; ~ leaf hojas
de oro
golden (ghoul-dön) adj dorado
goldmine (ghould-main) n mina de
oro
goldsmith (ghould-ssmiz) n orfebre m
golf (gholf) n golf m
golf-club (gholf-klab) n palo de golf
golf-course (gholf-kooss) n campo de
golf
golf-links (gholf-lingkss) n campo de
golf
gondola (ghon-dö-lö) n góndola f
gone (ghon) adv (pp go) ido
good (ghud) adj bueno
good-bye! (ghud-bai) ¡adiós!
good-humoured (ghud-hyuu-möd) adj
de buen humor
good-looking (ghud-lu-king) adj bien
parecido
good-natured (ghud-nei-chöd) adj
bondadoso
goods (ghuds) pl mercancías fpl, bienes mpl; ~ train tren de mercancías
good-tempered (ghud-têm-pöd) adj
de buen humor
goodwill (ghud-ᵘil) n buena voluntad
goose (ghuuss) n (pl geese) oca f
gooseberry (ghus-bö-ri) n grosella espinosa
goose-flesh (ghuuss-flêʃ) n carne de

gallina

**gorge** (ghoodʒ) *n* cañón *m*

**gorgeous** (ghoo-dʒöss) *adj* magnífico

**gospel** (*gho*-sspöl) *n* evangelio *m*

**gossip** (*gho*-ssip) *n* chisme *m*; *v* \*contar chismes

**got** (ghot) *v* (p, pp get)

**gourmet** (*ghu*ᵒ-mei) *n* gastrónomo *m*

**gout** (ghaut) *n* gota *f*

**govern** (*gha*-vön) *v* \*regir

**governess** (*gha*-vö-niss) *n* aya *f*

**government** (*gha*-vön-mönt) *n* régimen *m*, gobierno *m*

**governor** (*gha*-vö-nö) *n* gobernador *m*

**gown** (ghaun) *n* traje *m*

**grace** (ghreiss) *n* gracia *f*; perdón *m*

**graceful** (*ghreiss*-föl) *adj* gracioso

**grade** (ghreid) *n* grado *m*; *v* graduar

**gradient** (*ghrei*-di-önt) *n* pendiente *f*

**gradual** (*ghræ*-dʒu-öl) *adj* gradual; **gradually** *adv* paulatinamente

**graduate** (*ghræ*-dʒu-eit) *v* graduarse

**grain** (ghrein) *n* grano *m*, trigo *m*

**gram** (ghræm) *n* gramo *m*

**grammar** (*ghræ*-mö) *n* gramática *f*

**grammatical** (ghrö-*mæ*-ti-köl) *adj* gramatical

**gramophone** (*ghræ*-mö-foun) *n* gramófono *m*

**grand** (ghrænd) *adj* imponente

**granddad** (*ghræn*-dæd) *n* abuelo *m*

**granddaughter** (*ghræn*-doo-tö) *n* nieta *f*

**grandfather** (*ghræn*-faa-ðö) *n* abuelo *m*

**grandmother** (*ghræn*-ma-ðö) *n* abuela *f*

**grandparents** (*ghræn*-pêᵒ-röntss) *pl* abuelos *mpl*

**grandson** (*ghræn*-ssan) *n* nieto *m*

**granite** (*ghræ*-nit) *n* granito *m*

**grant** (ghraant) *v* conceder; *n* subvención *f*, beca *f*

**grapefruit** (*ghreip*-fruut) *n* pomelo *m*; toronja *fMe*

**grapes** (ghreipss) *pl* uvas *fpl*

**graph** (ghræf) *n* gráfico *m*

**graphic** (*ghræ*-fik) *adj* gráfico

**grasp** (ghraassp) *v* agarrar; *n* agarre *m*

**grass** (ghraass) *n* césped *m*

**grasshopper** (*ghraass*-ho-pö) *n* saltamontes *m*

**grate** (ghreit) *n* reja *f*; *v* rallar

**grateful** (*ghreit*-föl) *adj* agradecido

**grater** (*ghrei*-tö) *n* rayador *m*

**gratis** (*ghræ*-tiss) *adj* gratuito

**gratitude** (*ghræ*-ti-tyuud) *n* gratitud *f*

**gratuity** (ghrö-*tyuu*-ö-ti) *n* propina *f*

**grave** (ghreiv) *n* sepultura *f*; *adj* grave

**gravel** (*ghræ*-völ) *n* grava *f*

**gravestone** (*ghreiv*-sstoun) *n* lápida *f*

**graveyard** (*ghreiv*-yaad) *n* cementerio *m*

**gravity** (*ghræ*-vö-ti) *n* gravedad *f*; seriedad *f*

**gravy** (*ghrei*-vi) *n* salsa *f*

**graze** (ghreis) *v* \*pacer; *n* rozadura *f*

**grease** (ghriiss) *n* grasa *f*; *v* engrasar

**greasy** (*ghrii*-ssi) *adj* grasiento, grasoso

**great** (ghreit) *adj* grande; **Great Britain** Gran Bretaña

**Greece** (ghriiss) Grecia *f*

**greed** (ghriid) *n* codicia *f*

**greedy** (*ghrii*-di) *adj* codicioso; glotón

**Greek** (ghriik) *adj* griego

**green** (ghriin) *adj* verde; ~ **card** tarjeta verde

**greengrocer** (*ghriin*-ghrou-ssö) *n* verdulero *m*

**greenhouse** (*ghriin*-hauss) *n* invernadero *m*, invernáculo *m*

**greens** (ghriins) *pl* legumbres *fpl*

**greet** (ghriit) *v* saludar

**greeting** (*ghrii*-ting) *n* saludo *m*

**grey** (ghrei) *adj* gris

**greyhound** (*ghrei*-haund) *n* galgo *m*

**grief** (ghriif) *n* pesadumbre *f*; aflicción *f*, dolor *m*

**grieve** (ghriiv) *v* *estar afligido

**grill** (ghril) *n* parrilla *f*; *v* asar en parrilla

**grill-room** (*ghril*-ruum) *n* parrilla *f*

**grin** (ghrin) *v* *sonreír; *n* sonrisa sardónica

***grind** (ghraind) *v* *moler; triturar

**grip** (ghrip) *v* *asir; *n* agarradero *m*, agarre *m*; *nAm* maletín *m*

**grit** (ghrit) *n* polvo *m*

**groan** (ghroun) *v* *gemir

**grocer** (*ghrou*-ssö) *n* abacero *m*; abarrotero *mMe*; **grocer's** abacería *f*; abarrotería *fMe*

**groceries** (*ghrou*-ssö-ris) *pl* comestibles *mpl*

**groin** (ghroin) *n* ingle *f*

**groove** (ghruuv) *n* surco *m*

**gross**[1] (ghrouss) *n* (pl ~) gruesa *f*

**gross**[2] (ghrouss) *adj* grosero; bruto

**grotto** (*ghro*-tou) *n* (pl ~es, ~s) gruta *f*

**ground**[1] (ghraund) *n* fondo *m*, tierra *f*; ~ **floor** piso bajo; **grounds** terreno *m*

**ground**[2] (ghraund) *v* (p, pp grind)

**group** (ghruup) *n* grupo *m*

**grouse** (ghrauss) *n* (pl ~) gallo de bosque

**grove** (ghrouv) *n* soto *m*

***grow** (ghrou) *v* *crecer; cultivar; *hacerse

**growl** (ghraul) *v* *gruñir

**grown-up** (*ghroun*-ap) *adj* adulto; *n* adulto *m*

**growth** (ghrouz) *n* crecimiento *m*; tumor *m*

**grudge** (ghradʒ) *v* envidiar

**grumble** (*ghram*-böl) *v* refunfuñar

**guarantee** (ghæ-rön-*tii*) *n* garantía *f*; *v* garantizar

**guarantor** (ghæ-rön-*too*) *n* garante *m*

**guard** (ghaad) *n* guardia *f*; *v* guardar

**guardian** (*ghaa*-di-ön) *n* tutor *m*

**guess** (ghêss) *v* adivinar; *creer, conjeturar; *n* conjetura *f*

**guest** (ghêsst) *n* huésped *m*, invitado *m*

**guest-house** (*ghêsst*-hauss) *n* pensión *f*

**guest-room** (*ghêsst*-ruum) *n* habitación para huéspedes

**guide** (ghaid) *n* guía *m*; *v* guiar

**guidebook** (*ghaid*-buk) *n* guía *f*

**guide-dog** (*ghaid*-dogh) *n* perro lazarillo

**guilt** (ghilt) *n* culpa *f*

**guilty** (*ghil*-ti) *adj* culpable

**guinea-pig** (*ghi*-ni-pigh) *n* conejillo de Indias

**guitar** (ghi-*taa*) *n* guitarra *f*

**gulf** (ghalf) *n* golfo *m*

**gull** (ghal) *n* gaviota *f*

**gum** (gham) *n* encía *f*; goma *f*; cola *f*

**gun** (ghan) *n* fusil *m*, revólver *m*; cañón *m*

**gunpowder** (*ghan*-pau-dö) *n* pólvora *f*

**gust** (ghasst) *n* ráfaga *f*

**gusty** (*gha*-ssti) *adj* borrascoso

**gut** (ghat) *n* intestino *m*; **guts** coraje *m*

**gutter** (*gha*-tö) *n* cuneta *f*

**guy** (ghai) *n* tipo *m*

**gymnasium** (dʒim-*nei*-si-öm) *n* (pl ~s, -sia) gimnasio *m*

**gymnast** (*dʒim*-næsst) *n* gimnasta *m*

**gymnastics** (dʒim-*næ*-sstikss) *pl* gimnasia *f*

**gynaecologist** (ghai-nö-*ko*-lö-dʒisst) *n* ginecólogo *m*

# H

**haberdashery** (hæ-bö-dæ-ʃö-ri) n mercería f

**habit** (hæ-bit) n hábito m

**habitable** (hæ-bi-tö-böl) adj habitable

**habitual** (hö-bi-chu-öl) adj habitual

**had** (hæd) v (p, pp have)

**haddock** (hæ-dök) n (pl ~) bacalao m

**haemorrhage** (hê-mö-ridȝ) n hemorragia f

**haemorrhoids** (hê-mö-roids) pl hemorroides fpl

**hail** (heil) n granizo m

**hair** (hêᵒ) n cabello m; ~ **cream** brillantina f; ~ **piece** postizo m; ~ **rollers** rizadores mpl; ~ **tonic** tónico para el cabello

**hairbrush** (hêᵒ-braʃ) n cepillo para el cabello

**haircut** (hêᵒ-kat) n corte de pelo

**hair-do** (hêᵒ-duu) n peinado m

**hairdresser** (hêᵒ-drê-ssö) n peluquero m

**hair-dryer** (hêᵒ-drai-ö) n secador para el pelo

**hair-grip** (hêᵒ-ghrip) n horquilla f

**hair-net** (hêᵒ-nêt) n redecilla f

**hair-oil** (hêᵒ-roil) n aceite para el pelo

**hairpin** (hêᵒ-pin) n horquilla f

**hair-spray** (hêᵒ-ssprei) n laca para el cabello

**hairy** (hêᵒ-ri) adj cabelludo

**half¹** (haaf) adj medio

**half²** (haaf) n (pl halves) mitad f

**half-time** (haaf-taim) n descanso m

**halfway** (haaf-ᵘei) adv a mitad de camino

**halibut** (hæ-li-böt) n (pl ~) halibut m

**hall** (hool) n vestíbulo m; sala f

**halt** (hoolt) v pararse

**halve** (haav) v partir por la mitad

**ham** (hæm) n jamón m

**hamlet** (hæm-löt) n aldea f

**hammer** (hæ-mö) n martillo m

**hammock** (hæ-mök) n hamaca f

**hamper** (hæm-pö) n cesto m

**hand** (hænd) n mano f; v alargar; ~ **cream** crema para las manos

**handbag** (hænd-bægh) n bolso m

**handbook** (hænd-buk) n manual m

**hand-brake** (hænd-breik) n freno de mano

**handcuffs** (hænd-kafss) pl esposas fpl

**handful** (hænd-ful) n puñado m

**handicraft** (hæn-di-kraaft) n trabajo manual; artesanía f

**handkerchief** (hæng-kö-chif) n pañuelo m

**handle** (hæn-döl) n mango m; v manejar; tratar

**hand-made** (hænd-meid) adj hecho a mano

**handshake** (hænd-ʃeik) n apretón de manos

**handsome** (hæn-ssöm) adj guapo

**handwork** (hænd-ᵘöök) n obra hecha a mano

**handwriting** (hænd-rai-ting) n escritura f

**handy** (hæn-di) adj manejable

***hang** (hæng) v *colgar

**hanger** (hæng-ö) n percha f

**hangover** (hæng-ou-vö) n resaca f

**happen** (hæ-pön) v suceder, pasar

**happening** (hæ-pö-ning) n acontecimiento m

**happiness** (hæ-pi-nöss) n felicidad f

**happy** (hæ-pi) adj contento, feliz

**harbour** (haa-bö) n puerto m

**hard** (haad) adj duro; difícil; **hardly** apenas

**hardware** (haad-ᵘêᵒ) n quincalla f; ~ **store** ferretería f

**hare** (hêᵒ) n liebre f

**harm** (haam) n perjuicio m; mal m,

daño *m*; *v* perjudicar

**harmful** (*haam*-föl) *adj* perjudicial, dañoso

**harmless** (*haam*-löss) *adj* inocuo

**harmony** (*haa*-mö-ni) *n* armonía *f*

**harp** (haap) *n* arpa *f*

**harpsichord** (*haap*-ssi-kood) *n* clavicémbalo *m*

**harsh** (haaʃ) *adj* áspero; severo; cruel

**harvest** (*haa*-visst) *n* cosecha *f*

**has** (hæs) *v* (pr have)

**haste** (heisst) *n* prisa *f*

**hasten** (*hei*-ssön) *v* apresurarse

**hasty** (*hei*-ssti) *adj* apresurado

**hat** (hæt) *n* sombrero *m*; ~ **rack** percha *f*

**hatch** (hæch) *n* trampa *f*

**hate** (heit) *v* detestar; odiar; *n* odio *m*

**hatred** (*hei*-trid) *n* odio *m*

**haughty** (*hoo*-ti) *adj* altivo

**haul** (hool) *v* arrastrar

\***have** (hæv) *v* \*haber, \*tener; \*hacer; ~ **to** deber

**haversack** (*hæ*-vö-ssæk) *n* morral *m*

**hawk** (hook) *n* azor *m*; halcón *m*

**hay** (hei) *n* heno *m*; ~ **fever** fiebre del heno

**hazard** (*hæ*-söd) *n* riesgo *m*

**haze** (heis) *n* calina *f*; niebla *f*

**hazelnut** (*hei*-söl-nat) *n* avellana *f*

**hazy** (*hei*-si) *adj* calinoso; brumoso

**he** (hii) *pron* él

**head** (hêd) *n* cabeza *f*; *v* dirigir; ~ **of state** jefe de Estado; ~ **teacher** director de escuela

**headache** (*hê*-deik) *n* dolor de cabeza

**heading** (*hê*-ding) *n* título *m*

**headlamp** (*hêd*-læmp) *n* fanal *m*

**headland** (*hêd*-lönd) *n* promontorio *m*

**headlight** (*hêd*-lait) *n* faro *m*

**headline** (*hêd*-lain) *n* titular *m*

**headmaster** (hêd-*maa*-sstö) *n* director de escuela

**headquarters** (hêd-kᵘoo-tös) *pl* cuartel general

**head-strong** (*hêd*-sstrong) *adj* cabezudo

**head-waiter** (hêd-ᵘei-tö) *n* jefe de camareros

**heal** (hiil) *v* curar

**health** (hêlz) *n* salud *f*; ~ **centre** dispensario *m*; ~ **certificate** certificado de salud

**healthy** (*hêl*-zi) *adj* sano

**heap** (hiip) *n* montón *m*

\***hear** (hiᵒ) *v* \*oír

**hearing** (*hiᵒ*-ring) *n* oído *m*

**heart** (haat) *n* corazón *m*; núcleo *m*; **by** ~ de memoria; ~ **attack** ataque cardíaco

**heartburn** (*haat*-böön) *n* acidez *f*

**hearth** (haaz) *n* hogar *m*

**heartless** (*haat*-löss) *adj* insensible

**hearty** (*haa*-ti) *adj* cordial

**heat** (hiit) *n* calor *m*; *v* \*calentar; **heating pad** almohada eléctrica

**heater** (*hii*-tö) *n* calefactor *m*; **immersion** ~ calentador de inmersión

**heath** (hiiz) *n* landa *f*

**heathen** (*hii*-ðön) *n* pagano *m*

**heather** (*hê*-ðö) *n* brezo *m*

**heating** (*hii*-ting) *n* calefacción *f*

**heaven** (*hê*-vön) *n* cielo *m*

**heavy** (*hê*-vi) *adj* pesado

**Hebrew** (*hii*-bruu) *n* hebreo *m*

**hedge** (hêdʒ) *n* seto *m*

**hedgehog** (*hêdʒ*-hogh) *n* erizo *m*

**heel** (hiil) *n* talón *m*; tacón *m*

**height** (hait) *n* altura *f*; colmo *m*, apogeo *m*

**hell** (hêl) *n* infierno *m*

**hello!** (hê-*lou*) ¡hola!; ¡buenos días!

**helm** (hêlm) *n* timón *m*

**helmet** (*hêl*-mit) *n* casco *m*

**helmsman** (*hêlms*-mön) *n* timonero *m*

**help** (hêlp) *v* ayudar; *n* ayuda *f*

**helper** (*hêl*-pö) *n* ayudante *m*

**helpful** (*hêlp*-föl) *adj* servicial

**helping** (*hêl*-ping) *n* porción *f*

**hem** (hêm) *n* dobladillo *m*

**hemp** (hêmp) *n* cáñamo *m*

**hen** (hên) *n* gallina *f*

**henceforth** (hênss-*fooz*) *adv* de ahora en adelante

**her** (höö) *pron* la, le; *adj* su

**herb** (hööb) *n* hierba *f*

**herd** (hööd) *n* manada *f*

**here** (hiᵒ) *adv* acá; ~ **you are** tenga usted

**hereditary** (hi-*rê*-di-tö-ri) *adj* hereditario

**hernia** (*höö*-ni-ö) *n* hernia *f*

**hero** (*hiᵒ*-rou) *n* (pl ~es) héroe *m*

**heron** (*hê*-rön) *n* garza *f*

**herring** (*hê*-ring) *n* (pl ~, ~s) arenque *m*

**herself** (höö-*ssêlf*) *pron* se; ella misma

**hesitate** (*hê*-si-teit) *v* vacilar

**heterosexual** (hê-tö-rö-*ssêk*-ʃu-öl) *adj* heterosexual

**hiccup** (*hi*-kap) *n* hipo *m*

**hide** (haid) *n* piel *f*

\***hide** (haid) *v* esconder

**hideous** (*hi*-di-öss) *adj* horrible

**hierarchy** (*haiᵒ*-raa-ki) *n* jerarquía *f*

**high** (hai) *adj* alto

**highway** (*hai*-ᵘei) *n* carretera *f*; *nAm* autopista *f*

**hijack** (*hai*-dʒæk) *v* apresar

**hijacker** (*hai*-dʒæ-kö) *n* secuestrador *m*

**hike** (haik) *v* caminar

**hill** (hil) *n* colina *f*

**hillside** (*hil*-ssaid) *n* ladera *f*

**hilltop** (*hil*-top) *n* cima *f*

**hilly** (*hi*-li) *adj* montuoso

**him** (him) *pron* le

**himself** (him-*ssêlf*) *pron* se; él mismo

**hinder** (*hin*-dö) *v* \*impedir

**hinge** (hindʒ) *n* bisagra *f*

**hip** (hip) *n* cadera *f*

**hire** (haiᵒ) *v* alquilar; **for** ~ de alquiler

**hire-purchase** (haiᵒ-*pöö*-chöss) *n* compra a plazos

**his** (his) *adj* su

**historian** (hi-*sstoo*-ri-ön) *n* historiador *m*

**historic** (hi-*ssto*-rik) *adj* histórico

**historical** (hi-*ssto*-ri-köl) *adj* histórico

**history** (*hi*-sstö-ri) *n* historia *f*

**hit** (hit) *n* éxito *m*

\***hit** (hit) *v* pegar; tocar, \*acertar

**hitchhike** (*hich*-haik) *v* \*hacer autostop

**hitchhiker** (*hich*-hai-kö) *n* autoestopista *m*

**hoarse** (hooss) *adj* ronco

**hobby** (*ho*-bi) *n* afición *f*

**hobby-horse** (*ho*-bi-hooss) *n* comidilla *f*

**hockey** (*ho*-ki) *n* hockey *m*

**hoist** (hoisst) *v* izar

**hold** (hould) *n* bodega *f*

\***hold** (hould) *v* \*tener; \*retener; ~ **on** agarrarse; ~ **up** \*sostener

**hold-up** (*houl*-dap) *n* atraco *m*

**hole** (houl) *n* bache *m*, agujero *m*

**holiday** (*ho*-lö-di) *n* vacaciones *fpl*; fiesta *f*; ~ **camp** colonia veraniega; ~ **resort** lugar de descanso; **on** ~ de vacaciones

**Holland** (*ho*-lönd) Holanda *f*

**hollow** (*ho*-lou) *adj* hueco

**holy** (*hou*-li) *adj* santo

**homage** (*ho*-midʒ) *n* homenaje *m*

**home** (houm) *n* casa *f*; hospicio *m*; *adv* en casa, a casa; **at** ~ en casa

**home-made** (houm-*meid*) *adj* casero

**homesickness** (*houm*-ssik-nöss) *n* nostalgia *f*

**homosexual** (hou-mö-*ssêk*-ʃu-öl) *adj* homosexual

**honest** (*o*-nisst) *adj* honesto; sincero

**honesty** (*o*-ni-ssti) *n* honradez *f*

**honey** (*ha*-ni) *n* miel *f*

**honeymoon** (*ha*-ni-muun) *n* luna de miel

**honour** (*o*-nö) *n* honor *m*; *v* honrar, *rendir homenaje

**honourable** (*o*-nö-rö-böl) *adj* honorable; honesto

**hood** (hud) *n* capucha *f*; *nAm* capó *m*

**hoof** (huuf) *n* casco *m*

**hook** (huk) *n* gancho *m*

**hoot** (huut) *v* tocar la bocina

**hooter** (*huu*-tö) *n* bocina *f*

**hoover** (*huu*-vö) *v* pasar el aspirador

**hop¹** (hop) *v* brincar; *n* salto *m*

**hop²** (hop) *n* lúpulo *m*

**hope** (houp) *n* esperanza *f*; *v* esperar

**hopeful** (*houp*-föl) *adj* esperanzado

**hopeless** (*houp*-löss) *adj* desesperado

**horizon** (hö-*rai*-sön) *n* horizonte *m*

**horizontal** (ho-ri-*son*-töl) *adj* horizontal

**horn** (hoon) *n* cuerno *m*; bocina *f*

**horrible** (*ho*-ri-böl) *adj* horrible; terrible, atroz

**horror** (*ho*-rö) *n* espanto *m*, horror *m*

**hors-d'œuvre** (oo-*döövr*) *n* entremeses *mpl*

**horse** (hooss) *n* caballo *m*

**horseman** (*hooss*-mön) *n* (pl -men) jinete *m*

**horsepower** (*hooss*-pau⁰) *n* caballo de vapor

**horserace** (*hooss*-reiss) *n* carrera de caballos

**horseradish** (*hooss*-ræ-diʃ) *n* rábano picante

**horseshoe** (*hooss*-ʃuu) *n* herradura *f*

**horticulture** (*hoo*-ti-kal-chö) *n* horticultura *f*

**hosiery** (*hou*-ȝö-ri) *n* géneros de punto

**hospitable** (*ho*-sspi-tö-böl) *adj* hospitalario

**hospital** (*ho*-sspi-töl) *n* hospital *m*

**hospitality** (ho-sspi-*tæ*-lö-ti) *n* hospitalidad *f*

**host** (housst) *n* anfitrión *m*

**hostage** (*ho*-sstidȝ) *n* rehén *m*

**hostel** (*ho*-sstöl) *n* hospedería *f*

**hostess** (*hou*-sstiss) *n* azafata *f*

**hostile** (*ho*-sstail) *adj* hostil

**hot** (hot) *adj* caliente

**hotel** (hou-*têl*) *n* hotel *m*

**hot-tempered** (hot-*têm*-pöd) *adj* colérico

**hour** (au⁰) *n* hora *f*

**hourly** (*au⁰*-li) *adj* a cada hora

**house** (hauss) *n* casa *f*; vivienda *f*; inmueble *m*; ~ **agent** corredor de casas; ~ **block** *Am* manzana de casas; **public** ~ café *m*

**houseboat** (*hauss*-bout) *n* casa flotante

**household** (*hauss*-hould) *n* menaje *m*

**housekeeper** (*hauss*-kii-pö) *n* ama de llaves

**housekeeping** (*hauss*-kii-ping) *n* gobierno de la casa

**housemaid** (*hauss*-meid) *n* criada *f*

**housewife** (*hauss*-ᵘaif) *n* ama de casa

**housework** (*hauss*-ᵘöök) *n* faenas domésticas

**how** (hau) *adv* cómo; qué; ~ **many** cuánto; ~ **much** cuánto

**however** (hau-*ê*-vö) *conj* todavía, sin embargo

**hug** (hagh) *v* abrazar; *n* abrazo *m*

**huge** (hyuudȝ) *adj* formidable, enorme

**hum** (ham) *v* tararear

**human** (*hyuu*-mön) *adj* humano; ~ **being** ser humano

**humanity** (hyu-*mæ*-nö-ti) *n* humanidad *f*

**humble** (*ham*-böl) *adj* humilde

**humid** (*hyuu*-mid) *adj* húmedo

**humidity** (hyu-*mi*-dö-ti) *n* humedad *f*

**humorous** (*hyuu*-mö-röss) *adj* chistoso, gracioso, humorístico

**humour** (*hyuu*-mö) *n* humor *m*

**hundred** (*han*-dröd) *n* ciento

**Hungarian** (hang-*ghê*°-ri-ön) *adj* húngaro

**Hungary** (*hang*-ghö-ri) Hungría *m*

**hunger** (*hang*-ghö) *n* hambre *f*

**hungry** (*hang*-ghri) *adj* hambriento

**hunt** (hant) *v* cazar; *n* caza *f*; ~ **for** buscar

**hunter** (*han*-tö) *n* cazador *m*

**hurricane** (*ha*-ri-kön) *n* huracán *m*; ~ **lamp** lámpara sorda

**hurry** (*ha*-ri) *v* \*darse prisa, apresurarse; *n* prisa *f*; **in a** ~ de prisa

\***hurt** (hööt) *v* \*hacer daño, dañar; ofender

**hurtful** (*hööt*-föl) *adj* perjudicial

**husband** (*has*-bönd) *n* esposo *m*, marido *m*

**hut** (hat) *n* cabaña *f*

**hydrogen** (*hai*-drö-dʒön) *n* hidrógeno *m*

**hygiene** (*hai*-dʒiin) *n* higiene *f*

**hygienic** (hai-*dʒii*-nik) *adj* higiénico

**hymn** (him) *n* himno *m*

**hyphen** (*hai*-fön) *n* guión *m*

**hypocrisy** (hi-*po*-krö-ssi) *n* hipocresía *f*

**hypocrite** (*hi*-pö-krit) *n* hipócrita *m*

**hypocritical** (hi-pö-*kri*-ti-köl) *adj* hipócrita, mojigato

**hysterical** (hi-*sstê*-ri-köl) *adj* histérico

## I

**I** (ai) *pron* yo

**ice** (aiss) *n* hielo *m*

**ice-bag** (*aiss*-bægh) *n* bolsa de hielo

**ice-cream** (*aiss*-kriim) *n* helado *m*

**Iceland** (*aiss*-lönd) Islandia *f*

**Icelander** (*aiss*-lön-dö) *n* islandés *m*

**Icelandic** (aiss-*læn*-dik) *adj* islandés

**icon** (*ai*-kon) *n* icono *m*

**idea** (ai-*di*°) *n* idea *f*; pensamiento *m*; noción *f*, concepto *m*

**ideal** (ai-*di*°l) *adj* ideal; *n* ideal *m*

**identical** (ai-*dên*-ti-köl) *adj* idéntico

**identification** (ai-dên-ti-fi-*kei*-fön) *n* identificación *f*

**identify** (ai-*dên*-ti-fai) *v* identificar

**identity** (ai-*dên*-tö-ti) *n* identidad *f*; ~ **card** carnet de identidad

**idiom** (*i*-di-öm) *n* modismo *m*

**idiomatic** (i-di-ö-*mæ*-tik) *adj* idiomático

**idiot** (*i*-di-öt) *n* idiota *m*

**idiotic** (i-di-*o*-tik) *adj* idiota

**idle** (*ai*-döl) *adj* ocioso; vago; vano

**idol** (*ai*-döl) *n* ídolo *m*

**if** (if) *conj* si

**ignition** (igh-*ni*-fön) *n* encendido *m*; ~ **coil** bobina del encendido

**ignorant** (*igh*-nö-rönt) *adj* ignorante

**ignore** (igh-*noo*) *v* ignorar

**ill** (il) *adj* enfermo; malo; maligno

**illegal** (i-*lii*-ghöl) *adj* ilegal

**illegible** (i-*lê*-dʒö-böl) *adj* ilegible

**illiterate** (i-*li*-tö-röt) *n* analfabeto *m*

**illness** (*il*-nöss) *n* enfermedad *f*

**illuminate** (i-*luu*-mi-neit) *v* iluminar

**illumination** (i-luu-mi-*nei*-fön) *n* iluminación *f*

**illusion** (i-*luu*-ʒön) *n* ilusión *f*

**illustrate** (*i*-lö-sstreit) *v* ilustrar

**illustration** (i-lö-*sstrei*-fön) *n* ilustración *f*

**image** (*i*-midʒ) *n* imagen *f*

**imaginary** (i-*mæ*-dʒi-nö-ri) *adj* imaginario

**imagination** (i-mæ-dʒi-*nei*-fön) *n* imaginación *f*

**imagine** (i-*mæ*-dʒin) *v* imaginarse; figurarse

**imitate** (*i*-mi-teit) *v* imitar

**imitation** (i-mi-*tei*-[ön) *n* imitación *f*

**immediate** (i-*mii*-dyöt) *adj* inmediato

**immediately** (i-*mii*-dyöt-li) *adv* inmediatamente, de inmediato

**immense** (i-*mênss*) *adj* inmenso, enorme

**immigrant** (*i*-mi-ghrönt) *n* inmigrante *m*

**immigrate** (*i*-mi-ghreit) *v* inmigrar

**immigration** (i-mi-*ghrei*-[ön) *n* inmigración *f*

**immodest** (i-*mo*-disst) *adj* inmodesto

**immunity** (i-*myuu*-nö-ti) *n* inmunidad *f*

**immunize** (*i*-myu-nais) *v* inmunizar

**impartial** (im-*paa*-[öl) *adj* imparcial

**impassable** (im-*paa*-ssö-böl) *adj* intransitable

**impatient** (im-*pei*-[önt) *adj* impaciente

**impede** (im-*piid*) *v* *impedir

**impediment** (im-*pê*-di-mönt) *n* impedimento *m*

**imperfect** (im-*pöö*-fikt) *adj* imperfecto

**imperial** (im-*pi*ᵊ-ri-öl) *adj* imperial

**impersonal** (im-*pöö*-ssö-nöl) *adj* impersonal

**impertinence** (im-*pöö*-ti-nönss) *n* impertinencia *f*

**impertinent** (im-*pöö*-ti-nönt) *adj* grosero, descarado, impertinente

**implement**[1] (*im*-pli-mönt) *n* herramienta *f*

**implement**[2] (*im*-pli-mênt) *v* efectuar

**imply** (im-*plai*) *v* implicar

**impolite** (im-pö-*lait*) *adj* descortés

**import**[1] (im-*poot*) *v* importar

**import**[2] (*im*-poot) *n* importación *f*; ~ **duty** impuestos de importación

**importance** (im-*poo*-tönss) *n* importancia *f*

**important** (im-*poo*-tönt) *adj* impor-

tante

**importer** (im-*poo*-tö) *n* importador *m*

**imposing** (im-*pou*-sing) *adj* imponente

**impossible** (im-*po*-ssö-böl) *adj* imposible

**impotence** (*im*-pö-tönss) *n* impotencia *f*

**impotent** (*im*-pö-tönt) *adj* impotente

**impound** (im-*paund*) *v* confiscar

**impress** (im-*prêss*) *v* impresionar

**impression** (im-*prê*-[ön) *n* impresión *f*

**impressive** (im-*prê*-ssiv) *adj* impresionante

**imprison** (im-*pri*-sön) *v* encarcelar

**imprisonment** (im-*pri*-sön-mönt) *n* encarcelamiento *m*

**improbable** (im-*pro*-bö-böl) *adj* improbable

**improper** (im-*pro*-pö) *adj* impropio

**improve** (im-*pruuv*) *v* mejorar

**improvement** (im-*pruuv*-mönt) *n* mejora *f*

**improvise** (*im*-prö-vais) *v* improvisar

**impudent** (*im*-pyu-dönt) *adj* impudente

**impulse** (*im*-palss) *n* impulso *m*; estímulo *m*

**impulsive** (im-*pal*-ssiv) *adj* impulsivo

**in** (in) *prep* en; dentro de; *adv* adentro

**inaccessible** (i-næk-*ssê*-ssö-böl) *adj* inaccesible

**inaccurate** (i-*næ*-kyu-röt) *adj* inexacto

**inadequate** (i-*næ*-di-kᵘöt) *adj* inadecuado

**incapable** (ing-*kei*-pö-böl) *adj* incapaz

**incense** (*in*-ssênss) *n* incienso *m*

**incident** (*in*-ssi-dönt) *n* incidente *m*

**incidental** (in-ssi-*dên*-töl) *adj* imprevisto

**incite** (in-*ssait*) *v* incitar

**inclination** (ing-kli-*nei*-[ön) *n* inclinación *f*

**incline** (ing-*klain*) *n* inclinación *f*

**inclined** (ing-*klaind*) *adj* dispuesto, inclinado; *be ~ to *v* inclinarse
**include** (ing-*kluud*) *v* *incluir
**inclusive** (ing-*kluu*-ssiv) *adj* incluso
**income** (*ing*-köm) *n* ingresos *mpl*
**income-tax** (*ing*-köm-tækss) *n* impuesto sobre los ingresos
**incompetent** (ing-*kom*-pö-tönt) *adj* incompetente
**incomplete** (in-köm-*pliit*) *adj* incompleto
**inconceivable** (ing-kön-*ssii*-vö-böl) *adj* inconcebible
**inconspicuous** (ing-kön-*sspi*-kyu-öss) *adj* discreto
**inconvenience** (ing-kön-*vii*-nyönss) *n* incomodidad *f*, inconveniencia *f*
**inconvenient** (ing-kön-*vii*-nyönt) *adj* inoportuno; molesto
**incorrect** (ing-kö-*rêkt*) *adj* inexacto, incorrecto
**increase¹** (ing-*kriiss*) *v* aumentar; incrementar, *acrecentarse
**increase²** (*ing*-kriiss) *n* aumento *m*
**incredible** (ing-*krê*-dö-böl) *adj* increíble
**incurable** (ing-*kyuᵒ*-rö-böl) *adj* incurable
**indecent** (in-*dii*-ssönt) *adj* indecente
**indeed** (in-*diid*) *adv* por cierto
**indefinite** (in-*dê*-fi-nit) *adj* indefinido
**indemnity** (in-*dêm*-nö-ti) *n* indemnización *f*
**independence** (in-di-*pên*-dönss) *n* independencia *f*
**independent** (in-di-*pên*-dönt) *adj* independiente; autónomo
**index** (*in*-dêkss) *n* índice *m*; ~ **finger** índice *m*
**India** (*in*-di-ö) India *f*
**Indian** (*in*-di-ön) *adj* indio; *n* indio *m*
**indicate** (*in*-di-keit) *v* señalar, indicar
**indication** (in-di-*kei*-ʃön) *n* señal *f*, indicación *f*

**indicator** (*in*-di-kei-tö) *n* indicador *m*
**indifferent** (in-*di*-fö-rönt) *adj* indiferente
**indigestion** (in-di-*dʒêss*-chön) *n* indigestión *f*
**indignation** (in-digh-*nei*-ʃön) *n* indignación *f*
**indirect** (in-di-*rêkt*) *adj* indirecto
**individual** (in-di-*vi*-dʒu-öl) *adj* aparte, individual; *n* individuo *m*
**Indonesia** (in-dö-*nii*-si-ö) Indonesia *f*
**Indonesian** (in-dö-*nii*-si-ön) *adj* indonesio
**indoor** (*in*-doo) *adj* en casa
**indoors** (in-*doos*) *adv* en casa
**indulge** (in-*daldʒ*) *v* ceder
**industrial** (in-*da*-sstri-öl) *adj* industrial; ~ **area** zona industrial
**industrious** (in-*da*-sstri-öss) *adj* diligente
**industry** (*in*-dö-sstri) *n* industria *f*
**inedible** (i-*nê*-di-böl) *adj* incomible
**inefficient** (i-ni-*fi*-ʃönt) *adj* ineficiente
**inevitable** (i-*nê*-vi-tö-böl) *adj* inevitable
**inexpensive** (i-nik-*sspên*-ssiv) *adj* barato
**inexperienced** (i-nik-*sspiᵒ*-ri-önsst) *adj* inexperto
**infant** (*in*-fönt) *n* criatura *f*
**infantry** (*in*-fön-tri) *n* infantería *f*
**infect** (in-*fêkt*) *v* infectar
**infection** (in-*fêk*-ʃön) *n* infección *f*
**infectious** (in-*fêk*-ʃöss) *adj* contagioso
**infer** (in-*föö*) *v* *deducir
**inferior** (in-*fiᵒ*-ri-ö) *adj* inferior
**infinite** (*in*-fi-nöt) *adj* infinito
**infinitive** (in-*fi*-ni-tiv) *n* infinitivo *m*
**infirmary** (in-*föö*-mö-ri) *n* enfermería *f*
**inflammable** (in-*flæ*-mö-böl) *adj* inflamable
**inflammation** (in-flö-*mei*-ʃön) *n* inflamación *f*

**inflatable** (in-*flei*-tö-böl) *adj* inflable
**inflate** (in-*fleit*) *v* hinchar
**inflation** (in-*flei*-ʃön) *n* inflación *f*
**influence** (*in*-flu-önss) *n* influencia *f*; *v* *influir
**influential** (in-flu-*én*-ʃöl) *adj* influyente
**influenza** (in-flu-*én*-sö) *n* gripe *f*
**inform** (in-*foom*) *v* informar; comunicar
**informal** (in-*foo*-möl) *adj* informal
**information** (in-fö-*mei*-ʃön) *n* información *f*; informes *mpl*, comunicado *m*; ~ **bureau** oficina de informaciones
**infra-red** (in-frö-*rêd*) *adj* infrarrojo
**infrequent** (in-*frii*-kʷönt) *adj* infrecuente
**ingredient** (ing-*ghrii*-di-önt) *n* ingrediente *m*
**inhabit** (in-*hæ*-bit) *v* habitar
**inhabitable** (in-*hæ*-bi-tö-böl) *adj* habitable
**inhabitant** (in-*hæ*-bi-tönt) *n* habitante *m*
**inhale** (in-*heil*) *v* inhalar
**inherit** (in-*hê*-rit) *v* heredar
**inheritance** (in-*hê*-ri-tönss) *n* herencia *f*
**initial** (i-*ni*-ʃöl) *adj* inicial; *n* inicial *f*; *v* rubricar
**initiative** (i-*ni*-ʃö-tiv) *n* iniciativa *f*
**inject** (in-*dʒêkt*) *v* inyectar
**injection** (in-*dʒêk*-ʃön) *n* inyección *f*
**injure** (*in*-dʒö) *v* *herir; ofender
**injury** (*in*-dʒö-ri) *n* herida *f*; lesión *f*
**injustice** (in-*dʒa*-sstiss) *n* injusticia *f*
**ink** (ingk) *n* tinta *f*
**inlet** (*in*-lêt) *n* ensenada *f*
**inn** (in) *n* posada *f*
**inner** (*i*-nö) *adj* interior; ~ **tube** cámara de aire
**inn-keeper** (*in*-kii-pö) *n* posadero *m*
**innocence** (*i*-nö-ssönss) *n* inocencia *f*

**innocent** (*i*-nö-ssönt) *adj* inocente
**inoculate** (i-*no*-kyu-leit) *v* vacunar
**inoculation** (i-no-kyu-*lei*-ʃön) *n* inoculación *f*
**inquire** (ing-kʷ*ai*ö) *v* informarse, *pedir informes
**inquiry** (ing-kʷ*ai*ö-ri) *n* pregunta *f*, indagación *f*; encuesta *f*; ~ **office** oficina de informaciones
**inquisitive** (ing-kʷ*i*-sö-tiv) *adj* curioso
**insane** (in-*ssein*) *adj* lunático
**inscription** (in-*sskrip*-ʃön) *n* inscripción *f*
**insect** (*in*-ssêkt) *n* insecto *m*; ~ **repellent** insectífugo *m*
**insecticide** (in-*ssêk*-ti-ssaid) *n* insecticida *m*
**insensitive** (in-*ssên*-ssö-tiv) *adj* insensible
**insert** (in-*ssööt*) *v* insertar
**inside** (in-*ssaid*) *n* interior *m*; *adj* interior; *adv* adentro; *prep* en, dentro de; ~ **out** al revés; **insides** entrañas *fpl*
**insight** (*in*-ssait) *n* entendimiento *m*
**insignificant** (in-ssigh-*ni*-fi-könt) *adj* insignificante; irrelevante; baladí
**insist** (in-*ssisst*) *v* insistir; persistir
**insolence** (*in*-ssö-lönss) *n* insolencia *f*
**insolent** (*in*-ssö-lönt) *adj* insolente
**insomnia** (in-*ssom*-ni-ö) *n* insomnio *m*
**inspect** (in-*sspêkt*) *v* inspeccionar
**inspection** (in-*sspêk*-ʃön) *n* inspección *f*; control *m*
**inspector** (in-*sspêk*-tö) *n* inspector *m*
**inspire** (in-*sspai*ö) *v* inspirar
**install** (in-*sstool*) *v* instalar
**installation** (in-sstö-*lei*-ʃön) *n* instalación *f*
**instalment** (in-*sstool*-mönt) *n* plazo *m*
**instance** (*in*-sstönss) *n* ejemplo *m*; caso *m*; **for ~** por ejemplo
**instant** (*in*-sstönt) *n* instante *m*

**instantly** (*in*-sstönt-li) *adv* instantáneamente, inmediatamente, al instante

**instead of** (in-*sstêd* ov) en lugar de

**instinct** (*in*-sstingkt) *n* instinto *m*

**institute** (*in*-ssti-tyuut) *n* instituto *m*; institución *f*; *v* \*instituir

**institution** (in-ssti-*tyuu*-ʃön) *n* instituto *m*, institución *f*

**instruct** (in-*sstrakt*) *v* \*instruir

**instruction** (in-*sstrak*-ʃön) *n* instrucción *f*

**instructive** (in-*sstrak*-tiv) *adj* instructivo

**instructor** (in-*sstrak*-tö) *n* instructor *m*

**instrument** (*in*-sstru-mönt) *n* instrumento *m*; **musical ~** instrumento músico

**insufficient** (in-ssö-*fi*-ʃönt) *adj* insuficiente

**insulate** (*in*-ssyu-leit) *v* aislar

**insulation** (in-ssyu-*lei*-ʃön) *n* aislamiento *m*

**insulator** (*in*-ssyu-lei-tö) *n* aislador *m*

**insult**[1] (in-*ssalt*) *v* insultar

**insult**[2] (*in*-ssalt) *n* insulto *m*

**insurance** (in-*ʃuᵒ*-rönss) *n* seguro *m*; **~ policy** póliza de seguro

**insure** (in-*ʃuᵒ*) *v* asegurar

**intact** (in-*tækt*) *adj* intacto

**intellect** (*in*-tö-lêkt) *n* intelecto *m*

**intellectual** (in-tö-*lêk*-chu-öl) *adj* intelectual

**intelligence** (in-*tê*-li-dʒönss) *n* inteligencia *f*

**intelligent** (in-*tê*-li-dʒönt) *adj* inteligente

**intend** (in-*tênd*) *v* intentar, \*tener la intención de

**intense** (in-*tênss*) *adj* intenso

**intention** (in-*tên*-ʃön) *n* intención *f*

**intentional** (in-*tên*-ʃö-nöl) *adj* intencional

**intercourse** (*in*-tö-kooss) *n* trato *m*

**interest** (*in*-trösst) *n* interés *m*; rédito *m*; *v* interesar

**interesting** (*in*-trö-ssting) *adj* interesante

**interfere** (in-tö-*fiᵒ*) *v* interferir; **~ with** mezclarse en

**interference** (in-tö-*fiᵒ*-rönss) *n* interferencia *f*

**interim** (*in*-tö-rim) *n* ínterin *m*

**interior** (in-*tiᵒ*-ri-ö) *n* interior *m*

**interlude** (*in*-tö-luud) *n* intermedio *m*

**intermediary** (in-tö-*mii*-dyö-ri) *n* intermediario *m*

**intermission** (in-tö-*mi*-ʃön) *n* entreacto *m*

**internal** (in-*töö*-nöl) *adj* interno

**international** (in-tö-*næ*-ʃö-nöl) *adj* internacional

**interpret** (in-*töö*-prit) *v* interpretar

**interpreter** (in-*töö*-pri-tö) *n* intérprete *m*

**interrogate** (in-*tê*-rö-gheit) *v* interrogar

**interrogation** (in-tê-rö-*ghei*-ʃön) *n* interrogatorio *m*

**interrogative** (in-tö-*ro*-ghö-tiv) *adj* interrogativo

**interrupt** (in-tö-*rapt*) *v* interrumpir

**interruption** (in-tö-*rap*-ʃön) *n* interrupción *f*

**intersection** (in-tö-*ssêk*-ʃön) *n* intersección *f*

**interval** (*in*-tö-völ) *n* intervalo *m*

**intervene** (in-tö-*viin*) *v* \*intervenir

**interview** (*in*-tö-vyuu) *n* entrevista *f*

**intestine** (in-*tê*-sstin) *n* intestino *m*

**intimate** (*in*-ti-möt) *adj* íntimo

**into** (*in*-tu) *prep* dentro de

**intolerable** (in-*to*-lö-rö-böl) *adj* insoportable

**intoxicated** (in-*tok*-ssi-kei-tid) *adj* embriagado

**intrigue** (in-*triigh*) *n* intriga *f*

**introduce** (in-trö-*dyuuss*) *v* presentar; *introducir

**introduction** (in-trö-*dak*-ʃön) *n* presentación *f*; introducción *f*

**invade** (in-*veid*) *v* invadir

**invalid**[1] (*in*-vö-liid) *n* inválido *m*; *adj* inválido

**invalid**[2] (in-*væ*-lid) *adj* nulo

**invasion** (in-*vei*-ʒön) *n* irrupción *f*, invasión *f*

**invent** (in-*vênt*) *v* inventar

**invention** (in-*vên*-ʃön) *n* invención *f*

**inventive** (in-*vên*-tiv) *adj* inventivo

**inventor** (in-*vên*-tö) *n* inventor *m*

**inventory** (*in*-vön-tri) *n* inventario *m*

**invert** (in-*vööt*) *v* *invertir

**invest** (in-*vêsst*) *v* *invertir

**investigate** (in-*vê*-ssti-gheit) *v* investigar

**investigation** (in-vê-ssti-*ghei*-ʃön) *n* investigación *f*

**investment** (in-*vêsst*-mönt) *n* inversión *f*

**investor** (in-*vê*-sstö) *n* inversionista *m*

**invisible** (in-*vi*-sö-böl) *adj* invisible

**invitation** (in-vi-*tei*-ʃön) *n* invitación *f*

**invite** (in-*vait*) *v* invitar, convidar

**invoice** (*in*-voiss) *n* factura *f*

**involve** (in-*volv*) *v* *envolver; **involved** implicado

**inwards** (*in*-ᵘöds) *adv* hacia adentro

**iodine** (*ai*-ö-diin) *n* yodo *m*

**Iran** (i-*raan*) Irán *m*

**Iranian** (i-*rei*-ni-ön) *adj* iraní

**Iraq** (i-*raak*) Irak *m*

**Iraqi** (i-*raa*-ki) *adj* iraquí

**irascible** (i-*ræ*-ssi-böl) *adj* irascible

**Ireland** (*aiᵒ*-lönd) Irlanda *f*

**Irish** (*aiᵒ*-riʃ) *adj* irlandés

**Irishman** (*aiᵒ*-riʃ-mön) *n* (pl -men) irlandés *m*

**iron** (*ai*-ön) *n* hierro *m*; plancha *f*; de hierro; *v* planchar

**ironical** (ai-*ro*-ni-köl) *adj* irónico

**ironworks** (*ai*-ön-ᵘöökss) *n* herrería *f*

**irony** (*aiᵒ*-rö-ni) *n* ironía *f*

**irregular** (i-*rê*-ghyu-lö) *adj* irregular

**irreparable** (i-*rê*-pö-rö-böl) *adj* irreparable

**irrevocable** (i-*rê*-vö-kö-böl) *adj* irrevocable

**irritable** (*i*-ri-tö-böl) *adj* irritable

**irritate** (*i*-ri-teit) *v* irritar

**is** (is) *v* (pr be)

**island** (*ai*-lönd) *n* isla *f*

**isolate** (*ai*-ssö-leit) *v* aislar

**isolation** (ai-ssö-*lei*-ʃön) *n* aislamiento *m*

**Israel** (*is*-reil) Israel *m*

**Israeli** (is-*rei*-li) *adj* israelí

**issue** (*i*-ʃuu) *v* *distribuir; *n* emisión *f*, tirada *f*, edición *f*; cuestión *f*, punto *m*; consecuencia *f*, resultado *m*, conclusión *f*, término *m*; salida *f*

**isthmus** (*iss*-möss) *n* istmo *m*

**it** (it) *pron* lo

**Italian** (i-*tæl*-yön) *adj* italiano

**italics** (i-*tæ*-likss) *pl* cursiva *f*

**Italy** (*i*-tö-li) Italia *f*

**itch** (ich) *n* picazón *f*; prurito *m*; *v* picar

**item** (*ai*-töm) *n* ítem *m*; punto *m*

**itinerant** (ai-*ti*-nö-rönt) *adj* ambulante

**itinerary** (ai-*ti*-nö-rö-ri) *n* itinerario *m*

**ivory** (*ai*-vö-ri) *n* marfil *m*

**ivy** (*ai*-vi) *n* hiedra *f*

# J

**jack** (dʒæk) *n* gato *m*

**jacket** (*dʒæ*-kit) *n* americana *f*, chaqueta *f*; sobrecubierta *f*; saco *m*Me

**jade** (dʒeid) *n* jade *m*

**jail** (dʒeil) *n* cárcel *f*

**jailer** (*dʒei*-lö) *n* carcelero *m*

**jam** (dʒæm) *n* mermelada *f*; congestión *f*

**janitor** (*dʒæ*-ni-tö) *n* conserje *m*

**January** (*dʒæ*-nyu-ö-ri) enero

**Japan** (dʒö-*pæn*) Japón *m*

**Japanese** (dʒæ-pö-*niis*) *adj* japonés

**jar** (dʒaa) *n* jarra *f*

**jaundice** (*dʒoon*-diss) *n* ictericia *f*

**jaw** (dʒoo) *n* mandíbula *f*

**jealous** (*dʒê*-löss) *adj* celoso

**jealousy** (*dʒê*-lö-ssi) *n* celos

**jeans** (dʒiins) *pl* vaqueros *mpl*

**jelly** (*dʒê*-li) *n* jalea *f*

**jelly-fish** (*dʒê*-li-fiʃ) *n* medusa *f*

**jersey** (*dʒöö*-si) *n* jersey *m*

**jet** (dʒêt) *n* chorro *m*; avión a reacción

**jetty** (*dʒê*-ti) *n* muelle *m*

**Jew** (dʒuu) *n* judío *m*

**jewel** (*dʒuu*-öl) *n* joya *f*

**jeweller** (*dʒuu*-ö-lö) *n* joyero *m*

**jewellery** (*dʒuu*-öl-ri) *n* joyería *f*

**Jewish** (*dʒuu*-iʃ) *adj* judío

**job** (dʒob) *n* tarea *f*; puesto *m*, empleo *m*

**jockey** (*dʒo*-ki) *n* jockey *m*

**join** (dʒoin) *v* juntar; unirse a, asociarse a; ensamblar, reunir

**joint** (dʒoint) *n* articulación *f*; soldadura *f*; *adj* unido, en común

**jointly** (*dʒoint*-li) *adv* juntamente

**joke** (dʒouk) *n* broma *f*

**jolly** (*dʒo*-li) *adj* jovial

**Jordan** (*dʒoo*-dön) Jordania *f*

**Jordanian** (dʒoo-*dei*-ni-ön) *adj* jordano

**journal** (*dʒöö*-nöl) *n* revista *f*

**journalism** (*dʒöö*-nö-li-söm) *n* periodismo *m*

**journalist** (*dʒöö*-nö-lisst) *n* periodista *m*

**journey** (*dʒöö*-ni) *n* viaje *m*

**joy** (dʒoi) *n* delicia *f*, regocijo *m*

**joyful** (*dʒoi*-föl) *adj* contento, alegre

**jubilee** (*dʒuu*-bi-lii) *n* aniversario *m*

**judge** (dʒadʒ) *n* juez *m*; *v* juzgar

**judgment** (*dʒadʒ*-mönt) *n* juicio *m*

**jug** (dʒagh) *n* cántaro *m*

**Jugoslav** (yuu-ghö-*sslaav*) *adj* yugoslavo

**Jugoslavia** (yuu-ghö-*sslaa*-vi-ö) Yugoslavia *f*

**juice** (dʒuuss) *n* zumo *m*

**juicy** (*dʒuu*-ssi) *adj* zumoso

**July** (dʒu-*lai*) julio

**jump** (dʒamp) *v* saltar; *n* salto *m*

**jumper** (*dʒam*-pö) *n* jersey *m*

**junction** (*dʒangk*-jön) *n* encrucijada *f*; empalme *m*

**June** (dʒuun) junio

**jungle** (*dʒang*-ghöl) *n* selva *f*, jungla *f*

**junior** (*dʒuu*-nyö) *adj* menor

**junk** (dʒangk) *n* cachivache *m*

**jury** (*dʒuᵒ*-ri) *n* jurado *m*

**just** (dʒasst) *adj* justo; *adv* apenas; justamente

**justice** (*dʒa*-sstiss) *n* derecho *m*; justicia *f*

**juvenile** (*dʒuu*-vö-nail) *adj* juvenil

# K

**kangaroo** (kæng-ghö-*ruu*) *n* canguro *m*

**keel** (kiil) *n* quilla *f*

**keen** (kiin) *adj* entusiasta; agudo

*keep** (kiip) *v* *tener; guardar; continuar; ~ **away from** *mantenerse alejado de; ~ **off** no tocar; ~ **on** continuar; ~ **quiet** *estarse quieto; ~ **up** perseverar; ~ **up with** *seguir el paso

**keg** (kêgh) *n* barrilete *m*

**kennel** (*kê*-nöl) *n* perrera *f*; perrera *m*

**Kenya** (*kê*-nyö) Kenya *m*

**kerosene** (*ké*-rö-ssiin) *n* petróleo lampante

**kettle** (*ké*-töl) *n* olla *f*

**key** (kii) *n* llave *f*

**keyhole** (*kii*-houl) *n* ojo de la cerradura

**khaki** (*kaa*-ki) *n* caqui *m*

**kick** (kik) *v* patear; *n* patada *f*

**kick-off** (ki-*kof*) *n* saque inicial

**kid** (kid) *n* niño *m*, chico *m*; cabritilla *f*; *v* embromar

**kidney** (*kid*-ni) *n* riñón *m*

**kill** (kil) *v* matar

**kilogram** (*ki*-lö-ghræm) *n* kilogramo *m*

**kilometre** (*ki*-lö-mii-tö) *n* kilómetro *m*

**kind** (kaind) *adj* amable, bondadoso; bueno; *n* género *m*

**kindergarten** (*kin*-dö-ghaa-tön) *n* escuela de párvulos, jardín de infancia

**king** (king) *n* rey *m*

**kingdom** (*king*-döm) *n* reino *m*

**kiosk** (*kii*-ossk) *n* quiosco *m*

**kiss** (kiss) *n* beso *m*; *v* besar

**kit** (kit) *n* avíos *mpl*

**kitchen** (*ki*-chin) *n* cocina *f*; ~ **garden** huerto *m*

**Kleenex**® (*klii*-nêkss) *n* pañuelo de papel

**knapsack** (*næp*-ssæk) *n* mochila *f*

**knave** (neiv) *n* sota *f*

**knee** (nii) *n* rodilla *f*

**kneecap** (*nii*-kæp) *n* rótula *f*

**\*kneel** (niil) *v* arrodillarse

**knew** (nyuu) *v* (p know)

**knickers** (*ni*-kös) *pl* braga *f*

**knife** (naif) *n* (pl knives) cuchillo *m*

**knight** (nait) *n* caballero *m*

**\*knit** (nit) *v* \*hacer punto

**knob** (nob) *n* botón *m*

**knock** (nok) *v* golpear; *n* golpe *m*; ~ **against** chocar contra; ~ **down** derribar

**knot** (not) *n* nudo *m*; *v* anudar

**\*know** (nou) *v* \*saber, \*conocer

**knowledge** (*no*-lidʒ) *n* conocimiento *m*

**knuckle** (*na*-köl) *n* nudillo *m*

# L

**label** (*lei*-böl) *n* rótulo *m*; *v* rotular

**laboratory** (lö-*bo*-rö-tö-ri) *n* laboratorio *m*

**labour** (*lei*-bö) *n* trabajo *m*, labor *f*; dolores *mpl*; *v* ajetrearse, bregar; **labor permit** *Am* permiso de trabajo

**labourer** (*lei*-bö-rö) *n* obrero *m*

**labour-saving** (*lei*-bö-ssei-ving) *adj* economizador de trabajo

**labyrinth** (*læ*-bö-rinz) *n* laberinto *m*

**lace** (leiss) *n* puntilla *f*; cordón *m*

**lacquer** (*læ*-kö) *n* laca *f*

**lad** (læd) *n* joven *m*, muchacho *m*

**ladder** (*læ*-dö) *n* escalera de mano

**lady** (*lei*-di) *n* señora *f*; **ladies' room** lavabos para señoras

**lagoon** (lö-*ghuun*) *n* laguna *f*

**lake** (leik) *n* lago *m*

**lamb** (læm) *n* cordero *m*

**lame** (leim) *adj* paralítico, cojo

**lamentable** (*læ*-mön-tö-böl) *adj* lamentable

**lamp** (læmp) *n* lámpara *f*

**lamp-post** (*læmp*-pousst) *n* poste de farol

**lampshade** (*læmp*-ʃeid) *n* pantalla *f*

**land** (lænd) *n* país *m*, tierra *f*; *v* aterrizar; desembarcar

**landlady** (*lænd*-lei-di) *n* patrona *f*

**landlord** (*lænd*-lood) *n* propietario *m*, dueño *m*; patrón *m*

**landmark** (*lænd*-maak) *n* punto de re-

ferencia; mojón *m*
**landscape** (*lænd*-sskeip) *n* paisaje *m*
**lane** (lein) *n* callejón *m*; pista *f*
**language** (*læng*- gh^u idʒ) *n* lengua *f*; ~
  **laboratory** laboratorio de lenguas
**lantern** (*læn*-tön) *n* linterna *f*
**lapel** (lö-*pêl*) *n* solapa *f*
**larder** (*laa*-dö) *n* despensa *f*
**large** (laadʒ) *adj* grande; espacioso
**lark** (laak) *n* alondra *f*
**laryngitis** (læ-rin-*dʒai*-tiss) *n* laringitis
  *f*
**last** (laasst) *adj* último; precedente; *v*
  durar; **at** ~ al fin; al final
**lasting** (*laa*-ssting) *adj* duradero
**latchkey** (*læch*-kii) *n* llave de la casa
**late** (leit) *adj* tardío; retrasado
**lately** (*leit*-li) *adv* últimamente, recientemente
**lather** (*laa*-ðö) *n* espuma *f*
**Latin America** (*læ*-tin ö-*mê*-ri-kö)
  América Latina
**Latin-American** (læ-tin-ö-*mê*-ri-kön)
  *adj* latinoamericano
**latitude** (*læ*-ti-tyuud) *n* latitud *f*
**laugh** (laaf) *v* *reír; *n* risa *f*
**laughter** (*laaf*-tö) *n* risa *f*
**launch** (loonch) *v* lanzar; *n* buque a
  motor
**launching** (*loon*-ching) *n* botadura *f*
**launderette** (loon-dö-*rêt*) *n* lavandería
  de autoservicio
**laundry** (*loon*-dri) *n* lavandería *f*; ropa sucia
**lavatory** (*læ*-vö-tö-ri) *n* cuarto de aseo
**lavish** (*læ*-viʃ) *adj* pródigo
**law** (loo) *n* ley *f*; derecho *m*; ~
  **court** tribunal *m*
**lawful** (*loo*-föl) *adj* lícito
**lawn** (loon) *n* césped *m*
**lawsuit** (*loo*-ssuut) *n* proceso *m*, causa *f*
**lawyer** (*loo*-yö) *n* abogado *m*; jurista
  *m*

**laxative** (*læk*-ssö-tiv) *n* laxante *m*
* **lay** (lei) *v* colocar, *poner; ~ **bricks**
  mampostear
**layer** (lei^ö) *n* capa *f*
**layman** (*lei*-mön) *n* profano *m*
**lazy** (*lei*-si) *adj* perezoso
**lead**[1] (liid) *n* ventaja *f*; dirección *f*;
  trailla *f*
**lead**[2] (lêd) *n* plomo *m*
* **lead** (liid) *v* *conducir
**leader** (*lii*-dö) *n* jefe *m*, líder *m*
**leadership** (*lii*-dö-ʃip) *n* dirección *f*
**leading** (*lii*-ding) *adj* dominante, principal
**leaf** (liif) *n* (pl leaves) hoja *f*
**league** (liigh) *n* liga *f*
**leak** (liik) *v* gotear; *n* goteo *m*
**leaky** (*lii*-ki) *adj* que tiene escapes
**lean** (liin) *adj* magro
* **lean** (liin) *v* apoyarse
**leap** (liip) *n* salto *m*
* **leap** (liip) *v* saltar
**leap-year** (*liip*-yi^ö) *n* año bisiesto
* **learn** (löön) *v* aprender
**learner** (*löö*-nö) *n* principiante *m*
**lease** (liiss) *n* contrato de arrendamiento; arrendamiento *m*; *v*
  *arrendar, alquilar
**leash** (liiʃ) *n* correa *f*
**least** (liisst) *adj* mínimo, menos; **at** ~
  por lo menos
**leather** (*lê*-ðö) *n* cuero *m*; de piel
**leave** (liiv) *n* licencia *f*
* **leave** (liiv) *v* partir, dejar; ~ **out**
  omitir
**Lebanese** (lê-bö-*niis*) *adj* libanés
**Lebanon** (*lê*-bö-nön) Líbano *m*
**lecture** (*lêk*-chö) *n* curso *m*, conferencia *f*
**left**[1] (lêft) *adj* izquierdo
**left**[2] (lêft) *v* (p, pp leave)
**left-hand** (*lêft*-hænd) *adj* izquierdo, de
  izquierda
**left-handed** (lêft-*hæn*-did) *adj* zurdo

**leg** (lêgh) *n* pata *f*, pierna *f*

**legacy** (*lê*-ghö-ssi) *n* herencia *f*

**legal** (*lii*-ghöl) *adj* legítimo, legal; jurídico

**legalization** (lii-ghö-lai-*sei*-fön) *n* legalización *f*

**legation** (li-*ghei*-fön) *n* legación *f*

**legible** (*lê*-dʒi-böl) *adj* legible

**legitimate** (li-*dʒi*-ti-möt) *adj* legítimo

**leisure** (*lê*-ʒö) *n* ocio *m*; comodidad *f*

**lemon** (*lê*-mön) *n* limón *m*

**lemonade** (lê-mö-*neid*) *n* limonada *f*

**\*lend** (lênd) *v* prestar

**length** (lêngz) *n* longitud *f*

**lengthen** (*lêng*-zön) *v* alargar

**lengthways** (*lêngz*-ᵘeis) *adv* longitudinalmente

**lens** (lêns) *n* lente *m/f*; **telephoto ~** teleobjetivo *m*; **zoom ~** lente de foco regulable

**leprosy** (*lê*-prö-ssi) *n* lepra *f*

**less** (lêss) *adv* menos

**lessen** (*lê*-ssön) *v* \*disminuir

**lesson** (*lê*-ssön) *n* lección *f*

**\*let** (lêt) *v* dejar; alquilar; **~ down** decepcionar

**letter** (*lê*-tö) *n* carta *f*; letra *f*; **~ of credit** carta de crédito; **~ of recommendation** carta de recomendación

**letter-box** (*lê*-tö-bokss) *n* buzón *m*

**lettuce** (*lê*-tiss) *n* lechuga *f*

**level** (*lê*-völ) *adj* igual; plano, llano; *n* nivel *m*; *v* igualar, nivelar; **~ crossing** paso a nivel

**lever** (*lii*-vö) *n* palanca *f*

**Levis** (*lii*-vais) *pl* jeans *mpl*

**liability** (lai-ö-*bi*-lö-ti) *n* responsabilidad *f*

**liable** (*lai*-ö-böl) *adj* responsable; **~ to** sujeto a

**liberal** (*li*-bö-röl) *adj* liberal; generoso, dadivoso

**liberation** (li-bö-*rei*-fön) *n* liberación *f*

**Liberia** (lai-*bi*ᵒ-ri-ö) Liberia *f*

**Liberian** (lai-*bi*ᵒ-ri-ön) *adj* liberiano

**liberty** (*li*-bö-ti) *n* libertad *f*

**library** (*lai*-brö-ri) *n* biblioteca *f*

**licence** (*lai*-ssönss) *n* licencia *f*; permiso *m*; **driving ~** permiso de conducir

**license** (*lai*-ssönss) *v* autorizar

**lick** (lik) *v* lamer

**lid** (lid) *n* tapa *f*

**lie** (lai) *v* \*mentir; *n* mentira *f*

**\*lie** (lai) *v* \*yacer; **~ down** \*tenderse

**life** (laif) *n* (pl lives) vida *f*; **~ insurance** seguro de vida

**lifebelt** (*laif*-bêlt) *n* chaleco salvavidas

**lifetime** (*laif*-taim) *n* vida *f*

**lift** (lift) *v* levantar; *n* ascensor *m*; elevador *mMe*

**light** (lait) *n* luz *f*; *adj* ligero; pálido; **~ bulb** bulbo *m*

**\*light** (lait) *v* \*encender

**lighter** (*lai*-tö) *n* encendedor *m*

**lighthouse** (*lait*-hauss) *n* faro *m*

**lighting** (*lai*-ting) *n* alumbrado *m*

**lightning** (*lait*-ning) *n* relámpago *m*

**like** (laik) *v* \*querer; gustar; *adj* semejante; *conj* como

**likely** (*lai*-kli) *adj* probable

**like-minded** (laik-*main*-did) *adj* unánime

**likewise** (*laik*-ᵘais) *adv* así también, asimismo

**lily** (*li*-li) *n* azucena *f*

**limb** (lim) *n* miembro *m*

**lime** (laim) *n* cal *f*; tilo *m*; lima *f*

**limetree** (*laim*-trii) *n* tilo *m*

**limit** (*li*-mit) *n* límite *m*; *v* limitar

**limp** (limp) *v* cojear; *adj* inerte

**line** (lain) *n* renglón *m*; raya *f*; cordón *m*; línea *f*; cola *f*

**linen** (*li*-nin) *n* lino *m*; ropa blanca

**liner** (*lai*-nö) *n* vapor de línea

**lingerie** (*long*-ʒö-rii) *n* ropa interior de

mujer

**lining** (*lai*-ning) *n* forro *m*

**link** (lingk) *v* enlazar; *n* enlace *m*; eslabón *m*

**lion** (*lai*-ön) *n* león *m*

**lip** (lip) *n* labio *m*

**lipsalve** (*lip*-ssaav) *n* manteca de cacao

**lipstick** (*lip*-sstik) *n* lápiz labial

**liqueur** (li-*kyu*ᵒ) *n* licor *m*

**liquid** (*li*-kᵘid) *adj* líquido; *n* líquido *m*

**liquor** (*li*-kö) *n* bebidas alcohólicas

**liquorice** (*li*-kö-riss) *n* regaliz *m*

**list** (lisst) *n* lista *f*; *v* inscribir

**listen** (*li*-ssön) *v* escuchar

**listener** (*liss*-nö) *n* oyente *m*

**literary** (*li*-trö-ri) *adj* literario

**literature** (*li*-trö-chö) *n* literatura *f*

**litre** (*lii*-tö) *n* litro *m*

**litter** (*li*-tö) *n* desperdicio *m*; trastos *mpl*; lechigada *f*

**little** (*li*-töl) *adj* pequeño; poco

**live**¹ (liv) *v* vivir

**live**² (laiv) *adj* vivo

**livelihood** (*laiv*-li-hud) *n* sustento *m*

**lively** (*laiv*-li) *adj* vivo

**liver** (*li*-vö) *n* hígado *m*

**living-room** (*li*-ving-ruum) *n* sala de estar, living *m*

**load** (loud) *n* carga *f*; fardo *m*; *v* cargar

**loaf** (louf) *n* (pl loaves) pan *m*

**loan** (loun) *n* préstamo *m*

**lobby** (*lo*-bi) *n* vestíbulo *m*

**lobster** (*lob*-sstö) *n* langosta *f*

**local** (*lou*-köl) *adj* local; ~ **call** llamada local; ~ **train** tren ómnibus

**locality** (lou-*kæ*-lö-ti) *n* localidad *f*

**locate** (lou-*keit*) *v* localizar

**location** (lou-*kei*-ʃön) *n* ubicación *f*

**lock** (lok) *v* *cerrar con llave; *n* cerradura *f*; esclusa *f*; ~ **up** guardar con llave

**locomotive** (lou-kö-*mou*-tiv) *n* locomotora *f*

**lodge** (lodʒ) *v* alojar; *n* apeadero de caza

**lodger** (*lo*-dʒö) *n* huésped *m*

**lodgings** (*lo*-dʒings) *pl* alojamiento *m*

**log** (logh) *n* madero *m*

**logic** (*lo*-dʒik) *n* lógica *f*

**logical** (*lo*-dʒi-köl) *adj* lógico

**lonely** (*loun*-li) *adj* solitario

**long** (long) *adj* largo; ~ **for** anhelar; **no longer** ya no

**longing** (*long*-ing) *n* anhelo *m*

**longitude** (*lon*-dʒi-tyuud) *n* longitud *f*

**look** (luk) *v* mirar; *parecer, *tener aires de; *n* ojeada *f*, mirada *f*; aspecto *m*; ~ **after** ocuparse de, cuidar de; ~ **at** mirar; ~ **for** buscar; ~ **out** prestar atención, *tener cuidado; ~ **up** buscar

**looking-glass** (*lu*-king-ghlaass) *n* espejo *m*

**loop** (luup) *n* nudo corredizo

**loose** (luuss) *adj* suelto

**loosen** (*luu*-ssön) *v* *soltar

**lord** (lood) *n* lord *m*

**lorry** (*lo*-ri) *n* camión *m*

***lose** (luus) *v* *perder

**loss** (loss) *n* pérdida *f*

**lost** (losst) *adj* perdido; desaparecido; ~ **and found** objetos perdidos; ~ **property office** oficina de objetos perdidos

**lot** (lot) *n* suerte *f*, destino *m*; masa *f*, cantidad *f*

**lotion** (*lou*-ʃön) *n* loción *f*; **after-shave** ~ loción para después de afeitarse

**lottery** (*lo*-tö-ri) *n* lotería *f*

**loud** (laud) *adj* fuerte

**loud-speaker** (laud-*sspii*-kö) *n* altavoz *m*

**lounge** (laundʒ) *n* salón *m*

**louse** (lauss) *n* (pl lice) piojo *m*

**love** (lav) *v* amar; *n* amor *m*; **in ~** enamorado

**lovely** (*lav*-li) *adj* delicioso, precioso, bonito

**lover** (*la*-vö) *n* amante *m*

**love-story** (*lav*-sstoo-ri) *n* historia de amor

**low** (lou) *adj* bajo; profundo; deprimido; **~ tide** bajamar *f*

**lower** (*lou*-ö) *v* bajar; rebajar; arriar; *adj* inferior

**lowlands** (*lou*-lönds) *pl* tierra baja

**loyal** (*loi*-öl) *adj* leal

**lubricate** (*luu*-bri-keit) *v* lubrificar, lubricar

**lubrication** (luu-bri-*kei*-fön) *n* lubricación *f*; **~ oil** aceite lubricante; **~ system** sistema de lubricación

**luck** (lak) *n* éxito *m*, suerte *f*; azar *m*

**lucky** (*la*-ki) *adj* afortunado; **~ charm** talismán *m*

**ludicrous** (*luu*-di-kröss) *adj* ridículo, grotesco

**luggage** (*la*-ghidჳ) *n* equipaje *m*; **hand ~** equipaje de mano; **left ~ office** consigna *f*; **~ rack** portabagajes *m*, rejilla *f*; **~ van** furgón de equipajes

**lukewarm** (*luuk*-ᵘoom) *adj* tibio

**lumbago** (lam-*bei*-ghou) *n* lumbago *m*

**luminous** (*luu*-mi-nöss) *adj* luminoso

**lump** (lamp) *n* nudo *m*, grumo *m*, terrón *m*; chichón *m*; **~ of sugar** terrón de azúcar; **~ sum** suma global

**lumpy** (*lam*-pi) *adj* apelmazado

**lunacy** (*luu*-nö-ssi) *n* locura *f*

**lunatic** (*luu*-nö-tik) *adj* lunático; *n* alienado *m*

**lunch** (lanch) *n* almuerzo *m*

**luncheon** (*lan*-chön) *n* almuerzo *m*

**lung** (lang) *n* pulmón *m*

**lust** (lasst) *n* concupiscencia *f*

**luxurious** (lagh-ჳuᵒ-ri-öss) *adj* lujoso

**luxury** (*lak*-fö-ri) *n* lujo *m*

# M

**machine** (mö-*fiin*) *n* aparato *m*, máquina *f*

**machinery** (mö-*fii*-nö-ri) *n* maquinaria *f*; mecanismo *m*

**mackerel** (*mæ*-kröl) *n* (pl ~) escombro *m*

**mackintosh** (*mæ*-kin-tof) *n* impermeable *m*

**mad** (mæd) *adj* loco; rabioso

**madam** (*mæ*-döm) *n* señora *f*

**madness** (*mæd*-nöss) *n* locura *f*

**magazine** (*mæ*-ghö-siin) *n* revista *f*

**magic** (*mæ*-dჳik) *n* magia *f*; *adj* mágico

**magician** (mö-*dჳi*-fön) *n* prestidigitador *m*

**magistrate** (*mæ*-dჳi-ssträit) *n* magistrado *m*

**magnetic** (mægh-*nê*-tik) *adj* magnético

**magneto** (mægh-*nii*-tou) *n* (pl ~s) magneto *m*

**magnificent** (mægh-*ni*-fi-ssönt) *adj* magnífico; grandioso, espléndido

**magpie** (*mægh*-pai) *n* urraca *f*

**maid** (meid) *n* muchacha *f*

**maiden name** (*mei*-dön neim) apellido de soltera

**mail** (meil) *n* correo *m*; *v* enviar por correo

**mailbox** (*meil*-bokss) *nAm* buzón *m*

**main** (mein) *adj* principal; mayor; **~ deck** puente superior; **~ line** línea principal; **~ road** camino principal; **~ street** calle mayor

**mainland** (*mein*-lönd) *n* tierra firme

**mainly** (*mein*-li) *adv* principalmente

**mains** (meins) *pl* conducción principal

maintain (mein-*tein*) v *mantener

maintenance (*mein*-tö-nönss) n mantenimiento m

maize (meis) n maíz m

major (*mei*-dʒö) adj grande; mayor; n mayor m

majority (mö-*dʒo*-rö-ti) n mayoría f

*make (meik) v *hacer; ganar; *conseguir; ~ do with arreglarse con; ~ good compensar; ~ up redactar

make-up (*mei*-kap) n maquillaje m

malaria (mö-*lê*ᵒ-ri-ö) n malaria f

Malay (mö-*lei*) n malayo m

Malaysia (mö-*lei*-si-ö) Malasia f

Malaysian (mö-*lei*-si-ön) adj malayo

male (meil) adj macho

malicious (mö-*li*-ʃöss) adj malicioso

malignant (mö-*ligh*-nönt) adj maligno

mallet (*mæ*-lit) n mazo m

malnutrition (mæl-nyu-*tri*-ʃön) n desnutrición f

mammal (*mæ*-möl) n mamífero m

mammoth (*mæ*-möz) n mamut m

man (mæn) n (pl men) hombre m; men's room lavabos para caballeros

manage (*mæ*-nidʒ) v administrar; *tener éxito

manageable (*mæ*-ni-dʒö-böl) adj manejable

management (*mæ*-nidʒ-mönt) n manejo m; gestión f

manager (*mæ*-ni-dʒö) n jefe m, director m

mandarin (*mæn*-dö-rin) n mandarina f

mandate (*mæn*-deit) n mandato m

manger (*mein*-dʒö) n pesebre m

manicure (*mæ*-ni-kyuᵒ) n manicura f; v *hacer la manicura

mankind (mæn-*kaind*) n humanidad f

mannequin (*mæ*-nö-kin) n maniquí m

manner (*mæ*-nö) n modo m, manera f; manners pl modales mpl

man-of-war (mæ-növ-ᵘoo) n buque de guerra

manor-house (*mæ*-nö-hauss) n casa señorial

mansion (*mæn*-ʃön) n mansión f

manual (*mæ*-nyu-öl) adj manual

manufacture (mæ-nyu-*fæk*-chö) v fabricar

manufacturer (mæ-nyu-*fæk*-chö-rö) n fabricante m

manure (mö-*nyu*ᵒ) n abono m

manuscript (*mæ*-nyu-sskript) n manuscrito m

many (*mê*-ni) adj muchos

map (mæp) n carta f; mapa m; plano m

maple (*mei*-pöl) n arce m

marble (*maa*-böl) n mármol m; canica f

March (maach) marzo

march (maach) v marchar; n marcha f

mare (mê*ᵒ*) n yegua f

margarine (maa-dʒö-*riin*) n margarina f

margin (*maa*-dʒin) n margen m

maritime (*mæ*-ri-taim) adj marítimo

mark (maak) v marcar; caracterizar; n marca f; nota f; blanco m

market (*maa*-kit) n mercado m

market-place (*maa*-kit-pleiss) n plaza de mercado

marmalade (*maa*-mö-leid) n confitura f

marriage (*mæ*-ridʒ) n matrimonio m

marrow (*mæ*-rou) n médula f

marry (*mæ*-ri) v casarse; married couple cónyuges mpl

marsh (maaʃ) n pantano m

marshy (*maa*-ʃi) adj pantanoso

martyr (*maa*-tö) n mártir m

marvel (*maa*-völ) n maravilla f; v maravillarse

marvellous (*maa*-vö-löss) adj maravilloso

**mascara** (mæ-*sskaa*-rö) *n* rímel *m*

**masculine** (*mæ*-sskyu-lin) *adj* masculino

**mash** (mæʃ) *v* machacar

**mask** (maassk) *n* máscara *f*

**Mass** (mæss) *n* misa *f*

**mass** (mæss) *n* masa *f*; ~ **production** producción en serie

**massage** (*mæ*-ssaaʒ) *n* masaje *m*; *v* *dar masaje

**masseur** (mæ-*ssöö*) *n* masajista *m*

**massive** (*mæ*-ssiv) *adj* macizo

**mast** (maasst) *n* mástil *m*

**master** (*maa*-sstö) *n* maestro *m*; patrón *m*; profesor *m*; *v* dominar

**masterpiece** (*maa*-sstö-piiss) *n* obra maestra

**mat** (mæt) *n* estera *f*; *adj* mate, apagado

**match** (mæch) *n* cerilla *f*; partido *m*; cerillo *mMe*; *v* *hacer juego con

**match-box** (*mæch*-bokss) *n* caja de cerillas

**material** (mö-*ti*ö-ri-öl) *n* material *m*; tejido *m*; *adj* material

**mathematical** (mæ-zö-*mæ*-ti-köl) *adj* matemático

**mathematics** (mæ-zö-*mæ*-tikss) *n* matemáticas *fpl*

**matrimonial** (mæ-tri-*mou*-ni-öl) *adj* matrimonial

**matrimony** (*mæ*-tri-mö-ni) *n* matrimonio *m*

**matter** (*mæ*-tö) *n* materia *f*; asunto *m*, cuestión *f*; *v* *tener importancia; **as a** ~ **of fact** efectivamente, en realidad

**matter-of-fact** (mæ-tö-röv-*fækt*) *adj* desapasionado

**mattress** (*mæ*-tröss) *n* colchón *m*

**mature** (mö-*tyu*ö) *adj* maduro

**maturity** (mö-*tyu*ö-rö-ti) *n* madurez *f*

**mausoleum** (moo-ssö-*lii*-öm) *n* mau-

soleo *m*

**mauve** (mouv) *adj* malva

**May** (mei) *n* mayo

***may** (mei) *v* *poder

**maybe** (*mei*-bii) *adv* quizás

**mayor** (mêᵒ) *n* alcalde *m*

**maze** (meis) *n* laberinto *m*

**me** (mii) *pron* me

**meadow** (*mê*-dou) *n* prado *m*

**meal** (miil) *n* comida *f*

**mean** (miin) *adj* mezquino; *n* promedio *m*

***mean** (miin) *v* significar; *querer decir

**meaning** (*mii*-ning) *n* significado *m*

**meaningless** (*mii*-ning-löss) *adj* sin sentido

**means** (miins) *n* medio *m*; **by no** ~ en ningún caso, de ningún modo

**in the meantime** (in ðö *miin*-taim) entretanto

**meanwhile** (*miin*-ᵘail) *adv* entretanto

**measles** (*mii*-söls) *n* sarampión *m*

**measure** (*mê*-ʒö) *v* *medir; *n* medida *f*

**meat** (miit) *n* carne *f*

**mechanic** (mi-*kæ*-nik) *n* mecánico *m*

**mechanical** (mi-*kæ*-ni-köl) *adj* mecánico

**mechanism** (*mê*-kö-ni-söm) *n* mecanismo *m*

**medal** (*mê*-döl) *n* medalla *f*

**mediaeval** (mê-di-*ii*-völ) *adj* medieval

**mediate** (*mii*-di-eit) *v* mediar

**mediator** (*mii*-di-ei-tö) *n* mediador *m*

**medical** (*mê*-di-köl) *adj* médico

**medicine** (*mêd*-ssin) *n* medicamento *m*; medicina *f*

**meditate** (*mê*-di-teit) *v* meditar

**Mediterranean** (mê-di-tö-*rei*-ni-ön) Mediterráneo

**medium** (*mii*-di-öm) *adj* mediano, medio

***meet** (miit) *v* *encontrarse con

**meeting** (*mii*-ting) *n* asamblea *f*, reunión *f*; encuentro *m*

**meeting-place** (*mii*-ting-pleiss) *n* lugar de reunión

**melancholy** (*mê*-löng-kö-li) *n* melancolía *f*

**mellow** (*mê*-lou) *adj* suave

**melodrama** (*mê*-lö-draa-mö) *n* melodrama *m*

**melody** (*mê*-lö-di) *n* melodía *f*

**melon** (*mê*-lön) *n* melón *m*

**melt** (mêlt) *v* fundir

**member** (*mêm*-bö) *n* miembro *m*; **Member of Parliament** diputado *m*

**membership** (*mêm*-bö-ſip) *n* afiliación *f*

**memo** (*mê*-mou) *n* (pl ~s) apunte *m*

**memorable** (*mê*-mö-rö-böl) *adj* memorable

**memorial** (mö-*moo*-ri-öl) *n* monumento *m*

**memorize** (*mê*-mö-rais) *v* aprenderse de memoria

**memory** (*mê*-mö-ri) *n* memoria *f*; recuerdo *m*

**mend** (mênd) *v* reparar, *remendar

**menstruation** (mên-sstru-*ei*-jön) *n* menstruación *f*

**mental** (*mên*-töl) *adj* mental

**mention** (*mên*-jön) *v* nombrar, mencionar; *n* mención *f*

**menu** (*mê*-nyuu) *n* menú *m*

**merchandise** (*möö*-chön-dais) *n* mercancía *f*

**merchant** (*möö*-chönt) *n* comerciante *m*

**merciful** (*möö*-ssi-föl) *adj* misericordioso

**mercury** (*möö*-kyu-ri) *n* mercurio *m*

**mercy** (*möö*-ssi) *n* misericordia *f*, clemencia *f*

**mere** (mi⁰) *adj* puro

**merely** (*mi⁰*-li) *adv* solamente

**merger** (*möö*-dʒö) *n* fusión *f*

**merit** (*mê*-rit) *v* *merecer; *n* mérito *m*

**mermaid** (*möö*-meid) *n* sirena *f*

**merry** (*mê*-ri) *adj* alegre

**merry-go-round** (*mê*-ri-ghou-raund) *n* caballitos *mpl*

**mesh** (mêſ) *n* malla *f*

**mess** (mêss) *n* desorden *m*; ~ **up** estropear

**message** (*mê*-ssidʒ) *n* mensaje *m*

**messenger** (*mê*-ssin-dʒö) *n* mensajero *m*

**metal** (*mê*-töl) *n* metal *m*; metálico

**meter** (*mii*-tö) *n* contador *m*

**method** (*mê*-zöd) *n* método *m*; orden *m*

**methodical** (mö-*zo*-di-köl) *adj* metódico

**methylated spirits** (*mê*-zö-lei-tid sspirritss) alcohol de quemar

**metre** (*mii*-tö) *n* metro *m*

**metric** (*mê*-trik) *adj* métrico

**Mexican** (*mêk*-ssi-kön) *adj* mejicano; *n* mejicano *m*

**Mexico** (*mêk*-ssi-kou) Méjico *m*

**mezzanine** (*mê*-sö-niin) *n* entresuelo *m*

**microphone** (*mai*-krö-foun) *n* micrófono *m*

**midday** (*mid*-dei) *n* mediodía *m*

**middle** (*mi*-döl) *n* medio *m*; *adj* medio; **Middle Ages** Edad Media; ~ **class** clase media; **middle-class** *adj* burgués

**midnight** (*mid*-nait) *n* medianoche *f*

**midst** (midsst) *n* medio *m*

**midsummer** (*mid*-ssa-mö) *n* pleno verano

**midwife** (*mid*-ᵘaif) *n* (pl -wives) comadrona *f*

**might** (mait) *n* fuerza *f*

***might** (mait) *v* *poder

**mighty** (*mai*-ti) *adj* fuerte

**migraine** (*mi*-ghrein) *n* migraña *f*

**mild** (maild) *adj* suave

**mildew** (*mil*-dyu) *n* moho *m*

**mile** (mail) *n* milla *f*

**mileage** (*mai*-lidʒ) *n* millaje *m*

**milepost** (*mail*-pousst) *n* cipo *m*

**milestone** (*mail*-sstoun) *n* piedra miliar

**milieu** (*mii*-lyöö) *n* medio ambiente

**military** (*mi*-li-tö-ri) *adj* militar; ~ **force** fuerzas armadas

**milk** (milk) *n* leche *f*

**milkman** (*milk*-mön) *n* (pl -men) lechero *m*

**milk-shake** (*milk*-ʃeik) *n* batido de leche

**milky** (*mil*-ki) *adj* lechoso

**mill** (mil) *n* molino *m*; fábrica *f*

**miller** (*mi*-lö) *n* molinero *m*

**milliner** (*mi*-li-nö) *n* sombrerera *f*

**million** (*mi*-yön) *n* millón *m*

**millionaire** (mil-yö-*nê*ᵒ) *n* millonario *m*

**mince** (minss) *v* picar

**mind** (maind) *n* mente *f*; *v* *hacer objeción a; fijarse en, *tener cuidado con

**mine** (main) *n* mina *f*

**miner** (*mai*-nö) *n* minero *m*

**mineral** (*mi*-nö-röl) *n* mineral *m*; ~ **water** agua mineral

**miniature** (*min*-yö-chö) *n* miniatura *f*

**minimum** (*mi*-ni-möm) *n* mínimum *m*

**mining** (*mai*-ning) *n* minería *f*

**minister** (*mi*-ni-sstö) *n* ministro *m*; clérigo *m*; **Prime Minister** Presidente de Consejo de ministros

**ministry** (*mi*-ni-sstri) *n* ministerio *m*

**mink** (mingk) *n* visón *m*

**minor** (*mai*-nö) *adj* pequeño, escaso, menor; secundario; *n* menor de edad

**minority** (mai-*no*-rö-ti) *n* minoría *f*

**mint** (mint) *n* menta *f*

**minus** (*mai*-nöss) *prep* menos

**minute**[1] (*mi*-nit) *n* minuto *m*; **minutes** actas

**minute**[2] (mai-*nyuut*) *adj* menudo

**miracle** (*mi*-rö-köl) *n* milagro *m*

**miraculous** (mi-*ræ*-kyu-löss) *adj* milagroso

**mirror** (*mi*-rö) *n* espejo *m*

**misbehave** (miss-bi-*heiv*) *v* portarse mal

**miscarriage** (miss-*kæ*-ridʒ) *n* aborto *m*

**miscellaneous** (mi-ssö-*lei*-ni-öss) *adj* misceláneo

**mischief** (*miss*-chif) *n* diabluras *fpl*; mal *m*, daño *m*, malicia *f*

**mischievous** (*miss*-chi-vöss) *adj* travieso

**miserable** (*mi*-sö-rö-böl) *adj* miserable

**misery** (*mi*-sö-ri) *n* miseria *f*; necesidad *f*

**misfortune** (miss-*foo*-chên) *n* contratiempo *m*, infortunio *m*

*****mislay** (miss-*lei*) *v* extraviar

**misplaced** (miss-*pleisst*) *adj* inoportuno; fuera de lugar

**mispronounce** (miss-prö-*naunss*) *v* pronunciar mal

**miss**[1] (miss) señorita *f*

**miss**[2] (miss) *v* *perder

**missing** (*mi*-ssing) *adj* que falta; ~ **person** desaparecido *m*

**mist** (misst) *n* niebla *f*

**mistake** (mi-*ssteik*) *n* error *m*, equivocación *f*

*****mistake** (mi-*ssteik*) *v* confundir

**mistaken** (mi-*sstei*-kön) *adj* equivocado; *be ~ equivocarse

**mister** (*mi*-sstö) *n* señor *m*

**mistress** (*mi*-sströss) *n* señora *f*; dueña *f*; querida *f*

**mistrust** (miss-*trasst*) *v* desconfiar de

**misty** (*mi*-ssti) *adj* nebuloso

*****misunderstand** (mi-ssan-dö-*sstænd*)

*v* comprender mal

**misunderstanding** (mi-ssan-dö-*sstæn*-ding) *n* equivocación *f*

**misuse** (miss-*yuuss*) *n* abuso *m*

**mittens** (*mi*-töns) *pl* guantes *mpl*

**mix** (mikss) *v* mezclar; ~ **with** alternar con

**mixed** (miksst) *adj* mezclado

**mixer** (*mik*-ssö) *n* batidora *f*

**mixture** (*mikss*-chö) *n* mezcla *f*

**moan** (moun) *v* *gemir

**moat** (mout) *n* foso *m*

**mobile** (*mou*-bail) *adj* móvil

**mock** (mok) *v* burlarse de

**mockery** (*mo*-kö-ri) *n* burla *f*

**model** (*mo*-döl) *n* modelo *m*; maniquí *m*; *v* modelar

**moderate** (*mo*-dö-röt) *adj* moderado; mediocre

**modern** (*mo*-dön) *adj* moderno

**modest** (*mo*-disst) *adj* modesto

**modesty** (*mo*-di-ssti) *n* modestia *f*

**modify** (*mo*-di-fai) *v* modificar

**mohair** (*mou*-hê⁰) *n* mohair *m*

**moist** (moisst) *adj* mojado, húmedo

**moisten** (*moi*-ssön) *v* *humedecer

**moisture** (*moiss*-chö) *n* humedad *f*; **moisturizing cream** crema hidratante

**molar** (*mou*-lö) *n* muela *f*

**moment** (*mou*-mönt) *n* momento *m*

**momentary** (*mou*-mön-tö-ri) *adj* momentáneo

**monarch** (*mo*-nök) *n* monarca *m*

**monarchy** (*mo*-nö-ki) *n* monarquía *f*

**monastery** (*mo*-nö-sstri) *n* monasterio *m*

**Monday** (*man*-di) lunes *m*

**monetary** (*ma*-ni-tö-ri) *adj* monetario; ~ **unit** unidad monetaria

**money** (*ma*-ni) *n* dinero *m*; ~ **exchange** oficina de cambio; ~ **order** libranza *f*

**monk** (mangk) *n* monje *m*

**monkey** (*mang*-ki) *n* mono *m*

**monologue** (*mo*-no-logh) *n* monólogo *m*

**monopoly** (mö-*no*-pö-li) *n* monopolio *m*

**monotonous** (mö-*no*-tö-nöss) *adj* monótono

**month** (manz) *n* mes *m*

**monthly** (*manz*-li) *adj* mensual; ~ **magazine** revista mensual

**monument** (*mo*-nyu-mönt) *n* monumento *m*

**mood** (muud) *n* humor *m*

**moon** (muun) *n* luna *f*

**moonlight** (*muun*-lait) *n* luz de la luna

**moor** (mu⁰) *n* brezal *m*, turbera *f*

**moose** (muuss) *n* (pl ~, ~s) alce *m*

**moped** (*mou*-pêd) *n* bicimotor *m*

**moral** (*mo*-röl) *n* moral *f*; *adj* moral; **morals** costumbres

**morality** (mö-*ræ*-lö-ti) *n* moralidad *f*

**more** (moo) *adj* más; **once** ~ otra vez

**moreover** (moo-*rou*-vö) *adv* además

**morning** (*moo*-ning) *n* mañana *f*; ~ **paper** diario matutino

**Moroccan** (mö-*ro*-kön) *adj* marroquí

**Morocco** (mö-*ro*-kou) Marruecos *m*

**morphia** (*moo*-fi-ö) *n* morfina *f*

**morphine** (*moo*-fiin) *n* morfina *f*

**morsel** (*moo*-ssöl) *n* trozo *m*

**mortal** (*moo*-töl) *adj* fatal, mortal

**mortgage** (*moo*-ghidʒ) *n* hipoteca *f*

**mosaic** (mö-*sei*-ik) *n* mosaico *m*

**mosque** (mossk) *n* mezquita *f*

**mosquito** (mö-*sskii*-tou) *n* (pl ~es) mosquito *m*

**mosquito-net** (mö-*sskii*-tou-nêt) *n* mosquitero *m*

**moss** (moss) *n* musgo *m*

**most** (mousst) *adj* el más; **at** ~ a lo sumo, como máximo; ~ **of all** sobre todo

**mostly** (*mousst*-li) *adv* generalmente

**motel** (mou-*tê*l) *n* motel *m*

**moth** (moz) *n* polilla *f*

**mother** (*ma*-ðö) *n* madre *f*; ~ **tongue** lengua materna

**mother-in-law** (*ma*-ðö-rin-loo) *n* (pl mothers-) suegra *f*

**mother-of-pearl** (ma-ðö-röv-*pööl*) *n* nácar *m*

**motion** (*mou*-ʃön) *n* movimiento *m*; moción *f*

**motive** (*mou*-tiv) *n* motivo *m*

**motor** (*mou*-tö) *n* motor *m*; *v* *ir en coche; **starter** ~ motor de arranque

**motorbike** (*mou*-tö-baik) *n Am* motocicleta *f*

**motor-boat** (*mou*-tö-bout) *n* bote a motor

**motor-car** (*mou*-tö-kaa) *n* automóvil *m*

**motor-cycle** (*mou*-tö-ssai-köl) *n* motocicleta *f*

**motoring** (*mou*-tö-ring) *n* automovilismo *m*

**motorist** (*mou*-tö-risst) *n* automovilista *m*

**motorway** (*mou*-tö-ᵘei) *n* autopista *f*

**motto** (*mo*-tou) *n* (pl ~es, ~s) lema *f*

**mouldy** (*moul*-di) *adj* enmohecido

**mound** (maund) *n* montículo *m*

**mount** (maunt) *v* montar; *n* monte *m*

**mountain** (*maun*-tin) *n* montaña *f*; ~ **pass** paso *m*; ~ **range** cordillera *f*

**mountaineering** (maun-ti-*niö*-ring) *n* montañismo *m*

**mountainous** (*maun*-ti-nöss) *adj* montañoso

**mourning** (*moo*-ning) *n* luto *m*

**mouse** (mauss) *n* (pl mice) ratón *m*

**moustache** (mö-*sstaaʃ*) *n* bigote *m*

**mouth** (mauz) *n* boca *f*; hocico *m*; desembocadura *f*

**mouthwash** (*mauz*-ᵘoʃ) *n* enjuague bucal

**movable** (*muu*-vö-böl) *adj* movible

**move** (muuv) *v* *mover; trasladar; mudarse; *conmover; *n* jugada *f*, paso *m*; mudanza *f*

**movement** (*muuv*-mönt) *n* movimiento *m*

**movie** (*muu*-vi) *n* filme *m*

**much** (mach) *adj* mucho; **as** ~ tanto

**muck** (mak) *n* suciedad *f*

**mud** (mad) *n* lodo *m*

**muddle** (*ma*-döl) *n* dédalo *m*, embrollo *m*; *v* embrollar

**muddy** (*ma*-di) *adj* lodoso

**mud-guard** (*mad*-ghaad) *n* guardabarros *m*; salpicadera *f Me*

**mug** (magh) *n* vaso *m*, taza *f*

**mulberry** (*mal*-bö-ri) *n* mora *f*

**mule** (myuul) *n* mulo *m*

**mullet** (*ma*-lit) *n* mújol *m*

**multiplication** (mal-ti-pli-*kei*-ʃön) *n* multiplicación *f*

**multiply** (*mal*-ti-plai) *v* multiplicar

**mumps** (mampss) *n* paperas *f pl*

**municipal** (myuu-*ni*-ssi-pöl) *adj* municipal

**municipality** (myuu-ni-ssi-*pæ*-lö-ti) *n* municipalidad *f*

**murder** (*möö*-dö) *n* asesinato *m*; *v* asesinar

**murderer** (*möö*-dö-rö) *n* asesino *m*

**muscle** (*ma*-ssöl) *n* músculo *m*

**muscular** (*ma*-sskyu-lö) *adj* musculoso

**museum** (myuu-*sii*-öm) *n* museo *m*

**mushroom** (*maʃ*-ruum) *n* seta *f*; hongo *m*

**music** (*myuu*-sik) *n* música *f*; ~ **academy** conservatorio *m*

**musical** (*myuu*-si-köl) *adj* musical; *n* comedia musical

**music-hall** (*myuu*-sik-hool) *n* teatro de variedades

**musician** (myuu-*si*-ʃön) *n* músico *m*

**muslin** (*mas*-lin) *n* muselina *f*

**mussel** (*ma*-ssöl) *n* mejillón *m*

**\*must** (masst) *v* *tener que

**mustard** (*ma*-sstöd) *n* mostaza *f*

**mute** (myuut) *adj* mudo
**mutiny** (*myuu*-ti-ni) *n* amotinamiento *m*
**mutton** (*ma*-tön) *n* carnero *m*
**mutual** (*myuu*-chu-öl) *adj* mutuo, recíproco
**my** (mai) *adj* mi
**myself** (mai-*ssêlf*) *pron* me; yo mismo
**mysterious** (mi-*sstiᵒ*-ri-öss) *adj* misterioso
**mystery** (*mi*-sstö-ri) *n* enigma *m*, misterio *m*
**myth** (miz) *n* mito *m*

# N

**nail** (neil) *n* uña *f*; clavo *m*
**nailbrush** (*neil*-braʃ) *n* cepillo para las uñas
**nail-file** (*neil*-fail) *n* lima para las uñas
**nail-polish** (*neil*-po-liʃ) *n* barniz para las uñas
**nail-scissors** (*neil*-ssi-sös) *pl* tijeras para las uñas
**naïve** (naa-*iiv*) *adj* ingenuo
**naked** (*nei*-kid) *adj* desnudo
**name** (neim) *n* nombre *m*; *v* nombrar; **in the ~ of** en nombre de
**namely** (*neim*-li) *adv* a saber
**nap** (næp) *n* siesta *f*
**napkin** (*næp*-kin) *n* servilleta *f*
**nappy** (*næ*-pi) *n* pañal *m*
**narcosis** (naa-*kou*-ssiss) *n* (pl -ses) narcosis *f*
**narcotic** (naa-*ko*-tik) *n* narcótico *m*
**narrow** (*næ*-rou) *adj* angosto, estrecho
**narrow-minded** (*næ*-rou-*main*-did) *adj* mezquino
**nasty** (*naa*-ssti) *adj* antipático, desagradable
**nation** (*nei*-ʃön) *n* nación *f*; pueblo *m*

**national** (*næ*-ʃö-nöl) *adj* nacional; del Estado; **~ anthem** himno nacional; **~ dress** traje del país; **~ park** parque nacional
**nationality** (*næ*-ʃö-*næ*-lö-ti) *n* nacionalidad *f*
**nationalize** (*næ*-ʃö-nö-lais) *v* nacionalizar
**native** (*nei*-tiv) *n* indígena *m*; *adj* nativo; **~ country** patria *f*, país natal; **~ language** lengua materna
**natural** (*næ*-chö-röl) *adj* natural; innato
**naturally** (*næ*-chö-rö-li) *adv* naturalmente, por supuesto
**nature** (*nei*-chö) *n* naturaleza *f*; natural *m*
**naughty** (*noo*-ti) *adj* travieso
**nausea** (*noo*-ssi-ö) *n* náusea *f*
**naval** (*nei*-völ) *adj* naval
**navel** (*nei*-völ) *n* ombligo *m*
**navigable** (*næ*-vi-ghö-böl) *adj* navegable
**navigate** (*næ*-vi-gheit) *v* navegar
**navigation** (næ-vi-*ghei*-ʃön) *n* navegación *f*
**navy** (*nei*-vi) *n* marina *f*
**near** (niᵒ) *prep* cerca de; *adj* cercano
**nearby** (*niᵒ*-bai) *adj* cercano
**nearly** (*niᵒ*-li) *adv* casi
**neat** (niit) *adj* pulcro; puro
**necessary** (*nê*-ssö-ssö-ri) *adj* necesario
**necessity** (nö-*ssê*-ssö-ti) *n* necesidad *f*
**neck** (nêk) *n* cuello *m*; **nape of the ~** nuca *f*
**necklace** (*nêk*-löss) *n* collar *m*
**necktie** (*nêk*-tai) *n* corbata *f*
**need** (niid) *v* deber, necesitar; *n* necesidad *f*; **~ to** deber
**needle** (*nii*-döl) *n* aguja *f*
**needlework** (*nii*-döl-ᵁöök) *n* labor de aguja
**negative** (*nê*-ghö-tiv) *adj* negativo; *n*

negativo *m*

**neglect** (ni-*ghlêkt*) *v* descuidar; *n* negligencia *f*

**neglectful** (ni-*ghlêkt*-föl) *adj* negligente

**negligee** (nê-ghli-зei) *n* bata suelta

**negotiate** (ni-*ghou*-ʃi-eit) *v* negociar

**negotiation** (ni-ghou-ʃi-*ei*-ʃön) *n* negociación *f*

**Negro** (*nii*-ghrou) *n* (pl ~es) negro *m*

**neighbour** (*nei*-bö) *n* vecino *m*

**neighbourhood** (*nei*-bö-hud) *n* vecindad *f*

**neighbouring** (*nei*-bö-ring) *adj* contiguo, vecino

**neither** (*nai*-ðö) *pron* ninguno de los dos; **neither ... nor** ni ... ni

**neon** (*nii*-on) *n* neón *m*

**nephew** (*nê*-fyuu) *n* sobrino *m*

**nerve** (nöö v) *n* nervio *m*; audacia *f*

**nervous** (*nöö*-vöss) *adj* nervioso

**nest** (nêsst) *n* nido *m*

**net** (nêt) *n* red *f*; *adj* neto

**the Netherlands** (*nê*-ðö-lönds) Países Bajos *mpl*

**network** (*nêt*-ᵘöök) *n* red *f*

**neuralgia** (nyuⁿ-*ræl*-dʒö) *n* neuralgia *f*

**neurosis** (nyuⁿ-*rou*-ssiss) *n* neurosis *f*

**neuter** (*nyuu*-tö) *adj* neutro

**neutral** (*nyuu*-tröl) *adj* neutral

**never** (*nê*-vö) *adv* nunca

**nevertheless** (nê-vö-ðö-*lêss*) *adv* no obstante

**new** (nyuu) *adj* nuevo; **New Year** año nuevo

**news** (nyuus) *n* noticiario *m*, noticia *f*; noticias *fpl*

**newsagent** (*nyuu*-sei-dʒönt) *n* vendedor de periódicos

**newspaper** (*nyuus*-pei-pö) *n* diario *m*

**newsreel** (*nyuus*-riil) *n* noticiario *m*

**newsstand** (*nyuus*-sstænd) *n* quiosco de periódicos

**New Zealand** (nyuu *sii*-lönd) Nueva

Zelanda

**next** (nêksst) *adj* próximo; ~ **to** junto a

**next-door** (nêksst-*doo*) *adv* al lado

**nice** (naiss) *adj* agradable, bonito, ameno; rico; simpático

**nickel** (*ni*-köl) *n* níquel *m*

**nickname** (*nik*-neim) *n* mote *m*

**nicotine** (*ni*-kö-tiin) *n* nicotina *f*

**niece** (niiss) *n* sobrina *f*

**Nigeria** (nai-*dʒi*ⁿ-ri-ö) Nigeria *f*

**Nigerian** (nai-*dʒi*ⁿ-ri-ön) *adj* nigeriano

**night** (nait) *n* noche *f*; **by** ~ de noche; ~ **flight** vuelo nocturno; ~ **rate** tarifa nocturna; ~ **train** tren nocturno

**nightclub** (*nait*-klab) *n* cabaret *m*

**night-cream** (*nait*-kriim) *n* crema de noche

**nightdress** (*nait*-drêss) *n* camisón *m*

**nightingale** (*nai*-ting-gheil) *n* ruiseñor *m*

**nightly** (*nait*-li) *adj* nocturno

**nil** (nil) nada

**nine** (nain) *num* nueve

**nineteen** (nain-*tiin*) *num* diecinueve

**nineteenth** (nain-*tiinz*) *num* decimonono

**ninety** (*nain*-ti) *num* noventa

**ninth** (nainz) *num* noveno

**nitrogen** (*nai*-trö-dʒön) *n* nitrógeno *m*

**no** (nou) no; *adj* ninguno; ~ **one** nadie

**nobility** (nou-*bi*-lö-ti) *n* nobleza *f*

**noble** (*nou*-böl) *adj* noble

**nobody** (*nou*-bo-di) *pron* nadie

**nod** (nod) *n* cabeceo *m*; *v* cabecear

**noise** (nois) *n* ruido *m*; alboroto *m*

**noisy** (*noi*-si) *adj* ruidoso

**nominal** (*no*-mi-nöl) *adj* nominal

**nominate** (*no*-mi-neit) *v* nombrar

**nomination** (no-mi-*nei*-ʃön) *n* nominación *f*; nombramiento *m*

**none** (nan) *pron* ninguno

**nonsense** (*non*-ssönss) *n* tontería *f*

**noon** (nuun) *n* mediodía *m*

**normal** (*noo*-möl) *adj* normal

**north** (nooz) *n* norte *m*; *adj* septentrional; **North Pole** polo norte

**north-east** (nooz-*iisst*) *n* nordeste *m*

**northerly** (*noo*-ðö-li) *adj* del norte

**northern** (*noo*-ðön) *adj* norteño

**north-west** (nooz-*u*ésst) *n* noroeste *m*

**Norway** (*noo*-*u*ei) Noruega *f*

**Norwegian** (noo-*u*ii-dʒön) *adj* noruego

**nose** (nous) *n* nariz *f*

**nosebleed** (*nous*-bliid) *n* hemorragia nasal

**nostril** (*no*-sstril) *n* ventana de la nariz

**not** (not) *adv* no

**notary** (*nou*-tö-ri) *n* notario *m*

**note** (nout) *n* apunte *m*, esquela *f*; nota *f*; tono *m*; *v* notar; observar, *comprobar

**notebook** (*nout*-buk) *n* libreta de apuntes

**noted** (*nou*-tid) *adj* afamado

**notepaper** (*nout*-pei-pö) *n* papel de escribir, papel para cartas

**nothing** (*na*-zing) *n* nada *f*, nada

**notice** (*nou*-tiss) *v* observar, notar, *advertir; *ver; *n* aviso *m*, noticia *f*; atención *f*

**noticeable** (*nou*-ti-ssö-böl) *adj* perceptible; notable

**notify** (*nou*-ti-fai) *v* notificar

**notion** (*nou*-ʃön) *n* noción *f*

**notorious** (nou-*too*-ri-öss) *adj* de mala fama

**nougat** (*nuu*-ghaa) *n* turrón *m*

**nought** (noot) *n* cero *m*

**noun** (naun) *n* nombre *m*, substantivo *m*

**nourishing** (*na*-ri-ʃing) *adj* nutritivo

**novel** (*no*-völ) *n* novela *f*

**novelist** (*no*-vö-lisst) *n* novelista *m*

**November** (nou-*vêm*-bö) noviembre

**now** (nau) *adv* ahora; actualmente; **~ and then** de vez en cuando

**nowadays** (*nau*-ö-deis) *adv* hoy en día

**nowhere** (*nou*-*u*ê*ð*) *adv* en ninguna parte

**nozzle** (*no*-söl) *n* tobera *f*

**nuance** (nyuu-*angss*) *n* matiz *m*

**nuclear** (*nyuu*-kli-ö) *adj* nuclear; **~ energy** energía nuclear

**nucleus** (*nyuu*-kli-öss) *n* núcleo *m*

**nude** (nyuud) *adj* desnudo; *n* desnudo *m*

**nuisance** (*nyuu*-ssönss) *n* molestia *f*

**numb** (nam) *adj* entumecido; aterido

**number** (*nam*-bö) *n* número *m*; cifra *f*; cantidad *f*

**numeral** (*nyuu*-mö-röl) *n* numeral *m*

**numerous** (*nyuu*-mö-röss) *adj* numeroso

**nun** (nan) *n* monja *f*

**nunnery** (*na*-nö-ri) *n* convento *m*

**nurse** (nööss) *n* enfermera *f*; niñera *f*; *v* *atender a; amamantar

**nursery** (*nöö*-ssö-ri) *n* cuarto de niños; guardería *f*; vivero *m*

**nut** (nat) *n* nuez *f*; tuerca *f*

**nutcrackers** (*nat*-kræ-kös) *pl* cascanueces *m*

**nutmeg** (*nat*-mêgh) *n* nuez moscada

**nutritious** (nyuu-*tri*-ʃöss) *adj* nutritivo

**nutshell** (*nat*-ʃêl) *n* cáscara de nuez

**nylon** (*nai*-lon) *n* nylon *m*

# O

**oak** (ouk) *n* roble *m*

**oar** (oo) *n* remo *m*

**oasis** (ou-*ei*-ssiss) *n* (pl oases) oasis *f*

**oath** (ouz) *n* juramento *m*

**oats** (outss) *pl* avena *f*

**obedience** (ö-*bii*-di-önss) *n* obediencia *f*

**obedient** (ö-*bii*-di-önt) *adj* obediente

**obey** (ö-*bei*) *v* \*obedecer

**object**[1] (*ob*-dʒikt) *n* objeto *m*

**object**[2] (öb-*dʒêkt*) *v* objetar; ~ **to** \*oponerse a

**objection** (öb-*dʒêk*-ʃön) *n* objeción *f*

**objective** (öb-*dʒêk*-tiv) *adj* objetivo; *n* objetivo *m*

**obligatory** (ö-*bli*-ghö-tö-ri) *adj* obligatorio

**oblige** (ö-*blaidʒ*) *v* obligar; \***be obliged to** \*estar obligado a; \*tener que

**obliging** (ö-*blai*-dʒing) *adj* simpático

**oblong** (*ob*-long) *adj* oblongo; *n* rectángulo *m*

**obscene** (öb-*ssiin*) *adj* obsceno

**obscure** (öb-*sskyu*[o]) *adj* obscuro, misterioso, oscuro

**observation** (ob-sö-*vei*-ʃön) *n* observación *f*

**observatory** (öb-*söö*-vö-tri) *n* observatorio *m*

**observe** (öb-*sööv*) *v* observar

**obsession** (öb-*ssê*-ʃön) *n* obsesión *f*

**obstacle** (*ob*-sstö-köl) *n* obstáculo *m*

**obstinate** (*ob*-ssti-nöt) *adj* obstinado; pertinaz

**obtain** (öb-*tein*) *v* \*conseguir, \*obtener

**obtainable** (öb-*tei*-nö-böl) *adj* adquirible

**obvious** (*ob*-vi-öss) *adj* obvio

**occasion** (ö-*kei*-ʒön) *n* ocasión *f*; motivo *m*

**occasionally** (ö-*kei*-ʒö-nö-li) *adv* de vez en cuando, ocasionalmente

**occupant** (*o*-kyu-pönt) *n* ocupante *m*

**occupation** (o-kyu-*pei*-ʃön) *n* ocupación *f*

**occupy** (*o*-kyu-pai) *v* ocupar

**occur** (ö-*köö*) *v* suceder, ocurrir, \*acontecer

**occurrence** (ö-*ka*-rönss) *n* acontecimiento *m*

**ocean** (*ou*-ʃön) *n* océano *m*

**October** (ok-*tou*-bö) octubre

**octopus** (*ok*-tö-pöss) *n* pulpo *m*

**oculist** (*o*-kyu-lisst) *n* oculista *m*

**odd** (od) *adj* raro; impar

**odour** (*ou*-dö) *n* olor *m*

**of** (ov, öv) *prep* de

**off** (of) *adv* fuera; *prep* de

**offence** (ö-*fênss*) *n* falta *f*; ofensa *f*, escándalo *m*

**offend** (ö-*fênd*) *v* ofender; transgredir

**offensive** (ö-*fên*-ssiv) *adj* ofensivo; insultante; *n* ofensivo *m*

**offer** (*o*-fö) *v* \*ofrecer; presentar; *n* oferta *f*

**office** (*o*-fiss) *n* oficina *f*; cargo *m*; ~ **hours** horas de oficina

**officer** (*o*-fi-ssö) *n* oficial *m*

**official** (ö-*fi*-ʃöl) *adj* oficial

**off-licence** (*of*-lai-ssönss) *n* almacén de licores

**often** (*o*-fön) *adv* a menudo, frecuentemente

**oil** (oil) *n* aceite *m*; petróleo *m*; **fuel** ~ combustible líquido; ~ **filter** filtro del aceite; ~ **pressure** presión del aceite

**oil-painting** (oil-*pein*-ting) *n* pintura al óleo

**oil-refinery** (*oil*-ri-fai-nö-ri) *n* refinería de petróleo

**oil-well** (*oil*-[u]êl) *n* pozo de petróleo

**oily** (*oi*-li) *adj* aceitoso

**ointment** (*oint*-mönt) *n* ungüento *m*

**okay!** (ou-*kei*) ¡de acuerdo!

**old** (ould) *adj* viejo; ~ **age** vejez *f*

**old-fashioned** (ould-*fæ*-ʃönd) *adj* anticuado

**olive** (*o*-liv) *n* aceituna *f*; ~ **oil** aceite de oliva

**omelette** (*om*-löt) *n* tortilla *f*

**ominous** (*o*-mi-nöss) *adj* siniestro

**omit** (ö-*mit*) *v* omitir

**omnipotent** (om-*ni*-pö-tönt) *adj* omnipotente

**on** (on) *prep* sobre; a

**once** (<sup>u</sup>anss) *adv* una vez; **at ~** en seguida; **~ more** otra vez

**oncoming** (*on*-ka-ming) *adj* venidero

**one** (<sup>u</sup>an) *num* uno; *pron* uno

**oneself** (<sup>u</sup>an-*ssélf*) *pron* uno mismo

**onion** (*a*-nyön) *n* cebolla *f*

**only** (*oun*-li) *adj* solo; *adv* sólo, solamente; *conj* pero

**onwards** (on-<sup>u</sup>öds) *adv* adelante

**onyx** (*o*-nikss) *n* ónix *m*

**opal** (*ou*-pöl) *n* ópalo *m*

**open** (*ou*-pön) *v* abrir; *adj* abierto; sincero

**opening** (*ou*-pö-ning) *n* abertura *f*

**opera** (*o*-pö-rö) *n* ópera *f*; **~ house** teatro de la ópera

**operate** (*o*-pö-reit) *v* operar, funcionar

**operation** (o-pö-*rei*-[šö]n) *n* funcionamiento *m*; operación *f*

**operator** (*o*-pö-rei-tö) *n* telefonista *f*

**operetta** (o-pö-*ré*-tö) *n* opereta *f*

**opinion** (ö-*pi*-nyön) *n* parecer *m*, opinión *f*

**opponent** (ö-*pou*-nönt) *n* contrincante *m*

**opportunity** (o-pö-*tyuu*-nö-ti) *n* oportunidad *f*

**oppose** (ö-*pous*) *v* *oponerse

**opposite** (*o*-pö-sit) *prep* enfrente de; *adj* contrario, opuesto

**opposition** (o-pö-*si*-[šö]n) *n* oposición *f*

**oppress** (ö-*préss*) *v* oprimir

**optician** (op-*ti*-[šö]n) *n* óptico *m*

**optimism** (*op*-ti-mi-söm) *n* optimismo *m*

**optimist** (*op*-ti-misst) *n* optimista *m*

**optimistic** (op-ti-*mi*-sstik) *adj* optimista

**optional** (*op*-[šö]-nöl) *adj* opcional

**or** (oo) *conj* o

**oral** (*oo*-röl) *adj* oral

**orange** (*o*-rind[ž]) *n* naranja *f*; *adj* de color naranja

**orchard** (*oo*-chöd) *n* vergel *m*

**orchestra** (*oo*-ki-sströ) *n* orquesta *f*; **~ seat** *Am* butaca *f*

**order** (*oo*-dö) *v* ordenar; *pedir; *n* orden *m*; orden *f*, mandato *m*; pedido *m*; **in ~** en regla; **in ~ to** para; **made to ~** hecho a la medida; **out of ~** averiado; **postal ~** giro postal

**order-form** (*oo*-dö-foom) *n* hoja de pedido

**ordinary** (*oo*-dön-ri) *adj* común, ordinario

**ore** (oo) *n* mineral *m*

**organ** (*oo*-ghön) *n* órgano *m*

**organic** (oo-*ghæ*-nik) *adj* orgánico

**organization** (oo-ghö-nai-*sei*-[šö]n) *n* organización *f*

**organize** (*oo*-ghö-nais) *v* organizar

**Orient** (*oo*-ri-önt) *n* oriente *m*

**oriental** (oo-ri-*ên*-töl) *adj* oriental

**orientate** (*oo*-ri-ön-teit) *v* orientarse

**origin** (*o*-ri-d[ž]in) *n* origen *m*; descendencia *f*, procedencia *f*

**original** (ö-*ri*-d[ž]i-nöl) *adj* auténtico, original

**originally** (ö-*ri*-d[ž]i-nö-li) *adv* originalmente

**orlon** (*oo*-lon) *n* orlón *m*

**ornament** (*oo*-nö-mönt) *n* adorno *m*

**ornamental** (oo-nö-*mên*-töl) *adj* ornamental

**orphan** (*oo*-fön) *n* huérfano *m*

**orthodox** (*oo*-zö-dokss) *adj* ortodoxo

**ostrich** (*o*-sstrich) *n* avestruz *m*

**other** (*a*-ðö) *adj* otro

**otherwise** (*a*-ðö-<sup>u</sup>ais) *conj* si no; *adv* de otra manera

**ought to** (oot) *tener que

**our** (au<sup>ö</sup>) *adj* nuestro

**ourselves** (au<sup>ö</sup>-*ssélvs*) *pron* nos; nosotros mismos

**out** (aut) *adv* fuera; ~ **of** fuera de, de

**outbreak** (*aut*-breik) *n* explosión *f*

**outcome** (*aut*-kam) *n* resultado *m*

\***outdo** (aut-*duu*) *v* superar

**outdoors** (aut-*doos*) *adv* afuera

**outer** (au-tö) *adj* exterior

**outfit** (*aut*-fit) *n* equipo *m*

**outline** (*aut*-lain) *n* contorno *m*; *v* bosquejar

**outlook** (*aut*-luk) *n* previsión *f*; punto de vista

**output** (*aut*-put) *n* producción *f*

**outrage** (*aut*-reidȝ) *n* ultraje *m*

**outside** (aut-*ssaid*) *adv* afuera; *prep* fuera de; *n* exterior *m*

**outsize** (*aut*-ssais) *n* tamaño extraordinario

**outskirts** (*aut*-ssköötss) *pl* afueras *fpl*

**outstanding** (aut-*sstæn*-ding) *adj* eminente, destacado

**outward** (*aut*-ᵘöd) *adj* externo

**outwards** (*aut*-ᵘöds) *adv* hacia afuera

**oval** (*ou*-völ) *adj* ovalado

**oven** (*a*-vön) *n* horno *m*

**over** (*ou*-vö) *prep* encima de; más de; *adv* encima; abajo; *adj* acabado; ~ **there** allá

**overall** (*ou*-vö-rool) *adj* total

**overalls** (*ou*-vö-rools) *pl* mono *m*; overol *mMe*

**overcast** (*ou*-vö-kaasst) *adj* nublado

**overcoat** (*ou*-vö-kout) *n* abrigo *m*

\***overcome** (ou-vö-*kam*) *v* vencer

**overdue** (ou-vö-*dyuu*) *adj* atrasado

**overgrown** (ou-vö-*ghroun*) *adj* cubierto de verdor

**overhaul** (ou-vö-*hool*) *v* revisar

**overhead** (ou-vö-*hêd*) *adv* en alto

**overlook** (ou-vö-*luk*) *v* pasar por alto

**overnight** (ou-vö-*nait*) *adv* de noche

**overseas** (ou-vö-*ssiis*) *adj* ultramar

**oversight** (*ou*-vö-ssait) *n* descuido *m*

\***oversleep** (ou-vö-*ssliip*) *v* quedarse dormido

**overstrung** (ou-vö-*sstrang*) *adj* sobreexcitado

\***overtake** (ou-vö-*teik*) *v* recoger; **no overtaking** prohibido adelantar

**over-tired** (ou-vö-*taiᵒd*) *adj* exhausto

**overture** (*ou*-vö-chö) *n* obertura *f*

**overweight** (*ou*-vö-ᵘeit) *n* sobrepeso *m*

**overwhelm** (ou-vö-ᵘêlm) *v* \*desconcertar, subyugar

**overwork** (ou-vö-ᵘöök) *v* trabajar demasiado

**owe** (ou) *v* deber; **owing to** a causa de, debido a

**owl** (aul) *n* buho *m*

**own** (oun) *v* \*poseer; *adj* propio

**owner** (*ou*-nö) *n* propietario *m*

**ox** (okss) *n* (pl oxen) buey *m*

**oxygen** (*ok*-ssi-dȝön) *n* oxígeno *m*

**oyster** (*oi*-sstö) *n* ostra *f*

# P

**pace** (peiss) *n* andares *mpl*; paso *m*; ritmo *m*

**Pacific Ocean** (pö-*ssi*-fik *ou*-ʃön) Océano Pacífico

**pacifism** (*pæ*-ssi-fi-söm) *n* pacifismo *m*

**pacifist** (*pæ*-ssi-fisst) *n* pacifista *m*

**pack** (pæk) *v* embalar; ~ **up** empaquetar

**package** (*pæ*-kidȝ) *n* paquete *m*

**packet** (*pæ*-kit) *n* paquete *m*

**packing** (*pæ*-king) *n* embalaje *m*

**pad** (pæd) *n* almohadilla *f*; bloque *m*

**paddle** (*pæ*-döl) *n* remo *m*

**padlock** (*pæd*-lok) *n* candado *m*

**pagan** (*pei*-ghön) *adj* pagano; *n* pagano *m*

**page** (peidȝ) *n* página *f*

**page-boy** (*peidʒ*-boi) *n* paje *m*
**pail** (peil) *n* balde *m*
**pain** (pein) *n* dolor *m*; **pains** pena *f*
**painful** (*pein*-föl) *adj* dolorido
**painless** (*pein*-löss) *adj* sin dolor
**paint** (peint) *n* pintura *f*; *v* pintar
**paint-box** (*peint*-bokss) *n* caja de colores
**paint-brush** (*peint*-braʃ) *n* pincel *m*
**painter** (*pein*-tö) *n* pintor *m*
**painting** (*pein*-ting) *n* pintura *f*
**pair** (pêᵒ) *n* par *m*
**Pakistan** (paa-ki-*sstaan*) Paquistán *m*
**Pakistani** (paa-ki-*sstaa*-ni) *adj* paquistaní
**palace** (*pæ*-löss) *n* palacio *m*
**pale** (peil) *adj* pálido
**palm** (paam) *n* palma *f*
**palpable** (*pæl*-pö-böl) *adj* palpable
**palpitation** (pæl-pi-*tei*-ʃön) *n* palpitación *f*
**pan** (pæn) *n* sartén *f*
**pane** (pein) *n* cristal *m*
**panel** (*pæ*-nöl) *n* painel *m*, cuarterón *m*
**panelling** (*pæ*-nö-ling) *n* enmaderado *m*
**panic** (*pæ*-nik) *n* pánico *m*
**pant** (pænt) *v* jadear
**panties** (*pæn*-tis) *pl* braga *f*
**pants** (pæntss) *pl* calzoncillos *mpl*; *plAm* pantalones *mpl*
**pant-suit** (*pænt*-ssuut) *n* traje pantalón
**panty-hose** (*pæn*-ti-hous) *n* media pantalón
**paper** (*pei*-pö) *n* papel *m*; periódico *m*; de papel; **carbon** ~ papel carbón; ~ **bag** bolsa de papel; ~ **napkin** servilleta de papel; **typing** ~ papel para mecanografiar; **wrapping** ~ papel de envolver
**paperback** (*pei*-pö-bæk) *n* libro de bolsillo

**paper-knife** (*pei*-pö-naif) *n* abrecartas *m*
**parade** (pö-*reid*) *n* parada *f*, desfile *m*
**paraffin** (*pæ*-rö-fin) *n* parafina *f*
**paragraph** (*pæ*-rö-ghraaf) *n* párrafo *m*
**parakeet** (*pæ*-rö-kiit) *n* cotorra *f*
**paralise** (*pæ*-rö-lais) *v* paralizar
**parallel** (*pæ*-rö-lêl) *adj* paralelo; *n* paralelo *m*
**parcel** (paa-ssöl) *n* paquete *m*
**pardon** (paa-dön) *n* perdón *m*; indulto *m*
**parents** (*pêᵒ*-röntss) *pl* padres *mpl*
**parents-in-law** (*pêᵒ*-röntss-in-loo) *pl* padres políticos
**parish** (*pæ*-riʃ) *n* parroquia *f*
**park** (paak) *n* parque *m*; *v* estacionar
**parking** (*paa*-king) *n* aparcamiento *m*; **no** ~ prohibido estacionarse; ~ **fee** derechos de estacionamiento; ~ **light** luz de estacionamiento; ~ **lot** *Am* estacionamiento *m*; ~ **meter** parquímetro *m*; ~ **zone** zona de aparcamiento
**parliament** (*paa*-lö-mönt) *n* parlamento *m*
**parliamentary** (paa-lö-*mên*-tö-ri) *adj* parlamentario
**parrot** (*pæ*-röt) *n* loro *m*
**parsley** (*paa*-ssli) *n* perejil *m*
**parson** (*paa*-ssön) *n* pastor *m*
**parsonage** (*paa*-ssö-nidʒ) *n* curato *m*
**part** (paat) *n* parte *f*; pieza *f*; *v* separar; **spare** ~ recambio *m*
**partial** (*paa*-ʃöl) *adj* parcial
**participant** (paa-*ti*-ssi-pönt) *n* participante *m*
**participate** (paa-*ti*-ssi-peit) *v* participar
**particular** (pö-*ti*-kyu-lö) *adj* especial, particular; exigente; **in** ~ en particular
**parting** (*paa*-ting) *n* despedida *f*; raya *f*

**partition** (paa-_ti_-ʃön) _n_ tabique _m_

**partly** (_paat_-li) _adv_ en parte

**partner** (_paat_-nö) _n_ pareja _f_; socio _m_

**partridge** (_paa_-trid3) _n_ perdiz _f_

**party** (_paa_-ti) _n_ partido _m_; guateque _m_, fiesta _f_; grupo _m_

**pass** (paass) _v_ transcurrir, pasar; *aprobar; ~ **by** pasar de largo; ~ **through** *atravesar

**passage** (_pæ_-ssid3) _n_ pasaje _m_; travesía _f_; trozo _m_

**passenger** (_pæ_-ssön-d3ö) _n_ pasajero _m_; ~ **train** tren de pasajeros

**passer-by** (paa-ssö-_bai_) _n_ transeúnte _m_

**passion** (_pæ_-ʃön) _n_ pasión _f_; cólera _f_

**passionate** (_pæ_-ʃö-nöt) _adj_ apasionado

**passive** (_pæ_-ssiv) _adj_ pasivo

**passport** (_paass_-poot) _n_ pasaporte _m_; ~ **control** inspección de pasaportes; ~ **photograph** fotografía de pasaporte

**password** (_paass_-ᵘööd) _n_ santo y seña

**past** (paasst) _n_ pasado _m_; _adj_ pasado; transcurrido; _prep_ a lo largo de, más allá de

**paste** (peisst) _n_ pasta _f_; _v_ pegar

**pastry** (_pei_-sstri) _n_ pastelería _f_; ~ **shop** pastelería _f_

**pasture** (_paass_-chö) _n_ prado _m_

**patch** (pæch) _v_ *remendar

**patent** (_pei_-tönt) _n_ patente _f_

**path** (paaz) _n_ senda _f_

**patience** (_pei_-ʃönss) _n_ paciencia _f_

**patient** (_pei_-ʃönt) _adj_ paciente; _n_ paciente _m_

**patriot** (_pei_-tri-öt) _n_ patriota _m_

**patrol** (pö-_troul_) _n_ patrulla _f_; _v_ patrullar; vigilar

**pattern** (_pæ_-tön) _n_ diseño _m_

**pause** (poos) _n_ pausa _f_; _v_ *hacer una pausa

**pave** (peiv) _v_ pavimentar

**pavement** (_peiv_-mönt) _n_ acera _f_; pavimento _m_

**pavilion** (pö-_vil_-yön) _n_ pabellón _m_

**paw** (poo) _n_ pata _f_

**pawn** (poon) _v_ empeñar; _n_ peón _m_

**pawnbroker** (_poon_-brou-kö) _n_ prestamista _m_

**pay** (pei) _n_ salario _m_, sueldo _m_

*****pay** (pei) _v_ pagar; *rendir; ~ **attention to** prestar atención a; **paying** rentable; ~ **off** amortizar; ~ **on account** pagar a plazos

**pay-desk** (_pei_-dêssk) _n_ caja _f_

**payee** (pei-_ii_) _n_ favorecido _m_

**payment** (_pei_-mönt) _n_ pago _m_

**pea** (pii) _n_ guisante _m_

**peace** (piiss) _n_ paz _f_

**peaceful** (_piiss_-föl) _adj_ tranquilo

**peach** (piich) _n_ melocotón _m_

**peacock** (_pii_-kok) _n_ pavo _m_

**peak** (piik) _n_ pico _m_; cumbre _f_; ~ **hour** hora punta; ~ **season** apogeo de la temporada

**peanut** (_pii_-nat) _n_ cacahuete _m_; cacahuate _mMe_

**pear** (pêᵒ) _n_ pera _f_

**pearl** (pööl) _n_ perla _f_

**peasant** (_pê_-sönt) _n_ campesino _m_

**pebble** (_pê_-böl) _n_ guijarro _m_

**peculiar** (pi-_kyuul_-yö) _adj_ extraño; especial, peculiar

**peculiarity** (pi-kyuu-li-_æ_-rö-ti) _n_ particularidad _f_

**pedal** (_pê_-döl) _n_ pedal _m_

**pedestrian** (pi-_dê_-sstri-ön) _n_ peatón _m_; **no pedestrians** prohibido para los peatones; ~ **crossing** cruce para peatones

**pedicure** (_pê_-di-kyuᵒ) _n_ pedicuro _m_

**peel** (piil) _v_ pelar; _n_ piel _f_

**peep** (piip) _v_ espiar

**peg** (pêgh) _n_ percha _f_

**pelican** (_pê_-li-kön) _n_ pelícano _m_

**pelvis** (_pêl_-viss) _n_ pelvis _m_

**pen** (pên) *n* pluma *f*

**penalty** (*pé*-nöl-ti) *n* pena *f*; castigo *m*; ~ **kick** penalty *m*

**pencil** (*pên*-ssöl) *n* lápiz *m*

**pencil-sharpener** (*pên*-ssöl-ʃaap-nö) *n* sacapuntas *m*

**pendant** (*pé*-dönt) *n* pendiente *m*

**penetrate** (*pé*-ni-treit) *v* penetrar

**penguin** (*pêng*-ghᵘin) *n* pingüino *m*

**penicillin** (pê-ni-*ssi*-lin) *n* penicilina *f*

**peninsula** (pö-*nin*-ssyu-lö) *n* península *f*

**penknife** (*pên*-naif) *n* (pl -knives) cortaplumas *m*

**pension¹** (*pang*-ssi-ong) *n* pensión *f*

**pension²** (*pên*-ʃön) *n* pensión *f*

**people** (*pii*-pöl) *pl* gente *f*; *n* pueblo *m*

**pepper** (*pê*-pö) *n* pimienta *f*

**peppermint** (*pê*-pö-mint) *n* menta *f*

**perceive** (pö-*ssiiv*) *v* percibir

**percent** (pö-*ssênt*) *n* por ciento

**percentage** (pö-*ssên*-tidʒ) *n* porcentaje *m*

**perceptible** (pö-*ssêp*-ti-böl) *adj* perceptible

**perception** (pö-*ssêp*-ʃön) *n* percepción *f*

**perch** (pööch) (pl ~) perca *f*

**percolator** (*pöö*-kö-lei-tö) *n* cafetera filtradora

**perfect** (*pöö*-fikt) *adj* perfecto

**perfection** (pö-*fêk*-ʃön) *n* perfección *f*

**perform** (pö-*foom*) *v* ejecutar, desempeñar

**performance** (pö-*foo*-mönss) *n* representación *f*

**perfume** (*pöö*-fyuum) *n* perfume *m*

**perhaps** (pö-*hæpss*) *adv* quizás

**peril** (*pé*-ril) *n* peligro *m*

**perilous** (*pé*-ri-löss) *adj* peligroso

**period** (*piᵒ*-ri-öd) *n* época *f*, período *m*; punto *m*

**periodical** (piᵒ-ri-*o*-di-köl) *n* periódico *m*; *adj* periódico

**perish** (*pé*-riʃ) *v* \*perecer

**perishable** (*pé*-ri-ʃö-böl) *adj* perecedero

**perjury** (*pöö*-dʒö-ri) *n* perjurio *m*

**permanent** (*pöö*-mö-nönt) *adj* duradero, permanente; estable, fijo; ~ **press** planchado permanente; ~ **wave** ondulación permanente

**permission** (pö-*mi*-ʃön) *n* permiso *m*, autorización *f*; licencia *f*

**permit¹** (pö-*mit*) *v* permitir

**permit²** (*pöö*-mit) *n* permiso *m*

**peroxide** (pö-*rok*-ssaid) *n* peróxido *m*

**perpendicular** (pöö-pön-*di*-kyu-lö) *adj* perpendicular

**Persia** (*pöö*-ʃö) Persia *f*

**Persian** (*pöö*-ʃön) *adj* persa

**person** (*pöö*-ssön) *n* persona *f*; **per** ~ por persona

**personal** (*pöö*-ssö-nöl) *adj* personal

**personality** (pöö-ssö-*næ*-lö-ti) *n* personalidad *f*

**personnel** (pöö-ssö-*nêl*) *n* personal *m*

**perspective** (pö-*sspêk*-tiv) *n* perspectiva *f*

**perspiration** (pöö-sspö-*rei*-ʃön) *n* transpiración *f*, sudor *m*

**perspire** (pö-*sspai*ᵒ) *v* transpirar, sudar

**persuade** (pö-*ssᵘeid*) *v* persuadir; convencer

**persuasion** (pö-*ssᵘei*-ʒön) *n* convicción *f*

**pessimism** (*pê*-ssi-mi-söm) *n* pesimismo *m*

**pessimist** (*pê*-ssi-misst) *n* pesimista *m*

**pessimistic** (pê-ssi-*mi*-sstik) *adj* pesimista

**pet** (pêt) *n* animal doméstico; cariño *m*; favorito

**petal** (*pé*-töl) *n* pétalo *m*

**petition** (pi-*ti*-ʃön) *n* petición *f*

**petrol** (*pê*-tröl) *n* gasolina *f*; ~ **pump**

bomba de gasolina; ~ **station** puesto de gasolina; ~ **tank** depósito de gasolina

**petroleum** (pi-*trou*-li-öm) *n* petróleo *m*

**petty** (*pê*-ti) *adj* pequeño, fútil, insignificante; ~ **cash** calderilla *f*

**pewit** (*pii*-ᵘit) *n* avefría *f*

**pewter** (*pyuu*-tö) *n* estaño *m*

**phantom** (*fæn*-töm) *n* fantasma *m*

**pharmacology** (faa-mö-*ko*-lö-dʒi) *n* farmacología *f*

**pharmacy** (*faa*-mö-ssi) *n* farmacia *f*; droguería *f*

**phase** (feis) *n* fase *f*

**pheasant** (*fê*-sönt) *n* faisán *m*

**Philippine** (*fi*-li-pain) *adj* filipino

**Philippines** (*fi*-li-piins) *pl* Filipinas *fpl*

**philosopher** (fi-*lo*-ssö-fö) *n* filósofo *m*

**philosophy** (fi-*lo*-ssö-fi) *n* filosofía *f*

**phone** (foun) *n* teléfono *m*; *v* llamar por teléfono, telefonear

**phonetic** (fö-*nê*-tik) *adj* fonético

**photo** (*fou*-tou) *n* (pl ~s) foto *f*

**photograph** (*fou*-tö-ghraaf) *n* fotografía *f*; *v* fotografiar

**photographer** (fö-*to*-ghrö-fö) *n* fotógrafo *m*

**photography** (fö-*to*-ghrö-fi) *n* fotografía *f*

**photostat** (*fou*-tö-sstæt) *n* fotocopia *f*

**phrase** (freis) *n* frase *f*

**phrase-book** (*freis*-buk) *n* manual de conversación

**physical** (*fi*-si-köl) *adj* físico

**physician** (fi-*si*-jön) *n* médico *m*

**physicist** (*fi*-si-ssisst) *n* físico *m*

**physics** (*fi*-sikss) *n* física *f*

**physiology** (fi-si-*o*-lö-dʒi) *n* fisiología *f*

**pianist** (*pii*-ö-nisst) *n* pianista *f*

**piano** (pi-æ-nou) *n* piano *m*; **grand** ~ piano de cola

**pick** (pik) *v* recoger; escoger; *n* elec-

ción *f*; ~ **up** recoger; *ir a buscar; **pick-up van** camioneta de reparto

**pick-axe** (*pi*-kækss) *n* pico *m*

**pickles** (*pi*-köls) *pl* encurtidos *mpl*

**picnic** (*pik*-nik) *n* día de campo; *v* *hacer un día de campo

**picture** (*pik*-chö) *n* cuadro *m*; ilustración *f*, grabado *m*; imagen *f*; ~ **postcard** tarjeta postal ilustrada, postal ilustrada; **pictures** cine *m*

**picturesque** (pik-chö-*rêssk*) *adj* pintoresco

**piece** (piiss) *n* fragmento *m*, pedazo *m*

**pier** (piᵒ) *n* muelle *m*

**pierce** (piᵒss) *v* punzar

**pig** (pigh) *n* cerdo *m*

**pigeon** (*pi*-dʒön) *n* paloma *f*

**pig-headed** (pigh-*hê*-did) *adj* testarudo

**piglet** (*pigh*-löt) *n* cochinillo *m*

**pigskin** (*pigh*-sskin) *n* piel de cerdo

**pike** (paik) *n* (pl ~) lucio *m*

**pile** (pail) *n* montón *m*; *v* amontonar; **piles** *pl* hemorroides *fpl*

**pilgrim** (*pil*-ghrim) *n* peregrino *m*

**pilgrimage** (*pil*-ghri-midʒ) *n* peregrinación *f*

**pill** (pil) *n* píldora *f*

**pillar** (*pi*-lö) *n* columna *f*, pilar *m*

**pillar-box** (*pi*-lö-bokss) *n* buzón *m*

**pillow** (*pi*-lou) *n* almohadón *m*, almohada *f*

**pillow-case** (*pi*-lou-keiss) *n* funda de almohada

**pilot** (*pai*-löt) *n* piloto *m*; práctico *m*

**pimple** (*pim*-pöl) *n* grano *m*

**pin** (pin) *n* alfiler *m*; *v* clavar; **bobby** ~ *Am* horquilla *f*

**pincers** (*pin*-ssös) *pl* tenazas *fpl*

**pinch** (pinch) *v* pellizcar

**pineapple** (*pai*-næ-pöl) *n* piña *f*

**ping-pong** (*ping*-pong) *n* tenis de mesa

**pink** (pingk) *adj* rosado

**pioneer** (pai-ö-*ni*ᵒ) *n* pionero *m*

**pious** (*pai*-öss) *adj* pío

**pip** (pip) *n* pepita *f*

**pipe** (paip) *n* pipa *f*; conducto *m*; ~ **cleaner** limpiapipas *m*; ~ **tobacco** tabaco de pipa

**pirate** (*pai*ᵒ-röt) *n* pirata *m*

**pistol** (*pi*-sstöl) *n* pistola *f*

**piston** (*pi*-sstön) *n* pistón *m*; ~ **ring** aro de émbolo

**piston-rod** (*pi*-sstön-rod) *n* biela *f*

**pit** (pit) *n* hoyo *m*; mina *f*

**pitcher** (*pi*-chö) *n* cántaro *m*

**pity** (*pi*-ti) *n* piedad *f*; *v* \*tener piedad de, compadecerse de; **what a pity!** ¡qué lástima!

**placard** (*plæ*-kaad) *n* cartel *m*

**place** (pleiss) *n* lugar *m*; *v* \*poner, colocar; ~ **of birth** lugar de nacimiento; \***take** ~ \*tener lugar

**plague** (pleigh) *n* plaga *f*

**plaice** (pleiss) (pl ~) platija *f*

**plain** (plein) *adj* claro; corriente, sencillo; *n* llano *m*

**plan** (plæn) *n* plan *m*; plano *m*; *v* planear

**plane** (plein) *adj* plano; *n* avión *m*; ~ **crash** accidente aéreo

**planet** (*plæ*-nit) *n* planeta *m*

**planetarium** (plæ-ni-*tê*ᵒ-ri-öm) *n* planetario *m*

**plank** (plængk) *n* tablón *m*

**plant** (plaant) *n* planta *f*; instalación *f*; *v* plantar

**plantation** (plæn-*tei*-fön) *n* plantación *f*

**plaster** (*plaa*-sstö) *n* estuco *m*, yeso *m*; esparadrapo *m*

**plastic** (*plæ*-sstik) *adj* de plástico; *n* plástico *m*

**plate** (pleit) *n* plato *m*; chapa *f*

**plateau** (*plæ*-tou) *n* (pl ~x, ~s) meseta *f*

**platform** (*plæt*-foom) *n* andén *m*; ~ **ticket** billete de andén

**platinum** (*plæ*-ti-nöm) *n* platino *m*

**play** (plei) *v* \*jugar; tocar; *n* juego *m*; obra de teatro; **one-act** ~ pieza en un acto; ~ **truant** \*hacer novillos

**player** (plei ᵒ) *n* jugador *m*

**playground** (*plei*-ghraund) *n* patio de recreo

**playing-card** (*plei*-ing-kaad) *n* naipe *m*

**playwright** (*plei*-rait) *n* dramaturgo *m*

**plea** (plii) *n* defensa *f*

**plead** (pliid) *v* informar

**pleasant** (*plê*-sönt) *adj* agradable, simpático

**please** (pliis) por favor; *v* \*placer; **pleased** contento; **pleasing** agradable

**pleasure** (*plê*-ʒö) *n* placer *m*, diversión *f*

**plentiful** (*plên*-ti-föl) *adj* abundante

**plenty** (*plên*-ti) *n* abundancia *f*

**pliers** (plai ᵒs) *pl* alicates *mpl*

**plimsolls** (*plim*-ssöls) *pl* zapatos de gimnasia

**plot** (plot) *n* conjuración *f*, complot *m*; trama *f*; parcela *f*

**plough** (plau) *n* arado *m*; *v* arar

**plucky** (*pla*-ki) *adj* valiente

**plug** (plagh) *n* enchufe *m*; ~ **in** enchufar

**plum** (plam) *n* ciruela *f*

**plumber** (*pla*-mö) *n* plomero *m*

**plump** (plamp) *adj* regordete

**plural** (*plu*ᵒ-röl) *n* plural *m*

**plus** (plass) *prep* más

**pneumatic** (nyuu-*mæ*-tik) *adj* neumático

**pneumonia** (nyuu-*mou*-ni-ö) *n* neumonía *f*

**poach** (pouch) *v* cazar en vedado

**pocket** (*po*-kit) *n* bolsillo *m*

**pocket-book** (*po*-kit-buk) *n* bolsa *f*

**pocket-comb** (*po*-kit-koum) *n* peine de bolsillo

**pocket-knife** (*po*-kit-naif) *n* (pl -knives) navaja *f*

**pocket-watch** (*po*-kit-ᵘoch) *n* reloj de bolsillo

**poem** (*pou*-im) *n* poema *m*

**poet** (*pou*-it) *n* poeta *m*

**poetry** (*pou*-i-tri) *n* poesía *f*

**point** (point) *n* punto *m*; punta *f*; *v* señalar con el dedo; ~ **of view** punto de vista; ~ **out** apuntar

**pointed** (*poin*-tid) *adj* puntiagudo

**poison** (*poi*-sön) *n* veneno *m*; *v* envenenar

**poisonous** (*poi*-sö-nöss) *adj* venenoso

**Poland** (*pou*-lönd) Polonia *f*

**Pole** (poul) *n* polaco *m*

**pole** (poul) *n* poste *m*

**police** (*po*-*liiss*) *pl* policía *f*

**policeman** (pö-*liiss*-mön) *n* (pl -men) agente de policía, guardia *m*

**police-station** (pö-*liiss*-sstei-ʃön) *n* comisaría *f*

**policy** (*po*-li-ssi) *n* política *f*; póliza *f*

**polio** (*pou*-li-ou) *n* polio *f*, poliomielitis *f*

**Polish** (*pou*-liʃ) *adj* polaco

**polish** (*po*-liʃ) *v* pulir

**polite** (pö-*lait*) *adj* cortés

**political** (pö-*li*-ti-köl) *adj* político

**politician** (po-li-*ti*-ʃön) *n* político *m*

**politics** (*po*-li-tikss) *n* política *f*

**pollution** (pö-*luu*-ʃön) *n* contaminación *f*, polución *f*

**pond** (pond) *n* estanque *m*

**pony** (*pou*-ni) *n* pony *m*

**poor** (puᵒ) *adj* pobre; mediocre

**pope** (poup) *n* Papa *m*

**poplin** (*po*-plin) *n* popelín *m*

**pop music** (pop *myuu*-sik) música pop

**poppy** (*po*-pi) *n* amapola *f*; adormidera *f*

**popular** (*po*-pyu-lö) *adj* popular

**population** (po-pyu-*lei*-ʃön) *n* población *f*

**populous** (*po*-pyu-löss) *adj* populoso

**porcelain** (*poo*-ssö-lin) *n* porcelana *f*

**porcupine** (*poo*-kyu-pain) *n* puerco espín

**pork** (pook) *n* carne de cerdo

**port** (poot) *n* puerto *m*; babor *m*

**portable** (*poo*-tö-böl) *adj* portátil

**porter** (*poo*-tö) *n* mozo *m*; portero *m*

**porthole** (*poot*-houl) *n* portilla *f*

**portion** (*poo*-ʃön) *n* porción *f*

**portrait** (*poo*-trit) *n* retrato *m*

**Portugal** (*poo*-tyu-ghöl) Portugal *m*

**Portuguese** (poo-tyu-*ghiis*) *adj* portugués

**position** (pö-*si*-ʃön) *n* posición *f*; actitud *f*; puesto *m*

**positive** (*po*-sö-tiv) *adj* positivo; *n* positiva *f*

**possess** (pö-*sêss*) *v* *poseer; **possessed** *adj* poseído

**possession** (pö-*sê*-ʃön) *n* posesión *f*; **possessions** bienes *mpl*

**possibility** (po-ssö-*bi*-lö-ti) *n* posibilidad *f*

**possible** (*po*-ssö-böl) *adj* posible; eventual

**post** (pousst) *n* poste *m*; puesto *m*; correo *m*; *v* echar al correo; **post-office** casa de correos

**postage** (*pou*-sstidʒ) *n* franqueo *m*; ~ **paid** franco; ~ **stamp** sello de correos; timbre *mMe*

**postcard** (*pousst*-kaad) *n* tarjeta postal; tarjeta postal ilustrada

**poster** (*pou*-sstö) *n* cartel *m*, poster *m*

**poste restante** (pousst rê-*sstangt*) lista de correos

**postman** (*pousst*-mön) *n* (pl -men) cartero *m*

**post-paid** (pousst-*peid*) *adj* franco

**postpone** (pö-*sspoun*) *v* aplazar

**pot** (pot) *n* olla *f*

**potato** (pö-*tei*-tou) *n* (pl ~es) patata *f*; papa *fMe*

**pottery** (*po*-tö-ri) *n* cerámica *f*; loza *f*

**pouch** (pauch) *n* petaca *f*

**poulterer** (*poul*-tö-rö) *n* pollero *m*

**poultry** (*poul*-tri) *n* aves de corral

**pound** (paund) *n* libra *f*

**pour** (poo) *v* *verter

**poverty** (*po*-vö-ti) *n* pobreza *f*

**powder** (*pau*-dö) *n* polvo *m*; ~ **compact** polvera *f*; **talc** ~ talco *m*

**powder-puff** (*pau*-dö-paf) *n* borla para empolvarse

**powder-room** (*pau*-dö-ruum) *n* tocador *m*

**power** (pauô) *n* fuerza *f*, energía *f*; poder *m*; potencia *f*

**powerful** (*pauô*-föl) *adj* poderoso; fuerte

**powerless** (*pauô*-löss) *adj* impotente

**power-station** (*pauô*-sstei-∫ön) *n* central eléctrica

**practical** (*præk*-ti-köl) *adj* práctico

**practically** (*præk*-ti-kli) *adv* prácticamente

**practice** (*præk*-tiss) *n* práctica *f*

**practise** (*præk*-tiss) *v* practicar; ensayarse

**praise** (preis) *v* alabar; *n* elogio *m*

**pram** (præm) *n* cochecillo *m*

**prawn** (proon) *n* gamba *f*

**pray** (prei) *v* orar

**prayer** (prêô) *n* oración *f*

**preach** (priich) *v* predicar

**precarious** (pri-*kêô*-ri-öss) *adj* precario

**precaution** (pri-*koo*-∫ön) *n* precaución *f*

**precede** (pri-*ssiid*) *v* preceder

**preceding** (pri-*ssii*-ding) *adj* precedente

**precious** (*prê*-∫öss) *adj* precioso; querido

**precipice** (*prê*-ssi-piss) *n* precipicio *m*

**precipitation** (pri-ssi-pi-*tei*-∫ön) *n* precipitación *f*

**precise** (pri-*ssaiss*) *adj* preciso, exacto; meticuloso

**predecessor** (*prii*-di-ssê-ssö) *n* predecesor *m*

**predict** (pri-*dikt*) *v* *predecir

**prefer** (pri-*föö*) *v* *preferir

**preferable** (*prê*-fö-rö-böl) *adj* preferible

**preference** (*prê*-fö-rönss) *n* preferencia *f*

**prefix** (*prii*-fikss) *n* prefijo *m*

**pregnant** (*prêgh*-nönt) *adj* encinta, embarazada

**prejudice** (*prê*-dʒö-diss) *n* prejuicio *m*

**preliminary** (pri-*li*-mi-nö-ri) *adj* preliminar

**premature** (*prê*-mö-chuô) *adj* prematuro

**premier** (*prêm*-iô) *n* jefe de gobierno

**premises** (*prê*-mi-ssiss) *pl* finca *f*

**premium** (*prii*-mi-öm) *n* prima *f*

**prepaid** (prii-*peid*) *adj* pagado por adelantado

**preparation** (prê-pö-*rei*-∫ön) *n* preparación *f*

**prepare** (pri-*pêô*) *v* preparar

**preposition** (prê-pö-*si*-∫ön) *n* preposición *f*

**prescribe** (pri-*sskraib*) *v* prescribir

**prescription** (pri-*sskrip*-∫ön) *n* prescripción *f*

**presence** (*prê*-sönss) *n* presencia *f*

**present¹** (*prê*-sönt) *n* regalo *m*, presente *m*; *adj* actual; presente

**present²** (pri-*sênt*) *v* presentar

**presently** (*prê*-sönt-li) *adv* en seguida, dentro de poco

**preservation** (prê-sö-*vei*-∫ön) *n* conservación *f*

**preserve** (pri-*sööv*) *v* preservar; conservar

**president** (*prê*-si-dönt) *n* presidente *m*

**press** (prèss) *n* prensa *f*; *v* empujar, *apretar; planchar; ~ conference conferencia de prensa

**pressing** (*prê*-ssing) *adj* urgente

**pressure** (*prê*-jö) *n* presión *f*; tensión *f*; **atmospheric** ~ presión atmosférica

**pressure-cooker** (*prê*-jö-ku-kö) *n* olla a presión

**prestige** (prê-*sstii3*) *n* prestigio *m*

**presumable** (pri-*syuu*-mö-böl) *adj* presumible

**presumptuous** (pri-*samp*-jöss) *adj* presuntuoso; presumido

**pretence** (pri-*tênss*) *n* pretexto *m*

**pretend** (pri-*ténd*) *v* fingir

**pretext** (*prii*-têksst) *n* pretexto *m*

**pretty** (*pri*-ti) *adj* bonito; *adv* bastante

**prevent** (pri-*vênt*) *v* *impedir; *prevenir

**preventive** (pri-*vên*-tiv) *adj* preventivo

**previous** (*prii*-vi-öss) *adj* precedente, anterior, previo

**pre-war** (prii-*ᵁoo*) *adj* de la preguerra

**price** (praiss) *n* precio *m*; *v* fijar el precio

**priceless** (*praiss*-löss) *adj* inapreciable

**price-list** (*praiss*-lisst) *n* lista de precios

**prick** (prik) *v* pinchar

**pride** (praid) *n* orgullo *m*

**priest** (priisst) *n* cura *m*

**primary** (*prai*-mö-ri) *adj* primario; primero, primordial; elemental

**prince** (prinss) *n* príncipe *m*

**princess** (prin-*ssêss*) *n* princesa *f*

**principal** (*prin*-ssö-pöl) *adj* principal; *n* director de escuela, principal *m*

**principle** (*prin*-ssö-pöl) *n* principio *m*

**print** (print) *v* *imprimir; *n* positiva *f*; grabado *m*; **printed matter** impreso *m*

**prior** (prai⁶) *adj* anterior

**priority** (prai-*o*-rö-ti) *n* prioridad *f*

**prison** (*pri*-sön) *n* prisión *f*

**prisoner** (*pri*-sö-nö) *n* preso *m*, prisionero *m*; ~ **of war** prisionero de guerra

**privacy** (*prai*-vö-ssi) *n* intimidad *f*, vida privada

**private** (*prai*-vit) *adj* particular, privado; personal

**privilege** (*pri*-vi-lid3) *n* privilegio *m*

**prize** (prais) *n* premio *m*; recompensa *f*

**probable** (*pro*-bö-böl) *adj* probable

**probably** (*pro*-bö-bli) *adv* probablemente

**problem** (*pro*-blöm) *n* problema *m*

**procedure** (prö-*ssii*-d3ö) *n* procedimiento *m*

**proceed** (prö-*ssiid*) *v* *proseguir; proceder

**process** (*prou*-ssêss) *n* procedimiento *m*, proceso *m*

**procession** (prö-*ssê*-jön) *n* procesión *f*, comitiva *f*

**proclaim** (prö-*kleim*) *v* proclamar

**produce**¹ (prö-*dyuuss*) *v* *producir

**produce**² (*prod*-yuuss) *n* producto *m*

**producer** (prö-*dyuu*-ssö) *n* productor *m*

**product** (*pro*-dakt) *n* producto *m*

**production** (prö-*dak*-jön) *n* producción *f*

**profession** (prö-*fê*-jön) *n* profesión *f*

**professional** (prö-*fê*-jö-nöl) *adj* profesional

**professor** (prö-*fê*-ssö) *n* profesor *m*

**profit** (*pro*-fit) *n* beneficio *m*, ganancia *f*; ventaja *f*; *v* aprovechar

**profitable** (*pro*-fi-tö-böl) *adj* provechoso

**profound** (prö-*faund*) *adj* profundo

**programme** (*prou*-ghræm) *n* programa *m*

**progress**¹ (*prou*-ghrêss) *n* progreso *m*

**progress**[2] (prö-*ghréss*) v progresar

**progressive** (prö-*ghré*-ssiv) adj progresista; progresivo

**prohibit** (prö-*hi*-bit) v prohibir

**prohibition** (prou-i-*bi*-ʃön) n prohibición f

**prohibitive** (prö-*hi*-bi-tiv) adj exorbitante

**project** (*pro*-dǯĕkt) n plan m, proyecto m

**promenade** (pro-mö-*naad*) n paseo m

**promise** (*pro*-miss) n promesa f; v prometer

**promote** (prö-*mout*) v *promover

**promotion** (prö-*mou*-ʃön) n promoción f

**prompt** (prompt) adj inmediato, pronto

**pronoun** (*prou*-naun) n pronombre m

**pronounce** (prö-*naunss*) v pronunciar

**pronunciation** (prö-nan-ssi-*ei*-ʃön) n pronunciación f

**proof** (pruuf) n prueba f

**propaganda** (pro-pö-*ghæn*-dö) n propaganda f

**propel** (prö-*pêl*) v impeler

**propeller** (prö-*pê*-lö) n hélice f

**proper** (*pro*-pö) adj justo; debido, conveniente, apropiado

**property** (*pro*-pö-ti) n propiedad f; cualidad f

**prophet** (*pro*-fit) n profeta m

**proportion** (prö-*poo*-ʃön) n proporción f

**proportional** (prö-*poo*-ʃö-nöl) adj proporcional

**proposal** (prö-*pou*-söl) n propuesta f

**propose** (prö-*pous*) v *proponer

**proposition** (pro-pö-*si*-ʃön) n propuesta f

**proprietor** (prö-*prai*-ö-tö) n propietario m

**prospect** (*pro*-sspĕkt) n perspectiva f

**prospectus** (prö-*sspĕk*-töss) n pros-

pecto m

**prosperity** (pro-*sspê*-rö-ti) n prosperidad f

**prosperous** (*pro*-sspö-röss) adj próspero

**prostitute** (*pro*-ssti-tyuut) n prostituta f

**protect** (pro-*tĕkt*) v proteger

**protection** (prö-*tĕk*-ʃön) n protección f

**protein** (*prou*-tiin) n proteína f

**protest**[1] (*prou*-têsst) n protesta f

**protest**[2] (prö-*têsst*) v protestar

**Protestant** (*pro*-ti-sstönt) adj protestante

**proud** (praud) adj orgulloso

**prove** (pruuv) v *demostrar, *comprobar; resultar

**proverb** (*pro*-vööb) n proverbio m

**provide** (prö-*vaid*) v *proveer; **provided that** con tal que

**province** (*pro*-vinss) n provincia f

**provincial** (prö-*vin*-ʃöl) adj provincial

**provisional** (prö-*vi*-ʒö-nöl) adj provisional

**provisions** (prö-*vi*-ʒöns) pl provisiones fpl

**prune** (pruun) n ciruela pasa

**psychiatrist** (ssai-*kai*-ö-trisst) n psiquiatra m

**psychic** (*ssai*-kik) adj psíquico

**psychoanalyst** (ssai-kou-*æ*-nö-lisst) n psicoanalista m

**psychological** (ssai-ko-*lo*-dǯi-köl) adj psicológico

**psychologist** (ssai-*ko*-lö-dǯisst) n psicólogo m

**psychology** (ssai-*ko*-lö-dǯi) n psicología f

**pub** (pab) n taberna f

**public** (*pa*-blik) adj público; general; n público m; ~ **garden** jardín público; ~ **house** taberna f

**publication** (pa-bli-*kei*-ʃön) n publica-

ción f
**publicity** (pa-*bli*-ssö-ti) n publicidad f
**publish** (pa-bliʃ) v publicar
**publisher** (pa-bli-ʃö) n editor m
**puddle** (pa-döl) n charco m
**pull** (pul) v tirar; ~ **out** partir; ~ **up**
  pararse
**pulley** (pu-li) n (pl ~s) polea f
**Pullman** (pul-mön) n coche Pullman
**pullover** (pu-lou-vö) n pulóver m
**pulpit** (pul-pit) n púlpito m
**pulse** (palss) n pulso m
**pump** (pamp) n bomba f; v bombear
**punch** (panch) v *dar puñetazos; n
  puñetazo m
**punctual** (pangk-chu-öl) adj puntual
**puncture** (pangk-chö) n pinchazo m
**punctured** (pangk-chöd) adj pinchado
**punish** (pa-niʃ) v castigar
**punishment** (pa-niʃ-mönt) n castigo
  m
**pupil** (pyuu-pöl) n alumno m
**puppet-show** (pa-pit-ʃou) n teatro
  guiñol
**purchase** (pöö-chöss) v comprar; n
  compra f; ~ **price** precio de compra; ~ **tax** impuesto sobre la venta
**purchaser** (pöö-chö-ssö) n comprador
  m
**pure** (pyuᵒ) adj casto, puro
**purple** (pöö-pöl) adj purpúreo
**purpose** (pöö-pöss) n propósito m,
  fin m, intención f; **on** ~ intencionado
**purse** (pööss) n bolsa f, monedero m
**pursue** (pö-ssyuu) v *perseguir
**pus** (pass) n pus f
**push** (puʃ) n empujón m; v empujar
**push-button** (puʃ-ba-tön) n botón m
* **put** (put) v colocar, *poner; meter;
  plantear; ~ **away** guardar; ~ **off**
  aplazar; ~ **on** *ponerse; ~ **out** apagar
**puzzle** (pa-söl) n rompecabezas m;

enigma m; v confundir; **jigsaw** ~
  rompecabezas m
**puzzling** (pas-ling) adj embarazoso
**pyjamas** (pö-dʒaa-mös) pl pijama m

# Q

**quack** (kᵘæk) n curandero m, charlatán m
**quail** (kᵘeil) n (pl ~, ~s) codorniz f
**quaint** (kᵘeint) adj curioso; anticuado
**qualification** (kᵘo-li-fi-kei-ʃön) n aptitud f; reserva f, restricción f
**qualified** (kᵘo-li-faid) adj calificado;
  competente
**qualify** (kᵘo-li-fai) v *ser capaz de,
  *ser apto para
**quality** (kᵘo-lö-ti) n calidad f; característica f
**quantity** (kᵘon-tö-ti) n cantidad f;
  número m
**quarantine** (kᵘo-rön-tiin) n cuarentena f
**quarrel** (kᵘo-röl) v disputar, *reñir; n
  disputa f
**quarry** (kᵘo-ri) n cantera f
**quarter** (kᵘoo-tö) n cuarto m; trimestre m; barrio m; ~ **of an hour**
  cuarto de hora
**quarterly** (kᵘoo-tö-li) adj trimestral
**quay** (kii) n muelle m
**queen** (kᵘiin) n reina f
**queer** (kᵘiᵒ) adj singular, extraño
**query** (kᵘiᵒ-ri) n pregunta f; v indagar; *poner en duda
**question** (kᵘêss-chön) n pregunta f;
  cuestión f, problema m; v interrogar; *poner en duda; ~ **mark** signo
  de interrogación
**queue** (kyuu) n cola f; v *hacer cola
**quick** (kᵘik) adj rápido
**quick-tempered** (kᵘik-têm-pöd) adj

irascible

**quiet** (k$^u$ai-öt) *adj* quieto, tranquilo; *n* silencio *m*, paz *f*

**quilt** (k$^u$ilt) *n* colcha *f*

**quinine** (k$^u$i-niin) *n* quinina *f*

**quit** (k$^u$it) *v* cesar

**quite** (k$^u$ait) *adv* enteramente, completamente; bastante; muy

**quiz** (k$^u$is) *n* (pl ~zes) concurso *m*

**quota** (k$^u$ou-tö) *n* cuota *f*

**quotation** (k$^u$ou-tei-ſön) *n* cita *f*; ~ **marks** comillas *fpl*

**quote** (k$^u$out) *v* citar

# R

**rabbit** (ræ-bit) *n* conejo *m*

**rabies** (rei-bis) *n* rabia *f*

**race** (reiss) *n* carrera *f*; raza *f*

**race-course** (reiss-kooss) *n* pista para carreras, hipódromo *m*

**race-horse** (reiss-hooss) *n* caballo de carrera

**race-track** (reiss-træk) *n* pista para carreras

**racial** (rei-ſöl) *adj* racial

**racket** (ræ-kit) *n* alboroto *m*

**racquet** (ræ-kit) *n* raqueta *f*

**radiator** (rei-di-ei-tö) *n* radiador *m*

**radical** (ræ-di-köl) *adj* radical

**radio** (rei-di-ou) *n* radio *f*

**radish** (ræ-diſ) *n* rábano *m*

**radius** (rei-di-öss) *n* (pl radii) radio *m*

**raft** (raaft) *n* zatara *f*

**rag** (rægh) *n* trapo *m*

**rage** (reidʒ) *n* furor *m*, rabia *f*; *v* rabiar

**raid** (reid) *n* irrupción *f*

**rail** (reil) *n* barandilla *f*, barrera *f*

**railing** (rei-ling) *n* barandilla *f*

**railroad** (reil-roud) *nAm* vía del tren, ferrocarril *m*

**railway** (reil-$^u$ei) *n* ferrocarril *m*

**rain** (rein) *n* lluvia *f*; *v* *llover

**rainbow** (rein-bou) *n* arco iris

**raincoat** (rein-kout) *n* impermeable *m*

**rainproof** (rein-pruuf) *adj* impermeable

**rainy** (rei-ni) *adj* lluvioso

**raise** (reis) *v* alzar; aumentar; educar, cultivar, criar; recaudar; *nAm* aumento de sueldo

**raisin** (rei-sön) *n* pasa *f*

**rake** (reik) *n* rastrillo *m*

**rally** (ræ-li) *n* reunión *f*

**ramp** (ræmp) *n* rampa *f*

**ramshackle** (ræm-ſæ-köl) *adj* destartalado

**rancid** (ræn-ssid) *adj* rancio

**rang** (ræng) *v* (p ring)

**range** (reindʒ) *n* alcance *m*

**range-finder** (reindʒ-fain-dö) *n* telémetro *m*

**rank** (rængk) *n* rango *m*; fila *f*

**ransom** (ræn-ssöm) *n* rescate *m*

**rape** (reip) *v* violar

**rapid** (ræ-pid) *adj* rápido

**rapids** (ræ-pids) *pl* rápidos de río

**rare** (rê$^ö$) *adj* raro

**rarely** (rê$^ö$-li) *adv* raras veces

**rascal** (raa-ssköl) *n* pícaro *m*, pillo *m*

**rash** (ræſ) *n* erupción *f*; *adj* precipitado, irreflexivo

**raspberry** (raas-bö-ri) *n* frambuesa *f*

**rat** (ræt) *n* rata *f*

**rate** (reit) *n* precio *m*, tarifa *f*; velocidad *f*; **at any** ~ de todos modos, en todo caso; ~ **of exchange** cambio *m*

**rather** (raa-ðö) *adv* bastante; más bien

**ration** (ræ-ſön) *n* ración *f*

**rattan** (ræ-tæn) *n* rota *f*

**raven** (rei-vön) *n* cuervo *m*

**raw** (roo) *adj* crudo; ~ **material** materia prima

**ray** (rei) *n* rayo *m*

**rayon** (*rei*-on) *n* rayón *m*

**razor** (*rei*-sö) *n* máquina de afeitar

**razor-blade** (*rei*-sö-bleid) *n* hoja de afeitar

**reach** (riich) *v* alcanzar; *n* alcance *m*

**reaction** (ri-æk-fön) *n* reacción *f*

*read** (riid) *v* *leer

**reading** (*rii*-ding) *n* lectura *f*

**reading-lamp** (*rii*-ding-læmp) *n* lámpara para lectura

**reading-room** (*rii*-ding-ruum) *n* sala de lectura

**ready** (*rê*-di) *adj* preparado, listo

**ready-made** (rê-di-*meid*) *adj* confeccionado

**real** (ri⁰l) *adj* verdadero

**reality** (ri-*æl*-ö-ti) *n* realidad *f*

**realizable** (*ri⁰*-lai-sö-böl) *adj* realizable

**realize** (*ri⁰*-lais) *v* *reconocer; realizar

**really** (*ri⁰*-li) *adv* verdaderamente, en realidad; de veras

**rear** (ri⁰) *n* parte posterior; *v* criar

**rear-light** (ri⁰-*lait*) *n* luz trasera

**reason** (*rii*-sön) *n* causa *f*, razón *f*; sentido *m*; *v* razonar

**reasonable** (*rii*-sö-nö-böl) *adj* razonable

**reassure** (rii-ö-*fu⁰*) *v* tranquilizar

**rebate** (*rii*-beit) *n* reducción *f*, rebaja *f*

**rebellion** (ri-*bél*-yön) *n* sublevación *f*, rebelión *f*

**recall** (ri-*kool*) *v* *acordarse; llamar; revocar

**receipt** (ri-*ssiit*) *n* recibo *m*

**receive** (ri-*ssiiv*) *v* recibir

**receiver** (ri-*ssii*-vö) *n* receptor *m*

**recent** (*rii*-ssönt) *adj* reciente

**recently** (*rii*-ssönt-li) *adv* el otro día, recientemente

**reception** (ri-*ssêp*-fön) *n* recepción *f*; acogida *f*; ~ **office** oficina de recibo

**receptionist** (ri-*ssêp*-fö-nisst) *n* recepcionista *f*

**recession** (ri-*ssê*-fön) *n* retroceso *m*

**recipe** (*rê*-ssi-pi) *n* receta *f*

**recital** (ri-*ssai*-töl) *n* recital *m*

**reckon** (*rê*-kön) *v* calcular; considerar; *creer

**recognition** (rê-kögh-*ni*-fön) *n* reconocimiento *m*

**recognize** (*rê*-kögh-nais) *v* *reconocer

**recollect** (rê-kö-*lêkt*) *v* *acordarse

**recommence** (rii-kö-*mênss*) *v* *recomenzar

**recommend** (rê-kö-*mênd*) *v* *recomendar; aconsejar

**recommendation** (rê-kö-mên-*dei*-fön) *n* recomendación *f*

**reconciliation** (rê-kön-ssi-li-*ei*-fön) *n* reconciliación *f*

**record¹** (*rê*-kood) *n* disco *m*; récord *m*; registro *m*; **long-playing** ~ microsurco *m*

**record²** (ri-*kood*) *v* registrar

**recorder** (ri-*koo*-dö) *n* magnetófono *m*

**recording** (ri-*koo*-ding) *n* grabación *f*

**record-player** (*rê*-kood-plei⁰) *n* tocadiscos *m*

**recover** (ri-*ka*-vö) *v* recuperar; *restablecerse, curarse

**recovery** (ri-*ka*-vö-ri) *n* curación *f*, restablecimiento *m*

**recreation** (rê-kri-*ei*-fön) *n* recreación *f*, recreo *m*; ~ **centre** centro de recreo; ~ **ground** terreno de recreo público

**recruit** (ri-*kruut*) *n* recluta *m*

**rectangle** (*rêk*-tæng-ghöl) *n* rectángulo *m*

**rectangular** (rêk-*tæng*-ghyu-lö) *adj* rectangular

**rector** (*rêk*-tö) *n* pastor *m*, rector *m*

**rectory** (*rêk*-tö-ri) *n* rectoría *f*

**rectum** (*rêk*-töm) *n* intestino recto

**red** (rêd) *adj* rojo

**redeem** (ri-*diim*) *v* redimir

**reduce** (ri-*dyuuss*) *v* *reducir, *disminuir, rebajar

**reduction** (ri-*dak*-[ö]n) *n* rebaja *f*, reducción *f*

**redundant** (ri-*dan*-dönt) *adj* superfluo

**reed** (riid) *n* junquillo *m*

**reef** (riif) *n* arrecife *m*

**reference** (*rêf*-rönss) *n* referencia *f*; relación *f*; **with ~ to** con respecto a

**refer to** (ri-*föö*) remitir a

**refill** (*rii*-fil) *n* repuesto *m*

**refinery** (ri-*fai*-nö-ri) *n* refinería *f*

**reflect** (ri-*flêkt*) *v* reflejar

**reflection** (ri-*flêk*-[ö]n) *n* reflejo *m*; imagen reflejada

**reflector** (ri-*flêk*-tö) *n* reflector *m*

**reformation** (rê-fö-*mei*-[ö]n) *n* Reforma *f*

**refresh** (ri-*frêf*) *v* refrescar

**refreshment** (ri-*frêf*-mönt) *n* refresco *m*

**refrigerator** (ri-*fri*-dʒö-rei-tö) *n* refrigerador *m*

**refund**[1] (ri-*fand*) *v* reintegrar

**refund**[2] (*rii*-fand) *n* reintegro *m*

**refusal** (ri-*fyuu*-söl) *n* negativa *f*

**refuse**[1] (ri-*fyuus*) *v* rehusar

**refuse**[2] (*rê*-fyuuss) *n* desecho *m*

**regard** (ri-*ghaad*) *v* considerar; *n* respeto *m*; **as regards** en cuanto a, por lo que se refiere a

**regarding** (ri-*ghaa*-ding) *prep* relativo a, tocante a; respecto a

**regatta** (ri-*ghæ*-tö) *n* regata *f*

**régime** (rei-*ʒiim*) *n* régimen *m*

**region** (*rii*-dʒön) *n* región *f*

**regional** (*rii*-dʒö-nöl) *adj* regional

**register** (*rê*-dʒi-sstö) *v* inscribirse; certificar; **registered letter** carta certificada

**registration** (rê-dʒi-*sstrei*-[ö]n) *n* inscripción *f*; ~ **form** formulario de matriculación; ~ **number** matrícula *f*; ~ **plate** placa *f*

**regret** (ri-*ghrêt*) *v* *sentir; *n* arrepentimiento *m*

**regular** (*rê*-ghyu-lö) *adj* regular; corriente, normal

**regulate** (*rê*-ghyu-leit) *v* regular

**regulation** (rê-ghyu-*lei*-jön) *n* reglamento *m*, regulación *f*; regla *f*

**rehabilitation** (rii-hö-bi-li-*tei*-[ö]n) *n* rehabilitación *f*

**rehearsal** (ri-*höö*-ssöl) *n* ensayo *m*

**rehearse** (ri-*hööss*) *v* ensayar

**reign** (rein) *n* reinado *m*; *v* *gobernar

**reimburse** (rii-im-*bööss*) *v* reembolsar

**reindeer** (*rein*-di[ö]) *n* (pl ~) reno *m*

**reject** (ri-*dʒêkt*) *v* rehusar, rechazar; *reprobar

**relate** (ri-*leit*) *v* *contar

**related** (ri-*lei*-tid) *adj* emparentado

**relation** (ri-*lei*-[ö]n) *n* relación *f*; pariente *m*

**relative** (*rê*-lö-tiv) *n* pariente *m*; *adj* relativo

**relax** (ri-*lækss*) *v* descansar

**relaxation** (ri-læk-*ssei*-[ö]n) *n* relajación *f*

**reliable** (ri-*lai*-ö-böl) *adj* fiable

**relic** (*rê*-lik) *n* reliquia *f*

**relief** (ri-*liif*) *n* alivio *m*; ayuda *f*; relieve *m*

**relieve** (ri-*liiv*) *v* relevar

**religion** (ri-*li*-dʒön) *n* religión *f*

**religious** (ri-*li*-dʒöss) *adj* religioso

**rely on** (ri-*lai*) *contar con

**remain** (ri-*mein*) *v* quedarse; quedar

**remainder** (ri-*mein*-dö) *n* resto *m*

**remaining** (ri-*mei*-ning) *adj* demás, restante

**remark** (ri-*maak*) *n* observación *f*; *v* *hacer una observación

**remarkable** (ri-*maa*-kö-böl) *adj* notable

**remedy** (*rê*-mö-di) *n* remedio *m*

**remember** (ri-*mêm*-bö) *v* \*acordarse

**remembrance** (ri-*mêm*-brönss) *n* recuerdo *m*

**remind** (ri-*maind*) *v* \*recordar

**remit** (ri-*mit*) *v* remitir

**remittance** (ri-*mi*-tönss) *n* remesa *f*

**remnant** (*rêm*-nönt) *n* resto *m*, residuo *m*, remanente *m*

**remote** (ri-*mout*) *adj* remoto, lejano

**removal** (ri-*muu*-völ) *n* remoción *f*

**remove** (ri-*muuv*) *v* \*remover

**remunerate** (ri-*myuu*-nö-reit) *v* remunerar

**remuneration** (ri-myuu-nö-*rei*-fön) *n* remuneración *f*

**renew** (ri-*nyuu*) *v* \*renovar; alargar

**rent** (rênt) *v* alquilar; *n* alquiler *m*

**repair** (ri-*pêᵒ*) *v* arreglar, reparar; *n* reparación *f*

**reparation** (rê-pö-*rei*-fön) *n* reparación *f*

**\*repay** (ri-*pei*) *v* reintegrar

**repayment** (ri-*pei*-mönt) *n* reintegro *m*

**repeat** (ri-*piit*) *v* \*repetir

**repellent** (ri-*pê*-lönt) *adj* repugnante, repelente

**repentance** (ri-*pên*-tönss) *n* arrepentimiento *m*

**repertory** (*rê*-pö-tö-ri) *n* repertorio *m*

**repetition** (rê-pö-*ti*-fön) *n* repetición *f*

**replace** (ri-*pleiss*) *v* reemplazar

**reply** (ri-*plai*) *v* responder; *n* respuesta *f*; **in ~** en contestación

**report** (ri-*poot*) *v* relatar; informar; presentarse; *n* relación *f*, informe *m*

**reporter** (ri-*poo*-tö) *n* reportero *m*

**represent** (rê-pri-*sênt*) *v* representar

**representation** (rê-pri-sên-*tei*-fön) *n* representación *f*

**representative** (rê-pri-*sên*-tö-tiv) *adj* representativo

**reprimand** (*rê*-pri-maand) *v* reprender

**reproach** (ri-*prouch*) *n* reproche *m*; *v* reprochar

**reproduce** (rii-prö-*dyuuss*) *v* \*reproducir

**reproduction** (rii-prö-*dak*-fön) *n* reproducción *f*

**reptile** (*rêp*-tail) *n* reptil *m*

**republic** (ri-*pa*-blik) *n* república *f*

**republican** (ri-*pa*-bli-kön) *adj* republicano

**repulsive** (ri-*pal*-ssiv) *adj* repulsivo

**reputation** (rê-pyu-*tei*-fön) *n* reputación *f*; renombre *m*

**request** (ri-*kᵘêsst*) *n* ruego *m*; demanda *f*; *v* solicitar

**require** (ri-*kᵘaiᵒ*) *v* \*requerir

**requirement** (ri-*kᵘaiᵒ*-mönt) *n* requerimiento *m*

**requisite** (*rê*-kᵘi-sit) *adj* necesario

**rescue** (*rê*-sskyuu) *v* rescatar; *n* rescate *m*

**research** (ri-*ssööch*) *n* investigación *f*

**resemblance** (ri-*sêm*-blönss) *n* semejanza *f*

**resemble** (ri-*sêm*-böl) *v* asemejarse

**resent** (ri-*sênt*) *v* \*resentirse por

**reservation** (rê-sö-*vei*-fön) *n* reservación *f*

**reserve** (ri-*sööv*) *v* reservar; *n* reserva *f*

**reserved** (ri-*söövd*) *adj* reservado

**reservoir** (*rê*-sö-vᵘaa) *n* embalse *m*

**reside** (ri-*said*) *v* residir

**residence** (*rê*-si-dönss) *n* residencia *f*; **~ permit** permiso de residencia

**resident** (*rê*-si-dönt) *n* residente *m*; *adj* residente; interno

**resign** (ri-*sain*) *v* resignar

**resignation** (rê-sigh-*nei*-fön) *n* resignación *f*

**resin** (*rê*-sin) *n* resina *f*

**resist** (ri-*sisst*) *v* resistir

**resistance** (ri-*si*-sstönss) *n* resistencia

*f*

**resolute** (*rê*-sö-luut) *adj* resuelto, decidido

**respect** (ri-*sspêkt*) *n* respeto *m*; estimación *f*, reverencia *f*; *v* respetar

**respectable** (ri-*sspêk*-tö-böl) *adj* respetable

**respectful** (ri-*sspêkt*-föl) *adj* respetuoso

**respective** (ri-*sspêk*-tiv) *adj* respectivo

**respiration** (rê-sspö-*rei*-[ö]n) *n* respiración *f*

**respite** (*rê*-sspait) *n* dilación *f*

**responsibility** (ri-sspon-ssö-*bi*-lö-ti) *n* responsabilidad *f*

**responsible** (ri-*sspon*-ssö-böl) *adj* responsable

**rest** (rêsst) *n* descanso *m*; resto *m*; *v* *hacer reposo, descansar

**restaurant** (*rê*-sstö-ro[ng]) *n* restaurante *m*

**restful** (*rêsst*-föl) *adj* reposado

**rest-home** (*rêsst*-houm) *n* casa de reposo

**restless** (*rêsst*-löss) *adj* inquieto

**restrain** (ri-*sstrein*) *v* *contener, *impedir

**restriction** (ri-*sstrik*-[ö]n) *n* restricción *f*

**result** (ri-*salt*) *n* resultado *m*; consecuencia *f*; *v* resultar

**resume** (ri-*syuum*) *v* reemprender

**résumé** (*rê*-syu-mei) *n* resumen *m*

**retail** (*rii*-teil) *v* vender al detalle; ~ **trade** comercio al por menor

**retailer** (*rii*-tei-lö) *n* comerciante al por menor, minorista *m*; revendedor *m*

**retina** (*rê*-ti-nö) *n* retina *f*

**retired** (ri-*tai*[ö]d) *adj* jubilado

**return** (ri-*töön*) *v* *volver; *n* regreso *m*; ~ **flight** vuelo de regreso; ~ **journey** vuelta *f*, viaje de regreso

**reunite** (rii-yuu-*nait*) *v* reunir

**reveal** (ri-*viil*) *v* *manifestar, revelar

**revelation** (rê-vö-*lei*-[ö]n) *n* revelación *f*

**revenge** (ri-*vêndʒ*) *n* venganza *f*

**revenue** (*rê*-vö-nyuu) *n* ingresos *mpl*, renta *f*

**reverse** (ri-*vööss*) *n* contrario *m*; reverso *m*; marcha atrás; revés *m*; *adj* inverso; *v* *dar marcha atrás

**review** (ri-*vyuu*) *n* reseña *f*; revista *f*

**revise** (ri-*vais*) *v* revisar

**revision** (ri-*vi*-ʒön) *n* revisión *f*

**revival** (ri-*vai*-völ) *n* recuperación *f*

**revolt** (ri-*voult*) *v* sublevarse; *n* rebelión *f*, revuelta *f*

**revolting** (ri-*voul*-ting) *adj* repugnante, chocante, repelente

**revolution** (rê-vö-*luu*-[ö]n) *n* revolución *f*

**revolutionary** (rê-vö-*luu*-[ö]-nö-ri) *adj* revolucionario

**revolver** (ri-*vol*-vö) *n* revólver *m*

**revue** (ri-*vyuu*) *n* revista *f*

**reward** (ri-*ᵘood*) *n* recompensa *f*; *v* recompensar

**rheumatism** (*ruu*-mö-ti-söm) *n* reumatismo *m*

**rhinoceros** (rai-*no*-ssö-röss) *n* (pl ~, ~es) rinoceronte *m*

**rhubarb** (*ruu*-baab) *n* ruibarbo *m*

**rhyme** (raim) *n* rima *f*

**rhythm** (*ri*-ðöm) *n* ritmo *m*

**rib** (rib) *n* costilla *f*

**ribbon** (*ri*-bön) *n* cinta *f*

**rice** (raiss) *n* arroz *m*

**rich** (rich) *adj* rico

**riches** (*ri*-chis) *pl* riqueza *f*

**riddle** (*ri*-döl) *n* adivinanza *f*

**ride** (raid) *n* paseo *m*

* **ride** (raid) *v* *ir en coche; montar

**rider** (*rai*-dö) *n* jinete *m*

**ridge** (ridʒ) *n* cresta *f*

**ridicule** (*ri*-di-kyuuḷ) *v* ridiculizar

**ridiculous** (ri-*di*-kyu-löss) *adj* ridículo

**riding** (*rai*-ding) *n* equitación *f*

**riding-school** (*rai*-ding-sskuul) *n* picadero *m*

**rifle** (rait) *v* rifle *m*

**right** (rait) *n* derecho *m*; *adj* correcto; derecho; justo; **all right!** ¡de acuerdo!; * **be ~** *tener razón; **~ of way** prioridad de paso

**righteous** (*rai*-chöss) *adj* justo

**right-hand** (rait-hænd) *adj* derecho

**rightly** (rait-li) *adv* justamente

**rim** (rim) *n* llanta *f*; borde *m*

**ring** (ring) *n* anillo *m*; círculo *m*; pista *f*

* **ring** (ring) *v* *sonar; **~ up** llamar por teléfono

**rinse** (rinss) *v* enjuagar; *n* enjuague *m*

**riot** (*rai*-öt) *n* motín *m*

**rip** (rip) *v* rasgar

**ripe** (raip) *adj* maduro

**rise** (rais) *n* aumento de sueldo, aumento *m*; levantamiento *m*; subida *f*; nacimiento *m*

* **rise** (rais) *v* levantarse; subir

**rising** (*rai*-sing) *n* levantamiento *m*

**risk** (rissk) *n* riesgo *m*; peligro *m*; *v* arriesgar

**risky** (*ri*-sski) *adj* arriesgado

**rival** (*rai*-völ) *n* rival *m*; competidor *m*; *v* rivalizar

**rivalry** (*rai*-völ-ri) *n* rivalidad *f*; competencia *f*

**river** (*ri*-vö) *n* río *m*; **~ bank** ribera *f*

**riverside** (*ri*-vö-ssaid) *n* ribera *f*

**roach** (rouch) *n* (pl ~) escarcho *m*

**road** (roud) *n* calle *f*, camino *m*; **~ fork** *n* bifurcación *f*; **~ map** mapa de carreteras; **~ system** red de carreteras; **~ up** camino en obras

**roadhouse** (*roud*-hauss) *n* parador *m*

**roadside** (*roud*-ssaid) *n* borde del camino

**roam** (roum) *v* vagabundear

**roar** (roo) *v* mugir, rugir; *n* rugido *m*, retumbo *m*

**roast** (rousst) *v* asar, asar en parrilla

**rob** (rob) *v* robar

**robber** (*ro*-bö) *n* ladrón *m*

**robbery** (*ro*-bö-ri) *n* robo *m*

**robe** (roub) *n* traje largo

**robin** (*ro*-bin) *n* petirrojo *m*

**robust** (rou-*basst*) *adj* robusto

**rock** (rok) *n* roca *f*; *v* mecer

**rocket** (*ro*-kit) *n* cohete *m*

**rocky** (*ro*-ki) *adj* rocoso

**rod** (rod) *n* barra *f*

**roe** (rou) *n* huevos de los peces, hueva *f*

**roll** (roul) *v* *rodar; *n* rollo *m*; panecillo *m*

**roller-skating** (*rou*-lö-sskei-ting) *n* patinaje de ruedas

**Roman Catholic** (*rou*-mön *kæ*-zö-lik) católico

**romance** (rö-*mænss*) *n* amorío *m*

**romantic** (rö-*mæn*-tik) *adj* romántico

**roof** (ruuf) *n* techo *m*; **thatched ~** techo de paja

**room** (ruum) *n* habitación *f*; espacio *m*, sitio *m*; **~ and board** pensión completa; **~ service** servicio de habitación; **~ temperature** temperatura ambiente

**roomy** (*ruu*-mi) *adj* espacioso

**root** (ruut) *n* raíz *f*

**rope** (roup) *n* soga *f*

**rosary** (*rou*-sö-ri) *n* rosario *m*

**rose** (rous) *n* rosa *f*; *adj* rosa

**rosary** (*ro*-tön) *adj* podrido

**rouge** (ruuʒ) *n* colorete *m*

**rough** (raf) *adj* áspero

**roulette** (ruu-*lêt*) *n* ruleta *f*

**round** (raund) *adj* redondo; *prep* alrededor de, en torno de; *n* vuelta *f*; **~ trip** *Am* ida y vuelta

**roundabout** (*raun*-dö-baut) *n* glorieta *f*

**rounded** (*raun*-did) *adj* redondeado

**route** (ruut) *n* ruta *f*

**routine** (ruu-*tiin*) *n* rutina *f*

**row¹** (rou) *n* fila *f*; *v* remar

**row²** (rau) *n* bronca *f*

**rowdy** (*rau*-di) *adj* alborotador

**rowing-boat** (*rou*-ing-bout) *n* bote *m*

**royal** (*roi*-öl) *adj* real

**rub** (rab) *v* frotar

**rubber** (*ra*-bö) *n* caucho *m*; goma de borrar; hule *mMe*; ~ **band** elástico *m*

**rubbish** (*ra*-biʃ) *n* basura *f*; habladuría *f*, tontería *f*; **talk** ~ *decir tonterías

**rubbish-bin** (*ra*-biʃ-bin) *n* cubo de la basura

**ruby** (*ruu*-bi) *n* rubí *m*

**rucksack** (*rak*-ssæk) *n* mochila *f*

**rudder** (*ra*-dö) *n* timón *m*

**rude** (ruud) *adj* grosero

**rug** (ragh) *n* alfombrilla *f*

**ruin** (*ruu*-in) *v* arruinar; *n* ruina *f*

**ruination** (ruu-i-*nei*-ʃön) *n* hundimiento *m*

**rule** (ruul) *n* regla *f*; régimen *m*, gobierno *m*, dominio *m*; *v* *gobernar, *regir; **as a** ~ generalmente, por regla general

**ruler** (*ruu*-lö) *n* monarca *m*, gobernante *m*; regla *f*

**Rumania** (ruu-*mei*-ni-ö) Rumania *f*

**Rumanian** (ruu-*mei*-ni-ön) *adj* rumano

**rumour** (*ruu*-mö) *n* rumor *m*

***run** (ran) *v* correr; ~ **into** *encontrarse con

**runaway** (*ra*-nö-ᵘei) *n* fugitivo *m*

**rung** (ran) *v* (pp ring)

**runway** (*ran*-ᵘei) *n* pista de aterrizaje

**rural** (*ruᵒ*-röl) *adj* rural

**ruse** (ruus) *n* astucia *f*

**rush** (raʃ) *v* precipitarse; *n* junco *m*

**rush-hour** (*raʃ*-auᵒ) *n* hora de afluencia

**Russia** (*ra*-ʃö) Rusia *f*

**Russian** (*ra*-ʃön) *adj* ruso

**rust** (rasst) *n* herrumbre *f*

**rustic** (*ra*-sstik) *adj* rústico

**rusty** (*ra*-ssti) *adj* oxidado

# S

**saccharin** (*ssæ*-kö-rin) *n* sacarina *f*

**sack** (ssæk) *n* saco *m*

**sacred** (*ssei*-krid) *adj* sagrado

**sacrifice** (*ssæ*-kri-faiss) *n* sacrificio *m*; *v* sacrificar

**sacrilege** (*ssæ*-kri-lidʒ) *n* sacrilegio *m*

**sad** (ssæd) *adj* triste; afligido, melancólico

**saddle** (*ssæ*-döl) *n* silla *f*

**sadness** (*ssæd*-nöss) *n* tristeza *f*

**safe** (sseif) *adj* seguro; *n* caja fuerte, caja de caudales

**safety** (*sseif*-ti) *n* seguridad *f*

**safety-belt** (*sseif*-ti-bêlt) *n* cinturón de seguridad

**safety-pin** (*sseif*-ti-pin) *n* imperdible *m*

**safety-razor** (*sseif*-ti-rei-sö) *n* máquina de afeitar

**sail** (sseil) *v* navegar; *n* vela *f*

**sailing-boat** (*ssei*-ling-bout) *n* buque velero

**sailor** (*ssei*-lö) *n* marinero *m*

**saint** (sseint) *n* santo *m*

**salad** (*ssæ*-löd) *n* ensalada *f*

**salad-oil** (*ssæ*-löd-oil) *n* aceite de mesa

**salary** (*ssæ*-lö-ri) *n* sueldo *m*

**sale** (sseil) *n* venta *f*; **clearance** ~ liquidación *f*; **for** ~ de venta; **sales** rebajas *fpl*

**saleable** (*ssei*-lö-böl) *adj* vendible

**salesgirl** (*sseils*-ghööl) *n* vendedora *f*

**salesman** (*sseils*-mön) *n* (pl -men)

vendedor *m*

**salmon** (*ssæ*-mön) *n* (pl ~) salmón *m*

**salon** (*ssæ*-long) *n* salón *m*

**saloon** (*ssö-luun*) *n* bar *m*; cantina *fMe*

**salt** (ssoolt) *n* sal *f*

**salt-cellar** (*ssoolt*-ssê-lö) *n* salero *m*

**salty** (*ssool*-ti) *adj* salado

**salute** (ssö-*luut*) *v* saludar

**salve** (ssaav) *n* ungüento *m*

**same** (sseim) *adj* mismo

**sample** (*ssaam*-pöl) *n* muestra *f*

**sanatorium** (ssæ-nö-*too*-ri-öm) *n* (pl ~s, -ria) sanatorio *m*

**sand** (ssænd) *n* arena *f*

**sandal** (*ssæn*-döl) *n* sandalia *f*

**sandpaper** (*ssænd*-pei-pö) *n* papel de lija

**sandwich** (*ssæn*-ᵘidȝ) *n* bocadillo *m*; emparedado *m*

**sandy** (*ssæn*-di) *adj* arenoso

**sanitary** (*ssæ*-ni-tö-ri) *adj* sanitario; ~ **towel** paño higiénico

**sapphire** (*ssæ*-faiᵒ) *n* zafiro *m*

**sardine** (ssaa-*diin*) *n* sardina *f*

**satchel** (*ssæ*-chöl) *n* cartera *f*

**satellite** (*ssæ*-tö-lait) *n* satélite *m*

**satin** (*ssæ*-tin) *n* raso *m*

**satisfaction** (ssæ-tiss-*fæk*-fön) *n* satisfacción *f*

**satisfy** (*ssæ*-tiss-fai) *v* *satisfacer

**Saturday** (*ssæ*-tö-di) sábado *m*

**sauce** (ssooss) *n* salsa *f*

**saucepan** (*ssooss*-pön) *n* cacerola *f*

**saucer** (*ssoo*-ssö) *n* platillo *m*

**Saudi Arabia** (ssau-di-ö-*rei*-bi-ö) Arabia Saudí

**Saudi Arabian** (ssau-di-ö-*rei*-bi-ön) *adj* saudí

**sauna** (*ssoo*-nö) *n* sauna *f*

**sausage** (*sso*-ssidȝ) *n* salchicha *f*

**savage** (*ssæ*-vidȝ) *adj* salvaje

**save** (sseiv) *v* salvar; ahorrar

**savings** (*ssei*-vings) *pl* ahorros *mpl*;

~ **bank** caja de ahorros

**saviour** (*ssei*-vyö) *n* salvador *m*

**savoury** (*ssei*-vö-ri) *adj* sabroso; picante

**saw¹** (ssoo) *v* (p see)

**saw²** (ssoo) *n* sierra *f*

**sawdust** (*ssoo*-dasst) *n* serrín *m*

**saw-mill** (*ssoo*-mil) *n* serrería de maderas

*****say** (ssei) *v* *decir

**scaffolding** (*sskæ*-föl-ding) *n* andamio *m*

**scale** (sskeil) *n* escala *f*; escala musical; escama *f*; **scales** *pl* balanza *f*

**scandal** (*sskæn*-döl) *n* escándalo *m*

**Scandinavia** (sskæn-di-*nei*-vi-ö) Escandinavia *f*

**Scandinavian** (sskæn-di-*nei*-vi-ön) *adj* escandinavo

**scapegoat** (*sskeip*-ghout) *n* cabeza de turco

**scar** (sskaa) *n* cicatriz *f*

**scarce** (sskê°ss) *adj* escaso

**scarcely** (*sskê°*-ssli) *adv* apenas

**scarcity** (*sskê°*-ssö-ti) *n* escasez *f*

**scare** (sskê°) *v* asustar; *n* susto *m*

**scarf** (sskaaf) *n* (pl ~s, scarves) bufanda *f*

**scarlet** (*sskaa*-löt) *adj* escarlata

**scary** (*sskê°*-ri) *adj* alarmante

**scatter** (*sskæ*-tö) *v* esparcir

**scene** (ssiin) *n* escena *f*

**scenery** (*ssii*-nö-ri) *n* paisaje *m*

**scenic** (*ssii*-nik) *adj* pintoresco

**scent** (ssênt) *n* perfume *m*

**schedule** (*fé*-dyuul) *n* horario *m*

**scheme** (sskiim) *n* esquema *m*; proyecto *m*

**scholar** (*ssko*-lö) *n* erudito *m*; alumno *m*

**scholarship** (*ssko*-lö-fip) *n* beca *f*

**school** (sskuul) *n* escuela *f*

**schoolboy** (*sskuul*-boi) *n* alumno *m*

**schoolgirl** (*sskuul*-ghööl) *n* alumna *f*

schoolmaster ( *sskuul*-maa-sstö ) *n* maestro *m*

schoolteacher ( *sskuul*-tii-chö ) *n* maestro *m*

science ( *ssai*-önss ) *n* ciencia *f*

scientific ( ssai-ön-*ti*-fik ) *adj* científico

scientist ( *ssai*-ön-tisst ) *n* científico *m*

scissors ( *ssi*-sös ) *pl* tijeras *fpl*

scold ( sskould ) *v* reprender; insultar

scooter ( *sskuu*-tö ) *n* motoneta *f*; patín *m*

score ( sskoo ) *n* tanteo *m*; *v* marcar

scorn ( sskoon ) *n* escarnio *m*, desprecio *m*; *v* despreciar

Scot ( sskot ) *n* escocés *m*

Scotch ( sskoch ) *adj* escocés; **scotch tape** cinta adhesiva

Scotland ( *sskot*-lönd ) Escocia *f*

Scottish ( *ssko*-tiʃ ) *adj* escocés

scout ( sskaut ) *n* explorador *m*

scrap ( sskræp ) *n* pedazo *m*

scrap-book ( *sskræp*-buk ) *n* álbum *m*

scrape ( sskreip ) *v* raspar

scrap-iron ( *sskræ*-pai°n ) *n* chatarra *f*

scratch ( sskræch ) *v* \*hacer raeduras, rascar; *n* raedura *f*, rasguño *m*

scream ( sskriim ) *v* gritar, chillar; *n* grito *m*, chillido *m*

screen ( sskriin ) *n* mampara *f*; pantalla *f*

screw ( sskruu ) *n* tornillo *m*; *v* atornillar

screw-driver ( *sskruu*-drai-vö ) *n* destornillador *m*

scrub ( sskrab ) *v* \*fregar; *n* matorral *m*

sculptor ( *sskalp*-tö ) *n* escultor *m*

sculpture ( *sskalp*-chö ) *n* escultura *f*

sea ( ssii ) *n* mar *m*

sea-bird ( *ssii*-bööd ) *n* ave marina

sea-coast ( *ssii*-kousst ) *n* litoral *m*

seagull ( *ssii*-ghal ) *n* gaviota *f*

seal ( ssiil ) *n* sello *m*; foca *f*

seam ( ssiim ) *n* costura *f*

seaman ( *ssii*-mön ) *n* (pl -men) marino *m*

seamless ( *ssiim*-löss ) *adj* sin costura

seaport ( *ssii*-poot ) *n* puerto de mar

search ( ssööch ) *v* buscar; cachear; *n* búsqueda *f*

searchlight ( *ssööch*-lait ) *n* reflector *m*

seascape ( *ssii*-sskeip ) *n* marina *f*

sea-shell ( *ssii*-ʃêl ) *n* concha *f*

seashore ( *ssii*-ʃoo ) *n* orilla del mar

seasick ( *ssii*-ssik ) *adj* mareado

seasickness ( *ssii*-ssik-nöss ) *n* mareo *m*

seaside ( *ssii*-ssaid ) *n* orilla del mar; ~ **resort** playa de veraneo

season ( *ssii*-sön ) *n* temporada *f*, estación *f*; **high** ~ apogeo de la temporada; **low** ~ temporada baja; **off** ~ fuera de temporada

season-ticket ( *ssii*-sön-ti-kit ) *n* tarjeta de temporada

seat ( ssiit ) *n* asiento *m*; sitio *m*, localidad *f*; sede *f*

seat-belt ( *ssiit*-bêlt ) *n* cinturón de seguridad

sea-urchin ( *ssii*-öö-chin ) *n* erizo de mar

sea-water ( *ssii*-°oo-tö ) *n* agua de mar

second ( *ssê*-könd ) *num* segundo; *n* segundo *m*; instante *m*

secondary ( *ssê*-kön-dö-ri ) *adj* secundario; ~ **school** escuela secundaria

second-hand ( ssê-könd-*hænd* ) *adj* de segunda mano

secret ( *ssii*-kröt ) *n* secreto *m*; *adj* secreto

secretary ( *ssê*-krö-tri ) *n* secretaria *f*; secretario *m*

section ( *ssêk*-ʃön ) *n* sección *f*; división *f*, departamento *m*

secure ( ssi-*kyu*° ) *adj* firme; *v* lograr

security ( ssi-*kyu*°-rö-ti ) *n* seguridad *f*; fianza *f*

sedate ( ssi-*deit* ) *adj* sosegado

sedative (*ssê*-dö-tiv) *n* calmante *m*

seduce (ssi-*dyuuss*) *v* *seducir

*see (ssii) *v* *ver; comprender, *darse cuenta; ~ to *atender a

seed (ssiid) *n* semilla *f*

*seek (ssiik) *v* buscar

seem (ssiim) *v* *parecer

seen (ssiin) *V* (pp see)

seesaw (*ssii*-ssoo) *n* columpio *m*

seize (ssiis) *v* agarrar

seldom (*ssê*l-döm) *adv* pocas veces

select (ssi-*lêkt*) *v* seleccionar, *elegir; *adj* seleccionado, selecto

selection (ssi-*lêk*-jön) *n* elección *f*, selección *f*

self-centred (ssêlf-*ssên*-töd) *adj* egocéntrico

self-employed (ssêl-fim-*ploid*) *adj* independiente

self-evident (ssêl-*fê*-vi-dönt) *adj* evidente

self-government (ssêlf-*gha*-vö-mönt) *n* autonomía *f*

selfish (*ssêl*-fij) *adj* egoísta

selfishness (*ssêl*-fij-nöss) *n* egoísmo *m*

self-service (ssêlf-*ssöö*-viss) *n* autoservicio *m*

*sell (ssêl) *v* vender

semblance (*ssêm*-blönss) *n* apariencia *f*

semi- (*ssê*-mi) semi-

semicircle (*ssê*-mi-ssöö-köl) *n* semicírculo *m*

semi-colon (ssê-mi-*kou*-lön) *n* punto y coma

senate (*ssê*-nöt) *n* senado *m*

senator (*ssê*-nö-tö) *n* senador *m*

*send (ssênd) *v* enviar, mandar; ~ back *devolver; ~ for mandar a buscar; ~ off despachar

senile (*ssii*-nail) *adj* senil

sensation (ssên-*ssei*-jön) *n* sensación *f*

sensational (ssên-*ssei*-jö-nöl) *adj* sensacional

sense (ssênss) *n* sentido *m*; juicio *m*, razón *f*; *v* *sentir; ~ of honour sentido del honor

senseless (*ssênss*-löss) *adj* insensato

sensible (*ssên*-ssö-böl) *adj* sensato

sensitive (*ssên*-ssi-tiv) *adj* sensitivo

sentence (*ssên*-tönss) *n* frase *f*; sentencia *f*; *v* sentenciar

sentimental (ssên-ti-*mên*-töl) *adj* sentimental

separate[1] (*ssê*-pö-reit) *v* separar

separate[2] (*ssê*-pö-röt) *adj* separado

separately (*ssê*-pö-röt-li) *adv* por separado

September (ssêp-*têm*-bö) septiembre

septic (*ssêp*-tik) *adj* séptico; *become ~ infectarse

sequel (*ssii*-kᵘöl) *n* continuación *f*

sequence (*ssii*-kᵘönss) *n* sucesión *f*; serie *f*

serene (ssö-*riin*) *adj* sereno; claro

serial (*ssi*ᵃ-ri-öl) *n* novela por entregas

series (*ssi*ᵃ-riis) *n* (pl ~) serie *f*

serious (*ssi*ᵃ-ri-öss) *adj* serio

seriousness (*ssi*ᵃ-ri-öss-nöss) *n* seriedad *f*

sermon (*ssöö*-mön) *n* sermón *m*

serum (*ssi*ᵃ-röm) *n* suero *m*

servant (*ssöö*-vönt) *n* criado *m*

serve (ssööv) *v* *servir

service (*ssöö*-viss) *n* servicio *m*; ~ charge servicio *m*; ~ station puesto de gasolina

serviette (ssöö-vi-*êt*) *n* servilleta *f*

session (*ssê*-jön) *n* sesión *f*

set (ssêt) *n* juego *m*, grupo *m*

*set (ssêt) *v* *poner; ~ menu cubierto a precio fijo; ~ out partir

setting (*ssê*-ting) *n* escena *f*; ~ lotion fijador *m*

settle (*ssê*-töl) *v* arreglar; ~ down

arraigarse
**settlement** (ssê-töl-mönt) *n* acuerdo *m*, arreglo *m*, convenio *m*
**seven** (ssê-vön) *num* siete
**seventeen** (ssê-vön-*tiin*) *num* diecisiete
**seventeenth** (ssê-vön-*tiinz*) *num* decimoséptimo
**seventh** (ssê-vönz) *num* séptimo
**seventy** (ssê-vön-ti) *num* setenta
**several** (ssê-vö-röl) *adj* varios
**severe** (ssi-*vi⁰*) *adj* violento, rigoroso, severo
**sew** (ssou) *v* coser; ~ **up** *hacer una sutura
**sewer** (ssuu-ö) *n* desagüe *m*
**sewing-machine** (ssou-ing-mö-ʃiin) *n* máquina de coser
**sex** (ssêkss) *n* sexo *m*; sexualidad *f*
**sexton** (ssêk-sstön) *n* sacristán *m*
**sexual** (ssêk-ʃu-öl) *adj* sexual
**sexuality** (ssêk-ʃu-æ-lö-ti) *n* sexualidad *f*
**shade** (ʃeid) *n* sombra *f*; tono *m*
**shadow** (ʃæ-dou) *n* sombra *f*
**shady** (ʃei-di) *adj* sombreado
*shake** (ʃeik) *v* sacudir
**shaky** (ʃei-ki) *adj* vacilante
*shall** (ʃæl) *v* *tener que
**shallow** (ʃæ-lou) *adj* poco profundo
**shame** (ʃeim) *n* vergüenza *f*; deshonra *f*; **shame!** ¡qué vergüenza!
**shampoo** (ʃæm-*puu*) *n* champú *m*
**shamrock** (ʃæm-rok) *n* trébol *m*
**shape** (ʃeip) *n* forma *f*; *v* formar
**share** (ʃê⁰) *v* compartir; *n* parte *f*; acción *f*
**shark** (ʃaak) *n* tiburón *m*
**sharp** (ʃaap) *adj* afilado
**sharpen** (ʃaa-pön) *v* afilar
**shave** (ʃeiv) *v* rasurarse, afeitarse
**shaver** (ʃei-vö) *n* máquina de afeitar
**shaving-brush** (ʃei-ving-braʃ) *n* brocha de afeitar

**shaving-cream** (ʃei-ving-kriim) *n* crema de afeitar
**shaving-soap** (ʃei-ving-ssoup) *n* jabón de afeitar
**shawl** (ʃool) *n* chal *m*
**she** (ʃii) *pron* ella
**shed** (ʃêd) *n* cobertizo *m*
*shed** (ʃêd) *v* derramar; esparcir
**sheep** (ʃiip) *n* (pl ~) oveja *f*
**sheer** (ʃi⁰) *adj* absoluto, puro; fino, traslúcido
**sheet** (ʃiit) *n* sábana *f*; hoja *f*; chapa *f*
**shelf** (ʃêlf) *n* (pl shelves) estante *m*
**shell** (ʃêl) *n* concha *f*; cáscara *f*
**shellfish** (ʃêl-fiʃ) *n* marisco *m*
**shelter** (ʃêl-tö) *n* refugio *m*; *v* abrigar
**shepherd** (ʃê-pöd) *n* pastor *m*
**shift** (ʃift) *n* turno *m*
*shine** (ʃain) *v* *relucir; brillar, *resplandecer
**ship** (ʃip) *n* buque *m*; *v* transportar; **shipping line** línea de navegación
**shipowner** (ʃi-pou-nö) *n* armador *m*
**shipyard** (ʃip-yaad) *n* astillero *m*
**shirt** (ʃööt) *n* camisa *f*
**shiver** (ʃi-vö) *v* *temblar, tiritar; *n* escalofrío *m*
**shivery** (ʃi-vö-ri) *adj* estremecido
**shock** (ʃok) *n* choque *m*; *v* chocar; ~ **absorber** amortiguador *m*
**shocking** (ʃo-king) *adj* chocante
**shoe** (ʃuu) *n* zapato *m*; **gym shoes** sandalias de gimnasia; ~ **polish** betún *m*; grasa *fMe*
**shoe-lace** (ʃuu-leiss) *n* cordón *m*
**shoemaker** (ʃuu-mei-kö) *n* zapatero *m*
**shoe-shop** (ʃuu-ʃop) *n* zapatería *f*
**shook** (ʃuk) *v* (p shake)
*shoot** (ʃuut) *v* tirar
**shop** (ʃop) *n* tienda *f*; *v* *ir de compras; ~ **assistant** dependiente *m*; **shopping bag** saco de compras; **shopping centre** centro comercial

shopkeeper (ʃop-kii-pö) n tendero m

shop-window (ʃop-ᵘin-dou) n escaparate m

shore (ʃoo) n ribera f, orilla f

short (ʃoot) adj corto; bajo; ~ circuit cortocircuito m

shortage (ʃoo-tidʒ) n carencia f, escasez f

shortcoming (ʃoot-ka-ming) n deficiencia f

shorten (ʃoo-tön) v acortar

shorthand (ʃoot-hænd) n taquigrafía f

shortly (ʃoot-li) adv pronto, próximamente

shorts (ʃootss) pl pantalones cortos; plAm calzoncillos mpl

short-sighted (ʃoot-ssai-tid) adj miope

shot (ʃot) n disparo m; inyección f; secuencia f

*should (ʃud) v *tener que

shoulder (ʃoul-dö) n hombro m

shout (ʃaut) v gritar; n grito m

shovel (ʃa-völ) n pala f

show (ʃou) n representación f, espectáculo m; exposición f

*show (ʃou) v *mostrar; enseñar; *demostrar

show-case (ʃou-keiss) n vitrina f

shower (ʃauᵉ) n ducha f; aguacero m

showroom (ʃou-ruum) n salón de demostraciones

shriek (ʃriik) v chillar; n chillido m

shrimp (ʃrimp) n camarón m

shrine (ʃrain) n santuario m

*shrink (ʃringk) v encogerse

shrinkproof (ʃringk-pruuf) adj no encoge

shrub (ʃrab) n arbusto m

shudder (ʃa-dö) n estremecimiento m

shuffle (ʃa-föl) v barajar

*shut (ʃat) v *cerrar; ~ in *encerrar

shutter (ʃa-tö) n persiana f

shy (ʃai) adj esquivo, tímido

shyness (ʃai-nöss) n timidez f

Siam (ssai-æm) Siam m

Siamese (ssai-ö-miis) adj siamés

sick (ssik) adj enfermo; que tiene náuseas

sickness (ssik-nöss) n enfermedad f; náusea f

side (ssaid) n lado m; partido m; one-sided adj unilateral

sideburns (ssaid-bööns) pl patillas fpl

sidelight (ssaid-lait) n luz lateral

side-street (ssaid-sstriit) n calle lateral

sidewalk (ssaid-ᵘook) nAm acera f

sideways (ssaid-ᵘeis) adv lateralmente

siege (ssiidʒ) n sitio m

sieve (ssiv) n tamiz m; v tamizar

sift (ssift) v tamizar

sight (ssait) n vista f; aspecto m; curiosidad f

sign (ssain) n signo m, señal f; gesto m, seña f; v suscribir, firmar

signal (ssigh-nöl) n señal f; v *hacer señales

signature (ssigh-nö-chö) n firma f

significant (ssigh-ni-fi-könt) adj significativo

signpost (ssain-pousst) n poste de indicador

silence (ssai-lönss) n silencio m; v acallar

silencer (ssai-lön-ssö) n silenciador m

silent (ssai-lönt) adj callado; *be ~ callarse

silk (ssilk) n seda f

silken (ssil-kön) adj sedoso

silly (ssi-li) adj necio, bobo

silver (ssil-vö) n plata f; de plata

silversmith (ssil-vö-ssmiz) n platero m

silverware (ssil-vö-uêᵉ) n plata labrada

similar (ssi-mi-lö) adj similar

similarity (ssi-mi-læ-rö-ti) n semejanza f

simple (ssim-pöl) adj ingenuo, simple; ordinario

**simply** (*ssim*-pli) *adv* simplemente

**simulate** (*ssi*-myu-leit) *v* simular

**simultaneous** (ssi-möl-*tei*-ni-öss) *adj* simultáneo

**sin** (ssin) *n* pecado *m*

**since** (ssinss) *prep* desde; *adv* desde entonces; *conj* desde que; puesto que

**sincere** (ssin-*ssiº*) *adj* sincero

**sinew** (*ssi*-nyuu) *n* tendón *m*

**\*sing** (ssing) *v* cantar

**singer** (*ssing*-ö) *n* cantante *m*; cantadora *f*

**single** (*ssing*-ghöl) *adj* solo; soltero

**singular** (*ssing*-ghyu-lö) *n* singular *m*; *adj* singular

**sinister** (*ssi*-ni-sstö) *adj* siniestro

**sink** (ssingk) *n* pileta *f*

**\*sink** (ssingk) *v* hundirse

**sip** (ssip) *n* sorbo *m*

**siphon** (*ssai*-fön) *n* sifón *m*

**sir** (ssöö) *n* señor *m*

**siren** (*ssaiº*-rön) *n* sirena *f*

**sister** (*ssi*-sstö) *n* hermana *f*

**sister-in-law** (*ssi*-sstö-rin-loo) *n* (pl sisters-) cuñada *f*

**\*sit** (ssit) *v* \*estar sentado; ~ **down** \*sentarse

**site** (ssait) *n* sitio *m*

**sitting-room** (*ssi*-ting-ruum) *n* sala de estar

**situated** (*ssi*-chu-ei-tid) *adj* situado

**situation** (ssi-chu-*ei*-fön) *n* situación *f*; ubicación *f*

**six** (ssiks) *num* seis

**sixteen** (ssikss-*tiin*) *num* dieciséis

**sixteenth** (ssikss-*tiinz*) *num* decimosexto

**sixth** (ssikssz) *num* sexto

**sixty** (*ssikss*-ti) *num* sesenta

**size** (ssais) *n* tamaño *m*, número *m*; dimensión *f*; formato *m*

**skate** (sskeit) *v* patinar; *n* patín *m*

**skating** (*sskei*-ting) *n* patinaje *m*

**skating-rink** (*sskei*-ting-ringk) *n* pista de patinaje

**skeleton** (*sské*-li-tön) *n* esqueleto *m*

**sketch** (sskêch) *n* dibujo *m*, bosquejo *m*; *v* dibujar, bosquejar

**sketch-book** (*sskêch*-buk) *n* cuaderno de diseño

**ski¹** (sskii) *v* esquiar

**ski²** (sskii) *n* (pl ~, ~s) esquí *m*; ~ **boots** botas de esquí; ~ **pants** pantalones de esquí; ~ **sticks** bastones de esquí

**skid** (sskid) *v* patinar

**skier** (*sskii*-ö) *n* esquiador *m*

**skiing** (*sskii*-ing) *n* esquí *m*

**ski-jump** (*sskii*-dʒamp) *n* salto de esquí

**skilful** (*sskil*-föl) *adj* hábil, diestro

**ski-lift** (*sskii*-lift) *n* telesilla *m*

**skill** (sskil) *n* habilidad *f*

**skilled** (sskild) *adj* hábil; especializado

**skin** (sskin) *n* piel *f*; cáscara *f*; ~ **cream** crema para la piel

**skip** (sskip) *v* saltar; brincar

**skirt** (sskööt) *n* falda *f*

**skull** (sskal) *n* cráneo *m*

**sky** (sskai) *n* cielo *m*; aire *m*

**skyscraper** (*sskai*-sskrei-pö) *n* rascacielos *m*

**slack** (sslæk) *adj* lento

**slacks** (sslækss) *pl* pantalones *mpl*

**slam** (sslæm) *v* \*dar un portazo

**slander** (*sslaan*-dö) *n* calumnia *f*

**slant** (sslaant) *v* inclinarse

**slanting** (*sslaan*-ting) *adj* oblicuo, pendiente, inclinado

**slap** (sslæp) *v* pegar; *n* bofetada *f*

**slate** (ssleit) *n* pizarra *f*

**slave** (ssleiv) *n* esclavo *m*

**sledge** (sslêdʒ) *n* trineo *m*

**sleep** (ssliip) *n* sueño *m*

**\*sleep** (ssliip) *v* \*dormir

**sleeping-bag** (*sslii*-ping-bægh) *n* saco de dormir

**sleeping-car** (*sslii*-ping-kaa) *n* coche cama

**sleeping-pill** (*sslii*-ping-pil) *n* somnífero *m*

**sleepless** (*ssliip*-löss) *adj* desvelado

**sleepy** (*sslii*-pi) *adj* soñoliento

**sleeve** (ssliiv) *n* manga *f*; funda *f*

**sleigh** (sslei) *n* trineo *m*

**slender** (*sslên*-dö) *adj* esbelto

**slice** (sslaiss) *n* tajada *f*

**slide** (sslaid) *n* desliz *m*; tobogán *m*; diapositiva *f*

***slide** (sslaid) *v* deslizarse

**slight** (sslait) *adj* ligero; leve

**slim** (sslim) *adj* esbelto; *v* adelgazar

**slip** (sslip) *v* deslizarse, resbalar; *n* desliz *m*; combinación *f*; fondo *m*Me

**slipper** (*sslii*-pö) *n* zapatilla *f*

**slippery** (*sslii*-pö-ri) *adj* resbaladizo

**slogan** (*sslou*-ghön) *n* lema *m*, slogan *m*

**slope** (ssloup) *n* pendiente *f*; *v* inclinarse

**sloping** (*sslou*-ping) *adj* inclinado

**sloppy** (*sslo*-pi) *adj* chapucero

**slot** (sslot) *n* ranura *f*

**slot-machine** (*sslot*-mö-ʃiin) *n* máquina tragamonedas

**slovenly** (*sslo*-vön-li) *adj* descuidado

**slow** (sslou) *adj* lerdo, lento; ~ **down** desacelerar, *ir más despacio; frenar

**sluice** (sslluuss) *n* compuerta *f*

**slum** (sslam) *n* barrio bajo

**slump** (sslamp) *n* baja *f*

**slush** (sslaʃ) *n* aguanieve *f*

**sly** (sslai) *adj* astuto

**smack** (ssmæk) *v* pegar; *n* bofetada *f*

**small** (ssmool) *adj* pequeño; menudo

**smallpox** (*ssmool*-pokss) *n* viruelas *fpl*

**smart** (ssmaat) *adj* elegante; inteligente, listo

**smell** (ssmêl) *n* olor *m*

***smell** (ssmêl) *v* *oler; *heder

**smelly** (*ssmê*-li) *adj* hediondo

**smile** (ssmail) *v* sonreír; *n* sonrisa *f*

**smith** (ssmiz) *n* herrero *m*

**smoke** (ssmouk) *v* fumar; *n* humo *m*; **no smoking** prohibido fumar

**smoker** (*ssmou*-kö) *n* fumador *m*; compartimiento para fumadores

**smoking-compartment** (*ssmou*-king-köm-paat-mönt) *n* compartimiento para fumadores

**smoking-room** (*ssmou*-king-ruum) *n* sala para fumar

**smooth** (ssmuuð) *adj* llano, liso; dulce

**smuggle** (*ssma*-ghöl) *v* contrabandear

**snack** (ssnæk) *n* tentempié *m*

**snack-bar** (*ssnæk*-baa) *n* cafetería *f*

**snail** (ssneil) *n* caracol *m*

**snake** (ssneik) *n* culebra *f*

**snapshot** (*ssnæp*-ʃot) *n* instantánea *f*

**sneakers** (*ssnii*-kös) *plAm* zapatos de gimnasia

**sneeze** (ssniis) *v* estornudar

**sniper** (*ssnai*-pö) *n* francotirador *m*

**snooty** (*ssnuu*-ti) *adj* arrogante

**snore** (ssnoo) *v* roncar

**snorkel** (*ssnoo*-köl) *n* esnórquel *m*

**snout** (ssnaut) *n* hocico *m*

**snow** (ssnou) *n* nieve *f*; *v* *nevar

**snowstorm** (*ssnou*-sstoom) *n* nevasca *f*

**snowy** (*ssnou*-i) *adj* nevoso

**so** (ssou) *conj* por tanto; *adv* así; a tal grado, tan; **and** ~ **on** etcétera; ~ **far** hasta ahora; ~ **that** así que, a fin de

**soak** (ssouk) *v* empapar, remojar

**soap** (ssoup) *n* jabón *m*; ~ **powder** jabón en polvo

**sober** (*ssou*-bö) *adj* sobrio; ponderado

**so-called** (ssou-*koold*) *adj* así llamado

**soccer** (*sso*-kö) *n* fútbol *m*; ~ **team** equipo *m*

**social** (*ssou*-ʃöl) *adj* social

**socialism** (*ssou*-ʃö-li-söm) *n* socialismo *m*

**socialist** (*ssou*-ʃö-lisst) *adj* socialista; *n* socialista *m*

**society** (ssö-*ssai*-ö-ti) *n* sociedad *f*; asociación *f*; compañía *f*

**sock** (ssok) *n* calcetín *m*

**socket** (*sso*-kit) *n* casquillo *m*; sóquet *mMe*

**soda-water** (*ssou*-dö-ᵘoo-tö) *n* agua de soda, soda *f*

**sofa** (*ssou*-fö) *n* sofá *m*

**soft** (ssoft) *adj* blando; ~ **drink** bebida no alcohólica

**soften** (*sso*-fön) *v* ablandar

**soil** (ssoil) *n* suelo *m*; tierra *f*

**soiled** (ssoild) *adj* manchado

**sold** (ssould) *v* (p, pp sell); ~ **out** agotado

**solder** (*ssol*-dö) *v* \*soldar

**soldering-iron** (*ssol*-dö-ring-aiᵒn) *n* soldador *m*

**soldier** (*ssoul*-dჳö) *n* militar *m*, soldado *m*

**sole¹** (ssoul) *adj* único

**sole²** (ssoul) *n* suela *f*; lenguado *m*

**solely** (*ssoul*-li) *adv* exclusivamente

**solemn** (*sso*-löm) *adj* solemne

**solicitor** (ssö-*li*-ssi-tö) *n* procurador *m*, abogado *m*

**solid** (*sso*-lid) *adj* robusto, sólido; macizo; *n* sólido *m*

**soluble** (*sso*-lyu-böl) *adj* soluble

**solution** (ssö-*luu*-ʃön) *n* solución *f*

**solve** (ssolv) *v* \*resolver

**sombre** (*ssom*-bö) *adj* sombrío

**some** (ssam) *adj* algunos, unos; *pron* algunos, unos; un poco; ~ **day** uno u otro día; ~ **more** algo más; ~ **time** alguna vez

**somebody** (*ssam*-bö-di) *pron* alguien

**somehow** (*ssam*-hau) *adv* de un modo u otro

**someone** (*ssam*-ᵘan) *pron* alguien

**something** (*ssam*-zing) *pron* algo

**sometimes** (*ssam*-taims) *adv* a veces

**somewhat** (*ssam*-ᵘot) *adv* algo

**somewhere** (*ssam*-ᵘêᵒ) *adv* en alguna parte

**son** (ssan) *n* hijo *m*

**song** (ssong) *n* canción *f*

**son-in-law** (*ssa*-nin-loo) *n* (pl sons-) yerno *m*

**soon** (ssuun) *adv* rápidamente, pronto, en breve; **as** ~ **as** tan pronto como

**sooner** (*ssuu*-nö) *adv* más bien

**sore** (ssoo) *adj* doloroso; *n* llaga *f*; úlcera *f*; ~ **throat** dolor de garganta

**sorrow** (*sso*-rou) *n* tristeza *f*, sufrimiento *m*, pena *f*

**sorry** (*sso*-ri) *adj* apenado; **sorry!** ¡dispense usted!, ¡disculpe!, ¡perdón!

**sort** (ssoot) *v* clasificar, \*disponer; *n* clase *f*; **all sorts of** toda clase de

**soul** (ssoul) *n* alma *f*

**sound** (ssaund) *n* sonido *m*; *v* \*sonar, \*resonar; *adj* bueno

**soundproof** (*ssaund*-pruuf) *adj* insonorizado

**soup** (ssuup) *n* sopa *f*

**soup-plate** (*ssuup*-pleit) *n* plato para sopa

**soup-spoon** (*ssuup*-sspuun) *n* cuchara *f*

**sour** (ssauᵒ) *adj* agrio

**source** (ssooss) *n* fuente *f*

**south** (ssaus) *n* sur *m*; **South Pole** polo sur

**South Africa** (ssaus æ-fri-kö) África del Sur

**south-east** (ssaus-*iisst*) *n* sudeste *m*

**southerly** (*ssa*-ōō-li) *adj* meridional

**southern** (*ssa*-ōōn) *adj* meridional

**south-west** (ssauz-ᵘ*êsst*) *n* sudoeste *m*

**souvenir** (*ssuu*-vö-ni⁶) *n* recuerdo *m*

**sovereign** (*ssov*-rin) *n* soberano *m*

**Soviet** (*ssou*-vi-öt) *adj* soviético

**Soviet Union** (*ssou*-vi-öt *yuu*-nyön) Unión Soviética

*****sow** (ssou) *v* *sembrar

**spa** (sspaa) *n* balneario *m*

**space** (sspeiss) *n* espacio *m*; distancia *f*; *v* espaciar

**spacious** (*sspei*-jöss) *adj* espacioso

**spade** (sspeid) *n* azada *f*, pala *f*

**Spain** (sspein) España *f*

**Spaniard** (*sspæ*-nyöd) *n* español *m*

**Spanish** (*sspæ*-nij) *adj* español

**spanking** (*sspæng*-king) *n* zurra *f*

**spanner** (*sspæ*-nö) *n* llave inglesa

**spare** (sspê⁶) *adj* de reserva, disponible; *v* pasarse sin; ~ **part** pieza de repuesto; ~ **room** cuarto para huéspedes; ~ **time** tiempo libre; ~ **tyre** neumático de repuesto; ~ **wheel** rueda de repuesto

**spark** (sspaak) *n* chispa *f*

**sparking-plug** (*sspaa*-king-plagh) *n* bujía *f*

**sparkling** (*sspaa*-kling) *adj* centelleante; espumante

**sparrow** (*sspæ*-rou) *n* gorrión *m*

*****speak** (sspiik) *v* hablar

**spear** (sspi⁶) *n* lanza *f*

**special** (*sspê*-jöl) *adj* especial; ~ **delivery** por expreso

**specialist** (*sspê*-jö-lisst) *n* especialista *m*

**speciality** (sspê-ji-æ-lö-ti) *n* especialidad *f*

**specialize** (*sspê*-jö-lais) *v* especializarse

**specially** (*sspê*-jö-li) *adv* en particular

**species** (*sspii*-jiis) *n* (pl ~) especie *f*

**specific** (sspö-*ssi*-fik) *adj* específico

**specimen** (*sspê*-ssi-mön) *n* espécimen *m*

**speck** (sspêk) *n* mancha *f*

**spectacle** (*sspêk*-tö-köl) *n* espectáculo *m*; **spectacles** anteojos *mpl*

**spectator** (sspêk-*tei*-tö) *n* espectador *m*

**speculate** (*sspê*-kyu-leit) *v* especular

**speech** (sspiich) *n* habla *f*; discurso *m*; lenguaje *m*

**speechless** (*sspiich*-löss) *adj* atónito

**speed** (sspiid) *n* velocidad *f*; rapidez *f*, prisa *f*; **cruising** ~ velocidad de cruce; ~ **limit** límite de velocidad

*****speed** (sspiid) *v* *dar prisa; correr demasiado

**speeding** (*sspii*-ding) *n* exceso de velocidad

**speedometer** (sspii-*do*-mi-tö) *n* velocímetro *m*

**spell** (sspêl) *n* encanto *m*

*****spell** (sspêl) *v* deletrear

**spelling** (*sspê*-ling) *n* deletreo *m*

*****spend** (sspênd) *v* gastar; pasar

**sphere** (ssfi⁶) *n* esfera *f*

**spice** (sspaiss) *n* especia *f*

**spiced** (sspaisst) *adj* condimentado

**spicy** (*sspai*-ssi) *adj* picante

**spider** (*sspai*-dö) *n* araña *f*; **spider's web** telaraña *f*

*****spill** (sspil) *v* *verter

*****spin** (sspin) *v* hilar; *hacer girar

**spinach** (*sspi*-nidʒ) *n* espinacas *fpl*

**spine** (sspain) *n* espinazo *m*

**spinster** (*sspin*-sstö) *n* solterona *f*

**spire** (sspai⁶) *n* aguja *f*

**spirit** (*sspi*-rit) *n* espíritu *m*; humor *m*; **spirits** bebidas espirituosas; moral *f*; ~ **stove** calentador de alcohol

**spiritual** (*sspi*-ri-chu-öl) *adj* espiritual

**spit** (sspit) *n* esputo *m*, saliva *f*; espetón *m*

**\*spit** (sspit) *v* escupir

**in spite of** (in sspait ov) a pesar de

**spiteful** (*sspait*-föl) *adj* malévolo

**splash** (ssplæ∫) *v* salpicar

**splendid** (*ssplén*-did) *adj* magnífico, espléndido

**splendour** (*ssplên*-dö) *n* esplendor *m*

**splint** (ssplint) *n* tablilla *f*

**splinter** (*ssplin*-tö) *n* astilla *f*

**\*split** (ssplit) *v* \*hender

**\*spoil** (sspoil) *v* echar a perder; mimar

**spoke¹** (sspouk) *v* (p speak)

**spoke²** (sspouk) *n* radio *m*

**sponge** (sspand3) *n* esponja *f*

**spook** (sspuuk) *n* fantasma *m*

**spool** (sspuul) *n* bobina *f*

**spoon** (sspuun) *n* cuchara *f*

**spoonful** (*sspuun*-ful) *n* cucharada *f*

**sport** (sspoot) *n* deporte *m*

**sports-car** (*sspootss*-kaa) *n* coche de carreras

**sports-jacket** (*sspootss*-d3æ-kit) *n* chaqueta de deporte

**sportsman** (*sspootss*-mön) *n* (pl -men) deportista *m*

**sportswear** (*sspootss*-uê°) *n* conjunto de deporte

**spot** (sspot) *n* mancha *f*; lugar *m*, puesto *m*

**spotless** (*sspot*-löss) *adj* inmaculado

**spotlight** (*sspot*-lait) *n* proyector *m*

**spotted** (*sspo*-tid) *adj* moteado

**spout** (sspaut) *n* chorro *m*

**sprain** (ssprein) *v* \*torcerse; *n* torcedura *f*

**\*spread** (ssprêd) *v* \*extender

**spring** (sspring) *n* primavera *f*; muelle *m*; manantial *m*

**springtime** (*sspring*-taim) *n* primavera *f*

**sprouts** (ssprautss) *pl* col de Bruselas

**spy** (sspai) *n* espía *m*

**squadron** (*ssk*ᵘ*o*-drön) *n* escuadrilla *f*

**square** (ssk*ᵘ*ê°) *adj* cuadrado; *n* cuadrado *m*; plaza *f*

**squash** (ssk*ᵘ*o∫) *n* zumo *m*

**squirrel** (*ssk*ᵘ*i*-röl) *n* ardilla *f*

**squirt** (ssk*ᵘ*ööt) *n* chisguete *m*

**stable** (*sstei*-böl) *adj* estable; *n* establo *m*

**stack** (sstæk) *n* montón *m*

**stadium** (*sstei*-di-öm) *n* estadio *m*

**staff** (sstaaf) *n* personal *m*

**stage** (ssteid3) *n* escenario *m*; fase *f*; etapa *f*

**stain** (sstein) *v* manchar; *n* mancha *f*; **stained glass** vidrio de color; ~ **remover** quitamanchas

**stainless** (*sstein*-löss) *adj* inmaculado; ~ **steel** acero inoxidable

**staircase** (*sstê°*-keiss) *n* escalera *f*

**stairs** (sstê°s) *pl* escalera *f*

**stale** (ssteil) *adj* viejo

**stall** (sstool) *n* puesto *m*; butaca *f*

**stamina** (*sstæ*-mi-nö) *n* vigor *m*

**stamp** (sstæmp) *n* sello *m*; *v* sellar; patear; *n* estampilla *fMe*; ~ **machine** máquina expendedora de sellos

**stand** (sstænd) *n* puesto *m*; tribuna *f*

**\*stand** (sstænd) *v* \*estar de pie

**standard** (*sstæn*-död) *n* norma *f*; normal; ~ **of living** nivel de vida

**stanza** (*sstæn*-sö) *n* estrofa *f*

**staple** (*sstei*-pöl) *n* grapa *f*

**star** (sstaa) *n* estrella *f*

**starboard** (*sstaa*-böd) *n* estribor *m*

**starch** (sstaach) *n* almidón *m*; *v* almidonar

**stare** (sstê°) *v* mirar

**starling** (*sstaa*-ling) *n* estornino *m*

**start** (sstaat) *v* \*empezar; *n* comienzo *m*; **starter motor** arranque *m*

**starting-point** (*sstaa*-ting-point) *n* punto de partida

**state** (ssteit) *n* Estado *m*; estado *m*; *v* declarar; **the States** Estados Unidos

**statement** (*ssteit*-mönt) *n* declaración *f*

**statesman** (*ssteitss*-mön) *n* (pl -men) estadista *m*

**station** (*sstei*-ſ̶ön) *n* estación *f*; puesto *m*

**stationary** (*sstei*-ſ̶ö-nö-ri) *adj* estacionario

**stationer's** (*sstei*-ſ̶ö-nös) *n* papelería *f*

**stationery** (*sstei*-ſ̶ö-nö-ri) *n* papelería *f*

**station-master** (*sstei*-ſ̶ön-maa-sstö) *n* jefe de estación

**statistics** (*sstö*-*ti*-sstikss) *pl* estadística *f*

**statue** (*sstæ*-chuu) *n* estatua *f*

**stay** (sstei) *v* quedarse; hospedarse; *n* estancia *f*

**steadfast** (*sstéd*-faasst) *adj* constante

**steady** (*sstê*-di) *adj* firme

**steak** (ssteik) *n* biftec *m*

*steal** (sstiil) *v* hurtar

**steam** (sstiim) *n* vapor *m*

**steamer** (*sstii*-mö) *n* vapor *m*

**steel** (sstiil) *n* acero *m*

**steep** (sstiip) *adj* abrupto

**steeple** (*sstii*-pöl) *n* campanario *m*

**steering-column** (*sstiᵒ*-ring-ko-löm) *n* columna del volante

**steering-wheel** (*sstiᵒ*-ring-ᵘiil) *n* volante *m*

**steersman** (*sstiᵒs*-mön) *n* (pl -men) timonel *m*

**stem** (sstêm) *n* tallo *m*

**stenographer** (*sstê*-*no*-ghró-fö) *n* taquígrafo *m*

**step** (sstêp) *n* paso *m*; peldaño *m*; *v* pisar

**stepchild** (*sstêp*-chaild) *n* (pl -children) hijastro *m*

**stepfather** (*sstêp*-faa-ðö) *n* padrastro *m*

**stepmother** (*sstêp*-ma-ðö) *n* madras-

tra *f*

**sterile** (*sstê*-rail) *adj* estéril

**sterilize** (*sstê*-ri-lais) *v* esterilizar

**steward** (*sstyuu*-öd) *n* camarero *m*

**stewardess** (*sstyuu*-ö-dêss) *n* azafata *f*

**stick** (sstik) *n* palo *m*

*stick** (sstik) *v* pegar

**sticky** (*ssti*-ki) *adj* pegajoso

**stiff** (sstif) *adj* tieso

**still** (sstil) *adv* todavía; sin embargo; *adj* quieto

**stillness** (*sstil*-nöss) *n* silencio *m*

**stimulant** (*ssti*-myu-lönt) *n* estimulante *m*

**stimulate** (*ssti*-myu-leit) *v* estimular

**sting** (ssting) *n* picadura *f*

*sting** (ssting) *v* picar

**stingy** (*sstin*-dʒi) *adj* mezquino

*stink** (sstingk) *v* apestar

**stipulate** (*ssti*-pyu-leit) *v* estipular

**stipulation** (ssti-pyu-*lei*-ſ̶ön) *n* estipulación *f*

**stir** (sstöö) *v* *mover; *revolver

**stirrup** (*ssti*-röp) *n* estribo *m*

**stitch** (sstich) *n* punto *m*, punzada *f*; sutura *f*

**stock** (sstok) *n* existencias *fpl*; *v* *tener en existencia; ~ **exchange** bolsa de valores, bolsa *f*; ~ **market** bolsa *f*; **stocks and shares** acciones *fpl*

**stocking** (*ssto*-king) *n* media *f*

**stole¹** (sstoul) *v* (p steal)

**stole²** (sstoul) *n* estola *f*

**stomach** (*ssta*-mök) *n* estómago *m*

**stomach-ache** (*ssta*-mö-keik) *n* dolor de estómago

**stone** (sstoun) *n* piedra *f*; piedra preciosa; hueso *m*; de piedra; **pumice** ~ piedra pómez

**stood** (sstud) *v* (p, pp stand)

**stop** (sstop) *v* cesar; dejar de; *n* parada *f*; **stop!** ¡alto!

**stopper** (*ssto*-pö) *n* tapón *m*

**storage** (*sstoo*-ridʒ) *n* almacenaje *m*

**store** (sstoo) *n* repuesto *m*; almacén *m*; *v* almacenar

**store-house** (*sstoo*-hauss) *n* almacén *m*

**storey** (*sstoo*-ri) *n* piso *m*

**stork** (sstook) *n* cigüeña *f*

**storm** (sstoom) *n* tormenta *f*

**stormy** (*sstoo*-mi) *adj* tempestuoso

**story** (*sstoo*-ri) *n* cuento *m*

**stout** (sstaut) *adj* gordo, corpulento

**stove** (sstouv) *n* estufa *f*; cocina *f*

**straight** (streit) *adj* derecho; honesto; *adv* directamente; ~ **ahead** todo seguido; ~ **away** directamente, en seguida; ~ **on** todo seguido

**strain** (sstrein) *n* esfuerzo *m*; tensión *f*; *v* *forzar; filtrar

**strainer** (*sstrei*-nö) *n* escurridor *m*

**strange** (sstreindʒ) *adj* extraño; raro

**stranger** (*sstrein*-dʒö) *n* extranjero *m*; forastero *m*

**strangle** (*sstræng*-ghöl) *v* estrangular

**strap** (sstræp) *n* correa *f*

**straw** (sstroo) *n* paja *f*

**strawberry** (*sstroo*-bö-ri) *n* fresa *f*

**stream** (sstriim) *n* arroyo *m*; corriente *f*; *v* *fluir

**street** (sstriit) *n* calle *f*

**streetcar** (*sstriit*-kaa) *nAm* tranvía *m*

**street-organ** (*sstrii*-too-ghön) *n* organillo *m*

**strength** (sstrêngz) *n* fuerza *f*, vigor *m*

**stress** (sstrèss) *n* esfuerzo *m*; énfasis *m*; *v* acentuar

**stretch** (sstrêch) *v* estirar; *n* trecho *m*

**strict** (sstrikt) *adj* estricto; severo

**strife** (sstraif) *n* lucha *f*

**strike** (sstraik) *n* huelga *f*

**\*strike** (sstraik) *v* golpear; atacar; impresionar; *estar en huelga; arriar

**striking** (*sstrai*-king) *adj* impresionante, notable, vistoso

**string** (sstring) *n* cordel *m*; cuerda *f*

**strip** (sstrip) *n* faja *f*

**stripe** (sstraip) *n* raya *f*

**striped** (sstraipt) *adj* rayado

**stroke** (sstrouk) *n* ataque *m*

**stroll** (sstroul) *v* pasear; *n* paseo *m*

**strong** (sstrong) *adj* fuerte

**stronghold** (*sstrong*-hould) *n* plaza fuerte

**structure** (*sstrak*-chö) *n* estructura *f*

**struggle** (*sstra*-ghöl) *n* combate *m*, lucha *f*; *v* luchar

**stub** (sstab) *n* talón *m*

**stubborn** (*ssta*-bön) *adj* testarudo

**student** (*sstyuu*-dönt) *n* estudiante *m*; estudiante *f*

**study** (*ssta*-di) *v* estudiar; *n* estudio *m*; despacho *m*

**stuff** (sstaf) *n* substancia *f*; cachivache *m*

**stuffed** (sstaft) *adj* rellenado

**stuffing** (*ssta*-fing) *n* relleno *m*

**stuffy** (*ssta*-fi) *adj* sofocante

**stumble** (*sstam*-böl) *v* *tropezarse

**stung** (sstang) *v* (p, pp sting)

**stupid** (*sstyuu*-pid) *adj* estúpido

**style** (sstail) *n* estilo *m*

**subject**[1] (*ssab*-dʒikt) *n* sujeto *m*; súbdito *m*; ~ **to** sujeto a

**subject**[2] (ssöb-*dʒêkt*) *v* someter

**submit** (ssöb-*mit*) *v* someterse

**subordinate** (ssö-*boo*-di-nöt) *adj* subalterno; subordinado

**subscriber** (ssöb-*sskrai*-bö) *n* abonado *m*

**subscription** (ssöb-*sskrip*-ʃön) *n* suscripción *f*

**subsequent** (*ssab*-ssi-kᵘönt) *adj* posterior

**subsidy** (*ssab*-ssi-di) *n* subsidio *m*

**substance** (*ssab*-sstönss) *n* sustancia *f*

**substantial** (ssöb-*sstæn*-ʃöl) *adj* material; real; sustancial

**substitute** (*ssab*-ssti-tyuut) *v* \*substituir; *n* sustituto *m*

**subtitle** (*ssab*-tai-töl) *n* subtítulo *m*

**subtle** (*ssa*-töl) *adj* sutil

**subtract** (ssöb-*trækt*) *v* restar

**suburb** (*ssa*-bööb) *n* suburbio *m*

**suburban** (ssö-*böö*-bön) *adj* suburbano

**subway** (*ssab*-ᵁei) *nAm* metro *m*

**succeed** (ssök-*ssiid*) *v* \*tener éxito; suceder

**success** (ssök-*ssêss*) *n* éxito *m*

**successful** (ssök-*ssêss*-föl) *adj* de éxito

**succumb** (ssö-*kam*) *v* sucumbir

**such** (ssach) *adj* tal; *adv* tan; ~ **as** tal como

**suck** (ssak) *v* chupar

**sudden** (*ssa*-dön) *adj* súbito

**suddenly** (*ssa*-dön-li) *adv* repentinamente

**suede** (ssᵁeid) *n* gamuza *f*

**suffer** (*ssa*-fö) *v* sufrir

**suffering** (*ssa*-fö-ring) *n* sufrimiento *m*

**suffice** (ssö-*faiss*) *v* bastar

**sufficient** (ssö-*fi*-fönt) *adj* suficiente, bastante

**suffrage** (*ssa*-fridʒ) *n* derecho electoral, sufragio *m*

**sugar** (*fu*-ghö) *n* azúcar *m/f*

**suggest** (ssö-*dʒêsst*) *v* \*sugerir

**suggestion** (ssö-*dʒêss*-chön) *n* sugestión *f*

**suicide** (*ssuu*-i-ssaid) *n* suicidio *m*

**suit** (ssuut) *v* \*convenir; adaptar; \*ir bien; *n* traje *m*

**suitable** (*ssuu*-tö-böl) *adj* apropiado, apto

**suitcase** (*ssuut*-keiss) *n* maleta *f*

**suite** (ssᵁiit) *n* apartamento *m*

**sum** (ssam) *n* suma *f*

**summary** (*ssa*-mö-ri) *n* resumen *m*, sumario *m*

**summer** (*ssa*-mö) *n* verano *m*; ~ **time** horario de verano

**summit** (*ssa*-mit) *n* cima *f*

**summons** (*ssa*-möns) *n* (pl ~es) citación *f*

**sun** (ssan) *n* sol *m*

**sunbathe** (*ssan*-beið) *v* tomar el sol

**sunburn** (*ssan*-böön) *n* quemadura del sol

**Sunday** (*ssan*-di) *n* domingo *m*

**sun-glasses** (*ssan*-ghlaa-ssis) *pl* gafas de sol

**sunlight** (*ssan*-lait) *n* luz del sol

**sunny** (*ssa*-ni) *adj* soleado

**sunrise** (*ssan*-rais) *n* amanecer *m*

**sunset** (*ssan*-ssêt) *n* ocaso *m*

**sunshade** (*ssan*-feid) *n* quitasol *m*

**sunshine** (*ssan*-fain) *n* sol *m*

**sunstroke** (*ssan*-sstrouk) *n* insolación *f*

**suntan oil** (*ssan*-tæn-oil) aceite bronceador

**superb** (ssu-*pööb*) *adj* grandioso, soberbio

**superficial** (ssuu-pö-*fi*-föl) *adj* superficial

**superfluous** (ssu-*pöö*-flu-öss) *adj* superfluo

**superior** (ssu-*piᵒ*-ri-ö) *adj* mejor, mayor, superior

**superlative** (ssu-*pöö*-lö-tiv) *adj* superlativo; *n* superlativo *m*

**supermarket** (*ssuu*-pö-maa-kit) *n* supermercado *m*

**superstition** (ssuu-pö-*ssti*-fön) *n* superstición *f*

**supervise** (*ssuu*-pö-vais) *v* supervisar

**supervision** (ssuu-pö-*vi*-ʒön) *n* supervisión *f*

**supervisor** (*ssuu*-pö-vai-sö) *n* supervisor *m*

**supper** (*ssa*-pö) *n* cena *f*

**supple** (*ssa*-pöl) *adj* flexible, ágil

**supplement** (*ssa*-pli-mönt) *n* suplemento *m*

**supply** (ssö-*plai*) *n* abastecimiento *m*, suministro *m*; existencias *fpl*; oferta *f*; *v* suministrar

**support** (ssö-*poot*) *v* apoyar, \*sostener, soportar; *n* apoyo *m*; ~ **hose** medias elásticas

**supporter** (ssö-*poo*-tö) *n* aficionado *m*

**suppose** (ssö-*pous*) *v* \*suponer; **supposing that** dado que

**suppository** (ssö-*po*-si-tö-ri) *n* supositorio *m*

**suppress** (ssö-*prêss*) *v* reprimir

**surcharge** (ssöö-chaadʒ) *n* sobretasa *f*

**sure** (ʃuᵒ) *adj* seguro

**surely** (ʃuᵒ-li) *adv* seguramente

**surface** (*ssöö*-fiss) *n* superficie *f*

**surf-board** (*ssööf*-bood) *n* tabla para surf

**surgeon** (*ssöö*-dʒön) *n* cirujano *m*; **veterinary** ~ veterinario *m*

**surgery** (*ssöö*-dʒö-ri) *n* operación *f*; consultorio *m*

**surname** (*ssöö*-neim) *n* apellido *m*

**surplus** (*ssöö*-plöss) *n* sobra *f*

**surprise** (ssö-*prais*) *n* sorpresa *f*; *v* sorprender; extrañar

**surrender** (ssö-*rên*-dö) *v* \*rendirse; *n* rendición *f*

**surround** (ssö-*raund*) *v* rodear, cercar

**surrounding** (ssö-*raun*-ding) *adj* circundante

**surroundings** (ssö-*raun*-dings) *pl* alrededores *mpl*

**survey** (*ssöö*-vei) *n* resumen *m*

**survival** (ssö-*vai*-völ) *n* supervivencia *f*

**survive** (ssö-*vaiv*) *v* sobrevivir

**suspect**¹ (ssö-*sspêkt*) *v* sospechar

**suspect**² (ssa-sspêkt) *n* persona sospechosa

**suspend** (ssö-*sspênd*) *v* suspender

**suspenders** (ssö-*sspên*-dös) *plAm* ti-

rantes *mpl*; **suspender belt** portaligas *m*

**suspension** (ssö-*sspên*-ʃön) *n* suspensión *f*; ~ **bridge** puente colgante

**suspicion** (ssö-*sspi*-ʃön) *n* sospecha *f*; suspicacia *f*, desconfianza *f*

**suspicious** (ssö-*sspi*-ʃöss) *adj* sospechoso; suspicaz, desconfiado

**sustain** (ssö-*sstein*) *v* soportar

**Swahili** (ssᵘö-*hii*-li) *n* suahili *m*

**swallow** (ssᵘo-lou) *v* tragar; *n* golondrina *f*

**swam** (ssᵘæm) *v* (p swim)

**swamp** (ssᵘomp) *n* marisma *f*

**swan** (ssᵘon) *n* cisne *m*

**swap** (ssᵘop) *v* \*trocar

**\*swear** (ssᵘêᵒ) *v* jurar

**sweat** (ssᵘêt) *n* sudor *m*; *v* sudar

**sweater** (ssᵘê-tö) *n* suéter *m*

**Swede** (ssᵘiid) *n* sueco *m*

**Sweden** (ssᵘii-dön) Suecia *f*

**Swedish** (ssᵘii-diʃ) *adj* sueco

**\*sweep** (ssᵘiip) *v* barrer

**sweet** (ssᵘiit) *adj* dulce; lindo; *n* caramelo *m*; dulce *m*

**sweeten** (ssᵘii-tön) *v* endulzar

**sweetheart** (ssᵘiit-haat) *n* amor *m*, querida *f*

**sweetshop** (ssᵘiit-ʃop) *n* confitería *f*

**swell** (ssᵘêl) *adj* magnífico

**\*swell** (ssᵘêl) *v* hincharse

**swelling** (ssᵘê-ling) *n* hinchazón *f*

**swift** (ssᵘift) *adj* veloz

**\*swim** (ssᵘim) *v* nadar

**swimmer** (ssᵘi-mö) *n* nadador *m*

**swimming** (ssᵘi-ming) *n* natación *f*; ~ **pool** piscina *f*

**swimming-trunks** (ssᵘi-ming-trangkss) *n* calzón de baño

**swim-suit** (ssᵘim-ssuut) *n* traje de baño

**swindle** (ssᵘin-döl) *v* estafar; *n* estafa *f*

**swindler** (ssᵘin-dlö) *n* estafador *m*

swing (ssᵘing) n columpio m

*swing (ssᵘing) v oscilar; columpiarse

Swiss (ssᵘiss) adj suizo

switch (ssᵘich) n interruptor m; v cambiar; ~ off apagar; ~ on *encender

switchboard (ssᵘich-bood) n cuadro de distribución

Switzerland (ssᵘit-ssö-lönd) Suiza f

sword (ssood) n espada f

swum (ssᵘam) v (pp swim)

syllable (ssi-lö-böl) n sílaba f

symbol (ssim-böl) n símbolo m

sympathetic (ssim-pö-zê-tik) adj cordial, compasivo

sympathy (ssim-pö-zi) n simpatía f; compasión f

symphony (ssim-fö-ni) n sinfonía f

symptom (ssim-töm) n síntoma m

synagogue (ssi-nö-ghogh) n sinagoga f

synonym (ssi-nö-nim) n sinónimo m

synthetic (ssin-zê-tik) adj sintético

syphon (ssai-fön) n sifón m

Syria (ssi-ri-ö) Siria f

Syrian (ssi-ri-ön) adj sirio

syringe (ssi-rindӡ) n jeringa f

syrup (ssi-röp) n jarabe m

system (ssi-sstöm) n sistema m; decimal ~ sistema decimal

systematic (ssi-sstö-mæ-tik) adj sistemático

# T

table (tei-böl) n mesa f; tabla f; ~ of contents índice m; ~ tennis tenis . de mesa

table-cloth (tei-böl-kloz) n mantel m

tablespoon (tei-böl-sspuun) n cuchara f

tablet (tæ-blit) n pastilla f

taboo (tö-buu) n tabú m

tactics (tæk-tikss) pl táctica f

tag (tægh) n etiqueta f

tail (teil) n cola f

tail-light (teil-lait) n farol trasero

tailor (tei-lö) n sastre m

tailor-made (tei-lö-meid) adj hecho a la medida

*take (teik) v coger; tomar; llevar; comprender, *entender; ~ away quitar; llevarse; ~ off despegar; ~ out sacar; ~ over encargarse de; ~ place *tener lugar; ~ up ocupar

take-off (tei-kof) n despegue m

tale (teil) n cuento m

talent (tæ-lönt) n talento m

talented (tæ-lön-tid) adj dotado

talk (took) v hablar; n conversación f

talkative (too-kö-tiv) adj locuaz

tall (tool) adj alto

tame (teim) adj manso, domesticado; v domesticar

tampon (tæm-pön) n tapón m

tangerine (tæn-dӡö-riin) n mandarina f

tangible (tæn-dӡi-böl) adj tangible

tank (tængk) n tanque m

tanker (tæng-kö) n buque cisterna

tanned (tænd) adj tostado

tap (tæp) n grifo m; golpecito m; v golpear

tape (teip) n cinta f; adhesive ~ cinta adhesiva; esparadrapo m

tape-measure (teip-mê-ӡö) n centímetro m, cinta métrica

tape-recorder (teip-ri-koo-dö) n magnetófono m

tapestry (tæ-pi-sstri) n tapiz m

tar (taa) n brea f

target (taa-ghit) n objetivo m, blanco m

tariff (tæ-rif) n arancel m

tarpaulin (taa-poo-lin) n lona impermeable

**task** (taassk) *n* tarea *f*

**taste** (teisst) *n* gusto *m*; *v* \*saber a; \*probar

**tasteless** (*teisst*-löss) *adj* insípido

**tasty** (*tei*-ssti) *adj* rico, sabroso

**taught** (toot) *v* (p, pp teach)

**tavern** (*tæ*-vön) *n* taberna *f*

**tax** (tækss) *n* impuesto *m*; *v* \*imponer contribuciones

**taxation** (tæk-*ssei*-fön) *n* impuesto *m*

**tax-free** (*tækss*-frii) *adj* libre de impuestos

**taxi** (*tæk*-ssi) *n* taxi *m*; ~ **rank** parada de taxis; ~ **stand** *Am* parada de taxis

**taxi-driver** (*tæk*-ssi-drai-vö) *n* taxista *m*

**taxi-meter** (*tæk*-ssi-mii-tö) *n* taxímetro *m*

**tea** (tii) *n* té *m*; merienda *f*

**\*teach** (tiich) *v* enseñar

**teacher** (*tii*-chö) *n* profesor *m*, maestro *m*; profesora *f*; institutor *m*

**teachings** (*tii*-chings) *pl* enseñanza *f*

**tea-cloth** (*tii*-kloz) *n* trapo de cocina

**teacup** (*tii*-kap) *n* taza de té

**team** (tiim) *n* equipo *m*

**teapot** (*tii*-pot) *n* tetera *f*

**tear**[1] (tiö) *n* lágrima *f*

**tear**[2] (teö) *n* rasgón *m*; \***tear** *v* desgarrar

**tear-jerker** (*tiö*-dʒöö-kö) *n* cuplé lacrimoso

**tease** (tiis) *v* tomar el pelo

**tea-set** (*tii*-ssèt) *n* juego de té

**tea-shop** (*tii*-fop) *n* salón de té

**teaspoon** (*tii*-sspuun) *n* cucharilla *f*

**teaspoonful** (*tii*-sspuun-ful) *n* cucharadita *f*

**technical** (*têk*-ni-köl) *adj* técnico

**technician** (têk-*ni*-fön) *n* técnico *m*

**technique** (têk-*niik*) *n* técnica *f*

**technology** (têk-*no*-lö-dʒi) *n* tecnología *f*

**teenager** (*tii*-nei-dʒö) *n* jovencito *m*

**teetotaller** (tii-*tou*-tö-lö) *n* abstemio *m*

**telegram** (*tê*-li-ghræm) *n* telegrama *m*

**telegraph** (*tê*-li-ghraaf) *v* telegrafiar

**telepathy** (ti-*lê*-pö-zi) *n* telepatía *f*

**telephone** (*tê*-li-foun) *n* teléfono *m*; ~ **book** *Am* listín telefónico, guía telefónica; ~ **booth** cabina telefónica; ~ **call** llamada telefónica; ~ **directory** guía telefónica, listín telefónico; directorio telefónico *Me*; ~ **exchange** central telefónica; ~ **operator** telefonista *f*

**telephonist** (ti-*lê*-fö-nisst) *n* telefonista *f*

**television** (*tê*-li-vi-ʒön) *n* televisión *f*; ~ **set** televisor *m*

**telex** (*tê*-lêkss) *n* télex *m*

**\*tell** (têl) *v* \*decir; \*contar

**temper** (*têm*-pö) *n* cólera *f*

**temperature** (*têm*-prö-chö) *n* temperatura *f*

**tempest** (*têm*-pisst) *n* tempestad *f*

**temple** (*têm*-pöl) *n* templo *m*; sien *f*

**temporary** (*têm*-pö-rö-ri) *adj* provisional, temporal

**tempt** (têmpt) *v* \*tentar

**temptation** (têmp-*tei*-fön) *n* tentación *f*

**ten** (tên) *num* diez

**tenant** (*tê*-nönt) *n* inquilino *m*

**tend** (tênd) *v* \*tender a; cuidar de; ~ **to** \*tender a

**tendency** (*tên*-dön-ssi) *n* inclinación *f*, tendencia *f*

**tender** (*tên*-dö) *adj* tierno, delicado

**tendon** (*tên*-dön) *n* tendón *m*

**tennis** (*tê*-niss) *n* tenis *m*; ~ **shoes** zapatos de tenis

**tennis-court** (*tê*-niss-koot) *n* campo de tenis, cancha *f*

**tense** (tênss) *adj* tenso

**tension** (*tên*-ʃön) *n* tensión *m*
**tent** (tênt) *n* tienda *f*
**tenth** (tênz) *num* décimo
**tepid** (*tê*-pid) *adj* tibio
**term** (tööm) *n* término *m*; período *m*, plazo *m*; condición *f*
**terminal** (*töö*-mi-nöl) *n* estación terminal
**terrace** (*tê*-röss) *n* terraza *f*
**terrain** (tê-*rein*) *n* terreno *m*
**terrible** (*tê*-ri-böl) *adj* tremendo, terrible, pésimo
**terrific** (tö-*ri*-fik) *adj* tremendo
**terrify** (*tê*-ri-fai) *v* aterrorizar; **terrifying** aterrador
**territory** (*tê*-ri-tö-ri) *n* territorio *m*
**terror** (*tê*-rö) *n* terror *m*
**terrorism** (*tê*-rö-ri-söm) *n* terrorismo *m*, terror *m*
**terrorist** (*tê*-rö-risst) *n* terrorista *m*
**terylene** (*tê*-rö-liin) *n* terilene *m*
**test** (têsst) *n* prueba *f*, ensayo *m*; *v* *probar, ensayar
**testify** (*tê*-ssti-fai) *v* testimoniar
**text** (têksst) *n* texto *m*
**textbook** (*têkss*-buk) *n* libro de texto
**textile** (*têk*-sstail) *n* textil *m*
**texture** (*têkss*-chö) *n* textura *f*
**Thai** (tai) *adj* tailandés
**Thailand** (*tai*-lænd) Tailandia *f*
**than** (ðæn) *conj* que
**thank** (zængk) *v* *agradecer; ~ **you** gracias
**thankful** (*zængk*-föl) *adj* agradecido
**that** (ðæt) *adj* aquel, ese; *pron* aquél, eso; que; *conj* que
**thaw** (zoo) *v* descongelarse; *n* deshielo *m*
**the** (ðö,ði) *art* el *art*; **the ... the** cuanto más ... más
**theatre** (*ziô*-tö) *n* teatro *m*
**theft** (zêft) *n* robo *m*
**their** (ðêô) *adj* su
**them** (ðêm) *pron* les

**theme** (ziim) *n* tema *m*, sujeto *m*
**themselves** (ðöm-*ssêlvs*) *pron* se; ellos mismos
**then** (ðên) *adv* entonces; después; en tal caso
**theology** (zi-o-lö-dʒi) *n* teología *f*
**theoretical** (zi*ô*-*rê*-ti-köl) *adj* teórico
**theory** (zi*ô*-ri) *n* teoría *f*
**therapy** (*zê*-rö-pi) *n* terapia *f*
**there** (ðê*ô*) *adv* allí; hacia allá
**therefore** (ðê*ô*-foo) *conj* por lo tanto
**thermometer** (zö-*mo*-mi-tö) *n* termómetro *m*
**thermostat** (*zöö*-mö-sstæt) *n* termostato *m*
**these** (ðiis) *adj* éstos
**thesis** (*zii*-ssiss) *n* (pl theses) tesis *f*
**they** (ðei) *pron* ellos
**thick** (zik) *adj* espeso; denso
**thicken** (*zi*-kön) *v* espesar
**thickness** (*zik*-nöss) *n* espesor *m*
**thief** (ziif) *n* (pl thieves) ladrón *m*
**thigh** (zai) *n* muslo *m*
**thimble** (*zim*-böl) *n* dedal *m*
**thin** (zin) *adj* delgado; flaco
**thing** (zing) *n* cosa *f*
***think** (zingk) *v* *pensar; reflexionar; ~ **of** *pensar en; *recordar; ~ **over** considerar
**thinker** (*zing*-kö) *n* pensador *m*
**third** (zööd) *num* tercero
**thirst** (zöösst) *n* sed *f*
**thirsty** (*zöö*-ssti) *adj* sediento
**thirteen** (zöö-*tiin*) *num* trece
**thirteenth** (zöö-*tiinz*) *num* treceno
**thirtieth** (*zöö*-ti-öz) *num* treintavo
**thirty** (*zöö*-ti) *num* treinta
**this** (ðiss) *adj* este, esto; *pron* éste
**thistle** (*zi*-ssöl) *n* cardo *m*
**thorn** (zoon) *n* espina *f*
**thorough** (*za*-rö) *adj* minucioso
**thoroughbred** (*za*-rö-brêd) *adj* purasangre
**thoroughfare** (*za*-rö-fê*ô*) *n* ruta prin-

cipal, arteria principal

**those** (ðous) *adj* aquellos; *pron* aquéllos

**though** (ðou) *conj* si bien, aunque;
*adv* sin embargo

**thought**[1] (zoot) *v* (p, pp think)

**thought**[2] (zoot) *n* pensamiento *m*

**thoughtful** (*zoot*-föl) *adj* pensativo;
atento

**thousand** (*zau*-sönd) *num* mil

**thread** (zrĕd) *n* hilo *m*; *v* enhebrar

**threadbare** (*zrĕd*-bĕ⁰) *adj* gastado

**threat** (zrĕt) *n* amenaza *f*

**threaten** (*zrĕ*-tön) *v* amenazar;
**threatening** amenazador

**three** (zrii) *num* tres

**three-quarter** (zrii-*k*ᵘ*oo*-tö) *adj* tres
cuartos

**threshold** (*zrĕ*-ʃould) *n* umbral *m*

**threw** (zruu) *v* (p throw)

**thrifty** (*zrif*-ti) *adj* económico

**throat** (zrout) *n* garganta *f*

**throne** (zroun) *n* trono *m*

**through** (zruu) *prep* a través de

**throughout** (zruu-*aut*) *adv* por todas
partes

**throw** (zrou) *n* lanzamiento *m*

* **throw** (zrou) *v* tirar, arrojar

**thrush** (zraʃ) *n* tordo *m*

**thumb** (zam) *n* pulgar *m*

**thumbtack** (*zam*-tæk) *n Am* chinche *f*

**thump** (zamp) *v* golpear

**thunder** (*zan*-dö) *n* trueno *m*; *v* *tronar

**thunderstorm** (*zan*-dö-sstoom) *n* tronada *f*

**thundery** (*zan*-dö-ri) *adj* tormentoso

**Thursday** (*zöös*-di) jueves *m*

**thus** (ðass) *adv* así

**thyme** (taim) *n* tomillo *m*

**tick** (tik) *n* señal *f*; ~ **off** señalar

**ticket** (*ti*-kit) *n* billete *m*; multa *f*;
boleto *m Me*; ~ **collector** revisor
*m*; ~ **machine** máquina de billetes

**tickle** (*ti*-köl) *v* cosquillear

**tide** (taid) *n* marea *f*; **high** ~ pleamar
*f*; **low** ~ bajamar *f*

**tidings** (*tai*-dings) *pl* noticias *fpl*

**tidy** (*tai*-di) *adj* aseado; ~ **up** arreglar

**tie** (tai) *v* anudar, atar; *n* corbata *f*

**tiger** (*tai*-ghö) *n* tigre *m*

**tight** (tait) *adj* estrecho; angosto,
apretado; *adv* fuertemente

**tighten** (*tai*-tön) *v* estrechar, *apretar; estrecharse

**tights** (taitss) *pl* traje de malla

**tile** (tail) *n* azulejo *m*; teja *f*

**till** (til) *prep* hasta; *conj* hasta que

**timber** (*tim*-bö) *n* madera de construcción

**time** (taim) *n* tiempo *m*; vez *f*; **all
the** ~ continuamente; **in** ~ a tiempo; ~ **of arrival** hora de llegada; ~
**of departure** hora de salida

**time-saving** (*taim*-ssei-ving) *adj* que
economiza tiempo

**timetable** (*taim*-tei-böl) *n* horario *m*

**timid** (*ti*-mid) *adj* tímido

**timidity** (ti-*mi*-dö-ti) *n* timidez *f*

**tin** (tin) *n* estaño *m*; lata *f*; **tinned
food** conservas *fpl*

**tinfoil** (*tin*-foil) *n* papel de estaño

**tin-opener** (*ti*-nou-pö-nö) *n* abrelatas
*m*

**tiny** (*tai*-ni) *adj* menudo

**tip** (tip) *n* punta *f*; propina *f*

**tire**[1] (tai⁰) *n* neumático *m*; llanta
*f Me*

**tire**[2] (tai⁰) *v* cansar

**tired** (tai⁰d) *adj* cansado; ~ **of** harto
de

**tissue** (*ti*-ʃuu) *n* tejido *m*; pañuelo de
papel

**title** (*tai*-töl) *n* título *m*

**to** (tuu) *prep* hasta; a, para, en, hacia

**toad** (toud) *n* sapo *m*

**toadstool** (*toud*-sstuul) *n* hongo *m*

**toast** (tousst) *n* pan tostado; brindis

*m*

**tobacco** (tö-*bæ*-kou) *n* (pl ~s) tabaco *m*; ~ **pouch** petaca *f*

**tobacconist** (tö-*bæ*-kö-nisst) *n* estanquero *m*; **tobacconist's** estanco *m*

**today** (tö-*dei*) *adv* hoy

**toddler** (*tod*-lö) *n* párvulo *m*

**toe** (tou) *n* dedo del pie

**toffee** (*to*-fi) *n* caramelo *m*

**together** (tö-*ghê*-ðö) *adv* juntos

**toilet** (*toi*-löt) *n* retrete *m*; ~ **case** neceser *m*

**toilet-paper** (*toi*-löt-pei-pö) *n* papel higiénico

**toiletry** (*toi*-lö-tri) *n* artículos de tocador

**token** (*tou*-kön) *n* señal *f*; prueba *f*; ficha *f*

**told** (tould) *v* (p, pp tell)

**tolerable** (*to*-lö-rö-böl) *adj* tolerable

**toll** (toul) *n* peaje *m*

**tomato** (tö-*maa*-tou) *n* (pl ~es) tomate *m*; jitomate *mMe*

**tomb** (tuum) *n* tumba *f*

**tombstone** (*tuum*-sstoun) *n* lápida *f*

**tomorrow** (tö-*mo*-rou) *adv* mañana

**ton** (tan) *n* tonelada *f*

**tone** (toun) *n* tono *m*; timbre *m*

**tongs** (tongs) *pl* tenazas *f*

**tongue** (tang) *n* lengua *f*

**tonic** (*to*-nik) *n* tónico *m*

**tonight** (tö-*nait*) *adv* esta noche

**tonsilitis** (ton-ssö-*lai*-tiss) *n* amigdalitis *f*

**tonsils** (*ton*-ssöls) *pl* amígdalas *fpl*

**too** (tuu) *adv* demasiado; también

**took** (tuk) *v* (p take)

**tool** (tuul) *n* herramienta *f*; ~ **kit** bolsa de herramientas

**tooth** (tuuz) *n* (pl teeth) diente *m*

**toothache** (*tuu*-zeik) *n* dolor de muelas

**toothbrush** (*tuuz*-braʃ) *n* cepillo de dientes

**toothpaste** (*tuuz*-peisst) *n* pasta dentífrica

**toothpick** (*tuuz*-pik) *n* palillo *m*

**toothpowder** (*tuuz*-pau-dö) *n* polvo para los dientes

**top** (top) *n* cima *f*; parte superior; tapa *f*; superior; **on ~ of** encima de; ~ **side** parte superior

**topcoat** (*top*-kout) *n* sobretodo *m*

**topic** (*to*-pik) *n* asunto *m*

**topical** (*to*-pi-köl) *adj* actual

**torch** (tooch) *n* antorcha *f*; linterna *f*

**torment**[1] (too-*mênt*) *v* atormentar

**torment**[2] (*too*-mênt) *n* tormento *m*

**torture** (*too*-chö) *n* tortura *f*; *v* torturar

**toss** (toss) *v* echar

**tot** (tot) *n* niño pequeño

**total** (*tou*-töl) *adj* total; completo, absoluto; *n* total *m*

**totalitarian** (tou-tæ-li-*tê*ᵟ-ri-ön) *adj* totalitario

**totalizator** (*tou*-tö-lai-sei-tö) *n* totalizador *m*

**touch** (tach) *v* tocar; *concernir; contacto *m*, toque *m*; tacto *m*

**touching** (*ta*-ching) *adj* conmovedor

**tough** (taf) *adj* duro

**tour** (tuᵟ) *n* vuelta *f*

**tourism** (*tu*ᵟ-ri-söm) *n* turismo *m*

**tourist** (*tu*ᵟ-risst) *n* turista *m*; ~ **class** clase turista; ~ **office** oficina para turistas

**tournament** (*tu*ᵟ-nö-mönt) *n* torneo *m*

**tow** (tou) *v* remolcar

**towards** (tö-ᵘ*oods*) *prep* hacia; para con

**towel** (tauᵟl) *n* toalla *f*

**towelling** (*tau*ᵟ-ling) *n* tela para toallas

**tower** (tauᵟ) *n* torre *f*

**town** (taun) *n* ciudad *f*; ~ **centre** centro de la ciudad; ~ **hall** ayuntamiento *m*

**townspeople** ( *tauns*-pii-pöl ) *pl* ciuda-danos *mpl*

**toxic** ( *tok*-ssik ) *adj* tóxico

**toy** (toi ) *n* juguete *m*

**toyshop** ( *toi*-ʃop ) *n* juguetería *f*

**trace** (treiss ) *n* huella *f*; *v* rastrear

**track** (træk ) *n* via *f*; pista *f*

**tractor** ( *træk*-tö ) *n* tractor *m*

**trade** (treid ) *n* comercio *m*; oficio *m*; *v* comerciar

**trademark** ( *treid*-maak ) *n* marca de fá-brica

**trader** ( *trei*-dö ) *n* comerciante *m*

**tradesman** ( *treids*-mön ) *n* (pl -men) tendero *m*

**trade-union** (treid-*yuu*-nyön ) *n* sindi-cato *m*

**tradition** (trö-*di*-ʃön ) *n* tradición *f*

**traditional** (trö-*di*-ʃö-nöl ) *adj* tradicio-nal

**traffic** ( *træ*-fik ) *n* tránsito *m*; ~ **jam** embotellamiento *m*; ~ **light** semá-foro *m*

**trafficator** ( *træ*-fi-kei-tö ) *n* indicador *m*

**tragedy** ( *træ*-dʒö-di ) *n* tragedia *f*

**tragic** ( *træ*-dʒik ) *adj* trágico

**trail** (treil ) *n* rastro *m*, sendero *m*

**trailer** ( *trei*-lö ) *n* remolque *m*; *nAm* caravana *f*

**train** (trein ) *n* tren *m*; *v* amaestrar, entrenar; **stopping** ~ tren de cerca-nías; **through** ~ tren directo; ~ **ferry** transbordador de trenes

**training** ( *trei*-ning ) *n* entrenamiento *m*

**trait** (treit ) *n* rasgo *m*

**traitor** ( *trei*-tö ) *n* traidor *m*

**tram** (træm ) *n* tranvía *m*

**tramp** (træmp ) *n* vagabundo *m*; *v* va-gabundear

**tranquil** ( *træng*-kᵘil ) *adj* tranquilo

**tranquillizer** ( *træng*-kᵘi-lai-sö ) *n* cal-mante *m*

**transaction** (træn-*sæk*-ʃön ) *n* transac-ción *f*

**transatlantic** (træn-söt-*læn*-tik ) *adj* transatlántico

**transfer** (trænss-*föö* ) *v* *transferir

**transform** (trænss-*foom* ) *v* transfor-mar

**transformer** (trænss-*foo*-mö ) *n* trans-formador *m*

**transition** (træn-*ssi*-ʃön ) *n* transición *f*

**translate** (trænss-*leit* ) *v* *traducir

**translation** (trænss-*lei*-ʃön ) *n* traduc-ción *f*

**translator** (trænss-*lei*-tö ) *n* traductor *m*

**transmission** (træns-*mi*-ʃön ) *n* trans-misión *f*

**transmit** (træns-*mit* ) *v* transmitir

**transmitter** (træns-*mi*-tö ) *n* emisor *m*

**transparent** (træn-*sspêᵒ*-rönt ) *adj* transparente

**transport¹** ( *træn*-sspoot ) *n* transporte *m*

**transport²** (træn-*sspoot* ) *v* transportar

**transportation** (træn-sspoo-*tei*-ʃön ) *n* transporte *m*

**trap** (træp ) *n* trampa *f*

**trash** (træʃ ) *n* basura *f*

**travel** ( *træ*-völ ) *v* viajar; ~ **agency** agencia de viajes; ~ **agent** agente de viajes; ~ **insurance** seguro de viaje; **travelling expenses** gastos de viaje

**traveller** ( *træ*-vö-lö ) *n* viajero *m*; **traveller's cheque** cheque de viaje-ro

**tray** (trei ) *n* bandeja *f*; charola *fMe*

**treason** ( *trii*-sön ) *n* traición *f*

**treasure** ( *trê*-ʒö ) *n* tesoro *m*

**treasurer** ( *trê*-ʒö-rö ) *n* tesorero *m*

**treasury** ( *trê*-ʒö-ri ) *n* Tesorería *f*

**treat** (triit ) *v* tratar

**treatment** ( *triit*-mönt ) *n* tratamiento

*m*

**treaty** (*trii*-ti) *n* tratado *m*

**tree** (trii) *n* árbol *m*

**tremble** (*trêm*-böl) *v* \*temblar; vibrar

**tremendous** (tri-*mên*-döss) *adj* tremendo

**trespass** (*trêss*-pöss) *v* infringir

**trespasser** (*trêss*-pö-ssö) *n* intruso *m*

**trial** (trai⁰l) *n* proceso *m*; prueba *f*

**triangle** (*trai*-æng-ghöl) *n* triángulo *m*

**triangular** (trai-*æng*-ghyu-lö) *adj* triangular

**tribe** (traib) *n* tribu *m*

**tributary** (*tri*-byu-tö-ri) *n* afluente *m*

**tribute** (*tri*-byuut) *n* homenaje *m*

**trick** (trik) *n* truco *m*

**trigger** (*tri*-ghö) *n* gatillo *m*

**trim** (trim) *v* recortar

**trip** (trip) *n* excursión *f*, viaje *m*

**triumph** (*trai*-ömf) *n* triunfo *m*; *v* triunfar

**triumphant** (trai-*am*-fönt) *adj* triunfante

**trolley-bus** (*tro*-li-bass) *n* trolebús *m*

**troops** (truupss) *pl* tropas *fpl*

**tropical** (*tro*-pi-köl) *adj* tropical

**tropics** (*tro*-pikss) *pl* trópicos *mpl*

**trouble** (*tra*-böl) *n* preocupación *f*, molestia *f*; *v* molestar

**troublesome** (*tra*-böl-ssöm) *adj* molesto

**trousers** (*trau*-sös) *pl* pantalones *mpl*

**trout** (traut) *n* (pl ~) trucha *f*

**truck** (trak) *nAm* camión *m*

**true** (truu) *adj* verdadero; real, auténtico; leal, fiel

**trumpet** (*tram*-pit) *n* trompeta *f*

**trunk** (trangk) *n* baúl *m*; tronco *m*; *nAm* portaequipajes *m*; **trunks** *pl* pantalones de gimnasia

**trunk-call** (*trangk*-kool) *n* conferencia interurbana

**trust** (trasst) *v* confiar en; *n* confianza *f*

**trustworthy** (*trasst*-ᵁöö-ði) *adj* confiable

**truth** (truuz) *n* verdad *f*

**truthful** (*truuz*-föl) *adj* verídico

**try** (trai) *v* intentar; \*esforzarse; *n* tentativa *f*; ~ **on** \*probarse

**tube** (tyuub) *n* tubo *m*

**tuberculosis** (tyuu-böö-kyu-*lou*-ssiss) *n* tuberculosis *f*

**Tuesday** (*tyuus*-di) martes *m*

**tug** (tagh) *v* remolcar; *n* remolcador *m*; estirón *m*

**tuition** (tyuu-*i*-∫ön) *n* enseñanza *f*

**tulip** (*tyuu*-lip) *n* tulipán *m*

**tumbler** (*tam*-blö) *n* vaso *m*

**tumour** (*tyuu*-mö) *n* tumor *m*

**tuna** (*tyuu*-nö) *n* (pl ~, ~s) atún *m*

**tune** (tyuun) *n* tonada *f*; ~ **in** sintonizar

**tuneful** (*tyuun*-föl) *adj* melodioso

**tunic** (*tyuu*-nik) *n* túnica *f*

**Tunisia** (tyuu-*ni*-si-ö) Túnez *m*

**Tunisian** (tyuu-*ni*-si-ön) *adj* tunecino

**tunnel** (*ta*-nöl) *n* túnel *m*

**turbine** (*töö*-bain) *n* turbina *f*

**turbojet** (*töö*-bou-dʒêt) *n* avión turborreactor

**Turk** (töök) *n* turco *m*

**Turkey** (*töö*-ki) Turquía *f*

**turkey** (*töö*-ki) *n* pavo *m*

**Turkish** (*töö*-ki∫) *adj* turco; ~ **bath** baño turco

**turn** (töön) *v* girar; \*volver; *n* cambio *m*, vuelta *f*; curva *f*; turno *m*; ~ **back** \*volver; ~ **down** rechazar; ~ **into** \*convertirse en; ~ **off** \*cerrar; ~ **on** \*encender; abrir; ~ **over** \*volver; ~ **round** \*volver; \*volverse

**turning** (*töö*-ning) *n* vuelta *f*

**turning-point** (*töö*-ning-point) *n* punto decisivo

**turnover** (*töö*-nou-vö) *n* volumen de transacciones; ~ **tax** impuesto so-

bre la venta
**turnpike** ( *töön*-paik ) *nAm* autopista
de peaje
**turpentine** ( *töö*-pön-tain ) *n* trementina *f*
**turtle** ( *töö*-töl ) *n* tortuga *f*
**tutor** ( *tyuu*-tö ) *n* maestro particular;
tutor *m*
**tuxedo** (tak-*ssii*-dou ) *nAm* (pl ~s,
~es) smoking *m*
**tweed** (t<sup>u</sup>iid ) *n* lana tweed
**tweezers** ( *t<sup>u</sup>ii*-sös) *pl* pinzas *fpl*
**twelfth** (t<sup>u</sup>êlfz) *num* duodécimo
**twelve** (t<sup>u</sup>êlv ) *num* doce
**twentieth** ( *t<sup>u</sup>ên*-ti-öz) *num* vigésimo
**twenty** ( *t<sup>u</sup>ên*-ti) *num* veinte
**twice** (t<sup>u</sup>aiss ) *adv* dos veces
**twig** (t<sup>u</sup>igh ) *n* ramita *f*
**twilight** ( *t<sup>u</sup>ai*-lait ) *n* crepúsculo *m*
**twine** (t<sup>u</sup>ain ) *n* trenza *f*
**twins** (t<sup>u</sup>ins ) *pl* gemelos *mpl*; **twin
beds** camas gemelas
**twist** (t<sup>u</sup>isst ) *v* *torcer; *n* torsión *f*
**two** (tuu ) *num* dos
**two-piece** (tuu-*piiss* ) *adj* de dos piezas
**type** (taip ) *v* escribir a máquina, mecanografiar; *n* tipo *m*
**typewriter** ( *taip*-rai-tö ) *n* máquina de
escribir
**typewritten** ( *taip*-ri-tön ) mecanogra-
fiado
**typhoid** ( *tai*-foid ) *n* tifus *m*
**typical** ( *ti*-pi-köl ) *adj* característico, típico
**typist** ( *tai*-pisst ) *n* dactilógrafa *f*
**tyrant** ( *tai<sup>o</sup>*-rönt ) *n* tirano *m*
**tyre** (tai<sup>o</sup> ) *n* neumático *m*; ~ **pressure** presión del neumático

# U

**ugly** ( *a*-ghli ) *adj* feo
**ulcer** ( *al*-ssö ) *n* úlcera *f*
**ultimate** ( *al*-ti-möt ) *adj* último
**ultraviolet** (al-trö-*vai<sup>o</sup>*-löt) *adj* ultravioleta
**umbrella** (am-*brê*-lö) *n* paraguas *m*
**umpire** ( *am*-pai<sup>o</sup> ) *n* árbitro *m*
**unable** (a-*nei*-böl) *adj* incapaz
**unacceptable** (a-nök-*ssêp*-tö-böl ) *adj*
inaceptable
**unaccountable** (a-nö-*kaun*-tö-böl ) *adj*
inexplicable
**unaccustomed** (a-nö-*ka*-sstmd ) *adj*
desacostumbrado
**unanimous** (yuu-*næ*-ni-möss ) *adj* unánime
**unanswered** (a-*naan*-ssöd ) *adj* sin
contestación
**unauthorized** (a-*noo*-zö-raisd ) *adj* desautorizado
**unavoidable** (a-nö-*voi*-dö-böl ) *adj* inevitable
**unaware** (a-nö-*<sup>u</sup>ê<sup>o</sup>* ) *adj* inconsciente
**unbearable** (an-*bê<sup>o</sup>*-rö-böl ) *adj* insufrible
**unbreakable** (an-*brei*-kö-böl ) *adj*
irrompible
**unbroken** (an-*brou*-kön ) *adj* intacto
**unbutton** (an-*ba*-tön ) *v* desabotonar
**uncertain** (an-*ssöö*-tön ) *adj* incierto
**uncle** ( *ang*-köl ) *n* tío *m*
**unclean** (an-*kliin* ) *adj* sucio
**uncomfortable** (an-*kam*-fö-tö-böl) *adj*
incómodo
**uncommon** (an-*ko*-mön ) *adj* insólito,
raro
**unconditional** (an-kön-*di*-jö-nöl ) *adj*
incondicional
**unconscious** (an-*kon*-]öss ) *adj* inconsciente

**uncork** (an-*kook*) *v* descorchar

**uncover** (an-*ka*-vö) *v* destapar

**uncultivated** (an-*kal*-ti-vei-tid) *adj* inculto

**under** (*an*-dö) *prep* debajo de, bajo

**undercurrent** (*an*-dö-ka-rönt) *n* resaca *f*

**underestimate** (an-dö-*rê*-ssti-meit) *v* subestimar

**underground** (*an*-dö-ghraund) *adj* subterráneo; *n* metro *m*

**underline** (an-dö-*lain*) *v* subrayar

**underneath** (an-dö-*niiz*) *adv* debajo

**undershirt** (*an*-dö-jööt) *n* camiseta *f*

**undersigned** (*an*-dö-ssaind) *n* suscrito *m*

* **understand** (an-dö-*sstænd*) *v* comprender

**understanding** (an-dö-*sstæn*-ding) *n* comprensión *m*

* **undertake** (an-dö-*teik*) *v* emprender

**undertaking** (an-dö-*tei*-king) *n* empresa *f*

**underwater** (*an*-dö-ᵘoo-tö) *adj* subacuático

**underwear** (*an*-dö-ᵘêᵒ) *n* ropa interior

**undesirable** (an-di-*saiᵒ*-rö-böl) *adj* indeseable

* **undo** (an-*duu*) *v* desatar

**undoubtedly** (an-*dau*-tid-li) *adv* sin duda

**undress** (an-*drêss*) *v* desnudarse

**undulating** (*an*-dyu-lei-ting) *adj* ondulante

**unearned** (a-*nöönd*) *adj* inmerecido

**uneasy** (a-*nii*-si) *adj* inquieto

**uneducated** (a-*nê*-dyu-kei-tid) *adj* inculto

**unemployed** (a-nim-*ploid*) *adj* desocupado

**unemployment** (a-nim-*ploi*-mönt) *n* desempleo *m*

**unequal** (a-*nii*-kᵘöl) *adj* desigual

**uneven** (a-*nii*-vön) *adj* desigual; irregular

**unexpected** (a-nik-*sspêk*-tid) *adj* imprevisto, inesperado

**unfair** (an-*fêᵒ*) *adj* ímprobo, injusto

**unfaithful** (an-*feiz*-föl) *adj* infiel

**unfamiliar** (an-fö-*mil*-yö) *adj* desconocido

**unfasten** (an-*faa*-ssön) *v* desatar

**unfavourable** (an-*fei*-vö-rö-böl) *adj* desfavorable

**unfit** (an-*fit*) *adj* inadecuado

**unfold** (an-*fould*) *v* *desplegar

**unfortunate** (an-*foo*-chö-nöt) *adj* desafortunado

**unfortunately** (an-*foo*-chö-nöt-li) *adv* por desgracia, desgraciadamente

**unfriendly** (an-*frênd*-li) *adj* poco amistoso

**unfurnished** (an-*föö*-nijt) *adj* desamueblado

**ungrateful** (an-*ghreit*-föl) *adj* ingrato

**unhappy** (an-*hæ*-pi) *adj* desdichado

**unhealthy** (an-*hêl*-zi) *adj* insalubre

**unhurt** (an-*hööt*) *adj* ileso

**uniform** (*yuu*-ni-foom) *n* uniforme *m*; *adj* uniforme

**unimportant** (a-nim-*poo*-tönt) *adj* insignificante

**uninhabitable** (a-nin-*hæ*-bi-tö-böl) *adj* inhabitable

**uninhabited** (a-nin-*hæ*-bi-tid) *adj* inhabitado

**unintentional** (a-nin-*tên*-jö-nöl) *adj* no intencional

**union** (*yuu*-nyön) *n* unión *f*; liga *f*, confederación *f*

**unique** (yuu-*niik*) *adj* único

**unit** (*yuu*-nit) *n* unidad *f*

**unite** (yuu-*nait*) *v* unir

**United States** (yuu-*nai*-tid ssteitss) Estados Unidos

**unity** (*yuu*-nö-ti) *n* unidad *f*

**universal** (yuu-ni-*vöö*-ssöl) *adj* gene-

ral, universal
**universe** (*yuu*-ni-vööss) *n* universo *m*
**university** (yuu-ni-*vöö*-ssö-ti) *n* universidad *f*
**unjust** (an-*dʒasst*) *adj* injusto
**unkind** (an-*kaind*) *adj* desagradable, arisco
**unknown** (an-*noun*) *adj* desconocido
**unlawful** (an-*loo*-föl) *adj* ilegal
**unlearn** (an-*löön*) *v* desacostumbrar
**unless** (ön-*léss*) *conj* a menos que
**unlike** (an-*laik*) *adj* diferente
**unlikely** (an-*lai*-kli) *adj* improbable
**unlimited** (an-*li*-mi-tid) *adj* ilimitado
**unload** (an-*loud*) *v* descargar
**unlock** (an-*lok*) *v* abrir
**unlucky** (an-*la*-ki) *adj* desafortunado
**unnecessary** (an-*né*-ssö-ssö-ri) *adj* innecesario
**unoccupied** (a-*no*-kyu-paid) *adj* desocupado
**unofficial** (a-nö-*fi*-föl) *adj* extraoficial
**unpack** (an-*pæk*) *v* desempaquetar
**unpleasant** (an-*plê*-sönt) *adj* desagradable; antipático
**unpopular** (an-*po*-pyu-lö) *adj* impopular
**unprotected** (an-prö-*têk*-tid) *adj* indefenso
**unqualified** (an-*kᵘo*-li-faid) *adj* incompetente
**unreal** (an-*riᵒl*) *adj* irreal
**unreasonable** (an-*rii*-sö-nö-böl) *adj* irrazonable
**unreliable** (an-ri-*lai*-ö-böl) *adj* no confiable
**unrest** (an-*rêsst*) *n* desasosiego *m*; inquietud *f*
**unsafe** (an-*sseif*) *adj* inseguro
**unsatisfactory** (an-ssæ-tiss-*fæk*-tö-ri) *adj* poco satisfactorio
**unscrew** (an-*sskruu*) *v* destornillar
**unselfish** (an-*ssél*-fiʃ) *adj* desinteresado

**unskilled** (an-*sskild*) *adj* no especializado
**unsound** (an-*ssaund*) *adj* enfermizo
**unstable** (an-*sstei*-böl) *adj* inestable
**unsteady** (an-*sstê*-di) *adj* vacilante, inestable
**unsuccessful** (an-ssök-*ssêss*-föl) *adj* fracasado
**unsuitable** (an-*ssuu*-tö-böl) *adj* inadecuado
**unsurpassed** (an-ssö-*paasst*) *adj* sin igual
**untidy** (an-*tai*-di) *adj* desaliñado
**untie** (an-*tai*) *v* desatar
**until** (ön-*til*) *prep* hasta
**untrue** (an-*truu*) *adj* falso
**untrustworthy** (an-*trasst*-ᵘöö-ði) *adj* indigno de confianza
**unusual** (an-*yuu*-ʒu-öl) *adj* inusitado, insólito
**unwell** (an-*ᵘêl*) *adj* indispuesto
**unwilling** (an-*ᵘi*-ling) *adj* desinclinado
**unwise** (an-*ᵘais*) *adj* imprudente
**unwrap** (an-*ræp*) *v* *desenvolver
**up** (ap) *adv* hacia arriba, arriba
**upholster** (ap-*houl*-sstö) *v* tapizar
**upkeep** (*ap*-kiip) *n* manutención *f*
**uplands** (*ap*-lönds) *pl* altiplano *m*
**upon** (ö-*pon*) *prep* sobre
**upper** (a-pö) *adj* superior
**upright** (*ap*-rait) *adj* derecho; *adv* de pie
**upset** (ap-*ssêt*) *v* trastornar; *adj* trastornado
**upside-down** (ap-ssaid-*daun*) *adv* al revés
**upstairs** (ap-*sstêᵒs*) *adv* arriba
**upstream** (ap-*sstriim*) *adv* río arriba
**upwards** (*ap*-ᵘöds) *adv* hacia arriba
**urban** (*öö*-bön) *adj* urbano
**urge** (öödʒ) *v* estimular; *n* impulso *m*
**urgency** (*öö*-dʒön-ssi) *n* urgencia *f*
**urgent** (*öö*-dʒönt) *adj* urgente

**urine** (*yuᵒ*-rin) *n* orina *f*

**Uruguay** (*yuᵒ*-rö-gh*ᵘ*ai) Uruguay *m*

**Uruguayan** (yuᵒ-rö-gh*ᵘ*ai-ön) *adj* uruguayo

**us** (ass) *pron* nosotros

**usable** (*yuu*-sö-böl) *adj* utilizable

**usage** (*yuu*-sidʒ) *n* uso *m*

**use**¹ (yuus) *v* usar; **\*be used to** \*estar acostumbrado a; **~ up** consumir

**use**² (yuuss) *n* uso *m*; utilidad *f*; **\*be of ~** \*servir

**useful** (*yuuss*-föl) *adj* útil

**useless** (*yuuss*-löss) *adj* inútil

**user** (*yuu*-sö) *n* usuario *m*

**usher** (*a*-ʃö) *n* acomodador *m*

**usherette** (a-ʃö-*rêt*) *n* acomodadora *f*

**usual** (*yuu*-ʒu-öl) *adj* usual

**usually** (*yuu*-ʒu-ö-li) *adv* habitualmente

**utensil** (yuu-*tên*-ssöl) *n* herramienta *f*, utensilio *m*

**utility** (yuu-*ti*-lö-ti) *n* utilidad *f*

**utilize** (*yuu*-ti-lais) *v* utilizar

**utmost** (*at*-mousst) *adj* extremo

**utter** (a-tö) *adj* completo, total; *v* emitir

# V

**vacancy** (*vei*-kön-ssi) *n* vacante *f*

**vacant** (*vei*-könt) *adj* vacante

**vacate** (vö-*keit*) *v* vaciar

**vacation** (vö-*kei*-ʃön) *n* vacaciones *fpl*

**vaccinate** (*væk*-ssi-neit) *v* vacunar

**vaccination** (væk-ssi-*nei*-ʃön) *n* vacunación *f*

**vacuum** (*væ*-kyu-öm) *n* vacío *m*; **~ cleaner** aspirador *m*; **~ flask** termo *m*

**vagrancy** (*vei*-ghrön-ssi) *n* vagancia *f*

**vague** (veigh) *adj* vago

**vain** (vein) *adj* vanidoso; vano; **in ~** inútilmente, en vano

**valet** (*væ*-lit) *n* ayuda de cámara

**valid** (*væ*-lid) *adj* vigente

**valley** (*væ*-li) *n* valle *m*

**valuable** (*væ*-lyu-böl) *adj* valioso; **valuables** *pl* objetos de valor

**value** (*væ*-lyu) *n* valor *m*; *v* valuar

**valve** (vælv) *n* válvula *f*

**van** (væn) *n* camioneta *f*

**vanilla** (vö-*ni*-lö) *n* vainilla *f*

**vanish** (*væ*-niʃ) *v* \*desaparecer

**vapour** (*vei*-pö) *n* vapor *m*

**variable** (*vêᵒ*-ri-ö-böl) *adj* variable

**variation** (vêᵒ-ri-*ei*-ʃön) *n* variación *f*; cambio *m*

**varied** (*vêᵒ*-rid) *adj* variado

**variety** (vö-*rai*-ö-ti) *n* variedad *f*; **~ show** espectáculo de variedades; **~ theatre** teatro de variedades

**various** (*vêᵒ*-ri-öss) *adj* varios

**varnish** (*vaa*-niʃ) *n* barniz *m*; *v* barnizar

**vary** (*vêᵒ*-ri) *v* variar; cambiar; \*diferir

**vase** (vaas) *n* vaso *m*

**vaseline** (*væ*-ssö-liin) *n* vaselina *f*

**vast** (vaasst) *adj* vasto

**vault** (voolt) *n* bóveda *f*; caja de caudales

**veal** (viil) *n* carne de ternera

**vegetable** (*vê*-dʒo-tö-böl) *n* legumbre *f*

**vegetarian** (vê-dʒi-*têᵒ*-ri-ön) *n* vegetariano *m*

**vegetation** (vê-dʒi-*tei*-ʃön) *n* vegetación *f*

**vehicle** (*vii*-ö-köl) *n* vehículo *m*

**veil** (veil) *n* velo *m*

**vein** (vein) *n* vena *f*; **varicose ~** varice *f*

**velvet** (*vêl*-vit) *n* terciopelo *m*

**velveteen** (vêl-vi-*tiin*) *n* pana *f*

**venerable** (*vê*-nö-rö-böl) *adj* venerable

**venereal disease** (vi-*ni⁰*-ri-öl di-*siis*) enfermedad venérea

**Venezuela** (vê-ni-s*ʷei*-lö) Venezuela *f*

**Venezuelan** (vê-ni-s*ʷei*-lön) *adj* venezolano

**ventilate** (*vên*-ti-leit) *v* ventilar; airear

**ventilation** (vên-ti-*lei*-ʃön) *n* ventilación *f*; aireo *m*

**ventilator** (*vên*-ti-lei-tö) *n* ventilador *m*

**venture** (*vên*-chö) *v* arriesgar

**veranda** (vö-*ræn*-dö) *n* veranda *f*

**verb** (vööb) *n* verbo *m*

**verbal** (*vöö*-böl) *adj* verbal

**verdict** (*vöö*-dikt) *n* sentencia *f*, veredicto *m*

**verge** (vööd3) *n* borde *m*

**verify** (*vê*-ri-fai) *v* verificar

**verse** (vööss) *n* verso *m*

**version** (*vöö*-ʃön) *n* versión *f*

**versus** (*vöö*-ssöss) *prep* contra

**vertical** (*vöö*-ti-köl) *adj* vertical

**vertigo** (*vöö*-ti-ghou) *n* vértigo *m*

**very** (*vê*-ri) *adv* mucho, muy; *adj* preciso, verdadero; extremo

**vessel** (*vê*-ssöl) *n* embarcación *f*, buque *m*; vasija *f*

**vest** (vêsst) *n* camiseta *f*; *nAm* chaleco *m*

**veterinary surgeon** (*vê*-tri-nö-ri *ssöö*-dʒön) veterinario *m*

**via** (*vai⁰*) *prep* por

**viaduct** (*vai⁰*-dakt) *n* viaducto *m*

**vibrate** (vai-*breit*) *v* vibrar

**vibration** (vai-*brei*-ʃön) *n* vibración *f*

**vicar** (*vi*-kö) *n* vicario *m*

**vicarage** (*vi*-kö-rid3) *n* casa del párroco

**vice-president** (vaiss-*prê*-si-dönt) *n* vicepresidente *m*

**vicinity** (vi-*ssi*-nö-ti) *n* vecindad *f*

**vicious** (*vi*-ʃöss) *adj* vicioso

**victim** (*vik*-tim) *n* víctima *f*

**victory** (*vik*-tö-ri) *n* victoria *f*

**view** (vyuu) *n* vista *f*; parecer *m*, opinión *f*; *v* mirar

**view-finder** (*vyuu*-fain-dö) *n* visor *m*

**vigilant** (*vi*-dʒi-lönt) *adj* despierto

**villa** (*vi*-lö) *n* villa *f*

**village** (*vi*-lid3) *n* pueblo *m*

**villain** (*vi*-lön) *n* villano *m*

**vine** (vain) *n* vid *f*

**vinegar** (*vi*-ni-ghö) *n* vinagre *m*

**vineyard** (*vin*-yöd) *n* viña *f*

**vintage** (*vin*-tid3) *n* vendimia *f*

**violation** (vai⁰-*lei*-ʃön) *n* violación *f*

**violence** (*vai⁰*-lönss) *n* violencia *f*

**violent** (*vai⁰*-lönt) *adj* violento; impetuoso

**violet** (*vai⁰*-löt) *n* violeta *f*; *adj* morado

**violin** (vai⁰-*lin*) *n* violín *m*

**virgin** (*vöö*-dʒin) *n* virgen *f*

**virtue** (*vöö*-chuu) *n* virtud *f*

**visa** (*vii*-sö) *n* visado *m*

**visibility** (vi-sö-*bi*-lö-ti) *n* visibilidad *f*

**visible** (*vi*-sö-böl) *adj* visible

**vision** (*vi*-ʒön) *n* visión *f*

**visit** (*vi*-sit) *v* visitar; *n* visita *f*; **visiting hours** horas de visita

**visiting-card** (*vi*-si-ting-kaad) *n* tarjeta de visita

**visitor** (*vi*-si-tö) *n* visitante *m*

**vital** (*vai*-töl) *adj* esencial

**vitamin** (*vi*-tö-min) *n* vitamina *f*

**vivid** (*vi*-vid) *adj* vivo

**vocabulary** (vö-*kæ*-byu-lö-ri) *n* vocabulario *m*; glosario *m*

**vocal** (*vou*-köl) *adj* vocal

**vocalist** (*vou*-kö-lisst) *n* vocalista *m*

**voice** (voiss) *n* voz *f*

**void** (void) *adj* nulo

**volcano** (vol-*kei*-nou) *n* (pl ~es, ~s) volcán *m*

**volt** (voult) *n* voltio *m*

**voltage** (*voul*-tid3) *n* voltaje *m*

**volume** (*vo*-lyum) *n* volumen *m*; tomo *m*

voluntary (vo-lön-tö-ri) adj voluntario

volunteer (vo-lön-tiᵒ) n voluntario m

vomit (vo-mit) v vomitar

vote (vout) v votar; n voto m; votación f

voucher (vau-chö) n recibo m, comprobante m

vow (vau) n voto m, juramento m; v prestar juramento

vowel (vauᵘl) n vocal f

voyage (voi-idʒ) n viaje m

vulgar (val-ghö) adj vulgar; popular, ordinario

vulnerable (val-nö-rö-böl) adj vulnerable

vulture (val-chö) n buitre m

# W

wade (ᵘeid) v vadear

wafer (ᵘei-fö) n oblea f

waffle (ᵘo-föl) n barquillo m

wages (ᵘei-dʒis) pl paga f

waggon (ᵘæ-ghön) n vagón m

waist (ᵘeisst) n cintura f

waistcoat (ᵘeiss-kout) n chaleco m

wait (ᵘeit) v esperar; ~ on *servir

waiter (ᵘei-tö) n camarero m; mesero mMe

waiting n espera f

waiting-list (ᵘei-ting-lisst) n lista de espera

waiting-room (ᵘei-ting-ruum) n sala de espera

waitress (ᵘei-triss) n camarera f; mesera fMe

*wake (ᵘeik) v *despertar; ~ up *despertarse

walk (ᵘook) v *andar; pasear; n caminata f; andadura f; walking a pie

walker (ᵘoo-kö) n paseante m

walking-stick (ᵘoo-king-sstik) n bastón m

wall (ᵘool) n muro m; pared f

wallet (ᵘo-lit) n cartera f

wallpaper (ᵘool-pei-pö) n papel pintado

walnut (ᵘool-nat) n nogal m

waltz (ᵘoolss) n vals m

wander (ᵘon-dö) v vagar; *errar

want (ᵘont) v *querer; desear; n necesidad f; carencia f, falta f

war (ᵘoo) n guerra f

warden (ᵘoo-dön) n guardián m

wardrobe (ᵘoo-droub) n guardarropa m, vestuario m

warehouse (ᵘêᵒ-hauss) n almacén m

wares (ᵘêᵒs) pl mercancías fpl

warm (ᵘoom) adj caliente; v *calentar

warmth (ᵘoomz) n calor m

warn (ᵘoon) v *advertir

warning (ᵘoo-ning) n advertencia f

wary (ᵘêᵒ-ri) adj prudente

was (ᵘos) v (p be)

wash (ᵘoʃ) v lavar; ~ and wear no precisa plancha; ~ up *fregar

washable (ᵘo-ʃö-böl) adj lavable

wash-basin (ᵘoʃ-bei-ssön) n palangana f

washing (ᵘo-ʃing) n lavado m; ropa sucia

washing-machine (ᵘo-ʃing-mö-ʃiin) n máquina de lavar

washing-powder (ᵘo-ʃing-pau-dö) n jabón en polvo

washroom (ᵘoʃ-ruum) nAm cuarto de aseo

wash-stand (ᵘoʃ-sstænd) n lavabo m

wasp (ᵘossp) n avispa f

waste (ᵘeisst) v *perder; n desperdicio m; adj baldío

wasteful (ᵘeisst-föl) adj derrochador

wastepaper-basket (ᵘeisst-pei-pö-baasskit) n cesto para papeles

**watch** (ᵁoch) v mirar, observar; vigilar; n reloj m; ~ **for** acechar; ~ **out** *tener cuidado

**watch-maker** (ᵁoch-mei-kö) n relojero m

**watch-strap** (ᵁoch-sstræp) n correa de reloj

**water** (ᵁoo-tö) n agua f; **iced** ~ agua helada; **running** ~ agua corriente; ~ **pump** bomba de agua; ~ **ski** esquí acuático

**water-colour** (ᵁoo-tö-ka-lö) n color de aguada; acuarela f

**watercress** (ᵁoo-tö-krêss) n berro m

**waterfall** (ᵁoo-tö-fool) n cascada f

**watermelon** (ᵁoo-tö-mê-lön) n sandía f

**waterproof** (ᵁoo-tö-pruuf) adj impermeable

**water-softener** (ᵁoo-tö-ssof-nö) n ablandador m

**waterway** (ᵁoo-tö-ᵁei) n vía navegable

**watt** (ᵁot) n vatio m

**wave** (ᵁeiv) n ondulación f, ola f; v *hacer señales

**wave-length** (ᵁeiv-lêngz) n longitud de onda

**wavy** (ᵁei-vi) adj ondulado

**wax** (ᵁækss) n cera f

**waxworks** (ᵁækss-ᵁöökss) pl museo de figuras de cera

**way** (ᵁei) n manera f; camino m; lado m, dirección f; distancia f; **any** ~ de todos modos; **by the** ~ a propósito; **one-way traffic** dirección única; **out of the** ~ apartado; **the other** ~ **round** al revés; ~ **back** vuelta f; ~ **in** entrada f; ~ **out** salida f

**wayside** (ᵁei-ssaid) n borde del camino

**we** (ᵁii) pron nosotros

**weak** (ᵁiik) adj débil; flojo

**weakness** (ᵁiik-nöss) n debilidad f

**wealth** (ᵁêlz) n riqueza f

**wealthy** (ᵁêl-zi) adj rico

**weapon** (ᵁê-pön) n arma f

***wear** (ᵁêⁿ) v llevar; ~ **out** gastar

**weary** (ᵁiⁿ-ri) adj cansado

**weather** (ᵁê-ðö) n tiempo m; ~ **forecast** boletín meteorológico

***weave** (ᵁiiv) v tejer

**weaver** (ᵁii-vö) n tejedor m

**wedding** (ᵁê-ding) n matrimonio m, boda f

**wedding-ring** (ᵁê-ding-ring) n anillo de boda

**wedge** (ᵁêdʒ) n cuña f

**Wednesday** (ᵁêns-di) miércoles m

**weed** (ᵁiid) n mala hierba

**week** (ᵁiik) n semana f

**weekday** (ᵁiik-dei) n día laborable

**weekend** (ᵁii-kênd) n fin de semana

**weekly** (ᵁii-kli) adj semanal

***weep** (ᵁiip) v llorar

**weigh** (ᵁei) v pesar

**weighing-machine** (ᵁei-ing-mö-ʃiin) n báscula f

**weight** (ᵁeit) n peso m

**welcome** (ᵁêl-köm) adj bienvenido; n bienvenida f; v *dar la bienvenida

**weld** (ᵁêld) v *soldar

**welfare** (ᵁêl-fêⁿ) n bienestar m

**well¹** (ᵁêl) adv bien; adj sano; **as** ~ también; **as** ~ **as** así como; **well!** ¡bueno!

**well²** (ᵁêl) n pozo m

**well-founded** (ᵁêl-faun-did) adj fundamentado

**well-known** (ᵁêl-noun) adj notorio

**well-to-do** (ᵁêl-tö-duu) adj acomodado

**went** (ᵁênt) v (p go)

**were** (ᵁöö) v (p be)

**west** (ᵁêsst) n occidente m, oeste m

**westerly** (ᵁê-sstö-li) adj occidental

**western** (ᵁê-sstön) adj occidental

**wet** (ᵁêt) *adj* mojado; húmedo

**whale** (ᵁeil) *n* ballena *f*

**wharf** (ᵁoof) *n* (pl ~s, wharves) muelle *m*

**what** (ᵁot) *pron* qué; lo que; ~ **for** para que

**whatever** (ᵁo-tê-vö) *pron* cualquier cosa que

**wheat** (ᵁiit) *n* trigo *m*

**wheel** (ᵁiil) *n* rueda *f*

**wheelbarrow** (ᵁiil-bæ-rou) *n* carretilla *f*

**wheelchair** (ᵁiil-chêᵒ) *n* silla de ruedas

**when** (ᵁên) *adv* cuándo; *conj* cuando

**whenever** (ᵁê-nê-vö) *conj* cuando quiera que

**where** (ᵁêᵒ) *adv* dónde; *conj* donde

**wherever** (ᵁêᵒ-rê-vö) *conj* dondequiera que

**whether** (ᵁê-ðö) *conj* si; **whether … or** si … o

**which** (ᵁich) *pron* cuál; que

**whichever** (ᵁi-chê-vö) *adj* cualquiera

**while** (ᵁail) *conj* mientras; *n* rato *m*

**whilst** (ᵁailsst) *conj* mientras

**whim** (ᵁim) *n* antojo *m*, capricho *m*

**whip** (ᵁip) *n* azote *m*; *v* batir

**whiskers** (ᵁi-sskös) *pl* patillas *fpl*

**whisper** (ᵁi-sspö) *v* susurrar; *n* susurro *m*

**whistle** (ᵁi-ssöl) *v* silbar; *n* silbato *m*

**white** (ᵁait) *adj* blanco

**whitebait** (ᵁait-beit) *n* boquerón *m*

**whiting** (ᵁai-ting) *n* (pl ~) merluza *f*

**Whitsun** (ᵁit-ssön) Pentecostés *m*

**who** (huu) *pron* quien; que

**whoever** (huu-ê-vö) *pron* quienquiera

**whole** (houl) *adj* completo, entero; intacto; *n* total *m*

**wholesale** (houl-sseil) *n* venta al por mayor; ~ **dealer** mayorista *m*

**wholesome** (houl-ssöm) *adj* saludable

**wholly** (houl-li) *adv* totalmente

**whom** (huum) *pron* a quien

**whore** (hoo) *n* puta *f*

**whose** (huus) *pron* cuyo; de quien

**why** (ᵁai) *adv* por qué

**wicked** (ᵁi-kid) *adj* malvado

**wide** (ᵁaid) *adj* vasto, ancho

**widen** (ᵁai-dön) *v* ensanchar

**widow** (ᵁi-dou) *n* viuda *f*

**widower** (ᵁi-dou-ö) *n* viudo *m*

**width** (ᵁidz) *n* anchura *f*

**wife** (ᵁaif) *n* (pl wives) esposa *f*, mujer *f*

**wig** (ᵁigh) *n* peluca *f*

**wild** (ᵁaild) *adj* salvaje; feroz

**will** (ᵁil) *n* voluntad *f*; testamento *m*

***will** (ᵁil) *v* *querer

**willing** (ᵁi-ling) *adj* dispuesto

**willingly** (ᵁi-ling-li) *adv* gustosamente

**will-power** (ᵁil-pauᵒ) *n* fuerza de voluntad

***win** (ᵁin) *v* vencer

**wind** (ᵁind) *n* viento *m*

***wind** (ᵁaind) *v* serpentear; *dar cuerda, enrollar

**winding** (ᵁain-ding) *adj* tortuoso

**windmill** (ᵁind-mil) *n* molino de viento

**window** (ᵁin-dou) *n* ventana *f*

**window-sill** (ᵁin-dou-ssil) *n* antepecho *m*

**windscreen** (ᵁind-sskriin) *n* parabrisas *m*; ~ **wiper** limpiaparabrisas *m*

**windshield** (ᵁind-ʃiild) *nAm* parabrisas *m*

**windy** (ᵁin-di) *adj* ventoso

**wine** (ᵁain) *n* vino *m*

**wine-cellar** (ᵁain-ssê-lö) *n* cueva *f*

**wine-list** (ᵁain-lisst) *n* carta de vinos

**wine-merchant** (ᵁain-möö-chönt) *n* vinatero *m*

**wine-waiter** (ᵁain-ᵁei-tö) *n* camarero *m*

**wing** (ᵁing) *n* ala *f*

**winkle** (ᵁing-köl) *n* caracol marino

**winner** (ᵘi-nö) n vencedor m

**winning** (ᵘi-ning) adj ganador; **winnings** pl ganancias fpl

**winter** (ᵘin-tö) n invierno m; ~ **sports** deportes de invierno

**wipe** (ᵘaip) v enjugar

**wire** (ᵘaiᵒ) n alambre m

**wireless** (ᵘaiᵒ-löss) n radio f

**wisdom** (ᵘis-döm) n sabiduría f

**wise** (ᵘais) adj sabio

**wish** (ᵘiʃ) v desear; n deseo m

**witch** (ᵘich) n bruja f

**with** (ᵘið) prep con; de

*****withdraw** (ᵘið-droo) v retirar

**within** (ᵘi-ðin) prep dentro de; adv de dentro

**without** (ᵘi-ðaut) prep sin

**witness** (ᵘit-nöss) n testigo m

**wits** (ᵘitss) pl razón f

**witty** (ᵘi-ti) adj chistoso

**wolf** (ᵘulf) n (pl wolves) lobo m

**woman** (ᵘu-mön) n (pl women) mujer f

**womb** (ᵘuum) n matriz f

**won** (ᵘan) v (p, pp win)

**wonder** (ᵘan-dö) n milagro m; asombro m; v preguntarse

**wonderful** (ᵘan-dö-föl) adj estupendo, maravilloso; delicioso

**wood** (ᵘud) n madera f; bosque m

**wood-carving** (ᵘud-kaa-ving) n talla f

**wooded** (ᵘu-did) adj selvoso

**wooden** (ᵘu-dön) adj de madera; ~ **shoe** zueco m

**woodland** (ᵘud-lönd) n arbolado m

**wool** (ᵘul) n lana f; **darning** ~ hilo de zurcir

**woollen** (ᵘu-lön) adj de lana

**word** (ᵘööd) n palabra f

**wore** (ᵘoo) v (p wear)

**work** (ᵘöök) n obra f; trabajo m; v trabajar; funcionar; **working day** día de trabajo; ~ **of art** obra de arte; ~ **permit** permiso de trabajo

**worker** (ᵘöö-kö) n obrero m

**working** (ᵘöö-king) n funcionamiento m

**workman** (ᵘöök-mön) n (pl -men) obrero m

**works** (ᵘöökss) pl fábrica f

**workshop** (ᵘöök-ʃop) n taller m

**world** (ᵘööld) n mundo m; ~ **war** guerra mundial

**world-famous** (ᵘööld-fei-möss) adj de fama mundial

**world-wide** (ᵘööld-ᵘaid) adj mundial

**worm** (ᵘööm) n gusano m

**worn** (ᵘoon) adj (pp wear) gastado

**worn-out** (ᵘoon-aut) adj gastado

**worried** (ᵘa-rid) adj inquieto

**worry** (ᵘa-ri) v inquietarse; n preocupación f, inquietud f

**worse** (ᵘööss) adj peor; adv peor

**worship** (ᵘöö-ði öv) v venerar; n culto m

**worst** (ᵘöösst) adj pésimo; adv peor

**worsted** (ᵘu-sstid) n estambre m/f

**worth** (ᵘööz) n valor m; *****be** ~ *****valer; *****be worth-while** *****valer la pena

**worthless** (ᵘööz-löss) adj sin valor

**worthy of** (ᵘöö-ði öv) digno de

**would** (ᵘud) v (pl will) *****soler

**wound**[1] (ᵘuund) n herida f; v ofender, *****herir

**wound**[2] (ᵘaund) v (p, pp wind)

**wrap** (ræp) v *****envolver

**wreck** (rêk) n pecio m; v *****destruir

**wrench** (rênch) n llave f; tirón m; v dislocar

**wrinkle** (ring-köl) n arruga f

**wrist** (risst) n muñeca f

**wrist-watch** (risst-ᵘoch) n reloj de pulsera

*****write** (rait) v escribir; **in writing** por escrito; ~ **down** anotar

**writer** (rai-tö) n escritor m

**writing-pad** (rai-ting-pæd) n bloque m; bloc mMe

**writing-paper** ( *rai*-ting-pei-pö ) *n* papel de escribir

**written** ( *ri*-tön ) *adj* (pp write) por escrito

**wrong** (rong) *adj* impropio, erróneo; *n* mal *m*; *v* agraviar; *\*be* ~ no *tener razón

**wrote** (rout) *v* (p write)

# X

**Xmas** ( *kriss*-möss ) Navidad *f*

**X-ray** ( *êkss*-rei ) *n* radiografía *f*; *v* radiografiar

# Y

**yacht** (yot) *n* yate *m*

**yacht-club** ( *yot*-klab ) *n* club de yates

**yachting** ( *yo*-ting ) *n* deporte de vela

**yard** (yaad) *n* corral *m*

**yarn** (yaan) *n* hilo *m*

**yawn** (yoon) *v* bostezar

**year** (yi⁰) *n* año *m*

**yearly** ( *yi⁰*-li ) *adj* anual

**yeast** (yiisst) *n* levadura *f*

**yell** (yêl) *v* gritar; *n* grito *m*

**yellow** ( *yê*-lou ) *adj* amarillo

**yes** (yêss) sí

**yesterday** ( *yê*-sstö-di ) *adv* ayer

**yet** (yêt) *adv* aun; *conj* pero, sin embargo

**yield** (yiild) *v* producir; ceder

**yoke** (youk) *n* yugo *m*

**yolk** (youk) *n* yema *f*

**you** (yuu) *pron* tú; a ti; usted; a usted; vosotros; os; ustedes

**young** (yang) *adj* joven

**your** (yoo) *adj* de usted; tu; vuestro, tuyos

**yourself** (yoo-*ssêlf*) *pron* te; tú mismo; usted mismo

**yourselves** (yoo-*ssêlvs*) *pron* se; vosotros mismos; ustedes mismos

**youth** (yuuz) *n* juventud *f*; ~ **hostel** albergue para jóvenes

**Yugoslav** (yuu-ghö-*sslaav*) *n* yugoslavo *m*

**Yugoslavia** (yuu-ghö-*sslaa*-vi-ö ) Yugoslavia *f*

# Z

**zeal** (siil) *n* celo *m*

**zealous** ( *sê*-löss ) *adj* celoso

**zebra** ( *sii*-brö ) *n* cebra *f*

**zenith** ( *sê*-niz ) *n* cenit *m*; apogeo *m*

**zero** ( *si⁰*-rou ) *n* (pl ~s) cero *m*

**zest** (sêsst) *n* energía *f*

**zinc** (singk) *n* cinc *m*

**zip** (sip) *n* cremallera *f*; ~ **code** *Am* código postal

**zipper** ( *si*-pö ) *n* cierre relámpago

**zodiac** ( *sou*-di-æk ) *n* zodíaco *m*

**zone** (soun) *n* zona *f*; región *f*

**zoo** (suu) *n* (pl ~s) jardín zoológico

**zoology** (sou-*o*-lö-dʒi) *n* zoología *f*

# Léxico gastronómico

## Comidas

**almond** almendra

**anchovy** anchoa

**angel food cake** pastel confeccionado con clara de huevo

**angels on horseback** ostras envueltas en tocino, asadas y servidas en pan tostado

**appetizer** entremés

**apple** manzana
~ **charlotte** pastel de compota de manzanas y pan rallado
~ **dumpling** pastel de manzanas
~ **sauce** puré de manzanas

**apricot** albaricoque

**Arbroath smoky** róbalo ahumado

**artichoke** alcachofa

**asparagus** espárrago
~ **tip** punta de espárrago

**aspic** (en) gelatina

**assorted** variado

**aubergine** berenjena

**avocado (pear)** aguacate

**bacon** tocino
~ **and eggs** huevos con tocino

**bagel** panecillo en forma de corona

**baked** al horno
~ **Alaska** helado cubierto con merengue, dorado en el horno;
se sirve flameado como postre
~ **beans** judías blancas en salsa de tomates
~ **potato** patata sin pelar cocida al horno

**Bakewell tart** pastel de almendras con mermelada de frambuesas

**baloney** especie de mortadela

**banana** plátano
~ **split** dos mitades de plátano servidas con helado y nueces, rociadas con almíbar o crema de chocolate

**barbecue** 1) carne picada de ternera en una salsa a base de tomates, servida en un panecillo 2) comida al aire libre
~ **sauce** salsa de tomates muy picante

**barbecued** asado a la parrilla con carbón de leña

**basil** albahaca

**bass** lubina (pescado)

**bean** judía, haba, frijol

**beef** carne de ternera
~ **olive** rollo de carne de ternera

**beefburger** bistec de carne picada, asado y a veces servido en un panecillo

**beet, beetroot** remolacha
**bilberry** arándano
**bill** cuenta
  ∼ **of fare** lista de platos
**biscuit** 1) galleta (GB) 2) panecillo (US)
**black pudding** morcilla
**blackberry** zarzamora
**blackcurrant** grosella negra
**bloater** arenque salado, ahumado
**blood sausage** morcilla
**blueberry** arándano
**boiled** hervido
**Bologna (sausage)** especie de mortadela
**bone** hueso
**boned** deshuesado
**Boston baked beans** judías blancas con tocino y melaza
**Boston cream pie** torta rellena de nata en capas superpuestas, cubierta de chocolate
**brains** sesos
**braised** asado
**bramble pudding** pudín de zarzamoras (a menudo con manzanas)
**braunschweiger** salchichón de hígado ahumado
**bread** pan
**breaded** empanado
**breakfast** desayuno
**bream** brema (pescado)
**breast** pecho, pechuga
**brisket** pecho
**broad bean** haba
**broth** caldo
**brown Betty** especie de compota de manzanas, con especias y cubierta de pan rallado
**brunch** comida que reemplaza el desayuno y el almuerzo
**brussels sprout** col de Bruselas
**bubble and squeak** patatas y coles

picadas que se fríen, mezcladas a veces con trozos de carne de ternera (especie de tortilla)
**bun** 1) panecillo dulce confeccionado con frutas secas 2) especie de panecillo (US)
**butter** mantequilla
**buttered** con mantequilla
**cabbage** col, repollo
**Caesar salad** ensalada verde con ajo, anchoas, cuscurro y queso rallado
**cake** pastel, torta
**cakes** galletas, pastelillos
**calf** ternera
**Canadian bacon** lomo de cerdo ahumado que se corta en lonchas finas
**cantaloupe** melón
**caper** alcaparra
**capercaillie, capercailzie** urogallo grande
**caramel** caramelo
**carp** carpa
**carrot** zanahoria
**cashew** anacardo
**casserole** cacerola
**catfish** siluro (pescado)
**catsup** salsa de tomate
**cauliflower** coliflor
**celery** apio
**cereal** cereal
  **hot** ∼ gachas
**chateaubriand** solomillo de ternera
**check** cuenta
**Cheddar (cheese)** queso de textura firme y de sabor ligeramente ácido
**cheese** queso
  ∼ **board** bandeja de quesos
  ∼ **cake** pastel de queso doble crema, ligeramente azucarado
**cheeseburger** bistec de carne pica-

da, asado con una loncha de queso, servido en un panecillo

**chef's salad** ensalada de jamón, pollo, huevos cocidos, tomates, lechuga y queso

**cherry** cereza

**chestnut** castaña

**chicken** pollo

**chicory** 1) endibia (GB) 2) escarola, achicoria (US)

**chili pepper** chile, ají

**chips** 1) patatas fritas (GB) 2) chips (US)

**chitt(er)lings** tripas de cerdo

**chive** cebolleta

**choice** elección, surtido

**chop** costilla

~ **suey** plato hecho con carne picada de cerdo o de pollo, arroz y legumbres

**chopped** picado

**chowder** sopa espesa a base de mariscos

**Christmas pudding** pudín inglés hecho con frutas secas, a veces flameado, muy nutritivo y que se sirve en Navidad

**chutney** condimento indio muy sazonado, con sabor agridulce

**cinnamon** canela

**clam** almeja

**club sandwich** bocadillo doble con tocino, pollo, tomates, lechuga y mayonesa

**cobbler** compota de frutas cubierta con una capa de pasta

**cock-a-leekie soup** sopa de pollo y puerros

**coconut** coco

**cod** bacalao

**Colchester oyster** ostra inglesa muy afamada

**cold cuts/meat** fiambres

**coleslaw** ensalada de col

**compote** compota

**condiment** condimento

**cooked** cocido

**cookie** galleta

**corn** 1) trigo (GB) 2) maíz (US)

~ **on the cob** mazorca de maíz

**cornflakes** copos de maíz

**corned beef** carne de ternera sazonada

**cottage cheese** requesón

**cottage pie** carne picada que se cuece con cebollas y se cubre con puré de patatas

**course** plato

**cover charge** precio del cubierto

**crab** cangrejo de mar

**cracker** galletita salada

**cranberry** arándano agrio

~ **sauce** mermelada de arándanos agrios

**crawfish, crayfish** 1) cangrejo de río 2) langosta (GB) 3) langostino (US)

**cream** 1) nata 2) crema (sopa) 3) crema (postre)

~ **cheese** queso doble crema

~ **puff** pastelillo con nata

**creamed potatoes** patatas cortadas en forma de dados en salsa blanca

**creole** plato muy condimentado con tomates, pimientos y cebollas; suele servirse con arroz blanco

**cress** berro

**crisps** patatas a la inglesa, chips

**croquette** croqueta

**crumpet** especie de panecillo redondo, asado y untado de mantequilla

**cucumber** pepino

**Cumberland ham** jamón ahumado, muy conocido

**Cumberland sauce** jalea de grosellas sazonada de vino, jugo de naranja y especias

**cupcake** pastelillo, hojaldre

**cured** salado y ahumado

**currant** 1) pasa de Corinto 2) grosella

**curried** con curry

**custard** 1) crema 2) flan

**cutlet** 1) chuleta 2) escalope 3) fina lonja de carne

**dab** lenguado

**Danish pastry** pastellillos hojaldrados

**date** dátil

**Derby cheese** queso blando picante, de color amarillo claro

**dessert** postre

**devilled** con aliño muy fuerte

**devil's food cake** torta de chocolate muy nutritiva

**devils on horseback** ciruelas pasas cocidas en vino tinto, rellenas de almendras y anchoas, envueltas en tocino, asadas y servidas en una tostada

**Devonshire cream** crema doble muy espesa

**diced** cortado en daditos

**diet food** alimento dietético

**dill** eneldo

**dinner** cena

**dish** plato

**donut, doughnut** buñuelo en forma de anillo, rosquilla

**double cream** doble crema, nata

**Dover sole** lenguado de Dover, muy afamado

**dressing** 1) salsa para ensalada 2) relleno para aves (US)

**Dublin Bay prawn** langostino

**duck** pato

**duckling** anadón

**dumpling** albóndiga de pasta

**Dutch apple pie** tarta de manza-

nas, cubierta con una capa de azúcar negra y mantequilla

**éclair** pastelillo relleno de crema de chocolate o de café

**eel** anguila

**egg** huevo

   **boiled** ~ pasado por agua

   **fried** ~ frito

   **hard-boiled** ~ duro

   **poached** ~ escalfado

   **scrambled** ~ revuelto

   **soft-boiled** ~ poco pasado por agua

**eggplant** berenjena

**endive** 1) escarola, achicoria (GB) 2) endibia (US)

**entrecôte** solomo de ternera

**entrée** 1) entrada (GB) 2) plato principal (US)

**fennel** hinojo

**fig** higo

**filet mignon** solomillo

**fillet** filete de carne o de pescado

**finnan haddock** róbalo ahumado

**fish** pescado

   ~ **and chips** filetes de pescado y patatas fritas

   ~ **cake** albóndigas, galleta de pescado y patatas

**flan** tarta de frutas

**flapjack** hojuela espesa

**flounder** fleso (pescado)

**forcemeat** relleno, picadillo

**fowl** ave

**frankfurter** salchicha de Francfort

**French bean** judía verde

**French bread** pan francés

**French dressing** 1) vinagreta (GB) 2) salsa cremosa de ensalada con salsa de tomates (US)

**french fries** patatas fritas

**French toast** rebanada de pan, mojada en huevos batidos, frita en una sartén y servida con mermelada o azúcar

**fresh** fresco

**fried** frito, asado

**fritter** buñuelo

**frogs' legs** ancas de rana

**frosting** capa de azúcar garrapiñado

**fruit** fruta

**fry** fritura

**galantine** trozos de carne y picadillo cocidos en gelatina

**game** caza

**gammon** jamón ahumado

**garfish** anguila de mar

**garlic** ajo

**garnish** aderezo

**gherkin** pepinillo

**giblets** menudillos de ave

**ginger** jengibre

**goose** ganso

~ **berry** grosella espinosa

**grape** uva

~ **fruit** pomelo, toronja

**grated** rallado

**gravy** jugo de carne, salsa

**grayling** pescado de la familia del salmón

**green bean** judía verde

**green pepper** pimiento verde

**green salad** ensalada verde

**greens** verduras

**grilled** asado a la parrilla

**grilse** salmón joven

**grouse** urogallo

**gumbo** 1) legumbre de origen africano 2) plato criollo a base de *okra*, con carne o pescado y tomates

**haddock** róbalo

**haggis** panza de cordero rellena de copos de avena

**hake** merluza

**half** mitad, semi

**ham** jamón

~ **and eggs** huevos con jamón

**hamburger** hamburguesa

**hare** liebre

**haricot bean** alubia blanca

**hash** 1) carne picada 2) picadillo de carne de ternera cubierto con patatas y legumbres

**hazelnut** avellana

**heart** corazón

**herb** hierba aromática

**herring** arenque

**home-made** de confección casera

**hominy grits** crema espesa de harina de maíz, especie de polenta

**honey** miel

~ **dew melon** tipo de melón cuya carne es de color verde amarillento

**hors-d'œuvre** entremeses

**horse-radish** rábano picante

**hot** 1) caliente 2) con especias

~ **cross bun** bollito con pasas (que se come durante la Cuaresma)

~ **dog** salchicha caliente en un panecillo

**huckleberry** especie de arándano

**hush puppy** buñuelo a base de harina de maíz

**ice-cream** helado

**iced** helado

**icing** capa de azúcar garrapiñado

**Idaho baked potato** patata sin pelar cocida al horno

**Irish stew** guisado de cordero con cebollas y patatas

**Italian dressing** vinagreta

**jam** confitura

**jellied** en gelatina

**Jell-O** postre a la gelatina

**jelly** gelatina o jalea de frutas

**Jerusalem artichoke** aguaturma

**John Dory** especie de dorada

**jugged hare** estofado de liebre

**juice** jugo, zumo
**juniper berry** baya de enebro
**junket** leche cuajada azucarada
**kale** col rizada
**kedgeree** migajas de pescado aderezadas con arroz, huevos y mantequilla
**ketchup** salsa de tomates
**kidney** riñón
**kipper** arenque ahumado
**lamb** cordero
**Lancashire hot pot** guisado de chuletas y riñones de cordero, con patatas y cebollas
**larded** mechado
**lean** magro
**leek** puerro
**leg** pierna, muslo, corvejón
**lemon** limón
~ **sole** especie de platija
**lentil** lenteja
**lettuce** lechuga, ensalada verde
**lima bean** haba grande
**lime** lima (limón verde)
**liver** hígado
**loaf** pan, hogaza
**lobster** bogavante
**loin** lomo
**Long Island duck** pato de Long Island, muy afamado
**low-calorie** pobre en calorías
**lox** salmón ahumado
**lunch** almuerzo
**macaroni** macarrones
**macaroon** macarrón (almendrado)
**mackerel** caballa
**maize** maíz
**mandarin** mandarina
**maple syrup** jarabe de arce
**marinade** escabeche
**marinated** en escabeche
**marjoram** mejorana
**marmalade** mermelada de naranja

u otros sabores
**marrow** tuétano
~ **bone** hueso con tuétano
**marshmallow** dulce de malvavisco
**marzipan** mazapán
**mashed potatoes** puré de patatas
**mayonnaise** mayonesa
**meal** comida
**meat** carne
~ **ball** albóndiga de carne
~ **loaf** carne picada preparada en forma de un pan y que se cuece al horno
**medium (done)** a punto
**melted** derretido
**Melton Mowbray pie** especie de empanada de carne
**menu** lista de platos
**meringue** merengue
**milk** leche
**mince** picadillo
~ **pie** tarta de frutas confitadas cortadas en daditos, con manzanas y especias (con o sin carne)
**minced** picado
~ **meat** carne picada
**mint** menta
**mixed** mezclado, surtido
~ **grill** brocheta de carne
**molasses** melaza
**morel** morilla
**mousse** postre de nata aromatizada
**mulberry** mora
**mullet** mújol (pescado)
**mulligatawny soup** sopa de pollo muy picante de origen indio
**mushroom** champiñón
**muskmelon** tipo de melón
**mussel** mejillón
**mustard** mostaza
**mutton** carnero
**noodle** tallarín
**nut** nuez

**oatmeal (porrdige)** gachas de avena

**oil** aceite

**okra** fruto del *gumbo* utilizado generalmente para espesar las sopas y guisados

**olive** aceituna

**omelet** tortilla

**onion** cebolla

**orange** naranja

**ox tongue** lengua de buey

**oxtail** cola de buey (sopa)

**oyster** ostra

**pancake** hojuela espesa, torta de sartén

**paprika** pimiento

**Parmesan (cheese)** queso parmesano

**parsley** perejil

**parsnip** chirivía

**partridge** perdiz

**pastry** pastel, pastelillo

**pasty** empanadilla de carne

**pea** guisante

**peach** melocotón

**peanut** cacahuete, maní
~ **butter** manteca de cacahuete

**pear** pera

**pearl barley** cebada perlada

**pepper** pimienta

**peppermint** menta

**perch** perca

**persimmon** caqui

**pheasant** faisán

**pickerel** lucio pequeño (pescado)

**pickle** 1) legumbre o fruta en vinagre 2) pepinillo (US)

**pickled** conservado en salmuera o vinagre

**pie** torta a menudo cubierta con una capa de pasta, rellena de carne, legumbres, frutas o crema inglesa

**pig** cerdo

**pigeon** pichón

**pike** lucio

**pineapple** piña

**plaice** platija, acedía

**plain** natural

**plate** plato

**plum** ciruela, ciruela pasa
~ **pudding** pudín inglés hecho con frutas secas, a veces flameado, muy nutritivo y que se sirve en Navidad

**poached** escalfado

**popcorn** palomitas de maíz

**popover** panecillo esponjoso cocido en el horno

**pork** cerdo

**porridge** gachas

**porterhouse steak** lonja espesa de solomillo de res

**pot roast** carne de ternera asada y legumbres

**potato** patata, papa
~ **chips** 1) patatas fritas (GB) 2) chips (US)
~ **in its jacket** patata sin pelar

**potted shrimps** mantequilla sazonada, derretida y enfriada, servida con camarones

**poultry** ave de corral

**prawn** camarón grande

**prune** ciruela seca

**ptarmigan** perdiz blanca

**pudding** pudín blando o consistente hecho con harina, relleno de carne, pescado, legumbres o frutas

**pumpernickel** pan hecho con harina gruesa de centeno

**pumpkin** calabaza

**quail** codorniz

**quince** membrillo

**rabbit** conejo

**radish** rábano

**rainbow trout** trucha arco iris

**raisin** pasa

**rare** poco hecho

**raspberry** frambuesa

**raw** crudo

**red mullet** salmonete

**red (sweet) pepper** pimiento morrón

**redcurrant** grosella roja

**relish** condimento hecho con trocitos de legumbres y vinagre

**rhubarb** ruibarbo

**rib (of beef)** costilla (de ternera)

**rib-eye steak** solomillo

**rice** arroz

**rissole** croqueta de pescado o carne

**river trout** trucha de río

**roast(ed)** asado

**Rock Cornish hen** pollo tomatero

**roe** huevos de pescado

**roll** panecillo

**rollmop herring** filete de arenque escabechado con vino blanco, enrollado con un pepinillo en medio

**round steak** filete de pierna de ternera

**Rubens sandwich** carne de ternera en pan tostado, con col fermentada, queso suizo y salsa para ensalada; se sirve caliente

**rump steak** filete de lomo de ternera

**rusk** rebanadas tostadas de pan de molde

**rye bread** pan de centeno

**saddle** cuarto trasero

**saffron** azafrán

**sage** salvia

**salad** ensalada

  ~ **bar** surtido de ensaladas

  ~ **cream** salsa cremosa para ensalada, ligeramente azucarada

  ~ **dressing** salsa para ensalada

**salmon** salmón

  ~ **trout** trucha asalmonada

**salt(ed)** sal(ado)

**sandwich** bocadillo, emparedado

**sardine** sardina

**sauce** salsa

**sauerkraut** col fermentada

**sausage** salchicha

**sauté(ed)** salteado

**scallop** 1) venera 2) escalope de ternera

**scampi** langostino

**scone** panecillo tierno hecho con harina de avena o cebada

**Scotch broth** caldo a base de carne de carnero o de buey y legumbres

**Scotch woodcock** pan tostado con huevos revueltos y crema de anchoas

**sea bass** róbalo, lubina

**sea kale** col marina

**seafood** mariscos y peces marinos

**(in) season** (en su) época (estación del año)

**seasoning** condimento, sazón

**service** servicio

  ~ **charge** importe que se paga por el servicio

  ~ **(not) included** servicio (no) incluido

**set menu** menú fijo

**shad** alosa, sábalo

**shallot** chalote

**shellfish** marisco

**sherbet** sorbete

**shoulder** espalda

**shredded wheat** hojuelas de trigo en croquetas (se sirven en el desayuno)

**shrimp** camarón, gamba

**silverside (of beef)** codillo (de ternera)

**sirloin steak** bistec del solomillo
**skewer** brocheta
**slice** loncha, rodaja
**sliced** cortado en lonchas
**sloppy Joe** carne picada de ternera con una salsa picante de tomates, se sirve en un panecillo
**smelt** eperlano
**smoked** ahumado
**snack** comida ligera
**sole** lenguado
**soup** sopa, crema
**sour** agrio
**soused herring** arenque conservado en vinagre y especias
**spaghetti** espaguetis
**spare rib** costilla de cerdo casi descarnada
**spice** especia
**spinach** espinaca
**spiny lobster** langosta
**(on a) spit** (en un) espetón
**sponge cake** bizcocho ligero y esponjoso
**sprat** arenque pequeño, sardineta
**squash** calabaza
**starter** entrada
**steak and kidney pie** empanada de carne de ternera y riñones
**steamed** cocido al vapor
**stew** guisado
**Stilton (cheese)** queso inglés afamado (blanco o con mohos azules)
**strawberry** fresa
**string bean** judía verde
**stuffed** relleno
**stuffing** (el) relleno
**suck(l)ing pig** lechón
**sugar** azúcar
**sugarless** sin azúcar
**sundae** copa de helado con frutas, nueces, nata batida y a veces jarabe

**supper** comida ligera de la noche, cena
**swede** naba de Suecia
**sweet** 1) dulce 2) postre
~ **corn** maíz blanco
~ **potato** patata dulce
**sweetbread** lechecillas
**Swiss cheese** queso suizo (Emmenthal)
**Swiss roll** bizcocho enrollado y relleno de mermelada
**Swiss steak** lonja de ternera asada con legumbres y especias
**T-bone steak** bistec y filete de ternera separados por un hueso en forma de T
**table d'hôte** menú fijo
**tangerine** especie de mandarina
**tarragon** estragón
**tart** tarta de frutas
**tenderloin** filete de carne
**Thousand Island dressing** salsa para ensalada, sazonada, hecha de mayonesa y pimientos
**thyme** tomillo
**toad-in-the-hole** carne de ternera (o salchicha) cubierta de pasta y cocida al horno
**toast** pan tostado, tostada
**toasted** tostado
~ **cheese** pan tostado con queso derretido
**tomato** tomate
**tongue** lengua
**tournedos** bistec espeso del filete (ternera)
**treacle** melaza
**trifle** pastel con jerez o aguardiente, hecho con almendras, mermelada y crema batida o natillas y crema de vainilla
**tripe** tripas, callos
**trout** trucha
**truffle** trufa

**tuna, tunny** atún
**turbot** rodaballo, rombo
**turkey** pavo
**turnip** nabo
**turnover** pastelillo relleno de compota o mermelada
**turtle** tortuga
**underdone** poco hecho
**vanilla** vainilla
**veal** ternera
  ~ **bird** pulpeta de ternera
**vegetable** legumbre
  ~ **marrow** calabacín
**venison** caza, corzo
**vichyssoise** sopa fría preparada con puerros, patatas y crema
**vinegar** vinagre
**Virginia baked ham** jamón cocido al horno, adornado con clavos de especia, rebanadas de piña y cerezas; se le baña con el jugo de las frutas
**vol-au-vent** pastel de hojaldre relleno de salsa con crema, trozos de carne y champiñones
**wafer** barquillo
**waffle** especie de barquillo caliente

**walnut** nuez
**water ice** sorbete
**watercress** berro de agua
**watermelon** sandía
**well-done** bastante hecho
**Welsh rabbit/rarebit** queso derretido sobre una tostada
**whelk** buccino (molusco)
**whipped cream** nata batida
**whitebait** boquerón
**Wiener schnitzel** escalope de ternera empanado
**wine list** lista de vinos
**woodcock** becada
**Worcestershire sauce** condimento líquido picante a base de vinagre, soja y ajo
**yoghurt** yogur
**York ham** jamón de York (ahumado)
**Yorkshire pudding** especie de pasta de hojuelas que se sirve con el rosbif
**zucchini** calabacín
**zwieback** rebanadas tostadas de pan de molde

# Bebidas

**ale** cerveza negra, ligeramente azucarada, fermentada a elevada temperatura
  **bitter** ~ negra, amarga y más bien pesada
  **brown** ~ negra de botella, ligeramente azucarada
  **light** ~ dorada de botella

  **mild** ~ negra de barril, bastante fuerte
  **pale** ~ dorada de botella
**angostura** esencia aromática amarga que se añade a los cócteles
**applejack** aguardiente de manzanas

**Athol Brose** bebida escocesa hecha con whisky, miel, agua y a veces copos de avena

**Bacardi cocktail** cóctel de ron con ginebra, jarabe de granadina y jugo de limón

**barley water** bebida refrescante a base de cebada y aromatizada con limón

**barley wine** cerveza negra muy alcoholizada

**beer** cerveza
  **bottled** ~ de botella
  **draft, draught** ~ de barril

**bitters** aperitivos y digestivos a base de raíces, corteza o hierbas

**black velvet** champán mezclado con *stout* (acompaña con frecuencia las ostras)

**bloody Mary** vodka, jugo de tomate y especias

**bourbon** whisky americano, a base de maíz

**brandy** 1) denominación genérica de los aguardientes de uvas y otras frutas 2) coñac
  ~ **Alexander** mezcla de aguardiente, crema de cacao y nata

**British wines** vino fermentado en Gran Bretaña, fabricado a base de uvas o jugo de uvas importados

**cherry brandy** licor de cerezas

**cider** sidra
  ~ **cup** mezcla de sidra. especias, azúcar y hielo

**claret** vino tinto de Burdeos

**cobbler** *long drink* helado a base de frutas, al que se añade vino o licor

**coffee** café
  ~ **with cream** con nata
  **black** ~ solo
  **caffeine-free** ~ descafeinado

**white** ~ con leche, cortado

**cordial** licor estimulante y digestivo

**cream** nata

**cup** bebida refrescante a base de vino helado, sifón, un espirituoso y adornada con una raja de naranja, de limón o de pepino

**daiquiri** cóctel de ron con jugo de limón y de piña

**double** doble porción

**Drambuie** licor a base de whisky y miel

**dry martini** 1) vermú seco (GB) 2) cóctel de ginebra con algo de vermú seco (US)

**egg-nog** bebida de ron u otro licor fuerte con yemas de huevos batidas y azúcar

**gin** ginebra

**gin and it** mezcla de ginebra y vermú italiano

**gin-fizz** mezcla de ginebra, jugo de limón, sifón y azúcar

**ginger ale** bebida sin alcohol, perfumada con extracto de jengibre

**ginger beer** bebida ligeramente alcohólica, a base de jengibre y azúcar

**grasshopper** mezcla de crema de menta, crema de cacao y nata

**Guinness (stout)** cerveza negra, con gusto muy pronunciado y algo dulce, con mucha malta y lúpulo

**half pint** aproximadamente 3 decilitros

**highball** whisky o aguardiente diluido con agua, soda o *ginger ale*

**iced** helado

**Irish coffee** café con azúcar y whisky irlandés, cubierto con nata batida (Chantilly)

**Irish Mist** licor irlandés a base de whisky y miel

**Irish whiskey** whisky irlandés menos áspero que el whisky escocés *(scotch);* además de cebada contiene centeno, avena y trigo

**juice** jugo, zumo

**lager** cerveza dorada ligera

**lemon squash** zumo de limón

**lemonade** limonada

**lime juice** zumo de lima (limón verde)

**liqueur** licor, poscafé

**liquor** aguardiente

**long drink** licor diluido en agua o tónica y servido con cubitos de hielo

**madeira** vino de Madera

**Manhattan** whisky americano, vermú y *angostura*

**milk** leche

~ **shake** batido

**mineral water** agua mineral

**mulled wine** vino caliente con especias

**neat** bebida pura, sola, sin hielo y sin agua

**old-fashioned** whisky, *angostura*, cerezas con marrasquino y azúcar

**on the rocks** con cubitos de hielo

**Ovaltine** Ovomaltina

**Pimm's cup(s)** bebida alcohólica compuesta por alguno de los siguientes licores; se mezcla con zumo de fruta y algunas veces con agua de Seltz

~ **No. 1** a base de ginebra

~ **No. 2** a base de whisky

~ **No. 3** a base de ron

~ **No. 4** a base de aguardiente

**pink champagne** champán rosado

**pink lady** mezcla de clara de huevo, Calvados, zumo de limón,

jarabe de granadina y ginebra

**pint** aproximadamente 6 decilitros

**port (wine)** (vino de) Oporto

**porter** cerveza negra y amarga

**punch** ponche

**quart** 1,14 litro (US 0,95 litro)

**root beer** bebida edulcorada efervescente, aromatizada con hierbas y raíces

**rum** ron

**rye (whiskey)** whisky de centeno, más pesado y más áspero que el *bourbon*

**scotch (whisky)** whisky escocés, mezcla de whisky de trigo y de whisky de cebada

**screwdriver** vodka y zumo de naranja

**shandy** *bitter ale* mezclada con zumo de limón o con una *ginger beer*

**sherry** jerez

**short drink** todo licor no diluido, puro

**shot** dosis de cualquier licor espirituoso

**sloe gin-fizz** licor de endrina con sifón y zumo de limón

**soda water** agua gaseosa

**soft drink** bebida sin alcohol

**spirits** aguardientes

**stinger** coñac y crema de menta

**stout** cerveza negra con mucho lúpulo y alcohol

**straight** alcohol que se bebe seco, sin mezcla

**tea** té

**toddy** ponche hecho de ron, agua, limón y azúcar

**Tom Collins** ginebra, zumo de limón, sifón y azúcar

**tonic (water)** (agua) tónica, agua gaseosa, a base de quinina

**vermouth** vermú
**water** agua
**whisky sour** whisky, zumo de limón, azúcar y sifón
**wine** vino
   **dessert** ~ de postre

**dry** ~ seco
**red** ~ tinto
**rosé** ~ clarete, rosado
**sparkling** ~ espumoso
**sweet** ~ dulce (de postre)
**white** ~ blanco

# Verbos irregulares ingleses

En la siguiente lista damos los verbos irregulares ingleses. Los verbos compuestos o los que llevan un prefijo se conjugan como los verbos simples, por ej.: *mistake* y *overdrive* se conjugan como *take* y *drive*.

| *Infinitivo* | *Pret. indefinido* | *Participio pasado* | |
|---|---|---|---|
| **arise** | arose | arisen | *levantarse* |
| **awake** | awoke | awoken | *despertarse* |
| **be** | was | been | *ser, estar* |
| **bear** | bore | borne | *soportar* |
| **beat** | beat | beaten | *batir* |
| **become** | became | become | *llegar a ser* |
| **begin** | began | begun | *comenzar* |
| **bend** | bent | bent | *doblar* |
| **bet** | bet | bet | *apostar* |
| **bid** | bade/bid | bidden/bid | *pedir* |
| **bind** | bound | bound | *atar* |
| **bite** | bit | bitten | *morder* |
| **bleed** | bled | bled | *sangrar* |
| **blow** | blew | blown | *soplar* |
| **break** | broke | broken | *romper* |
| **breed** | bred | bred | *criar* |
| **bring** | brought | brought | *traer* |
| **build** | built | built | *construir* |
| **burn** | burnt/burned | burnt/burned | *quemar* |
| **burst** | burst | burst | *reventar* |
| **buy** | bought | bought | *comprar* |
| **can**\* | could | — | *poder* |
| **cast** | cast | cast | *arrojar* |
| **catch** | caught | caught | *coger* |
| **choose** | chose | chosen | *escoger* |
| **cling** | clung | clung | *adherirse* |
| **clothe** | clothed/clad | clothed/clad | *vestir* |
| **come** | came | come | *venir* |
| **cost** | cost | cost | *costar* |
| **creep** | crept | crept | *arrastrar* |
| **cut** | cut | cut | *cortar* |
| **deal** | dealt | dealt | *distribuir* |
| **dig** | dug | dug | *cavar* |
| **do (he does)** | did | done | *hacer* |
| **draw** | drew | drawn | *dibujar* |
| **dream** | dreamt/dreamed | dreamt/dreamed | *soñar* |
| **drink** | drank | drunk | *beber* |
| **drive** | drove | driven | *conducir* |
| **dwell** | dwelt | dwelt | *habitar* |
| **eat** | ate | eaten | *comer* |
| **fall** | fell | fallen | *caer* |

\* presente de indicativo

| | | | |
|---|---|---|---|
| **feed** | fed | fed | *alimentar* |
| **feel** | felt | felt | *sentir* |
| **fight** | fought | fought | *luchar* |
| **find** | found | found | *encontrar* |
| **flee** | fled | fled | *huir* |
| **fling** | flung | flung | *lanzar* |
| **fly** | flew | flown | *volar* |
| **forsake** | forsook | forsaken | *renunciar* |
| **freeze** | froze | frozen | *helar* |
| **get** | got | got | *obtener* |
| **give** | gave | given | *dar* |
| **go** | went | gone | *ir* |
| **grind** | ground | ground | *moler* |
| **grow** | grew | grown | *crecer* |
| **hang** | hung | hung | *colgar* |
| **have** | had | had | *tener* |
| **hear** | heard | heard | *oír* |
| **hew** | hewed | hewed/hewn | *cortar* |
| **hide** | hid | hidden | *esconder* |
| **hit** | hit | hit | *golpear* |
| **hold** | held | held | *sostener* |
| **hurt** | hurt | hurt | *herir* |
| **keep** | kept | kept | *guardar* |
| **kneel** | knelt | knelt | *arrodillarse* |
| **knit** | knitted/knit | knitted/knit | *juntar* |
| **know** | knew | known | *saber* |
| **lay** | laid | laid | *acostar* |
| **lead** | led | led | *dirigir* |
| **lean** | leant/leaned | leant/leaned | *apoyarse* |
| **leap** | leapt/leaped | leapt/leaped | *saltar* |
| **learn** | learnt/learned | learnt/learned | *aprender* |
| **leave** | left | left | *marcharse* |
| **lend** | lent | lent | *prestar* |
| **let** | let | let | *permitir* |
| **lie** | lay | lain | *acostarse* |
| **light** | lit/lighted | lit/lighted | *encender* |
| **lose** | lost | lost | *perder* |
| **make** | made | made | *hacer* |
| **may*** | might | — | *poder* |
| **mean** | meant | meant | *significar* |
| **meet** | met | met | *encontrar (personas)* |
| **mow** | mowed | mowed/mown | *segar* |
| **must*** | — | — | *tener que* |
| **ought (to)*** | — | — | *deber* |
| **pay** | paid | paid | *pagar* |
| **put** | put | put | *poner* |
| **read** | read | read | *leer* |
| **rid** | rid | rid | *desembarazar* |
| **ride** | rode | ridden | *cabalgar* |

---

\* presente de indicativo

| ring | rang | rung | *sonar* |
|------|------|------|---------|
| **rise** | rose | risen | *ascender* |
| **run** | ran | run | *correr* |
| **saw** | sawed | sawn | *aserrar* |
| **say** | said | said | *decir* |
| **see** | saw | seen | *ver* |
| **seek** | sought | sought | *buscar* |
| **sell** | sold | sold | *vender* |
| **send** | sent | sent | *enviar* |
| **set** | set | set | *poner* |
| **sew** | sewed | sewed/sewn | *coser* |
| **shake** | shook | shaken | *agitar* |
| **shall*** | should | — | *deber* |
| **shed** | shed | shed | *desprenderse* |
| **shine** | shone | shone | *brillar* |
| **shoot** | shot | shot | *tirar* |
| **show** | showed | shown | *mostrar* |
| **shrink** | shrank | shrunk | *encogerse* |
| **shut** | shut | shut | *cerrar* |
| **sing** | sang | sung | *cantar* |
| **sink** | sank | sunk | *hundir* |
| **sit** | sat | sat | *sentarse* |
| **sleep** | slept | slept | *dormir* |
| **slide** | slid | slid | *resbalar* |
| **sling** | slung | slung | *lanzar* |
| **slink** | slunk | slunk | *escabullirse* |
| **slit** | slit | slit | *rajar* |
| **smell** | smelled/smelt | smelled/smelt | *oler* |
| **sow** | sowed | sown/sowed | *sembrar* |
| **speak** | spoke | spoken | *hablar* |
| **speed** | sped/speeded | sped/speeded | *apresurarse* |
| **spell** | spelt/spelled | spelt/spelled | *deletrear* |
| **spend** | spent | spent | *gastar* |
| **spill** | spilt/spilled | spilt/spilled | *derramar* |
| **spin** | spun | spun | *girar* |
| **spit** | spat | spat | *escupir* |
| **split** | split | split | *rajar* |
| **spoil** | spoilt/spoiled | spoilt/spoiled | *estropear* |
| **spread** | spread | spread | *extender* |
| **spring** | sprang | sprung | *saltar* |
| **stand** | stood | stood | *estar de pie* |
| **steal** | stole | stolen | *robar* |
| **stick** | stuck | stuck | *hundir* |
| **sting** | stung | stung | *picar* |
| **stink** | stank/stunk | stunk | *apestar* |
| **strew** | strewed | strewed/strewn | *esparcir* |
| **stride** | strode | stridden | *andar a pasos largos* |
| **strike** | struck | struck/stricken | *golpear* |
| **string** | strung | strung | *atar* |

---

* presente de indicativo

| | | | |
|---|---|---|---|
| **strive** | strove | striven | *esforzarse* |
| **swear** | swore | sworn | *jurar* |
| **sweep** | swept | swept | *barrer* |
| **swell** | swelled | swollen | *hinchar* |
| **swim** | swam | swum | *nadar* |
| **swing** | swung | swung | *balancearse* |
| **take** | took | taken | *tomar* |
| **teach** | taught | taught | *enseñar* |
| **tear** | tore | torn | *desgarrar* |
| **tell** | told | told | *decir* |
| **think** | thought | thought | *pensar* |
| **throw** | threw | thrown | *arrojar* |
| **thrust** | thrust | thrust | *impeler* |
| **tread** | trod | trodden | *pisotear* |
| **wake** | woke/waked | woken/waked | *despertar* |
| **wear** | wore | worn | *llevar puesto* |
| **weave** | wove | woven | *tejer* |
| **weep** | wept | wept | *llorar* |
| **will\*** | would | — | *querer* |
| **win** | won | won | *ganar* |
| **wind** | wound | wound | *enrollar* |
| **wring** | wrung | wrung | *torcer* |
| **write** | wrote | written | *escribir* |

---

\* presente de indicativo

# Abreviaturas inglesas

| | | |
|---|---|---|
| **AA** | *Automobile Association* | Asociación Automovilística |
| **AAA** | *American Automobile Association* | Asociación Automovilística de los Estados Unidos |
| **ABC** | *American Broadcasting Company* | Sociedad Privada de Radio-difusión y Televisión (EE.UU.) |
| **A.D.** | *anno Domini* | año de Cristo |
| **Am.** | *America; American* | América; americano |
| **a.m.** | *ante meridiem (before noon)* | de la mañana (de 00.00 a 12.00 h.) |
| **Amtrak** | *American railroad corporation* | Sociedad Privada de Com-pañías de Ferrocarriles Americanos |
| **AT & T** | *American Telephone and Telegraph Company* | Compañía Americana de Teléfonos y Telégrafos |
| **Ave.** | *avenue* | avenida |
| **BBC** | *British Broadcasting Corporation* | Sociedad Británica de Radio-difusión y Televisión |
| **B.C.** | *before Christ* | antes de Cristo |
| **bldg.** | *building* | edificio |
| **Blvd.** | *boulevard* | bulevar |
| **B.R.** | *British Rail* | Ferrocarriles Británicos |
| **Brit.** | *Britain; British* | Gran Bretaña; británico |
| **Bros.** | *brothers* | hermanos |
| **¢** | *cent* | 1/100 de dólar |
| **Can.** | *Canada; Canadian* | Canadá; canadiense |
| **CBS** | *Columbia Broadcasting System* | Sociedad Privada de Radio-difusión y Televisión (EE.UU.) |
| **CID** | *Criminal Investigation Department* | Oficina de Investigación Criminal |
| **CNR** | *Canadian National Railway* | Ferrocarriles Canadienses |
| **c/o** | *(in) care of* | al cuidado de |
| **Co.** | *company* | compañía |
| **Corp.** | *corporation* | compañía |
| **CPR** | *Canadian Pacific Railways* | Compañía Privada de Ferrocarriles Canadienses |
| **D.C.** | *District of Columbia* | Distrito de Columbia (Washington, D.C.) |
| **DDS** | *Doctor of Dental Science* | Dentista |

| | | |
|---|---|---|
| **dept.** | *department* | departamento, división |
| | | administrativa |
| **EEC** | *European Economic* | Comunidad Económica |
| | *Community* | Europea |
| **e.g.** | *for instance* | por ejemplo, verbigracia |
| **Eng.** | *England; English* | Inglaterra; inglés |
| **excl.** | *excluding; exclusive* | no incluido |
| **ft.** | *foot/feet* | pie/pies (medida: 30,5 cm.) |
| **GB** | *Great Britain* | Gran Bretaña |
| **H.E.** | *His/Her Excellency;* | Su Excelencia; |
| | *His Eminence* | Su Eminencia |
| **H.H.** | *His Holiness* | Su Santidad |
| **H.M.** | *His/Her Majesty* | Su Majestad |
| **H.M.S.** | *Her Majesty's ship* | navío de guerra británico |
| **hp** | *horsepower* | caballos de vapor |
| **Hwy** | *highway* | carretera principal |
| **i.e.** | *that is to say* | a saber, es decir |
| **in.** | *inch* | pulgada (medida: 2,54 cm.) |
| **Inc.** | *incorporated* | Sociedad Anónima |
| **incl.** | *including, inclusive* | incluido |
| **£** | *pound sterling* | libra esterlina |
| **L.A.** | *Los Angeles* | Los Angeles |
| **Ltd.** | *limited* | Sociedad Anónima |
| **M.D.** | *Doctor of Medicine* | médico |
| **M.P.** | *Member of Parliament* | Miembro del Parlamento |
| **mph** | *miles per hour* | millas por hora |
| **Mr.** | *Mister* | Señor |
| **Mrs.** | *Missis* | Señora |
| **Ms.** | *Missis/Miss* | Señora/Señorita |
| **nat.** | *national* | nacional |
| **NBC** | *National Broadcasting* | Sociedad Privada de Radio- |
| | *Company* | difusión y Televisión |
| | | (EE.UU.) |
| **No.** | *number* | número |
| **N.Y.C.** | *New York City* | Ciudad de Nueva York |
| **O.B.E.** | *Officer (of the Order)* | Caballero de la Orden del |
| | *of the British Empire* | Imperio Británico |
| **p.** | *page; penny/pence* | página; 1/100 de libra |
| **p.a.** | *per annum* | por año |
| **Ph.D.** | *Doctor of Philosophy* | Doctor en Filosofía |
| **p.m.** | *post meridiem* | de la tarde/noche |
| | *(after noon)* | (de 12.00 a 24.00 h.) |
| **PO** | *Post Office* | Oficina de Correos |
| **POO** | *post office order* | giro postal |

| | | |
|---|---|---|
| **pop.** | *population* | población |
| **P.T.O.** | *please turn over* | vuelva la página, por favor |
| **RAC** | *Royal Automobile Club* | Real Club Autómovil (Gran Bretaña) |
| **RCMP** | *Royal Canadian Mounted Police* | Policía Montada de Canadá |
| **Rd.** | *road* | carretera |
| **ref.** | *reference* | referencia |
| **Rev.** | *reverend* | Reverendo (pastor de la Iglesia Anglicana) |
| **RFD** | *rural free delivery* | distribución del correo en el campo |
| **RR** | *railroad* | ferrocarril |
| **RSVP** | *please reply* | se ruega contestación |
| **$** | *dollar* | dólar |
| **Soc.** | *society* | sociedad |
| **St.** | *saint; street* | santo(a); calle |
| **STD** | *Subscriber Trunk Dialling* | teléfono automático |
| **UN** | *United Nations* | Organización de las Naciones Unidas |
| **UPS** | *United Parcel Service* | Compañía Privada de Expedición de Paquetes (EE.UU.) |
| **US** | *United States* | Estados Unidos de América |
| **USS** | *United States Ship* | navío de guerra (EE.UU.) |
| **VAT** | *value added tax* | tasa al valor añadido |
| **VIP** | *very important person* | persona importante que beneficia de ventajas particulares |
| **Xmas** | *Christmas* | Navidad |
| **yd.** | *yard* | yarda (medida: 91,44 cm.) |
| **YMCA** | *Young Men's Christian Association* | Asociación Cristiana de Muchachos |
| **YWCA** | *Young Women's Christian Association* | Asociación Cristiana de Muchachas |
| **ZIP** | *ZIP code* | número de distrito postal |

# Numerales

| Cardinales | | Ordinales | |
|---|---|---|---|
| 0 | zero | 1st | first |
| 1 | one | 2nd | second |
| 2 | two | 3rd | third |
| 3 | three | 4th | fourth |
| 4 | four | 5th | fifth |
| 5 | five | 6th | sixth |
| 6 | six | 7th | seventh |
| 7 | seven | 8th | eighth |
| 8 | eight | 9th | ninth |
| 9 | nine | 10th | tenth |
| 10 | ten | 11th | eleventh |
| 11 | eleven | 12th | twelfth |
| 12 | twelve | 13th | thirteenth |
| 13 | thirteen | 14th | fourteenth |
| 14 | fourteen | 15th | fifteenth |
| 15 | fifteen | 16th | sixteenth |
| 16 | sixteen | 17th | seventeenth |
| 17 | seventeen | 18th | eighteenth |
| 18 | eighteen | 19th | nineteenth |
| 19 | nineteen | 20th | twentieth |
| 20 | twenty | 21st | twenty-first |
| 21 | twenty-one | 22nd | twenty-second |
| 22 | twenty-two | 23rd | twenty-third |
| 23 | twenty-three | 24th | twenty-fourth |
| 24 | twenty-four | 25th | twenty-fifth |
| 25 | twenty-five | 26th | twenty-sixth |
| 30 | thirty | 27th | twenty-seventh |
| 40 | forty | 28th | twenty-eighth |
| 50 | fifty | 29th | twenty-ninth |
| 60 | sixty | 30th | thirtieth |
| 70 | seventy | 40th | fortieth |
| 80 | eighty | 50th | fiftieth |
| 90 | ninety | 60th | sixtieth |
| 100 | a/one hundred | 70th | seventieth |
| 230 | two hundred and thirty | 80th | eightieth |
| | | 90th | ninetieth |
| 1,000 | a/one thousand | 100th | hundredth |
| 10,000 | ten thousand | 230th | two hundred and thirtieth |
| 100,000 | a/one hundred thousand | | |
| 1,000,000 | a/one million | 1,000th | thousandth |

# La hora

Los británicos y los americanos utilizan el sistema de 12 horas. La abreviatura *a.m. (ante meridiem)* designa las horas anteriores al mediodía, *p.m. (post meridiem)* las de la tarde o de la noche. Sin embargo, en Gran Bretaña existe la tendencia, cada vez más acentuada, a indicar los horarios como en el continente.

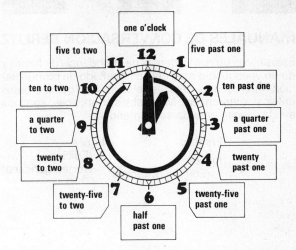

*I'll come at seven a.m.*      Vendré a las 7 de la mañana.
*I'll come at two p.m.*        Vendré a las 2 de la tarde.
*I'll come at eight p.m.*      Vendré a las 8 de la noche.

# Los días de la semana

| | | | |
|---|---|---|---|
| *Sunday* | domingo | *Thursday* | jueves |
| *Monday* | lunes | *Friday* | viernes |
| *Tuesday* | martes | *Saturday* | sábado |
| *Wednesday* | miércoles | | |

# MANUALES DE CONVERSACION BERLITZ

Estos libros ofrecen, además de abundancia de frases y de un vocabulario muy útil acompañado de pronunciación, interesantes detalles relativos a propinas, datos útiles y sugerencias. Manejables y eficaces, son una ayuda valiosa para darse a entender.

Francés

Inglés
(Edición Británica)

Inglés
(Edición Norteamericana)

## CASSETTES BERLITZ

La mayoría de los Manuales de Conversación pueden combinarse con una cassette que le ayudará a mejorar su acento. Cada cassette, grabada en alta fidelidad, va acompañada de un folleto de 32 páginas impresas con el texto completo de la grabación.